"It never happened. Noting ever happened. Even while it was happening it wasn't happening. It didn't matter. It was of no interest. The crimes of the United States have been systematic, constant, vicious, remorseless, but very few people have actually talked about them. You have to hand it to America. It has exercised a quite clinical manipulation of power worldwide while masquerading as a force for universal good. It's a brilliant, even witty, highly successful act of hypnosis."

~ Harold Pinter – Nobel Lecture (2005)

"Everything that is written about human rights in your world, and in the world of your allies who share in plundering the world, is an enormous lie. Billions of human beings live in infrahuman conditions starving, without enough food, medicine, clothes, shoes or shelter and without even a minimum amount of knowledge or enough information to understand their tragedy and that of the world in which they live."

~ Fidel Castro's speech regarding Bush's "War on Terrorism"

Exposing Lies of the Empire

Andre Vltchek

Badak Merah
2015

EXPOSING LIES OF THE EMPIRE

Written by: Andre Vltchek
Cover Design and Layout by: Rossie Indira
Cover Art by: George Burchett
Portrait photo by: Alejandro Wagner
Photos by: Andre Vltchek
Proofread by: Arthur Temungwa

First edition, 2015

Published by PT. Badak Merah Semesta
Jl. Madrasah Azziyadah 16, Jakarta
http://badak-merah.weebly.com
email: badak.merah.press@gmail.com

ISBN: 978-602-70058-6-0

"Not long ago I met count Dracula in Buenos Aires. He was looking for an Argentinean psychoanalyst... Dracula was told by someone that he can still be cured by an Argentinean psychoanalyst. I found count Dracula in a terrible state; really depressed, thin, terrible... He was suffering from a tremendous complex of inferiority, seeing how the great corporations of the modern world are behaving."

~ Eduardo Galeano

in conversation with Andre Vltchek, in Montevideo, Uruguay, 2005

"Western countries see the rest of the world as their playing field fit only for exploitation."

~ Pramoedya Ananta Toer

in conversation with Andre Vltchek, in Jakarta, 2004

TABLE OF CONTENTS

PREFACE: Exposing Lies of the Empire

The Empire lies. It lies about the present, about the past, even about the future. It lies day and night, relentlessly.

Its founding dogmas are based on deception, its history on false pathos and insincere heroism.

Europe is where it is now, still filthy rich (although always complaining), because of those hundreds of millions of people all over the world who were robbed and murdered, those who become victims of the very madness of colonialism, of the crusades and the slave trade. Cathedrals and palaces, museums and theatres, train stations – all had been constructed on horrid foundations of bones and blood, and amalgamated by tears. There were so many centuries of plunder that the acts of looting the world for the sole benefit of the few, turned into inseparable part of the 'Western existence and culture', something that gets almost never addressed, let alone criticized.

The Europe's offshoot - North America - developed into 'the richest part of the world' as a result of the extermination campaign by the 'pioneers' arriving from the 'old continent'. The land and the riches underneath it were confiscated; most of the 'natives' were either murdered or forced into Christianity by overzealous 'God-fearing' morally defunct 'puritans'. Simultaneously, millions of back people who were hunted down like animals all over Africa were shackled, thrown to terrible ships, brought to America and turned into slaves. Black women were chained in the middle of the fields, in devilish heat or cold, for those Protestant righteousness bigots to sexually relief themselves into them, at will. The rights of some minorities were protected, true, but mainly the rights of few rich individuals and families, against the majority that has been poor.

'Pious' fanaticism, unmatchable greed and extreme brutality are behind that 'great success' of the West and of the Christendom. The world was conquered, people enslave, riches confiscated and used for building series of Western capitalist and imperialist Empires, then finally one single one, that is usurping and controlling the planet until now.

Total control has been administered, through both concrete and abstract fear, and through the constant injection of primitive but very effective doctrines and perceptions. Propaganda, 'education', 'culture', entertainment and even science have been mobilized. Target of elaborate brainwashing became both the lower and middle classes from the nations-victimizers, as well as the great majority of the people in the conquered countries.

Distortion of the reality has been extreme. Even those nations that used to have much greater and deeper culture than Europe are now viewing and judging themselves by imported Western tools and twisted perceptions. The brightest sons and daughters are sent from the colonies to the capitals of the Empire for 'education' and reeducation, and made to become conformist, obedient, in order to serve the Empire better.

Even those countries that are now brave enough to face the Empire – China, Russia, Venezuela, Ecuador, Iran or Zimbabwe – have their own 'fifth column', its 'elite' or at least a substantial fraction of it, which is fully propagandized by, and loyal to the Empire. More 'educated' it is, more indoctrinated. As a rule, more titles and years of schooling its members carry back home from abroad (or from those local, private, and mostly religious schools), more servility they demonstrate.

Colonialists are now controlling the planet completely, and the control has many layers; it is not just military and economic, but also ideological, mental, intellectual and emotional.

How naive are those who believe that the Empire mainly wages wars for oil and other natural resources! Oil is just the means – the end, the goal, is much more monumental: it is the unopposed, total rule over the planet!

***

Since my early childhood, I had been living all over this beautiful but scarred planet. At first, moving from one place to another was not my decision, it was dictated by the circumstances. But later it became my choice.

Until now, I have no 'homeland', no country that I could or would want to call my own; the place that I would put above others.

I was born in Leningrad, in the Soviet Union, grew up in Plzen (then it was still Czechoslovakia), and later in New York. I lived in Mexico and Chile, Costa Rica and Vietnam, Samoa, Japan, Indonesia, Kenya and Lebanon.

More I witnessed, more I became convinced that nothing is more shocking, more ridiculous, than those quietly proclaimed and concealed rights and privileges of the conquerors, as well as the profound humiliation and forced 'irrelevance' of billions of those who are here to serve, after losing all their rights. Corruption of global arrangement is obvious, but only to those who were not fully indoctrinated, yet.

While the Empire constantly brags about 'democracy', it is running the most totalitarian regime ever known to mankind. Popular, progressive, responsible leaders and governments worldwide, determined to serve its people, have been habitually overthrown, murdered and then demonized *postmortem*. To call such regime a 'mafia-style' would be great insult even to *Cosa Nostra*.

I witnessed brutal and arrogant acts of the Empire, in all corners of the globe. Indignant, I began writing essays and books about the neo-colonialism and imperialism, and again, I began making documentary films on the subject.

There was very little support and many betrayals along the way, but by then, I could not and would not turn back.

As the global grip on power has been tightening, I found myself working day and night, producing, what one reader described an 'amount of work usually made by a battalion'. It was not because I am extraordinarily hard working by nature, but because the fate of the world has been hanging on a thread.

Paradoxically, more concerned I felt, more determinately I fought; more scared I felt, more courageous became my struggle.

I have been trying to follow examples of great people who were much older than me: fighters against the Empire and its horrors: Noam Chomsky, John Pilger, and Eduardo Galeano.

I have been well aware of the fact that after seeing what I saw, after knowing what I knew, I had no right to stop: the Empire has been manufacturing 'opposition movements', from Latin America to Ukraine, Russia, China, Cuba, Syria, Eritrea. It has been sending Pentecostal religious fanatics to all corners of the globe; it has been using drones to murder people from the distance, while using pop and communication gadgets and social media to turn people all over the world into one monolithic, submissive, idiotic, pinkish, and unthinking mass.

As in dark ages as in horror stricken Calvin's Protestant Geneva, the Empire made trust and communication among people almost impossible. Many could not trust their wives or their neighbors, anymore. The essence of existence shrank to fear, irrational obedience and feelings of guilt.

People, as well as entire nations, have been attempting to anticipate the next move and forthcoming mood of the Empire. They were trying to appease it, to make it content and proud of them, as if it would be a sadistic father and they would be its 'children'.

Rationality collapsed. Relatively young tyrant was now ruling over ancient cultures. It was behaving like some religious paternal figure, spreading fear, as it was judging and punishing. Entire structure of global regime felt suddenly extremely twisted, incestuous, endlessly depressing.

Revolutionary songs were silenced, poetry forgotten, dreams and desires to live in much better world ridiculed.

Such depressing nihilism and tyranny could not have been tolerated, any longer. It had to be confronted!

***

Since roughly the beginning of 2012, I abandoned attempts to save money, to build reserves, and to own anything tangible: whatever I gained from my films, books or reports, I immediately recycled into journeys to the most battered and the most endangered corners of the globe. Everything went to the cost of hotels, tickets, and equipment. There was hardly any time for personal life – the world has been in flames, and deranged market and post-Christian fundamentalists, imperialists, racists and bigots seemed to be fully in charge of the carnage.

I have been visiting battlefields and countries destabilized and assaulted by Western neo-colonialist and neo-conservative warmongers: Iraq, Ukraine, Cuba, Venezuela, China, Zimbabwe, the Democratic Republic of Congo (DRC), Eritrea, Uganda, Yemen, Palestine, to name just a few. I continued to study and to analyze the system, the mechanisms used by the Empire. One country after another has been being destroyed, for serving its own people, instead of the Empire and its corporations.

I have filmed, photographed, and wrote; day and night.

***

In 2012, I discussed the state of the world with Noam Chomsky, in a dialogue, which formed the foundation of our book "On Western Terrorism: From Hiroshima to Drone Warfare", (Pluto, 2013, and so far translated to 14 languages).

At one point, Noam asked about my childhood and the impact Western propaganda had on my early years.

It was extremely important question. Suddenly I remembered clearly what took place many years ago: growing up in Eastern Europe, with Western media of indoctrination pointing directly across the 'Iron Curtain'. We, young people, were conditioned to reject Communism, to give up on the entire 'project' of bi-polar world, on the fight against Western colonialism and imperialism. We were discouraged from trying to reform and improve our imperfect but hopeful system.

We became dissidents. We attacked the essence of our system. We left our countries.

I had been thoroughly brainwashed by 'The Radio Free Europe", Voice of America, the BBC and countless other propaganda outlets of the Empire. It happened when I was 14 or 15 years old – that young.

It took me couple of years, living, paradoxically, in the New York City, to de-indoctrinate myself. I was lucky that several bright young and not so young, exceptionally knowledgeable New York intellectuals were then around me. Others in my position were not as fortunate.

The Empire's weapons of mass destruction do not only consist of nuclear bombs, stealth fighters and drones. Even more effective are indoctrination, propaganda and 'culture', or more precisely 'anti-culture'.

Putting form over substance and keeping it there, in the brains of creative people and consumers, could be much more destructive than thousands of tanks. Pop tunes and Hollywood bizarre, toxic 'entertainment' (as are its local equivalents like Bollywood, K-pop or soap operas) is giving birth to entire generations of atomized, shallow, confused, depressed, self-centered, insecure and uncreative people.

Rebelliousness is repressed. Everybody consumes the same things, moves to the same rhythm, and thinks the same thoughts. It is one horrid site!

Determination, optimism, and solidarity – everything essentially human and progressive crumbles, and gets off the way of the Empire.

And then come the tanks, and nukes and drones!

And almost nobody has any ability to fight back, to organize, to defend humanity and the progress, anymore.

***

This book is challenging many dogmas. It is trying to uncover propaganda of the Empire, its dogmas, as well as its crimes.

It is a long book, but so has been the list of crimes committed in front of my eyes.

The book is erratic when it comes to its style – there are philosophical essays shoulder to shoulder with hardcore pieces of investigative journalism, from places like Iraq, Cuba, Eritrea and India. I did not manage to polish it to some stylistic perfection, and frankly, I did not want to. There is no time for perfection, and no need! Let us think together, laugh together, cry, plan and struggle! Let each and every chapter be different; let it be surprising, as are our lives and the places scattered all over the planet.

This book is a direct result of several years on the road, in the trenches, in countless slums, metropolises, and frontlines. Working on all continents, I have been moving from top to bottom, mingling with the elites of the client states, with the poorest of the poor, with gangsters and soldiers, academics, artists, miners and farmers. I also met several great thinkers, Presidents, corrupt officials and businessmen, battalion commanders, mass murderers and fake prophets. In many poor countries, I met the most cynical breed of human beings - the servants and butlers of the Empire.

It has been one long, hair-raising ride and I do not regret one single step, one single second of it.

This book is part of the process. It looks substantial, but it concludes nothing. There will be many more books to come: this year, during the following years and decades. I swear: as long as there are great stories to tell, we will keep publishing, keep struggling. Reason will not be defeated! Optimism will not be broken. Oppression will be fought. Humanity will prevail.

Yokkaichi, Japan,

7 January 2015

Photo 1. Ebeye Marshall Islands – pollution from nearby US military base at Kwajalein, Mashall Islands

1

Fascism Will be Fought

2015: DEFENDING HUMANITY BY REASON OR FORCE

One more step, one more explosion of insanity, and all that humanity fought for, what it labored for and has been aiming at for years, centuries and millennia, may disappear in a monstrous series of blasts. Our planet might break into pieces, or it may get poisoned and become uninhabitable, forever.

Hyperbolic? Not at all, given the track record of the Empire: war after war, invasion after invasion, with hundreds of destabilized countries, murdered leaders, and overthrown governments.

The storyline may be similar to that of the famous novella by Gabriel Garcia Marquez: “Chronicle of a Death Foretold”. We can foresee what may soon happen, we are warning that carnage is likely to take place in a very near future and on a grand scale, but our warnings, while registering, are not propelling almost anyone to action. But this may soon change.

Those who are now pushing the world to an irreversible

disaster are clearly identifiable: they are market fundamentalists, conservative Christian dogmatists who believe in the superiority of their doctrine and of the 'chosen nature' of the Western people and culture, as well as the millions of their lackeys and minor cohorts: thousands of CEO's and deranged 'military strategists'.

If they are allowed to choose: to destroy the world or to lose control over it, they would opt for destruction. And they would have no regrets in ending billions of human lives, because their 'logic' and 'morality' have foundations in some bizarre and hazy 'holy righteous' dogmas, and because, during the long and dark centuries, they managed to cultivate countless arguments, designed to justify their lunacy.

The only circumstance, under which they would let the rest of us survive and exist, would be, if we were to become their unconditional slaves; not just servants, but slaves.

They want to rule over us and simultaneously they demand to be feared, admired and adored. Yes, the control, the submission, has to be total. And all those servile, shameful feelings we are expected to demonstrate have to be absolute, 'pure' and unconditional.

You are guessing correctly: it all has its roots somewhere 'back there' – in the era of the 'Holy Inquisition'.

If we dare to resist, they are capable of nuking us, reducing all of us to dust, even if they and their families would also vanish in that fire.

It is because these people are true extremists and fanatics, because they want absolutely everything, because they are maniacs in possession not only of tremendous propaganda, surveillance and security apparatuses, but also of nukes.

***

After this regime and its rulers colonized and enslaved almost the entire planet Earth, there is very little decency left in the places that have fallen into their hands, as almost everything that used to be pure, everything natural and human, has been spat on, perverted, trivialized and commercialized.

People all over the world used to dream and desire things like solidarity, beauty, love, justice for all, equality and brotherhood, as well as permanent lack of fear.

Knowledge was supposed to have one and only purpose: to give people the intellectual tools to build better societies.

Now, children and adults go to schools to become obedient ants and half-wits, ready for the corporate drill. The more schooling and diplomas they receive the more stereotypical and conditioned their brains become.

In most of countries, medicine is nothing more than a well-remunerated business, while almost all pharmaceutical companies are busy plundering rainforests and registering their patents, instead of curing people.

Great science died, after being locked behind the doors of predominantly corporate laboratories or private universities and research centers. The best scientific brains are working for the military, or they are busy developing 'products' for markets, instead of advancing humanity.

The Arts, once the vanguard of human thought and progress, has been reduced to entertainment, into mainly indistinguishable mass of pop, as soulless and brainless, as the supermarkets or shopping malls. Instead of leading people to the barricades, instead of making them aim at something higher, artists have been reduced to the level of cheap entertainers.

Deliberately, form was put high above the substance. In all the major world cities ruled by the Empire, people in buses and trains now stare at the screens of their latest mobile phones, exchanging increasingly incomprehensible, idiotic and abbreviated infantile and self-centered messages. Hardly anyone reads books. Hardly anyone thinks. Hardly anyone has any feelings. Even love has become like that mass-produced pinkish pop cover of confetti.

Nobody seems to be happy. In the Empire itself, people are miserably atomized, lonely and lost. They are too scared to open their hearts to each other, to love, to give everything to others. In the colonies, horrendously retarded family and religious structures are put to work, to serve oppression, which in turn serves the Empire.

Ideals are being spat on, dragged through dirt by the omnipotent manufacturers of obedience and by their most powerful tools – the mass media, religious entrepreneurs, the private education system, and the pop entertainment machine. Only consumerism, commercialism, business achievements and loyalty to the regime are glorified. There is nothing that encourages people to dream of a much better world, or to struggle for a new, just and egalitarian society.

Any society or ideology that dares to put people first, is demonized, and ridiculed. It is ideologically attacked. If it refuses to succumb, it gets attacked militarily, it gets bombed, and eventually, it ends up being thoroughly destroyed.

***

The Western Empire insists on controlling everything of any substance. It has even managed to radicalize non-Christian religions, most strikingly Islam: first through the British support of *Wahhabis*, then through Western creation of the Mujahedeen in Afghanistan, that subsequently gave birth to Al-Qaeda, and recently by NATO's creation of ISIS.

The Empire is only interested in controlling the world, not in its wellbeing or continued existence. It is actually showing a spectacular disinterest towards the survival of the human race and of our planet.

I have seen entire nations 'sinking', or becoming uninhabitable due to global warming: Kiribati, Tuvalu, and Marshall Islands. I have seen enormous islands like Sumatra or Borneo totally logged out, covered by black toxic rivers, thoroughly destroyed.

I have seen unimaginable horrors – cities that were fully abandoned to 'market forces' – Jakarta, Nairobi, Tegucigalpa...

I talked to people in New York City who were scared that they could get sick one day; not because of illness itself, but because they would not be able to pay their medical bills. I saw young people squashed under the deadly weight of student loans. I talked to armies of people who have 'no idea what to do with their lives' – all reason, all meaning for existence simply lost!

I have seen dozens of battlefields, cities and villages bombed to the ground. I saw millions of refugees. All this, so the Empire can maintain this monstrous self-serving and self-promoting system – a system which nobody really wants, and never really wanted.

And now, one more step, and it will trigger conflict with Russia, China, perhaps Iran...

***

The more I see, the more I think: We have to find a way how to disarm those maniacs who are ruling the world, as well finding a way how to disarm their servants and lackeys in the 'client-states'.

This is absolute madness! This is not where humanity should be, right now. They have kidnapped humanity, detained progress, murdered dreams and covered entire continents with a dark, sarcastic, depressing blanket of nihilism.

Instead of creating beautiful music and poetry, instead of building public parks and ecological cities, we are choking our urban centers with cars; we are murdering millions of people over access to natural resources. We live for over-production and over-consumption, while billions are rotting alive in a gutter. We are overthrowing decent political leaders and murdering journalists who refuse to lie. We are spying on each other, cheating on each other, and torturing each other, intimidating each other, murdering each other and hating each other.

Most of the people have been made to forget that human beings are essentially optimistic, sharing and loving creatures. Most people have been made to forget, or were never allowed to know, that building better societies is much more glorious and fun than living in some extreme individualistic nightmare. Living for humanity, not for profit, not for a 'me-me-me-goes first' dogma, is fulfilling and actually gives meaning to one's existence.

***

Our so-called 'leaders', political, religious and economic/ business, belong in a mental institution.

How to get them there, would require, doubtlessly, an extremely delicate maneuver.

I suggest: let us promise them; let us give them, all the imaginable golden parachutes they desire. Anything: just to get rid of them; push them away from power.

They should be behind bars, of course, facing charges ranging from fraud to genocide, but punishing them is not my priority, at least not right now.

The priority is for humanity to survive – to survive as a multitude of free people, not as slaves.

Those maniacs know that they can thrive only in a world, which they have created. They have no kindness, no creative power. Their system can only flourish because of deception, intimidation, and terror.

That is why they and their system will never go voluntarily, and peacefully.

Life is business, for them. They don't exist for humanity; they exist as slave-owners (slavery is a business for them, too, ever since the beginning) and as religious inquisitors; and they also exist for their deadly business games: for deals, for markets.

Let us find a way to buy back our world from them!

Let us find a way to buy grass and rivers, oceans and rainforests, ancient cities, creatures, trees and flowers.

Let us find a way to buy back the respect for human race. Let's buy it from them and then, let us never sell it again. Let us not sell it to anyone, no matter how beautifully he plays his flute!

Let us recover, even at a price, logic and reason: let love be love again; let pain be pain, let justice be exactly that – justice – and nothing else!

Any price will do, as long as they leave this planet alone.

For millennia, their Crusades, their colonialism, their plunder has turned our world into an enormous globe of fear, of torture, of smoke and of grotesque parody on morality.

And after all that madness and terror that has been committed, some people are still taking this regime, this Molotov Cocktail of fundamentalist Christianity, imperialism and capitalism, seriously!

Please, let us not take it seriously, anymore. It is just a terrible joke, a nightmare, and an insult to the very essence of humanity.

Let us laugh at it, let us throw up looking at it, or, as I suggested: let us negotiate an immediate deal, even if we become thoroughly broke for some time.

But, under no circumstances, should we take it 'seriously', anymore. And let us not continue living like this, any longer!

This regime has perverted all great aspirations of humanity. It has derailed progress and destroyed hope. It has choked kindness and solidarity. It has robbed the great majority of people, and then suggested that 'poverty should be eased through charity'. And it has murdered hundreds of millions of people, perhaps billions.

Let us insult it. Let us laugh at it. Let us throw money in its face.

If it refuses to leave: let us fight it!

***

Look at all that nihilism surrounding us!

The Empire has no beautiful songs – songs about building the nations; it has no poetry that could cover our backs with goose bumps. It has no leaders who could, with hardly any security; stand on a balcony facing a crowd, sharing with people their passion for building a great world for all of us.

It has no loyalty, and it offers no certainty. 'Love' it produces is 'interest and business oriented', it does not last, and it is cannot be counted on.

The Empire cannot even fight, anymore, because it is sickly and cowardly. It murders millions, yes; but it murders them by pushing buttons and by flying drones, and by using proxy regimes – its colonies.

It is because the ideals of the Empire are low, because its religious dogmas are depressing, because capitalism is shallow, because neo-colonialism is immoral!

***

If the Empire kills us, we would all die for nothing – only so the Empire and its maniacs could thrive!

Therefore, let us not die! Let us fight for life, against the fascism that is now choking our throats.

Let us unite and shout:

"We Want This Earth Back!"

"We Want Kindness, Decency And Love Back!"

But these shouts should not be slogans at some protest marches. Protest marches do not work.

We either fight, or we change nothing. These should be the demands on our banners, our battle cries!

Ask anywhere in Latin America and Africa, in Asia and

Oceania, in the Middle East, even in the epicenters of the Empire – in Europe and North America: the people want to live in a world free of constant fear and irrational guilt. They want hospitals to cure the sick and to prevent others from getting ill, schools to really educate, and housing to give a roof and shelter to people, cities and villages to offer a great quality of life to their inhabitants. They want certainty.

People want life to have meaning again... and to be full of beauty, of hope and dreams! They want to watch the stars above, and to dream. Sometimes they can't even define it, anymore, but if you talk to them, this is what most of them really want.

"A journey of a thousand *li* begins with a single step", said great Chinese philosopher, Lao-tzu, some 25 centuries ago.

But in order to make that very first step, one has to stand up, to be erect.

And in order to stand up, one has to be alive; one has to be determined.

True, it is sometimes easier to kneel or to prostrate, than to stand, than to walk forward, than to struggle. Sometimes it is easier to betray, than to remain loyal to one's dream, to one's love, to the essential principles.

But one truly lives only when he or she is upright, when marching forward and aiming at a better world, when keeping promises and pledges.

The Empire broke many; it bought many, or scared them into submission. But others are standing up. Not everyone is for sale, neither is everyone ready to serve.

The first steps are being made, everywhere. Many thousand *li* distances will soon be covered.

Fascism will be fought. Humanity will be defended! By reason or by force, the regime would have to yield to the interests of humanity. It will not be allowed to make that final, the most destructive step!

2 January 2015

*****

2

Last of the Independents

THE DEATH OF INVESTIGATIVE JOURNALISM

Fifteen years ago, in 1997, my Haitian friends helped to arrange my visit to Cite Soleil, then the largest and the most brutal slum (or 'commune') in the Western hemisphere, on the outskirts of Port-au-Prince. The arrangement was simple: my F-4 camera and I were to be loaded onto the back of a van. The driver and two guards promised to take me there for a two-hour photo shoot. The condition was simple: I was supposed to stick to the back platform of the pickup truck.

Once we arrived, I broke the agreement: I simply couldn't resist the temptation. I jumped off from the van and began walking; photographing all that was in the radius of my lenses.

The guards refused to follow me and when I came back to the intersection, the van was gone. I was later told that my driver was simply too scared to remain in the area. The reputation of Cite Soleil was, and probably still is, that one could easily enter but could never leave.

Abandoned, young and moderately insane, I continued working for more than two hours. I encountered no hindrance: the locals appeared to be stunned seeing me walking around with a professional camera. Some were smiling politely; others were waving to me, and even thanking me.

At some point I noticed two Humvees and US military men and women with machine guns facing a desperate crowd. Local people were queuing to enter a compound behind tall walls, and the US soldiers were screening those who were eligible.

Nobody bothered to screen me – I just walked in with no interference. One of the US soldiers even gave me an enormous grin. What I found inside, however, was far from hilarious: a Haitian middle aged woman was lying on her stomach on some provisory operation table, her back split open, while several US military doctors and nurses poked into her body with scalpels and something that appeared like a pair of pliers.

"What the hell are they doing?" I asked her husband who was sitting nearby, his face covered by the palms of his hands. He was crying.

"They are removing her tumor", he said.

There were flies all over the place, as well as certain much mightier species of insects that I had never had a chance to encounter before. The stench was nauseating – that of illness, open bodies, blood and disinfectant.

"We are training for a combat scenario", explained one of the military nurses. "Haiti is as close to real combat as one can get."

"These are human beings, buddy", I tried to argue, but he had his own way of looking at this. "We don't come, they die. So we are helping them, in a way."

All I could do was to photograph the mess. No diagnostic equipment was used to determine what was really wrong with the patients. No x-rays were taken. I took a mental note that animals in almost any urban veterinarian clinic in the US were definitely treated much better than those unfortunate people.

The lady was in pain, but she didn't dare to complain. They were operating on her with only local anesthesia. After it was over, they stitched her up, and put bandages around her body.

"What now?" I asked her husband.

"We will take a bus back home", he replied.

Eventually the lady had to get up and walk, leaning on her husband who was lovingly supporting her. I couldn't believe my own eyes: the patient was made to walk after having her tumor removed.

I befriended a doctor who eventually took me to the series of tents that served as a military installation for the US soldiers and staff deployed in Haiti. The facilities were air-conditioned, spotless, equipped with a real operating theatre, and above all, empty. There were dozens of comfortable cots available.

"Why don't you let your patients stay here", I asked.

"Not allowed", replied doctor.

"You use them as guinea pigs, don't you?"

He didn't reply. He considered my question to be rhetorical one. Soon after, I arranged a car and left.

* * *

I never managed to publish the story, except in one newspaper in Prague. I sent photos to the New York Times, to the Independent, but received no reply.

I was not really surprised as one year earlier, after hanging from a ceiling with my arms tied, in some god-forsaken Indonesian military facility in occupied East Timor, and after being finally released with the words of "We didn't realize that you were such an important man" (they found a letter from ABC News stating that I was on a research assignment as an 'independent producer') I couldn't find any Western mass media outlet that showed interest in publishing reports about the mass rapes and other atrocities the Indonesian military had routinely unleashed against the defenseless population of East Timor.

But several others had already described these types of scenarios before me, including Noam Chomsky and John Pilger. One could easily summarize the dogma of 'free Western press' as: "Only those atrocities that serve the geopolitical and economic interests of the West can be considered as true atrocities and therefore allowed to be reported and analyzed in our mass media outlets."

But for this article I would like to look at the situation from a slightly different angle.

* * *

In 1945, this report appeared on the pages of Express:

> THE ATOMIC PLAGUE
>
> "I Write This as a Warning to the World"
>
> DOCTORS FALL AS THEY WORK
>
> Poison gas fear: All wear masks

Express Staff Reporter Peter Burchett was the first Allied staff reporter to enter the atom-bomb city. He traveled 400 miles from Tokyo alone and unarmed [this was incorrect but the Daily Express could not know that] carrying rations for seven meals – food is almost unobtainable in Japan – a black umbrella, and a typewriter. Here is his story from –

> "HIROSHIMA, Tuesday.
>
> In Hiroshima, 30 days after the first atomic bomb destroyed the city and shook the world, people are still dying, mysteriously and horribly – people who were uninjured by the cataclysm – from an unknown something which I can only describe as atomic plague. Hiroshima does not look like a bombed city. It looks as if a monster steamroller had passed over it and squashed it out of existence. I write these facts as dispassionately as I can in the hope that they will act as a warning to the world. In this first testing ground of the atomic bomb I have seen the most terrible and frightening desolation in four years of war. It makes a blitzed Pacific island seem like an Eden. The damage is far greater than photographs can show."

In Burchett's report there were no footnotes and almost no quotes. He came to Hiroshima 'armed' with his pair of eyes and ears, with his camera and a tremendous urge to define and describe some of the most appalling chapters in contemporary human history.

That's how it was done in those days: journalism was a passionate activity, and a war correspondent had to be bright, brave and extremely quick. It was also expected from him or from her, to be independent.

Burchett was one of the best, maybe the best and he had to pay a very high price, as at one point he had been declared 'an enemy of the Australian people', even stripped of his passport. He wrote about the US atrocities against the people of Korea during the Korean War, about the US atrocities against its own soldiers (after being exchanged, those prisoners of war who had dared to speak about the humane treatment they received from their North Korean and Chinese captors, were often taken away, brainwashed, and even tortured). He also wrote about the courage of the Vietnamese people who fought for their freedom and ideals against the mightiest military power on Earth.

What is remarkable is that even as he had to live in exile, even as his children had to be born outside Australia because of the vicious political witch-hunt unleashed against him, in those days there were still many publications ready to print his extraordinary writing. There were periodicals and publishing houses commissioning his reports and books, and then publishing them and paying for his work.

It is obvious that in those days censorship was not as absolute and consolidated as it is now.

What is even more remarkable is that he did not have to constantly defend what his eyes saw and his ears heard. His work was original and ground-breaking. He was not forced to quote countless sources, indexing everything that he was going to publish. He was not asked to recycle others. He came to a place he wanted to describe, he spoke to people, got some important quotes, described the background, and then the story would get published.

There was no need to quote some 'Professor Green' saying that it was raining if Burchett knew and saw that it really was. No need for some 'Professor Brown' to confirm that the ocean water was salty or that the Earth was round.

It is impossible to write like this now. All individualism, all passion, and all intellectual courage has disappeared from mass media reporting and from a great majority of non-fiction books. There are almost no manifestos, and no *j'accuse*. Reports are restrained, made 'safe', 'inoffensive'. They don't provoke readers; don't send them to the barricades.

* * *

The mass media monopolizes the coverage of the most important, the most explosive topics of today: the wars, occupations and the horrors that billions of people of the world have to suffer as a result of our neo-colonialist regime and its market fundamentalism.

Independent reporters are not being hired, anymore. Those who are still around and working are well 'tested' and even then, the numbers are much smaller than several decades ago.

It all makes sense. The coverage of conflicts is at the core of the 'ideological battle' and the propaganda mechanism of the Western globally imposed regime is fully in control of it. Naturally it would be naïve to believe that the mainstream media and academia are not essential parts of the system.

To understand the world in depth, one has to be familiar with the plight and horrors of war and conflict zones. That's where colonialism and neo-colonialism show their awful and sharp teeth. And by conflict zones, I don't only mean the places that are bombed from the air and shelled by artillery. There are 'conflict zones' where tens of thousands, even millions of people are dying as a results of sanctions, misery or internal battles fueled from outside (like in the present day Syria).

In the past, the best coverage of such conflicts was done by independent reporters, most of them coming from the ranks of progressive writers and independent thinkers. The stories and images of the wars, coups and the plight of refugees were on the 'daily menu', served with eggs and cereals to the citizenry of the culprit countries.

At one point, thanks to the independent reporters, the public in the West was becoming increasingly aware of conditions around the world.

Citizens of the Empire (North America and Europe) were given no place to escape the reality. Top writers and intellectuals spoke on prime television and radio shows about the terror we were spreading around the world. Newspapers and magazines regularly bombarded the public with anti-establishment reports. Students and citizens who felt great solidarity with the victims (that was before they became too busy with Facebook, Twitter and other social media that has pacified them and made them shout at smart phones instead of trashing city centers) periodically marched, building barricades and fighting the security forces on the streets. Some, inspired by the reports they read and watched, travelled abroad, not just to hit beaches but to see with their own eyes the living conditions of the victims.

Countless independent reporters were Marxists but some were not. Many of them were brilliant, passionate and unapologetically political. Most of them never pretended to be 'objective' (in the sense implanted by today's Anglo-American mass media, which insists on quoting several 'diverse' sources, but suspiciously leads their stories to uniformed conclusions). They were mostly intuitively antagonistic to the Western imperialist regime.

As even then there was consistent flow of propaganda disseminated by well-paid (and therefore well disciplined) reporters and academics, the independent reporters, photographers and filmmakers heroically served the world by producing an 'alternative narrative'.

Among them there were people who decided to exchange their typewriters for weapons, as in the case of Antoine Exupery. There was Hemingway holed in Madrid, drunkenly damning Spanish Fascists in his reports, while later endorsing the Cuban Revolution and providing it with financial support. There was Andre Malraux who, while covering Indochina, managed to get arrested by the French colonial authorities and later launched an anti-colonialist magazine. There was Orwell and his intuitive disgust for colonialism and then there were the masters of war and conflict-zone journalism: Ryszard Kapuscinski, Wilfred Burchett and lately John Pilger.

There is one very important point to be made about them and about hundreds of the others: they were able to support themselves – they lived, travelled and worked – from the incomes their reports generated, no matter how anti-establishment their work had been. Writing great articles and books was a solid profession; in fact one of the most respected and exciting professions one could hope for. What they were doing was seen by society as an essential service to humanity. In those days they were not expected to teach or to do something else in order to survive.

* * *

Things definitely have changed in the last few decades!

Today it feels like we are living in a different universe when we read from the book of Ryszard Kapuscinski, The Soccer War.

It is 1960, Congo, previously plundered by its Belgian colonizers (it lost millions in the most brutal reign of King Leopold

II and afterwards) gains independence and Belgian paratroopers arrive: "the anarchy, the hysteria, the slaughter".

Kapuscinski was in Warsaw. He wanted to go (Poland gave him enough hard currency to travel) but he had a Polish passport and in yet more proof of the great Western love for freedom of speech and information, "everyone from socialist countries was being thrown out of the Congo". Kapuscinski flew to Cairo. He teamed up with the Czech journalist, Jarda Boucek. They decided to go via Khartoum and Juba:

> "...In Juba we will have to buy a car, and everything that will happen after that is a big question mark. The goal of the expedition is Stanleyville, the capital of the eastern province of the Congo, in which the Lumumba government has taken refuge (Lumumba himself has already been arrested and his friend Anoine Gizenga is leading the government). I watch as Jarda's index finger journeys up in Nile, stops briefly for a little tourism (here there is nothing but crocodiles; here the jungle begins), turns to the south-west, and arrives on the banks of the Congo river where the name 'Stanleyville' appears beside a little circle with a dot in it. I tell Jarda that I want to take part in this expedition and that I have official instructions to go to Stanleyville (which is a lie). He agrees, but warns me that I might pay for this journey with my life (which later turns to be close to the truth). He shows me a copy of his will, which he has deposited with his embassy. I am to do the same."

What this fragment of the book indirectly shows is that those two adventurous and brave reporters had full confidence in what was waiting back in their home countries (Poland and Czechoslovakia). They were following the most important story of the greatest African pro-independence figure, Patrice Lumumba, a man who had eventually been slaughtered by joint Belgian – US efforts. (Lumumba's assassination tossed Congo into hell, one that has lasted until the very day when this article is written). They were not sure that they would survive the journey, but they were confident that their work would be respected and enumerated. They had to risk their lives, use their ingenuity, and to write brilliantly. But the 'rest was taken care of'.

The same was true for Wilfred Burchett and to some extent, of several other brave reporters who dared to cover the Vietnam War independently, hitting hard at public conscience in Europe and North America, not allowing the passive mainstream of citizenry to later claim that 'they did not know'.

That era did not last forever. Mass media outlets and opinion-makers of the Empire eventually realized that this sort of writing is unacceptable as it only creates dissidents and people that will search for alternative angles and sources of information, in the end undermining the regime.

When I read Kapuscinski, I involuntarily think about my own work in DR Congo, in Rwanda and Uganda.

Once again, one of the most important stories in the world is taking place in Congo. 6 to 10 million people have already died a result of Western greed, and the unbridled obsession with controlling the world. The entire historical narrative has been twisted, and two appalling African dictatorships fully supported by the US and UK are murdering and plundering Congo on behalf of the West and its companies.

Whenever I risk my life there, whenever I thrown into some hole from which I know I may never leave, I know there is no 'home base' waiting for me or backing me up. I get out because of some UN ID, because of some impressive (to my captors, but not to me) piece of accreditation. My work as an investigative journalist or a filmmaker guarantees nothing. I am not sent by anybody. Nothing is paid. I am on my own.

When Kapuscinski used to return home, he was welcomed as a hero. Half a century later, those of us who do the same work are nothing more than outcasts.

* * *

At one point, most of the major newspapers and magazines, as well as television channels, stopped relying on brave, mildly insane and independent 'freelancers'. They went on a hiring spree, turning reporters into corporate employees. Once this 'transition' had been achieved, it was extremely easy to convey to the 'employees' still called 'journalists' how to cover the events, what to write and what to avoid. Often nothing had to be said in detail – corporate staff is known to behave intuitively.

Funds for hiring independent writers, photographers or producers on freelance basis were cut drastically. Or they disappeared altogether.

Many starved freelancers were forced to apply for jobs. Others began writing books, hoping to keep the information flowing. But very soon they were told that 'these days there is no money in books, either'. The best was to apply for 'teaching jobs'.

Several universities were still absorbing and tolerant to some degree of intellectual dissent, but the price they 'charged' was steep: former revolutionaries and dissidents could teach but were allowed no emotional outbursts, no manifestos, and no calls to arms. They had to 'stick to the facts' (the way the facts were now customarily presented); they had to begin recycling the thoughts of their 'influential' colleagues, to overburden their books with quotes, indexes, and indigestible over-intellectualized pirouettes.

And by then we were already entering the internet era. Thousands of sites popped-up but many great alternative and Left-wing paper publications had to close down. After a few years of enthusiasm and hopes, it became clear that the regime and its mass media had consolidated control over the brains of the public with the help of the internet, not despite it. Main search engines implanted mainstream right-wing news agencies onto their front pages. Unless the individual really knew what he or she was looking for, unless he or she was very educated and very determined, there was very little hope in just stumbling over opposition coverage or interpretation of the world and local events.

Now, most in-depth articles have to be written with no funding, as if writing them has become some sort of a hobby.The glory of war correspondence is over, the grandeur of the adventure called the "search for truth", gone, all that has been replaced with hipness and 'lightness', social networking, entertainment.

The bliss of 'lightness' was at first reserved only for those in the driving seat – for the citizens of the Empire and for the outrageously corrupt (the West's doing) elites in faraway colonies. Needless to say, the majority of the world has still been submerged in an extremely 'heavy' reality, mostly living in shantytowns serving colonial economic interests, surviving in brutal dictatorships implanted mercilessly and then sadistically sustained by Washington, London or Paris.

But eventually, even many of those dying in the slums of Southeast Asia and Africa have been successfully injected with the "lightness", with the entertainment drug, and with absolute spite for serious analyses of their own condition.

* * *

Those few independent writers that were still left fighting – the war correspondents educated on the works of Burchett and Kapuscinski – were losing both the audience and the means to perform their work.

Practically, to cover wars, to cover real conflicts, is extremely expensive, especially if they are to be covered thoroughly. One has to deal with unreasonably pricey tickets on chartered or erratic flights, with heavy professional equipment, with bribes one has to spread in order to get anywhere near the action, with constant changes of plans, and with delays. One has to arrange visas and permits. One has to communicate and once in a while one gets injured.

Access is now much more controlled than in the days of the Vietnam War. While I still managed to get myself to the front line in Sri Lanka some ten years ago, it would be unthinkable in the latter years of the conflict. Although I had been successfully smuggling myself into East Timor in 1996, those independent reporters who are now trying to sneak in to Papua where Indonesia – a great partner in crime of the West – is perpetrating yet another genocide, are regularly arrested, imprisoned and deported.

In 1992 when I covered the war in Peru, once I got my accreditation from the Ministry of Foreign Affairs, it was basically up to me whether I wanted to stay in Lima or to risk my life and drive to Ayacucho, fully aware that the military or *Sendero Luminoso* could choose to blow my brains out on the way (which once actually almost happened).

But in these days to enter Iraq or Afghanistan, or any place that is occupied by US and European forces would be close to impossible, especially if the aim was to investigate crimes against humanity committed by the Western regime.

Frankly: these days it is hardly possible to get anywhere, unless you are what they call it 'embedded' (actually a very colorful but correct description: you let 'them' do it to you and 'they' let you write, as long as you write what 'they' tell you). To be allowed to cover the war a reporter would have to be mainstream; with some powerful organization covering his or her back, getting required accreditations and passes, and vouching for the writer's output. Independent reporters are considered unpredictable and they are therefore unwelcome.

There is a way to sneak in to several conflict zones. Those of us with years of experience know how to do it. But imagine that you are 'on your own', that you are volunteering, writing almost for free. Unless you are independently wealthy and willing to spend it all on your own writing, you better analyze things 'from a distance'. And that's exactly what the regime wanted to achieve: no first-hand reports from the Left. Only 'rambling' from far away.

* * *

As if the bureaucratic and institutional barriers erected by the regime were not sufficient enough to prevent some hardened independent reporters (from those few who are still around) from visiting the conflict areas, the financial constraints are always ready to kick in: almost no one outside the mainstream media is able to match the fees for drivers, fixers and interpreters that have been inflated by the corporate media operating on expense accounts.

The results are clear: the opposition to the neo-colonialist regime is losing the media war as it is unable to bring reporting from places where the Empire is continuously committing genocides and crimes against humanity, to the wider public. As we established earlier, of recent there has been no unceasing flow of images and dispatches that should bombard the millions in culprit nations – a flow similar to the one that managed to outrage and shock the public, and stopped the Vietnam War several decades ago.

The consequences are shocking. European and North American public are generally unaware of even the most appalling horrors that are taking place around the world. One of them is the brutal genocide that is taking place against the people of DR Congo. Another is the terrible destabilization campaign against Somalia; with almost one million refugees literally rotting in overcrowded camps in Kenya (I recently made a 70 minute documentary film "One Flew Over Dadaab" on the topic).

There are hardly any words available to describe the cynicism of the Israeli occupation of Palestine, but the US public is fed with 'objective' reports and is therefore 'pacified'.

While the propaganda machine is being unleashed against all countries that stand firm against Western colonialism – China, Russia, Cuba, Venezuela to name just a few – the crimes against humanity committed by the West and its allies (including Uganda,

Rwanda, Indonesia, India, Philippines, Colombia and many others) go unreported.

Millions are displaced; hundreds of thousands are killed, due to the Western geopolitical maneuvers in the Middle East, Africa and elsewhere. Very little had been reported on the disgraceful destruction of Libya in 2011 (and on the terrible aftermath) and on the way the West has been working tirelessly to overthrow the government in Syria.

There is hardly any reporting on how Turkish 'refugee camps' on the Syrian border are actually used to feed, train and arm the Syrian opposition, a fact well-documented by several leading Turkish journalists and filmmakers. Needless to say, for independent Western reporters such camps are off-limits, as my colleagues in Istanbul explained to me recently.

* * *

While there are several great publications like CounterPunch, "Z" and the New Left Review, those thousands of 'displaced' independent war correspondents should have more domiciles they could call 'home' or an 'institutional home'.

They are great assets, great potential guns and ammunition in the fight against imperialism and neo-colonialism. That's why the regime has made sure to sideline them, to make their work irrelevant.

But without their knowledge, no objective analyses of the present global conditions are possible. Without their reports and images, both victims and victimizers would not be able to understand the depth of insanity into which the world has been thrown.

Without them, as millions of human lives are being lost and billions of lives ruined, the citizenry of the Empire could possibly still be dying of laughter in their entertainment parlors and with their electronic gadgets in hand, once again fully ignoring the terrible smoke coming from proverbial funnels. And in the future, if confronted, they would be able to say again, as they have done so many times in history: "We didn't know".

16 March 2012

3

The Perfect Fascist City

TAKE A TRAIN IN JAKARTA

If you take a train in Jakarta, be warned: the images that will unwind outside your windows could be too disturbing to bear for someone who is not a war correspondent or a medical doctor. It will often feel as if hundreds of thousands of the wretched of the earth decided to camp along the tracks, as if garbage from the entire East Asia had been dumped along the rails, as if hell had really materialized here on earth, instead of threatening us from some imaginary religious realm.

From the unwashed windows of the train you will see people suffering from all imaginable diseases. You would probably spot exposed wounds, faces burned by fires, terrible hernias, untreated tumors and omnipresent swollen bellies of children suffering from malnutrition. And there would also be some ailments and deformities that are simply too terrible to describe or to photograph.

Jakarta, the capital city of a country hailed by the Western mainstream media as 'democratic', 'tolerant' and 'the largest economy in Southeast Asia', is actually a place where the majority of the population has absolutely no control over its future. On closer inspection it becomes evident that the city is stuck with social indicators that are more common in Sub-Saharan Africa than in East Asia. And the place is increasingly violent and intolerant towards religious and national minorities as well as those who are demanding social justice. It takes great discipline not to notice.

Slavoj Zizek, Slovenian philosopher, once wrote in his book *The Violence*:

> "Here we encounter the Lacanian difference between reality and the Real: 'reality' is the social reality of the actual people involved in interaction and in the productive processes, while the Real is the inexorable 'abstract', spectral logic of capital that determines what goes on in social reality. One can experience this gap in a palpable way when one visits a country where life is obviously in shambles. We see a lot of ecological decay and human misery. However, The Economist's report that one reads afterwards, informs us that the country's economic situation is 'financially sound' – reality doesn't matter, what matters is the situation of capital..."

Indonesian capital and its elites are doing well, although exactly at a price of the country being in shambles. But let's go back to the trains.

I decided to take the commuter rail, from Manggarai Station to the suburban city of Tangerang (the same place which, just a few years ago, unconstitutionally but with absolute impunity imposed Sharia Law on its population), for one simple reason: to see whether there was any real progress in 'fighting' against what many describe as the imminent collapse of Jakarta's infrastructure, alas final gridlock.

The gridlock, like everything in Indonesia, has its colorful history:

Since 1965 (the year of the brutal US-backed military coup which brought General Suharto to power and took between 800,000 and 3 million lives. Those murdered were the leftists, intellectuals, people of the Chinese minority, unionists and atheists as well, or simply those who had a more beautiful wife, a better plot of land or fatter cow) the government worked hard to make sure that Indonesian cities would have no public transportation, no sizeable parks and no sidewalks. Public places in general were considered very dangerous, as that is where the people used to gather discussing 'subversive' issues like their plans for the country.

Public parks were taken away from the people by 'developers' who built their private golf courses for the elites. Sidewalks had to go, too, as they were not profitable and 'too social'. And the public transportation became private and eventually got reduced to polluting minivans and appalling second hand Indian Bajaj rickshaws that haven't even run for decades in India.

And that was in Jakarta. Other cities with 1 to 2 million inhabitants like Palembang, Surabaya, Medan and Bandung have had no public transportation whatsoever, apart from dirty and tiny minivans and dozens of dilapidated, rusty and smelly buses.

That was of course the plan: car manufacturers were regurgitating old Japanese car models, selling them at inflated prices (cars in Indonesia sell for 50 to 120 percent higher prices than in the United States), forcing the people of Indonesia – some of the poorest in East Asia – to buy their own private vehicles. Cars were the first to be inserted, followed by dangerous, environmentally fatal and inefficient scooters that are actually banned in all major Chinese cities and in many other Asian ones.

Government officials and People's Representatives (DPR) have been having their palms greased by the car industry, quietly but consistently. The car lobby became extremely powerful, blocking all attempts to improve rail and maritime travel between the various ports in Java, the most overpopulated major island in the world.

On 14th August 2011, the Jakarta Post reported:

> "Indonesian Democratic Party of Struggle member Nusyirwan Soedjono, a deputy chairman of House of Representatives' Commission V overseeing transportation affairs, has long questioned the government's reluctance to allocate more state funding for the improvement of the country's railway network, blaming its submission to "high-level" political lobbying arranged by the automotive industry, which has received direct advantages from the rapid development of the country's road infrastructure.
>
> There has been no story of us [the Commission V] rejecting the government's budget proposal for developing railway infrastructure," Nusyirwan told The Jakarta Post. "But it seems like there have been certain 'powerful groups' which always oppose every attempt to advance the services of our mass transportation, especially trains."

As they would in any extreme fascist or feudal society, 'elites' have been enjoying their chauffeured limousines, while the poor have been breaking their legs when falling into open sewers, getting raped and air-poisoned in private, dreadful and unregulated minivans, or risking having their brains spilled on uneven pavements after frustrating maneuvers on their scooters between aggressively-driven cars and trucks.

With impunity and impressive consistency, Jakarta has been stripped of almost all public spaces, while it became clear that the government was becoming increasingly unmotivated, incompetent, overfed and lazy, and determined to block all long-term solutions.

The total length of the rail tracks has actually shrank since Dutch colonial power; Jakarta became the only city of its size (over 10 million inhabitants, more during the weekdays) in the world without any type of a mass rapid transportation system.

A few years ago there was a feeble attempt to build two lines for an urban monorail, not the most efficient mass public system to begin with. Streets were blocked, dust and dirt everywhere, citizens were asked to be patient as this was 'being built for them,' although not really, as this was going to be a for-profit transportation system.

The project was given to a private consortium and then, predictably, the public money had been embezzled. Construction stopped without any warning, leaving ugly concrete piles sticking up in the middle of avenues. No heads were seen rolling as a result of that scandalous fraud and the press remained predictably disciplined, reporting only what was officially declared, which is always the case when too much money gets robbed by those who are 'too important to be disturbed' by investigations.

To be fair, there were other attempts to save Jakarta: for instance the introduction of so-called water taxis on the hopelessly polluted canals. But floating objects easily broke the engines of these primitive and unattractive open dinghies plus the stench from the surface of the canals that are permanently covered by a thick and consistent layer of garbage and toxic substances was so repulsive, that the 'project' was scrambled after only several weeks.

The East Flood Canal was supposed to change everything, to revolutionize the entire approach to public works and to bring about the development of the city to at least that of the basic Asian standard of the 21st century. For decades, Jakarta has been suffering from epic floods; sometimes two thirds of the city would find itself under water, the result of clogged canals, annihilated green areas and unbridled over-development. A decision was finally made to acquire land and to dig a canal that could take the excessive water out to the sea. It was promised that there would be public parks or at least some pathways along the shores. Romantics even dreamed about bicycle lanes and promenades, and there were calls for water transport and, how daring (!), tramlines.

Those who were still harboring some hopes for Jakarta were to experience an extremely hard landing. In 2010 and 2011, as work on the canal was still far from completion, the reality began to surface.

Construction quality was truly appalling and even before the work was near finishing stage; garbage had already covered the entire length of the project. And then came the shock: the government obviously had no plan to place any public transportation on the banks of the canal. In fact it made sure (as always) to steer away from building any "evil" public areas. Strips of land were as recently as the beginning of 2012, converted into yet another set of roads that were immediately reclaimed by the polluting and noisy scooters. As yet unfinished (although officially it is already operational), the entire canal looks just too familiar a hybrid of a spontaneously created garbage dump and the wet dream of the scooter/car lobby.

Along all those wasted square kilometers of urban space (although officially the administration calls it a true success) there is not even a tiny path for people to walk on, not one single playground for children.

How do the officials manage to survive in position after such evident fiascos and after betraying and robbing their own people? After all what the city administration allowed to happen, in most circumstances would be considered 'treason' in several other countries in Asia.

The answer is: in 'democratic Indonesia' there is no accountability. There is none; zero, zip! Corruption is endemic and the citizens have no mechanism to organize protest (obsession with social networks like Facebook is mainly for status reasons only, as well as for empty chat: even the murder of people of different beliefs by hard-line religious cadres does not bring 'educated and middle class' people onto the streets).

It feels that the entire nation, including its capital, gave up a long time ago. People are just living their lives in this monstrous megacity, and not even bothering to demand, to protest or to complain.

Of course in Indonesia complaining leads nowhere, letters addressed to the DPR go unanswered, even unopened, while letters to the press get published only if they stay within undefined but intuitively understood limits. 'Projects' are not open for debate (too much money is often involved and the government and private companies divide the loot among themselves in accordance with well established rules and formulas) and would never risk allowing the system to be endangered by the interference of the citizens): the people are simply informed (once in a while) about what is going to be built; when and where. If money disappears, as it does with predictable consistency, there are no repercussions. If plans 'change' or if schedules are not kept, nobody is held responsible.

Indonesia is a perfect dictatorship with periodically-held elections (the electorate can choose freely between either corrupt candidates with business interests or other corrupt candidates with business interests): a leader in the new breed of countries controlled and sponsored by Western interests with absolutely no power given to the people.

Passengers who would fall through the rusty floors of trains to their death or those who fall through unmarked holes that are to be found all over the city get no apology, let alone compensation.

When asked to compare Indonesia and China, Professor Dadang M. Maksoem, a former lecturer at UPM (University Putra Malaysia), who now works for the government of West Java, got furious: "Very simple: they [the Chinese] are committed to doing their best for their nation. There is no dedication like that here. How come, in this part of the world, governments can't even provide decent public transportation? People are forced to buy their own motorcycles in order to transport themselves – forced to risk their lives, having terrible accidents. Now there are traffic gridlocks everywhere. You can say that our system is stupid, idiotic, brain-dead, or greedy. Just go on and fill the gap!"

But that's not what one reads in the Western mainstream

media. Officially the West admires Indonesia. How could it not: Indonesian rulers and its servile elites sacrificed their own people, their own islands, even their own capital city for the goods and profits of Western multi-national companies and imperial geopolitical interests. Which foreign corporation or government would not appreciate such a generosity?

But once again, back to public transportation.

Around the time when the administration and the private sector were flirting with the construction of the monorail (or at least they told the people that they were), the city began to build so called 'busways'; projects based on an absolutely misunderstood concept of the public transportation project of the city of Bogota in far away South American Columbia.

Instead of building a heavy-duty train system, Jakarta slashed off two lanes from some major thoroughfares and supplied locally and very badly made narrow busses where passengers sit on either side of the aisle facing each other. Each bus had only one door. Monstrous stations were made of metal sheets that were rusting and full of holes. Most of the automatic platform doors have broken down and many people ended up being pushed out onto the road and to their deaths or serious injuries.

As with anything else in Jakarta, the system is not designed to improve the life of ordinary citizens; in this case to ease traffic congestion and to move millions of people in safety and comfort. It is structured as a 'project' designed to enrich private companies that share their profits with corrupt officials.

The busway system is inefficient, aesthetically unacceptable and it is actually not helping to connect the city – it is fragmenting it further. There are hardly any sidewalks adjacent to the stations. People arriving at the stop have to risk their lives reaching their homes walking through streets congested with traffic, or by other means of transportation.

Even if the busway stops are near the train stations, planners make sure that there is no direct connectivity. For decades, Jakarta's rulers made sure to disconnect all transportation structures, including the Dutch-era train stations from the rest of the city. The city has almost no sidewalks, almost no underpasses (there is just one in the whole city, near 'Kota', that took several years to build and which has already began to resemble a hellhole long before its completion) linking the stations to the avenues. Not that Jakarta actually has many avenues – most of them were converted into terrible poor replicas of Houstonian suburban throughways: with elevated and surface highways, almost no walkways, services fenced and separated from one another.

The stupidity of the city planning can be only matched by the idiocy of the development of the country as a whole – Jakarta is a microcosm. To make a U-turn, one has to often drive for one kilometer or more, adding to traffic jams, fuel consumption and pollution. But the city is designed in such a way, that one has to often drive even in order to cross the street, as there are hardly any passable sidewalks or street crossings. Nothing is connected here and no matter what, one has to use a car or the increasingly 'popular' cheap polluting scooter (locals wishfully call them 'motorbikes') and then rot in "macet" – the legendary traffic jam – as the car lobby has managed to buy and corrupt several layers of the government, and as a result forming resistance to the construction of any efficient public transportation network.

There are clearly many financial interests involved. To analyze Indonesia, it is necessary to remember that 'normal' considerations and moral principles have long disappeared from the lexicon of the rulers.

A small group of business people and politicians here have already plundered most of the country's natural resources; they have destroyed rainforests and turned this vast archipelago into an environmental disaster. The majority of Indonesians have never come close to sharing any of the profits earned from the destruction of their country.

Jakartans are no exception. The city is being developed 'against its people', as was noted by a significant Australian artist, George Burchett, who had visited it more than two years ago.

The population is uninformed and phlegmatic after decades of a pro-business brainwashing campaign and after the destruction of inquisitive thought in this city, that at this point in time has no art cinemas, permanents theatres, a socially-oriented press or art galleries specializing in unveiling Indonesia's tragedy through art. Instead, billions of bits of social rubbish fly from one Blackberry to another: elites chat and listen to outdated pop music, stuffing themselves on Western and Japanese junk food. There is not much else to do. In the meantime, the city is collapsing, blanketed in poisonous fumes, with enormous slums filling the space between giant but repetitive malls and office buildings. There is no water in its once glorious canals – just toxicity.

The most horrifying aspect is that there seems to be no space for people. People have become irrelevant. Even children: no playgrounds, no parks. Even poor Port Moresby, the capital of PNG does incomparably more for its citizens.

"To hell with your aid!" shouted President Sukarno publicly at the US ambassador, more than half a century ago. A terrible vendetta promptly ensued. After the US-sponsored coup that brought in a fascist regime that has held the reigns of power until this very day, Jakarta was changed into a "To hell with the people!" kind of place.

"When I come to Jakarta, I don't want to leave the house", explains Nabila Wibowo, the daughter of an Indonesian diplomat. She decided to stay in Portugal after her mother's posting came to an end. "There is no culture here, no concerts, and no good music. I can't even walk or move around the city. There are no sidewalks. I just stay for some time, locked in my room, and read my books".

Now the city is 'threatening' to build MRT, a subway system that is expected to have two lines upon completion. The project had been postponed for decades, but if it finally goes ahead, many analysts including some ITB (Bandung Institute of Technology) professors are too terrified to even imagine what the results will be, considering the track record of the city authorities and the quality of other transportation projects all over the country.

It is most likely that the money will be allocated and then embezzled again. In Indonesia there is absolutely no mechanism to guarantee transparency and impartial supervision. That's in a striking contrast to other complex countries like India where the New Delhi subway system was actually built on time and below the original estimated cost.

It appears that the embezzlement of public funds is a profession staffed by the most talented people of Indonesia. This is where the city and the country hold the world premier spot.

There is no serious pressure from the public to stop this madness. Nowadays the public is used to choking and dying prematurely from pollution, living in slums without clean water and basic sanitation, and sitting in endless traffic jams. The majority of the people of Jakarta have never left the country and therefore do not know that a 'different world is possible', that there are actually cities built for the people, not against them. Elites that travel know reality very well, but do not reveal it.

The vicious cycle is omnipresent: new projects are announced, then launched, and finally scrambled after enough pockets get filled. People are left with nothing and don't even demand anything. It had been like that, to a greater or lesser extent, during feudal times and during the Dutch colonial administration. Although before passing away, the greatest Indonesian writer Pramoedya Ananta Toer told me "the situation was never as bad as it is now."

Those who know or should know what is going on behind the scenes are either complicit in it, or simply refuse to face the reality.

In February 2012 I asked Ms Ririn Soedarsono, a professor at the prestigious ITB, whether the MRT project has any chance of being completed.

"We will start building MRT this year", she replied. "By the end of 2013 the first phase will be completed. Technically there should be no problem. But I don't know what the political climate will be..."

2013? Even in technologically-developed countries like Japan, China or Chile, one subway line could easily take between 4 to 10 years to construct, depending on the terrain. But maybe I misunderstood the 'first phase' definition.

Trains are still better in Jakarta than in Nairobi, some are even air-conditioned, as they come imported second-hand from Japan, but they tend to deteriorate rapidly due to lack of maintenance: a year in Jakarta, a 30 year-old Japanese train that has arrived in perfect condition will end up having its doors broken, seats slashed and air-conditioning system clogged with dirt.

"We go by train twice a week", explain Ms. Enny and Ms. Susie from Bogor. "It's unbearable during the weekdays, especially during peak hours. It is almost impossible to find a space to stand. It is quite scary and traumatic, especially for us, women, especially when passengers scramble in hordes, fighting to enter the car."

The superiority of Jakarta's trains over those in Nairobi, the capital of one of the poorest nations on earth and another 'capitalist democratic miracle' may not last for long. By the beginning of 2013, Nairobi is poised to finish renovating its rail tracks and to put into service the first modern line, followed by the second one in 2014. The stations will come with parking lots, shops and modern facilities, connecting neighborhoods inhabited by the middle-class and the poor.

Chinese construction firms that are involved in building highways, overpasses and other infrastructural projects in East Africa are also constructing sidewalks, rail tracks and within two years are planning to connect Jomo Kenyatta International Airport with the Nairobi rail network. The collapsing Sukarno Hatta Airport on the outskirts of Jakarta has been waiting for a rapid rail service for decades but so far only got extra lanes of highway.

One question that comes logically to one's mind is: could Indonesia be so far behind places like Cairo, Nairobi, Johannesburg and Lagos or is something else going on? Could it be possible that the Indonesian elites are actually sacrificing tens of millions of people for their own profits? They have done it before: could they be doing it again?

Along the tracks, half-naked dirty children and infants play in garbage and open sewers. Rubbish is burnt here in the open, as Jakarta doesn't have a comprehensive waste-management system. Garbage collection and its management is by definition a public service, therefore is nothing that would make profits and excite the officials. Only a fraction of Jakarta resident's has access to truly clean water, and only 30 percent to basic sanitation.

It is living hell all around the train cars that slowly make their way from one monstrous station to another.

Read the Indonesian press that has perfected its art of deception and you would think that there is at least some basic rail system already in place, in need of serious improvement but in place, nevertheless. You can even find some maps of the 'system' on the internet. But try to reach a station, try to use the network, and you would be forced to have many second thoughts about its existence as a dignified transportation option.

There are no schedules and no information. Unreceptive, slow and inefficient employees sell tickets manually. To get to a platform is dangerous. But despite everything, it is mainly the Indonesian middle-class that rides the trains.

The middle-class as it is locally defined are, using the definition of the World Bank and Indonesian government, according to whom, are those who live on more than US$2.00 a day. And that applies even to the city, which is by many standards one of the most expensive in East Asia.

According to that calculus, the 'middle class' forms the majority of the city in Jakarta. A great part of it lives in what would be considered elsewhere as 'slums'. Some of its members don't have access to clean water; most of them live in unacceptable hygienic conditions.

Some members of Jakarta's 'middle class' ride on the roofs of the trains because they can't afford the train fare; several people get electrocuted each year, others fall to their deaths. To keep them off the roofs, the compassionate government began hanging concrete balls above the tracks to break their skulls, as well as spraying them with colors, and even with excrement. Several stations, including Manggarai, attached razorwire to the ceilings of the platform, so that people who tried to jump off the roof would get shredded.

Herry Suheri – a cigarette seller at Manggarai Station does not think people will be deterred by all those drastic measures: "There are still people riding on the roofs of economy trains, especially during the peak hours. And it is not only about the free ride. There are simply not enough trains to accommodate people who have to get home or to work."

The train system, the 'green areas', the 'plan to improve the city' – everything is fake, an imaginary world of deceptions. The reality is brutal but clear: Jakarta does not fall under any definition of a city. It is a laboratory, an experiment of market fundamentalism. Guinea pigs are people. They are being studied: how much discomfort can they take, how much of an unhealthy environment, and what doses of depressing vistas would it take to make them finally run away?

For now, all hopes for Jakarta should be abandoned. 'The most unlivable major city in Asia-Pacific' will not improve, not anytime soon, not in the foreseeable future, not under this administration and this regime.

In South America the right-wingers used to shout: "Jakarta is Coming!" to frighten left-wing governments in Chile and elsewhere in the world. Jakarta is now here, in its full glory; a monument to unbridled capitalism; the monster, the warning, and a case study for those who want to understand how low the elites will sink in their overwhelming greed and selfishness.

17 February 2012

*****

4

The Electronic Menace

IN DEFENSE OF PAPER BOOKS

Do not trust them when they repeatedly tell you that the era of paper books is ending, that they are soon to become as obsolete as vinyl records or coal-fired train-engines. Books, printed on paper and sold in bookstores, have been our best friends for many centuries. They have educated billions of people worldwide, they have strengthened resistance, and have made people dream about better political and economic systems. There would have been no revolution without them, no intellectual development, and no deep understanding of the world.

Fascist dictators – from German Nazis to the Indonesian cronies who took power after the Western-sponsored coup of 1965 – were known to burn books, publicly and shamelessly. To them the books stank of progress, of the aim for social justice, and of the 'nightmare', the specter, of egalitarian societies.

Of course, not all books have been written and published for the purpose of educating the masses, calling for revolution, or exposing inequalities. There are the memoirs of people like Henry Kissinger as well as countless volumes on the economic theories of Milton Friedman, Friedrich von Hayek and their ilk calling for the implementation of market fundamentalism and its global dictatorship. There are even books written by people who were mass murderers, such as Adolf Hitler. But this generalized formula is probably indisputable: more books, more knowledge, more desire for progress and therefore better societies.

Now we are being told that the era of paper books is over, that in a few decades we should not even hope to have books as we have known them, which have helped to shape our lives. We are being warned to get ready for life without books.

* * *

I was sitting in one of Bangkok's cafes, staring at the slow flow of the Chao Phraya River, watching its fascinating old barges and long-tail boats. I had been typing a new chapter for my 1,000 page long political novel, "Winter Journey", which brings together stories about the countless slaughters and genocides performed by the 'Western Democracies' after WWII, acts, which according to my rough calculations, have taken approximately 45 million human lives worldwide, and probably many more.

At one point, my eyes fell on a copy of the International Herald Tribune and on an article titled "The bookstore's battle for survival", written by Julie Bossman.

I put my computer aside and began reading. Not only did it spoil my day, but it led to an incredible outburst of anger of which this commentary is the result.

It was not just what I read that shocked me, but also the tone of the piece. It was projecting an Orwellian inevitability, a total lack of options being given to the people of the world on this issue. Obviously, whether traditionally printed books will survive much longer, is not just a battle between corporations such as Amazon.com and Barnes & Noble. We are reminded, subliminally but powerfully, that it is big business that dictates how we should live, what we should consume and how we should think.

Living far away from the Western epicenters of corporate terror, I often forget how undemocratic Europe and North

America has really become and how submissive, how obedient their population is nowadays. Encounters with logic like that described in the article bring me face to face with reality.

Have we gone mad? Are we going to see and watch while some private companies dismante the intellectual fabric that has for centuries helped our societies to move forward? Are we going to entrust out intellectual future to the corporate minds of Amazon or Barnes & Noble, to allow them to decide what we read and how?

* * *

I actually left the Empire in 1996. I used to live on the Upper West Side in New York. All around me the old services and eateries were collapsing, giving way to chain outlets like Starbucks and GAP. The last blow came when the grand old Shakespeare & Company had to close down, giving way to yet another Barnes & Noble. I lost my interest in chain culture. I threw my computer and clothes into the trunk of my car and moved permanently to Merida, Yucatan, Mexico, and from there later on to Santiago de Chile.

And now it appears that Barnes & Noble that sharked everything around is now itself being eaten by a tremendous barracuda with a limitless appetite.

Julie Bossman writes in her piece from Palo Alto:

> "...Barnes & Noble, the giant that had helped put so many independent booksellers out of business, now finds itself locked in the fight of its life. What its engineers dreamed up was the Nook, a relative latecomer among e-readers that has nonetheless become the great e-hope of Barnes & Noble and, in fact, of many in the book business."

Seriously? So the chain book-store giant that made me leave my home is now taking an enormous and horrid step further – it's going electronic!

Sure, there is always a justification. Julie Bossman continues:

> "...Lurking behind all of this is Amazon, the dominant force in books online and the company that sets teeth on edge in publishing. From their perches in New York, many publishing executives, editors and publicists view Amazon as the enemy – an adversary that, if unchecked, could threaten their industry and their livelihoods."

What follows are business analyses, the stock prices, business appetites and trends. There are no moral, philosophical or educational issues addressed in the article. It is as if the people in the US and Europe have been fully surrendered to the markets, and as if the people have no other choice but to sit and wait while the corporate giants decide on how they should be given their information.

I really don't want to live in such a world, I don't, but that's not the point. What matters is that the West is eventually going to export its business concepts all over the world, as it always does. If bookstores close down in London, Paris and New York, the chances are that the new 'trend' will be pushed down the throats of the people in Kuala Lumpur, Johannesburg, Buenos Aires and elsewhere. And readers will have little choice in what they hold. And that matters to me.

What appears to be truly at stake here is definitely much more than the pathetic bottom lines of some corporate brethren. The chase for profits could deeply, irreversibly and negatively affect one of the most important and noble of human activities: the entire culture of reading and of learning. How could such principal decisions be left to a bunch of businessmen in their corporate institutions?

In many cultures, and particularly in some of the most educated ones, such as Cuba, Venezuela and China, books are not only 'protected', their publishing is actually subsidized by the state. And subsidized it should be. Like education and health, book publishing and distribution should be a basic public service. Books can't be and should not be only for profit.

Public parks and sidewalks are also 'unprofitable'. Of course in some countries, such as Indonesia, where Jakarta and other cities have implemented a virtually absolute western market-regime, such 'unnecessary' entities have almost completely disappeared. But is this what we want: a world without parks and forests, without sidewalks and public places, without books? Have we totally surrendered ourselves to corporate terror?

You see – if we allow business to take over everything, there will soon be nothing worth living for. We would be reduced to being pre-programmed robotic consumers, locked in efficient, air-conditioned and ultimately sterile malls, watching never-ending soap operas on television, eating and drinking pre-digested factory-produced meals made from floor scraps, reading computer-generated 'novels' and comic strips, watching movies with computer-generated plots. We would never be without our music-storing, camera-toting 'smart phones', headphones permanently jammed on our ears, listening to the same copyright-protected, mass-produced synthesized voices and rhythms!

Yet such a society, attempting to change the global system to its own ends, is self-defeating in that it is failing to understand, to deplore and to prevent the atrocities it is committing, atrocities which are reducing the number of potential consumers.

I can offer a good example from my 'field of expertise'. I am making a documentary film on the massacres in Congo committed by our proxies. To date, between six to ten million people have died, just so we can stick the rare earth Coltan (columbite-tantalite) in our mobile phones, and so we can also have access to uranium. Our business interests murdered those people, although the killing itself has been done predominantly by two vicious (but friendly to the West) African dictatorships.

In spite of the number of articles and books published about this, how many people in Europe or in the United States know about this? Now imagine that there were to be no books by Naomi Klein or John Pilger or by others like them. It would be back to the days of Joseph Conrad, back to the free reign of unchecked colonialism.

Maybe that's the plan!

How dandy: we would all be reading the same books, approved by the regime: on the screens of Nooks and iPads, and other similar gadgets. And of course there would be no dissident literature, no samizdat, as samizdat would be brutally crushed; not by the state but by copyright laws and electronic surveillance.

This would take some time. We would first be told that we would get a greater choice this way. But then, after they put all bookstores out of commission, there would suddenly be no choice, just pre-selected, mainstream, brain-numbing, 'one style lobotomizes all' pop.

Would you like to live in a world where you have to give away your complete personal information just in order to 'download' books by Hemingway or Sartre?

And once the electronic publishing companies possess all the electronic rights for all books and once there is no more paper book publishing – and you know that once electronic publishers get their hands on the rights, they will copyright everything and then ensure that there are no conventional publishing houses left – they will be able to decide what you are able to, and should read!

Diversity? For a sneak preview, consider iTunes. Log on and try to order Soviet Red Army Choir tracks or tunes from some off beat but great tango club in Buenos Aires, try to stock up on brilliant bands from the Congo or Zanzibar, or Chinese and Indian classical music. You can't? So you verge on being a criminal as you are forced to download illegal programs just to convert the music that you bought earlier, so it can actually play on your iPhone. But even then you can't use it as your own ringtone.

The music industry, hand in hand with electronic manufacturers, has turned hundreds of millions of those in Europe and North America who would probably be listening to 'rebellious', 'revolutionary' or 'opposition' music into pop music junkies. They have actually managed to do the same to people in Southeast Asia. Do you really and honestly want the same to happen with books?

Do you think, if the companies have their say, you would in the future be able to read those rebellious books by Noam Chomsky, or by Michael Parenti, or even by me? Do you think that once I finish my 1,000 page novel encouraging resistance against market fundamentalist and the Western neo-colonialist regime now controlling the world, it would be sold in Nook-compatible format? Think twice!

Once Barnes & Noble, Amazon or whoever 'wins', and decides what should be published and read, the book publishing industry would end up just like our great Western propaganda-regurgitating mass media. It would be totally monopolistic in manufacturing a vision of the world. As the propaganda machine already controls the media, film production and distribution, as well as music, books are the last loopholes, the only real opportunity to learn the truth.

I will never forget a conversation I had some ten years ago in New Delhi with Sudhanva Deshpande, the publisher of the "Left Word". Sudhanva with his mischievous smile stood next to the printing press in one of the slums and proudly explained: "We make our books very durable. We actually make them so durable that people can copy them at least ten times on a copier machine, page by page." I still consider this the greatest statement I have ever heard from any publisher.

I keep thinking about those gigantic bookstores, fully subsidized, in all the major Chinese cities; I have found much more political diversity on the shelves there than in the Barnes & Noble shop which I recently visited in a middle-class suburb of Chicago.

I also think about the bookstores in Venezuela, where all great works of poetry and classical literature are sold for just a few cents. Every year the government distributes millions of books for free to all corners of the country. It doesn't distribute propaganda; it distributes classics such as Cervantes' Don Quixote. And all people can read them, not just those with an iPad or Kindle.

What also comes to mind are the enormous publishing houses in the former Soviet Union, those that translated and distributed books worldwide for free, or for a nominal sum of money; they were published in all languages, including some minor ones in terms of the number of native speakers, in Africa and Asia. These books helped Africans and Asians to gain independence from Western colonial powers. They also helped colonized nations rediscover their own previously suppressed cultures.

A book is knowledge and knowledge is power. Books are one of the greatest cultural heritages. Be they printed in the corner of an oil-stained workshop in a poor country, or by a state-subsidized publishing house of an anti-imperialist nation, books can be a weapon for the oppressed who gain the knowledge and ideas contained therein.

Books are some of the mightiest weapons in revolutionary struggles and in resistance. To abandon them, to let them get captured would mean that everything is lost. It would be an acceptance that market fundamentalism and imperialism should now be allowed to possess, digitize and manipulate all knowledge, all verbalized dreams and the hopes that our humanity has created throughout the centuries. By no means should this be allowed to happen!

7 February 2012

*****

5

Kenya: Tricks, Intrigues and the Somali War

GRAB EVERYTHING AND JUSTIFY IT BY WAR

Welcome to Kenya. Karibu Sana! And welcome to the world of Kenyan politics, of intrigues and cruelty. Welcome to a world where 'seemingly' unconnected events like the Kenyan invasion to Somalia, the kidnapping of Western tourists and aid workers, gigantic infrastructural projects and brutal land grabs are all bundled into a cynical and deadly chain of events.

The Kidnappings and the War

On October 2011, Kenyan soldiers moved across the border to Somalia, backed by the air force as well as local and foreign propaganda campaigns.

"MOGADISHU, Somalia (AP) October 16, 2011 — Kenyan military forces moved into southern Somalia on Sunday, an official and residents said, a day after top Kenyan defense officials said the country has the right to defend itself after a rash of militant kidnappings of Europeans inside Kenya."

Of course any real war always needs a big justification. The war could be, after all, an embarrassing affair. It is all about crossing international borders, about violating territory belonging to a neighboring state, and often about the killing of hundreds or even thousands of innocent and defenseless people. The leaders who are ready to bring their country to war should have at least some solid and credible reason prepared, or at least they should have something that could be pulled out from their sleeves, capable of convincing the nation and the rest of the world that there is one.

The events that later helped to justify the Kenyan invasion of Somalia arrived conveniently (some would say suspiciously so) and in full force: without any warning Kenya experienced a spectacular string of kidnappings against foreigners.

A British citizen David Tebutt was killed while resisting attackers at the Kiwayu beach resort near the Somali border. His wife Judith was taken to Somalia and held hostage for several months before being released in March 2012. A few days after the tragedy, a wheelchair bound 66 year old French woman who was recovering from cancer – Marie Dedieu – was kidnapped from her rented home on Manda Island. She died in captivity. The absolute lack of compassion on the part of her kidnappers shocked the world. But that was not the end of the events: two Spanish aid workers (employed by *Medecins Sans Frontieres* (MSF)) were kidnapped from the heart of the Dadaab refugee camp on October 13, 2011.

All these actions occurred one after another, literally back to back, in October 2011.

The news of the kidnappings quickly spread all over the world, partially because of the sensationalist coverage of the local and international media. This dealt the Kenyan tourism industry a deadly blow. The bookings almost dried up, especially on the Lamu Archipelago. Foreigners began to evacuate the coast.

There was hardly any serious investigation done by the Kenyan press to find out who was really behind the kidnappings. As if by some invisible command, all fingers were suddenly pointing at Al-Shabaab. The Kenyan government declared that it had no choice but to take immediate action. And act it did, with surprising speed and a level of organization hardly seen in this endemically corrupt and disorganized State.

Al-Shabaab was designated as the culprit. The official mission was defined, briskly: 'To liberate the hostages from Al-Shabaab and to push the Islamist militants as far back as possible from the Kenyan border.'

The problem was that there was absolutely no proof that Al-Shabaab had been involved in any of the above-mentioned kidnappings. Its leaders strongly denied any participation.

As Kenyan troops first penetrated Somalian territory north of the border, even the Western-backed Transitional Federal Government of Somalia (TFG) began protesting against the invasion, and Somalia's President Sharif Sheikh Ahmed declared that his "administration and people in Somalia opposed the presence of Kenyan troops since the Somalian federal government 'had no agreement with Kenya beyond helping us with logistics'", as was reported by the ABC News (Australia) on October 25, 2011.

The experts were also skeptical (kidnappings were different from the usual Al-Shabaab strategy), but when the whole scenario began to look like a pre-arranged farce, the West suddenly threw its support behind Kenya (its long-time ally and its 'client' state) and almost all critical voices fell silent within a few days, including those from the TFG.

The few voices of dissent in the mainstream media were overwhelmed by the personal and hardly spontaneous attacks:

Alex Perry wrote for the Time Magazine's "Global Spin" on October 31, 2011:

> "Kenya's hasty invasion of its northern neighbor Somalia took a tragic turn late Sunday, when, according to witnesses on the ground, the Kenyan air force bombed a refugee camp sheltering those fleeing Somalia's famine, killing three children and two adults."

His piece was met with a barrage of vicious and vitriolic rounds. Almost all the comments were negative, some outrightly insulting.

* * *

The Operation "Linda Nchi" (Protect the Nation in Swahili) was awarded full legitimacy by the West and has been going on with no challenge ever since, of course with a tremendous cost to Somalia and its people.

While the actual fighting has been done by troops from Kenya, Ethiopia, the Transitional Federal Government of Somalia (TFG) and a few pro-Western factions inside Somalia, support has been mainly coming from the United States, Denmark, Israel and France – a country which in the last few years has desperately been trying to reestablish itself as one of the major neo-colonialist powers on the African continent.

* * *

According to Micah Zenko from CFR.org: "Initially, many believed that Kenya coordinated its invasion with the Pentagon, in a similar fashion as Ethiopia in December 2006, when the United States provided detailed intelligence, military training, and naval support. This perception was further reinforced when the U.S. ambassador to Kenya, Scott Gration, told the Financial Times: "We are looking to see how, as an ally in this conflict on terrorism, can we help the Kenyans.""

Several US officials went out of their way to deny any involvement of their country in the invasion, but based on the track record of Kenyan foreign policy almost since its independence (for decades, Kenya has been a bastion of fundamentalist capitalism and a staunch ally of the West against all independent-minded movements and governments in the region) it would be hard to imagine that Nairobi would dare to take a unilateral action of such magnitude without consulting the Empire.

The Guardian Weekly's Jean-Philippe Rémy reported on 8 November 2011:

> "Several sources agree, however, that the Kenyan intervention plan was discussed and decided in 2010, then finalized with input from western partners, including the US and to a lesser extent France. Nairobi seems to have seized on kidnappings of foreign nationals by Somali groups on Kenyan territory as an excuse to launch an operation ready and waiting.
>
> ... Nairobi plans to set up a semi-autonomous region, Jubaland. A puppet government would be used to control resources and facilities, starting with Kismayo, a port used by smuggling networks with Kenyan links, according to a UN report published in July..."

Were Kenya to manage to control Kismayo and one day to even reap the benefits of participating in the 'peacekeeping' mission in Mogadishu, "Lamu, Kenya's traditional port, mainly used for luxury tourism until now, would be converted into an oil terminal, providing an outlet for the as yet unexploited oilfields of southern

Sudan and northern Kenya. Radiating out from Lamu, a rail and road network would connect Ethiopia and Sudan to the Indian Ocean," concludes The Guardian.

To listen and believe the discourse of Kenyan officials, in a few years the port of Lamu could well become the jewel in the East African (otherwise desperately shabby) infrastructural grid.

The project called LAPSSET, would cost up to 25 billion dollars (depending who is quoting the figures) and was officially launched by the President of Kenya, Mwai Kibaki, the President of the Republic of Southern Sudan's Salva Kiir and Ethiopia's Prime Minister Meles Zenawi. LAPSSET is an abbreviation for the "Lamu Port and Lamu Southern Sudan-Ethiopia Transport Corridor". In theory, the project is supposed to be funded by Kenya and its landlocked neighbors – Ethiopia and South Sudan, although there is no transparency in exactly how. The plans are grandiose and include high-speed trains, highways, new airports, pipelines, a refinery and brand new resort towns.

The locals and foreigners are equally skeptical.

"South Sudan and Kenya signed a 'Memorandum of Understanding' for the 'option' of a pipeline. Oh, it is a nice idea", says Frank Feremans, the Belgian owner of a legendary 'Lamu House' hotel. "There is no plan; it is this 'You build the port and the market will follow' theory. The Permanent Secretary of the Ministry of Public Works arrives, explains to people through a meeting that the port will be very small, and that the pipeline will emerge at sea where ships will dock. It will not be intrusive. When the plans arrive some time later, they are for 32 berths. 'Why not build the new port in Mombasa?'"

At night, at a moonlit beach on Manda Island, expatriates frequently gather at Lamu House Beach Club, savoring the culinary delights consisting of Indian and Belgian fares. Italian wine flows freely, as does the conversation. This crowd consists of many hardened part-time and permanent residents, investment bankers, and business people as well as rich retirees. Some live here permanently, some for a few months a year only.

In this company hardly anybody actually believes that the port can be built at any point in the foreseeable future, and these are people who have access to enough "inside" information to support their theories.

"Raila (referring to Prime Minister Odinga) was recently in Europe", says one of the guests. "He visited the EU but secured no money. Corruption here is what matters. Everybody knows that if they get 1 billion dollars, hundreds of millions would simply disappear."

Someone who recently drove along the coast chips in: "They can't even build the road from Malindi. They put in the foundations, but they did not pave it... there is just tarmac. Once it rains, it will be all gone."

Back in town, a skipper with the nickname 'Lemon' just shakes his head lost in thought:

> "Here we all know that the kidnappings were not perpetrated by Al-Shabab, by gangs, yes; by gangs from outside this island – most definitely, but not by Al-Shabab. The kidnappings destroyed our livelihood; there is hardly any tourism here, now. It means that we are desperate. Now suddenly everybody wants the new port to be built. Even those who protested a few months ago are now ready to accept the project."

I ask him whether he thinks that everything is interconnected; the kidnappings, the war and the port?

"It is possible," he answers. "It is very likely. That is what the people are saying."

Another skipper, Mohammed, is bitter and unusually outspoken:

> "Here in Kenya, corruption is everywhere. Look at Kibaki himself, or at our MPs. When you are trying to get elected; well, you had better have a coffer full of money."

As he speaks, desperate touts and beggars are pitching mostly imaginary services or simply asking for bob – slang for 'shillings'.

"All eyes are now on the port," continues Mohammed. "For me, even if I don't like it, things are already in motion. But where they are going, I don't know. Billions of dollars are involved and people are worried. The majority here are scared that jobs will disappear to those in Nairobi, exactly as has happened several times in the past."

I walk to the Ministry of Lands and Settlements, straight to the Department of Land Adjudication And Settlement. I stumble across Mr. Bosko (when it comes to the port and kidnappings, everyone suddenly forgets his or her second name). He is evasive but in the end decides to speak:

> "98 to 99 percent of the people support the new port project. Those who do not support the project are being manipulated by those rich people who are not involved in the project but would like to be."

Mr. Bosko did not mention the fact that some Heads of States of the East African Community (EAC) do not seem to be at all ecstatic about the project.

On March 4, 2012 "All Africa" ran an opinion piece by Allan Brian Ssenyonga: "Will the EAC Be Upset By Lapsset?":

> "Considering what the LAPSSET transport corridor looks like on paper. It may not be insane to speculate that the ultra capitalist Kenyans will overtime develop a more northern outlook and thus 'upset' the direction of the EAC project. Over to you Uganda, Rwanda, Burundi and of course Tanzania!"

Lamu Archipelago

Lamu is lush and tropical, with a nostalgic and ancient 'Stone Town' designated as a world heritage site by UNESCO in 2001, and with dozens of ancient villages and settlements. Lamu Town is a Swahili settlement with narrow streets, traditional boats docked at the waterfront, old mosques and an imposing fort. This place had been for years a powerful magnet for well-heeled foreign visitors with deep pockets and an adventurous streak.

The town itself is very poor and full of touts, but it somehow manages to maintain a certain medieval charm, not unlike that of Zanzibar. UNESCO describes it as "the oldest and best-preserved Swahili settlement in East Africa, retaining its traditional functions." There are no cars and no scooters on the island – everybody walks or rides donkeys and cargo is moved over water.

In Lamu, local poverty rubs shoulders with foreign hedonism reflected in ridiculously overpriced hotels, 'homestays' and restaurants; most of them owned and managed by expatriates.

Clean white-sand beaches and mangroves; narrow and wide waterways, and humble fishing communities dot the archipelago. Many foreigners call all this a 'paradise', although only few local people would describe their living as divine.

The Muslim Swahili coast of Kenya of which Lamu Archipelago

is a firm part, has been brutally marginalized by Nairobi ever since independence. The great and ancient Swahili culture was viewed with suspicion and envy by rival tribes from the highlands and by the first government of Jomo Kenyatta.

To complicate things further, the 'paradise' is located right on the doorstep of Somalia, a war-torn country that has for decades been destabilized by Western interests.

And Somalia has for years struggled without any permanent and effective government. Its present foreign-backed administration is locked in combat with an Islamist group, Al-Shabaab, which the West accuses of being closely linked to Al-Qaida. According to the reports from mainstream media, the sea off the coast of Somalia is constantly 'congested with the pirates' who attack many international cargo vessels for ransom.

* * *

After almost an hour of tough negotiation I rent a speedboat with a crew and attempt to venture towards the construction site of the new port, and then out to sea and the Island of Shanga, which lies on the way to Somalia. But the skipper and his crew are confused and thoroughly impoverished. They don't have fuel on board. They begin to play games, demand money in advance, and then fail to secure necessary amount of fuel for our long journey. Changing the crew takes another hour.

Everything appears to be thoroughly disorganized, dysfunctional, and desperate.

Finally we shoot towards the narrow waterway rimmed by mangroves on both shores. The heat is awful. The ships carrying workers look like ghosts; they are overcrowded, and move slowly and majestically in depressing silence.

An enormous and pristine bay suddenly opens out in front of our eyes, the bay that is, according to the plan, supposed to be converted into container and tanker port.

Now our boat literally flies over the water, the engine roaring. Ancient Swahili settlements some more than 1,000 years old, emerge and disappear by the side, the fantastic rock formations of Kiunga Marine Park are on the horizon.

With every wave that the boat has to negotiate, Somalia gets closer and closer.

Then Shanga Island appears, a lost world of ancient Islamic ruins, and as an increasingly credible theory indicates, an island once inhabited by the crew of a boat that sailed from Shanghai and got shipwrecked in this area.

One of my missions here is to photograph the ruins for a major daily newspaper in Beijing. I hire a guide and begin my exhausting walk towards the lost city.

But not even two minutes into the journey, and my guide begins to speak in an agitated voice:

"People here are so scared! They are afraid to sail after dawn. They are afraid of foreigners, of white people."

But why would foreigners come here?

"They patrol the waters", he explains. "These are joint patrols between the Kenyan NAVY and Americans. Here they call foreigners the FBI. They say the white people are all Americans, but they are from many other countries, including England and Israel. But people here are illiterate. More than 90 percent in the village can't read and write. For them, every big white person is an American, an FBI."

What happens to the fishermen who are stopped?

"They are questioned. Some disappear for 2 to 4 days."

"Does everybody come back, eventually?"

He doesn't know. This is an enormous area.

Two years ago I debated the same issue with my friend, the leader of the Social Democratic Party of Kenya, Mwandawiro Mghanga, a former MP and a member of the Foreign Relations Committee. This was long before the invasion, although the direction in which the US – Kenyan relations was moving even then was crystal clear. Mr. Mwandawiro then openly explained the situation:

> "What you have to know is that these things are clouded in secrecy. When I was in Parliament, I repeatedly asked about the military agreements that Kenya had signed with the US and Britain. I demanded that they should be put on the table. Even as a member of the Defense and Foreign Affairs Committee of this country, I could not get access to this information. So things are done behind closed doors and people know very well that the Kenyan national intelligence and the army cooperate very closely

with the US."

He then continued with his prophecy:

> "Even though the US bases are not here, US planes land and operate from the Kenyan Ocean at Lamu on the Kenyan Coast and even at Wajir, in the northern part of Kenya, where the British and the American built a big airport... Yes where their planes can land. Even Jomo Kenyatta International Airport is often used for other than civilian purposes...
>
> ...Like I have told you: there is plenty to hide, including the cooperation between the CIA, FBI and Kenyan agencies when arresting our people... Also, look at our foreign policy: our involvement with Somalia on behalf of the US – and the way it is going right now. It can only cause us much harm. We are the ones who will pay a big price for following instructions and defending the interests of the US in the region...."

At the end of March 2012, almost half a year into the war, the faces of the people of Lamu reflected exhaustion, hopelessness and a deep sadness. The concept; the scenario that "the Kenyan government accused Al-Shabab of kidnappings in order to justify the invasion of Somalia on behalf of the West, while starving the Lamu archipelago so that the population would accept the construction of the new port" has been simply too complex for most of the people to grasp.

Mr. Kijogo Sikandara, a 74-year old captain, and a native of Lamu, seemed fully resigned:

> "People here were sidelined and they suffered very much in the past because of Nairobi. But now, I don't know what we would do without the port project. Some people don't like it; many don't. They say that their land will be taken away because of the port, connecting roads and other infrastructure... They say that culture will change. I had been a boat captain for many years. I have been transporting people between the mainland and this island for decades. I say: I don't mind anymore if this town becomes like Nairobi; at least young people will have some opportunity in life."

But does the captain believe that the project will really be completed and that the benefits will go to the people. I ask, he doesn't know.

Then I am on the water again, the roar of the engine, the mangroves, the narrow channel, the tiny Kililana community, and then again another tremendous bay, and then a sharp left turn. I see the destruction of the forest and of mangroves everywhere, but there seem to be no massive construction.

"They are doing nothing, just building some port authority building away from the shore", I was told by Frank Feremans before I left Lamu. "The thing is: there is no funding. The World Bank – nothing. They thought that the Chinese would invest, but there is no sign of it. The Chinese are always interested in concrete and well-defined projects, not in abstract schemes. Like right now: the Chinese are building a power plant – they will do 80% and the locals 20%. Conditions are set. But what Kenya is suggesting regarding the port: "You build it and contracts will come" is not serious."

After there was no interest from China and the European Union, the Kenyan government approached Indian companies, and then China again, apparently to no avail.

My speedboat approached a floating pontoon jetty. From there, a road goes seemingly nowhere, into the jungle. There is no traffic, nor even any movement. This is where President Kibaki made a speech about the greatness and the benefits of the new port. This is where most of the speeches by politicians are made.

A man is sitting at the edge of the pontoon, a fishing rod in his hand. He pays no attention to us. Apart from two guards aimlessly walking around and a fisherman, there are no people.

"Do you know about any groups of people working around here?" My skipper asks.

A fisherman waves his hand towards the jungle. Some workers are building some building there. Nothing spectacular, nothing that looks like 25 billon dollars is being spent.

"They destroyed Lamu for nothing", I hear back in town. "They ruined it on the chance that they would be able to pull this project through."

I have nothing to reply to that. That's how the country has been functioning for decades, nothing new.

Many parts of the country are already destroyed, but one doesn't often read about it.

The Western economic and geo-political interests are dividing Africa once again into several camps. At two extremes are the 'client' states (or 'allies') like Rwanda, Senegal, and Kenya, and 'disobedient' ones (described as evil) nations that include Eritrea, Zimbabwe and until it was destroyed – Libya.

The 'client' states could be in a state of total disarray, even social collapse, but they can always count on support from the Western propaganda machine.

For instance, Kenya is one of the most corrupt nations on earth, 154th (2011 data) out of 182 countries surveyed by the Berlin-based Transparency International. It also ranks 16th from the top on so-called "Failed States Index" (2011), one point better than Niger but worse than Burundi. And these are statistics and perception indexes amassed by relatively friendly organizations. But this reality is not often highlighted in the mass media.

Despite the upbeat macro-economic statistics, Kenya is facing some of the most serious problems in the world; it has the biggest slums in Africa, some of the highest homicide rates, tribal tensions and outright violence. Kenya is overflowing with internally-displaced people from the post-election violence, which took the lives of approximately 3,000 people in 2007/8.

Somali refugees are all over the country; there are approximately one million of them living in terrible and overcrowded camps, the largest one of which is called Dadaab, holding over 500,000 people. Hundreds of thousands of Somalis also live in all parts of Kenya legally; many of them taking advantage of the endemically corrupt local administration, which is happy to sell "under the table", thousands of residence permits, and even citizenship.

The fate of Somali refugees is mostly awful. Dadaab and other camps are overcrowded, and the conditions are terrible. Some refugees have lived here for two decades, with no right to work, with extremely basic education and other services mainly provided by UNHCR, no hope of return to their war-torn nation and a very slim chance of being allowed to settle in Kenya or a third country.

"Do you know that we have a policy here that says no refugee can be returned to Dadaab as conditions there amount to cruel and degrading punishment?" Dr. Barbara E. Harrell-Bond, Director Fahamu Refugee Programme, wrote to me recently from Oxford. Last year I had been working in the camp, producing and directing my 70-minute feature documentary film, "One Flew Over Dadaab".

"I arrived here one week ago and my impressions are more or less the same as they were back in 2007", explained Eva Andre from Community Services of UNHCR, as we were driving through along a red-earth road in a convoy of UN Land Cruisers.

"Since 2007 the situation has actually deteriorated and this is now the biggest camp in the world and it's no secret that the camp is overcrowded. Fewer children are going to school now than before..."

And there was drought and hunger in the area as I was filming. Then I was told stories; endless stories of overcrowding, idleness, and acute lack of hope, illnesses, brutal rapes, and permanent despair. Hospitals were full of new arrivals clinging to life with unimaginable determination.

Officially, Kenya periodically threatens to close the border with Somalia, claiming that it can no longer accept more refugees on its soil. It blames the international community for 'not doing more', or more precisely, for not 'paying more'.

In reality, all the refugee camps combined house more than 1 million people, and Kenya gains enormously from 'servicing' them. The camps are not only great sources of income for corrupt officials; they also provide great job opportunities for the entire country. Truck and bus drivers bring supplies and people, farmers sell their produce, teachers are expected to receive extra bonuses for working in Dadaab, and then there is an entire army of security guards, translators, fixers, medical staff as well as construction workers. There is also an army of badly-trained but well paid bureaucrats.

The more destabilized Somalia becomes, the more refugees are forced to venture into Kenya across the porous and dangerous border. The more overcrowded the camps become, the more 'emergencies' there are and inevitably, more job opportunities.

Only those with plenty of money can count on settling in Nairobi or elsewhere beyond the barbed-wire fences. Only substantial bribes can guarantee freedom.

Poor Somalis – true refugees – those that are escaping a country destabilized by the West (and now by Ethiopia and Kenya), are confined to awful tents and slum-style (or prison-style) accommodation, to basic rations and almost no hope for a decent education and upward or onward mobility.

"They don't want you to drive all the way to the border", explained a medic at Dadaab who did not want to be named. "Kenyan border guards rape Somali women, they often take all they have before allowing them to enter the country. Some people come fully dehydrated. Sometimes wild animals eat children alive or just attack the victims and let them die in the middle of the desert."

The misery of a once-proud nation – Somalia – appears almost beyond imagination, while the cynicism of the West unsurpassable. But then one remembers that there are other 'comparisons', such as Afghanistan, DR Congo, Iraq, Libya and Palestine.

One refugee, a lady, a mother, spoke to my camera: "We miss a lot our Somalia. We miss the land, we miss freedom of movement, and we miss the longest coastline in Africa. We miss so many things. And there was no rape in Somalia. Here there are so many rape cases. There, we spoke our language and we were bound by the same religion. We all miss the way Somalia was prior to 1991. Here we feel like in a prison where we are given food or more precisely, where we have to beg for food."

Foreign Interests

There seems to be no way out for Somalia, squeezed inbetween Western colonies or the 'client states' of Djibouti (not much more than a military base of the US, France and other Western nations), Ethiopia, Kenya and the sea.

The West has its long-term plans for the entire vast region, from DR Congo (which has already lost at least 6 million people in its recent history, through the plunder of its resources by the regional neo-colonies of the West), to the newly 'independent' South Sudan, Rwanda, Kenya and Somalia itself.

It is presumed that Somalia has enormous untapped oil reserves. It is also strategically located. Therefore, following the logic of Western neocolonialism, it cannot be allowed to go free. An attempt to fragment its territory (not unlike the scenario already implemented in Iraq and Sudan) is well under way. The Kenyan invasion is yet another 'practical' step in that direction.

Time wise, the Kenyan military action preceded the so-called London Conference on Somalia hosted by the UK government in

February 2012. It also gave some time for the Western analysts to calculate the impact.

Rasna Warah argues in The East African (March 5-11, 2012) that Western countries facing massive unemployment and recession at home have 'woken up to the fact that Somalia represents an untapped source of natural resources and a destination for Western goods.'

She assumes that Somali leaders could be persuaded to give rights and concessions to Western companies in exchange for aid. The question also remains who will be those leaders, as the mandate of TFG expires in August 2012.

"The task of managing Somalia's economy", writes Rasna Warah, "appears to rest with the newly-established Joint Financial Management Board, comprising representatives from Britain, France, The European Union, the World Bank and TPG (and later any future government which aims to 'increase transparency and accountability in the collection and accountability in the collection and efficient use of public revenues, as well as international development aid, and which will help strengthen Somali public financial management institutions.'"

The article mentions The Shock Doctrine by Naomi Klein, and it eventually comes to ask one powerful question: "The presence of the World Bank on the Board also raises questions about the philanthropic intentions of Western donors. Is Somalia going to be revived through loans from the Bank, and if so, will Somalia be in debt before it is on its feet?"

However, Ms Warah stops short of addressing participation of both Ethiopia and Kenya in Western plans to fragment, shackle and exploit Somalia.

Grab Everything And Justify It by War

Not long after the invasion, Kenyan officials performed a spectacular 'security' operation. Thousands of families in Nairobi – both Kenyan and Somali – have become victims of what the Kenyan officials decided to call 'war on terror'. In the days and weeks following the attack on Somalia, police and army officials accompanied by excavators and bulldozers, have torn down slum dwellings as well as multi-storey buildings. The official explanation was that these buildings intrude on the flight path of military planes. Nairobi has three major airports. Since these military planes could approach from at least two directions, it allows the government to destroy the dwellings of tens of thousands of people if it chooses to do so.

Visiting one of the demolition sites in Eastleigh in October 2011, I was told by Gilbert, a former resident: "There is no discussion and no negotiation. That's how it is in Kenya. They call it democracy, but in fact the government can come and throw us onto the street. If we protest, they shoot to kill."

The situation was desperate: there were German shepherd dogs, some 'special units' fully armed, both military and police. Bulldozers and excavators backed by the army. It did remind me of something but I was not sure of what! I kept photographing the intruders and they kept photographing me. Then it hit me: it was exactly like in Israel during the demolition of Palestinian dwellings: the methods, the dogs, the postures.

Then I talked to the people, or more precisely they talked to me, over each other. Over the roar of the engines and human voices, I managed to recognize words like 'land grab', 'injustice', 'terror'.

"We were paying the mortgage", cried a lady wearing a house dress, pulling her tiny daughter against her chest. "This is all we have, my husband and I and our 3 children. We both were working to pay for this place – for our home. These people came at night and told us to leave, immediately. Children were crying but they couldn't care less. They dragged us out. They treated us like animals, like criminals. Our clothes, books, toys, phones, television set – everything is there, destroyed."

It was done to thousands of people. No serious investigation took place.

During my repeated attempts to secure comments from the well-staffed UN Habitat in Nairobi (The United Nations Human Settlements Programme), it was made clear to me that there will be no official communiqué or criticism of Kenya coming from the United Nations.

The Nation reported posted on its blog on November 22nd, 2011:

> "...What actually happened was, tenants in a several large Eastleigh apartment buildings woke up to police demanding they vacate the premises immediately. Ten minutes max to grab their

stuff before all access was denied, or so I am told. Riot police and various army-looking dudes were crawling all over the place... Then the bulldozers came in and did their thing.

...There are at least a couple hundred hapless Eastleigh residents who are newly homeless tonight... Building owners I talked to swear they had the proper permits. The government swears it's simply cracking down on security risks and taking its land back. Former tenants swear that it's either discrimination against Eastleigh residents, many of whom are Somali, or that it's a simple case of the rich exploiting the poor, i.e. a land grab."

For some heads of the private and public sector, these atrocious land grabs were possibly the payment for their support of the invasion. But as always here, there is no proof, only rumors. No facts, just a logical deduction.

Photo 2. Beauty from Dadaab camp

I went back to Eastleigh on March 31st, 2012. I talked to a mason, Mr. Kelly Mbinda:

"We were forced out of our houses by police accompanied by dogs. The army was supervising eviction, claiming that the land is theirs."

I asked a housewife, Agnes Kaleche, what happened to the

people from the lower middle-class who used to live in those buildings? She shrugged her shoulders: "They moved to the neighboring slums; to Biafra and Kinyago."

"Just like that?" I asked.

"Just like that."

* * *

The war goes on. A few embedded reporters are travelling with the Kenyan army. There are rumors of atrocities being committed by the troops, but as there is no independent reporting allowed in this conflict ('for our safety', of course), no evidence can be provided.

All the issues mentioned above, appear to be inter-connected: the kidnappings, the port, the war and the evictions.

Another related topic is poverty, as well as an absolute lack of rights and protection for the average Kenyan citizens.

Elites in Kenya are corrupt and the corruption here is taken to the extreme, almost to madness. Elites are also absolutely indifferent towards the plight of their citizens. If money can be made through mega projects (imaginary or real), or from the war, or from the eviction of thousands of defenseless people, or from refugees, there will absolutely be no hesitation. People matter nothing to the 'rulers' here; lives are dispensable, worthless.

The project of the Port of Lamu may go ahead or not. The war may continue, it may expand or it may eventually wind down. The land confiscated from the poor people in Nairobi may be converted into a private real estate development project. Dadaab camp may stop growing one day, or it may burst.

But there is one thing that is certain: the greed and brutality of Kenyan (and those others in the region) elites and their foreign masters will not simply disappear. The country and the region will continue to suffer unless the entire system goes through a massive overhaul. The sooner the people of Kenya realize what twisted system they have been forced to exist in, the sooner they will be inspired to act. Once there is an understanding of the conditions, there will also be demands for justice. And then even the remnants of the monstrous system of intrigues and plots that has been killing tens of thousands of innocent people will be successfully smashed and placed where they belong – in the virtual museum of neocolonialism.

After that, there will probably be no kidnappings, no wars, and no refugees. The ports, railroads and highways will finally be built – for the people.

6 April 2012

*****

6

Down the Mean Streets of Central America

WHERE WOUNDS REFUSE TO HEAL

It is getting dark and my friend Manuel, a local journalist, is driving me in his battered old pick up truck through the ruined streets of the tough and violent Panamanian city on the Caribbean coast – Colon.

Near the first corner where we stop, I spot an old woman puffing on something wrapped in a makeshift paper cone. The smoke is heavy and it stinks: it is neither tobacco nor marijuana; it is something unidentifiable and thoroughly vile. She spits on the ground and then looks straight at me with provocative and bloodshot eyes. I say nothing, she says very little; but those few words that she utters represent the lowest grade of the language that used to serve such great poets like Cervantes and Octavio Paz. Her Spanish is indeed as degraded as the stuff she is smoking, but she does not care, nothing seems to matter to her anymore.

Two kids aged roughly 8 and 12, are carrying some dirty carton boxes on their heads. They first salute me with the thumb-up sign, then with some complex gangster finger-twisting gestures. I try to imitate them but cannot match the complexity and so I reply with a grin, which evokes bewilderment on their faces and which they refuse to return.

The stench all around us is bad – of rotting food, an open sewer, or probably a decomposing rat or other unfortunate creature that passed away somewhere nearby.

"Work quickly and get into the car!" says Manuel. "This is 'red zone' – 'zona roja.'"

"What is red zone?" I ask. "A brothel district?"

Almost every country in Latin America has its own terminology, at least, for brutality, sex, and poverty and for public buses.

"No", he replies. "Simply the most dangerous part of the city. The epicenter of gang violence."

I take a few more still images, then film for two minutes and finally get into the car.

"The best is still to come. Frankly you saw nothing, yet", explains Manuel. "But for the time being, let's follow some common sense: don't buckle up, don't roll down the windows unless you are really ready to film; don't make any eye contact and please keep an extremely low profile. You are in the most dangerous place in the Western Hemisphere."

Of course you hear the same warnings all over the region: "The meanest streets of the Western hemisphere are those of Port-Au-Prince in Haiti, of Tijuana in Mexico, of San Salvador, Tegucigalpa, Rio de Janeiro, Cali or Medellin. And if you buy into the Western defamation coverage of El Proceso in Venezuela, you would certainly believe that the murder capital of the Western hemisphere was Caracas.

But no matter how bad the other contenders are; Colon is unique in its hopeless decay and ferocity.

The city has never truly recovered from the brutal US invasion of December 1989, cynically code-named "Operation Just Cause". The operation was launched to oust the strongman Manuel Noriega, who used to be backed by the US, but at some point opted for the worst crime imaginable in the eyes of the Empire: to part ways with the West, embarking on a semi-independent course. To do it in the country that literally sits on one of the most important waterways in the world – the Panama Canal – proved to be synonymous with committing ritual suicide.

There had to be some figleaf to justify the unlawfulness of the invasion, in this case the drug-trafficking in which Noriega was involved.

During the invasion, thousands of people died. Entire cities, towns and neighborhoods were leveled to the ground. The people of Panama and the entire Latin America were once again reminded that the 'Monroe Doctrine' was still the main 'law' by which the Western Hemisphere has been governed. And so, in 1989, Panama joined the long list of devastated countries that experienced the brutality of direct or indirect invasions from the North: Granada, the Dominican Republic, Cuba, Guatemala, Brazil, Colombia, Bolivia, Chile, Argentina, Uruguay to name at least a few.

The city of Colon was never rebuilt. Until now it feels as if the US jets and helicopters are still periodically flying over its roofs, as if the armored vehicles were driving through the fronts of cafes and bars, as if gunshots could be heard right behind the next corner. Colon does not actually resemble a city, but more like a huge shipwreck, a frightening monument to destruction.

* * *

We cruise slowly and despite Manuel's warning I keep my window down, photographing and filming all along the way.

"If you use professional cameras: Leica or big Nikons, everything looks better than in the real life", I explain to Manuel. "You have to get very close if you want to capture things accurately; if you want your images to make an impact."

He ignores my musing; he is scared. And I have no heart to tell him that the Leica I am now using has almost no zoom; the zoom is my own body, so I have to actually get very close to the street scenes of his battered native city of Colon.

I see a girl – as she walks by; she almost levitates. Her legs are fully and provocatively exposed, but the entire upper part of her body is covered in white. She looks like a fragile ghost, or, from the waste up, a saint, but with provocatively painted lips. There is definitely a strong dose of poetry in all that I see around me. She smiles at me; I nod.

And then the children appear, young girls, as young as ten. They make suggestive motions while I am trying to look the other way. The poetry is gone. The images become extremely raw –

everything here seems to be overexposed.

There are young boys with the stares as sharp as knives. And there are two old men having a dispute, their fingers pointing in each other's faces menacingly. There are entire families with children living on the streets.

The decay is everywhere and it is quite an unimaginable decay; entire blocks of houses turned into skeletons, half-fallen churches, open garbage dumps, child sex-workers and gangs of desperate-looking tiny boys. I see no guns but I see knives and gang symbols, I hear extremely violent music, the toughest grade of Panamanian rap.

"The violence came with the invasion", says Manuel. "It never left. The tanks left but the violence did not. Then gang culture got its inspiration from the streets of LA and other US cities, as hopelessness translated itself into increased immigration to the North where many families ended up living in the toughest ghettos. The children became the foot soldiers of the gangs, moving back and forth between the North American inner-cities and their native Panama."

It did not sound unfamiliar at all. I have witnessed the same pattern for years in places as far apart as Honduras, Samoa and Cambodia.

"This building was bombed by the US forces", Manuel points at a huge, ghost-like, still surprisingly inhabited skyscraper. "If you want to film it, do so, but do it very quickly."

To Manuel's desperation I take my time. The building and its past fascinate me: the story is just incredible – the US forces bombed the tower inhabited by hundreds of civilians simply because it was tall and because it was 'there'. I recall my work in Grenada, a decade after the US invasion. I studied in disbelief what was left of the mental hospital blasted to pieces in 1983, in the so-called Operation Urgent Fury, with all its patients inside, simply because it had a green roof, unlike the rest of St. George's with its iconic red roof tops.

We pass by a place of worship belonging to Jehovah Witnesses. Houses of Christian sects are all over the city, and there are also mosques, even a huge Hindu temple. As always, wherever there is no hope left and fear reigns, religions move in, quickly and efficiently, instantly filling the void.

What is striking, is that in Colon, even the houses of worship are fortified: with several layers of barbed wire, some armed with surveillance systems.

* * *

In the very center of the city I hear the howl of ambulance sirens. I spot a tall hospital, not far from the ridiculously out of place Radisson Hotel and decaying cruise ship port. There is a crowd of desperate relatives at the entrance to the medical facility. Everything in Colon seems to be over-anxious, loud and unsettling. Observing the state of its infrastructure and services, it is astonishing and hardly credible that the country ranks 58 on the Human Development Index (UNDP, HDI, 2011), above nations like Kuwait and Malaysia.

The contrasts are everywhere and they are monstrous – on one side is a port designed for cruise ship liners, with several empty restaurants and the Radisson Hotel. Not far away is the dark and frightening city overrun by violence, desperation and permanent decay.

As we come closer to the port, it strikes me that there are no civilian ships. Instead I see one huge US battleship docked at the pier.

"But they are not supposed to be here, are they?" I drop my naïve rhetorical question, listing Philippines and other places where the US marines are actually 'not supposed to be' docking their ships.

"But they are", Manuel shrugs his shoulders.

"Is this a cruise ship?" Two well-groomed women with very good middle class accents approach me after spotting me filming the vessel. I smile and reply that this is actually a war ship, with cannons sticking out in all directions. For a moment I think they have come for sightseeing: two nice and naïve teachers or young doctors or office workers. But then I see miniskirts and incredibly high heels, and the piercing scent of cheap perfume penetrates my nostrils.

I move to the main entrance of the jetty: "No dogs" it says: "The Entrance".

I film for just a few seconds, before a tough-looking and uniformed US marine comes running towards me: "No filming!"

he screams.

I try a Kafkaesque approach on him: "But can I photograph?"

"Yes, but not too much", he barks at me, whatever that means. I switch one of my still cameras to an HD video mode and film a little bit more.

The ship is being refueled.

"How many people died during the invasion?" I ask an old man who is smoking a cheap cigar, right next to a huge plastic replica of a bottle of local rum serving as an advertisement.

"Thousands, sonny", he says, laconically.

"Some say 3,500 in the whole country," I suggest.

"More", he says. "I think more died in Colon alone".

"Father, but how is life now?" I ask him with my exaggerated Chilean accent, to make sure he does not take me for a gringo.

He pretends that he is thinking; although we both know the answer that is coming. He spits tobacco on the ground before speaking.

"Life is shit, sonny", he replies pensively, leaving no space for further inquiries. "*Una mierda, hijo.*"

* * *

Night descends and I feel hungry. All that is open near my hotel are only several North American fast food joints, and a disproportionally huge casino. I go through security, and then enter the casino. It is Friday but nobody is gambling. The roulette and blackjack tables are empty and so are the stools in front of the flashing and noisy slot machines.

The live music in the café is very loud but good; a corpulent local starlet pours out her heart in classic boleros, and then teases the audience with good Columbian *cumbias*. It is all as it should be on a Friday night: "I die without you... You are my life... If you leave me..." It all goes well, and the dish of shredded beef and friend plantains is delicious. One could easily forget that the city outside resembles a war-zone, and that gangs and child prostitutes are roaming the streets.

But then the music stops and the expression on the face of the singer changes. Something is about to happen, I think. With a bizarre, unnecessary and vulgar gesture, she lifts up her skirt above her waist. The audience roars.

As I leave the casino, I clearly hear the gunshots nearby.

* * *

That same night I stalk a police officer, whose name is D. Rodriguez. He is bored, guarding nothing more exciting than a large parking lot. He is eager to talk, as there is nothing better to do than to talk. I ask him how bad life in Colon, really is? He thinks for a few seconds than begins his long litany:

> "To tell you the truth, earlier, things were much better for the poor. No matter what they say, Noriega was actually helping many poor people. In his days, most of the families were able to get by easily. Now they squeeze you with taxes and regulations but you get almost nothing in return. In the past, one could encounter plenty of respect. One man; just one police officer would be able to guard an entire prison... Now forget it: security forces are being taken hostage; there is no safety in this country, anymore."

I ask him about the terrible state which his city appears to find itself in, but he does not seem to understand my question. He is a man of concrete questions and answers. He was born and raised here and this is all he knows; there is no point to comparisons.

"It is falling apart, I know", he says. "They – the administration – do nothing. But it has been like this for decades, at least since the invasion..."

* * *

But others do seem to know and they compare.

In January 2009 Grisel Bethancourt wrote for La Critica:

> "The City of Colón is the most violent in the Republic of Panama, according to an analysis of crime statistics taken from around the entire country announced by the Minister of Government and Justice Dilio Arcia. According to Arcia, this conclusion is derived from the numbers of homicides in Colón during 2008. There were 33 homicides for every 100,000 residents, which is greater than the 27 homicides for every 100,000 residents in Panama City. This report on the violence occurring along the Atlantic coast forms part of the diagnosis of the criminal situation faced by the entire country. Most of the murders in Colón are tied to gang activity, said Arcia. In 2008 there were a total of 652 homicides in the entire Republic of Panama, where gang activity,

> the settling of accounts, quarrels between rival groups and revenge are the main causes. Even though Panama is not a drug-producing country, most crime is tied to drug trafficking and 80% of the murders are caused by firearms. The statistics also indicate that in prisons the average age of the inmates is 30 years, and more than two thirds of the inmates started their criminal careers at age 12, where school drop-outs are a big part of the problem."

The editor of the publication replied:

> "At 33 murders per 100,000 inhabitants, Colón could very well be the most dangerous city in Latin America."

In his book What Uncle Sam Really Wants, Noam Chomsky wrote about the state of post-invasion Panama:

> "The US put the bankers back in power after the invasion. Noriega's involvement in drug-trafficking had been trivial compared to theirs. Drug-trafficking there has always been conducted primarily by the banks – the banking system is virtually unregulated, so it's a natural outlet for criminal money. This has been the basis for Panama's highly artificial economy and remains so – possibly at a higher level – after the invasion. The Panamanian Defence Forces have also been reconstructed with basically the same officers.

In general, everything's pretty much the same, only now more reliable servants are in charge. The same is true of Grenada, which has become a major centre of drug money laundering since the US invasion. Nicaragua, too, has become a significant conduit for drugs to the US market, after Washington's victory in the 1990 election. The pattern is standard – as is the failure to notice it."

* * *

One of the managers working at the Hotel Four Points run by Sheraton in a suburb of Colon called Rainbow City originally comes from the capital. He is ready to compare and to talk, but he does not want to be named:

> "Life here is very tough. Not much seems to be working here now: the medical care is terrible and so is education... Noriega was no saint, but during his government the poor and the middle class were just fine. The rich of course hated him, as he was making their life difficult. Like the President that we have now – for decades he was an arch-enemy of Noriega."

The name "Rainbow City" from where we are talking comes from the days when the North Americans were building the

Panama Canal. It is said that when they came here, they began housing and racially-segregating local workers, in the same way as they were doing at home in the United States.

"Of course I did not experience those days of segregation", says Manuel. "It all happened before I was born, but my parents and grandparents told me all about the past. There were shops, even supermarkets for "whites only" and others for the rest of the people."

Then he returned back to the invasion:

> "It all depends on whom you decide to talk to, of course. You hear one thing from the military and from the official press, which is owned by the rich, and you hear opposite things from those whose children were killed during the bombing and invasion. What I can tell you is that this country was used as an enormous training ground by the US military. They tested all sorts of the latest and their most sophisticated equipment here, to check it and to see how it would work in much more challenging war scenarios. They even brought some stealth bombers to this backwater. Why, to fight against the owners of Laundromats and mini-markets? And don't forget that we have a very good jungle here. You know what I mean by 'good' – it fits thousands of diverse war scenarios."

"Many Panamanian people died", concluded Manuel. "Yes, many people died here – in Colon; they were bombed, they were shot. But you know what? You will hardly find anything that would remind you of those horrors. Although now the whole city looks like one enormous war-zone, like something that has been bombed into the ground, there are almost no bullet holes left and no remnants of the structures that were bombed. All evidence of the crimes was painstakingly removed."

Manuel does not want to have his real name mentioned. He would lose his job if he were to be associated with the opposition intellectuals and their reports.

Before we part, he drives me to a former police station in the center of the battered city.

"It was totally destroyed; bombed. Now you only see the gate."

"Apparently everything has been destroyed around here", I say.

He nods.

* * *

The next day I drive around, to the posh marinas outside the city, where to speak Spanish is clearly considered déclassé and where catamarans fly the flags of the United States, Canada and the European Union. I drive to the series of ancient fortifications now designated as a world heritage sites by UNESCO.

Above all I want to see the Panama Canal; that fortified monster, the engineering masterpiece, the pride and damnation of this country.

As enormous ships are majestically being pulled through the locks, as tugboats and locomotives are performing their precision work, as the flags of dozens of countries from around the world fly above the vessels and along the Canal, one cannot avoid thinking about the striking contrast between this ribbon of high technology and precision connecting two oceans, and the naked misery just a few miles away.

Between the city of Colon and the Gatun Locks, there is frenetic construction under way: the new canal, new locks and a new waterway that will increase maritime traffic through Panama.

The companies that were awarded the construction contract belong to Belgium, Spain, Italy and other nations. And the ownership of the original Canal was officially transferred from the United States to Panama, in 1999.

But it is no secret that the sole superpower is firmly in charge of this strategically crucial country with only around 3.5 million inhabitants. The super-conservative, pro-US supermarket magnate Ricardo Martinelli has run the country since May 2009.

"Panama's Torrijos was succeeded by the right-wing Ricardo Martinelli, who comes from one of Panama's oldest economic and political oligarch families", Annie Bird wrote for The Red Phoenix. "JIATF-S, a unit under the U.S. military's Southern Command (SouthCom), left Panama for Miami 19 years ago when the U.S. left the Canal Zone. Last year JIATF-S came back to Panama providing "Operational Support" in a newly reopened U.S. military base which serves as the Center of Operations for the Central American System for Regional Integration's Regional Security Strategy (SICA-COSR). COSR will most likely be the regional center for the JIATF-S's C4I border surveillance program, which creates technology canals of radars and other electronic surveillance equipment linked to Colombian and Mexican border control technology."

Elsewhere in Central America

The legacy of the US invasions and interventions is still visible all over Central America, it scars entire communities, entire nations.

"Gang violence, drug culture, extremely high crime rates: these are all legacies of the imported conflicts and wars", the legendary Spanish priest, padre Pepe explained to me several years ago, who has, since 1985, fought against gang violence in El Salvador by trying to bring opportunities and skills to the youngsters who were recruited into some of the most brutal gangs in the world, particularly "M18" and Mara Salvatrucha (MS13).

In San Salvador, at Polígono Industrial Don Bosco, I witnessed hundreds of young men and women learning trades and trying to find their place in society. Some of them had terrible histories that have shattered their young lives: they had to kill, to murder in cold blood, in order to survive and to prove their allegiance to the gang. Many of them lost relatives during the civil war, some were 'sent' to the United States for education. Some joined the gangs here and others in California or elsewhere.

The gang wars in El Salvador, Honduras, Guatemala, and Mexico and to a much smaller extent in other Central American countries, have been reaching epic proportions for many years. The activities of the gangs range from extortion, killings, rape, arson and illegal gambling, to bank robberies and property fraud. The brutality is unimaginable: beheading and body-part dismemberment are the usual forms of executions. A former member of MS13 once confessed to me that after being gang-raped, a female victim had her chest cut open with a knife and her heart eaten by the gang members while she was still alive.

In Central America, as in a real war, there are usually two sides to the 'conflict'. It could be a war between two gangs, or as it was for years in El Salvador, a war between the gangs and the equally (or even more) brutal vigilante paramilitary groups like the Sombra Negra ("Black Shadow") death squad, which consists of members of the military and police, and executes on-the-spot anyone suspected of belonging to the Maras.

As brutal as the gangs are, their members are products of the violence that was often brought back to this part of the world from outside. This was clearly the point being made by the great French filmmaker Christian Poveda who spent years documenting

Salvadorian gangs and who himself was murdered by Maras in 2009. Poveda often described Maras as "Victims of society".

In June I drove to the same neighborhood of Soyapango where the filmmaker was allegedly murdered. I filmed the gang insignias and then I asked the driver to come back so as to allow me to take still photographs. As we were making the second approach, our car came under fire.

The same afternoon I visited the town of Guazapa, a place where some of the most terrible atrocities during the civil war took place. I was shown electric poles with the bullet holes, places where the military and death squads (many of them trained in the United States) charged against the civilians. I was taken to the places where people were murdered in broad daylight.

I crossed the river, stopping at the concrete wall where the names of the victims were once engraved onto the simple monument, but were now fading. The river flowed lazily by and it was getting dark and eerie.

"This was the border between the land controlled by the revolutionary FLMN and the rest of the country", explained my guide, a basketball trainer, Henrique (not his real name). "Thousands of people were massacred here by the military, by paramilitaries, by the US covert operations. The slopes of the volcano are like a massive graveyard. And why? It's because the majority of our people wanted their left-wing government!"

The area is dotted with craters from the intensive bombing (very similar to those I saw in Laos and Cambodia), with some remnants of schools and peasant houses.

The civil war in El Salvador (1980-1992) took, according to official counts, between 70,000 and 75,000 lives, but it is widely believed that many more than 100,000 people were killed or "disappeared" in this small country with just slightly over 6 million inhabitants (2012 estimate).

I visited an old man – the only member of the family of over 30 that was massacred during the war. "They came with a truck, loaded all of us onto the back of it and then shot and killed everybody just a few kilometers away. I was the only one who survived." We agree on a formal interview and filming in the future. As the darkness began to descend on the villages around Guazapa, my driver began to panic. "This area is controlled by

Maras", he explained.

Henrique calmed him down. "They will not attack us. I coach many of their members. We play basketball together." Sport is his way to draw young people away from violence.

"Most of them are good kids", he says. "But look at this country: when they were children, their parents and relatives were disappearing, being slaughtered like animals. Weapons were everywhere. Death was hiding behind every corner and life was cheap; it had hardly any value."

Now former FMLN guerillas are governing El Salvador, and things are slowly beginning to improve. But the legacy of violence will remain with the country for many long decades.

The US involvement in El Salvador (and in the rest of the region) has had a devastating impact on local societies. Even with the new winds blowing though Latin America, it is very difficult to change the old power structures that are firmly in place. Not only financial, but also moral corruption has been implanted here for generations.

In 1987, John Stockwell, former high-ranking CIA agent, gave a powerful speech on the Secret Wars of the CIA. He mentioned El Salvador where the war was then still in full swing:

> "They don't meet the death squads on the streets where they're actually chopping up people or laying them down on the street and running trucks over their heads. The CIA people in San Salvador meet the police chiefs, and the people who run the death squads, and they do liaise with them, they meet them beside the swimming pool of the villas. And it's a sophisticated, civilized kind of relationship. And they talk about their children, who are going to school at UCLA or Harvard and other schools, and they don't talk about the horrors of what's being done. They pretend like it isn't true."

But it was true and it is true even now. In El Salvador the civil war fought for ideals and sovereignty ended two decades ago, but the violence never stopped – it mutated into senseless gang wars and endless assassinations. There are thousands of literally sick elements of society, including members of the Sombra Negra, who are simply too accustomed to killing and too sure of their impunity.

* * *

In Guatemala, one of the most racially divided and feudal countries on earth, the civil war (1960-1996) took almost a quarter of a million people: 200,000 were killed and 50,000 “disappeared”. The conflict was mainly between the right-wing governments, the military and the indigenous Mayan groups, which actually represented the great majority of the country. The left-wing guerilla group, MR-13, fought both the pro-Western fascist governments and the US direct (Green Berets “advisors”, for instance) and indirect interventions, for 36 years.

Even before the war, the U.S. government ordered the Central Intelligence Agency to launch Operation PBSUCCESS (1953–54) and halt Guatemala’s “communist revolt”, basically progressive forces – “October Revolutionaries” – who took control of the country after 1944, implementing countless socially- oriented reforms; another terrible crime in the eyes of the Empire.

In neighboring Honduras, the United States established its continuing military presence and from there it supported (illegally, even according to the US Constitution) the terrorist Contras across the border in Nicaragua.

The military of Honduras for years took direct orders from the United States and entire waves of extra-judicial killings in the country’s history took place, backed by the CIA. The notorious “Battalion 316” perpetrated the worst ones. There were also kidnappings and “disappearances” of countless Left wing opposition figures (including members of ‘Cinchoneros Popular Liberation Movement’) orchestrated by the armed forces.

Recently, in 2009, the Left-Wing President Manuel Zelaya was deposed in what was widely believed to be a US-backed coup.

Both Guatemala and Honduras suffer from some of the highest levels of gang violence and delinquency anywhere in the world, a fact linked directly to the militias and death squads supported and trained for decades by the United States, as well as by the past wars ignited and fueled from the North.

* * *

Nicaragua is different.

There is no other country in Central America that has suffered more in the hands of the Empire. An adventurer William Walker declared himself a King here in 1856 before being driven from his ‘throne’ by other Central American countries one year later.

At the beginning of the 20th Century, President Zelaya dared to make an attempt to regulate foreign access to Nicaraguan natural resources and the United States reacted with predictable fury, invading the country in 1909 and staying, with one brief interval, until 1933. Nicaragua was converted into a *de facto* colony. Shortly after the Marines left, the long and horrible era of the Somoza Dynasty (1936 – 1979) was installed and sponsored from the North. Anastasio Somoza García was a strange brew, a fascist and caudillo, but above all the fateful servant of the Empire. His offspring followed the same line; Anastasio Somoza Debayle, was first the Head of the notorious National Guard and later the President, he was 'educated' at West Point.

During the brutal dictatorship of the Somoza clan, Nicaragua lost almost all of its coastal pines; there was unbridled deforestation, soil erosion and 'land grabs' by ruling elites. Hundreds of thousands of people were constantly on the move – relocated, displaced, and forced to abandon their land. Lethal pesticides like DDT and Dieldrin poisoned the land. The US interests and local elites ruined the country, systematically and without mercy.

The violence of the destruction reached unimaginable heights.

But unlike elsewhere, the opposition was well-organized and disciplined. The fight against fascism did not only include weapons, it encompassed education, revolutionary pathos ventilated through poetry, as well as literature and music.

After the devastating "Managua Earthquake" which killed 10,000 people and left 500,000 homeless on December 1972, the government stole much of the money from international relief funds. This was the last straw and on the 27th December 1974, a group of FSLN guerrillas went into action and the war for the liberation of Nicaragua erupted.

For almost seven years the government used death squads and bombed civilians. Martial law was declared and entire villages were razed. The US was unconditionally supported its ally. The Soviet Union and Cuba felt obliged to join the fight and support FSLN.

On July 19, 1979, the Somoza dictatorship finally came to an end. The new – Sandinista – government was proclaimed, led by the 35 year old, Daniel Ortega. Young revolutionaries took over the city, with their songs and good humor, and brought hope to a ghostly capital.

A fabulous creative energy was unleashed; several years of rebuilding the nation began. After the brutal pro-US dictatorship, the Sandinistas had to fight malnutrition, pollution, widespread misery and illiteracy.

But success and an independent course unleashed, as always, a furious reaction from the United States, who embraced the Contras, established by Somoza's National Guard and strongly supported by the former Nicaraguan business elites. The Contras were allegedly funded by the CIA elements involved in the cocaine trade in Central America, and the United States itself.

During the Reagan years, the US unleashed nothing short of a war against the poor Central American nation, destroying its ports, infrastructure and terrorizing civilians. The Contras brutalized the local population, making excursions from their bases in Honduras and Costa Rica.

As always in similar scenarios, the US enjoyed absolute impunity. Although the International Court of Justice (ICJ) condemned its actions in 1986, the U.S. refused to pay restitution to Nicaragua, even after The United Nations General Assembly passed a resolution in order to pressure the U.S. to pay the fine. Only El Salvador and Israel voted against it.

The brutality of the civil war exhausted the country and broke its revolutionary spirit. The Sandinistas lost the elections in 1990, and then again in 1996.

I drove all around the country in October 1996. The remnants of the violence were everywhere, destroyed towns and villages; the bullet holes. In Rama, I hired a small boat and sailed down the Rio Escondido. There, some of the most vicious fighting had taken place during the war. And it was there where I witnessed the most symbolic remnant of the war – a long and ghostly wreck of a cargo boat rotting in the middle of the river; a boat sank by the Contras. Its name was "Hope".

Imagine "Free and fair" elections (that is how they were described by the Western mass media) where most of the people you ask say they would vote for the Sandinistas, but vote for the Right-wing instead, too scared of the threats that were coming from the US embassy that was almost openly suggesting that the war would resume should the Left win again in democratic elections.

In those years I tried to make sense of all that was happening in Nicaragua, I spoke to Daniel Ortega and I spoke to Eden Pastora, "Commander Zero", the first hero of the Revolution and later the leader of a faction of the Contras, a man who apparently refused to accept the US command and tactics, and suggested to his North American counter-parts to "eat shit".

One thing was clear to me: no matter how broken the country felt, no matter how depressing the regressive policies were of the right wing governments, it was obvious to anyone that Nicaragua was "different" from other Central American nations. It was a place where people still knew how to dream about a better world. There was much more solidarity and awareness there than anywhere else in the region.

When the Left (Republicans) lost the civil war in Spain, they used to say: "We lost, but we had better songs!" Even when I worked for a year in Costa Rica, the 'region's star", I felt a great relief driving across the border to Nicaragua. They always had better jokes and much better songs there.

To have good songs and a good education certainly helps. The nation finally pulled together and in November 2006, Daniel Ortega won the elections once again. Of course he is far from being a perfect leader. Pastora, who came back and is now a cabinet minister, is also far from being 'clean', but what a difference between Nicaragua and those other Central American countries that also went through the deadly spiral of violence, such as Guatemala, Honduras, or Panama!

* * *

After coming under fire in San Salvador, after seeing all that hopelessness and the decay of the city of Colon in Panama, I arrived in Nicaragua. I came for just two days, for the film-roll I had to collect for one of my documentary films. I rented a car and after checking into my hotel in Managua, I drove to splendid Granada on the Lake Nicaragua.

It was already late afternoon when I arrived. Before entering the city center, I noticed a large and welcoming park in front of the historic train station. It was dotted with the impressive modern sculptures of the great Nicaraguan poets. Each sculpture had one poem engraved in white color on its black surface. I read the names and the poems with reverence: Ernesto Cardenal, Enrique Fernandez Morales, Manolo Cuadra, Jose Coronel Urtecho, Joaquin Pasos...

Children were playing all around the park and lovers were sat underneath those engraved poems, holding hands, embracing and kissing, whispering promises that were whispered by those who are in love, ever since the very beginning of the world.

There was something moving and good about this entire atmosphere. It was an image of peace, of simple joy, of goodness.

It hit me that this was all very symbolic – this was the spirit of Central America, a beautiful and tender part of the world, with its great ancient civilizations and communal and sharing spirit. In this world many great poems and songs were born. The couples would dance here until the early morning hours while stories would flow often for days and nights. The beautiful land and the sea produced more than enough to sustain those few millions who lived here.

But outside Nicaragua and Costa Rica, the violence is still torturing and scarring the people; blood still flows, women are still crying at night remembering all those horrors they had to witness, remembering the men they loved and lost, the children they breastfed and lost, and all the injustice that is impossible to ever forgive and forget.

All that injustice... And all that violence unleashed by generations of those who only knew wars and monstrous dictatorships, the death squads.

Chances are that the child who grows up playing on a metal replica of old steam train under the statues of great writers will grow up to recite poems to his first love, somewhere in a park like this one in Granada. Chances are that a child who played with knifes and grew up witnessing indescribable violence will join some gang, and will turn to killing and raping with not a second's thought.

In Guatemala, in El Salvador, in Nicaragua: people were certain what societies they wanted to live in. At one point or another they opted for progressive, humane governments. But their choices were drowned in blood. The Empire; the United States of America, put business and colonial interests ahead of any considerations for human lives. Hundreds of thousands of men, women and children were slaughtered. No apologies and no compensation ever came.

Entire nations ruined, entire cities ruined. The gangs, the violence, the misery – this is what has replaced hope and natural strife, for justice.

Two countries, two places only in this tortured strip of land between Mexico and the Darien Gap are now rising from the ashes again: Nicaragua and El Salvador. Honduras tried but was cut down the middle by yet another US-backed shameless coup. The only way for Nicaragua and El Salvador to survive is to join hands, to cling with all their strength to their bigger brothers in South America, those that are uniting, those who are finally coming through, those who after centuries of servility, are standing proudly on their own feet.

3 August 2012

*****

7

BOLIVIAN DOCTORS FIGHTING FOR SOCIALISM

It is late morning, May 27th, 2012, and one of the squares of the Bolivian city of Cochabamba is colorful and festive. The police and army are patrolling the area, but they are apparently also enjoying the Sunday morning, looking more like characters from an Italian comical opera than the strict upholders of the law.

The square is full. It is packed with indigenous women, some carrying children on their backs, some with cotton sacks in their hands, almost all wearing hats.

Hundreds of local women have come to the square to register their babies and children inside the provisory tents erected by the government. Most of these kids were born out of wedlock; something that would have just a few years ago been deplored by society, even considered immoral and shameful. Things are changing now and fingers point accusatively in different directions, while the state is trying to register everybody regardless of how he or she came onto this earth, as without the proper registration, children and adults have no right for government assistance.

In 2005, Evo Morales became for the first time, the President of

Bolivia and despite some vicious and determined resistance, and attempts to destabilize his government from both the West and the ranks of the Bolivian elites, things have begun changing rapidly for this nation with the greatest indigenous majority in South America. And "The Process" has never stopped, or never even slowed down.

Now in Cochabamba like in most other parts of the country, both the city and the state are encouraging women to come forward: to list their children, to talk about the abuse they have faced from family and society, to check themselves for breast cancer, for tuberculosis, to learn how to prepare healthy food themselves and for their children.

In the past I would have never dared to take photographs of Bolivian women and their children point blank. There were legends about stealing the soul through the lenses of cameras, and there was a creeping lack of trust. If I had attempted to ask questions, most of them would have gone unanswered. Now, it is as if the fog has been lifted, the dam has burst, and the bitterness accumulated over the past years and decades has began to flow, transforming, begging to lend itself to stories. The fear has miraculously vanished, replaced by hope, and the stories that have begun emerging were full of force.

Most of the stories were simple and they spoke of pain, of simple and faithful women being abandoned by their husbands, spouses, for no apparent reason when they were pregnant or when other women crossed their path. But there were also other stories, those of injustice and abuse, of social wrongs, full of outrage and rebelliousness.

"Two of my children died when they were little", one of the mothers said, facing me defiantly as if I had been designated to bear at least some part of the responsibility. She showed me with her harsh, hard-working hands how small they were: "that little", she kept repeating in disbelief, "that tiny". Then looking straight into my eyes: "Why?"

I knew why and so did she. There was nothing to be said, but looking at me she somehow knew that I heard what she was saying and that her words would be carried from this square to the wide world.

A few meters away, the mobile clinics were parked at the kerb - several of them. They were actually huge ingeniously converted trucks. I went up the stairs of one of them, knocked at the door. Someone opened and I was let inside where a woman was giving her full breast to her baby, while a doctor and a nurse showered her with medical advice.

And here, what stunned me was the trust – absolutely and powerfully expressed: between the mother and the doctor, the nurse and the woman and between all of them and me. It took me just a few seconds to explain what I was doing here. We exchanged polite greetings. I asked whether I could film. "Yes, of course", all of them nodded. It was up to me to set the limits. I was expected to be discreet, but I was not told to be. It was understood that all of us were gathered here for an important reason: to help Bolivia and its people. The doctor was probably Cuban, and the nurse was local. I did not ask; it did not matter. A true internationalist should not care much about one's geographical, cultural or other roots.

What mattered though was that right in front of my eyes something that would have been unimaginable just a few years ago was suddenly taking place: in once impoverished and racially divided and classist Bolivia, a white man, a doctor, was looking with simple warmth and human compassion at a suffering indigenous woman breastfeeding her baby, asking her "When was the last time you felt pain, mother?"

He behaved in a simple, kind, decent and humane way, but in a world increasingly kidnapped by financial and personal interests his humanism felt like an extreme, like a reminder of different era. He was a doctor and he behaved like one, as doctors were expected to behave in that not so distant past. But here as in so many other places all over the world, it has been common that instead of inquiring, "Where does it hurt?" but to ask instead for a credit card number or cash deposit, that normal behavior therefore felt something of an anomaly.

At one point the doctor patted the woman's arm, kindly. He was of a different race and background, and he behaved as her equal, making her feel calm and confident. After a while she began answering his questions quietly and boldly, as if she were speaking to a member of her own family.

At this point I knew I was witnessing a revolution. I had witnessed quite a few of them, as well as many civil wars all over the world. But this was different. There were no Kalashnikovs, no combat zones, but this was as big as the Sandinistas in Nicaragua "going up", taking the Congress, some decades ago.

Unlike the doctors who are concerned with their inflated salaries – in Bolivia and all over the world – the doctors working here appeared cool and confident, at ease and clearly at peace with themselves and the world and above all, with their own conscience. They seemed to have no need for complex philosophical somersaults explaining why they were stuffing their purses instead of serving the needy. They were doing exactly what they were trained to do: saving lives, offering advice, and being there for those that were in pain and in distress, nothing more, nothing less.

Just watching these doctors working in the middle of Cochabamba I felt overwhelmed and at the same time endlessly grateful. It was like coming home from an extremely long and unsettling journey, dotted with nightmarish images depicting perversely but accurately the direction the world was heading in, or rather to where its kidnappers were taking it. Coming back from a journey where commercial interests stand above compassion, where 'helping' those in need and in pain is simply a good business and has its price-tag, mostly ridiculously inflated.

To me these sights in the middle of the Bolivian Andes were like the essence of the human nature – by now almost extinct but still the essence – played in front of my eyes. And I was very much aware of the fact that this was exactly the socialism in which I have believed in for decades; it was right here, in action, in front of my eyes. And it was simple, natural and undogmatic.

Then I recalled one of the greatest novels ever written -The Plague (La Peste) - by Albert Camus, and the unforgettable phrase "And unable to become saints, they became doctors". I thought about the main character, a simple doctor named Bernard Rieux, who when the plague began ravishing the Algerian city of Oran, stood against the unimaginable horror and destruction, and against all odds fought the illness with all his knowledge and might, losing his wife, losing everybody he loved in the process, but in the end winning the battle and saving his city. As I watched the doctors working in the center of Cochabamba, it was evident that they, as Dr Rieux in The Plague, were not only fighting diseases, they were fighting fascism! In Cochabamba and in Oran, they were struggling for all humanity.

Then I looked around some more. I realized that I knew these women well. I had covered the civil war in neighboring Peru for more than a year in the 90s, I had driven through Bolivia – the poorest country in South America - from North to South, and from East to West so many times I lost count. They were always 'there', these women in colorful dresses and black hats - silently watching, standing by the side of the roads, selling fresh fruits and cheap imported goods on the sidewalks: the indigenous women of Peru, of Ecuador, of Bolivia.

The women of Altiplano used to appear to me as an incarnation of pain and stoicism, of a once tremendous and now destroyed culture, of hopelessness and the miraculous ability of human beings to survive the worst that life can serve on its dirty and cracked plates.

In the past, I always tried to avoid their eyes, because I felt shame and because I did not know how to help them. In Bolivia, for decades, a revolution had been postponed indefinitely. The country was silently bleeding, governed by the shameless and Euro-centric elites. It was a man's world, but in which, even the men – or more precisely a great majority of them, were going through a dehumanizing and constant humiliation. A decisive revolution appeared to be the only act capable of offering some hope; capable of overthrowing the feudal fascist system.

Decades ago, Che Guevara died for this country; one of the greatest revolutionaries of all times had fallen alone here, helpless, abandoned and betrayed. But for him not to fight in Bolivia and for Bolivia, would have been like not fighting at all; it would have been a thorough hypocrisy. Because it was precisely here– in these cold, inhospitable but endlessly beautiful mountains, in the clay huts of Altiplano, in the hot, humid and predominantly feudal settlements lost in the middle of selva – the jungle – that more than 500 years of colonial and post-colonial brutality, and the madness that showed its most terrible face, had stripped of all humanity and humanism.

This is where Potosi's veins were opened, this is where she was stripped naked and robbed of everything, her children dying in the mines for the glory of European civilization. The richest city on earth, the city of silver, with its people forced to die likes animals for the Crown, and for the brave and glorious European culture!

The plight of these women was hidden. Many of those journalists who were writing in Bolivia and Peru were paid, directly or indirectly, not to expose the harsh realities of the local people.

Of course there were some sparks of outrage, of fury, like those in the films by Francisco Lombardi, the greatest Peruvian filmmaker. He directed his “La boca del lobo” (‘Wolf's Mouth’, 1988), depicting the ‘Dirty War’ in the Peruvian Andes, which I had covered and which changed me forever, and the terror the indigenous people had to face. There, he showed a rape of a simple indigenous girl. It was a rape that was not even considered a rape by the soldiers who committed it, because the girl was indigenous – and in the eyes of city folks hardly human. Lombardi shows half-mad soldiers believing they were on the mission to get all local women pregnant.

And then he dared to show the horror of extra-judiciary execution, a mass murder of the villagers killed simply for being there, and at the end, he showed a boy called Vitin Luna; a boy who joined the army to serve his country as his father had done in the past. He showed Luna drunk, shattered and disillusioned, suddenly risking his career and his life, challenging the lieutenant who oversaw the rape and a killing during a game of Russian roulette, in one of the greatest and most powerful moments in Latin American cinema. Waving a gun and smashing down the door of the house in the middle of the night, screaming in the darkness: “Come down, lieutenant! Come down if you really have balls!”

Many years ago I showed the film to my acquaintance in La Paz, the owner of a major daily newspaper and the son of a Senator. I asked him: “Don't you think that one day there will be people banging at the gate of your mansion?” He gave me a big smile, as he was packing his golf bag. “They will come”, he said. “Of course one day they will come. But before that, I will be having plenty of fun while they will be eating shit.”

“Try this”, I was handed a cup of yoghurt with local herbs. “It is really good for you – all natural”. Several nutritionists have explained to local people how to incorporate healthy things they have and grow into their daily diet.

I moved further and was asked to register my family for some government health program. I tried to reproduce the most outrageous Chilean accent I could muster, but it didn't deter the enthusiastic government employee. “You don't live here? But you definitely know some people who do. Bring them here, we will tell them to sign up; it is for their own good."

The entire atmosphere was of socialist realism at its best. It was naïve, sincere and to be in the middle of it felt extremely good and warm. People working in the square appeared to be fully stripped of any cynicism, sarcasm and self-interest. The government, medical staff and hundreds of women who were on the receiving end of it, interacted naturally and confidently. There was calm and plenty of goodwill, but there was no artificiality – not many pre-fabricated smiles and no unnecessary or extreme courtesy.

Many years ago a friend of mine, a translator and writer Kevin Mathewson who presently lives in Brazil, recalled the first days of the Nicaraguan revolution that he experienced in Managua:

> "What I found the most powerful was not the revolution itself, but what it unleashed. One day I was standing at the side of the road. A bus was passing. It was full of girls from the countryside, dressed in their best. The bus was packed. Some girls were barefoot, but they were all very clean and very excited. You see, they were going to downtown Managua; they were going to dance. For the first time in their lives they were going to be allowed to enter the places that were just few days earlier reserved only for the elites. Suddenly, they knew they could... There was so much anticipation and hope and excitement radiating from their faces... This was the moment when I understood that this revolution was right, when I saw those shy countryside girls going to the capital city which was suddenly theirs."

The music erupted. Many women spontaneously moved towards its source; the provisional stage. Until then, most of them had known only hard work; they had no opportunity to learn how to dance, but they wanted to be included, they wanted to live. They moved their feet clumsily, they smiled apologetically, and they kept trying and trying to dance. Some outsiders may have found their movements ridiculous, but here, nobody was laughing. It was their square, their city and their country. They were testing and tasting the first steps of their own hard-earned freedom, not the type of freedom prefabricated and pushed down peoples' throats by the West.

For some of them, their new life was starting at the age of 18 or even sooner, but many were well into their 60s. It did not seem to matter much. They were all learning how to walk, how to take the first steps – the steps of people who suddenly realized that the country and the society in which they lived now actually belonged to them, and not the other way around.

I travelled throughout the country and I heard the voices of those in favor as well as those who were against the revolution, as I had earlier in Venezuela and elsewhere. I spoke to the medics who were throwing red paint onto their clothes, opposed to the reforms introduced by the government. I spoke to those who were deeply involved in the protest against the new highway that was being carved through the jungle.

I disagreed with the protesters, because many were using the indigenous card for their own commercial and political interests, or more precisely the opposing local media and international media were using these cards. It was also clear that there were striking similarities between the protests that were antagonistic to the progressive changes in today's Bolivia and the protests that have been rocking Venezuela since Chavez became the President, as well as in Allende's Chile before the US-sponsored military coup on 9-11-1973. Many of those protests were orchestrated and sponsored by the right-wing and by those who, as Eduardo Galeano once said to me, "were paid by somebody, but would not tell by whom".

I do not want to go into the details of my investigation –the details are disturbing, often appalling. In this essay I am simply offering a glimpse into those few moments that I lived in one of the squares of Cochabamba -moments that in their simplicity and epic beauty made me, once again, refuse impartiality. After those few moments, in my own way I joined 'the Process', offering my full support to the Bolivian revolution of Evo Morales.

As I was leaving Cochabamba for La Paz, the military transport BAE-146 jet encountered great difficulty gaining altitude. It was obviously overloaded and taking off at great altitude, its four engines seemed to be roaring in vain, unable to pull the airplane up. After the takeoff, it had frozen at an extremely low height, almost licking the roofs of the houses. The mountains were directly in front of us and I knew enough about flying to realize that either we would manage to go up or we would crash. I was clearly aware of the fact that if the plane were to make an attempt to make a turn to avoid the mountain range, it would slide to the side and lose the altitude sharply, as it was flying too slowly through the air that was too thin at this altitude.

There was no panic - I realized that many people on board were probably flying for the first time, unaware of the danger. And I was simply too tired to feel anything as I had worked for several days and nights without rest.

After several tense minutes, the pilots managed to gain altitude and we flew over the mountains, but just about.

The metaphor was clear, I thought. It was exactly what Bolivia was going through at this historic period. It was beyond the point of no return, and it could not change its direction. If the country were to leave its path towards an egalitarian society - historically its essence before European colonial terror smashed all the local cultures - it would simply crash. There would be almost nothing that could support its wings. The only way was to go forward, to clench the fists and fly over those enormous mountains of resistance taken away here by those from abroad; to fly above all that bad inertia and saturated hopelessness.

The old BAE-146 and its pilots were like Bolivia, far from perfect. Errors have been made every month, every week, and every day. But the path has been correct and well-defined. Now everything depended on their will, skills and guts. Full throttle, take off the flaps and up we go, carambas! Dangerous? Yes it was dangerous, as anything worth living and fighting for always is.

"No matter what happens to Evo", a young Argentinian philosopher said, whom I met onboard a mini-van plying at breakneck speed between the border at Desaguadero and the Peruvian city of Puno, "Bolivia will never go back. It may stumble, slow down, but after what is happening here right now, return is not an option."

But a day before that conversation, approaching the city of La Paz, I was thinking about the doctors I had encountered in Cochabamba. People like them were on the frontline of the Bolivian 'Process'. They were fighting for the country; they were pushing it forward. They were healing and simultaneously they were building trust and confidence, redefining relationships in this profound and ancient part of the world. They were not saints and they did not claim to be – they were simply revolutionaries.

At El Alto International Airport a young doctor had picked me up, my driver. He was just finishing his degree and driving a cab was one way to stay afloat.

"It is good you saw it", he said. "Westerners: most of them want this government to fail. They want to grab our natural resources again, to enslave us. They don't want Bolivia to be able to govern itself, to show an example to the world. This is one of the richest countries on earth, which was made to be one of the poorest. I want to be a doctor, yes. But not for the status – I want to become one so I will be able to cure, and also because I want to serve my people."

I recalled a poster in Santiago de Chile, several years ago, with a photo of a student and a few simple words: "I am studying to be a doctor, so I can take away the pain from which my country is suffering."

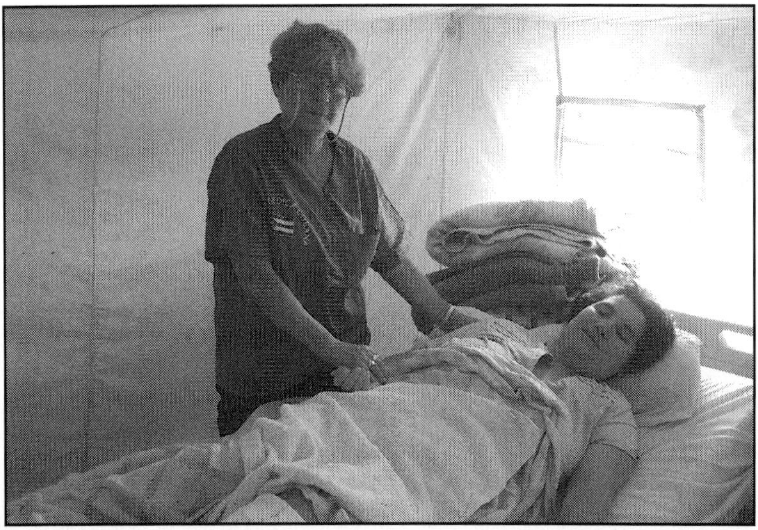

Photo 3. Cuban doctor at work in Rancagua, Chile, after deadly earthquake.

Everything is changing in South America. This is what its people have wanted for decades and centuries; this is what they struggled for. Their will was broken, literally raped by outside forces. Now a new era of solidarity, of a powerful and determined drive towards building compassionate and social states is sweeping colonial and post-colonial mentality and their other elements, aside. The continent is taking off in an elegant, confident, and majestic fashion.

It was a very dangerous takeoff, but it was already in the process. It was now or never, after more than 500 years of humiliation, theft and plunder.

"Please stop", I asked my young friend, the doctor, as we descended from El Alto, from more than 4,000 meters, towards that enormous crater of La Paz. I spotted a huge piece of graffiti demanding 'Medical care for all' and next to it a corpulent indigenous lady wearing her traditional outfit. I wanted to film the scene. As I was shooting, the lady suddenly moved aside, exposing the rest of the slogan her body had been sheltering before: "and it should be free!"

I liked the sight. I liked the lady, looking at me sarcastically but with a friendly spark in her eyes. I liked this enormous city of La Paz down below. I liked Mount Illimani covered by snow on the horizon, the symbol of this glorious and injured culture that was just beginning to heal. I liked the indigenous flags flying next to those of Bolivia.

"Whom would you like to heal?" I asked my friend, lighting up my Cuban cigarillo.

He did not answer; just waved his hand at the city and at the hills of El Alto, covered by slums.

"Good", I said. "There will be plenty of work for you here."

He nodded confidently and proudly, before shifting gear.

18 June 2012

*****

8

In the Heart of the DR Congo

THE MOST BRUTAL GENOCIDE MONEY CAN BUY

The camp for Congolese refugees in Kisoro is overcrowded, and people keep flowing in. The border between Uganda and DR Congo is just a few kilometers away, and right behind the border the vicious fighting goes on; there is true bloodshed and carnage.

The border is called Bunagana. I drive there, I film, and I talk to a few people. There is tension, everybody is edgy – locals and refugees. One cannot tell who is who. Both Ugandans and Congolese know, but, an outsider cannot tell the difference; it is one region, one area. People have been going back and forth for years and decades; people mixied, stayed on both sides of the border legally and illegally.

But now, there is almost nothing left to go back to at the other side of the border. The murderous militia, M23, recently went on a rampage – killing, raping and looting with no mercy, and with absolute impunity.

M23 is supported by Rwanda, by President Kagame and by his RPF (Rwandan Patriotic Front). Rwanda and Uganda are old allies. They are looting DR Congo and its natural riches, mostly in unison, and with deadly precision. Their forces are supported, armed and trained by the West (Europe and the United States). So in the lexicon of political indoctrination and disinformation that is being spread by the mass media on both sides of the Atlantic, the governments and armed forces of Uganda and Rwanda are defined as the 'good guys', they are even encouraged to serve in the lucrative 'peacekeeping missions' in Somalia, South Sudan and elsewhere.

It is widely believed that around 6 to10 million Congolese people have lost their lives since the 90's – which makes it the deadliest genocide since WWII. One of the richest countries on earth in terms of natural wealth has been reduced to the lowest ranking on HDI (Human Development Index of UNDP, 2011).

What is shocking is that almost nobody in Europe or North America seems to know about the situation. Some have heard about 'the civil war' in the Great Lakes region; some have heard about the refugees and the victims; some have even read about the pathetic bunch of stoned lunatics, running around the jungle with Kalashnikovs and hand grenades.

But of the genocide, committed on behalf of Western business and geo-political interests? There is not a clue.

Reports coming out of several Western press agencies depict the situation in Kisoro in gloomy and abstract terms, which are full of clichés. "Hospitals are overcrowded", reads one of them.

Kisoro hospital that I visited two days after the appearance of the reports, could hardly be described as overcrowded, but the 'crowds' were outside, consisting of dozens of people trying to make their way through the gate and the wire grid-protected perimeter, into the medical facility. The Hospital is staffed with confused international doctors and local nurses. After some negotiation, I am taken to several wounded Congolese soldiers, who are resting on cots. They are too frightened, and resolutely refuse to be interviewed.

"Nobody would say it openly, but no refugee would end up in this hospital", explains my driver who is from the capital city of Kampala. "Locals are instructed to report all Congolese people to the authorities. Those who escape DRC, end up in the camps. Unless they have some private arrangement with the authorities..."

"Yesterday I saw 20 Congolese soldiers walking down the road away from the border", explained an elementary school teacher, who speaks to me just a few minutes drive from Bunagana border. "They were not armed: they usually leave their weapons at the border crossing."

I wonder what that means? The regular Congolese army is supposed to be fighting the Rwanda-backed M23. So what are they doing here? At least in theory, shouldn't they be immediately returned to DR Congo, or treated as deserters? After all, everybody now agrees that the ravaging of East Kivu, right across the border, could amount to genocide. And these well-nourished men in uniforms are supposed to be defending their women, children and men, instead of getting sanatorium treatment in Uganda.

But it is obvious that Congolese soldiers in East Kivu are not encouraged to stay in their country, and fight the pro-Rwandan and therefore pro-Western militias.

As I mentioned, the cyberspace is constantly fed by reports from major Western press agencies, but I appear to be the only foreigner around, with professional still and video equipment. And I am here in order to put the final touches, to my documentary film, not for some mass media-related assignment. There are obviously no uncomfortable questions being asked. The authorities are alert but generally at ease, they show no fear. They don't shoot at me; they don't try to arrest me this time. They just shoo me away as if I was some annoying fly. But I persistently make my rounds, shuttling between the border from which I now clearly hear the fighting, to the camp, IRC post and the airstrip where a Russian piloted UN MI-8 helicopter is parked, ready for immediate departure.

"The UN is shuttling a Ugandan minister between Kampala and Kisoro", I am told by an onlooker, in a whisper.

"Minister of what?" I ask cautiously, but nobody knows. And I have no way of verifying. Uganda is a country of rumors.

I park the car and enter Nyakabande refugee camp, the one on the outskirts of Kisoro. I immediately begin to work, knowing the risk, and realizing that every second counts. It takes just a couple of minutes, and a security guard intercepts me.

Soon I am facing the head of the camp, a thoroughly arrogant individual, with a spiteful way of talking. He refers to me as "darling", despite my beard. I confront him; demanding to be allowed to film and take photographs. Several of my official IDs are rejected without any closer scrutiny. He demands for some 'special permits' from Kampala, which is around 500 kilometers away. I demand that he backs up and let me film, photograph and talk to the refugees. He laughs at me. He feels so certain of himself, that he shouts in my face that he will not identify himself, and will not give his name. When I insist, he calls the armed forces and orders them to throw me out of the camp. In DR Congo I would be lucky to survive such a confrontation.

"He is Rwandese", somebody whispers in my ear as I climb into the vehicle.

"What?" I scream. I really do.

"His name and the way he speaks. Maybe he grew up here, in Uganda, but he speaks like a Rwandese."

Rumors again?

I am trying to make the story simple. Not really simple, because there is no way to do it, but just a bit simpler.

The other day I spoke to the co-producer and the editor of our huge 150-minute documentary film "Rwandan Gambit". We discussed the complexity of the Great Lakes story. I have made films and written books on the Indonesian genocide of 1965/66, on the entire system of neo-colonialism in Oceania, on Chile and many other places. But nowhere else is the story is so complex and so blurred; nowhere else, I feel that I have to begin from zero.

What does the West know? What do the people in New York, London, Paris or Sydney imagine when one utters the names Rwanda, Burundi, Uganda or DR Congo separately or in one single breath? And I am talking about the educated people, not the crowd that gets the news from the network television stations.

Chances are they saw "Hotel Rwanda": a film about the 1994 genocide in Rwanda. About how Hutus suddenly went bananas, and began massacring innocent Tutsis. And how one good, heroic man – (in real life, his name is Paul Rusesabagina, and the hotel in Kigali is named Mille Collines) – saved hundreds of innocent lives.

A few months ago, I went back to Mille Collines for a cup of coffee, and had a chat with the headwaiter. Of course he had no clue that my editor spoke to Paul Rusesabagina and found out, that he was forced to leave Rwanda. “Do you know where Mr. Rusesabagina is?” I asked naively. “In South Africa”, was the reply. “Why do you ask?” “Just being curious”, I said.

So, how do I summarize what I found, during those three years of intensive work on the film on Rwanda and Congo?

First of all, all four countries involved: Rwanda, Burundi, DR Congo and Uganda have been suffering from the worst cases of colonialism and neo-colonialism. To begin with, Congo (then Zaire) had Patrice Lumumba, one of the greatest African leaders, assassinated by the West.

Emira Woods, Co-Director of Foreign Policy In Focus, explained in the film:

> “You had this liberation fighter Patrice Lumumba, who came to power as a leader of a unionist movement, a visionary who wanted to have the resources of the continent, as well as the country, serve the interests of the continent; to feed the children of the continent. And he was assassinated at the hands of the US and the UK – two key geopolitical actors, who wanted to deny the right of the Congo to truly seek its own destiny, to have a future determined by its own people.”

When the President of Rwanda – Paul Kagame – was living in exile in Uganda, he became a close friend of the now Ugandan President, Yoweri Museveni. They even went to the same high school together – in Mbarara. Eventually Kagame became the head of Ugandan military intelligence, and his RPF had been funded by Western sources through Ugandan channels, as was confirmed to us by the former US Ambassador to Rwanda – Robert Flaten.

At that period of time, one prominent Ugandan businessman who wants to remain anonymous for now at least, told me: “In Uganda, Paul Kagame is known as Pilato(after Pontius Pilate). He was the most sadistic killer and torturer, when he was the head of the Military Intelligence of Uganda.”

One of the many victims (in Uganda) who were under the supervision of Paul Kagame, declared to me in an interview, in Kampala on August 27, 2012: “I was electrocuted through my testicles as I was tied. Interrogators were using the so called kandoya. The kandoya involved tying forcefully, both of my hands behind my back, thus forcing my chest to widen, and in the process causing internal bleeding. After that I was again tied in a way that made me swing like a pendulum, and that is when electric torture was applied again. All this took place in Katabi Military Barracks in Entebbe, in 1987, when Paul Kagame was in charge. I spotted him on several occasions in the background. Most of the interrogators were Rwandese."

The dreadful human rights record of Paul Kagame naturally did not deter the US and its allies from supporting Kagame and the RPF, as it did not deter the West from supporting other sadistic murderers in Indonesia, the Arab world, El Salvador, Argentina, Chile, South Africa and elsewhere.

By the beginning of the 1990's, the RPF had been penetrating Rwandan territory from Uganda for years, killing civilians and forcing hundreds of thousands of refugees to flee their homes. There were already hundreds of thousands of refugees from Burundi – mainly Hutu – living in Rwanda, most of them arriving after the bloody and near-genocidal crackdown, of the Burundian Tutsi elites against Hutus.Two months ago, I ventured to Kirundo Province of Burundi, together with an interpreter, and the villagers recalled vividly and on the record (for my film) the horrors of the 1979 exodus from their country. "The situation inside Burundi was so dreadful, that Hutus would not even want to bury their dead in their own country. They were carrying them across the border to Rwanda."

In their books, Andrew Wallis (Silent accomplice), Barbara F. Walter, and Jack L. Snyder (Civil Wars, Insecurity, and Intervention) argue:

> "In 1990, the Rwandan Patriotic Front, a rebel group composed mostly of Tutsi refugees, invaded northern Rwanda from Uganda in an attempt to defeat the Hutu-led government. They began the Rwandan Civil War, fought between the Hutu regime, with support from Francophone Africa and France... and the RPF, with support from Uganda. This exacerbated ethnic tensions in the country. In response, many Hutu gravitated toward the Hutu Power ideology, with the prompting of state-controlled and independent Rwandan media."

The racist rhetoric and agitation had been mounting across the country. The leitmotif was that, Tutsi were enslaving Hutu and had to be resisted at all cost.

The IMF was not idle either. It did its best to destabilize Rwanda, impoverished it and devalued its currency.

In his penetrating analysis of the economic and social causes behind the Rwandan holocaust, Michel Chossudovsky, a Canadian economist and a professor of economics (emeritus) at the University of Ottawa, focused his attention on how the Structural Adjustment Policies of the IMF and the World Bank contributed to the disaster in the Great Lakes Region:

> "To lay the blame solely on deep-seated tribal hatred not only exonerates the great powers and the donors, it also distorts an exceedingly complex process of economic, social and political disintegration affecting an entire nation of more than seven million people... Rwanda, however, is but one among many countries in sub-Saharan Africa (not to mention recent developments in Burundi where famine and ethnic massacres are rampant) which are facing a similar predicament. And in many respects the Rwandan 1990 devaluation appears almost as a 'laboratory test-case' as well as a threatening 'danger signal' for the devaluation of the CFA franc implemented on the instructions of the IMF and the French Treasury in January 1994 by the same amount, 50%."

And, in a report prepared for the defense team at the ICTR, on June 2002, German analyst Uwe Frieseckewent, went even further by arguing that:

> "Western powers, most prominently the Anglo-American powers with the Francophone powers acting as competing junior partners, have caused the crises in the Great Lakes region of Africa during the 1980s and 1990s in a twofold manner and are therefore responsible for the human catastrophe that followed. First, they ruined the region like the rest of the continent through the International Monetary Fund's (IMF's) Structural Adjustment Policy economically. Secondly, they intervened with cover operations to manipulate simmering conflicts for the purpose of political control. The combination of both led to the disaster in Rwanda in 1994."

In 1994 the country was in total disarray, hit by misery, by RPF raids across the border and by the mounting refugee crises.

And then, on April 6, 1994, the airplane carrying the Rwandan President Juvénal Habyarimana and Cyprien Ntaryamira, the Hutu president of Burundi, was shot down on its final approach to Kanombe airport, Kigali, its debris scattering all over the backyard of Habyarimana's mansion, killing everyone onboard, including the French crew. The country erupted.

The Hutu militia groups, including the notorious

"Interahamwe", began massacring members of Tutsi minority, including women and children. In just 100 days, between 500,000 and 1 million people died, although it is uncertain what the exact demographics of the victims were, as by then the RPF was already on Rwandan territory, and according to many experts, deeply involved in the slaughter as well, as it marched towards the capital city of Kigali.

The 100 days of genocidal terror are very well documented, although some are arguing that it is partial and one-sided.

The essential question remains – "Who downed the plane with two Presidents?" – As this was clearly the trigger to the consequent events.

In my film, I worked closely with the Australian attorney Michael Hourigan, the former ICTR investigator, who clearly indicated that he was approached by trustworthy sources close to Kagame's regime. They were scared but determined to tell the truth. It was the RPF that downed the plane. Then, Hourigan was summoned to The Hague, and his testimony was disputed and eventually he was forced to resign, as he believes, because of pressure from some of the Western powers.

Until now, not one RPF official or soldier has stood trial at the ICTR (International Criminal Tribunal for Rwanda) in Arusha, Tanzania. The tribunal is one-sided, dealing exclusively with the crimes committed by Hutu against Tutsi.

During the 1994 Rwandan Genocide, between 500,000 and 1 million people lost their lives, in the neighboring DR Congo the number of victims fluctuates between 6 and 10 million, between 1996 and to date, depending on the sources.

People are literally murdered over Coltan, Uranium, Gold, Diamonds, and other strategic and precious minerals and gems.

Both Rwanda and Uganda – key Western allies – have been involved. After the Rwandan genocide, President Paul Kagame and the RPF found a very good excuse to penetrate neighboring DRCongo – there were Hutu genocide cadres hiding among the refugees, and the new Rwandan government, had the moral mandate, to pursue them across the border.

Although the RPF was involved in some gruesome reprisal massacres, including the 1995 Kibeho Massacre of thousands, possibly tens of thousands of mainly Hutu refugees (in my film I use the powerful testimony of Terry Pickard – an Australian military medic who in 1995 witnessed the carnage) –the real horror was reserved for Congo.

Both Rwandan and Ugandan forces have been plundering this enormous and rich (in terms of natural resources) part of Africa, staging military coups and supporting/aiding some of the most appalling militias in the world, including forces of former Congolese Tutsi army General – Laurent Nkunda – who later became one of the most brutal warlords in Africa, as well as the notorious militia, M23, led by General Bosco Ntaganda, former commander of the CNDP and the FARDC.

Pro-Rwandan and pro-Ugandan proxy militias have periodically clashed, sometimes changing allegiances, or even going on their own. The mass slaughter of civilians was regularly accompanied by mass rape, like that in the city of Bukavu.

The West, and particularly the US and UK have been firmly supportive of the regimes, in both Rwanda and Uganda.

In my film, several personalities ranging from the former Congolese Presidential candidate Ben Kalala, to one of the leading African affairs analyst from Ghana, Nii Akuetteh, as well as Prof. Masako Yonekawa, former UNHCR Head of Field Office in Goma, confirmed that Western governments and companies have great economic interests in DR Congo. And that both Rwanda and Uganda have been utilized in plundering the neighboring country on their behalf.

While the Western mass media has on most occasions remained 'disciplined', and silent about the background of the conflict in DR Congo, the UN has managed to publish two damning reports. The first one was called the "UN Mapping Report" published by OHCHR in June 2010. Amongst other things it boldly states:

> "The intention to destroy a group in part is sufficient to constitute a crime of genocide and the international courts have confirmed that the destruction of a group can be limited to a particular geographical area.[28] It is therefore possible to assert that, even if only a part of the Hutu population in Zaire was targeted and destroyed, it could nonetheless constitute a crime of genocide if this was the intention of the perpetrators. Several incidents listed in this report point to circumstances and facts from which a court could infer the intention to destroy the Hutu ethnic group in the DRC in part, if these were established beyond

all reasonable doubt.

The scale of the crimes and the large number of victims, probably several tens of thousands, all nationalities combined, are illustrated by the numerous incidents listed in the report (104 in all). The extensive use of edged weapons (primarily hammers) and the systematic massacres of survivors after the camps had been taken show that the numerous deaths cannot be attributed to the hazards of war or seen as equating to collateral damage.[30] The majority of the victims were children, women, elderly people and the sick, who were often undernourished and posed no threat to the attacking forces.[31] Numerous serious attacks on the physical or mental integrity of members of the group were also committed, with a very high number of Hutus shot, raped, burnt or beaten."

The second, the most recent report released in June 2012, is called "Addendum to the interim report of the Group of Experts on the Democratic Republic of the Congo (S/2012/348)" concerning violations of the arms embargo and sanctions regime by the Government of Rwanda. It reads:

> "Since the outset of its current mandate, the Group has gathered evidence of arms embargo and sanctions regime violations committed by the Rwandan Government. These violations consist of the provision of material and financial support to armed groups operating in the eastern Democratic Republic of the Congo, including the recently established M23, in contravention of paragraph 1 of Security Council resolution 1807 (2008).

The arms embargo and sanctions regimes violations include the following:

- Direct assistance in the creation of M23 through the transport of weapons and soldiers through Rwandan territory
- Recruitment of Rwandan youth and demobilized ex-combatants as well as Congolese refugees for M23
- Provision of weapons and ammunition to M23
- Mobilization and lobbying of Congolese political and financial leaders for the benefit of M23
- Direct Rwandan Defence Forces (RDF) interventions into Congolese territory to reinforce M23
- Support to several other armed groups as well as *Forces armées de la République démocratique du Congo* (FARDC) mutinies in the eastern Congo

• Violation of the assets freeze and travel ban through supporting sanctioned individuals."

This latest report hit so hard, that even the closest allies of Rwanda – the US and UK – felt obliged to issue warnings and threats, that military aid could be withdrawn from Kigali.

I took my last trip to Rwanda in July 2012. The atmosphere in the country did not feel good. All types of military groups were controlling Kigali, from the notorious Presidential Guards to the regular military, police and all sorts of paramilitary guards.

I had to collect the latest footage for my film, and I was once again ready to risk everything, and once again traveling to the extremes of the country. It helped that my driver (I used to drive my own car from Nairobi, Kenya, but such an approach was becoming increasingly dangerous) was Tutsi, but it helped only to some extent.

The fear could be felt everywhere. The street near my hotel was blocked by heavy barricades. It was one of the access roads to the Presidential mansion. There were metal detector checks, even into the Genocide Memorial in Kigali.

I saw potential recruits for the Congolese M23, near the Rwandan city of Musanze, in deep discussion with uniformed Rwandan soldiers.

I was arrested in Goma, right at the old border crossing. Of course I filmed and the Congolese guard spotted me – he emerged, enormous like a mountain – grabbed my hand and pulled me back into his country for interrogation. That prospect truly terrified me, having spent endless hours in a bunker of the Congolese intelligence two years earlier, when all my possessions gradually began to disappear into the deep pockets of my interrogators. Only my numerous ID's, most likely saved me from the worst.

I shouted to the Rwandese soldiers, who came – two of them – grabbed my other arm and began pulling me towards Rwanda, obviously eager to avoid an international scandal.

I immediately instructed my driver to approach the second border. We crossed, illegally, as I filmed, going back and forth.

The insanity of the last days of filming...

There was a refugee camp near Gisenyi, empty, just a few months ago, now overflowing with refugees. There were UNHCR insignias on the tents; there were UNHCR trucks, as well as countless aggressive guards. There were thousands of 'repatriated' Rwandan refugees and refugees escaping from the fighting in Kivu.

What I had observed in Uganda, Rwanda and DR Congo, was that the population of this part of Africa was once again on the move.

Rwanda, a Prussian-style militaristic 'client' state of the West was in a dismal condition – skyscrapers and clean streets in the center of the capital, but absolute misery off the main roads in the countryside, with its electrification in single digit –in a stark contrast to what the politicians like Tony Blair (an advisors to Paul Kagame), want the world to believe.

There was discontent, oppression and fear in all corners of the nation. Grenades were going off, the main opposition leader Victoire Ingabire had, had her head shaved and was in prison. Kagame was acting increasingly like some manic mass murderer, striking at dissent, and even at his former cohorts, with increasing desperation.

"Kagame believes that it is ok to kill anybody he dislikes. He kills Hutus, he kills Tutsis, and there are all those crimes that are piling upon him. He seems not to care. I think he has reached the point of no return...", Dr. Theogene Rudesingwa explained in my film , a former Chief of Staff of RPF and Ambassador to the US in 1995-1999, and in the past, one of the closest allies of Paul Kagame.

Another member of what used to be known as the "Gang of Four" in the RPF hierarchy, Dr. Gerald Gashima (former Prosecutor General in 1999-2003), talks in the film about disappearances and extra-judicial killings, claiming, that now, Kagame is "above the law; in Rwanda he is what is the law..."

The accusations are mounting, but there seems to be no determined pressure from the West to call for free elections (RPF keeps winning elections by either liquidating or intimidating the opposition members), let alone to stop the genocide in DR Congo.

It took around 3 years to make the film – "Rwandan Gambit". I had to risk my life repeatedly, driving all over the country, filming despite clear restrictions and prohibitions.

I had to talk to hundreds of people on five continents. My editor and I could hardly count on any substantial financial support. The film proved to be a monster, and a financially ruinous one. It has exhausted me financially, emotionally and intellectually.

We were addressing, unveiling the roots of the worst genocide since WWII; presenting it to the public all over the world, that had almost no knowledge about the occurrences in the Great Lake region.

We felt under pressure to finish the film and to finish it as soon as possible.

"6 million people! " The Congolese Presidential candidate, Ben Kalala, shouted, to our camera. "……6 million innocent men, women and children, what is the world waiting for?"

Some now say 10 million. It is an unimaginable number. I covered Chile, and the horrors of the Pinochet era. There, 3-4 thousand people died. In Indonesia, during the US-sponsored military coup of 1965, between 800,000 and 3 million people vanished. The Great Lakes genocide is the worst topic I have ever had to cover, and the most complex, too.

One has to look at colonialism and then move to the Cold War, one has to revisit the IMF practices and then the direct support of the West of potentially murderous but loyal regimes. One has to study the circumstances of the assassination of Lumumba and then to understand how, a few decades later, Paul Kagame was brought to power.

And now the film is finished. But the slaughter in Congo goes on. I only hope that our work of three years could trigger an outcry, and help to stop the genocide.

14 September 2012

*****

9

Turkish Secularists

BLAMING IT ALL ON THE MUSLIMS

In many aspects, Turkey is much like Indonesia – on paper the country's economic growth is truly impressive, but talk to the people, and they will tell you that the place is collapsing, becoming unlivable in, overpriced, and that daily life is now extremely brutal. In both countries, a big portion of the wealth disappears into the deep pockets of the super-rich ruling elites: to obnoxiously glitzy yacht docks and marinas dotted around Istanbul, and in the glitzy shopping malls of Jakarta.

There is suppressed anger and frustration on the streets of Istanbul. My good friend, a writer, had recently been injured in a public bus, as two buses raced through the narrow streets, with a total disregard for the passengers onboard. Last night I witnessed how a veiled woman was almost crushed by the doors of the metrobus; she begged and screamed to be released, whilst the driver obviously seemed to be enjoying her agony, and all in full view of the passengers. There were several people near the doors, but no one came to her rescue.

People don't shout here, but they elbow each other, walk

through each other, and often show absolute spite for their fellow citizens. There is generally a 'bad mood' everywhere at street level; there is an apparent diminishment of kindness, as well as something that could only be defined as, chronic fatigue.

Come as a tourist, to see the great ancient mosques and palaces, museums and traditional baths, and you will fall in love with the city in one instant. Live here for a while, and the chances are, that you will soon be exhausted and defeated.

***

Istanbul is a ferociously divided city. There is a clear distinction, between those who think that the greatest human right, is to be able to booze up in the open, at tables placed right on the sidewalk, and between those who choose faith over worldly pleasures.

To be precise: the city is divided between those secular (and historically, although not of recent, governing) upper and middle-classes, and their hated adversaries: the practising Muslims of Turkey, who form the majority of the nation.

"Woman who wear headscarves have no brains", a renowned Turkish author shouts at me, a woman, and needless to say, 'a secular' one. We are on the shores of the Bosporus, in a public place, at a café. People were looking at us and I felt embarrassed. There was no chance of even beginning to argue with her. She was having one of those Istanbul fits – a familiar outburst of: "I have no sympathy, no use for the Muslim religion. Have you ever read their Book?"

I did. And just a few days ago, I had the great pleasure of discussing the Book with the great British Muslim scholar, Ziauddin Sardar in London. I am better off keeping the fact to myself, for fear of being quartered, and my body-parts thrown into the darkness of the legendary waterway dividing Europe, and Asia.

She is not the only person I know in Istanbul who has those moments. In 'the City of Dreams', to show spite for Islam and for practicing Muslims, is clearly some commonly used secret 'password' to the universe of what is acceptable here as brainy and hip.

As she speaks, a Ferrari races along the narrow road connecting two posh neighborhoods on the shores of the Bosporus – Arnavutköy and Bebek. It only slows down when confronted by the massive body of a public bus. If it could torpedo the bus, it would. Stripped of its muffler, the car is making an obnoxious roaring noise, frightening the seagulls, children and old passers-by. The man driving it is definitely not a religious type: sporting a crew-cut, and a cool, bored Italian-actor-from-the 1960s look, with a woman sitting next to him, her hair flowing in the wind, wearing a sleeve-less blouse, with designer glasses lifted up her forehead, and a cigarette between two slender fingers.

Turkey is segregated. In a way, it is more divided than either Israel or South Africa before the collapse of apartheid. But you would never hear anyone talking about it here.

***

I have three books translated into, and published in the Turkish language; several of their television stations often interview me. I know many men and women in Istanbul. Some are secular, others are Muslim; but I never see them 'mixing together'. Most of the secularists I know here, despise Islam; they make sure to demonstrate how Western, how pro-Western, how 'European' they are. In their eyes, being religious equates to being a degenerate, an idiot, and even 'unpatriotic'.

Try to define Turkey as a Middle Eastern country, and you will lose all your friends and acquaintances in an instant.

The Muslim-bashers don't hide their ideas: they actually advertise them; firing up each other in what to an outsider, may easily appear as bigotry.

Not once did my publisher, my fellow writers, acquaintances, or those pro-Western intellectuals ever invite out to dinner or a night out, someone who happened to be a religious man or a woman. Not once in Istanbul did I have a chance to talk to a woman wearing a headscarf. Practicing Muslims are 'un-people' in all those 'literary' and 'intellectual' circles; they are not included, not talked to, not consulted. "One can learn nothing from them," a 'secular' poet once told me in a posh café overlooking the Bosphorus.

To me all this is particularly shocking, because, for a big part of my life I live in Southeast Asia and in East Africa, in two places where people mix readily. In Malaysia, there could hardly be any party, or night out with friends, without people of different races and religions sitting at the same table. To be Malaysian is to be

Malay, Chinese or Indian, Muslim or Buddhist or Hindu or secular. Of course even there it is not easy; it is not smooth, there are outbursts of intolerance, and even institutionalized discrimination, especially towards the Indian minority. But there is definitely no 'segregation'. And if one attacks or puts down entire nationalities or religious beliefs, he or she is considered 'uncool' and very badly brought up. It would not be tolerated, especially in the company of educated people.

I have to repeat once again: I have only observed segregation such as that in Istanbul, in South Africa before the collapse of apartheid (and in some parts of the country after the collapse), in several parts of Israel and for different reasons, in Central Australia.

***

Secularists point fingers at Muslims, accusing the present religious Government of taking away their 'sacred' liberties (including, the so often quoted, the right to booze up in full view of pedestrians).

But much more serious issues can be detected.

For instance, the West has been a determined sponsor of the present Turkish regime of Prime Minister Recep Tayyip Erdogan and President Abdullah Gul. There have been massive arrests and disappearances of many top "Kemalist" generals and intellectuals, including those who have been demanding that Turkey breaks up with the US political and military diktat, and instead forging alliances in the east.

So here is a paradox that is hardly understood in the West, even amongst some well meaning and left-leaning intellectuals: while promoting Islamic ideals, the present government is taking direct orders from the West, destroying anti-imperialist intellectuals and the top military brass.

At the same time as banning exposed drinking establishments and encouraging women to cover up, the present government is helping to train the Israeli air force within Turkish territory, as well as arming and training the so called 'Syrian opposition', in specially-designated camps.

***

It is not only Turkey's present that is complex; it is also its past.

Turkey harbors many grievances from by-gone eras. Simultaneously, it is accused of inflicting pain on many in the region. There are hardly any simple answers to the historical questions.

One of the most burning and controversial ones is that of the PKK and 'the Kurdish issue': are Kurds really the victims of Turkish discrimination, brutality and neglect? Or are they allies of the West, and themselves the perpetrators in the drive to fragment and destabilize the region, which includes the Turkish state (the case of pro-Western Iraqi Kurdistan is often quoted)? The common wisdom in the West is that the Kurds are victims, but talk to Left-wing intellectuals and analysts in Istanbul or in the Middle East, and you will learn that the potential Greater Kurdistan (with its seeds in Iraq) is nothing less than a sinister Western plot.

It is also true that the most dedicated fighters against Western imperialism are the secular generals, the high-ranking officers and intellectuals, many of them now imprisoned, most without any charges or trials.

Turkish reality is often paradoxical

***

"The society should aim at the wellbeing of its entire people. It is absurd to discriminate against citizens for being Kurdish, for being believers or non-believers, atheists or Islamists. These things should not matter and they take attention away from the real problems this country is facing: issues, like the unbridled privatization of the national wealth of the country, the skyrocketing prices and the deteriorating conditions of the common people, as well as the Western imperialist interests in the region," declares Sezer (even he prefers not to use his full name), a Turkish intellectual who believes in Turkish unity and who embraces the ideals of Kemal Ataturk, whose nationalist ideas as he says, never relied on the ethnic origin of the people, but instead on their citizenship; on belonging to the country.

No matter how noble his ideas, they appear to resonate in the mind of only a tiny minority of this fragmented nation. Sezer is expressing progressive, secular, urban views. But there is very little communication and understanding between the Turkish cities and the countryside, between the posh neighborhoods on the Bosporus and the humble dwellings of the have-nots, between those who wear headscarves and pray five times a day, and those that are sipping wine in the ridiculously overpriced and smart cafes, sitting cross-legged and wearing imported designer outfits.

The founding father of the Turkish state – Mustafa Kemal Ataturk – would probably find it difficult to fit into the nation he was trying so painstakingly to unite. No matter how secular his beliefs, it is unlikely that he would join that upper-class, the Bosphorus/Ferrari anti-Islamic choir.

But Ataturk would also certainly clash bitterly with the present government, which combines religious practices with servitude to the West. In fact both camps would be reluctant to accept Ataturk for what he truly believed in. In today's world, his nationalism would be seen as inconvenient. Both sides – the Islamic government and the secular elites – are in two different ways collaborating with the West.

It is actually probable that, were he to be living now, Ataturk would end up like many other brave Turkish opponents of Western imperialism, in jail.

5 October 2012

*****

10

Will This Tiny Nation Sink?

CLIMATE CHANGE VS KIRIBATI

There is just a narrow 'defense line' of mangroves and a coral bottom under the shallow water, right next to the coast. This is all that separates the stretched but narrow archipelago of Tarawa – the most populated (and overcrowded) chain of islands of the Republic of Kiribati – from the vast expanse of the Pacific Ocean.

The mangroves were planted a few years ago. They were introduced near the airport and at several other areas along the coast. The rest of the Tarawa Atoll appears to be exposed and unprotected, despite the fact that numerous sea walls have only just been constructed recently.

It is said that Tarawa is 'sinking', but actually it is precisely where it always has been; it is just that the sea-level is rising due to climate change, triggered by the unrestrained consumption of the industrialized nations thousands of miles away.

Some experts say that if the trend is not reversed soon, or if a solution is not found, at least three countries in the South Pacific – Tuvalu, the Marshall Islands (RMI) and Kiribati – will soon become 'uninhabitable'. That does not mean that they will just disappear under the surface of the ocean in one or two decades; the islands and atolls will still be there. But life on them will simply become unsustainable. It will become cheaper and more effective to move the people to other parts of the world: to Australia, New Zealand, Fiji, or anywhere else, rather than to import food, water and all the other basic necessities.

Various scientists disagree, offering a much more optimistic reading of the future. But all these debates are either too theoretical, or of a strictly practical and pragmatic nature. They don't take into consideration the most important factor: the decisions whether to go or to stay are being made right now, or they had been already made. And in most of the cases the people have not been consulted.

'Relocation' or the so called 'environmental migration', would mean that these tiny but fully legitimate nations, with their own culture, identity, languages, history, oral tradition and immense beauty, would simply cease to exist. Taken away from their geographical context and uprooted, the people and their nations would mutate into something absolutely different. Their present essence would be irreversibly lost. And our planet would become more homogeneous and culturally poorer.

Alexander Teabo, an opposition MP from the Kiribati Way Forward Party (he represents Butaritari Island) agreed to speak to me in his home at Bairiki. And when he spoke, he did so, with determination, urgency and often with outrage:

> "People should be consulted first. Those who are supposed to be moved from their homes and islands are all human beings, not objects. We all know that climate change is occurring, but if we roll up our sleeves, we could surely be here for a very long time!"

Many, including my friend and a prominent expert on climate change, Espen Ronneberg (Ronneberg was Vice-President of the Kyoto Conference of 1997 that adopted the Kyoto Protocol on the environment) would support his views: "We haven't yet reached the point where it's time to give up. I think there is still a window of opportunity to reverse the trend."

But Mr. Ronneberg also warns:

> "Some of the atoll countries around the Pacific are no more than a couple of meters above sea-level. They are currently experiencing some very serious king tides and storm surges. These are associated with cyclones and storms that may not

impact them directly, but the wave patterns they create tend to go over the top of the atolls leaving salt water behind, which is damaging to crops, to houses and other infrastructure. It also contaminates the fresh water supply if they use well-water. Those are some very serious impacts that are actually being observed. In some islands, if the sea-level rises by as much as the maximum that is suggested by scientists, there wouldn't be really much possibility of saving them."

***

It appears that instead of getting busy with efforts to save their nations, the governments of Kiribati and Tuvalu are doing good 'business' abroad by marketing their islands as terminally ill; impossible to save. It is only the RMI that has been counting on some determined promoters, for the 'fight' for survival.

Periodically and frequently, government officials embark on their epic overseas voyages, crying over the fate of their disappearing countries, and then reaping a rich harvest of foreign aid, which as a rule almost never reaches the average citizens. There is also this so-called *per-diem* inspiring factor, which arouses so many government officials, into constantly circling around the globe in search of sympathetic donors.

"Our President talks a lot about our plight... on the international level," explains Alexander Teabo. "But he seems to have no policies when he returns home."

Others say that the President Anote Tong actually implements at home, what he learns abroad. Recently, during a speech competition on climate change, a student successfully paraphrased him, elegantly grasping the essence of his reflections: "If we have to move out of the country, we must not leave like refugees but as marketable people."

'Marketable people' can hardly be described as a local traditional expression with its origins in Oceania.

To criticize or to ridicule the President and his government can be very dangerous here: several journalists had been fired and the opposition intimidated. There is a law permitting the government to shut down newspapers. On several occasions during my recent work in Kiribati, the country was described to me as a 'police state'.

The funding government is securing (part of it to feed

corruption in its own ranks) is simply too substantial to be jeopardized by a nuisance like the independent press. Transparency would inspire a free flow of 'uncomfortable' questions. Or even worse: it could help to create a group of well-informed citizens demanding the survival of their country! That would be unacceptable, as Mr. Tong has already made up his mind (and many deals): "The country has reached "the point of no return... To plan for the day when you no longer to have a country is indeed painful, but I think we have to do that..." "While being paid for such planning," he forgot to add.

It is now illegal to film or to engage in investigative journalism in Kiribati, unless one fully submits to government surveillance and supervision, pays the fee and fills all the 'necessary' forms. Such regulations are unheard of in most of the South Pacific nations.

In the Ministries (including the Ministry of Education) where I used to circulate freely, I have been asked repeatedly for permits and authorizations. At the tiny National Museum, Mr. Natan Ilonga, a 'cultural officer', began interrogating me after I had managed to ask just one question: "How do the local artists react to government policies on the climate change?"

"We want to help you," pressed Mr. Ilonga, with what he probably thought was a genuine MI5 grin: "Of course, before you talk to me you have to speak to my boss. However, before you speak to my boss, you have to pay 350 AUD and fill out these forms... just a few pages, as you can see... and you have to study what you are allowed and not allowed to document... And then we have to wait for a decision from "above" ... Only a few days... But we are really here to facilitate your work..."

To make his day, I asked him whether he really was a curator, or an intelligence agent. Finally he gave me a big broad smile: "Both, of course."

I happened to be less corpulent than this out-of-shape local 007, and more agile. I brutally outmaneuvered him. I jumped into the car and in no time got away from Mr. Ilonga, who was probably significantly slowed down by the avalanche of his own forms

***

Fortunately I still had some friends and allies on the island. I used to live in Oceania, and had done so for more than three years, studying and documenting the plight of almost all the countries and territories of Polynesia, Melanesia and Micronesia, with the exception of Niue and Nauru. The result of my research was a book named Oceania.

***

After outmaneuvering Mr. Ilonga, I drove to the Ministry of Education in search of Ms Teekoa Letaake, who used to be the Permanent Secretary of Education. I worked with her during my last visit and was impressed by her determination and honesty. But she did not hold the same position anymore.

It was Friday early afternoon, and payday on top of it. The offices of the Ministry were desperately empty.

"You see, it would never have been like this when Ms. Letaake was in charge," explained a young professional lady, who did not want to be named. "During lunch hour, the staff used to take turns. We used to work a lot... Now I am the only one who is still here..."

I asked her whether people of Tarawa discuss global warming and the rising sea-level at home.

"It is not usually discussed," she replied. "Only when something big happens, like when there is a tsunami warning. The probability of a tsunami is discussed at governmental and Parliamentary level, but not in public and not in people's dwellings."

"You know," she continued, "We don't really know what is going on here, or what game it is that this government is playing. Kiribati is our home. There is no place like home. We don't want to go anywhere. Well, some people do, but I don't and the great majority of our people don't. The government keeps scaring us, threatening us with tsunami, but we have never had any tsunami here, not since the day I was born, not since the days when my parents and grandparents were born. They say a tsunami would wipe us all out. If that is the case, why don't they build shelters?"

"Why aren't they building shelters?" I ask the local MPs, government officials, and common people. The answers come in different forms, with various nuances, but the meaning appears to be the same: there is no political will. There are funds, but no determination. Some people say that tsunami threats are fabricated. "They are frightening us. The government tries to convince the people that a tsunami is around the corner, so that they will run away, or at least agree to leave the country. But it is just the President's utopian world that is being imposed on us," says Alexander Teabo.

Back at the Ministry of Education, a lady I spoke to is defiant: "We don't believe this government, anymore. You know what my father did the last time there was a tsunami warning? He just sat in his chair and laughed, saying: 'if the tsunami hits, we wait until we are all dry, then we pack our things and take a boat to another island. But we will not abandon Kiribati.'"

As so many other people I spoke to, she explains that many citizens of the outer islands are forced to migrate to Tarawa, as there are no jobs and no educational facilities (apart from primary schools) or well-equipped hospitals on their islets and atolls. This is the same story that I heard in Tuvalu three years earlier.

"Are there any educational programs?" I insist. "Is there some part of the curriculum that deals with global warming, the rising sea-level, with climate change?"

"No," she replies.

As I walk to the car, I see a young woman rushing towards the school. She smiles at me. I run after her. "Are you a teacher?" She nods. "Can we talk?" I literally drag her to the car. It feels like we are doing something very nasty, very much forbidden in this country. Once we are inside, I get straight to the point: "Listen, do you teach the kids.... You know... about climate change and about the options that Kiribati has?"

Her name is Veronica. She has a tender smile, but has absolutely no clue about what I am talking about. "I am not sure," she says. "Maybe at social classes... I am new here... I am sorry... I really don't know." I have a feeling that I have disappointed her: she expected a much better script, much better lines from me.

***

The less the information there is on climate change, the more the attempts to make people 'believe' in the mostly nihilistic outcomes – in the inevitability of a future exodus or in some Armageddon scenario. Education is not allowed or encouraged, to address the most essential matters.

In the meantime, the country is becoming home to countless

religious extremist implants, mainly from the US, represented by their emissaries dressed in white shirts and armed with name-tags and bibles. Sterile prefabricated houses of various faiths, ranging from Mormons to Jehovah Witnesses are penetrating the slums.

Social issues are hardly discussed and political movements and parties have no ideologies. Kiribati remains one of the poorest countries on earth and it is scarred by a scale of social problems, staggering unemployment, illnesses ranging from AIDS to leprosy, child abuse and child prostitution.

After Kiribati yielded to Western advice and switched its 'allegiance' from China (PRC) to Taiwan, corruption (particularly on the outer islands) has increased. Instead of building infrastructure as China does all over Oceania, in Kiribati most of the Taiwanese aid ends up in the pockets of local government with very little tangible results for the community.

By the time the country gained independence, its reserves of sulfites had been exhausted. There is copra on the outer islands, but the old cargo ship 'donated' by Spain mysteriously broke down before it could be put to use and now rots idly, almost one mile offshore.

The tiny airport, with its grotesquely oversized runway, is used to refuel US military and coastguard planes, and could be easily converted into a military base at short notice, would the sole Empire find it desirable.

The industrialized world, the one that put most of Oceania into this dire condition, seems to do close to nothing. There are ineffective aid programs, as well as "wining and dining trips" for government officials. But shockingly there are hardly any substantial infrastructural projects that could protect the affected nations from disappearing.

***

Tarawa has several villages that can be described as sitting right on the frontline of the battle against the devastating climate change. At Temaiku Village, people lament that climate change is already knocking on their doors. The salty water is coming to the edges of their dwellings, which are now built on stilts. People sleep on elevated platforms. There is a new seawall made of stones and bags. It all looks like a fortification and it stands at the worst affected part of the island.

"We do worry about the rising sea-level," says Mr. Terobimo. "But we know very little about what is ahead of us. Look at the water: it is right next to our houses. We all want to leave Kiribati, and at the same time we don't; we want to stay. We are not sure... We are confused... We are not told what is going on."

The Deputy-Secretary of Environment seems to sympathize with the plight of his people, although he is clearly being diplomatic. Long after his work-hours we sit in his office, having a face-to-face discussion:

"I think the people of Kiribati are doing their best to fight coastal erosion and other climate change-related problems... But I can't be sure whether Kiribati will survive."

He mentions the integrated environmental policy that is now being designed and approved by the government, but which cannot be understood by anyone I spoke to on the atoll.

MP Teabo goes much further: "We can survive as a nation on these islands. We shall and will, fight! And if we lose, there is always the UN – we are part of the international community after all – we are part of the world. But let's not frighten our people before they even have a chance to fight. Let's defend the country. And let us retrieve only if everything else fails."

12 October 2012

*****

11

Solitude of an Internationalist

OUR LENINGRAD

"No one is forgotten and nothing is forgotten." That is what is engraved in gold on the granite stone, right behind the statue of the Motherland, spreading her arms in grief.

The Piskariovskoye Memorial Cemetery is in the city of St. Petersburg –186 mass graves and about half a million people are buried there, including most of my family from the maternal side.

During World War II, for 900 days (2 and a half years), the city of Leningrad stood firm, and defied the most horrific siege in modern history. It stopped the advance of the Nazi troops, withstood constant aerial bombardments, bitter cold, hunger and the lack of all basic necessities. Almost half the population vanished, was burnt by bombs, frozen in trenches and in unheated flats, or was starved to death.

The cultural capital of Russia delivered the ultimate sacrifice: rising in defiance and courage, playing an important role in defeating Nazism, and thus in saving the world.

All of this while most of the West, either collaborated with Nazism or tried to 'appease' it.

Naturally the USSR in general and Leningrad in particular, did not save the world that belonged to the white race; it saved the world of "non-humans", according to the German Fascists, of exterminable beings: people from the Indian sub-Continent, Africans, Jews, Roma (Gypsies), Slavs, most of the Asians and Arabs.

And by smashing Fascism, colonialism also received a decisive blow (as fascism and colonialism are made of similar stuff), allowing dozens of nations in Asia and Africa to gain independence, and freedom. At least for a time and at least until the Western nations managed to regroup.

This was, naturally, never forgiven in the European and North American capitals. The Soviet Union and all its ideals and principles have been dragged through the dirt and vilified. Although it saved the world from Nazism, it became common to compare it to Fascist Germany, and many progressive Western intellectuals adopted this twisted and insulting judgment.

As I sat on a bench near the Statue Of The Motherland, I was in the company of Artem Kirpichenok, one of the leading Russian historians; a Jew who lived in Israel for 15 years, but decided to return to his native St Petersburg after becoming disillusioned with the racism and institutionalized discrimination of the minorities living in the Jewish State.

"It is incredible that Western propaganda has succeeded in making most people all over the world believe that Nazism and Soviet Communism are comparable", I said. "Even some progressive intellectuals are pronouncing both '–isms' in one single breath."

"Nazi Germany, the same as England, USA and France, was based on a racist and colonialist mindset, widely accepted principles among the Western bourgeoisie in the 1930s," uttered Artem Kirpichenok. "Hitler built his empire in Eastern Europe on the British colonial design in India. Nazi racial theories did not differ too much from the racism of the US South or from the racial theories of French, Belgian, British or Dutch empires implemented in the colonies. The collapse of the Third Reich hit hard on all those ideals of colonialism and racism. And the Soviet Union was mainly to 'blame' for that collapse. The ideological basis of the European dominance over Asia, Africa and Latin America had been damaged."

That could of course never be forgiven. As a result, no country on earth has ever been so hated by the West as the Soviet Union, and now Russia.

* * *

During the siege, my maternal grandmother dug trenches on the outskirts of the city. She fought the Germans, and was decorated for her courage on several occasions. I have no idea how she did it, how she managed to fight and to survive – she was so gentle, fragile and very shy. Many years after the war, years after I was born, whilst she was reading me poems and fairy tales, I would find it very difficult to imagine her holding a Kalashnikov, hand grenades or even a shovel. But she did; she fought, and she was ready to die for what she then thought, was the epic battle for the survival of humanity. And she came very close to dying on several occasions.

She was an Orthodox Christian lady, but also a firm supporter of Communism, a rare combination. She married my grandfather, a brilliant Muslim man from the Chinese minority in Kazakhstan, Husain Ischakov, a linguist and a Commissar of Health and later for Food Supply (basically a ministerial post in the old days).

What followed was a fragment that appeared as if it had been cut out directly from official Western propaganda. My grandfather fell out of favor with Stalin, was arrested and executed. In 1937, (the first earliest memory my mom had of her 'childhood') this tall and elegant man was bent over the cradle, lifting my mom in his arms, and pressing her against his chest, before being led away by the agents of the State, to oblivion and eternity. He cried as he looked at her face; he knew exactly what was ahead. He never came back.

My grandmother fought. She was decorated. But nonetheless, after the War was over, she was arrested and thrown into jail for 'marrying an enemy of the State". She spent years in prison, while my mother went through hell, virtually an orphan. When my grandma was released from prison, she said to my mother: "It was so terrible that I thought; two more weeks and I would hang myself there." But she never betrayed my grandfather: all she had to do was to sign that she 'regretted' marrying him. She never did. Obviously, her loyalty was more important to her, than her own life.

She left that jail, still an Orthodox Christian, and still a Communist!

My grandfather's name was eventually 'cleared'; he was made a 'hero' again posthumously. Books were written about him, and my mother was allowed to study architecture.

* * *

What happened to my family was of course brutal and terrible.

But we are talking about 1930s and 1940s. After the revolution, Soviet Union had to defend itself on various ocasions, from several attackes conducted by the US, France, UK, even by Czech 'legions' that at one ponit managed to occupy almost entire Transsiberian Railrod, fighting its way towards the east.

German nazi spy network infiltrated Soviet intelligence, feeding it with names of the most loyal officials, cadres and army generals. False messages were sent to Moscow - messages saying that these dedicated and brave men and women were actually working for Germany, Japan and the West. This way, Soviet Union got weakened and divided. Many great Communists, including my grandfather, lost their lives.

Despite everything, the USSR was definitely more humane than Western Europe or the United States. To dispute that would be to deny the most basic statistics.

"Let us compare," I was repeatedly told by the greatest Southeast Asian novelist Pramoedya Ananta Toer, who was nominated countless times for the Nobel Prize for literature but never received one because, unlike Solzhenitsyn, he was imprisoned in the wrong – pro-Western – concentration camps. "Let us remember that everything occurs in some historical context."

Western propaganda has managed to put to work some tremendously effective lies, half-truths and outright fabrications, that could not be checked or disputed (not that most of the people would even try): the numbers of victims in the gulags were exaggerated, and were regularly combined with the numbers of both political and common criminals (in the Stalin era, everybody convicted of any crime was put to work, in some sort of labor camp with very bad conditions, as the country was still poor).

Anyone with a drop of objectivity would have to admit (unless he or she would be set on denying the basic principle of humanism, which declares that all people are equal, regardless of their race and or nationality) that the Communist Soviet Union committed far fewer crimes than those by Western countries under the banner of 'constitutional monarchies' or 'multi-party democracies'.

While the Soviets were busy pulling tens of millions out of poverty (and we are talking, for instance, about the Muslims of the Soviet Central Asia, areas where the standard of living eventually reached that of the European parts of Russia, as well as the other countless minorities inhabiting that enormous country), in approximately the same era, the Belgians managed to kill around 10 million people in Congo, chopping off their hands and burning women and children in their huts alive.

The Germans committed a monstrous genocide (or call it Holocaust) against the Herero tribe in Namibia. In Africa, the British and German empires built the first concentration camps on Earth. And the French colonial onslaughts are well documented in Southeast Asia, in West and North Africa, and elsewhere. The Dutch plundered, raped, killed and enriched themselves on the great archipelago that is now called Indonesia.

The genocides, mass murder and terror that were spread by the West, in the rest of the world, have been countless, but of course under-reported by Western academia and mass media.

Even the end of World War II did not bring to an end, the bestial treatment of 'the natives' at the hands of the European and North American colonialists. One should recall the treatment, from bombing to gassing, of the people of the Middle East, by Winston Churchill and other glorified British leaders. All this is of course well documented, including in the books written by Churchill himself.

There are countless statues of Winston Churchill or the Belgian King Leopold II, all over capitals in Europe. Why should there be no statues of great Soviet leaders, who saved the world from both Nazism and colonialism?

In the second half of the 20th Century, during the so called 'Cold War', the Soviet Union stood firmly on the side of the oppressed, on the side of the liberation struggles, for freedom in Africa, Asia and Latin America. One has to wonder how mighty has been the propaganda that has made it all to be forgotten?

While Europe and the United States (and their constitutional monarchies and multi-party 'democracies') cultivated despots in

Iran, Egypt, the Gulf, the Middle East, South Vietnam, Cambodia, South Korea, Chile, Argentina, Guatemala, Nicaragua, Uruguay, the Dominican Republic, Haiti, Brazil, Kenya, South Africa, Indonesia and so many other unfortunate places, the Soviet Union stood by the Cuban, Nicaraguan, Tanzanian and North Vietnamese revolutions, it supported the leaders, true heroes and liberators like Patrice Lumumba and President Salvador Allende.

And both of us – Noam Chomsky and I – came to the conclusion during our recent discussion at MIT, that the standards of living in Riga, Prague or East Berlin were allowed to be significantly higher than in Moscow, while those of Tashkent or Samarkand were just marginally lower. The standard of living in the colonies and the 'client' states of the West were ten, twenty, even a hundred times lower than those in Washington, Paris or London. New colonies lost millions of men, women and children because of extreme misery.

I calculated that some 55 million lives have been lost since World War II as a result of Western colonialism, neo-colonialism, direct invasions, sponsored coups and other acts of international terror. I have probably grossly under-estimated the numbers, as there were also lives lost to famines, terrible mismanagement, and the outright misery triggered by Western imperialism.

Tens of millions of lives were further lost as a result of the terrible seeds planted by imperialism and colonialism, the most obvious case being the Partition of the Sub-Continent.

I would suggest that instead of comparing Fascism and Soviet Communism, the Left and the entire thinking world should begin comparing what is truly comparable: the Fascism, Western colonialism and market fundamentalism (the most violent fundamentalist faith on Earth today), served and represented by "Western multi-party systems" and "Constitutional monarchies".

* * *

When I meet a new person, which happens with a great frequency, to me there is nothing more frightening than the most simple and natural question: "Where are you from?"

I don't know what to say, I cannot answer and even if I could, the reply would be too blurry, too complex, and too philosophical. On top of that, unless I opted for a long and detailed answer, the information I would give would be very inaccurate.

I am a dedicated Internationalist, but the majority of those that I meet does not take it as an identity.

My interviewers and reviewers often choose Prague, the former Czechoslovakia or the present day Czech Republic as the center of my identity, but it is thoroughly false. Prague was never my home. Czechoslovakia was where I endured a hellish childhood, where during the winter, I had my shoes filled with urine and then the other kids would let them freeze outside the school or gym, one of countless punishments for my having an "Asian mother". Former Czechoslovakia is where I had to fight after each class for my life from the age of six, simply because my mother was not just half Asian, but because she was also half Russian.

My identity is truly spread all around: it lies deep and high in the Peruvian and Bolivian Andes where I faced death on several occasions while covering the Peruvian "Dirty War". It is in Chile, bouncing from the walls of the narrow, winding and often haunted streets of the coastal city of Valparaiso – it lies with Chilean poets and with the songs of fishermen on its coast. My identity is spread throughout that enormous body of water of the South Pacific Ocean dotted with tiny specks of land – now 'island nations' that were colonized and utterly destroyed by the traditional colonial powers.

My identity is from the Swahili coast of Africa and around the Great Lakes of the continent, in all those places that experienced the worst genocide in modern history, a genocide triggered by the European and North American political and economic interests. My identity also lies in the deserts of the Middle East, and if I knew the Sub-Continent in just a bit more in detail, it would be there as well. I am at home in Havana, Caracas, Buenos Aires, Onomichi, Beijing, Cape Town and Kuala Lumpur. And I also live in Japan, Indonesia and Kenya.

It is a total mess, I know, it is very confusing and I cannot explain it, but that's how it is.

For years, even decades, my home was where there was a struggle for justice and independence; I have been writing books and articles, making films or getting directly involved in the struggle. I can hardly identify my race, culture or national identity, anymore and I don't even try to. I go where I am needed. And in the end, also, as Garcia Marquez wrote: "my home is where they read my books."

* * *

I was born in Russia, in Leningrad (I am sorry, but I simply cannot call it St. Petersburg, as it is called now, it will always remain Leningrad to me). I have never lived there, because my parents took me to Czechoslovakia when I was just a few months old. But every year, my mother would put me on a plane, one of those old Soviet Tupolev jets with mahogany tables, lampshades and black caviar served on all the international flights, in just one single class, to send me to Leningrad where my grandmother would be waiting for me, armed with a set of keys to some humble rented room in the Bay Of Finland, a room which, for me, was like a paradise. My grandmother was always armed with endless tickets and passes to the opera houses, ballet performances and art exhibitions. In the Communist days they cost nothing, but it was not easy to get them.

And she had piles of books waiting for me. I let her read to me, even though I was able to read myself. She read to me until it was late into the night and when it rained outside, the moments were especially magic.

From the moment I left Leningrad, I began counting the days left till my return. I had my special secret book where I marked each day that had passed. The cold deep water of the Neva River, its bridges, the open spaces, the beauty of this former Russian capital so often covered by fog, the pathos of Russian and then Soviet history, the pathos of the history of my own family – all this captivated my mind, made me dream, made me prematurely adult.

In Czechoslovakia, my mother missed Russia terribly. She cried almost every night. She read books to me, too, and a lot of poetry.

Like this, I had no childhood naturally, but they managed to make a writer out of me at an extremely early age. I inherited their struggle, their 900 days of Siege, their war, their Russia.

Both women passed everything on to me, but it was not just the suffering, the prisons and the wars, but also great hope, the ability to dream, enthusiasm, optimism, as well as great solidarity. They taught me that one could always build from nothing or rebuild from the ashes. And that love, if it is true love, is not something that does disappear, nor does it vanish in one month or even in several years.

They also passed on to me the love for their city; their lost but never forgotten love.

* * *

Now, after all those years I have returned to Leningrad. By now I was much more Latin American or Asian, than Russian. My native tongue was suddenly feeling so heavy and rusty: it was still perfect in terms of pronunciation but archaic and over-polite.

I returned exhausted, after launching my big book in London – a book about Indonesia, and how the West had ruined it after the 1965 US-sponsored coup. I returned after just finishing my 160 minutes documentary film on the genocide in DR Congo, and after working at the Ugandan and then on the Turkish-Syrian border.

I suddenly felt lonely and I was desperately longing to tell my story to someone dear to me. But it so happened that no one joined me in Leningrad.

I wandered through the streets, so beloved and yet so foreign.

I went to the old beach at Zelenogorsk, but it had changed, the marina was dotted with private boats and yachts instead of my old tugboats and patrol vessels.

I went to visit the forest where the dead body of my grandfather was thrown from the train. Now it was a memorial cemetery, in fact a haunted forest with the names and photographs nailed to the trees. I did not want to travel here from the city where I was born, from Leningrad. I wanted to come here from Helsinki, from a neutral place, but it was not meant to be.

The forest was quiet. There were a few mourners, but otherwise total silence. My Muslim, Communist, Chinese grandfather was here. My grandfather, a linguist, the Minister of Health of Kazakhstan, a man who gave his entire life to the revolution, but fell out of favor and was killed, and thrown into this quiet forest, without any respect or any rituals.

It was easy to draw conclusions, to condemn everything. But I had heard enough about him to know that he would not betray his beliefs, just as my grandmother had never done.

Before she died, I asked my grandmother: "You never re-married. You remained beautiful for decades after my grandfather died. Why?"

She smiled her unpretentious smile: "Your grandfather," she

said, "Was a very big man. It is extremely rare to meet a man like that. Others never even came up to his shoulder". And she did not mean my grandfather's height.

He was a Communist, and what it meant to him, was simply the process of building a much better world than the one he knew from his childhood.

In the forest, I sat on the grass. It was cold. After all those wars that I had covered, after the 145 countries I had visited, the dozens of books and films I had produced, after all that struggle, I suddenly felt the need to cling to someone, just for this moment; I needed to speak, to be held, to tell the story, from the beginning to the end. I was never the one into autobiographies, but now I needed to be understood. But in the end I came alone, with just my Leica and a tiny book of poetry written by Antonio Guerrero Rodriguez, one of the Cuban 5 – patriots imprisoned brutally in Miami.

My entire maternal family was broken and scattered. But we were all fighters. Like my grandmother and grandfather I had to go on: I had to struggle and fight for what I believe in. Like them I knew how short life is, how little time there is, and how precious it is, how mighty the enemy is.

* * *

Later I traveled on the legendary Leningrad metro, with all those underground palaces, and the old Soviet-era dilapidated carriages.

I kept reading Antonio Guerrero Rodriguez, the bi-lingual Spanish and Russian, edition that was given to me in Kiev, by the translator of my writing.

El amor que expira no esamor

El verdadero amor pertenece

A todo el tiempo, a la tierra toda,

Sin temor enfrenta tempestades,

Resiste hasta el filo de la muerte

Y, como la natura, es eterno.

In this stunning poem written in a Miami prison, Rodriguez argues that love that can pass is not really love. That true love could resist even death itself and is, like nature, eternal.

I noticed that a young lady was reading over my shoulder. After a while, she asked me in passable Spanish: "Is it true what it says?" Also in Spanish I replied: "Yes, they are in prison, all of them. It is terrible."

"It is not what I mean," she said with certain urgency. "Is it true what it says? That love is eternal or it is not love?"

I was stunned, as this would not have happened even in Buenos Aires, this exchange could only take place in Havana... and here. Then I realized that after all, this was my city, the city where poets were read by the millions, and the city that made me a writer. I looked at the girl, looked her straight in the eyes and replied in Russian: "My grandparents thought so. I don't know if it is the truth but I always lived as if it is."

The girl nodded. She said nothing, but as she was leaving the car at the next station, she gave me the most brilliant smile I had received in years. Obviously the city had its way to give me strength.

Outside, on the bank of the Neva River, I briefly put my forehead on the granite wall that separated the sidewalk from the enormous waterway. The stone was cold, refreshing.

Leningrad did not try to hold me. It was too proud, too enormous. But I felt it was embracing me, before sending me back to war, to the battle. I had to carry on the legacy of those who were fighting for the survival of humanity in the 1940s. I knew all those places that were under siege; I knew so many places on this Earth that were worse than any hell professed by religious theories. I really knew so many of them. I was obliged to fight and to work, day and night.

As Rodriguez and others realized, one has to fight when men, women and children are being slaughtered, when entire nations and cultures are being destroyed. When injustice is called justice and in the name of it, cruelty reigns.

With the deep waters of the Neva in front of me, I whispered as I had when I was a child addressing the city: "Now I will go, but I will come back. Please wait for me."

19 October 2012

12

Written in Blood and Dreams

POETRY AND LATIN AMERICAN REVOLUTION

The world is once again in turmoil. Several Arab nations are clearly in a state of mayhem, rebelling against decades of injustice. But their struggle is not always based on ideology, and it is not well defined. The West is taking full advantage of the confusion. Lybia is destroyed, while Syria is being destabilized.

Africa is bleeding, demolished by a new wave and breed of European and North American colonialism. About 10 million people in the Congo have died in the last few years during a slaughter encouraged by the economic and geo-political interests of former and present colonial powers.

The West is hailing both India and Indonesia for their high economic growth, but both countries are squarely failing to deliver social justice, both clinging to the appalling ogre of feudalism.

"Possibly the Arab countries are now where Latin American nations were ten years ago," Noam Chomsky suggested during our encounter, in June 2012 at MIT in Boston.

Possibly, but there also appear to be so many differences, both historical and cultural.

The South American continent is winning its struggle for independence and for real freedom. There are some setbacks, like the Western-backed coup in Paraguay and the state in which the hopelessly divided Colombia exists. But on the whole, the South American continent has won its long and epic battle against imperialism, or at least for now it has.

The question is – can Latin America share its experiences with the rest of the world? Will it be able to inspire the Arab people, Indians, Pakistanis, Indonesians, or Africans?

I don't know the answer, but I think we have to try. It is our responsibility, our duty. Our goal, our struggle, our people are not petty. Our revolutions have been based on brightness, internationalism and solidarity.

Let us be naïve if sharing and spreading hope is the proof of naiveté; let us fight the negativity and defeatism that are helping to throw billions of lives into a permanent state of misery – let us fight them with our goodwill and with our big hearts, as we fought for so long in the mountains, plains and jungles of Latin America itself.

If the official Western press laughs at us, so be it. Today Latin America has plenty to share with the world: it is building tens of millions of dwellings for the poor, it is immunizing children, feeding those who are hungry and educating those who have for centuries been confined to the darkness of ignorance. It votes at the United Nations against neo-colonialist designs. And it is increasingly supportive of the countries that are threatened by the Empire.

But let us not lecture; let us just share.

I am inviting my Latin American comrades and colleagues to produce an inspiring series of analyses of our struggle, our revolutions. I invite them to explain the decades of the determined fight for social justice and for freedom as we (not the West) see it.

Let those reports be written by us – by Latin Americans and by those (like myself), who have lived in Latin America for years, decades, until we got Latinized and gained a new identity.

Let these reports be distributed by some of the great progressive publications and sites, and especially by the new progressive and anti-imperialist media all over the world.

And I am appealing to our comrades and colleagues in the Arab countries, Africa, Indonesia, Pakistan and India to translate our reports into their local languages, and distribute them widely in their countries. Then, let us engage in a direct discussion.

Let us see if the South American success can be duplicated; if Cuba, Venezuela, Ecuador, Bolivia, Argentina and Brazil might inspire the men and women of Egypt, Morocco, Bahrain, India, Uganda, DR Congo, Indonesia, and Pakistan.

* * *

I am writing this essay in order to talk about the poetry, and about the songs, that have had such a decisive influence on the changes and revolutions in South America. We did not win because of our brains only; we won because of our hearts, and because of the great talent of our creative men and women, their ability to move others, to inspire and often to enrage the people all over the continent.

I am not sure whether the cultural differences are too big or whether our songs are too distinct. I don't know whether the same things that had touched us and brought us onto the streets and to the barricades, will manage to touch the people in Karachi or Cairo. I swear I don't know. But let us try. Our songs and poems are good and they helped us to win. Sharing them would cause no damage!

What I can testify, is that whenever I go to India, to North or sub-Saharan Africa or to the Middle East, I am relentlessly questioned about Venezuela, Bolivia, Cuba and Brazil.

Many people have 'heard something', but they instinctively distrust Western sources. Let there be no go-betweens; let them receive the information from us directly.

And instead of just talking, let us write. Let us share our victories and the complexities of our struggle. Let us explain what it took for our beloved Latin America to raise, and to stand tall, as it is standing now.

POETRY AND REVOLUTION

There are three houses, three dwellings, that used to belong to one of the greatest poets of the 20th Century, to 'Don Pablo' as he was known in Chile, or Pablo Neruda as he has been known all over the world. All three houses are stunning, all three he helped to build with his own hands.

One house is attached to a hill, in a bohemian neighborhood of Bellavista, in Santiago de Chile. The second one is in the port city of Valparaiso, commanding a stunning view of the bay, the port and the open ocean, spreading towards the horizon. The last one stands in what used to be a humble coastal village, called Isla Negra, 'Black Island', which is actually not an island at all but a cluster of houses, near a marvelous rocky coast. This is where Pablo Neruda wrote some of his most powerful poems, in a tiny wooden shack facing the enormous waves of the Pacific.

Many of Neruda's poems were full of outrage; they were like a passionate call to arms. Don Pablo was a Communist, and he believed in the Latin American struggle for true independence, he believed in revolution and above all –in the unity of this continent. His, arguably the greatest and the most monumental poem, is called "The Heights of Machu Picchu". It ends in spectacular rebelliousness and solidarity:

> And give me silence, give me water, hope.
>
> Give me the struggle, the iron, the volcanoes.
>
> Let bodies cling like magnets to my body.
>
> Come quickly to my veins and to my mouth.
>
> Speak through my speech, and through my blood.

But despite its power, this was not the poem that had been chosen to be engraved on the columns in front of La Sebastiana, and it is not the poem that, during the long years of fascist darkness, inspired young men and women to fight the horrible dictatorship installed from abroad. It is not the poem that made them risk their lives, to die for Chile and for its freedom.

Surprisingly, some of the most simple and the most humble verses written to a woman he loved actually became that symbol; one of the battle cries of the resistance:

> ...The fifth thing is your eyes,
>
> my Matilda, my beloved,
>
> I do not want to sleep without your eyes,

I do not want to live without you looking at me:

I will give the spring

for that you'll keep watching me.

And here exactly lies the secret! The Latin American Revolution and its recent victories have not been constructed solely on the ideals related to the struggle for social justice. Those who think that it is only the Left-Wing rationale, dialectics, and well-defined pragmatic goals or principles, that brought the recent successes and the victories to almost the entire continent, are fully misunderstanding 'The Process'.

The revolutions in this part of the world have been equally about the pathos, about poetry, about sentimental outbursts, about the arts: they are, and were expected to be essentially quixotic, emotional and beautiful.

* * *

The arts and the world of dreams play an essential role in the Latin American struggle for justice, an egalitarian society, and even in the armed struggle.

Here, the rebellion often foments from the lines of the poems, from songs, from canvases. The Theatres of Buenos Aires and of Santiago de Chile can be as explosive as car trunks packed with semtex.

Often there is no borderline between the revolution and poetry; they blend together.

"In the novel 'Love in the Time of Cholera', a man, Florentino Ariza, had all his dreams shattered when the love of his life refused him," a theatre actor in a Chilean port city of Valparaiso once told me.

He was supposed to act in my play and we met to discuss his role, but instead the meeting turned out to be philosophical.

"Fermina Daza married someone else, and Florentino had only two options: to give up his love for her or to fight... and to wait... no matter how long it took, just wait... He decided to fight and to wait. He waited for fifty-one years, nine months and four days... But in the end he won. The woman he loved became his... at the age of seventy something, but his. Do you understand?"

"He was obsessed..." I began to analyze.

"No!" shouted the actor in desperation. How could I be so thick? He ordered another round of white wine with cherimoya juice "Don't you see? It is like with the revolution! We waited; we fought. We sacrificed so much... But it is here. The victory is finally ours."

Of course Gabriel Garcia Marquez is a great Communist novelist. And of course his 'Love in the Time of Cholera' is a tremendous literary achievement, powerful and complex. But I never thought about the parallel – Fermina Daza and the revolution. "But why not?" I thought, downing the wine, as the accordionist began playing another desperate tango right behind my back, "Why not? Waiting for Fermina Daza is like waiting for the revolution..."

* * *

Stories, books, poetry, music, dance, and theatre – they are all very essential here. No revolution in Latin America could happen without them.

Before deciding to go to the barricades, the people of this continent have to be touched, moved, not just 'convinced'.

A few years ago, while visiting my Australian friend Tamara Pierson, in the Venezuelan city of Merida in the middle of the Andes (Tamara is a person who has given plenty to Venezuela and to the revolution), my visit coincided with a government campaign of giving away millions of books to the poor, to the masses. Classics like Don Quixote were literally handed out by the tons and all for free, all over the country. This was in addition to the almost complimentary editions of poetry and the masterpieces of world literature available in all the government run bookshops.

The gesture was a great one, but it was not just a gesture! It was a very logical and strategic move, because what Venezuela, Bolivia, Uruguay, Ecuador and other countries were fighting for were actually the very basic principles of humanism. One did not have to go all the way to Karl Marx, Chairman Mao, or Lenin or Chavez; the essence was all there – in the classics of Victor Hugo, Cervantes, Maxim Gorki, Tolstoy and Tagore.

Under the pretext that working class people and peasants were simply brainless beasts who could never understand intellectual peaks like poetry and novels, elites in much of the world, 'reserved' the right for philosophical thought and 'noble emotions' strictly to themselves. In direct contrast, in some of the countries in Latin America, we said that everyone could and should have the right to think, and to feel, as we began distributing the great books to everybody. By defying all the elitist theories, even the most humble people actually began to read the great classics, enjoying and easily understanding them.

Then the more they understood, the more they supported those who treated them as equals. They came to the revolution not through ideology, but through natural human instincts. They simply embraced those who respected them, were sharing with them, and treated them with kindness.

Exposing society to the arts also began to have a very positive and deep influence on the many trends in progressive Latin American societies. What is the point, for instance, of 'fighting' against domestic violence, if people are only exposed from their early age to brutal, vulgar videos, and standardized, mostly soulless and commercially-driven entertainment? Isn't it clear that a man who reads Marti, Neruda or Tagore will less likely beat and terrorize his wife and children?

People accustomed to comparing good and evil, not superficially, or because they are obliged to by their religion or ideology, but voluntarily and in depth, would logically also refuse to observe idly, as marginalized people rot away alive in the slums or directly on the streets, in front of their eyes.

* * *

"Tamara, have you liked my theatre play 'Ghosts of Valparaiso'?" I asked my friend before departing from Merida.

"My boyfriend and I read it aloud, twice, for two nights in a row," she explained with an absolutely serious face, this tough activist with a revolutionary spirit. "And we cried for two nights straight". There was nothing more to add and I was happy; by South American standards she gave me some of the highest marks of appreciation, pure and sincere.

I knew men in Peru and Colombia and in other places of the continent who would cry when reading the poems of Marti or Cesar Vallejo at night, then wake up in the morning, and go without any hesitation into the most beastly battles, with absolutely no fear. I knew men who would write poems to their wives or girlfriends in the trenches. Here, in Latin America, to feel, to be emotional is not something that is considered shameful or ridiculous, as long as a person is strong and tough when the strength and toughness are truly essential and necessary.

* * *

Arts teach people how to dream, and in turn the dreams push societies forward.

Poetry is not only about passionate outbursts; it is often about compassion, kindness and pensiveness. The emotional, melancholic cushion wrapped around many poems, can habitually absorb the most piercing pain, and encourage forgiveness.

But it is not only poetry that shapes the Latin psyche and helps to form the complex, fascinating national and continental identity; it is the entire wide-scale of artistic expressions: from cinema and theatre to literature and music.

It is also a lifestyle – those endless Friday and Saturday nights when big groups of friends gather, staying up till the morning, exchanging ideas, information, dreams and sorrows, migrating from one theatre to another, from one cinema to another, moving between exhibitions and galleries, sometimes dancing and sometimes drinking, but always talking.

No social networking, no Skype or Internet communication can replace those direct exchanges and stormy debates, as no electronic media can replace the warmth of human hands, or the expression of a friend's eyes, or movement of the lips.

Many great social and political concepts of Latin America were created during nights around café tables, after watching with friends some great works of art either on the stage or on the screen.

The arts not only educate, they encourage people to think and to feel, helping them to make essential distinctions between good and evil. Any revolution stripped of these qualities can simply lead to carnage, as it already has in so many unfortunate places.

Not surprisingly, almost all Latin American revolutions were based on poetry and the longing for love and beauty. Their demands were extremely 'decent' and 'moderate'. It was the Western-backed fascist backlash that employed beastliness, slaughter and rape.

* * *

It is a small wonder that, in almost all the countries that have fallen under Western neo-colonial rule, the arts were immediately marginalized or destroyed, with artists and many great intellectuals imprisoned or directly liquidated. It is logical; as the last thing that the fascist rulers want, is to have cultured and well informed passionate masses.

But even more destructive and effective than the gallows and executioner's noose has been the relentless campaigns aimed at discrediting the arts as something irrelevant, on par with 'entertainment'. This was extremely successful in Southeast Asia, but I also believe, in many countries of the Arab world.

Thinking had been described as tiring and outdated, 'serious topics' (read: everything that could improve the country or fate of its people) as boring, and pure feelings as negatively 'sentimental'.

To be 'hip' and 'cool', one has to be 'light'. And it means accepting the dogma by watching Hollywood and Disney, listening to pre-selected tunes, eating pre-fabricated food.

Latin America resisted. It turned serious topics into beautiful masterpieces. Poets and bards kept packing the stadiums, while cinemas on the main streets of Buenos Aires and Santiago de Chile routinely and stubbornly showed Iranian or Chinese art releases. The continent continued producing long poems and long books, as well as over-sized essays. To be frivolously 'light' commanded no respect here. 'Live to the fullest, but keep thinking and creating' could easily pass as a local motto.

* * *

Before the Argentinean military dictatorship went to the dogs in 1982, one of the greatest singers of all time – Mercedes Sosa – returned home from exile. Loved by the entire continent, admired for her powerful, prophetic voice, she was a striking opposite to what the mass media all over the world had been promoting for decades as the 'perfect female'. Ms Sosa was plump, and she was indigenous. But this was not Sunset Boulevard; this was El Puerto.

In the evening she entered, in a determined manner, the supreme temple of 'European culture' in Argentina – and one of the greatest opera houses in the world: Teatro Colon in Buenos Aires.

The theater was packed. Some of the songs she was going to sing were still banned. But her appearance was, in a way, a promise that the horrors of fascism were going to be over soon. Those who attended the concert later recalled that the atmosphere in the theatre was electrifying. She was expected to challenge Videla and the other rapists and murderers from the ranks of ruling military junta, to challenge them with her powerful but bare voice. She was expected to sing all those tunes that kept men, women and children alive, emotionally and spiritually, during the long years of darkness. And she did. She sang as no one else in the world could have done.

She sang a song about the burning sun and about a girl called Maria, Maria va; 'Maria is going'. And then other songs, and it was all there, the entire resistance, passion, love, Revolution – it was there in one single night, in the single voice of this exceptional lady.

The recording of the concert became one of the greatest classics of all times. The audience cried and it roared. It was over – the suffering was over. The songs, for years sung in the cellars and backyards, hummed in prisons and torture chambers, whistled at night – those beloved songs were now purring like tears and like blood, freely, from the stage of the Buenos Aires opera house.

But what is it, in what she sang, that challenged the entire system? Was it a call to battle, an insult to the system; was it politics?

She sang a ballad composed by Violetta Parra, the Chilean founder of the *Nueva Cancion* movement, a great musician and poet who committed suicide in 1967.

Gracias a la vida que me ha dado tanto

Me dio dos luceros, que cuando los abro,

Perfecto distingo lo negro del blanco

Y en el alto cielo su fondo estrellado

Y en las multitudes el hombre que yo amo

(Thanks to the life that has given me so much

It gave me two bright stars and when I open them

I distinguish perfectly the black from the white

And in the high sky its starred bottom

And in the crowd the man I love)

She sang a stunning and melancholic song, about an Argentinean poet Alfonsina Storni, "Alfonsina and The Sea", who threw herself in desperation into the sea at Mar de Plata:

> You are leaving Alfonsina
>
> With your loneliness
>
> Which new poems
>
> Did you go find?
>
> An ancient voice
>
> Made of wind and salt
>
> Breaks your soul
>
> And takes it away
>
> And you float away
>
> As in dreams
>
> Asleep, Alfonsina
>
> Dressed by the sea

"So where is the revolution?" an impatient young reformer in Cairo or Casablanca may ask. "All that sadness, and longing for love, and melancholy and beauty... all that parting... despair... but where is the call to the barricades, where is the rebellion?"

"But it is there... it is present... in all those love poems, don't you hear?" the Latin Americans would argue.

All of a sudden things get more direct.

As if hearing this discussion in Colon, Mercedes Sosa abruptly changes the rhythm. She begins singing an old beautiful *melonga* from Uruguay:

> I have so many brothers,
>
> I can't even count

The audience stops breathing. It knows what is coming. The night is approaching its climax.

Sosa sings about the warm hands of the poor people, and then suddenly about death, about 'our death, the death of our people that are following us' no matter where we go.

There is absolute silence, which gradually changes to a deafening roar. Mercedes Sosa makes one single strike, short, perfect and deadly, like the most refined move of a Samurai's sword:

> I have so many brothers,
>
> I can't even count
>
> And I have one sister
>
> The most beautiful one
>
> Whose name is freedom!

Several months later military junta is forced to step down.

Mercedes Sosa passed away in 2009, but the Latin American revolution survived. Before Ms Sosa's final journey, Cristina Kirchner – her greatest admirer and by then the President of Argentina – parted with her on behalf of the nation, and the entire Latin America, in a symbolic and highly emotional ceremony. In many ways these two powerful women transformed, and became the symbol of modern Argentina. It is likely that in their youth, Mercedes Sosa transformed Cristina Kirchner.

* * *

Without the emotional outbursts; without the poetry and the powerful lyrical songs, without the desperation and exposed emotions, without the ability to dream... there would never have been a victorious struggle for true freedom and justice in Latin America.

We are sentimental, yes. And we are dreamers. But we are also tough. And our world is mostly abstract. We are... so many things, so many diverse things.

Even in Cuba, one of the most talented and popular of the musicians and bards, Sylvio Rodriguez, very rarely sings about the revolution in direct terms. Even he is predominantly abstract. Almost all his great songs are philosophical, and very few openly are calls to arms, although somehow after listening to them, one would go and die defending Cuba, with no regrets. In La Maza he is asking what it would be like:

> If I didn't believe in the toughest
>
> If I didn't believe in the desire
>
> If I didn't believe in what I believe
>
> If I didn't believe in something pure

If I didn't believe in every wound
If I didn't believe in what comes around
If I didn't believe in what hides behind
Making oneself brother with life
If I didn't believe in whoever listens to me
If I didn't believe in what hurts
If I didn't believe in what stays
If I didn't believe in what fights!

We learnt that the dreams, the emotional education; are all necessary, even essential preparatory work for the revolution. How could one go into battle without the words of poetry on his or her lips, without the person he loves in his heart, and with total dedication to the country he wants to defend and reshape? It is the Latin American way. And it is working here. Whatever the world thinks, it is working here!

For years we had better poems and we had better songs than our opressors. For years our goals and the humanism were like two inseparable twins. For years we fought and lost, because they had more tanks and more money to corrupt our military and our 'elites'.

And then, suddenly, things began to change.

You see; it is all about values. One steals from the nation, because expensive cars and villas bring more 'respect' than honesty, knowledge, kindness, or beauty. There is simply no way one can fight corruption without making a determined attempt to change the value system.

To bring this thesis to its extreme: if one well-written poem could evoke more admiration from the people, from the nation, than a bright-red Ferrari, people would stop stealing and begin writing. In Cuba, the majority would opt for a poem. In countries like Venezuela, there is an entire generation of people growing up on the same principles.

* * *

One of the most iconic poems of the Latin American revolution is "The Parrots" by the Nicaraguan poet Ernesto Cardenal:

My friend Michel is an army officer
In Somoto up near the Honduran border,
And he told me he had found some contraband parrots
Waiting to be smuggled to the United States
To learn to speak English there.
There were 186 parrots
With 47 already dead in their cages.
He drove them back where they'd been taken from
And as the lorry approached a place known as The Plains
Near the mountains which were these parrot's home
(behind those plains the mountains stand huge)
the parrots got excited, started beating their wings
and shoving against their cage-sides.
When the cages were let open
They all shot out like an arrow shower
Straight for their mountains.
The Revolution did the same for us I think:
It freed us from the cages
Where they trapped us to talk English,
It gave us back the country
From which we were uprooted,
Their green mountains restored to the parrots
By parrot-green comrades.
But there were 47 that died.

I met Ernesto Cardenal only once. I was very young then, the Chilean dictatorship had only recently collapsed, and I was taking a break in Santiago, after spending several terrible months covering the brutal civil war in neighboring Peru, for several European publications.

Cardenal came to read at a prominent Book Fair, at the magnificently restored train station, turned into one of the major cultural centers of the city: Estacion Mapocho.

There wasn't really a stampede – Chilean crowds are too polite for that – but one had to use elbows to secure entry. The enormous space was packed, mostly with young people.

This author was one of the icons of the Latin American Left –a poet, later a revolutionary, later the Minister of Culture of Nicaragua during the first Sandinista government, later a priest but still a revolutionary, still a poet... he spoke very little. He lifted his huge book – his then latest and monumental 'Cosmic Chants' – and began to recite.

Each poem evoked a similar reaction, as that to goals scored by the 'revolutionary footballer,' Diego Maradona. This was sheer madness. People were screaming, hugging each other, and crying.

Cardenal's voice was like that of a prophet, of a prosecutor, and a bard – all in one.

I had to speak to him; I had to understand where all this strength, this magic, was coming from. After his appearance I ran backstage. There were girls; there were middle-aged women, journalists, and photographers. All of them pushing, all of them desperately besieging the poet.

Photo 4. Ernesto Cardenal – great Nicaraguan revolu-tionary poet.

From the first moment it appeared that I had no chance. But I was not ready to give up.

"Don Ernesto!" I screamed. "Don Ernesto, I have to talk to you!"

He noticed me. "Then talk if you *have to*!" He shouted over the heads of the crowd.

"But..." I pointed at the people. "Could we set up a meeting; an appointment?"

"Kid!" He screamed in despair. "Kid, did I hear you say appointment? The planet is burning, and people are suffering everywhere. There is no time for appointments! Speak up now or get lost!"

I spoke. And after that I virtually have never asked for any appointment again, usually losing all my interest if someone suggested setting one up for me. I concluded that Cardenal was essentially correct: If something is urgent and it can't wait, then one should speak and act immediately, or it is not urgent and dealing with it is simply a waste of time.

* * *

Latin America is full of legends, fairytales, supernatural beings, and stories. Just go to the old Chilean port city of Valparaiso, go to the Peruvian and Bolivian Andes, to the Brazilian and Venezuelan jungles. Go there and listen.

As with those love poems, on the surface of it the stories and fairytales have nothing in common with the revolution, but that is only on the surface. Look and listen much closer and you will realize that the imaginary universe of many thinkers and revolutionaries, their world of dreams, is often made up of similar stuff, such as the ideas for a better world; a better society.

In South America, there are legendary creatures, ghosts, and fantastic past events, all in multitude, and all over the continent. There are many people living 'in their own world' here, or more precisely in two distinct worlds: one that belongs in reality, and one that belongs to their dreams.

"And why not?" many would say. It is not that the world that we humans created is always so precious, so wonderful. Each man, each woman and each child should not feel guilty or ashamed of searching for inspiration in their own imagination; in a secret universe made to accommodate their desires and sensitivities.

While what I am describing now is absolutely the same in North Asia – in China, Japan and Korea – I am often misunderstood in North Africa, in the Middle East, and even on the Sub-Continent. I don't know why.

But back to Latin America: people here, are, as we have determined earlier, passionate dreamers.

And their inner universe, their universe of dreams often opens; dreams overflow, and try to improve the reality of this world.

Arguably the greatest living South American writer is Eduardo Galeano, the author of two monumental works on the conquest and plunder of the continent: "Open Veins of Latin America" and the trilogy called "Memory of Fire".

Once, as we sat in his Café Brazilero in Montevideo, I asked him, sarcastically, whether "The Veins of Latin America were still open, after all those years after his book was first published?"

But Galeano, an author of dreams, has a tendency not to answer the question in a concrete manner: "The other day I was walking through the streets of Buenos Aires and I bumped into Count Dracula," he explained with a stone-serious face, which made me think that in his own way he was actually not joking. "Dracula looked very thin, undernourished, destroyed. I asked him what happened and he replied: 'Times are tough'. With the US and UK on the loose, plundering and sucking blood out from the world, a decent vampire has no chance. The competition is too stiff."

That is how many men and women speak here; often some of the greatest of them; and the majority of the people have no difficulty in understanding them. The language of dreams and imagination is one of the main idioms of this vast continent – language that is understood and spoken in all of its corners!

Unless it has escaped some of my readers – all, or at least the great majority of those great men who are leading the continent in the revolutionary direction – Fidel Castro, Evo Morales, Hugo Chavez – are incurable dreamers or what could be described as determined 'romantics'. Listen to their speeches, read their essays; it is so obvious.

Ernesto 'Che' Guevara was clearly a quixotic figure. Cuba in general is a quixotic state. That is one of the main reasons why they, both 'Che' and Cuba, are loved and respected to such a great extent in so many parts of the world.

Wasn't it the supreme expression of idealism, the great and powerful poem of its own style, for a small Caribbean nation under siege and under attack from the mightiest empire on the earth, to send its best sons to fight and to die for the freedom of the far away African nations of Angola, Namibia and Congo; or to send some of the most talented men and women –doctors – to serve the poorest nations of the world without expecting anything in return?

* * *

It is all intertwined here, the poetry and the struggle, the pathos, the music and the revolution.

Poems are written with ink and in blood, while verses and the strings of guitars carry on the revolution.

The imagination of the continent is limitless, and its creativity astonishing. But there are limits, too; there are limits to the art.

One of the greatest Argentinean painters, Alberto Bruzzone, once said: "I cannot paint flowers or motherhood, when they are killing my students on the street!"

Bruzzone was so much ahead of his times – especially ahead of most of the artists in the West. How many artists in California or in London could exclaim: "I refuse to produce frivolous, brainless films, while my empire is keeping half of the world in virtual servitude and misery!"

But back to poetry: some men and women here wrote enormous verses with their own lives. Be it Che or Hugo Chavez, Sub-Commandant Marcos, Fidel or now the young leader of the student revolt in Chile – Camila Vallejo.

And of course, Pablo Neruda, Jose Marti, President Salvador Allende.

President Allende died in the flames at the old baroque palace – La Moneda – as the Chilean airforce bombed the place, and busily committed treason on 9-11-1973, serving the interests of the United States and its corporations.

They say Allende committed suicide. But I am much too Latino by now, and I have my own interpretation of events, my own imaginary world, and I am determined to stick to it.

Allende knew about the coup. Many in Chile that were close to him told me that he was well informed... But being a real democrat, he refused to arrest anyone based on just suspicion. So far these are the facts.

Now comes my own interpretation of the history, which I freely implement in all my fiction work: When the fighter jets began bombing the Presidential Palace, Allende stood up and began walking towards the huge baroque windows, towards the jets and towards his certain death. He was still the President of Chile; he was the democratically elected President of one of the oldest democracies on earth, until that day, of one of the most decent countries under the sun. He walked towards those pilots who betrayed him; who betrayed Chile, because no matter what they were doing, they were citizens of the country that he was entrusted to govern. He was walking towards them because he was not going to run away – he saw no point in running. He died walking proudly, undefeated, towards the roaring jets, towards the muzzles of their guns, towards the rockets attached under their wings a man wearing thick-framed glasses, a very kind man, a true humanist.

As Allende made his first steps, Pablo Neruda was dying not far from La Moneda, from cancer. During the elections, Don Pablo was supposed to run as a candidate of the Communist Party of Chile, but he instead endorsed Allende, who represented La Unidad Popular.

Two great men, two towering personalities of Chile and the world were then, dying at the same time, not far from each other, although not exactly side-by-side. Their country, their most beautiful country on Earth, was being ravaged and was going to be raped for almost two decades, by hideous forces consisting of Western neo-colonialists and a local gang of spiteful and mediocre servants of the North.

Don Pablo had already written his final poem. He parted with Matilda; he parted with his friends and with his nation. Allende was still writing his poem with his own body, his own flesh, and his blood.

This is one good example of how some of our best poems are written. This is where poetry and revolution merge; this is how they become a single and solid entity.

* * *

After the coup, the military packed the National Stadium in Santiago de Chile with thousands of prisoners. One of the greatest bards of Latin America – Victor Jarra – had his ribs and both of his hands broken. Soldiers threw a guitar at him: "Now sing for us," they laughed. He did. He sang *Venceremos* straight to their faces. They machine-gunned him down. The way this great and proud life ended – that was another poem that inspired us, and finally led us to victory. You don't cry for mercy when confronted by Fascism. You spit in its face and die, if you cannot win. Full stop!

And almost 30 years later, there was another beautiful 'poem' written by General Raúl Baduel, who headed Chávez's old paratrooper division in Maracay, as he and others defeated, against all odds, the US-sponsored coup in Caracas, in 2002. Some poems are, and have to be written with steel.

* * *

So now we know what role poetry plays in Latin American revolutions. And of what the poetry consists of, here.

And how it merges with this continent, one, that has been waiting for all those long decades and centuries to be truly liberated. The continent that kept fighting and losing, fighting again and again, and saw its legitimate leaders murdered or overthrown by the North: in Guatemala, Dominican Republic, Brazil, Chile, Nicaragua, and in so many other places.

It is all history now. The unity, solidarity, and tremendous force of creativity – all is alive and boiling, all is suddenly possible, reachable, and achievable.

But there are no celebrations yet, no fireworks, and there are tears and sadness all around, a melancholy. Both hopeful smiles and tears can be seen, often on the same face.

The revolution won, finally, on most of the continent.

But there were tens of millions that died.

26 October 2012

*****

13

'Tolerant' Indonesia

"SHI'A BLOOD IS HALAL!"

Co-written with ROSSIE INDIRA

As darkness hastily falls on the heart of Madura Island, uniquely shaped traditional wooden houses and hamlets begin to throw long shadows in an eastward direction. Traffic, which during the day is extremely light by Indonesian standards, is now ceasing entirely. Just a few noisy scooters remain on the road, avoiding the poor peasants slowly dragging their tired feet home from the fields.

Almost no one here speaks Bahasa Indonesia– the official language that was supposed to unite this sprawling archipelago, during and after the declaration of independence from the ruthless Dutch colonial rulers. The local languages and dialects are unfortunately unintelligible to all three of us – occupants of the car. Even our driver, a native from Surabaya, the second largest Indonesian city whose suburbs spread across on the opposite shore right across the narrow strait, and only a few minutes ferry ride from Madura, understands close to nothing when the natives speak.

We ask for directions, we receive unintelligible answers; we don't know whether we are on the right track.

But then the powerful lights penetrate the dusk, and we see dozens of police trucks, like ghosts, appearing from nowhere, at the side of the road.

"Where are you going?"

There is no point in pretending. We are going to..., we are searching for the Shi'a village, a hamlet, called Nangkernang that was recently attacked, and savagely destroyed by local Sunni religious bigots.

"It is not safe and you can't go there," explains an officer who appears to be in charge. "And it is far..." He waves his hand; he waves ahead, somewhere towards the great distance.

We talk, we argue, but the security forces are giving us clear orders: We can drive straight on, but without leaving the main road.

At the next village, we ask and miraculously we are understood. We are told that the path to the destroyed village begins right where the police vans are parked. "They lied to you. Just leave the car here, rent two motorbikes and a local guide and go back."

We do exactly that. We hire two shaky scooters, one driven by a kid who could not be older than fourteen, and the other one, by an old man. Our lights are turned off and we manage to pass unnoticed near the police post. Then we turn into a tight path between two rice fields. There is a narrow, wooden, half destroyed bridge and a creek below: all of that could be sensed in almost absolute darkness, but hardly seen. From here we have to abandon our stinky two-wheelers and walk.

***

The village is called Nangkernang, Karang Gayam, and the nearest city is Sampang, an hour's drive away, and on the coast. To our surprise, the village has at least some weak and unsteady supply of electricity.

We are expected here. Reluctantly we all introduce ourselves.

Then we are shown the devastation: dozens of houses totally ruined, burned down. And these were not just some small houses, but entire hamlets. The nearest house is right in front of a small wooden platform where we sit and talk, and it used to belong to a Shi'a imam.

Pak (Mr) Sinal is a man aged about 50 years, who speaks to us, hesitantly:

> "I myself am a Shi'a, but now I keep it hushed. There are approximately 50 houses belonging to Shi'a people that were burned and destroyed on 26th August 2012. One person died after being attacked with a machete. From what I know, one family, that of Ustadz Tajul, was driving in a mini-van to Sampang jail. On the way, they were harassed by a group of Sunnis. The family decided to return, but the gang followed them all the way to the village. One of the perpetrators called for reinforcements and soon more than a thousand people gathered, and eventually attacked the Shi'a community. They burned and destroyed houses here, they killed and injured people."

Just as the children and adults were beginning to relax, a man walked briskly up towards the platform. Everyone fell silent. The village is mixed: Sunni and Shi'a, living side by side. In August, it was the locals, not just those that came from outside, that attacked their neighbors.

***

On the way back to Surabaya, the driver begins telling a long and complicated tale about two brothers, two Imams – one Shi'a and one Sunni. The Sunni Imam apparently fell in love with a girl from a local boarding Shi'a school. His brother interfered and married the girl off to a boy of her own age.

"The Sunni Imam was so angry, that he began agitating the crowd against his own brother, and the violence erupted."

I have covered enough conflicts all over Indonesia, to know their simple and true causes – racism, intolerance and bigotry – are never accepted here. There is always some 'unpaid bus fare', just as in Ambon, or an obscure love story, or at least a bunch of 'provocateurs' triggering violence.

The reality is simple and terrible: since the 1960s, Indonesia has lived through at least 3 genocides: that of 1965/66, in which between 2 and 3 million people died as a result of the Western-backed military coup against President Sukarno and the moderate, constitutional PKI (the Communist Party of Indonesia, which had widely been expected to win the elections), the genocide in East Timor, in which approximately 30% of the local people lost their lives, and the ongoing genocide in West Papua.

The religion of the majority played a decisive role in all these 'events'. In 1965, as was confirmed by our friend, the former progressive President of Indonesia, Abdurrahman Wahid ('Gus Dur'), that religious cadres joined the military in an indiscriminate slaughter of 'atheists'; killing members of the PKI, intellectuals and members of the Chinese minority. East Timor and Papua, two Christian and animist nations had been put through forced Islamization and unimaginable discrimination and horrors. Papua is suffering; literally bleeding into extinction, until this very day.

But the West insists that Indonesia is a 'tolerant' nation, and even an example that should be followed by the leaders of the Arab Spring.

Who can ever forget the memorable phrase that Hilary Clinton dropped, while visiting Indonesia, in the same period when the secularists were being assaulted and beaten by the Islamic Defender's Front, in front of the idle police standing by, as Sharia Law was unconstitutionally imposed on several pockets of West Java and elsewhere, as the members of Ahmadiyah sect were being murdered, churches burnt, and non-Muslims brutally attacked, harassed and punished for their beliefs, all over the archipelago: "If you want to know if Islam, democracy, modernity and women's rights can co-exist, go to Indonesia."

Why would she utter such unfounded chimeras?

The answer is obvious: because the West in general and the US in particular, are infinitely grateful to this the fourth most populous country on Earth; grateful for murdering the Communists and members of Chinese minority, for murdering intellectuals, artists, and teachers.

Grateful to the Indonesian religious cadres that went to fight the Soviet Union and its 'client', the secular government in Afghanistan (who in the West could ever imagine tolerating women in Kabul being educated and empowered under Russian rule?), joining the Mujahedin, Pakistani jihadis and intelligence forces, as well as foreign legionnaires paid for by the West (including those embryonic cells of the future Al Qaida); all united and most of them stoned, putting an end to the only relatively hopeful period of modern Afghan history, while helping to bleed the USSR to extinction, militarily and financially!

And let us not forget how grateful the West is to the Indonesian people for allowing their natural resources to be plundered by multi-national companies, and by their own corrupt elites!

What would the West do without obedient countries like Indonesia: how could it maintain its ridiculously high level of consumption and its standard of living? And isn't obedience the basis of any religious and feudal society?

In Indonesia there is a clear paradox: most of the people think that the country is tolerant and moderate; they quote Western politicians and Western mass media. In the meantime the number of deaths caused by intolerance and bigotry is mounting.

"The problem with the majority of Indonesian Muslims is that they don't have their own opinion. They follow what their leaders say, or follow what the Qur'an says, or what the *hadiths* say. They don't exercise critical thinking at all. Therefore, when their leaders say; we are moderate and tolerant followers of Islam, most of the believers will say yes and think that is the case," explained Noor Huda Ismail, a Muslim thinker, analyst and an author of the book "My Friend a Terrorist".

***

The covered tennis court in the city of Sampang, is where the refugees from the area that we had earlier visited, had been given as a temporary shelter. There were armored vehicles parked at the gate and security personnel that forbade anyone to enter.

We 'gate crash'; park the car and I dash in, with a total disregard of the shouts and attempts to stop me – hardened by my work in the refugee camps of DR Congo, Uganda, Rwanda, Kenya and Turkey.

Here, refugees talk. They are outraged, and hurt. It feels like they have nothing to lose:

"We feel damaged, angry and disappointed, and we hold the government responsible," explains a young man– Nur Kholis. "Our rights were stolen from us. We did nothing wrong to those who killed and destroyed us."

> "We are now waiting for justice. As the Shi'a minority, we are discriminated against.
>
> We only have a few differences with Sunnis, and there is no reason for conflict. We always have to remember that we have more similarities than differences. But Shi'a people are now called *kafirs*; we are labeled as *najis*. They say that, Shi'a people change wives like animals. All these are lies, but people here believe it."

And then he, in his own words, comes to the same conclusion as Nur Huda Ismail:

> "Madurese believe what their big Imams say. There is no questioning them, even if they are wrong and obviously totally corrupt! Do you know that MUI Sampang (The Council of Ulemas in Sampang) issued a fatwa (Islamic edict), that Shi'a teaching is squarely misguided and heretical? The government did nothing! And now they want us to leave, instead of returning home; they are trying to relocate us to another island – far away Sulawesi!"

Hanny, a sister to the two Imams who were in a dispute over the fate of the girl from the boarding school, is even more explicit:

"I think that the majority of the people of Madura know very little about the differences between Sunni and Shi'a Muslims. But their Imams told them that the teaching of Shi'a is heretical, un-Islamic and that the Sunni teachings are the only correct ones. Sunni Imams want us to disappear from Madura Island; we are becoming political refugees. For them, the violence directed at us is justifiable; it is *halal* because they think we are like dirt, like shit, *haram, najis*. I saw one of the attackers, Seniwan, at the police station when he was detained. Later I was told that he was seen at the market! Maybe he has a double...," she adds sarcastically.

During interviews with the victims, I film and photograph the refugees. An old couple catches my eye. A woman and a man radiate terrible grief. I don't know what it is that I feel, but it is almost as if my hand, the one holding the camera, keeps turning the lens towards them. I follow my instinct and begin photographing, discreetly, somehow embarrassed. The woman moves. She utters a heart-wrenching sound. I suddenly have goose bumps on my back.

"Who are they?" I ask Hanny. "Who is she?"

"She is the mother of a man who was killed... they are his parents," she replies.

As always, in such situations, a short stab of hopelessness is soon replaced with a desire to inform, and to change things.

I bow to the old woman and go back to work.

***

Two young women, two Shi'a teachers, are literally holed-up in their girl's boarding school. They are so cute, defenseless and kind-hearted, that I instantly feel these could be two women I would like to have as my sisters.

But they are tough. They know that they are besieged, in danger, and exposed, but they do not abandon their posts.

Across the road is a small Sunni mosque, a *Mussola*, full of heavy guns pointing at the Shi'a boarding school. 'Guns' consist of powerful loudspeakers, belonging to part of the overwhelming Sunni majority, which is showered with money from the Gulf.

Naila Zakiyah is a lecturer at the Shi'a school for girls: Al Mahadul Islami:

> "In light of recent events, we are naturally worried about the safety of our students. We are supposed to educate girls here, but there is a group of people that is trying to undermine our efforts... Yes, we feel discriminated against... Before this year's Ramadhan, *the Mussola Al Anwar* from across the street broadcasted their sermon twice a week. They had their loudspeakers directed towards our school. They were shouting that Shi'a teaching is misguided, and that our blood is *haram*. It is said that those who are attacking us, are being funded by money from Saudi Arabia. I don't have any proof but that is what people say. In 2007, there were 500 people demonstrating in front of our boarding school; that time the funds came from KSA. Each person was given US$2. These were uneducated people; I doubt they knew what they were being used for."

We and the teachers exchanged mobile numbers, and then we simply crossed the road, and went directly to their torturers; to men known for shooting hate-coated verbal missiles towards those nice Shi'a teachers and their students. We marched to the *Mussola Al Anwar*, and fetched Mr. Atoilah.

While somehow embarrassed whilst visiting the Shi'a boarding school, I suddenly felt extremely *halal* here, with my US passport sticking out from my pocket. I was aware that I was entering a territory that was so kindly embraced and caressed by *Wahhabi* wisdom and by its guardian, the KSA – one of the closest allies of our dear and gentle, starred and striped Empire.

Mr. Atoilah was at first surprised by our interest, then he played shy, but by the end he had regained his natural militant and boorish self, and as expected, went ballistic:

> "The teaching of Shi'a deviates from Islamic teaching; therefore

> we have so many essential differences. The Shi'a minority once promised that they will convert to Sunni, but they lied to us... And so it seemed that we couldn't talk to them in a subtle way, anymore. If they don't want to convert, then we have to use violence. In our opinion, they are *kafir*. We will not be at peace with them until we die, even if our lives are at stake. They have already insulted Islam! If the police do not take action against the Shi'a, we will resort to violence."

He produces an amateur brochure, a photocopy of a pamphlet proclaiming, "The Truth About Shi'a" on its cover.

"Here, read this," he hands us a copy. It reads: 'sponsored by LPPI (Institute for Islamic Research and Study) based in Jakarta'. Then he adds: "We are part of NU, you know."

NU is one of the biggest, if not the biggest independent Muslim organization in the world, with an estimated membership base of 30 million people.

"*Astaga*", we think; which could be loosely translated as 'Oh damn it!'

Mr. Atoilah smiles, victoriously.

***

People from the Shi'ite minority are petrified. Many are now practising their faith in secret; most of them keep it to themselves. Even in the big cities, it is now difficult to make people go on the record and identify themselves as Shi'a.

It is said that there are approximately 1 million Shi'a Muslims in Indonesia, the official number quoted by the Indonesian press. But at all the religious Shi'a schools that we visited, teachers laugh at those numbers. They say that there are several millions of their brothers and sisters all over the archipelago, although nobody bothers to keep a count. And despite the persecution, their numbers are growing.

Naturally those millions cannot count on the protection of the State, and the same can be said about the other religious and ethnic minorities. In Indonesia the majority rules and it rules ruthlessly.

Here, the assassins go free and the victims end up in prisons.

According to the Jakarta Globe, it was actually two people, not one, killed on August 2012. As was reported a day later.

Around 30 Shi'ites, most of them children, were traveling from Nangkernang village... they were stopped by around 500 men from the mainstream Muslim groups...", said Umi Kutsum, who was at the scene... "Two people died," she said. "Five were wounded as they were trying to protect the women and children. I was petrified... The mob had swords and machetes..." Umi's children were among the group, who were taken away from her. The mob then torched four homes belonging to the Shi'ite community, including one belonging to Umi and her husband, the Shi'a cleric Tajul Muluk..."

The August attack was the second one in this area. On the 29th December 2011, hard-line Muslim groups burned down hundreds of homes in and around Nangkernang, displacing around 500 people. The Shi'a Islamic School was destroyed as well.

In a move that illustrates the 'impartiality' of the Indonesian justice system, instead of pursuing the mob leaders (everybody in the area knows who they are); the police instead charged a Shi'a cleric with blasphemy. And, as was even reported by the Jakarta Globe, the Ministry of Religious Affairs office in Sampang, said it would 'supervise' hundreds of Shi'a to learn Sunni Islam.

That proved too much for some.

On 13th July 2012, Amnesty International released its report on Indonesia:

> "**Shi'a leader imprisoned for blasphemy must be released**:
>
> The Indonesian authorities must immediately and unconditionally release Tajul Muluk, a Shi'a Muslim religious leader from East Java, who was today sentenced to two years' imprisonment for blasphemy by the Sampang District Court. Amnesty International considers Tajul Muluk to be a prisoner of conscience, imprisoned solely for the peaceful exercise of his right to freedom of thought, conscience and religion."

Tajul Muluk was displaced with over 300 other Shi'a villagers on 29th December 2011, when an anti-Shi'a mob of some 500 people attacked and burned houses, a boarding school and a Shi'a place of worship in Nangkrenang village, Sampang, Madura Island. Only one person was charged and sentenced to three months' imprisonment for the attacks.

Afterwards most of the Shi'a displaced by the attack returned to Nangkrenang village. But Tajul Muluk and about 20 other villagers, including his family, were prevented from returning to the village by the attackers, who reportedly threatened to kill them if they returned, and by the police.

On the 1st January 2012 a religious decree (*fatwa*) was issued by the Sampang branch of the Indonesia Ulema Council (MUI) about what they described as Tajul Muluk's "deviant teachings", and two days later a police report was filed against him. On 16th March, the East Java regional police charged Tajul Muluk with blasphemy under Article 156(a) of the Indonesian Criminal Code, and with "offensive actions" under Article 335 of the Code.

The New York-based Human Rights Watch joined those who called on the government to drop all the charges against Tajul Muluk.

The Indonesian government, stubbornly and defiantly, did absolutely nothing.

As it has been doing for years, it silently sided with the religious bigots.

***

A leading Indonesian fiction writer and journalist, Linda Christanty, is one of the few who are willing to speak about the conflict:

> "The *Wahabbis* from Saudi Arabia are very much against the Shi'a... One of the reasons is because they revere the Prophet Muhammad. For *Wahabbis*, it is forbidden to venerate any human being, including Muhammad. KSA actually even wanted to destroy Muhammad's grave. None of the Arab countries dared to oppose the plan. Turkey was the only country that interfered, and threatened Saudi Arabia with total destruction should they dare to destroy Muhammad's grave. That's why we can still see Muhammad's grave, thanks to Turkey."

But this is not just about religious differences. It is increasingly clear, that proud and independent-minded Shi'a are opposing Western imperialism in the Middle East, in the Gulf and elsewhere. Predominantly Shi'a Iran is now the arch-enemy of the West, and the ally of progressive Latin America. Saudi and Qatari cadres, and their clients are targeting Shi'a in KSA, Bahrain, and also in Turkey, and it seems now, in Indonesia as well.

In a short interview, Prof. Azyumardi Azra, a director at the Graduate School of State Islamic University in Jakarta, explained:

> "Since the early 1980s, Saudi Arabia with their *Wahabbism*, using some Indonesian alumni from Saudi Arabia, has tried to destroy Shi'a teaching, but they haven't been successful. And not all of these alumni are against Shi'a. Many of them belong to moderate streams of Muslim scholars here, such as the previous Minister of Religious Affairs, Said Agil Husin Al Munawar."

It is true about the previous Minister, but what he did not say, is that the present Minister of Religious Affairs, Suryadharma Ali throws pearls that could hardly be matched by his counterparts in other countries: "Converting Shi'ite Muslims to the Sunni Islam followed by most Indonesians would be the best way to prevent violent outbreaks..."

The more brutal the rule of the majority in Indonesia is; the more difficult it is to find people willing and ready to speak up about injustice. Mr. Sangaji from Jakarta is one of the few Shi'ites willing to go on record:

> "There have been many attacks on the Shi'a community, in the last few years here in Indonesia. It is so unfortunate that our Sunni brothers and sisters have little knowledge about Shi'a. But whenever we open the door for dialogue, they shut it in our face and refuse to come in. Our Shi'a intellectuals are always ready for a peaceful dialogue... Of course I feel discriminated against...
>
> Is there any influence from abroad? It is not really allowed to discuss this issue openly, but one should always be on the alert, as there is always such a possibility. Our country is in a deep crisis, economically and politically; reforms have failed. Indonesians are now so easily influenced."

Before leaving Madura, driving towards the new bridge, we see the same scenes as in most of the poor parts of the country. There is destitution and misery, next to tremendous new mosques, some of which are still under construction, made of marble and granite. Who pays for them? Who needs all that marble when the children run barefoot?

At Surabaya airport we spotted two jumbo-jets; two Boeing 747-400 belonging to Saudi Airlines – one arriving and one leaving – taking pilgrims on *Haj*. What else comes and what else leaves with these airplanes? For years, almost everything in Indonesia has been for sale. Since 1965, the lives of victims ceased to matter; the lives of the weak and of the minorities became worthless.

Last year I visited the enormous Syekh Muhammad Kholil Mosque, in the city of Bangkalan, on Madura Island – built like some lavish palace in the Gulf. I found the caretaker – Mohammad Hasan – and asked him what he thought about the recent events in West and Central Java, where members of the *Ahmadiyah* sect were lynched to death, and churches burnt. Without hesitation, he replied, straight to my face:

> "*Ahmadiyah* members should be killed. It is about faith. In Indonesia, we don't want *Ahmadiyah* because it deviates from the teaching of the Sharia. They deserved to be killed because they are destroying the true faith of the people. When it comes to burning churches, I am against it. We are a peaceful religion."

Such humility!

I felt like bowing in front of such humanism, 'tolerance' and 'moderation'.

And I felt like sending a letter to the State Department saying:

"Congratulations! You did to Indonesia what you could have never done to Vietnam, you and your bearded clients in the Gulf. It is not just that the country is being plundered, miserable and corrupt, and its environment ruined. But you have also destroyed their entire civilization, and now the people of this once great Asian culture – once really tolerant and deep – are listening to your pop, stuffing themselves on your fast food, driving your cars, and murdering each other over religion and ethnicity. Congratulations, really! Another nation down the drain! And who is next?"

2 November 202

*****

14

I Had No Idea Americans Were Voting Today ... Really!

SCREW THE ELECTIONS!

Nairobi.

I am not inventing this: I really did not know; I had no clue! Until today, which is the 6th of November 2012, ...1PM... Nairobi time... I had no clue that they were once again sticking those pieces of paper into boxes... far away – in the USA.

And how did I find out? I went to my favorite bookstore in East Africa and my friend, an Indian bookseller, simply pointed at a book written by Quintus Tullius Cicero. It was written some 2,100 years ago, and was called, “How to Win an Election”.

“Practice your Latin,” my Indian friend smiled. He somehow suspected that quite some time ago I had to suffer through a classics education. Traces of it have probably never left my face.

“It sucks,” I admitted. “My Latin sucks.”

“This...” he pointed his finger at a magazine cover, with the grinning face of Obama, and of some other guy that I did not recognize, “This surely sucks much more than your Latin... And don’t you worry; the book is a by-lingual edition, so you can cheat.”

And so I did. I purchased Cicero and some Kenyan novel, and then descended to a Congolese/French café, ordered a powerful espresso macchiato and a bottle of sparkling water. Then I began to read the English language side:

> "Promise everything to everybody. Except in the most extreme cases, candidates should say whatever the particular crowd of the day wants to hear. Tell traditionalists you have consistently supported conservative values. Tell progressives you have always been on their side. After the election you can explain to everyone that you would love to help them, but unfortunately circumstances beyond your control have intervened..."

Elections?

What elections?

Then I began to recall something. My ex-wife, a concert pianist and a professor of music at Columbia University, wrote to me just yesterday, from New York City. She was urgently trying to get some dirt on Obama for her friend, who appeared to be in the terminal stages of dark depression over the entire US political establishment.

Without giving it much thought, I happily complied and forwarded to her the manuscript of my book on Indonesia, called "Archipelago of Fear" (published by Pluto, UK, 2012). The book contains some toxic flashes, illuminating Obama's childhood in a fascist post-1965 Indonesia, as well as some revivals and vignettes on his Kenyan father – one of the luminous US-trained economists, who busily helped the West destroy everything slightly resembling 'socialist' or 'social' in Kenya, and the entire East Africa).

Then I wrote to my ex-wife, now a good friend; summarizing my moderate opinion on the President of the United States: "Regarding Obama: I do not have any particularly negative feelings towards him. He is a criminal, a war criminal, like all of those guys, from the days of Washington and Lincoln. He is a crook, but not an exceptional one... just a regular bandit. But in reality, just a sad clown serving Western market fundamentalism and imperialism."

But why was everyone so obsessed with the elections and with our dear leader Obama right now?

* * *

I confess that at some point in time, I stopped watching television and reading the newspapers. Writing and filming in all corners of the world, I live most of my life in hotels and onboard passenger airplanes; therefore periodically some glimpse of the headlines catches me. Most of the time, I avert my eyes from the screens or the front-pages, as I am not really that interested in who had been eaten by a shark, somewhere in Florida, who slept with whom and in what position, and who has been running for the US Senate or the White House.

I find it irrelevant. I ignore pop music, all Hollywood and Bollywood films, as well as most of the mass media. I also ignore all the coverage by all the news outlets, of what is occurring in the US and the European political scene, as I find this information totally unrelated to the suffering of the world which I am witnessing everywhere.

Western politicians are just like some pre-selected puppet theatre dolls, and whoever of them is occupying the throne, influences nothing of what is happening in the world, and even in their own countries – in the US and Europe. To borrow an expression of the great British playwright – Hanif Kureishi: "These guys are not even in charge of the farts coming out of their rectums."

Since the beginning of this year, I decided to go back to the basics, to do it all – or at least in the field of investigative journalism – in an old-fashioned way; the way it was done a long time ago, by Orwell, but especially by people like Wilfred Burchett and Ryszard Kapuściński. I decided to go to war-zones, to conflict areas, and there, listen to people, use as few quotes from the establishment as possible, and to be totally opinionated and ideological. This, I was convinced, would bring me as close as possible to real 'objectivity' and the 'truth' as one could get.

There, in the places where the real suffering was, people did not care who was in the White House: whether Clinton or Bush, or Obama. For them it was always the same: big multi-national companies cut down their forests, polluted their rivers, robbed their natural resources and bought their labor for a song. And overthrew their democratically elected governments (yes, in many countries there were attempts to establish democracy) if they tried to serve, to prioritize the people.

Whether it was done under the Democrats or Republicans is

soon forgotten, but the suffering remains in the memory.

In this year – in 2012 – I traveled to the cities and through the countryside of China and Latin America, to the border between Syria and Turkey, to Rwanda/DR Congo border, to Bahrain, Uganda, to the sites of religious violence in Indonesia, to the villages built on and near the garbage dumps in and right outside Kolkata, to the 'sinking' nation of Kiribati, to the Kenyan/Somali border, as well as to the biggest refugee camp on earth – Dadaab.

I made films, and worked on books and reports. There was no time for watching the news. The system: the Empire, the regime, savage capitalism, was murdering all over the world. Why waste time studying its mascots replaced once every four or eight years?

* * *

And then suddenly I was here, in Nairobi, a day before my departure for Cairo and Kuala Lumpur. I was here, struck by the revelation, that I had absolutely no clue that there were elections taking place, in the country whose citizenship I held: the United Sates of America. And I had no idea who the candidates were, although once I found out there was actually an election taking place, I was certain that Mr. Obama would be one of them, as he would not want to deprive us of his luminous presence at the zenith, for another four years.

I called, texted and "Whatsapped" several people who confirmed that, yes, indeed, there were Presidential elections taking place in the US. They all thought that this was a cute joke on my part. It wasn't.

I opened the Yahoo.uk page and it was there! Yes: Obama and Romney (who the hell was he? But as Obama is a Democrat, this dude must be a Republican, by definition, right?).

While I was hibernating, those guys in Washington had already managed to nominate each other, pre-select two loyalists from their ranks, run background checks (make sure that nobody is going to rock the boat) and then allow the voters of the USA to decide whether they, and much of the world, would be 'governed' for the next four years, by a Mickey Mouse with a pink nose or by the one with the orange one.

2+2 were suddenly gathered together: I now recalled that some Senate candidates recently wrote to me. They complimented my work, and then suggested that we 'should work together'. There was a candidate for Governor of one of the major States, too. I mainly ignored such letters, or very politely declined the offers. I was absolutely not interested in the establishment, too busy with my books, films, reports, personal turmoil and the Latin American Revolution.

* * *

Slowly, waking up to reality, I began to realize how dangerous and how subversive my refusals were of taking an interest in the luminous, shining path of the Western 'democratic' election process.

I recalled one of the greatest post-war novels, "Seeing", written by the Portuguese author, Jose Saramago. In its pages he described a 'peaceful' and 'democratic' European country, and the sudden turmoil, when its citizens began spoiling the ballots, and refusing to participate in the charade of voting for pre-selected and pre-approved corporate clients, called 'candidates'. The state immediately reacted by imposing Martial law; it began to kidnap, and to murder and torture the population.

To refuse to play the game – to take these depressing and poorly choreographed tragi-comedies called 'elections' seriously – was probably a very dangerous undertaking, a punishable crime. The Western regime likes to be taken seriously. Or else...!

I suddenly had felt so wicked, and so dangerous!

But what could I do? I really couldn't care lesser (same as most of the people I met felt all over the world), which candidate would be warming the chair in the White House. Obama's foreign policy has been appalling – from the Middle East to the Gulf States, from Latin America to Africa. There is nothing positive that he has been offering to the world, as there has been nothing positive offered by any of the White House dudes since WWII. As there would certainly be nothing positive in what Mr. Romney (whoever he is) would offer were he to become the President.

Cicero wrote:

> *Qua re etiamatqueetiampergetenereistamviam quam instititisti, ex-celledicendo. Hoc ettenentur Romae et adliciuntur et abimpediendo ac laedendorepelluntur.*
>
> "In such a chaotic world, you must stick to the path you have chosen. It is your unmatched skill as a speaker that draws the Roman people to you and keeps them on your side."

'Unmatched skill as a speaker', maybe, but 'sticking to the chosen path'?

I went upstairs, and cleansed myself by listening to a couple of good revolutionary Latin American songs. And later I took a shower, defining this moment in history, under a hot stream of water, as an erotic day: "Fuck their elections!" I mumbled merrily before departing for the airport and Cairo.

I still didn't know, and had no interest of knowing, who that guy called Romney really was.

6 November 2012

*****

15

Burchett's in Vietnam

'ENEMIES OF AUSTRALIAN STATE' AND HANOI

The Vietnam Fine Arts Museum in Hanoi is confident and elegant, surrounded by ancient trees, historic villas and a celebrated cultural icon – the Temple of Literature. It puts on display numerous masterpieces of Vietnamese Art, from its earliest days to the revolutionary and Socialist Realism period.

The socialist nation is growing.

This museum is all that its counterparts in Indonesia, Malaysia or India are not. It is because the artists of Vietnam fought for the survival of their nation during the darkest period of French colonial rule; they called upon the masses to go onto the battlefields and barricades during the struggle for independence, and they inspired and supported this proud land, when it was thrown into hell on earth – enduring carpet-bombings, napalm, agent orange, mass rapes and extermination campaigns during the "American War".

After victory, hundreds of eminent artists rolled up their sleeves and went to work, inspiring tens of millions in their effort to rebuild their ravaged country, and to create an egalitarian,

Socialist society. The great modern art of Vietnam was never decorative. It was as utilitarian as anti-aircraft guns, as cranes, and as classrooms.

***

I lived for almost three years in this city – not a particularly easy three years, as Hanoi then, was still recovering from the chain of devastating wars and from the collapse of its closest ally – the Soviet Union and its East European satellite states. By then, both Vietnam and Cuba were in the middle of an epic struggle for survival, battered by the shameful withdrawal of commitments and obligations by the group of countries that succeeded the USSR.

"Where do we go; what do we do?" I was told many years ago by one of the government officials. "We have to make sure that our people survive."

'Reforms' had to be introduced, the economy became mixed, and foreign companies were allowed to enter and to form joint ventures. Bill Gates came to visit, while LV and Gucci began opening their boutiques all over HCMC and Hanoi.

It was all confusing then, as the 'Hero Mothers' – those old and proud women who lost their sons and daughters in the wars fought against the French and US colonialists – were seen walking through Hanoi and HCMC streets to their free honor seats at the opera houses, avoiding the Bentleys of the *nouveau riche*. 'New Vietnam' was suddenly all about symbols – the latest models of mobile phones, then the hippest types of motorbikes, and later Bentleys. It is said that there are more of them in Hanoi now, than in the city of London.

It was confusing then and it is still confusing now.

But what matters, is that this country survived the terror it was put through, that it got on its feet, retained its culture, its creativity and its thirst for social justice... And that it preserved its own form of socialism, no matter how battered the emblems might have appeared from time to time.

***

But back, to the Vietnam Fine Arts Museum....

I used to come here often, alone – to dream, and to admire those great Vietnamese masters of the past; artists who lived and created during the eras when what are today called Indonesia, Thailand and Cambodia, were culturally and economically closely connected with Japan, Korea and China. Vietnam was then firmly present on almost all the major trade routes of Asia Pacific. It was influenced by dozens of the great Asian cultures, whilst influencing them in return.

But above all, I used to come here in search of some good, healthy and optimistic shots of Socialist Realism.

This time, in December 2012, I was in the company of my good friend, the Australian artist George Burchett, who had moved to this city almost two years ago. Or more precisely, he didn't move here; he returned here, as this was the city where he was born.

Now this museum was 'his'; he knew it much better than I ever did. He now became my guide. This is where he has been searching for inspiration, where he has been connecting the past – his own, that of his family and of this nation – with the present.

We walked side-by-side, admiring ancient Vietnamese art, so closely linked with Buddhism, with the Khmers and with China.

But it was understood that both of us came here anticipating the real joy of being confronted by those powerful images, depicting the struggle of the Vietnamese people against the Western onslaught, and by the tremendous euphoria of building the country afterwards.

"Look at those factories, the trains, and the boats on the river!" shouted my friend George, eventually switching from English to Russian: "Here! This is Hai Phong City: factory, steam engine, people; life!"

"It looks like some utopian paradise," he continued. "Beautiful, really beautiful: it is all here, right here: nature, the work, and enthusiasm..."

I saw it; I could also stare at those canvases for hours. And when I did, the meaning would return to life. The nihilism of imperialism, of individualism, of religions: all those things that were ruining our beautiful planet would soon be fading away, or at least they would hide for a while, in some dark corners.

The message was clear and powerful, and after many long years of circling the globe, of covering wars and the 'human condition' in general, I couldn't agree with it more: 'It is glorious to fight for real freedom, as it is wonderful to dedicate one's life to building a nation'.

George and I stood in respectful silence in front of the paintings depicting the Ho Chi Minh Trail and 'Uncle Ho' himself; in front of the paintings portraying soldiers and strong, determined women, confronting some beefy and arrogant French soldiers. And we smiled at one of my favorite canvases by Nguyen Sang: 'Admitting a New Member into the Party'.

Our enchantment with; our love for this optimistic universe full of devoted work for humanity, was very different from the set of dogmatic official Western doctrines (even, or especially, from the 'new Left') and we knew it would be extremely difficult to translate and to transmit all this, even to some of the people we cared about a lot: to our colleagues and friends somewhere in faraway Canada or California.

It goes without saying that both George Burchett and I, were melting perfectly into this milieu – we grew up under very similar and very 'unusual' circumstances. Those circumstances formed us and convinced us that real art has to be engaged, that it has to be ideological; and no matter what, it has to be about the people and for the people.

***

George Burchett is not a typical 'Aussie', very far from that.

He was born in Hanoi, in Vietnam, almost a decade before I was born in Leningrad.

And he did not come into this Earth by landing in some plush realm; into a universe where a kindhearted Australian diplomat would visit the maternity ward where he was born, give him a big smile, pat him on the diaper and whisper: "Welcome to this wonderful world, our friend; you are now our mate, our brand new little Australian fellow citizen."

Far from that: George Burchett, son of Wilfred Burchett, was born as an exile. His father was considered an enemy of his own nation and for many years could not even get his hands on an Australian passport. Some called him the "Number one public enemy".

As quoted by 123HelpMe.com:

"The discontent that was felt towards Burchett by the

> conservative powers of the US and Australia was so extreme that in an unprecedented move, Burchett's Australian passport was revoked, leaving him and his children living in exile for seventeen years. The Commonwealth repeatedly refused to renew Burchett's passport that was lost in North Vietnam in 1955, on the grounds that 'he was a communist and in 1961 decided that Burchett would not be admitted to the country. This decision was recognised as in conflict with the Universal Declaration of Human Rights, and was almost certainly unconstitutional'..."

An official doctrine aside, the reason for this charade was very simple: Wilfred Burchett was probably the greatest journalist writing in the English language in the entire 20th Century. He was a giant of letters, a truly independent thinker and reporter, unwilling to follow the rigid rules of the anti-Communist Western propaganda.

Burchett was the first one to cover the Hiroshima nuclear holocaust. In his powerful report, "I write this as a warning to the world," as all his colleagues stood in line for the official communiqués on Japan's surrender, he traveled alone by local trains, almost 1,000 kilometers through the devastated country, to the ruins of Hiroshima. He felt he had to do it – in order to witness and to report the impact of what was later described as one of the most awful experiments on human beings in World history.

But there was much more to Burchett's 'crimes' than Hiroshima.

A true internationalist, and a man with a deep understanding of, and love for Asia Pacific, he wrote on the Korean War and on the brutal killing of civilians, by the US and its satellites. He also uncovered several taboo stories: for instance how the released US prisoners of war, who insisted that they were treated humanely by their Chinese and North Koreans captives, had been "disappeared" by their own army, and locked in mental institutions.

A close friend of China's Premier Chou En-lai, of Ho Chi Minh and Fidel Castro, Burchett wrote entire books on China, on Cambodia, on Vietnam and on the Soviet Union.

He produced dozens of powerful books of an alternative narrative, all of them written as eyewitness accounts. His range of topics was impressive: from the first man in space – Yuri Gagarin – to Ho Chi Minh and his struggle for independence, in books that included "North of the Seventeenth Parallel".

He put into his reports and books his own experiences; what he saw with his own eyes, heard with his ears, felt with his entire being; on the battlefields and in all those places that were devastated by Western imperialism. He wrote and he photographed: he documented what was not supposed to reach the eyes of the people inhabiting the US, Australia and Western Europe.

That could not be allowed to go on forever.

Not only was Wilfred Burchett stripped of his passport, he was demonized in the complacent Australian media; called a Communist (a terrible crime!), he was also described as an agent of the Soviet Union, and finally, as someone who was involved in interrogating Western prisoners of war in Korea, taking down their testimonies about the West and its engagment in chemical warfare.

Jamie Miller wrote for the prestigious academic journal, "Asia Pacific Journal":

> Japan Focus" ('The Forgotten History War: Wilfred Burchett, Australia and the Cold War in the Asia Pacific'):
>
> "Wilfred Burchett was one of the twentieth-century's most important journalists. Amid official denials and conventional reports to the contrary, his were the first accurate accounts of nuclear fallout in Hiroshima and American use of chemical warfare in Vietnam, among many other scoops... Consequently, he was reviled in Australia's anti-communist circles... Ideological antipathy towards Burchett took root easily in a specific factual basis; the classic anti-communist fear of subversion from within found an intriguing counterpoint in Burchett's subversion from without. From the Korean War until his death in 1983, he was, as the title of David Bradbury's film aptly put it, the nation's Public Enemy Number One. Every aspect of his life was painstakingly recorded by ASIO. And from 1955, a succession of Coalition Governments refused to issue Burchett with an Australian passport for seventeen years – it would take the accession of the Whitlam Labor Government in 1972 to reverse the policy – and even refused to register his children as Australian citizens for fifteen years."

It often appeared that the entire Western propaganda machine went into overdrive on one single character assassination project.

Burchett's case clearly demonstrated how 'dangerous' the truth is, how vindictive the Western regime is, and how powerful one single person can be, if armed with talent, courage and integrity.

***

George and I met several years ago. He and Ilza, his Bulgarian wife who is also a well-accomplished artist, were then still living in Sydney, while I was based, among other places, in Samoa, writing on the devastating impact of Western imperialism on Polynesia, Melanesia and Micronesia. My political novel about war correspondents – Point of No Return – was already out.

I think it was the great Australian historian Gavan McCormack (professor at ANU), who suggested that George reads my novel: "He writes like your father". Which made me swell with pride.

We began corresponding; then we met and became good friends. It turned into a habit of ours, to take long strolls together, and to discuss politics and history, whenever I flew through Sydney.

Then we embarked on an enormous journey together – all over Indonesia – from Jakarta to the terribly poor and isolated island of Sumba, in the eastern part of the archipelago. We traveled and talked about the past, about our families, but also about the enormous US and European propaganda machine, and the distortion of world history. But even then, above all, we were discussing revolutionary art.

All around us was the wasteland called Indonesia, a country that fell the victim of savage capitalism and neo-colonialism. It had no zeal and no revolutionary spirit left in its veins and decaying flesh, and all the way as we drove it was frightening us with its open wounds and smell of decay.

I wanted to know all about Wilfred Burchett. To me his work was like a multi-faceted inspiration: it had both the firmness of a rock, and the pioneering spirit and mobility of a rocket, taking off towards the stars.

Now I needed to understand the man – what was behind all that great work? To put it metaphorically: I comprehended, I loved the song; but I also desired to understand the singer.

I read what the regime did to him when he was still alive; I read it as a powerful warning, a message: that those holding the reins of power of the Empire would not stop at anything. They were ready to go all the way to prevent people from writing the truth.

I was not scared. For years I have been trying to do what Wilfred did so long before me. And like him, I was determined not to stop.

But I wanted to know the consequences of my actions; I had to be prepared.

George was generous: he was always willing to supply me with stories; sharing the struggle and pain of his father, as well as his own.

Thanks to him, I often felt as if I was part of the family. I never met his father – we were generations apart. But thanks to the stories I heard from his son, I often felt that I did – that we met; and that Wilfred Burchett managed to pass something essential on to me.

***

"Wilfred loved Hanoi." George often referred to his father by his first name. "But wherever we were living, he never stayed in one place for long. He always traveled. He came and went. He wrote beautifully about the city, especially in his book 'Vietnam North'. The way he wrote; it was not always verbally lyrical... however the lyricism could be seen in his photos... But then, it was Hanoi of 1966."

Now we were in Hanoi of 2012, sitting in one of those subdued but unmistakably elegant and artsy cafes, called Cong Caphe. The walls were decorated with paintings – some sort of mild parody on Socialist Realism. The humor was kind, it was not full of the brutality that many Western galleries love to import from China; the comrade-girls with military hats, leather boots, exposed nipples and pubic hair, spreading their legs in front of the portraits of legendary leaders.

In Hanoi things were soft, the past respected. We were drinking a delicious yoghurt coffee, a local specialty.

"I saw several Western teenagers skateboarding at the bottom of the Lenin statue," I said. "That's 2012... Nobody tried to stop them. You can imagine what they would do to them in London if they were banging the legs of Generalissimo Churchill with their boards..."

"Of course, things have changed," replied George. "But the city is still beautiful and the essence is still there. Now I want to bring back the reality that my dad reported and to combine it with what exists now."

"I went back to Hanoi in 2011, to organize my dad's exhibition at Ho Chi Minh Museum. To have it, the exhibition, there; it is as prestigious as it gets in Vietnam. It turned out to be a very big event. At the end, I was received by the President and he told me that I am always welcomed in Vietnam."

I recalled the email George wrote to me right after the exhibition. The words of the President unleashed emotions and they led to the dramatic decision: "I am going back."

In a way, it was like saying, "I am coming home." And sure, in so many ways Vietnam and the city of Hanoi were that real home that George had carried in his heart for decades. When referring to Vietnamese men and women, he always calls them 'my people'.

"When I was born, Wilfred tried to register me as an Australian citizen, but they refused me. The Prime Minister personally decided that I'm not to be an Aussie," George told me on several occasions. "I only became an Australian citizen in 1969, when my dad got his passport back."

Before that, Wilfred Burchett had to travel on a Vietnamese laissez-passer and later on a Cuban passport that was given to him by Fidel Castro.

George tried to live in Australia, with his family, for more than a decade. "I tried to love it," he told me. "I tried to be a real Aussie."

He went from one extreme of that vast country to another, living and working in the Aboriginal communities of the Northern Territories and later in the most cosmopolitan city of the nation – Sydney. "I made an effort, but I never felt at home there. It all felt pretentious and empty."

And so he spoke to the President of Vietnam, and then he went home, in 2011.

***

"This is my Hanoi," he smiled. Now we were sitting at a table in a small restaurant, in the historic center of the city. There were bird cages, small flower pots, ancient trees and yellow facades of old houses, everything arranged elegantly, as if it was a set on one of Tran Anh Hung's films.

Except that this was for real, it was real life, not a film.

And I felt happy that my friend George Burchett had finally returned home. At least one of us knew where he belongs.

***

One day during my visit, we went to the notorious Hoa Lo Prison, a place where French colonizers tortured and executed hundreds of Vietnamese patriots. During the American War, this place was nicknamed Hanoi Hilton by several US pilots who were held here as prisoners of war, after being shot down.

This area was my home for three years; the building where I lived was literally growing out from the prison premises, and from my windows I could clearly see an old French guillotine.

This time I had to film for my movie/dialogue with Noam Chomsky. I filmed the prison, now a museum, and then George filmed me, for yet another film I was working on.

Then we went to a local beer pub, ate mountains of roast pork and did some serious drinking. Life was good.

At one point, he exclaimed: “So many people don’t understand what this country went through! They had to fight the French to gain their independence. Then they were attacked, ravaged by the Americans. The West and China supported the Khmer Rouge, which was continuously attacking Vietnam. Then Vietnam liberated Cambodia, stopped the genocide and deposed the Khmer Rouge. The US protested. China invaded in a punitive excursion. Years later the Soviet Union collapsed.”

He snapped at the Western Left: “After 1975, Vietnam suddenly became the ‘bad guy’. It was not a hero anymore, after it liberated Cambodia. Some people even claimed that it occupied Phnom Penh. A chunk of the Left began singing that old tune about human rights... until Vietnam had to open itself to Western money and to multi-nationals. And then Hanoi was once again wrong for doing so... What alternatives did it have? Only Cuba stood by it.”

By then we had a few beers in our stomachs. “The Western Left, or at least a substantial part of it, hates all Left-wing countries and movements that have ever managed to come to power,” I clarified. “It hates China and Vietnam, it hates Cuba and Venezuela. It wants to stay pure: doesn’t want to govern, and it probably doesn’t even want any Left wing country to exist... When one governs, one makes errors, but how else to move forward? A big chunk of the Left in Western countries only wants to cry about how it is being marginalized, it hates taking risks..."

On that we patently agreed.

The night was young. At one point, my old friend Dzung joined us in one of the cafes facing the lake.

"Your motorbike is beautiful," I offered, a good old Hanoi compliment.

"It is actually much cheaper than the one that is parked next to it," she smiled, politely. She used to study in Moscow, during the 'good old days'.

We went on talking about Doi Moi and about the growing army of the *nouveau riche*.

Suddenly I did not want to leave either.

***

Jamie Miller continued in her report:

> "One of the pillars of Warner's depiction of Burchett was his seeming monopoly on the facts. When a large amount of government material on Burchett was declassified in the mid-1980s and released into the hands of maverick academic Gavan McCormack, that pillar collapsed forever. In his ground-breaking 'An Australian Dreyfus?' and subsequent forays over the next two years, McCormack systematically deconstructed the evidence underpinning Warner's articles, the testimony given in court against Burchett, ASIO's files, and the staple rumours on which the Australian press relied. The reverberations were so profound because the facts supporting each of these, due to Warner's involvement at every turn, were much the same.
>
> Some of the blows McCormack landed were devastating. His analysis of the declassified ASIO affidavits of Australian POWs, which Warner had been privileged to for years, revealed that the allegations that Burchett had interrogated Australian soldiers in Korea were unfounded. The affidavits in fact showed that Burchett had deliberately sought out Australian POWs, discussed the war with them (even if they rarely saw eye to eye), wrote home to their families on their behalf, and even drank whisky with them. As for British POWs, McCormack embarrassed Warner by revealing that the 1953 British Ministry of Defense

> report which Warner had cited as confirming that Burchett was involved in brainwashing, was actually published in 1955 and contained no such allegation, let alone the supporting quote that Burchett was 'actively involved in brainwashing procedures'."

***

Before I boarded my taxi to the airport, George told me the most essential:

> "When I went to Australia, I heard them calling my father 'a traitor', 'a Communist', 'a torturer of POW's', all that nonsense. I had enough, and that is when I turned to painting seriously... I have done it for my father and for humanity. For all those people who still believe in a dream... That great dream called internationalism."

He paused.

> "Vietnam represents the history that my family shares... And it is a truly heroic country."

"Your dad..." I said. "What really was the chemistry between him and Vietnam?"

> "My dad was formed by that great moment when Ho liberated the country. It was all enormous then: the Soviet Union, China..."

He waved as I was leaving.

I looked at his slender figure disappearing into the thick fog coming from West Lake.

There was one only thought on my mind: Australia fucked up endlessly: It produced and then pushed away the greatest journalist of the 20th century, a man so big that even a criminal like Henry Kissinger could not do without him when negotiating the peace agreement with North Vietnam; a man who single-handedly wrote an alternative narrative of the entire continent.

And then it lost his son, a great artist, one of the very few genuine internationalists that I have ever met.

Vietnam, quietly but with strength and affection, embraced them both.

7 December 2012

16

Robert Clive and the Forbidden

POLICE STATE INDIA

In the middle of December 2012, New Delhi was once again choking on a thick stratum of smog. Everyone around me was coughing, while I was supposed to be filming, for one of my documentaries. But in such conditions, filming became almost impossible, unless one was yearning for some peculiar special effects.

While I was modifying my script, the President of India, Shri Pranab Mukherjee, was attending a meeting of a group of local industrialists, somewhere on the ground floor of the hotel where I was staying. Security that was always tight suddenly became impenetrable.

Between the smog and the overzealous security personnel, I felt that I had almost no breathing space left; I was choking.

Since my first visit to India more than a decade ago, I noticed that the country has been radiating some sort of militarized Djibouti-style vibes. Occasionally it felt as if some sadistic security freaks had been running the place, after vigorous training on Mars or at West Point, or somewhere else – one would not dare to ask where.

I was intending to film the Indian Parliament, as well as several other government buildings, from the 20th floor of my hotel. I needed 'perspective' from which to observe the local hubs of power.

I took the elevator to the top floor and entered the bar; and, from there, a Chinese restaurant. It was long before opening hours and the staff were aimlessly hanging around and chatting.

I approached the window. It was dirty, but behind it, I spotted a narrow tiled terrace. I tried the door, but it was hopelessly locked. I pushed, but it did not give.

"Could you let me out?" I asked the flock of waiters.

They exchanged sarcastic glances. I probably said something thoroughly idiotic.

"You can't go out, sir," I was told. Then I waited for more. In India, there was always 'more' coming, after the initial rejection. This was no exception. "For your own security, for the security of other guests, and for..."

"And for?" I insisted.

A young lady uttered something related to the country.

"On Independence Day and during all other important holidays, we have snipers on these terraces, and also on the roof," explained her colleague. There was a clear flair of pathos in his words. His chest swelled with pride. As he uttered the word 'snipers', his voice shook with emotion; I had no clue why. It was obvious that snipers moved him, as others would be, by the verses of Neruda or Tagore.

"Look," I tried to reason. "The window is filthy, there is smog outside, and I need to film... Just open the stuff for a few minutes would you?" I tried to make light of it; I added: "I will not jump. I promise."

"It is forbidden, sir," explained the waiter, stone-faced. "Please forgive me for hurting your feelings."

I have never mastered those archaic expressions India was saturated with. Questions like, "Where do you belong?" translates as, "What is your nationality, or where do you come from?" a very rude opening question to start with, but the most common here. And now this: "hurting my feelings." He was not hurting my feelings; he was simply getting on my nerves.

"Forbidden by whom?" I wanted to know.

"Forbidden by the Government of India!" And again, came that swelling of the chest and breaking of the voice.

Of course one could not argue against the orders of such a supreme authority.

The government of India was an extremely busy entity. It diligently forbids people like me to film anything in this country: military and naval bases, Government buildings, public and private offices, the bridges, posh restaurants, and the trains.

The Museums were out of reach, too. And many of the statues! Before travelling to Mumbai and New Delhi, I stopped off in Kolkata, to film the Victoria Monument and the statues of all those British bandits and mass murderers, who used to rule and plunder this country.

"They maintain their monuments," Noam Chomsky, who came to give talks here some time earlier, told me. "Many Indian people actually still admire them."

I located the statue of the arch thug, Robert Clive, as well as of the kings, queens and viceroys of the British Empire.

"No filming and no photographs inside the monument!" The guard that looked like a member of some Reagan-days Central American death squad, shouted at me. The Victoria Monument was full of them. I offered to film his mug; but he showed me his gun. I backed up, strategically, and filmed Clive – sir, from behind the corner.

The statue of Robert Clive was wrapped: it was resting inside some huge see-through plastic condom.

Local women found it amusing; they were giggling and making cheeky jokes. But one could not film it. I did of course, employing some very basic guerrilla tactics of a seasoned war correspondent, although a museum appeared to be quite a bizarre place to put my experience from the trenches to practice.

* * *

In India, wherever I went, it was always 'no, no and no!' There were some slight variations, like: "Definitely not, Sir", "Please stop!" or "I will have to arrest you!" Sometimes "Sir" was uttered, sometimes not, and periodically my eyes would meet a neat, polished and round muzzle of a gun.

"Get a special permit" was the repeated advice that I was often offered.

Of course I knew what that meant. 'Getting a special permit' was synonymous with an erect finger pointing at the endless blue sky. And to endless hours burned in some shabby government office, while facing an incompetent and often semi-illiterate clerk, who would have not the slightest clue what I was asking for, while pretending that he was parked on top of the world. 'Getting a permit', meant losing hope in humanity. Doing it the 'official way' in India, one would need several lifetimes, in order to complete one single feature-length documentary film.

* * *

The Indian state appears to be thoroughly paranoid, scared of anyone trying to document the reality.

It has developed an allergy to writers, investigative journalists, filmmakers and photographers, especially those that happen to be 'independent', therefore 'unpredictable' and potentially capable of challenging the clichés fabricated in Washington, London and New Delhi, depicting the country as the 'largest democracy on Earth'.

To fight against such threatening elements, the Indian regime, which consists of the moneyed elites, feudal lords, religious fanatics and the military brass, have become pathologically obsessed with security, with surveillance, with relentless checking on things, and people. I have never witnessed such security zeal, even in the countries that are under direct threat from the West: such as Cuba or China. In both those countries, I film everywhere and freely, including opera houses, museums, trains, and even some military ships if they are in open waters.

In the slums, film as much as you want.

* * *

Security in India is everywhere: you go through metal detectors when entering the metro (subway) in New Delhi, before arriving at the lobbies of hotels, office buildings, upmarket malls, even some outdoor monuments like The Gate to India in Mumbai, or India Gate in New Delhi.

At the New Delhi Metro, a guard with a rifle stands at every entrance. Below the surface, there are mountains of sandbags with machine gunners behind them, then an armed guard after you purchase a token, and then another. There are many unarmed and sometimes plain-clothed security personnel on the platforms. That entire charade is spiced up with metal detectors.

I suspect that the security apparatus in India must be employing tens of millions of people.

Police barricades are all over the capital, as well as in Mumbai and Kolkata; entire roads are periodically blocked. The Army patrols the highways; armed forces (so many different types, that one can hardly keep track of who is who) operate on the streets, national roads, everywhere.

At the major train stations, not only are there the 'normal' hordes of police and security personnel; there are entire units of the army, holed up behind sandbags, heavily armed and obviously ready to shoot at the slightest pretext.

And the security at Indian airports, even when one is about to take a domestic flight, would put to shame most of the 'Homeland Security' dudes in the US, and could only find a match with the airport security in Israel.

When you fly from Kolkata to Mumbai, you have to show your printed 'E-ticket'. Arguing that the E-ticket is by definition electronic will get you nowhere. Forget about the word 'logic'. And remember – an image of your ticket on your iPhone would not do. If you don't have the printout; there is an office at the kerb that will supply you with one, for a fee.

Then your luggage goes through an X-ray; pre-screening so to speak. Then you show your passport and the ticket again. A few steps later, you do it once more, so you might as well keep your ticket and passport in your mouth if you have several pieces of luggage to carry.

Then you check in – passport required; and the chances are – it will be photocopied. Later you go through the real security, and that is heavy. Forget about just taking your computer out of your bag: you will be put on a wooden pedestal and thoroughly manually checked. Then your boarding pass and your carry-on luggage tag will be stamped. You will be ordered (not asked, but ordered) to produce your ID again, and once more at the gate and once again right at the entrance to the aircraft.

I have worked in 145 countries, on all continents, but I never experienced security-mania that would come close to that in India.

The police are watching you everywhere you turn.

* * *

But where is the Indian security apparatus when it is desperately needed?

When women are harassed, even gangraped on public transportation or right in the middle of the street, they are nowhere to be found.

I once witnessed 'the largest democracy' at work, right after the massacres in Ahmedabad, Gujarat in 2002.

People spoke to me of the religious-motivated slaughter, of the stomachs of pregnant woman being cut open, of brutal mass rapes. They were not protected. What were those tens of millions of parasitical armed forces doing during those massacres?

But during the Gandhi Nagar standoff, which came a short time later, when the attack was attributed to Muslims and some fingers began to point at Pakistan, hordes of the military personnel suddenly descended on Gujarat.

The grotesquely Fascist leaders of RSS and VHP, were all of a sudden opening their doors, inviting me to their long tea sessions, during which they explained and promoted their 'programs' of hate and bigotry: "You are white and Aryan, you should understand us..." I was part Asian and happy to be one, but I let them talk, asking questions and taking notes for posterity.

All that hate-speech! These Nazi organizations have been operating in the open, and are fully accepted by a great majority of Indian people. The Security apparatus knows about them, and does absolutely nothing to put an end to their existence.

It was when I was working in Gujarat, during the Swaminarayan Temple complex massacre, the then Prime Minister Atal Bihari Vajpayee and the maverick politician Sonia Gandhi, decided to visit, in order to boost their popularity. Enormous crowds of people came to welcome them, or maybe just to catch a glimpse of their famous faces. Before the motorcades reached the site, the police began 'softening up the crowd' –

basically beating up the citizens with sticks, and herding them behind barriers. Security at work!

I also observed that fabled 'Indian democracy' at work in Dalit (Untouchable) villages outside Kanchipuram in Tamil Nadu, listening to the stories about how the elections were conducted there; how entire towns are bought; literally purchased, or simply scared into submission by those who are holding the reins of power. No security apparatus ever intervened, upholding free and fair elections for the poor.

And there were no soldiers and no police, when the owners of Indian companies kicked the poor farmers off their land. Or actually, I am wrong: they were there, but to protect the interests of the rich bandits, against the poor and vulnerable.

Where are the police when you need them?

* * *

Torture, rapes, disappearances and political killings mark India, and so does the total spite for the great majority of its population. In India the security forces perform most of those beastly crimes.

The situation is so bad that even some mass media outlets are beginning to take notice.

The Guardian ran Seema Sengupta's story, "India's human rights record makes a farce of its democracy" on 22nd July 2011:

> "...The Asian Centre for Human Rights has documented a jump in cases of custodial deaths by 41.66% over the last decade, including 70.72% in prison and 12.60% in police custody. It is indeed a paradox that the largest democracy is defiled by frequent cases of illegal detention, torture, extra-judicial execution and forced disappearances. Moreover, nothing could be more disgraceful than the incarceration of thousands of people for political reasons in this multiparty democracy. Unfortunately, the state seems to be competing with the outlaws in trampling the basic rights of its citizens guaranteed by the Indian constitution. The common people, particularly minorities and the underprivileged, are enduring all forms of inhuman and degrading treatment at the hands of security personnel..."

Both Amnesty International and Human Rights Watch periodically report on the situation in Kashmir and elsewhere in India:

> "...Thousands of Kashmiris have reported to be killed by Indian security forces in custody, extra-judicial executions and enforced disappearances and these human right violations are said to be carried out by Indian security forces under total impunity. Civilians including women and children have been killed in "reprisal" attacks by Indian security forces and as a "collective punishment", villages and neighborhoods have been burnt down and women raped..."

After reading such reports and after having been acquainted with India for so many years, one does not feel necessarily safe when being stopped at some roadblock by the police or the military, especially at night.

Frankly, I feel much safer in the middle of the toughest slums of Mumbai, than in the company of the Indian armed forces, although I acknowledge that this could be a matter of personal preferences.

* * *

In sharp contrast to most of other Asian countries, in India there is nothing like 'free Internet'. You go to some café or to a hotel for lunch, and if you ask for the Internet password, you are told that there is no way to get on line.

It is, of course, for your own security, and for the security of the nation.

If you insist, some luxury hotels will ask for your passport, they will photocopy it, and then supply you with several pages of long forms that you will be encouraged to fill. The forms include requests for all your personal data, phone numbers, home address, passport number, perhaps even the names of your spouse and parents. To fill them takes approximately 20 minutes. I tried, at the ITC Hotel in Kolkata.

Try to purchase a local SIM for your mobile phone, and the process will be even more traumatic. As one person posted on Whirlpool:

> "Getting a simcard in India is a bit of a nightmare, with all sorts of identification and personal information requirements. They need a photo ID document with your current INDIAN address. So my Australian drivers license/passport etc. won't work and I have no photo ID doc with Indian address."

* * *

"Taj," I was told in a whisper. "Taj", I was winked at. "It is because of Taj!" I was yelled at. Almost everyone, with whom I met and discussed the security situation in India, was referring to the 2008 Mumbai terrorist attacks in which 166 people died.

The Mumbai assaults are supposed to offer a blanket explanation for all the extreme security measures. But I knew India before 2008, and it was not much different then, from what it is now. And after all, the last surviving participant in the Mumbai attacks –Kasab – had already been executed by hanging, on November 20th, 2012.

I gather it is pointless to argue, that, even those Asian countries that are in the midst of a civil war – like the Philippines and Thailand – are much less obsessed with security than India.

* * *

After arriving in Mumbai, I ate at one of those tasteless, and terribly over-decorated '6-star' hotels. I could not avoid it; I was invited.

There, 4 pieces of paneer (Indian cottage cheese), and one local beer went for 1,900 Rp, which is approximately US$35. And that was just a tiny and not so tasty appetizer. All around me, the local elites were on a power trip, stuffing themselves on kebabs and washing them down with grotesquely overpriced Champagne. A dinner for two could easily cost US $2,000.

The staff of the restaurant, as well as the guests, radiated unmatchable vulgarity and arrogance, most of them looked frightening – both the men and the women. I would not want to meet most of the diners at night on an empty country road.

Naturally, security was extremely tight. To get to the hotel was not easy; one had to be a foreigner or an ostensibly wealthy Indian.

The next day I filmed and photographed inside the Dharavi Slums.

There was no security at Dharavi and the people were extremely civil and relaxed. They did not bother me. When they realized that I came for a purpose, and not to spy on their misery, they returned to their routine, and allowed me to work. Kids went back to playing cricket, housewives got busy washing laundry, and men got back to building things or to smoking, or chatting.

Here, I was told, US$35 could feed entire family for two weeks, and probably for much longer.

* * *

The restaurant where I had dinner in Mumbai represents the reality of less than 1% of Indians, but that 1% is in full control; it is ruling the country, and plundering it mercilessly.

The great majority of Indian people lives in an absolutely different realm, it is still very poor and absolutely unprotected; it doesn't drink champagne and does not travel in chauffeured Bentleys and SUV's. And it is seen as a threat.

All that security apparatus is essential for maintaining the *status quo*; all those soldiers, police, and guards are there to protect the upper class, upper castes, and upper rank, from the masses down below. It guarantees that the lives of V-VIPs and demi-gods, flows comfortably, far from the maddening roar of the illiterate, sick and ragged majority.

The word 'democracy' comes from the Greek language and it means 'rule of the people', not 'a multi-party Western-style Parliamentary system'. 'Democracy is a form of government in which all citizens have an equal say in the decisions that affect their lives'. India appears to represent exactly the opposite.

* * *

Interestingly, the India of the rich is not ashamed of the misery of the majority of its citizens. Here, one can film the misery day and night, with no interference.

But the regime strongly objects to any visualization of the power.

Film the beggars but not the flowing champagne bought with money stolen from the poor. Film the slums but not the military bases and police posts that are there to oppress the majority. Film the people that are rotting on the streets but not the office buildings housing investment companies and major multi-nationals.

Film the people decomposing on the streets; film their gangrene and sores, but not the private hospitals equipped with the latest operating theatres charging some of the highest prices on earth. Film the illiterate slum dwellers, but not the arrogant faces of kids, attending the elite private schools.

And do not even think about filming statues, portraits of Robert Clive, and the rest of the gang from the 'good old days' – as some viewers could draw certain uncomfortable parallels, between the past and the present rulers of India.

21 December 2012

*****

17

OKINAWA: NOTES FROM THE “EVIL ISLAND”

It is all about the barbed wire, warnings and checkpoints. And to make it worse, the Futenma air force base is right in the middle of an extremely densely populated urban area.

Several middle-aged Japanese citizens are besieging the sedans and SUV’s driven by the US military personnel who are leaving their barracks for an outing. As cars wait at the intersection to join the traffic flow on the main road, elderly men and women, clench their fists, shouting slogans and waving their posters. There is a lone Japanese cop making sure that nothing goes wrong. But everything is orderly, routine.

“Close down the base!” Scream the demonstrators. “US army – out of Okinawa!”

American GI’s and military pilots avert their eyes. It is all somehow embarrassing. It is not like these American bombers and top guns are facing some stone-throwing body builders or aces from the local karate club. These ageing people, vocal adversaries of the Empire, can do no harm to the soldiers or to their vehicles; they could probably not even be able to kill a fly.

I approach one of the leaders of this small group of protesters.

The lady puts down her placard and listens to my questions, attentively. It is all so Japanese! I hand her my name card, with both hands; she, with both hands, accepts it. We bow to each other.

"Miyoko-san," I begin. "What is it exactly that irks you about this base?"

"It is so noisy and so dangerous," she replies. "There are all sorts of terribly treacherous airplanes flying from Futenma. We are never consulted. We are not informed."

I drive a bit further from Naha, to the tall Matsuki Building. It hosts several nightclubs on its premises; probably whorehouses, too, that come to life at night. However, during the day this entire structure is quiet and empty. And, by Japanese standards, it is very dingy. I take the elevator to the top floor, and climb onto the roof, stopping next to an enormous Canon security camera. All of a sudden, the Futenma base is in front of me.

This place feels insane: nobody really cares what I am doing. No guards, no deterrence. I just take out my video and stills cameras and begin working.

It is all so easy, so uneventful, that I almost feel 'disappointed'. There is no security drama, no charade.

I hear the engines, and look up towards the sky. A four-engine Hercules turns abruptly towards the runway, then literally drops from the sky, levels up at the last moment, then touches down, rolls for a few seconds down the runway, then takes off again: a 'touch and go' maneuver. I film it. Then I film another airplane, and then another.

I call my film editor in Tokyo.

"It all looks and feels weird," I tell him.

"Like some Third World country?" he volunteers.

"Yes," I confirm. "But that's not all. It is all totally spooky. With this new administration and the passionate love *boleros* it sings to US... All this can of course easily trigger WWIII. These bases are actually here, most likely, to trigger a conflict... to provoke China or North Korea, or both. Yet it is all so quiet and serene and in open."

"That's Okinawa," my editor confirms.

In his recent article, which appeared in the Australian magazine Arena, a leading Australian historian and Professor Emeritus at ANU, Gavan McCormack, calls Japan "The Servile State" and The US Marine Corps based in Okinawa "a force designed for attack deep within enemy territory." He mentions one of the best-selling books in Japan- The Truth of Postwar History–written by Magosaki Ukeru, a former head of the Intelligence and Analysis Bureau of the Japanese Ministry of Foreign Affairs:

> "...Magosaki and I also agree in seeing Okinawa, the island prefecture off the China coast where US occupation has been unbroken for sixty-seven years and where three-quarters of US military installations in Japan are concentrated, as crucial. Nowhere else can such a concentrated expression of the US-Japan relationship, be found. There, the fact that the Japanese national government is determinedly servile, and that all Okinawa policy is predicated on priority to US military interests, is the inescapable reality of everyday life. Required to serve as the arch upon which the Asia-Pacific security system as a whole can rest, Okinawa became something of an Achilles heel, because it is denied the very values the alliance is supposed to uphold. Its people feel threatened, not protected, by it, and discrimination against them in the name of 'East Asian security' has reached the point of being no longer tolerable."

* * *

While filming the Futenma Base from the roof of the Matsuki Building is somehow tolerated, to film the Kadena Base, a monster that brought so much grief to the rest of Northeast Asia during the Korean War, is something that is considered as thoroughly ordinary, even encouraged. The area is equipped with an open viewing terrace, which faces the runway, and comes complete with powerful coin-consuming binoculars, a coffee shop and spotless public bathrooms.

After working in India where one could not even film military ships openly docked at the Mumbai shore, Okinawa feels like the other extreme: the US military might here has been converted into a violent tourist attraction. It draws entire groups of schoolchildren, as well as camera people and photographers, both amateur and those working for the various Japanese media outlets.

Ms. Kato sells coffee and refreshments on the terrace. I point at the impenetrable bunkers protecting US fighter jets of the latest generation, from who knows whom, and ask her about what she thinks about all that, a horror show turned into entertainment. She replies with a pragmatic grin: "Business is great! But then, of course, as an Okinawan, I despise the base."

One has to wonder which the leading part of the sentence is.

As she speaks, a deafening thunderous sound erupts from somewhere inside the base. In anticipation of a tremendous flying monster ready to take to the air, I intuitively grab my cameras, ready to run towards the railings. But, Ms. Kato overpowers the roar, by her well-trained voice, as she shouts at me: "Relax, nothing is moving! They are just testing an engine."

Do they do this every day? They do, as everyone in Okinawa tells me. Airplane engines are tested almost every day, sometimes until ten at night, until the eardrums of the people are ready to burst.

Driving through Okinawa, one has to be ready for truly Kafkaesque images. There are endless perimeters consisting of barbed wire and concrete pillars. Division lines are everywhere. Little wonder, as the US bases cover some 18% of the territory of the main island.

There are literally hundreds of protected gates separating the civilian world from the universe of militarized zones. There are playgrounds for American children only, right behind the grid-irons; there are small arcades with Baskin Robins and Subway's, as if those fast-food joints cannot be found on the Japanese mainland territory.

There are Japanese public buses converted into vehicles designated for bussing American children to, and back from their schools. And there are Japanese fire stations, as well as US fire stations built on Japanese territory, with North American trucks and emergency phone numbers.

And there are 'American Villages' – depressing theme parks with the lowest grade of architecture and yet more Red Lobster's, KFC's, seedy bars, and some of the tackiest souvenir shops on earth. These are actually not for GI's, but for the Japanese tourists trying to catch a glimpse of the enormous flesh-and-blood American soldiers.

Influenced by the occupation forces, Okinawa has the worst food in Japan – a country famed for the finest gastronomy in the world.

Apart of one monorail line, Okinawa has no mass public transportation, yet another anomaly in a country that relies on the most intensive and efficient train network on Earth. In and outside Naha, everything moves by road, and overwhelmingly by private vehicles. As a result, the roads in the cities are often congested, and the entire Main Island has the feel of an ethnic Asian suburb somewhere in the United States.

Countless advertisements for real estate agencies seduce those who are ready to do business with the devil: "If you want to buy or sell land for military purposes, please let us know."

Sadly, all this bad taste and militarism can be found in the middle of what once was the great Ryukyu Kingdom, known for its glorious history of five hundred years, spanning between the 12th and 17th centuries. UNESCO designated several ruins of its castles and sites as world heritage sites. Okinawa was famous all over Asia for its advanced social structure, for its economic structure and its culture.

David McNeill, a professor at Sophia University in Tokyo and the coordinator of the academic Asia-Pacific Journal, explained for this report:

> "Like many places that have become dependent on external largesse, Okinawa can seem schizophrenic. Polls consistently show that most people on the island oppose the presence of US bases, but thousands of people, including civilian base-workers, bar and shop-owners, depend on the bases for part or most of their income. US popular culture has filtered down over the last 60+ years giving the island a look, feel and even a diet closer to contemporary America, than the Japanese mainland."

The fate of Okinawa and Okinawans seems to be tightly linked to US-Japan relations, I asked Ms. Satoko Norimatsu, a Japan Focus Coordinator and Director of the Peace Philosophy Centre, what changes could be expected in Japan's foreign policy, particularly in its relations with the United States, as it is expected that Japan will now move even 'closer to US'?

> "There won't be much change, as the previous DPJ (Democratic Party of Japan) Governments under Kan and Noda had already made concessions in the original DPJ agenda and the Party and the Government looked no different from the administrations led by LDP (Liberal Democratic Party). Those who attempted to initiate the change, namely Hatoyama and Ozawa, lost power and withdrew".

Then Ms. Satoko Norimatsu summarized:

> "The new LDP government will be as much US-leaning and US-subservient as the last-stage DPJ government was, if not more. One significant change will be their serious attempt to change Japan's post-war pacifist Constitution either nominally, or virtually, so that Japan can exercise its "right to collective self-defense," i.e. to engage in aggressive wars in conjunction with the US. That was Abe's unfinished business and long-sought after goal, from his previous term in 2006/2007."

* * *

In its modern history, Okinawans have been made to suffer immensely.

In 1945 a quarter of the civilian population died during the Battle of Okinawa. 200,000 tons of bombs, according to NHK, were dropped on the island by the US army, in total disregard for lives of the local people.

Then this stunning archipelago consisting of hundreds of Ryukyu Islands fell under US occupation. During the 27-year colonial reign, called 'the trustee-ship rule', the United States Air Force established numerous military bases all over the archipelago. From here, mainly using the Kadena Base, during the Korean War, B-29 Super Fortresses flew bombing missions, ravaging both Korea and China.

Thousands of Okinawan women were brutally raped, by the US army, after the Battle of Okinawa, and sexual violence continues to this day.

In 1972, the islands were returned to Japan under the Treaty of Mutual Cooperation and Security, but the United States Forces Japan (USFJ) has maintained a large military presence.

According to John Chan, since 1960, Japan has been honoring an agreement that "allows the U.S. to secretly bring nuclear weapons into Japanese ports, and there is speculation that some nuclear weapons may be located in Okinawa. Both tactical and strategic weapons have been maintained in Okinawa."

The Sakima Art Museum sits right on the perimeter of the Futenma Base. It even offers a view of it, from the roof.

The Museum houses some of the most politically-charged paintings found on the archipelago, most notably some 50 works by husband and wife, Iri and Toshi Maruki, who are now both in their 90's. On a wall, hangs their famous "The Battle of Okinawa".

Here, through art, the tragedy of the past is revealed, in all its brutality and force. Bodies are shown floating on the ocean surface, there are terrified faces of women, and mass suicide.

Kiyoko Sakima, Director of the Sakima Art Museum may often sound bitter, but she is also very active, full of determination to resist and struggle against injustice:

> "We fought a legal battle to get this place back from the base and we won, but only 3 years ago. 800 farms and homes were taken away from the local people; taken by force, when the bases were being constructed. There was no compensation – similar to what goes on in Palestine these days. Some people were forced to leave for Brazil, because they lost all that they had."

Ms. Sakima continues: "They see us as the 'Evil Island'; all over Asia, because everything that is dangerous and flies, takes off from here. Only 1% of the population of Japan lives in Okinawa, but we have 75% of the US military bases on our territory."

I recall the words of a veteran professor from Beijing, who educated hundreds of members of the Chinese diplomatic corps. He explained to me several years ago: "If China was attacked by the United States from its bases on Japanese territory, China would not hit back at the US, it will retaliate against Japan, as the attack would be coming from its soil."

That would not be a very attractive prospect for Okinawa.

* * *

Ms Satoko Norimatsu and other leading experts on Japan believe that the new Japanese administration will now try to 'maximize the perception of fear of China, while also maximizing the profits of the military-industrial complex'. The military 'cooperation' between the US and Japan will accelerate, including the so-called 'co-basing'.

Bad news for Okinawa once again! In pre-election speeches, local politicians made promises to scale down some military activities here, and move the bases, or at least part of their operations, to Guam, an 'unincorporated territory of the United States', located in the western Pacific Ocean, which is basically a colony.

But Ms. Sakima does not think that would be fair either: "These bases should be shut down, not moved elsewhere. Poor Guam: Japan used to occupy it, now the US does. Why should they inherit what we want to get rid of?"

One of the plans both the US and Japan are pushing for, is the eventual closure of the Futenma Base and the opening of a new enormous one – Henoko.

Gavan McCormack argues in his "Servile State Japan"; "The designated area is one classified by Okinawa as requiring the highest level of protection because of its unique and precious marine and forest environment, and the idea that a large military base could be imposed on it was inherently as impossible as if someone had suggested the same for the United States' Grand Canyon or Australia's Kakadu."

* * *

"Okinawans are united, from left to right, in opposing the construction of a new base in Henoko, and the four newly-elected LDP Lower House members of Okinawa, clarified that point too, after the recent elections," said Ms Norimatsu. "The Okinawan political climate remains the same: resisting the construction of the Henoko base, the closure of the Futenma air base, as well as resisting the deployment of the Osprey aircraft."

But it has been made clear to the people of Okinawa that even if they win; if any of the bases closed down, the Japanese Government and the US will pay absolutely nothing in compensation; the locals will have to rely on their own resources.

It is paradoxical, but the new Japanese 'Nationalist' Government is actually pro-American, as much as it is anti-Chinese. Is it a contradiction in terms? Most definitely, but in Japan anything goes – nobody seems to care much about foreign policy.

This may prove to be a tremendous blunder. Japan is betting on the most dangerous, aggressive and destabilizing force in the world. It is hosting the army and the air force of the country that is seen, all over the world, as the main threat; the army from which it suffered itself, in the past, immensely.

As my plane readies to depart for Nagoya, I observe Japanese military jets ready for takeoff, jets landing; jets all over the sky. The US air force uses the Funtenma and Kadena; Japan's air force shares the Naha International Airport with ANA, JAL and other civilian carriers.

Of course, 'Japan does not have its own army or air force'. To have them would still be unconstitutional. Those latest and fully armed jets are nothing, just an illusion. And the US does not have any aggressive imperialist plans in this part of the world.

Let's all keep pretending. Until it is too late!

26 December 2012

*****

18

THE IRRATIONAL, RACIST FEAR OF CHINA

Iraq, Afghanistan, Palestine, and Libya are in shambles, crushed by the heavy boots of Western imperialism.

But we are told to fear China.

The entire nations of Indochina were bombed back to the stone age, because the Western demi-gods would not tolerate, and felt they did not have to tolerate, what some yellow un-people in Asia were really longing for. Vietnam, Cambodia, Laos – millions of tons of bombs were dropped on them from strategic B-52's, from dive-bombers, and from jet fighters. The falling bombs rained on the pristine countryside, murdering children, women, and water buffalo – millions of people perished. No apologies, no admission of guilt, and no compensation came from the tyrant-nations.

Indonesia, then leader of the non-aligned world, with a huge constitutional Communist Party, was destroyed in the coup of 1965, through an alliance of Western governments, the Indonesian fascist military and the elites, as well as religious bigots from the largest Muslim organization – NU. 2-3 million people died, including those belonging to the Chinese minority. Teachers, artists, thinkers – all killed or silenced. Here, imperialism created a submissive nation with almost no intellectual base; unable even to analyze its own downfall.

But now we are ordered to be conscious of China's rise.

Latin America: raped again and again, from Mexico to the Dominican Republic, from Cuba to Granada, Panama, Haiti, Brazil, Argentina, Colombia and Chile, for years, decades and centuries. Almost all the countries in Central and South America, as well as the Caribbean, were ravaged at some point in history, by the racist and outrageous implementation of the 'Monroe Doctrine'.

The latest coups against the progressive governments of Honduras and Paraguay were enacted under the 'soft leadership' of the liberal West's supreme leader and 'upholder of global democracy' – President Barack Obama.

But it is China that has to be deterred, we are told! Not us – not the West – but China.

In the Middle East, entire kingdoms and emirates are bending over themselves, competing with each other over who will become the most subservient collaborator with Western business interests, who will place more US military bases on its soil, who will kill, arrest or torture more people – the opponents of global Western dictatorship.

But it is China, naturally, which is unacceptably endangering the European and North American's inherited right, to reign over the world. Or to be precise, the 'danger' is shared among China, Russia and Latin America – three places that managed to wrestle themselves from Western shackles, and to embark on their own political, social, cultural and developmental paths. Whatever they are, but their own!

But China is the 'worst', because those Russkies and Latinos still look kind of white, or at least most of them do. But to imagine that the world's most important country would be firmly placed in Asia is unthinkable, unacceptable, and truly sacrilegious.

In Africa, which of course does not matter much, as it is, in the eyes of multi-nationals and the Western governments, inhabited by the lowest breed of 'un-people' (to borrow Orwell's lexicon), entire enormous geographical areas and cultures had been plundered, divided, debilitated, virtually canceled. Ridiculous borders were erected, great peoples' rulers like Patrice Lumumba of Congo, assassinated. Murderous maniacs such as Paul Kagame and Museveni were groomed in and by the West, armed and brought to power, then sent on various missions; to plunder and police on behalf of Western interests.

Congo lost some 10 million people during the reign of Belgian genocidal king, Leopold II (now the national hero of Belgium, celebrated by countless statues all over Brussels). It is losing a similar amount of people now, as Washington and London's military darlings from Rwanda and Uganda are invading freely, overthrowing governments and pillaging that vast and battered nation on their doorsteps.

Somalia is virtually no more – forcefully divided, and regularly invaded by Western allies – Kenya and Ethiopia. Europeans are dumping toxic waste near its coast and then appear to be outraged by the piracy – one more justification for the continuous militarization of the entire region. The proud 'African Cuba' – Eritrea – is being tortured by sanctions; while the country/military base called Djibouti has been glorified and pampered, standing as a polluted, frustrated and grotesque symbol of French and US militarism; of Western imperialism, in the region that gave birth to the human race.

In West Africa, in Algiers, in Angola and Namibia, in Congo and Somalia, and in dozens of other countries of Africa, tens of millions of people have been slaughtered by Western imperialists in the 20th and 21st Centuries. And the dreadful count was not any better in the preceding eras, with a direct holocaust against native populations, with genocides like the one perpetrated by the Germans in what is now Namibia, with slavery, torture, rape and the absolute disrespect for non-white human lives.

But would such a legacy make Western nations humble, reflective, and apologetic? Would there at least be some pathos of profound guilt that could give birth to hope for global reconciliation? No – far from that! There is no remorse in London, Paris, Berlin, Brussels and Washington, or in the French countryside, the US Midwest or South. Or if there is some, it is concentrated in small, mainly urban pockets, disconnected from the mainstream.

But it is China, which is now blamed for 'doing business with African dictators'! And it is China whose guilt is being manufactured, inflated and implanted in the brains of people all over the world, by the Western propaganda apparatus, and by local media outlets, owned and 'trained' by and in the West.

Take for instance a mining accident in Zambia, whenever a Chinese company is involved, the situation gets overblown to tremendous proportions. The result is that dozens of people who died due to negligence are put on the same scale as dozens of millions who have perished because of savage Western imperialism, the slave trade, colonialism and neo-colonialism.

The same propaganda tactics are used all over the world. For instance, the Goethe Institute in Jakarta, Indonesia, not long ago, arranged a photo exhibition of Polish workers in Gdansk clashing with police, during the Solidarity days. Few people died then. But the Goethe Institute arranges no exhibitions commemorating the millions of Communists, atheists, intellectuals and Chinese people who died in 1965 and later, in Indonesia! It is almost like saying: "You see, those 3 million Indonesian lives had to be sacrificed, to prevent the scenario in which 30 people were later killed in Poland." Interesting logic, but supported by mountains of cash, and it works!

In Oceania – in Polynesia, Melanesia and Micronesia – the British, US, French, Spanish, German and other colonial masters, smashed and then reshaped the complex universe that used to belong to the proud people inhabiting tens of thousands of islands, islets and atolls of the South Pacific.

The local inhabitants were then pushed into slavery, effectively; their kingdoms, their geo-political entities were first divided into colonies, and then into nation-states. Their leaders were killed, sidelined, threatened, finally corrupted and bought.

Western nations fought battles over the islands, performed nuclear experiments on the local people, and then invented a so called 'strategic deterrence doctrine', making sure that no 'enemy' ships, no unsuitable ideas and anti-imperialist ideology could enter this tremendous universe, encompassed by an endless mass of water.

In the end, huge military bases were constructed, US, British and French; all sorts of toxic waste was dumped, and pristine atolls like Kwajalein, were converted into missile testing grounds.

Waste, radiation, junk food; all led to countless medical emergencies, which became so great that only climate change and the consequent rising level of the seawater, could realistically be considered as a greater threat to the survival of the people and states of Oceania.

I lived in the South Pacific for more than four years, and I traveled and worked in all the countries there, except in Niue and Nauru. I wrote about the struggle of the islanders inhabiting the South Pacific in my non-fiction book Oceania.

Several countries – Kiribati, the Marshall Islands, the Federated States of Micronesia, as well as the various islands and atolls now belonging to other states – are rapidly becoming uninhabitable. The seawater is rolling over their low-lying land, and the vegetation is dying.

The West, which is responsible for most of the pollution, the carbon dioxide emission and global warming, has been doing close to nothing to save these countries from vanishing.

The foreign aid the US, EU, Australia and New Zealand provide, is often as damaging as the poisonous gasses themselves. It is habitually being used to corrupt local government officials; to fly them around the world, embedding the so called '*per-diem* mentality'. Tamed and corrupt, the local rulers don't demand real compensation and real solutions for their suffering countries. 'Foreign aid' is also being used to pay for foreign experts to visit, to 'analyze' and to write countless and mostly futile reports. All that, just in order to create a perception that something is being done: and just to make sure that nothing ever will!

The people of Oceania do not want to be evacuated; most of them want to fight for the survival of their islands. I talked to them: in Kiribati, Tuvalu, FSM, RMI and elsewhere. But the West and local governments are insisting on idiotic evacuation schemes, for many unsavory reasons.

At one point, China began helping, in the spirit of internationalism; the way a socialist country would. It rolled up its sleeves and started to construct schools, hospitals, government buildings, roads, and stadiums, as well as protective walls and other heavy infrastructure, designed to defend the endangered populated areas.

The West immediately attacked all those efforts, injecting nihilism, dragging through the dirt, everything pure and decent. The first stage of Western propaganda, the same that has been used in Africa and elsewhere, consisted of a barrage of negative messages that China does 'nothing altruistically, ever'; it simply follows its dark self-interests and designs.

The 'philosophical' and propaganda punchlines are predictable and simple: "If we are shits, if our culture sends us to plunder and enslave the world, then humanity should be convinced that others have the same essence as we do. This way, what we are doing would not be seen as extraordinary. We are all human, all the same!"

It is rubbish, of course, and even people like Gustav Jung saw Western culture as exceptionally aggressive, as some sort of pathology. But, as was proven many times by Western propagandists like Joseph Goebbels and Rupert Murdoch, if propaganda is repeated 1,000 times, and if we corrupt/pay enough people all over the world to repeat what we tell them to, the rubbish converts itself into shining diamond nuggets of truth, and eventually to unchallengeable common wisdom.

But back to China and Oceania:

When the blitzkrieg of discrediting China failed to work, or at least it failed in the countries benefiting from China's assistance, the West invented a unique strategy: it went to Taipei and began 'encouraging' Taiwan' to get 'involved'. The Taiwanese were willing and ready, and began offering bribes to the leaders of Oceania, in exchange for recognition of Taiwan as an independent country. Whenever Taiwan is 'recognized', something that even US or EU refuse to do, on most occasions China (PRC) retaliates by breaking diplomatic relations.

And that was, most definitely, the plan of the sly old colonial powers.

While countries that stuck with China, like Samoa, got their protective seawalls, stadiums and parliament buildings constructed in solidarity and with socialist optimism, countries like Kiribati, a place that could be easily described as one of the true basket-cases in Oceania, were flooded with Taiwan-inflicted nihilism. Cash flowed in, but not to the people; into the deep pockets of the government.

While entire small countries in Oceania are near extinction, their leaders, mostly groomed and trained in Australia and the US, are busy selling their UN votes: voting in support of Israel's occupation of Palestine, in support of US invasions all over the world, or against the environmental resolutions that could have a direct and positive effect on the plight of their countries!

"One day I was besieged by an Israeli television crew," I was told by a priest in the capital of Federated States of Micronesia (FSM). "The Israeli public wanted to know: who are these creatures that are constantly voting in support of Israel, alongside the US and against the entire world?"

Well, the same (corrupt) ones who are welcoming those Taiwanese battleships, and their crews, allowing them to play their "national anthems" on the beaches, and to march all over the place like maniacs, holding flags! Just in order to satisfy the West, just in order to antagonize China, ignoring the fact that all this is harming immensely entire Oceania!

***

And, by the way, those who think that China cannot act altruistically, should read Fidel Castro, and his powerful, grateful words describing how Cuba got rescued by the Chinese nation, following Gorbachev's fit of madness and Yeltsin's Western-encouraged glorified alcoholic orgy, with its destruction of the USSR and several dreadful years of the unopposed plunder of the world by the Western Empire, as its aftermath.

***

When the Chinese media interviews me, I am often asked the same question: "What can China do to appease the West?"

And my reply is always the same: "Nothing!"

Western propaganda is not looking for objective ways to analyze China; it is not looking for China's good will. It is there, to twist and to harm any country that insists on its own development model, on serving its own people instead of submissively succumbing to the interests of the West, and those of multi-national companies.

The West tries to destroy socialist China as it had been trying to destroy Vietnam, during what is called in Asia, "The American War". Just as in the same way it expended a tremendous effort to ruin Moscow, right from the 1917 Revolution, till the very end. As it has tried to destroy all the countries that insisted on their own principles: Cuba, Egypt, Indonesia, Chile, Nicaragua, Eritrea, and Iran before Shah, to name just a few.

Some, like North Korea, were first ravaged and then pushed to the extreme, forced to radicalize and then ridiculed and paraded on television screens as a freak example of Communist gaga-land.

What the West has in store for China is clear, and it is not much different from its designs during the Opium War. The perfect scenario would be a crippled, divided and submissive, West-admiring nation. The best ruler would be some Chinese Yeltsin who would agree to commit treason, break the country into pieces, open it up to oligarchs and foreign interests, cancel all social aspirations and bomb the Parliament full of the people's representatives that still believe in socialism.

Then we could 'do business with China', and give it full ideological and propaganda support.

***

My usual advice to the Chinese media is: "Use numbers! Numbers are on your side."

But it appears that China's propaganda team is no match for the Western apparatchiks.

China is too timid, too soft, as actually almost the entire world is, compared to Western political and economic gangsters.

In a series of deadly strokes, the West can bomb a country, poison its people with depleted uranium, impose sanctions that kill hundreds of thousand of defenseless women and children, then bomb the place once again, invade it, plunder it, and make sure that its own companies will make billions in a reconstruction process that actually shows no concrete results.

Such an approach cannot be matched by anybody; neither by China nor by the Soviet Union, which always made sure that its satellite states had higher standards of living than Moscow!

***

If China doesn't do it, let me do it, in brief. Let's use numbers and show to the world, especially to those 'concerned' Western citizens, how China is really doing. Let's compare. And let's do it on a per capita basis, the only fair way.

How many people have been murdered by the West beyond its boundaries, since WWII; in the Arab World, in Asia Pacific, in Africa, Latin America, Oceania; actually almost everywhere? I calculated, and my conservative estimate is between 50 and 60 million. Well over 200 million in indirect actions.

China – a few thousand, during its punitive and erroneous invasion of Vietnam, after Vietnam liberated Cambodia from Khmer Rouge. But that was the worst China ever did! And it withdrew rapidly. And it never bombed Vietnam back to the stone ages!

So if, let's say, the Chinese invasion took 10,000 lives, the West killed at least 5,000 times more people than China. Simple math, isn't it?

How many governments has the West overthrown, including those that were elected through painstaking and enthusiastic democratic processes? I don't have the patience to go through all of them: Nicaragua, Chile, Brazil, Dominican Republic, Indonesia, Iran, Zaire, Paraguay, and dozens of others. Basically, any government that Western companies and politicians did not approve of went up in flames.

China: zero.

The West has really given the world great lessons in democracy!

But let's continue our comparisons.

Who is vetoing UN resolutions on Palestine and on other key international issues?

Who puts itself out of the reach of international courts of justice, even threatening to invade the Netherlands in case its citizens are brought to the international court in The Hague?

Who is the greatest polluter, on a per capita basis? China does not even match the Scandinavian nations, and it becomes the number two environmental threat, after the US, only if absolute numbers are applied, a totally bizarre way to utilize statistics. To use the same logic, one would conclude: 'there are more people smoking in France than in Monaco'.

Even the former US Vice-President, Al Gore, hardly a China-lover, wrote that China has tougher environmental laws than US.

But let's return to defense, to that 'threat' which China is allegedly posing to the rest of the world.

According to the Stockholm International Peace Research Institute (SIPRI 2012 Yearbook), The United Sates, with a population of 315 million, spends (officially) approximately 711 billion dollars per annum on military expenditure. Many analysts insist that the number is really over 1 trillion dollars; others say that the amount is even higher than that, but incalculable, because of a complex and non-transparent interaction between government and the private sector. But let us stick to official numbers and accept, for argument's sake, the lowest estimate of 711 billion dollars.

Close allies of US are all great spenders as well; they all zealously shop for their nukes, missiles and jet fighters: The UK with 63 million people spends 62.7 billion dollars on 'defense'. France with 65 million people spends 62.5 billion. Japan with 126 million people, forks out 59.3 billion, although, officially it does not even have an army. Two of the closest Western allies in the Middle East, are even more radical:

Saudi Arabia with 28 million people spends 48.2 billion dollars, and Israel with population of only 8 million, spends 15 billion, proportionally similar amounts.

China, the most populous country on Earth, with 1,347 million people, spends 143 billion dollars, approximately as much as UK and France combined, but with over 10 times more people to defend!

On a per capita basis, the US spends over 21 times more on defense than China. UK more than 9 times and Saudi Arabia more than 16 times!

And one has to wonder: whom do France and the UK have to 'defend' themselves from? Could it be Andorra, Monaco or Ireland, or maybe that outlying bit of Europe, Iceland?

In contrast, China, which has been attacked on several occasions; which was occupied, colonized and plundered by Western powers, notably by the UK and France (whose barbarity in ransacking Beijing was legendary), now has hundreds of strategic bombers and nuclear missiles pointed at its face, from the directions of Okinawa and Guam, from the US fleets in the region, and from the bases in the nearby former Soviet Central Asian Republics.

The US, in defiance of the Constitution of the Philippines, is conducting military exercises at the Clark base and other military installations on the territory of its former colony. It has a heavy military presence in South Korea, just a stone's throw from China, and is making overt and covert overtures towards Vietnam, trying to, bizarrely; lease some its old bases, which were last used during the war. And it is no secret that Mongolia is now one of the staunchest Western allies, with thousands of kilometers of a long border with China.

What justifies such contrasting military expenditures between the West and China?

The answer is – nothing! Just as in the case of the 'Monroe Doctrine', the West does not need some silly justifications. Its presumption of racial and cultural superiority, unpronounced but assumed, seems to suffice in silencing all internal skeptics and critics.

The elites, 'intellectuals' and media in most of the world are trained and paid to kneel and bow to that obvious but unchallenged farce.

What I am doing here; asking all these questions, is not only unacceptable in Europe and US, it is considered impolite!

And China, many times a victim of Western aggressions, now finds itself on the defensive, accused of 'flexing its muscle', despite its disproportionally low defense budget and almost zero history of invasions and imperialism.

***

China is portrayed as a threat, when it stands shoulder-to-shoulder with most of the progressive Latin American nations and with Russia, blocking UN resolutions designed to open the door to the Western invasion of Syria.

In the eyes of the Western regime, trying to prevent an invasion, amounts to a supreme crime, almost akin to terrorism. Countries that stand in its way become vilified through the most vitriolic propaganda.

One has to recall that the same rhetoric was used by Nazi Germany, during the war. Members of any resistance, partisans, and opposing forces – were all called terrorists. And who can forget those colorful insults reserved for the nations that were about to be attacked! Or for the Soviet Union that faced the Nazis, finally defeating them!

According to my investigations in the region, Western forces are training not only the 'Syrian opposition', but also Saudi and Qatari jihadists as well as mercenaries, in the so-called 'refugee camps' in Turkey, near Hatay, and at the US air force base in Adana.

But who will forgive China, Russia and Latin America for trying to prevent yet another Libya-style, horror scenario?

And then, there are those Spratly Islands; that *tour de force* of Western propaganda!

The Spratly Islands could actually be the only evidence that China is 'flexing its muscle', or that it is ready to defend its interests.

The Government of the Philippines, a former US colony, is at the forefront of the harsh criticism directed at China.

I went to talk to the Philippine academia, to top scholars in Manila, and I managed to speak to several of them.

Opinions were generally similar, summarized by Roland G. Simbulan, a Senior Fellow and a Professor in Development Studies and Public Management at the University of the Philippines, he explained:

> "Frankly speaking, those Spratly Islands are not so significant to us. What's happening is that our political elites are clearly encouraged by the US to provoke China, and there is also the big influence of the US military on our armed forces. I would say that the Philippine military is very vulnerable to such type of 'encouragement'. So the US is constantly nurturing those confrontational attitudes. But continuing with this type of approach could be disastrous for our country. Essentially we are very close to China, geographically and otherwise."

In Vietnam, the US is clearly exploiting old rivalries, pitching two socialist states against each other.

***

Then the human rights issue.

Again, let's compare.

There are more people in jail in US than in China. Not just more, but incomparably more.

Photo 5. Communist victory in Beijing.

According to the International Centre for Prison Studies, the US has the highest number of people in prisons, more than anywhere in the world: 730 per 100,000 of population! Out of 221 countries and territories from which data was collected, China ranks 123th, with 121 prisoners per 100,000 of its population. That's six times less than the US, and even less than Luxembourg (ranked 120th with 124 prisoners per 100,000 of population) or Australia (ranked 113th with 129 prisoners per 100,000 of population).

It is a known fact that in the US, many prisons are privatized and prisoners are basically held as free or cheap labor. If it is not a violation of human rights, to hold millions of people in jail, for minor offenses, just in order to keep the coffers of private companies full, then what is?

The use of torture is accepted and used by US interrogators all over the world.

China still executes more people than the US, even on a per capita basis, which is unfortunate, but the number of executions in China is decreasing, as is being reduced the list of crimes punishable by death.

But while the death penalty in China is often mentioned in connection with human rights violations, it is rarely stated that the US is carrying out extra-judicial executions in several parts of the world, including Afghanistan and Pakistan, where it uses so-called drones, to arbitrarily target terrorist suspects, including women and children.

And what about the main propaganda chip – Tibet? If we compare the situation there to that in the territories ruled by Western allies, like Indonesia and India, we arrive at extremely uncomfortable conclusions; uncomfortable for the Western demagogues.

Indian rule over Kashmir can only be described as outright carnage, with the most conservative estimates indicating that at least 70,000 lives were lost there, in the last two decades alone. Indonesian rule over Papua, with over 120,000 people killed (also a very conservative estimate) is nothing short of genocide.

But India and Indonesia are never described as nations that should be deterred because of the record of gross violations of human rights. Nor are the Western nations for their endless crimes against humanity on all the continents.

Are human rights only for those at home? Are those 50, 60 or even 200 million people that the West has murdered mostly in poor countries, not 'human'?

***

To claim that there is no racism in the way China is perceived would be ludicrous.

I have friends, otherwise sensible and progressive men and women, who, when China is mentioned, close their ears and begin to scream: "No, I never want to go there. It is terrible!"

Communist, socialist, or capitalist, the success of Asian nations is never taken lightly in the West.

Who can ever forget the sarcasm and 'mistrust' directed towards Japan when it bypassed, economically and socially, most of the European nations. And until now, when someone mentions that Singapore has many social indicators that are better than those in Australia, he or she is immediately countered by derogatory outbursts, directed at the tropical city-state.

Both Singapore and Japan are staunch Western allies and highly developed market economies that have been integrated into the global capitalist system.

China is different. It is developing its own model; it is clearing and creating its own path through unknown territory. It is unwilling to follow orders from others. It is too big, its culture too old.

In the past, like Japan, China was closed, living in its own realm, never externally aggressive, with no expansionist ambitions.

Westerners arrived and forced it to open up. What followed were bloodbaths and deceits, confusion and a long period of national humiliation and stagnation.

Then came the struggle for independence, and revolution. Not easy, not smooth, but China once again grew, began rising to its feet, educating its people, housing and healing the poor.

It went its own way; a complex way of balancing between its own culture and global conditions, between socialism and the capitalist reality that is dominating the world.

It has experienced some setbacks but many more accomplishments. And it did not really 'rise'; it just began regaining its rightful place in the world, a place that was denied to it for so long, after years of plunder and debilitating invasions.

It is generally a benign nation inhabited by kind-hearted people. Almost all those that know China, agree on that.

But it is also an extremely determined and proud nation. It is wise, and in search of harmony, always willing to compromise.

To try to corner it, to provoke it, to attack it, would be insane, and almost suicidal. This time China will not yield, not when essential issues are involved. There is still the fresh memory there, of what happened when it did.

The West, blinded by the fear that it could lose the privileges of the dictator, is doing the unthinkable: sticking an iron rod into the dragon's mouth. Here in Asia, dragons are respected and loved – mythical creatures of great wisdom and power.

But dragons can also be fierce when goowill is broken, and invaders are threatening to ravage the nation.

***

China is growing and trying to understand the world, to interact with it. Its people are enthusiastic about what they see; they want to make friends.

The West is acting in the most antagonistic way: once again triggering an arms race, spreading the most vitriolic propaganda, corrupting entire nations in Asia and Oceania into adopting an anti-Chinese stand.

Understandably, the West did not sacrifice all those millions of people, all around the world, just to abandon its dictatorial and exclusive grip on power. It did not destroy dozens of freedom-seeking countries; it did not bomb tens of millions into oblivion, just to back up now.

In the future, confrontation cannot be excluded, and it is clear who will be at fault.

China will not abandon its course. There will be no Chinese Yeltsin. By standing firm, China is showing an example to the world.

As these words are being written, Latin America is resisting and winning. Russia is resisting while searching for its own direction. And others may join. Africa is dreaming about resisting, but still does not dare; still too damaged. Arab countries dare, but have yet to decide in which direction to place their dreams.

But discontent with neo-colonialist boots that are crushing freedom all over the world is growing. And China is not the one who is wearing them!

The irrationality and racism of the West will soon backfire.

4 January 2013

19

TAHRIR SQUARE DIED, BUT NOT THE REVOLUTION

Cairo.

Tahrir Square is dark, and all of a sudden, endlessly sad. There are still countless tents in the middle of the roundabout, banners carried by the wind, even a small and provisory 'Museum of Revolution'. From time to time one can hear, as if by some echo of bygone and glorious times, passionate music and the fiery speeches of protesters. Once in a while the sparks of the past euphoria explode in a delicate and short-lived firework, only just to melt swiftly away into the night.

But this is not the same Tahrir Square that had attracted electrified crowds, some two years ago. Now, glances are suspicious, and trust is in short supply. And there is an omnipresent fear all over the place; too much fear, too much...

Most of the kindness and solidarity evaporated, and what replaced it is horrifying. Local gangs have developed precise tactics, allowing them to isolate single women from the crowd, who are then dragged to tents or abandoned spaces, and brutally raped. It has already happened on several occasions, in just the few recent weeks.

Many shops around the square have been looted, some repeatedly. Gangs insult and harass reporters, in fact anyone with a camera, anyone asking questions. After sunset, I am often the only foreign-looking person working in the vicinity of Tahrir Square.

"No!" screams a young boy frighteningly, penetrating me with his adult and criminal glances, just as I point my cameras towards the tall wall that cuts the center of the city in half, 'protecting' the US Embassy. I know that to show weakness would be deadly and I move on the kid, literally clearing him out of my way. He backs up and shouts some loud insults. A few seconds later an entire gang of 10 to 14 year-olds begins surrounding me, tugging at my sleeves, slapping my coat. It goes on for almost a minute. I keep working. I ignore them. Then some genuine adult protesters intervene.

The nauseating smell of urine is everywhere. Garbage covers the square. It used to be relatively clean area - the pride of the Revolution. Now it is all filthy, rubbish strewn everywhere.

"The US is involved, no doubt," explains my friend, Dr. Mohammed Shafik. Before I return to the square, we are lounging at the psychiatric ward where he is on his 24-hour duty shift. He attends to the patients, but in between his work we drink coffee, debating Egypt, and my reports that he would like to translate into Arabic.

"The United States is indirectly saying: You had your revolution, your elections; you have your political parties," continues Dr. Shafik. "Now go and consume! And vote every four years for parties that do not represent you at all... The US has been supporting both the Muslim Brotherhood and the Liberals, including El-Baradei. It even helped to push Mubarak out of the way. As long as the opposition has no strong social message, the US is fine with 'regime change'. And with the Muslim Brotherhood, the 'free market' system is guaranteed. Two Brotherhood leaders were even flown to the US; one of them was Khairat El-Shater."

* * *

But is everything lost?

On Tahrir probably yes, but not in all of Egypt.

The masses that move back and forth appear to be fragmented. Friday is their big day, but by now, most of the people have run out of steam and are confused. A few youngsters paint graffiti. The artwork on the walls is increasingly violent: depicting people shot through their heads, with parts of their jaws missing. Optimism has disappeared: bloody and frightening wounds have become the topics depicted by contemporary art. Martyrdom is in vogue, but it is not invented; it is real. There are paintings and photos of the martyrs of the revolution – those who died, those who died young, those who died very young. At least 59 people were killed in the recent wave of violence, and everybody knows that the real numbers are much higher.

I ask Mr. Ali, a local painter who sits at the entrance of the Revolution Museum, what comes next?

"Mubarak, the military and Islamic Brotherhood are the same," he replies, gloomily. "And the Islamic Brotherhood has close ties with both Israel and the United States. Mubarak is now in prison, locked up for a quarter of a century, for murdering people. So what? Morsi took over! He is now the one who is doing the killing."

"People voted for him," I utter.

"Half, yes. 51%. And the elections were a sham. But even if they weren't a sham, you know that people in Egypt are not educated, they don't know how to think politically. The Brotherhood was elected, yes. But once they began murdering people, morally speaking, their mandate expired!"

I wait for my friends from the Revolutionary Socialists organization.

As I film and photograph the scene, a woman approaches me and begins screaming in my face: "Who are you? What is your nationality? For whom are you working?" I give her my card, but she continues screaming, not even bothering to read it. She wants to insult me, not to know.

An old man with black rotten teeth comes from behind: "She thinks that you are an Israeli spy... Are you a journalist? Do you want to interview El-Baradei?"

"No," I reply sarcastically. "What about Khaled Ali, from the labor movement?"

"Good choice! I can arrange. I can arrange Morsi, El-Baradei and Khaled Ali. Me – I have contacts everywhere. Me – I am the director of the museum. Everybody knows me here; my name is Mr. Magdy."

I know who he is. I am not new here. Mr. Magdy owns a gallery that used to sell fake papyrus to tourists. It is called monumentally, the 'Pharaoh's Museum'. It is quite a big institution and Mr. Magdy is a big con-artist. But I have some time to kill before my friends arrive, and so I ask him: "Mr. Magdy, what is becoming of Tahrir Square? It used to be such a joyful place, full of hope..."

He is being diplomatic. He is neither with nor against the protestors: "The people of Egypt have no education. They don't know what they want. They have no idea what a true revolution is."

"Do you, Mr. Magdy? Do you know what a true revolution is?"

He gives me a sly and a bit crooked smile. "Let's go to my museum," he says, finally.

"Bye Mr. Magdy," I wave at him. He swears under his breath.

* * *

And then they arrive – my friends. Three men and two ladies, all smiles, determined, honest, pure. They are all young; they are socialists, all educated and all giving their lives to the revolution, unconditionally.

They are not overly optimistic; they clearly see the monumental challenges ahead. They all live in Cairo, except for Manal who has just returned from London, where she works for a major Arabic newspaper.

I ask her the same question: what happened to Tahrir Square?

"It changed," she answers with a sad smile. "Since I left, just a few months ago, it has changed. It is gloomy now. We had such hopes after our revolution, but now there is so much violence inside Egyptian society. And it is very dangerous violence, with absolutely no rules. Before, the police used force against civilians. Now civilians are attacking civilians. There is something dirty going on; something terrible is taking place... There are hidden forces. And look at the leadership of the army: the violence they are using against us is even worse than the one that was applied by Mubarak."

We take a break at a local café. Young people are outraged by the media coverage of Egypt in the Western media. "It's a total disaster, especially what is being spread by the BBC. They act as if they are not familiar with Islam and its culture. And they have fully adopted Morsi's terminology. They call protesters 'thugs'. They confuse everything, they generalize..."

Before leaving the hospital, I asked Dr. Shafik, who those people occupying Tahrir Square are?

He shrugged his shoulder: "Us – leftists – but also Mubarak supporters who are now protesting against Morsi and the Muslim Brotherhood... There are secret service agents all over the place. There are gangs as well as some ordinary people, simply venting their grievances against the Brotherhood..."

I look at Manal, and then I look at her 2-meter tall friend – Ahmed.

"Listen," I say. "Nothing feels right, here, somehow..."

"You noticed... Tahrir is no more; it was destroyed. It is not the symbol of our Revolution, anymore."

"So let's go to the Palace," I suggest.

Manal has just returned from London. She is tired. We are all tired, exhausted. She hesitates for just a few seconds, but then she nods.

* * *

We hire a beat-up minivan and cram ourselves inside. There are more and more of us; the group is rapidly expanding. Young men and women sing on top of each other; they are joking and teasing. We photograph each other, pat each other, and encourage those who appear to be scared.

Before, I used to ask, whether our Latin American Revolutions had any similarities with the Revolution in Egypt. I don't have to ask now; I see it with my own eyes. These people, my new comrades; this young Egyptian vanguard, is as determined and self-sacrificing as those who brought down the right-wing regimes in Bolivia, Venezuela and Ecuador.

While Egypt descends into chaos, while brutality, dishonesty and immorality are ravaging both the capital and the provinces, while hopelessness mutates to violence, I am roaming the streets of Cairo with a group of determined revolutionaries.

"These young men," whispers Ms. Wesam, a sister of Manal, "They have been fighting for Egypt ever since the first days of the Revolution; for the last two years. They have never stopped. And they never will."

'Until the final victory,' I smile.

The light inside the van is blinking. The sirens outside are howling. And suddenly we are arriving, at Heliopolis.

* * *

Tires are burning and distant explosions penetrate the night.

"Keep your cameras hidden," I am told. "There are snipers all around. They killed our friend – a reporter – right in front of the Palace.

At the pitch-dark intersection, an old man surrounded by a small group of people extends his hands to us.

"His son was murdered by Morsi's regime," says Manal, in a matter-of-fact voice. "He needs to be outside; with other people. Otherwise his grief will become unbearable."

We hug the man and we go in the direction of the palace, along the tram tracks, towards the fire and explosions. I photograph ambulances and then a spectacular sight – an Egyptian flag waving in front of the fire.

Thousands of protesters are moving like ghosts, up and down the avenue. I don't want to use the flash; it is unsafe for the protesters; flashlight triggers an unwanted reaction from the armed forces. But without it, even at the speed of 2.500, everything comes out too dark.

Then suddenly we hear screams. They are coming from ahead of us, and thousands of people are running in our direction. I have no idea what is going on: for a moment I think that the army is sending in tanks, or that the police have begun using live ammunition, as I saw them do in Port Said just a few days earlier.

"They are using tear gas," screams Wesam.

Tear gas? I wonder. I have covered dozens of conflicts and wars all over the world; tear gas is definitely one of the least frightening things one can face in a conflict zone. I am slightly disappointed, even annoyed by the speed and determination with which the crowd is running away.

And then I feel it. The gas... First just a bit, as it enters my nostrils and eyes. Then I get a full dose of it. I begin to swear. I almost lose my balance – almost faint. 'What the hell is this?' I think. This is not any old Peruvian or Indonesian tear gas; this is not a gentle Chilean brew. It is not even what I smelt on the banks of Nile, on January 28th, earlier this year. This is monstrous, potent, and deadly!

I stumble, regain my balance and stumble again. Ahmed throws his towel my way. I press it to my nose. It helps just a bit.

"Bastards!" I scream.

"It's poisonous and carcinogenic, we are running analyses of it in the lab"; somebody offers an explanation, on the run. "They are poisoning us..."

I remember what I was told: many protesters consist of young doctors, engineers, and teachers.

"A kid has fainted," screams Ahmed, half outraged, half laughing. "So his friends begin reviving him, but as he opens his eyes, two tear gas canisters explode right next to him, so he faints again... "Take him away!" I yelled at them.

It is all both drama and fiesta. The side streets are full of people. Ahmed and his friends form a circle, embrace each other and begin jumping and singing: "We love to sing to our dear dead friends: Morsi, Morsi, Morsi!"

The night is still young. Later, in Cairo and the provinces, almost 100 protesters get arrested and 120 are injured. Those who are arrested in Egypt are often tortured; some disappear.

* * *

Late at night we walk towards the subway station. We are tired and hungry, but still joking. Ahmed and his friends are playing around, chasing each other, acting silly. Our group is like a ball of light in the depressing darkness of this decaying city.

Tahrir Square died; it is no longer the symbol of the Revolution.

But that night in Cairo I understood that the Revolution has not been defeated here, that it may never be defeated, that it may continue until the final victory.

I also realized that it is time to stop asking silly questions about the 'lack of leadership' here. There are strong leaders – Khaled Ali and others – and there is a strong socialist agenda embedded in the several groups that are participating in this Revolution. The battles will not be fought the same way as they were fought in Bolivia or Venezuela. Egypt is not Latin America. But they are and will be fought – things will be done and all of us who can help should be helping now. Because those brave men and women that I met on the streets of Cairo, whether they know it or not, are struggling for Egypt and the rest of the oppressed world, one smashed by imperialism.

* * *

In June 2012, during my debate with Noam Chomsky, I expressed skepticism about the future of the Arab revolutions. I was wrong. Noam listened to me and then uttered: "Two decades ago, the situation in Latin America was terribly depressing. You would never think that people there could win, that they would achieve what they achieved now. It is the same with the Arab countries now."

* * *

Let this essay be a requiem for Tahrir Square. But let it not be some hopeless and sad requiem. One place had fallen, but the struggle goes on!

Two years ago, people came here, to Tahrir, to fight for a better world, against a brutal pro-Western dictatorship. They were ready to risk their lives, to sacrifice their jobs, and their daily routine.

At some point they won, or they were told that they had won. In reality, it was all just an illusion. One man stepped down, the system survived.

Then the Square became like an old oak tree; a fairy-tale place, like a space where people come to remember, to feel sadness and nostalgia for that swelling in their hearts, for all those beautiful dreams that never came through.

Like lovers whose love is forbidden by the clan or family, old revolutionaries have been coming here to repeat in whispers their innermost and unfulfilled wishes, to renew their pledges; to mourn, to bring messages and deposit them into the safety of the hollow trunk of the imaginary three. After all, how could one forget all that euphoria, that sudden anticipation, the promise of a better future that colored, for a few months, that impenetrable greyness into the bright colors of spring?

The rebellion, the revolution – it was all happening just about two years ago or even just one year ago, or for some people only a few months ago. And for almost everybody who fought here and dreamt of better world, it feels like that it all took place just yesterday...

Some say: 'and suddenly everything was over. Everything changed. Hope slowly and agonizingly died. It was cancelled, like a secret email address containing the entire universe that used to give meaning to life.' Just like that, hope disappeared; it was switched off. The emptiness that followed was much worse than the anger that brought people onto the streets two years ago. Betrayed hope is the most terrible thing imaginable; better to live in darkness one's entire life, than to be embraced by brightness for just a few moments and then go back to the gloom.

But I know and my friends know that, not everything has been lost. It simply can't be. No matter how brief, the dream was too beautiful; it was worth living and fighting for. It still could return; it has to return, and it will. Mistakes were made, and so much was damaged, but the very core remains intact.

My eyes are burning and my lungs are contracting after taking in too much poisonous gas. But the brilliance of the people, who are relentlessly fighting for a better Egypt, made me stay up all night and to write this simple essay, an eyewitness account.

Once again, the prisons of Egypt are full. The hospitals are overflowing with injured men and women. But the fight, the 'process' goes on; it is not dying. Tahrir Square died, but the revolution is getting stronger.

12 February 2013

*****

20

Deep in the Rectum

WESTERN ART IS BARKING AT CHINA

In Europe and the US, for years and decades, art has become sclerotic, toothless, and somehow synonymous with grant applications, ego trips, identical-looking museum buildings, hordes of tourists and the constant glorification of form over substance.

Like Gucci and Prada, Impressionists and the "3 Tenors", for instance, have been elevated to status symbols, or to something one is expected to see, and listen to periodically, in order to show some basic signs of sophistication.

The Western propaganda apparatus spent a great deal of energy and tremendous funds on extracting all the teeth from the artists, eventually turning them into well groomed poodles. Sex, gore, booze, drugs and nihilism: yes, yes! Politics, revolution and attempts to overthrow the Western imperialist regime: no, no!

We used to believe that at least those guys and gals sitting in Paris, were somehow different. Then in a May 27th, 2008 interview with Charlie Rose, Matthiessen stated that he "invented The Paris Review as cover" for his CIA activities.

By then, of course, nobody with a working brain believed that the European and other Western cultural institutions in Asia, Africa and elsewhere, were just 'promoting artistic activities'. But who would 'bite the hand that feeds you'.

At that point, all creativity was gone. In the West, collectors, capitalist propagandists, the entertainment business and those who just needed to have their dwellings and businesses 'decorated', already controlled the majority of 'art'.

***

In China, 'things' are different. And the more different they are, the more cash and energy is spent by Western governments, propagandists and cultural institutions, in order to make it exactly the same – toothless and sclerotic – as its counterparts in the West.

Chinese art is combative and fully engaged politically, and socially. For years and decades it has been on the vanguard, relentlessly pushing boundaries, asking uncomfortable questions, loudly accusing and demanding.

It also evolves: as it is increasingly involved in a tremendous project – helping to build and to improve the country with the largest population on earth.

Much of Chinese art, at least the best of it, is still undeniably socialist.

But Western propaganda is continuously barking at China.

"Censorship!" it screams. "Freedom of speech!"

Anyone who attacks socialism or the leading role of the Communist Party is immediately elevated to the status of a cultural icon, a divine being, by Western critics and their media. It does not really matter how well the artist paints, singer sings or filmmaker directs – becoming a dissident, an anti-Communist, gains immediate access to fame, limitless grants and funding.

Like those few artists in Caracas, Maracaibo and Havana who are willing to sell their souls and the revolution for hard cash, several Chinese artists have also joined the pre-orchestrated choir of supporters of Western cultural imperialism, after calculating and coming to the delicate conclusion, that the soft leather seats of luxury sedans under their backsides compensate for a lack of conscience, even for treason.

Some dissident 'heroes' are subtle, but most of them, so beloved by Western galleries, are actually increasingly vulgar: delivering endless flow of paintings depicting Chinese comrade ladies in military and police uniforms and Mao pants, in near pornographic poses, with huge erect nipples and hairy crotches between widely-spread legs. Such images do not require a great imagination or exceptional talent, Otto Dix and others better, executed them in the West, many decades ago. But they sell very well in New York, Paris and Sydney. And they are considered, 'oh my god, so risqué!'

Were it not to be so gross, barking at China's art scene could actually be seen as very comical, as on closer inspection, Western art is actually much more rigidly regulated than art in China, the same as the so-called "Western Democracy".

It is already living in some post-censorship (not just in post-modernist) era, resting lazily on slightly stinky compost that covers the green pastures over a hill. It doesn't even need to be threatened by censors; it is amazingly auto-repressive, remarkably disciplined; it regulates itself with great sensibility, intuition and precision.

Much of Western art is positioned deeply and firmly inside and far up the odorless rectums of the sponsors and owners of the galleries, of funding agencies and political and 'cultural' institutions.

Its colorful tubes and triangles, stains and phantasmagoric curves are all self-serving. An old woman who can't afford to pay electric bills, a man who has his house repossessed because he can't pay the mortgage after falling ill, children killed by US drones in far away countries: all these realities are almost never represented by the complex lines and curves, stripes and explosions of colors.

The milieu of Western art is egoistic; self-serving, as it has been paid, for decades, to be.

Go to London galleries and go to Chelsea in New York, and you will see: much of the contemporary art is about failed erections, about the fear of ageing and lonely death, or about outbursts of selfishness: self esteem, self-admiration and 'self-discovery'. Most of it is all 'me-me-me', plus, as mentioned above, about those experimentations with a quantity of extremely abstract forms, with no meaning or use.

***

Then visit the "798 Art District" in Beijing or "50 Moganshan Art District" in Shanghai. There, so much appears to be in direct contrast to what takes place in the galleries of the West.

Chinese artwork is engaged, full of humanism, compassion and wrath against injustice. Many artists exhibiting there are clearly searching for solutions and ways forward. Not for themselves – for their country!

In January 2013 I visited dozens of art galleries in Shanghai, with my friend Yuan Sheng, a leading Chinese concert pianist from Beijing. We planned to call on "50 Moganshan" for only two hours, but in the end decided to stay there for almost the entire day, climbing the stairs to the attics, discussing the artwork, engaging in conversations with the local curators and artists.

While "798 Art District" in Beijing (also known as "Dashanzi Art District"), is based among enormous 50-year old decommissioned military factory buildings, in Shanghai, the artists work and exhibit in the former industrial area along the Suzhou Creek.

In both cities, hundreds of galleries and art studios now mix with *avant-garde* theatres, unique cafes and eateries, and with outdoor sculptures. The former industrial landscape offers a neutral and unsentimental backdrop.

Both places are dramatic and full of creative energy. And they are not the only art 'temples' of these great cities; just important 'additions' to the countless concert halls, opera houses, museums, music districts and cultural centers.

The government provides space, but the galleries are run independently, with very little interference.

And just as in Venezuela and Cuba, the Chinese state puts great emphasis on the arts.

"I think the arts are now getting tremendous, unprecedented attention from the government and from the common people alike," explained Yuan Sheng, a concert pianist, a graduate of the Manhattan School of Music and a professor of piano at the Central Conservatory of Music in Beijing. "During the 6th National Meeting of the 17th National Congress, the government passed a resolution, which emphasizes greatly the importance of cultural development, decisively increasing financial and other support for the arts and cultural development of the country."

Galleries in Beijing may be the most radical, but even those in Shanghai are clearly engaged, and in combative mode.

The oil paintings of Wei Yi at 523 Art Zone Gallery expose the problems of rural laborers. The Art Zone's powerful exhibition "We Are All Bachelors" shows 'men without women' aged 40-70, in the poor mountainous Miao towns.

"We have already dedicated many years of our lives, to exposing the social problems our country is facing," explained an employee of the gallery, while packing for me several free catalogues and DVD's of related documentaries. "If people are not interested, we have to make them change, so they get involved. We are working with some very famous artists like Lin Xiaodong, who is exposing the plight of farmers and immigrants from the countryside. He, of course, also exhibits his work in several major museums and at the 798 Art District in Beijing."

At ShangART Gallery, a naked man is crawling on a horizontally placed ladder, going nowhere.

There are impressive photos from Tibet and Nepal by Xiao Lin and there is the scarred urban landscape, destroyed *hutons* and kitschy modern developments and abandoned mosques at OFOTO Gallery.

Then we visit yet another enormous exhibition from rural China, this one at the Suzhouhe Art Center. "Our artwork is part of the huge social investigation conducted in Western Hunan Province", explains an employee of this multi-storey gallery. "Hunan still has so many poor people. What you see here is the result of our two-year work; work which we plan to continue for at least ten more years." On display are brilliantly executed full-size portraits depicting both men, and women from the countryside. One wall is fully dedicated to "The Village Committee". Each portrait has an explanation. Yuan translates for me: 'Head of Party in the Village, Yu Huang Gang: 5 acres of land, 7 people in the family, 2 cows, 7 ducks, 3 sons who are still single, 70 years old."

Across the road is the Aike-Dellarco Gallery. There, a powerful work of art has two images embedded in one painting; the images change depending from which side one looks. What is permanent is the huge fire in the distance, but seen from the right, one faces Palestine or maybe Egypt, with people running away from the flames and smoke. Moving to the left, the fire remains, but now we are in the middle of some pedestrian street in Shanghai, where people are actually moving slowly towards the blaze.

And nearby, there is yet another gallery, with an enormous eerie painting of a monstrous and appalling-looking aircraft carrier, seen through the absolute environmental destruction on the slopes of the mountains.

The variety and force of the local paintings is remarkable; their creativity is breathtaking.

Here, almost everything has meaning, the stories are real and urgent, almost all of them global.

Before leaving the district, we enter the Pata Gallery that is exhibiting the work of Zheng Hong Xiang. On one of them, there is an executioner's noose hanging from the ceiling, and a half-naked man with his head covered by a red box. There are fragments from the US Declaration of Independence printed on the surface of the box, in white letters.

Yuan and I approach Ms Ivy, a young art student who works in the gallery. What does she imagine when she see these paintings?

"This is called 'Misunderstanding'," she explains, without any hesitation. "A man is soon going to commit suicide. It is like what the Declaration of Independence says, versus the reality. You can read quotes from Jefferson and other US founding fathers on the box, but that is not what the life of this man is all about. And look at the next painting – look at this: it depicts this tremendous carcass of "McDonald's man", one of the cultural icons of US, that is exported to the whole world."

I look around the gallery and notice another covered head, this one by Chairman Mao's quotes, with a statuette of a rhinoceros standing in front of the painting.

***

In China, of course, it is not all exclusively about socialist zeal and social consciousness; and art is not always engaged, progressive and political. There is plenty of repetitiveness and commercialism, too, although it is clear that artistic integrity and a willingness to address essential issues is incomparably more alive here than in the West.

An undeniable dose of Western nihilism can also be detected here; it has already penetrated local art. It is somehow tolerated, even admired in certain circles.

Dozens of 'top Western artists' have migrated to China, for many different reasons. Some are here to share, some to learn, although there are those who are here clearly on a mission – to neutralize political messages, to discredit socialism and to separate local art from reality.

We took a close look at one of the galleries run by several Western artists residing in Shanghai. They were not showing anything ground-breaking. What we found was just the usual diet of derogatory pop that is often passed off in the West, as Chinese New Wave: female police officers with heavy make-up, performing erotic dances inside their police car, as well as the sexy poses of female soldiers. All Communist symbols put down, diminished, dragged through dirt.

***

It is not only in China: the West is working hard at trivializing all Latin American revolutions, and it pays heavily for any attempt to de-politicize local artists, from Central to South America, from Southeast Asia to the Middle East.

While walking through the Shanghai Art District, what kept coming to my mind were the ridiculous graffiti now decorating Tahrir Square in Cairo, and what I was told about their origin. It was definitely not homegrown Middle Eastern stuff; it was actually not unlike the 'artwork' of the period of the 'Orange Revolution' in Ukraine and elsewhere.

But here I was, to the highest degree, impressed by how many great Chinese artists are resisting, in fact flatly rejecting those Western implants, designed to destroy all social and socialist messages.

It is obvious that leading Chinese art galleries are capable of, and ready and willing to exhibit works of art that combat all types of problems that China and the world are presently facing; from the plight of rural workers, to the changing urban landscape, social inequalities and Western imperialism.

It is also clear that their approach is constructive and socialist, not nihilistic and destructive, trying to serve the country, not to destroy it.

"Art critics admit that Chinese art now leads the world," I was recently told by Peter King, a Professor at Sydney University.

And it is leading through its substance, not just through its form.

It is not the Chinese government, but the West that tries to muzzle local artists; to strip them of political fervor and social consciousness. And it is doing it cannily, covertly and persistently

***

Sydney interacts with Chinese artists more than any other 'Western' city in the world. It is due to its relative geographical proximity to Asia, and also because of the growing number of Chinese students here.

The Ray Hughes Gallery in Surrey Hills was one of the first art institutions to react to the 'new wave' in Chinese art. It now possesses one of the greatest collections of Chinese contemporary paintings in Australia, and arguably in the world. It actually began exhibiting China's *avant-garde* soon after the first journey of Ray Hughes to China, in 1999. He was quick to identify the tremendous commercial potential of China's 'new wave', and now his gallery hosts several vintage pieces of the iconic Luo Brothers from Nanning, as well as of Qi Zhi Long, Lin Xiaodong, Li Jin and several other famous artists.

Evan Hughes, the son of Ray Hughes, is a Cambridge-educated art collector. He is pragmatic and honest and told me during our encounter:

"Chinese art is definitely much more politically and socially-engaged than that in the West, where there are hardly any political artists left. Western art has been invaded by apathy, particularly in 70's and 80's. In China there is a revolution in what can be now exhibited – political content has been liberalized.

We are offering the work of many important Chinese artists; some of them are political, some are not. But what makes several of them so impressive is that they went through training at the great Chinese Art academies including the Guangzhou Academy. Their technique is simply brilliant."

The most striking example of the prominence of Chinese Art in Sydney is just a few years old, the magnificent White Rabbit Gallery in the Chippendale neighborhood. It is the first large art institution in Australia fully dedicated to modern Chinese art. It is called a gallery, but in reality it is a large multi-storey cultural center, which consists of a library, tea-room, boutique, Film Club and several enormous spaces, exhibiting some of the best contemporary artists from China.

"At White Rabbit, the art is not necessarily political," explained Liz Keenan, Press and Publicity Director of White Rabbit Gallery. "We are aiming to bring here the best of Chinese contemporary art of the 21st century".

Ms. Keenan walked me from floor to floor and from one *avant-garde* masterpiece to another. Inside White Rabbit there are canvasses, statues, structures and other art works by Cao Xiaodong, Chen Fei, Feng Yan, Gade, Xiong Wenyun and many others. There are large and often controversial works, like Wang Zhiyuan's "Thrown to the Wind", an 11meters tall, tornado of plastic containers or Ai Weiwei's Sunflower Seeds.

But it is striking how great the difference is between the Chinese art exhibited abroad, and the art on display in Beijing, Guangzhou and Shanghai galleries!

It is as if they came from different countries, from different galaxies.

Instead of selecting canvasses that would inspire Western audiences and dormant Western artists, instead of presenting great Chinese political and social art as an example, almost all Western galleries choose either abstract experimental or decorative works.

Of course they are great, too, but they will not change the world!

***

But the most celebrated, the most propagated in the West, are artists like Ai Weiwei; a staunchly anti-Communist artist and a vocal advocate of 'Western democracy'.

Ai Weiwei, a darling of the Western mass media, recently attacked the great Chinese novelist, a winner of the Nobel Prize for Literature, Mo Yan. What was Mo Yan's greatest sin? Apparently, being an unapologetic socialist and the the Vice Chairman of the Chinese Writers Association.

In the West, no shadow of doubt can be cast on Ai Weiwei himself. He is allowed to be political, he is encouraged to regurgitate propaganda; 'our propaganda', of course.

Was he arrested because he was a dissident, or because he really broke the laws of his country? And when we are told that 'police broke into his million dollar studio', should we not ask how he made those millions, and who was propagating his work? Of course, in the West, such questions are labeled as 'unacceptable', and 'impolite', almost sacrilegious!

Don't get me wrong: I do believe that artists have to be political. It is actually their obligation to be political – to be engaged. Therefore, it should be Ai Weiwei's right to be anti-Communist, anti-Mo Yan, while propagating Western imperialism.

As it is my right to be anti-Ai Weiwei-ian!

The problem is that those Chinese artists who believe in socialism but criticize the system in order to improve it, are generally ignored, and even ridiculed in the West, unless they opt for some compromise and at least show a few exposed nipples and the legs of their female comrades in military or police uniforms!

***

Western art has always prostituted itself, serving those who happen to be holding the reins of power. This has gone on since the Greeks and Romans; and has continued for centuries, even millennia.

That glorified tradition of Western 'freedom of expression'; exists only for as long as most of the artists, media people and thinkers agree to march in closed ranks, serving the regime. For as long as they repeat that the idiocy of the 'multi-party' system that upholds the dictatorship of elites, is superior to all other forms of governance.

Most Western operas and symphonies of the past, were written for some narcissistic king or a bunch of twisted aristocrats, and were premiered in front of a closed circle of powerful spectators. Composers had patrons, they were 'sponsored', or they starved, not unlike now.

And painters? Almost all fell one over another, crawling up the rear of the moneyed-classes; kissing hands and other bodily parts of bishops and cardinals, dukes and emperors; those bandits, and early-day 'patrons of the arts'.

Last year, once again, I went to the Museo de Prado in Madrid, just for a few hours, before departing for Santiago de Chile. I could not last for long there: I felt dizzy from unbridled Christian fundamentalism. I observed in disbelief, all the panoptics of Iberian kings, dukes, queens, kids from the palaces, top ranking religious crooks; all painted by Velasquez, Murillo, El Greco – the demi-gods of Spanish art. Compared to what is on exhibition at Prado, the Taliban look fairly secular.

And at the Louvre? Once again, all those carpets hanging from the walls, depicting hunting scenes, all that amassment of furniture, old musical instruments, mugs of crooked aristocrats, religious motifs... There are a few curvy nudes, of course. If of war, it is mostly glorious.

Walking through the Prado or the Louvre, one would never think that Spain and France were two great colonial, imperialist powers, which caused the deaths of tens, probably hundreds of millions of innocent people in the Caribbean, Central and South America, Africa, Asia and the Middle East.

Where were those free spirits, those great Western artists? Were they too busy dying from syphilis and cirrhosis of liver, at the same time as entire tribes and nations were being reduced to dust by the patrons of the arts?

Did we ever see artwork named: "French soldiers are slaughtering the last women and children of Grenada", or "Spanish priests are torturing and raping Inca villagers"?

In one of the most visited museums in the world – Musée d'Orsay in Paris – all the artists seem to be engaged in having breakfast on the grass, salivating over curvy or cubist models sitting on wooden chairs, cutting off their own ears, finishing their intestines with absinthe, or flying over Paris or Vitebsk with their dreamy lovers. If in 'far away places', then they are depicted through the shining eyes of tigers or other animals, peeking from an impenetrable bush, in so called 'primitive art'. If Polynesia is being shown; then it is through its corpulent nudes and not through some French mini-genocide committed by Jean-Baptiste Dutrou-Bornier on Easter Island.

Western artists have a history of being much more submissive than their counterparts anywhere else in the world. And there should be no doubt that the Western regime has corrupted or forced into silence many more creative people than any other dictatorship in the history of mankind!

According to the Stuttgart-based painter and political cartoonist, Marina Wiedemann:

> "Contemporary art in Europe is a total debacle. Exceptions: sure there are some. But it all feels like some polluted swamp: on the surface are those handpicked artists you are expected to stuff your face with... the art that you are being fed with, by the establishment... underneath, a brutal fight for joining those who are already floating and visible. And artists who are really talented and have plenty to say: they have no chance to surface at all, as they are kept under, by the most celebrated shit covering the surface."

The greatest political artist of Southeast Asia, Djokopekik from Indonesia, commented for this essay:

> "I am not too interested in Western art, but from the little that I know, it seems that Western artists really like to paint without considering the situation in their part of the world and in the world in general. And the world is now in mourning because of so many ills and so many deaths, while Western artists still continue to live happily, making lots of money, and not thinking about other people who are suffering."

Djokopekik, who is of course a much greater artist than Ai Weiwei, spent years in brutal imprisonment during the pro-Western dictatorship of General Suharto. It goes without saying that there was no mass campaign in the West to free him, or to demand 'freedom of expression' in Indonesia.

But back to the rectum: let's fetch those free and proud Western artists from its depth, and ask them 'why on earth', or more precisely 'why the hell' they ended up on their pathetic ego-trips, instead of dedicating their lives to showing the horrors their governments and cultures have been committing all over the world?

In the past, the West had at least a few great painters, like Goya, Delacroix, and Picasso. Now? Where are those daring to paint Belgrade or Baghdad after bombing, of the Laotian and Cambodian countryside after receiving millions of tons of bombs, or the torture chambers in Chile, Argentina? Do we know of any great Western painter who could be working in East Kivu in DR Congo or in Palestine?

I will tell you who does it: the Latin Americans and the Chinese! Not gringos and Europeans.

I was recently filming in the tremendous museum in Santiago de Chile: the Museum of Memory and Human Rights. There is everything there that one has to know about the US violation of human rights, by the manufacturing and support of Latin American dictatorships. The architecture of the museum is splendid, combining an old villa and several stories of imposing glass and steel.

And in one of the exhibition halls: I discovered paintings by one of the greatest contemporary artists – Fernando Botero; that very Botero from Colombia, who is famous all over the world for his paintings and sculptures of fat and nude women. But this time there were no buttocks and breasts, just Muslim men with their hands tied behind their backs, blindfolded; their bodies tortured, with dogs jumping on their exposed chest.

Abu Ghraib; the horrors of Abu Ghraib! I stood in front of the paintings, motionless, for many long minutes, and my glasses got foggy; I was overwhelmed. Not because what I saw was telling me something new: I have covered Western wars and atrocities for many years. But I was overwhelmed with gratitude towards this grand Colombian artist, because here, once again, he had demonstrated what exactly art is capable of doing and should be doing.

If he, if others like him, had something to say about Chinese art, I would listen. And I am sure that China would listen as well.

But there is absolutely nothing we can learn from the artistic cowardice and impotence coming out from London and New York, Paris and Berlin! There is nothing we can learn about 'human rights' and 'democracy' from cultures responsible for hundreds of millions of people murdered on all continents.

Artists of the world should unite against the nihilism and spinelessness coming from Europe and North America. To hell with their money, and as Sukarno used to say: "To hell with their aid!" and their 'funding'.

Let them paint their lines and ovals. Let them piss on canvases, spread it all over and call it art. Let them cover their internal emptiness with abstractions. Alternatively, let them paint flowers for luxury hotels and the villas of the millionaires.

The great Argentine painter, Alberto Bruzzone, once said: “I cannot paint flowers or motherhood, when they are killing my students on the street!”

Many Chinese painters feel the same: they have no time to deal with their sexuality, with personal fears and desires, while there are still hundreds of millions of their fellow citizens living in poverty, and billions all over the world living in slavery!

15 February 2013

*****

21

The "Perfect" Wicked Occupation

FACING SYRIA FROM AN ISRAELI BUNKER

Golan Heights

It is late afternoon and I am standing on top of an active, temporarily abandoned, Israeli bunker.

Through my Nikon lens I can clearly see a huge Syrian flag waving majestically in the wind. The flag is near, damn near, but why should it not be there? – This is after all Syria, according to international law.

Where the flag is waving, is part of Syria. Behind the flag, it is Syria; and Syria is where I am standing now, exposed and shivering in the chilly wind blowing from the mountains.

It is quite a sight, all around me, quite a sight! Right ahead – destroyed and abandoned – are the remains of houses and buildings of the Syrian town of al- Qunaitra. On the left, the UN, or more precisely, is the UNDOF base. There are white trucks and light armored vehicles behind their perimeter; almost like those outside Goma, East Kivu, in DR Congo.

But here, the UN base is sitting on what is called a Demilitarized Zone, or DMZ. It is right between the ceasefire 1974 UNDOF lines, Alfa and Bravo. Through the DMZ runs a shiny and new Israeli barbed, high-voltage, stereotypical, and despite its glow – melancholy – wire fence.

Above all that mess, on top of the mountain, an enormous Israeli military post hums, equipped with dozens of radars, listening devices and antennas. It is far, maybe one kilometer away, but the sound it produces is like that of a giant beehive. It is really obnoxious stuff – like some cartoon about over-militarization; a battleship placed on top of the mountain.

I photograph the trenches of the bunker; the mountaintop turned surveillance fortress, and then some old rusty, as well as those new shiny wires. “Danger! Mines!” It is written, I guess in the spirit of international understanding, in Hebrew, English and Arabic. These signs are all around me. I am trying not to step too far from the main paths, although here and there I stray – the images are too powerful, too tempting.

An Israeli human rights lawyer, Ms Lynda Brayer, who drove with me from Haifa, sits put inside the car. She must be thinking that I am at least moderately insane. Despite her concern and objections, I drove this small Nissan to the several hills, overlooking Syria; I drove it near the Israeli military installations; road or no road.

But I really can’t get enough – the images are intensely perverse. The whole reality of this occupation – the Israeli occupation of Golan Heights – is mad, surreal, and in its own wicked way – ‘perfect’.

And then it also hits me that I am mad. Just a few days earlier, on January 30th, 2013, Israel attacked Syrian territory, damaging a facility outside Damascus, using fighter jets. According to Reuters:

> “The foreign ministry summoned the head of the U.N. force in the Israeli-occupied Golan Heights to deliver the protest a day after Israel hit what Syria said was a military research centre and diplomats said was a weapons convoy heading for Lebanon.”

“Syria holds Israel and those who protect it in the Security Council, fully responsible for the results of this aggression and affirms its right to defend itself, its land and sovereignty,” Syrian television was quoted as saying.

The Syrian President, Bashar el-Assad, declared few days later: "Syria can defend itself from current threats... and aggression."

So here I am, totally exposed, wearing my green coat, standing on top of an Israeli bunker, facing Syria through my big photo lens. 'That is perhaps not very wise', I mumbled, running down the hill for cover.

How beautiful the Golan Heights are, how beautiful! How lovely the green gentle slopes and dramatic stormy clouds are, embracing, like a soft comforter, the tops of the hills.

How sad, how scarred, how ravaged the Golan Heights are! Those mighty stone military barriers, resembling the walls of old Inca castles; that constant flow of Israeli military hardware – those trucks, 4×4's and tanks – and all around, those anonymous stonewalls that used to encircle the local houses and hamlets and towns.

It is all so empty now. I stop the car, kill the engine and listen: I don't hear any birds, just that constant humming from the surrounding hills.

"In the occupied territory of Golan Heights, the majority of people were expelled; brutally and unceremoniously," I was told by Joul Jammal, an Israeli lawyer. "This Syrian territory occupied by Israel, is predominantly populated by the Arab Druze people; those brave and proud inhabitants, who, for decades, have not succumbed to the occupation." The Druze people form an extremely close-knit society, and like Bohras, they represent one of the branches of *Ismailis*. Some theories claim that Druze people are actually Muslims, others that they are not at all.

Some say that the occupation of the Golan Heights is 'soft', that Druze people enjoy a high standard of living, much higher than in most countries of the region, including Syria itself. The Economist even argued that were Israel to return the Golan Heights to Syria, many of its inhabitants would suffer from the 'Hong Kong syndrome'.

British propaganda truly knows how to twist things around.

Prior to the 1967 Six Day War, the population of the Golan Heights consisted of 145,000 inhabitants, including several thousand Palestinian refugees. The Israelis forced the great majority of local people to flee. Only 7,000 remained, and these were concentrated in a handful of villages.

Hundreds of villages and hamlets were demolished and much of the land was given to Jewish settlers.

Even the biggest Syrian city in the region – Al-Quneitra – was occupied in 1967, returned to Syria in 1974, but before that, it was dynamited and bulldozed to the ground.

Now *kibbutzim* and Israeli settlements scar the landscape. There is more than just agro-industry. Merom Golan and Ein Zivan, not far from the border and the UN camp, look like some sort of modern-day fortifications, heavily protected gated communities.

An "Organic beef" farm is being advertised on the main road. The sign is idyllic and you turn the wheel and drive up to the hill, only to be welcomed by a closed gate and barbed wire. The Ortal Winery is advertised right at the intersection with the road that leads to the Ortal Community. You drive in that direction, but soon, instead of some elegant wine cellar you discover a huge, heavy metal gate, with surveillance cameras and an eerie feel to it.

"This is an outpost," protests Ms Brayer, "not part of communal infrastructure. It is totally different from what we can see on the West Bank."

We have to tank. The gas station is self-service, with no attendants in sight. It is fully computerized, and hidden behind a fence. Even for me, this is too technologically advanced.

Soon, a military vehicle stops next to us. "Are you OK?" we are asked.

"Fine," I say. "Do you know how to operate this?" I point at the pump. The soldier eagerly explains. He asks no questions about the reasons of our presence in this area. He is confident, reserved, but friendly. My window is open and there are three cameras openly resting on the back seat. It would take some discipline not to notice. The soldier notices. But he doesn't seem to care.

In India, in Pakistan, in Congo – I would already have been detained and escorted to the barracks for interrogations. Here, the army is in total control and has no fear. I was certainly observed as I stood on top of their bunker, photographing. Nobody seems to be bothered.

I ask the soldier about the bunker.

"It's an abandoned one; at least for now. You are asking about a

> conflict around here? No, nothing – there is nothing going on. There are no provocations from the Syrian side... No provocations for years."

"Even as the Israeli jets crossed into Syria, just a few days ago?"

"It was absolutely quiet here," he reconfirms. "It's as if nothing happened."

He is a young kid, bespectacled, timid. He replies to my questions briefly and to the point, as if he was standing in front of a class. His friend is impatient; he seems to be in a hurry.

"Sorry, I have to run," the soldier waves at me.

We drive by a monument commemorating something called "679 Brigade". There is a bellicose artwork, and some history engraved on the stone. There is a decommissioned Israeli tank parked nearby. I need some exercise. I jump and grab the cannon with both hands, and then I hang on it for a while. I do some pull-ups. The whole place, as well as my presence here, is bizarre, Kafkaesque.

A nearby base is overflowing with Israeli vehicles carrying tall antennae. I make a u-turn, return to the entrance and photograph the entire place. Everything is in the open; there seem to be no secrets.

But back in Haifa, Joul Jammal warned me: "It appears that the army does not fear reporters. They want to present all of this as an 'enlightened occupation'. You can film and photograph what is really 'in the open'. But when they kill and when they destroy houses, they also periodically kill reporters."

We admire apples at a small stall. There is a brilliant direct view into unoccupied Syria from here. Apples and cherries – that's what the Golan Heights is famous for.

And it is also renowned for the mass expulsion of its population! There is yet another vineyard nearby, right before the terrible barbed-wire fence. I suddenly lose all my love for a good wine, at least for some time.

"It is all quiet here," smiles the seller. "The only sounds we get here are those of car engines, as well as the humming of the radios and radars on top of the hill over there."

Further down we discover a tower and the cannon of some old

tank, facing the valley and the Syrian city of al-Quneitra. It is buried deep in the earth, and now 'decorated' with graffiti. A few minutes drive north and there are the gloomy ruins of a former Syrian military outpost. The grass is tall here, and the silence complete.

A kilometer further, and I suddenly spot the huge multi-storey ruins of a building: a military compound, or maybe an abandoned school?

I park the car and walk around the deep puddles. Then I see them: Israeli soldiers, an entire commando, machine guns at the ready, climbing the walls, playing some weird war games. They are exercising.

At some point they become aware of me. A soldier walks towards me, slowly.

"Is everything OK?" Here comes the same question, and the same friendly indifference.

"Fine," I say, pointing at the monstrous decomposed structure. "What was this?"

"An old Syrian base," he replies.

"Can I?" I point the lens at the commando.

"Sure," he shrugs his shoulders and goes away.

"Hey", I scream at him. "How close can I get to the borderline if I walk this way?"

"The puddles are deep," he smiles. "And you are not wearing boots. Drive further north and you can actually sit on the fence."

"And burn my ass on thousands of your volts," I say.

"Precisely," he laughs.

'A joke', I think; 'a military joke'. "Thanks," I say.

I return to the car. I drive north.

***

"Yes, you can go all the way to the border," says a man, a giant, guarding the entrance to the military road that leads towards the border with Lebanon. He is a Druze, a local. He does not smile; he is not joking. We are at Majdal al-Shams, a divided town with nine thousand inhabitants, and the largest Druze 'urban area' in Golan.

"You can go and see the Shouting Hill. That's where the separated, broken families meet; that's where they at least can exchange glances, and shout at each other through the barbed wire."

I ask him about the occupation of the Golan Heights. He does not hesitate one single moment:

"I am Syrian," he says. "I want this place to be returned to Syria!"

I am amazed; the man is not afraid to express his feelings. He is proud, tall and coherent. He even gives me his name, which I prefer not to use.

Unlike the Palestinians of the West Bank and Gaza, people here do not have to beg for work permits to go to Israel. This is 'annexed, incorporated territory'. Ever since 1981 the Golan Heights have fallen under Israeli civil law, and are incorporated into the Israeli system of local councils. People can go as they please; they can work in Haifa or Tel Aviv. They can apply and get Israeli citizenship, an ID card, even a passport. Less than 10 percent choose this option. They are proud and they are stubborn: their home is Syria. They are waiting to 'return home', have been waiting already, for many long decades.

"Are there many divided families?" I ask the guard.

"Yes, many, houses are on both sides and the border runs in between them."

I ask him whether he has some family members on the other side of the fence.

"Yes, in Jaramana, east of Damascus. We all meet in Jordan, once in a while. Jordan is where the families from Syria and the occupied Golan Heights can meet."

The borderline is a kilometer away from the center. It is monstrous, horrendous. Compared to this, the old Cold War borders looked like promenades. And even the border between North and South Korea somehow has a more 'civil' appearance; at least they grow gingseng at the DMZ.

This frontier – between Syria and occupied Syria –now has three tall layers of electric fences, equipped, traditionally, with barbed wire. In between is a narrow road for Israeli military vehicles. And only then, only behind all this, there are the UN watchtowers.

Paradoxically, it appears that there is absolutely no fortification on the Syrian side.

Before mobile phones became affordable, people used to come here, to the border, from both sides; they used to line up with bullhorns to make small talk with their relatives. I am told that they still come, occasionally, just to look at each other, through the barbed-wire grid. They come here to see, to recognize the faces of their loved ones.

I wave at a cargo vehicle; I stop it, and ask the driver when this ugly stuff was actually constructed.

"It's new," he says. "But this is still nothing. Come back in a few months: the Israelis are planning to build the real wall – tall and concrete. It will be going up very soon."

***

We speak to several people in Majdal al-Shams and the other villages and towns of the area.

The Druze could be described as open and friendly people. They live in their own universe. They have their own religion and philosophy of life. They believe in reincarnation and they almost never marry out of their clan.

By the standards of the region, the Golan Heights is a very rich area. The health system and education are of a similar quality as those in Israel, and so are the other social services.

But this is occupied land, from which most of the native people were expelled right after the war. Now Jewish settlements dot the plateau.

Israel tried to use the uniqueness of the Druze culture and religion to its own advantage: convincing the natives that they are not part of Syria; that they are a separate nation.

As Mr. Jammal explained: "Israel has been using the divide and rule strategy; it tried to create the notion of a superficial Druze state, using the fact that Druze people have their own faith, which is far from the mainstream of Islam."

But the Druze resisted, at least the great majority of them. Returning to Syria is their goal, even after several decades of so-called 'soft' occupation.

We are told that many people from the Golan Heights aim to study in Syria. Some 200 are now attending universities there, to become doctors, dentists and lawyers. The UN is facilitating their border crossing, their journeys.

Before the recent escalation of hostilities between Israel and Syria, the UN even facilitated the sale of apples and cherries from the Golan Heights to unoccupied Syria. Now things are on hold, after the 'excursion' of Israeli fighter jets and the bombing of Syria, an act that breached international law and caused an explosion of anger all over the region.

"People here live as if everything is just a temporary arrangement. As if one day there will be no border, anymore," we are told by many in Majdal al-Shams.

Some wealthy residents are even building their villas right next to the borderline, facing the wall. Because behind the wall are those magnificent mountains. And one day, who knows, there might be, once again, an unobstructed view.

***

There are collaborators in the Golan Heights, some are local and some are 'imported'. Indeed, there are plenty of collaborators in the Golan Heights!

In a small restaurant, Falafel Abu, in the center of Majdal al-Shams, two men are sharing their evening meal. They ask questions; want to know all about us and they don't even try to conceal their identities, supplying us with their names, email addresses and mobile numbers.

One person is a local; a tall man who spent many years in the United States, in Idaho, before returning back to the Golan Heights. The other one is a Christian, from Beirut, Lebanon.

> "My father emigrated from Lebanon to Toronto, Canada, in 1990, after the war. I lived there for some time, and after I got my Canadian passport, I visited Israel and fell in love with this country. Then I came to the Golan Heights and I made good friends among Druze people. I married a Christian girl here, got a residence permit, and stayed."

"That would not be so simple," Lynda whispers.

At one point, both men begin pushing the official Israeli line. They are aware that I am an investigative journalist. This fact appears to be actually firing them up – they apparently want to talk and they don't mind being quoted.

"The entire community is now Israeli. We all have an Israeli mentality – we are open minded, educated; we travel..."

"Look at this man," they point at the owner of the falafel restaurant who, sporting an Ottoman-style moustache, with small, intelligent eyes, observes us from the distance. "His son is a lawyer. His daughter studied special education and now she works with mental patients in Spain."

I ask them about Syria.

"We are with the revolution! We'd like to see a difference in the region. We don't want people to be calling for jihad." Both men are in full agreement. "Israel will never return the Golan Heights to Syria; unless the water issue is resolved and the UN is involved. And even then, for security reasons, Israel will have to retain the hills."

The tall man has an Israeli passport. The Lebanese man has Israeli permanent residency.

How many people here support President Assad?

"Half and half," they say. I know it is not true. Most of people we spoke to support him.

Then it begins: the barrage of clichés, they had been holding back for almost an hour. The Lebanese man begins his speech:

"It is clear that Islam aims at being the enemy of the world... Look at what is happening in Egypt... I am even afraid to go back to Lebanon, now - afraid to even visit. All those Hezbollah spies there! I love Israel!"

The tall, local/'Idaho Man' joins this serenading of Israel: "People here know how to live in peace with the Jewish community. Sure, some 10% protest against the occupation. But almost all young people believe that Israel is their home. Now the Golan Heights is the quietest and the most peaceful area of Israel."

Eventually, both men depart. Yes, the Golan Heights is an extremely quiet part of the world. It is because some 80% of the local people were kicked out of their homes. It is because their hamlets, villages and towns were destroyed. It is because monstrous fences were erected. Both men also forgot to mention that terrible humming from the tops of all the local hills – the radars, radios, listening devices. And they forgot to mention the tanks and armored vehicles, moving up and down the narrow roads.

The Golan Heights – the land of cherries and apples, of ruins of villages and towns, of Israeli commandoes playing war games inside destroyed Syrian buildings.

As the two men leave, we go straight to the owner of falafel restaurant.

"You make the best falafel on Earth," I tell him, which is the undeniable truth. "Now please, tell me what do you think about what is happening in Syria?"

"I am very upset about the situation there," he replies, slowly. "There is so much damage, so much suffering, again. It is not correct what is happening there. I worry about my family across the border. Many people here call those 'revolutionaries' in Syria – the terrorists. Was the situation better before the 'uprising' began? Most definitely!"

It is our second day here, the end of the second day.

A small group gathers inside of the sweets' shop. The food in Majdal al-Shams is exquisite. The outspokenness of the local people is simply remarkable.

And what we hear from the local people is exactly the opposite from what is served to us by the official Israeli propaganda:

> "We want to go back to Syria. The rebels are terrorists. Assad is in the West's way to Iran; the West and Israel want to push him aside and have their path cleared towards Teheran. We all know that Qatar is paying for the 'rebels'. If Russia and China do not give in to the West, Assad will never fall."

Before we parted the previous day, the guard at the road to Lebanon clarified: "We are all connected with Syria here. We watch Syrian television; we are following the events. Most of the local people here identify themselves with Assad. We like Assad here. But in the West and in Israel, they simply hate intelligent Arab leaders. They like and support those idiots in Qatar, Bahrain and Saudi Arabia!"

It is actually exactly the same point of view that I heard from the people of Hatay, on the border between Turkey and Syria, where I investigated the Western training camps that are manufacturing the so-called 'Syrian Opposition'.

People also complain about the Israeli control of the housing stock. There has to be an official permit to build any new house, and that permit costs a fortune. This town, alone, lacks some 1,000 houses; Israelis simply do not allow Druze towns to grow – growth is reserved only for Jewish settlements. People live in crammed conditions. The houses built without official permits get demolished.

And then we are told about the structure of 'democracy' in this occupied territory: "Syrian citizens – the great majority – have no right to vote. Israel imposes its own handpicked Druze representatives, to form so-called 'village or town councils'. They all consist of collaborators and they carry Israeli passports and identification cards. It goes without saying that those councils are not here to serve the interests of the local population."

***

As I drive towards the border with Lebanon, I am confronted by one of the most beautiful sceneries on Earth: Mt. Hermon or Jabal al-Shaykh in Arabic – the tallest peak of Syria and now the 'buffer zone' between Syria and Israeli-occupied Golan Heights. The top of the mountain is on the border between Syria and Lebanon.

Then I drive further, and my eyes fall on the enormous Nimrod Fortress, built around 1229 by Al-Aziz Uthman, a nephew of Saladin and younger son of Al-Adil I. It was named *Qala'at al-Subeiba*, "Castle of the Large Cliff" in Arabic and it was supposed to prevent an attack on Damascus by the participants of the Sixth Crusade. How paradoxical this is! An enormous, powerful structure that used to protect the Muslim world from aggression and terror that came from early Western imperialists, is still there, standing almost intact, but now it appears helpless and obsolete, sadly hugging the cliff, unable to offer any protection to local people.

I am thinking about Joul Jamal. He told me, in Haifa: "Israel will be forced to return the Golan Heights, one day. But it will not do it voluntarily. Colonialists have to be forced to withdraw. Palestine and the Golan Heights, they are very important: as they are on the frontline of the war against imperialism."

I am also thinking about the great Israeli novelist Amos Oz and what I read just recently:

> "One of the things which makes this conflict particularly hard is the fact that the Israeli-Palestinian, the Israeli-Arab conflict, is essentially a conflict between two victims. The two are victims of the same oppressor. Europe, which colonized the Arab world, exploited it, humiliated it, trampled upon its culture, controlled it and used it as an imperialistic playground, is the same Europe which discriminated against the Jews, persecuted them, harassed them, and finally, mass-murdered them in an unprecedented crime of genocide. Now, you would have thought that two victims immediately develop between themselves a sense of solidarity – as, for instance, in the poetry of Berthold Brecht. But in real life, some of the worst conflicts are precisely the conflicts between two victims of the same oppressor..."

Then I reach the borderline with Lebanon: yet another terrible fence consisting of barbed wire, an electric grid, and signs warning against landmines. There is a broken tree, a monument to a dead soldier, to a lost life.

I leave the car and walk along the dreadful perimeter. I think about all those borders I saw in this part of the world, which, centuries ago, did not exist. The borders between Israel and Lebanon, between the occupied Golan Heights and Syria, between Turkey and Syria, between Jordan and Saudi Arabia, Jordan and the Palestinian West Bank, the border between Egypt and Gaza, and so many other unnecessary frontiers.

It was all thoroughly messed up. There were no easy solutions. Western imperialism was fueling conflicts in the entire region; conflicts over oil, conflicts over geo-political interests. The closest Western allies: Saudi Arabia, Israel, Qatar and Turkey – all doing their share of destructive work, reducing and dividing this ancient part of our planet into some miserable, tiny facets of land separated by endless kilometers of barbed wire.

I began photographing the border perimeter. I did it intuitively. I felt very tired and sad.

Then a Israeli military vehicle stopped near me.

"Are you OK?" Again.

At this point I had enough. I waved my hand at the endless fence, at the minefields and I shouted at patrol car: "No, I am not. Are you?"

Like near Al-Qunaitra, the soldier was just a kid, a conscript, wearing glasses.

He grimaced. He moved his lips; as if saying ‘I know, I know, so what do we do?’

Then he smiled at me, before stepping on the accelerator.

“Are you sure you will be OK?”

“I will be OK,” I replied. And I added under my breath: ‘you and I will be OK. But I am not sure about the others.’

19 February 2013

*****

22

A Landscape of Wires

ISRAEL'S WALL OF MADNESS

Co-written with LYNDA BURNSTEIN BRAYER

Golan Heights.

If someone were to say: "Israel, Palestine and Golan Heights! And you have only two seconds to describe what first comes to your mind."

Then I would immediately put into words two images that would enter my mind: "Mental asylum, and an enormous bag full of intertwined professional wires."

Mental asylum, because how else could one describe those long decades of lies, half-truths, and deceptions? How else could one describe a state of affairs when language loses its meaning, words turn into fragmented squeaks and shouts, and people just don't seem to get through to each other?

The wires would come to mind, because I am not only a writer, but also a filmmaker and photographer. Not by choice, but simply because sometimes, actually quite often, I also feel that the words do not suffice in describing reality. While working, I have to use wires, many of them. And I hate wires: all those chargers and fire-wires, the USB wires and other stuff. You put them into a bag and they tangle; you can never separate them, straighten them, and find the two ends.

And that's what this ancient part of the world has become: an enormous web of wires, coated with insanity.

Photo 6. Israeli fences at Golan Heights

***

Let's not talk politics, for a while. Let's address the most practical issues – how to move from point A to point B.

How do I go from Rafah to Ramallah? You see, even now, my Word is giving me two spelling error signals for both names, so maybe they do not really exist or they carry no significance?

How do Palestinians travel from Bethlehem to Gaza City?

How do men and women from Israeli-occupied Golan Heights go to their homeland – Syria, and how do they meet their relatives? And let's not make any technical mistakes – by international law the people of the Golan Heights are actually *de jure* living in Syria as no government has recognized the Israeli occupation.

But we all know, of course, that in order to reach Majdal al-Shams, the biggest town of the Golan Heights, one does not fly to Damascus but to Tel Aviv.

Are you getting a headache, already? Take a deep breath, as it gets much worse.

What country do Jordanians or Saudis enter if they decide to visit the West Bank? Do they enter Palestine or Israel? Saudis can hardly even pronounce the word 'Israel' (a dirty word, although, paradoxically, one of their *de facto* close allies in the region), let alone travel there. And could they, at least theoretically, enter the West Bank?

If you have an Israeli stamp in your passport, you can never visit most of the Arab countries. But the West Bank is Palestine, although it is still occupied and fragmented, and controlled by Israel. So what do you get stamped into your passport? Would a Saudi visitor get the Star of David stamped into his or her passport pages?

As a foreigner, I can land in Tel Aviv and go to Gaza or the West Bank. Israeli citizens cannot!

I remember, at the beginning of the last Intifada, I hired a car driven by an Israeli communist driver, a brilliant student of history, who dropped me at the fortified border with Gaza and right away began his epic fight with the Israeli border guards, calling them names and repeating one simple and legitimate point, in English, certainly for my entertainment. It went like this: "Assholes, we are bombing this place from mine and my parent's tax money. I have the right to go and see how my own army is murdering civilians!"

The conversation eventually mutated into Hebrew, and I couldn't follow. But I got the point.

The Israeli border guards eventually let me pass. Not that I had a ball in Gaza, mind you! Not long after the crossing, my shared taxi came under fire from an Israeli helicopter, and just a few hours later I found myself working in the notorious Shifa hospital, full of men shot through their testicles, heads and limbs.

Several days later I managed to cross into the Egyptian Sinai, while poor Palestinians in Gaza were pickled, sealed and unable to go anywhere. Their brand new airport was at first closed down, and then later destroyed.

* * *

While Israelis cannot go to the West Bank or Gaza, except in their armored vehicles and with their guns sticking out in all directions, the people of Gaza and the West Bank can go, at least in theory, to Israel, but, only if they manage to secure the necessary permits. And to get them, for the inhabitants of the West Bank, it is difficult and humiliating, while for the population of Gaza – the process is sadistic, insulting and the outcome almost certainly negative.

"They have made Palestinians fully dependent on Israel," explained Tami Sheleff who helps Palestinian people to get Israeli work permits. She is a volunteer in a Jewish volunteer organization called Border Watch. "Whether you live, or die, often depends on whether you work in Israel or not. One poor man recently told me: 'I know I should not cross illegally. If they catch me, I am finished! But I have no choice.' And even if you get a permit, life does not always get easier. Workers are at the mercy of their bosses: both Jewish and Arab, and Arabs do not necessarily make better employers. Arab collaborators are often those who hire Palestinian workers. Then, they have absolute power over them."

* * *

It is all a total mess. My annoying imaginary wires are replaced, in real life, by razor-sharp border wire, by several layers of high-voltage wire, by the wires 'decorating' the tall concrete walls dividing entire communities, dividing schools from towns, towns from towns, fields from towns.

I wrote that for the Israelis it is forbidden to enter the occupied territories, except when they come aboard their tanks. But of course even for Israeli civilians, there is one exception: they can go to Palestine if they grab Palestinian land and become 'settlers', which many of them choose to do. In that case, they can use special roads and flash their special ID cards.

* * *

As we drive on toll road 6, from Haifa to Jerusalem, my CP

colleague and the human rights lawyer Lynda Brayer, is obviously beginning to harbor a secret desire to murder me with her bare hands.

I see Palestinian towns on the left side and I demand that we leave the motorway and drive on the local road. My argument is that I need to drive through Palestinian towns, again and again, to get a better feel of the situation. Lynda's point is that 'we would never make it to Jerusalem', as there are endless checkpoints on the secondary roads passing through the West Bank.

We argue. Lynda yells: "My children googled you and they warned me that if I work with you, I would probably return home in a body bag". Satisfied with the fact that my good reputation had reached all the way to Israel and Palestine, I adopt a conciliatory approach. I ask: "Why on earth can't we take a local road, really?"

"I can't go there," she replies. "You can, but not me."

At some point we leave Route 6 and enter Route 423. And I get what I was asking for: the visuals of the insanity of the occupation. The motorway is squeezed between two tall concrete walls, so tall that the Berlin Wall would look like a midget in comparison. Watchtowers are everywhere – tall and mean – and the barbed wire is like icing on a cake, decorating all those monstrosities.

We have to go through a checkpoint. Then, a few minutes later, Lynda explains: "Here, the school you see on the left-hand side... the children have to go through an underground tunnel to reach it from their homes. There are Jewish settlements in between, and kids are not allowed to pass through them."

I see more wires, wires everywhere. I can hardly recognize the school.

* * *

From the terrace of the Tantur Ecumenical Institute in Jerusalem, there are two brilliant vistas one can enjoy: one of the Israeli Secret Service headquarters, and the other, of the monstrous wall that encircles the Palestinian city of Bethlehem.

By now I am tired of walls; sick of the walls; walls make me want to vomit.

For several days we covered the Israeli-occupied Golan Heights, with almost nothing but walls and wires. There are several layers of barbed high-voltage wire between the occupied Golan and Syria, between Israel and Lebanon. There are wires and minefields; there are rusty old wires and shiny new wires, all sorts of wires. The Israeli steel industry must be doing tremendously well!

After days and days of facing the wires, you begin wondering where the people are – they appear to be so small; they are hiding somewhere behind the wires, they are humiliated by the wires, intimidated by the wires, separated by the wires.

At some point you begin getting crazy from all those wires, you wonder how it would feel to wed a wire, to make love to a wire, to have some cute wire as a pet.

Then you know it is time to leave Israel and the occupied territories; and to leave them very quickly. Of course you can do it, any time, but the Palestinians cannot! They are stuck with those bloody wires!

* * *

During the last evening, which I spent in this part of the world, before returning to Cairo, I wandered around the old city of Jerusalem. As always, the city was magnificent, one of the greatest urban areas on Earth.

Jerusalem or Al-Quds? According to Word on my computer, it was definitely Jerusalem, because 'Al-Quds' was, as were all Palestinian cities, underlined in red, therefore shown as an error.

But even Jerusalem was divided. Here, the wires were imaginary, not real, or at least most of them.

I asked an Arab shopkeeper for the directions to the Al-Aqsa Mosque. He asked me whether I am a Muslim. I replied that I had no religion, but I wanted to see the mosque. He began shouting insults in Arabic. Then I was approached by a kid who offered to take me to the Temple Mount and to the Dome of the Rock. Some old woman overheard us, and began scolding the kid; lecturing him that taking me there would be *haram.*

Eventually, I walked alone, asking for the directions. I found the main entrance, manned by two Israeli guards. "Are you Muslim?" they asked. "No", I replied, "no religion." "You can't go," they said: "It is only for them."

I called my friends. "They will not let you through," they

explained. “A few days ago, a group of Jews entered Al-Aqsa Mosque and they tried to pray there.”

‘That would have been normal during the Caliphate of Cordoba’; I was going to utter, but changed my mind. These were very different times.

I felt the mistrust and the heavy, stiff atmosphere all over the old city.

At some point I reached one of the gates leading to the Temple Mount. A sympathetic guard let me come as close as the entrance. “Don’t cross. Don’t enter.” Perimeters were everywhere, some imaginary, some real; and prohibitions, piling on top of each other.

To reach the Western Wall or ‘Wailing Wall’, one has to go through an elaborate metal detector, through real security.

As I walk, I wonder whether this city will ever live in peace, whether it will ever feel comfortable.

Near the Wall, in a small café, I ask for directions. I am meeting Lynda at Salah al Din Street, which is in East Jerusalem. The owner gives me a dirty look. “No idea where it is!” he replies, rudely.

I walk, and then I ask an Arab-looking vendor for directions. “Just walk straight, all the way to the end, for fifteen minutes,” he replies. “Exit through the Damascus Gate and follow the ancient wall.”

I follow his advice. I exit; I walk through the Damascus Gate and then I see the Wall – beautiful and historic. But I don’t care. At this point, to me, a wall is a wall. They all make me feel sick, nauseated. My stomach is rebelling, I feel like throwing up.

I lower my gaze; I apologize to this wonderful wall, which is part of a UNESCO-designated world heritage site. But there is nothing I can do – this wall is one too many. I walk, quickly, towards the street named after the great anti-imperialist Sultan who, many centuries ago, drove the Europeans from these tragic lands – the Sultan Salah al Din.

* * *

“Let’s dash to Bethlehem; to Palestine,” I suggest, to Lynda, when she picks me up with the car in front of a police station.

"I can't," she says. Then, after a few moments of hesitation "OK, let's; I know back roads."

It is dark and we have to stop on the highway, at one more of those sophisticated checkpoint. We make a U-Turn, then exit the motorway; drive up to the hill. The police stop us. Lynda speaks Hebrew. An elaborate hat is covering her headscarf. They think we are two Jewish settlers and they let us pass.

"I used to live here," explains Lynda. "I was the lawyer who set up the 'Society of St. Yves; the Catholic Human Rights Center'."

We make it. Now we are driving through Bethlehem and Lynda is swearing. "They changed everything. All these roads are one-way, now. I don't recognize anything."

But now I am just laughing. After days in the Golan Heights, after all those walls, the relics of occupation, and after the latest gadgets of the occupation, it is the most logical thing to do, to end my work here – in Palestine – at night.

"We will now splurge," Lynda informs me. "Let's inject something into the Palestinian economy. It is my treat. Let's visit the magnificent Jacir Palace hotel, built during the Ottoman Empire and more than one hundred years old."

She shows me her Human Rights Center from which the Roman Catholic Church summarily removed her because Israel thought she was "hostile"! And we stop for a few seconds at some roundabout.

Then I see it. "Damn it!" I scream. There is THE WALL, the Israeli wall, from the Palestinian side. It is enormous, it is bigger than life, and it is sicker than any wall I have ever seen before. There is a watchtower incorporated into it. Somehow it looks like a piranha, only without the teeth!

There is graffiti. "This Is Illegally Occupied Land: State of Palestine. 194."

Then a few more signs like: Leave This Palestine – "End Up Terror!"

And: "Revolution Started Here! And will continue..."

I think about Egypt, about Port Said, Tahrir Square and the fights in front of the Presidential Palace in Cairo. I think about President Morsi and his government, which, with absolute spite for the Palestinian people, just recently inundated the tunnel connecting Gaza and Sinai. He destroyed the only lifeline that the people of Gaza had been counting on. 'What solidarity!' I think. Revolution Started Here!

In Jacir Palace, which now belongs to the Intercontinental chain, a waiter – Hassan – tries to put into perspective all this insanity, the restrictions, prohibitions, and divisions of the occupation.

"When I do, I travel on my Palestinian passport," he replies to our question. "I cannot travel to Israel without a permit."

What about to the capital of Palestine – to Ramallah?

"I can go, via Wadi Naar, the 'Valley of Fire', through Israeli checkpoints. It can easily take almost 2 hours, although it is very near as the crow flies."

Lynda mutters that just to get from Ramallah to Jerusalem for those who have a permit; it can sometimes take three hours! One way!

What about when you want to go to Gaza?

"That of course is quite a different story. We cannot go, unless we get an Israeli permit, which is close to impossible."

"We – Israelis – cannot go at all," says Linda. "You can go, in theory, but you have to get a permit and that requires the effort of Sisyphus."

"Do you know anyone from here; from Bethlehem, who has managed to travel to Gaza?" I ask.

"No, I don't," replies the waiter.

We are told that during the high season, this magnificent Ottoman-style hotel is filled with Russian, Korean and Japanese visitors. But there are hardly any Arabs that come here. Can they come or can't they?

My head is spinning from all those wires, walls and restrictions.

We walk by two Palestinian police officers.

"Take a photo," says Lynda. I photograph the two young boys in uniforms, helmets in their hands. They smile; they even pose for us.

"Welcome to Palestine!" they repeat again and again.

"Thank you," we reply, as our eyes fall on the humongous Israeli watchtower just a few steps away.

Later, late at night, inside the car, as we are approaching the Israeli checkpoint before entering Jerusalem, I ask Lynda:

"When you are in Tel Aviv or in Haifa, you may shut yourself off from all this reality and live in one of the richest and the most comfortable countries on Earth, right?"

"That's correct," she replies. "If you forget about what Israel is doing to the Palestinians and others, you can have your high culture, sophistication, and comfort."

"Do people know? Do they care?"

"Most of them live in denial," she replies. "They prefer to live in what is called here "the bubble"! I consider them selfish. They prefer not to see, not to know."

For a while we drive in silence.

"All those walls that we saw," I say. "All those wires... It will not be easy to dismantle them."

"Not easy at all," she agrees.

"That's where non-fiction fails," I suggest. "So many people know, in theory, that this is wrong. We can give them numbers, analyses, UN resolutions backed by the whole world, but blocked by the US... We can state and repeat all those moral conclusions, over and over again... But such an approach has failed for years and decades. Nothing changes."

"So what would help?"

"I have no idea. Poems, songs, films, a fiction..." I think out loud. "The wall, The Walls; they don't feel real, do they? They don't exist, do they? If they do, it would be too insane. Maybe we should try to prove that they exist only in our imagination; that they are not real, just a nightmare. And if we manage to prove it, they would, eventually, disappear..."

"Try it," she says.

"It is just an idea," I say. "We are all running out of schemes, aren't we?"

* * *

Departing Israel, I felt suddenly loved, understood and appreciated.

Two Mossad (or whichever agency they belonged to) agents wanted to know all about my life. About how many children I have, all about my marriages, and divorces.

They wanted to know everything. They studied my passport, my press cards, my residency cards, my driver's licenses and my ground passes.

"On this," one of them said, with a melancholic smile, pointing at the ID of the Foreign Correspondent's Club of Thailand, "You don't look like yourself..."

"You know," I confessed, "This one was taken 9 years ago... I have aged."

"Oh no," they both began consoling me. "You look great! It's just that the photo somehow does not match..."

We discussed my childhood, my youth, my books, and my films.

They asked questions, and they listened. I have never been in a relationship with any woman who has asked so many important and personal questions and who would listen so attentively to all my answers. These people were even taking notes!

It all lasted some 30 minutes, at least. Their boss arrived and asked me more questions. We cracked some jokes. They acted as if they were my mates.

After they concluded that they had learnt enough about me, they allowed me to proceed towards the Royal Jordanian counter. I felt a bit disappointed: I was beginning to enjoy our conversation about my books and films. But by then I already felt pure; moved almost to tears. Like after a confession. Not that I know much about confessions, as I have no religion... But that's how I imagined it must feel...

"Now", I thought, "all is pronounced and forgiven. All sins have disappeared into thin air."

So now, dudes, we can start from the very beginning. I will kick your backsides, with all my strength, until you let your colonies go free. Until we meet again; until the next confession!

"You can return the car", I sent a text message to Lynda, my CounterPunch mate, my 'Jewish mother'. "And tell your children you are coming home in one piece, not in a body bag."

22 February 2013

*****

23

Long Live Revolution...Damn It!

CHAVEZ'S TRIUMPH

Nairobi.

When we lose people that are indispensible to us, nothing may change on the surface: we are still walking, eating, sleeping, working, even fighting. The void, the gaping hole is what dominates our hearts and our souls.

Yesterday, the President of Venezuela and one of the greatest revolutionaries in the history of mankind – Hugo Chavez – passed away, and the world is still moving by inertia. Buildings did not collapse, continents did not sink, and the wars and misery ravaging many parts of the world did not stop.

Yet something changed. Three beautiful muses that have been inspiring so many millions all over the world, turned into widows, at least for one day or two. Their names are: Love, Faith and Hope.

Some ask: is it really wise to make an entire country, an entire revolution dependent, and reliant on one single man?

My answer is simple: people like Chavez are born infrequently, too rarely. It would be a historical anomaly for two giants of his size to live in the same period of time, in the same city, and even in the same country

***

Yet his words and deeds were simple and pragmatic: poor people have to be housed, fed, educated and given medical care, and above all, they have to be armed with dignity. And the wealthy world, which became rich through plunder, colonial expansions and unmatchable brutality, has to stop terrorizing and looting; the countries of Europe and North America have to be forced to behave like members of the international community consisting of states with equal rights, instead of what they have been accustomed to for decades and centuries: a bunch of thugs living above the law.

Hugo Chavez was a man who appeared to come from a different era, where Western propaganda, indoctrination and surveillance had not yet broken the free spirit of men and women. He stood tall, spoke loudly and coherently, naming names, and pointing fingers. He was not afraid of his own people: he drank gallons of coffee and talked to them from the balcony of the Presidential Palace, and at street corners.

"And it smells of sulfur still today," he laughed, at the UN, after George W. Bush left the stage. He was not the only one who smelt it, but he was the only one who dared to say it.

In his universe, no tyrant, no hypocrite was above the law, and immune from his attacks. He was not scared to say what he believed, publicly, even about such characters like the King of Spain, or the President of the United States of America.

***

Not everybody liked him, not all 'natural allies' stood by him.

It is mainly because he spoke the truth when others did not dare to. It is because he was constantly taking action while most of the others who were 'resisting' the global regime, were content with shouting at the television and exchanging conspiracy theories through electronic chats, while taking no risks. It is because, in a way, he became the bad conscience of those who have been playing it both ways: simultaneously criticizing power and collaborating with it.

Those who were morally bankrupt hated him the most. Western mainstream media, and Arab mainstream media like Al-Jazeera, detested him relentlessly.

Chavez wrote history as one writes an epic and daring poem – with his own mind, heart and flesh. He lifted the flag with his own hands; he straightened his back, shouted a few essential words to the wind, and walked forwards. He was always at the front. He never hid behind the backs of others. This is how the legendary Samurais fought, or closer home – the great warriors of the Andes.

How few, how very few now dare! One can make a list that would fit into a handful of pages. And most of those who do dare – often fall, silently and anonymously. And those who fall even for one single moment, from exhaustion or suffering from wounds, are chased and bayonetted by the regime; bayonetted mercilessly, to death.

President Hugo Chavez to the people of Venezuela, or Commander Chavez to some brave men and women all over the world, wrote his poem while standing on thin ice. Decisions he made were never simple; never comfortable. His life was always in danger.

To be a young officer, a paratrooper/philosopher, and to attempt a coup in a country locked in a horrible embrace with the North was not easy. But his country, his beloved la patria, was like a woman who had been raped and then forced to offer her body to the same men who ravished her. To free her, that beloved land of his, from such misery and humiliation, one had to fight decisively, with all the means available. There was no time to theorize.

And he fought. And was captured and imprisoned. But his courage gained him admiration and support unknown in his country for centuries.

That suffering woman he was ready to die for – Venezuela – finally opened her arms; decided to believe again, to hope, to dream one more time. She embraced him, pressed him against her body with all her strength. And then, with one powerful stroke she broke the walls of his prison, and elevated him, almost literally, on the outstretched arms of her people, to the Presidential Palace.

Three muses, three celestial beings, stood by him throughout that mortal fight for genuine freedom of Venezuela and Latin America; during those endless days and nights he was locked in a dungeon:

Love – for Venezuela, for Latin America, for humanity itself.

Faith – in justice, in his strength and in the vigor and determination of his people.

Hope – which whispered in his ear, relentlessly, that the present brutal arrangement of the World is not final; that it could be fought and changed.

And they won!

Venezuela washed tears from her face; she put on her modest but clean dress, and stood up, at the northern tip of South America, stunningly beautiful and despite the past, proud and daring.

Chavez and his people won. His three Muses won. Entire Latin America fell silent. Then it cheered. Hundreds of years of servitude were over. All unified, this beautiful continent was finally liberated. Because, as we all know by now, people when united and inspired, when aiming at great goals and ideals, are always victorious, no matter how immense is the sacrifice!

***

Optimism, enthusiasm and determination: there could be no more dangerous or deadlier enemies to the present inhuman global dictatorship, which is imposed on the world by the Western colonial and neo-colonial nations.

The Empire is spreading nihilism, fragmentation, financial and moral corruption, fear, and compliance with mainstream thoughts and 'ideas', manufactured by its ideologues, propagandists and the advertising industry. Life is reduced to a form, which devours all substance. A depressing breed of individualism, egotism, passivity, and obedience is constantly promoted and advertised.

The Venezuelan Revolution offered exactly the opposite: optimism, solidarity, hope, and a great opportunity to fight for, to create and to live for humanity as a whole. Against some callous Hollywood-style horror movie, it placed simplicity and beauty, against Armageddon, a few simple flowers and the promise to return to the essence of humanism.

***

I write this dispatch in Nairobi, in Kenya; in Africa, which is being ravaged and chained once again. Every word causes me pain and I know that the pain is coming unmistakably from the direction of Venezuela. The pain is sharp; it is immense. Only love can hurt like this; only true love.

But there is no time for laments and tears. One false step, one month, even one day of letting down our guards, and everything that Chavez and Venezuela fought for, everything that we fought for, may disappear in one simple instant.

Photo 7. Here nobody surrenders!

Evo Morales, the President of Bolivia, declared: “Chavez is More Alive than Ever”.

That is true. But our determination to support, to defend the Latin American Revolution, should also be more alive than ever. Chavez did not believe in goals only, he believed in journey, in the process – en el proceso. That is what the revolution is: determined, selfless, an optimistic journey; it is the indefatigable fight against fascism – for a better world, and for justice.

During that long but beautiful journey, some people fall, but then others rise and lift up the banners. Those who fall will be never left behind: they will be carried in our hearts and in our songs, because their achievements are everlasting.

So back from where I began: when we lose a person who appeared indispensable, we may double from pain. It is only human. But then it is our duty to straighten our backs again, remembering the way Hugo Chavez did. There is Caracas, Havana,

La Paz, Buenos Aires, Montevideo, Quito, Managua and so many other beloved cities behind us; depending on us for their defense. Asuncion in Paraguay has already fallen, and so has Tegucigalpa, Honduras. We cannot afford to lose more!

Human life is short, but dreams of humanism, and the love for humanity, are eternal. And one can only love humanity and fight for it with a straight back; never doubled over, and never on one's knees.

The man who freed Venezuela is no more. But she will go forward, no doubt, with him inside her heart, with his words on her lips.

Yesterday, a true hero of the Latin American Revolution, President Hugo Chavez, fell. And long live freedom, long live Venezuela, long live Latin America, and the Revolution, damn it!

6 March 2013

*****

24

Out and About in Zimbabwe's Capital

HARARE: IS IT REALLY THE WORST CITY ON EARTH?

For a change, I don't want to discuss politics. I don't want to debate whether big bad Mugabe is actually an African national hero, as many on this continent believe, or some brutal dictator, as we are told relentlessly by the BBC, The Economist and virtually the entire Western establishment media.

'Data' about Zimbabwe is developed somewhere, to serve Western political interests, and then it is recycled, repeated by hundreds of websites all over the Internet.internet. Old reports are not updated when the situation improves. Incorrect statistics are hardly challenged.

I don't want to discuss all this now. One day I will, I promise, and in detail.

* * *

Now the world is in turmoil: President Hugo Chavez is dead; he passed away or, as some believe, he was assassinated. And this poor and ravaged continent – Africa – is experiencing the latest wave of carnage sponsored and organized by several Western nations. From West Africa to Somalia, from Mali to DR Congo, flames, tanks, aircraft, drones, and also misery and hopelessness are once again killing millions.

As Chavez, the proud leader of the global opposition and a favorite punchbag of Western propaganda, was put to rest, I took off from Nairobi. Three hours later I found myself approaching Harare International Airport, with endless plains and fantastic rock formations under the wing of the Brazilian-made Embraer of Kenyan Airways.

I had to do it; I had to come, as a gesture, as my tribute to the Latin American revolution, as my internationalist duty towards Africa. Instead of mourning Chavez, I decided to continue working for the revolution that he triggered and which I have always tried to be part of.

'The world's least livable city on Earth', I read before coming here, 'The worst city on Earth'. There were expat surveys, surveys by The Economist, and at some point surveys that 'leniently' depicted Harare as the 4th worst city on Earth, not the worst, in 2012.

I am used to working in warzones and in the most hopeless and dangerous slums. I am used to the cities of the sub-Continent, of DR Congo, of Haiti. I survived many Western outposts all over the world, officially glorified but collapsed urban centers like Jakarta, Nairobi, Kampala, Djibouti, Phnom Penh, and Cairo.

I was not afraid of 'horrible' Harare. But I was not convinced by reports coming out of the West. That's why I decided to return to Zimbabwe. Once again, I would use my own eyes and ears and my own brain, challenging the official propaganda emanating from London and Washington.

* * *

Harare International Airport is simple but modern. The staff appear to be unmotivated and slow, but they are friendly and in possession of great sense of humor. There is no tension and there are no insults, no power games, as at Nairobi airport, or in Phnom Penh. No throwing of passport in your face and no fingerprinting and photographing, as is done at all third world airports that are known for sending intelligence to the West; from Bangkok to Nairobi.

After I purchase my visa-on-arrival, the immigration officers can't find change. I have to wait for five minutes. While I am waiting, we chat about the Kenyan elections.

Soon after, I am driven through the green and quiet streets, some carrying fairly interesting names like Benghazi and Julius Nyerere, towards Harare's modern and elegant city center.

Right from the beginning, something just does not feel right. The worst city on Earth: I search for sandbags and gunners like in New Delhi or Mumbai, for gangs roaming the streets like in Colon in Panama, for the garbage-clogged rivers and horrid pollution of Jakarta or Alexandria. I see nothing like that here; no appalling slums and no burning fires, real or metaphorical.

There are a few beggars on the sidewalks, but fewer than there are in New York or Paris. The pavement is often broken, uneven, even potholed, but it is nothing compared to Kampala.

And then, as I slowly approach my hotel in the center of the city, it strikes me that, at least through the window of a car, Harare could be described as a beautiful city! Of course, it is not as stunning as Cape Town, it is on a much smaller scale, but in a very modest way it is very attractive.

I pinch myself. I blink a few times, quickly. I ask my driver to slap my face, but he refuses.

"Why, sir?" he appears bewildered.

"But..." I mumble. "Harare appears to be a very nice place."

"It is," replies the driver.

"But..." I continue to wonder, "It is supposed to be the most terrible town on Earth."

"Who says?"

"The newspapers in the West... The reports, surveys..."

"Oh," the driver smiled. "Then we should slap their faces, not yours. For lying, you know..."

* * *

I suggest this: let's not talk about the President and about the past and political present of the country. Let me just take you for a long walk through Harare, so you can get to know the city described by our propagandists as the worst, absolutely the worst, in the world. And let me throw a few images into the bargain.

Just stay by my side and let's walk, for several days, searching for the truth.

But before we stroll, let's listen to some voices from the UK and the US – those that are manufacturing public opinion all over the world.

On September 7th, 2011, iAfrica reported:

> "A top research group on Thursday rated Zimbabwe's capital as the worst of 140 world cities in which to live. The British-based Economist Intelligence Unit said its researchers excluded cities in Libya, Iraq and other war-zones. Harare, where power and water outages occur daily, scored a 38 percent "livability rating," the group said.

The group said the threat of civil unrest and the availability of public healthcare and public transport in Harare were intolerable. Energy and water supplies were undesirable, it said, calling phones and Internet services uncomfortable..."

In 2009 the BBC claimed that Zimbabwe's women had an average life expectancy of 34 years and that men on average did not live past 37. That information was duplicated by countless websites.

Other BBC reports were republished word for word by thousands of news and reference outlets, including Wikipedia:

> "The health system has more or less collapsed. By the end of November 2008, three of Zimbabwe's four major hospitals had shut down, along with the Zimbabwe Medical School, and the fourth major hospital had two wards and no operating theatres working. Due to hyperinflation, those hospitals still open are not able to obtain basic drugs and medicines."

Predictably, the official propaganda news agency of the UK threw in colorful words like 'genocide' and 'tragedy', and pre-selected quotes from several medics who blamed the situation on the Zimbabwean government.

Not one glimpse of diversity, no arguments from 'the other side'.

Not even a word about what the majority of those in the Southern part of Africa believe, or even what some members of the Western establishment have recently confirmed.

According to African Globe [November 17th, 2012]:

> "The United States government has, for the first time, admitted that the illegal sanctions it imposed destroyed Zimbabwe's economy and were hurting ordinary people.

Incoming US Ambassador to Zimbabwe David Bruce Wharton made the admission yesterday at a media round-table discussion in Harare and pledged to work with authorities in Zimbabwe and the US to normalize relations.

The admission comes after the World Diamond Council said it was also engaging the US government and the European Union to lift sanctions they imposed on Marange diamonds, despite Zimbabwe having received the Kimberly Process Certification Scheme nod to export the gems."

But I promised: no politics... Let's just walk and see.

* * *

The 'Trauma Centre & Hospital, Harare' is in a quiet part of the city and it could easily qualify as one of the most elegant medical facilities I have seen elsewhere in the world. It is stylish; full of artwork, and at the same time high-tech and immaculately clean.

I greet two representatives working at the reception area. One of them is Ana – a young, sophisticated lady who came to Zimbabwe from Serbia.

"I came here to see whether Harare has any operation theatres," I mumble, suddenly feeling embarrassed. "You see, there are some reports that say that the capital shut down all of its hospitals, or at least all its operation theatres."

"Now it's out," I thought, expecting blows. Instead I receive a big and welcoming smile.

"Would you like some water, of coffee? We can show you around. Before you came, we had already had a film crew here that was investigating the same issue."

I am taken to a high-tech emergency room, equipped with the latest technology. Then I am asked to take off my shoes, and to change my clothes. The next thing I realize, I am wearing a white coat and being taken through a sterilization room into two operation theatres that look more like the interior of a space ship. Surgery rooms are not the places where I would normally choose to spend my evenings, but these are damn beautiful surgery rooms! And, above all, despite what they say in London, they actually do exist!

"Let me take one photo of you, standing next to the operation theatre, so they don't say in England or the US that the images are pirated from some medical journal," Ana says laughing.

"We have specialized Laminar flow theatres used for Key Hole surgery, and Orthopedics..." I keep taking notes. I have no clue what is she talking about, but what I see looks definitely impressive. Ana continues: "Thoracic and Vascular Surgeons are available at the Hospital. We have neurosurgeons on call..."

After the tour I am invited to drink coffee with Dr Vivek Solanki, the owner of the hospital.

"I should not be speaking about the competition," he smiles, "but in Harare we have plenty of operational hospitals, with decent to excellent operation theatres. It is all propaganda, about the medical care in this country. Of course, there was a very short and tough period around 2008, but it did not last long."

I ask doctor Solanki whether this super modern and efficient hospital is only for the richest of the rich.

"I have introduced a new concept here," he explains, passionately. "Of course this is a private hospital, but we are determined to serve the Zimbabwean people. So, in contrast to what happens in the US, here, when an ambulance, taxi or relatives bring a patient to us, a patient who needs emergency treatment... no matter how complicated the case is, we treat the patient, regardless of whether he or she has money or insurance. We never ask, and never check whether he or she can pay. We stabilize the patient first, and only after he or she is out of danger, a choice is given: if he or she chooses to pay, we keep the patient. If not, we transfer him or her to a state hospital, and charge nothing for saving their life. We also treat babies under 6 months, as well as the elderly over 70, for free."

"We lose money," whispers Ana, expressing outrage, half-jokingly. "But he owns the place, and there is nothing we can do about it."

"I became a doctor thanks to the President," volunteers Doctor Solanki. "The education in this country is free. I am Zimbabwean, a third generation Indian. I received help when I needed it. Now I have to give back to my country. I build hospitals. I am a doctor. I know how to cure people, save lives. That's what I have to do."

In the car, as I am being driven towards the city center, I receive a text message from Nairobi: "Life expectancy in Zimbabwe for women is 34 and for men it is 37 – is incorrect. Even according to the CIA Factbook 2012, the life expectancy at birth in Zimbabwe was 51.82 est., higher than South Africa, where it stands at 49.41 est."

"Low life expectency is all because of AIDS," sighs my driver. "That nose-dived our life expectancy. But you know, things are getting much better here, lately, and everyone who is honest would tell you that, no matter what they think about the President. For instance, we get all that anti-retroviral treatment for free here. We also get free condoms, as well as plenty of information from the government."

"They also get help from China," I am told later, by one of the UN staffers working in Harare. "China provides doctors and free medicine. It has helped this country a lot."

Suffering from Western sanctions, the Zimbabwean economy collapsed. Since then it has been undergoing a slow but steady recovery.

I am sorry, again; we said 'no politics'. We said 'let's just go for a walk'. So here is my arm. Let's resume our stroll slowly through the city.

Right next to my hotel is the entrance to a magnificent swimming complex, Les Brown Municipal Pool. I don't know whether it is public or not, and I forgot to ask, but it appears to be. Right next to it are the Harare Gardens, a beautiful English-style park with people resting on the grass, enjoying picnics, and reading.

To have such public and 'open' areas like parks is unthinkable in Jakarta, where there is only one public green area of a substantial size, MONAS. And Jakarta is a monster with 12 million inhabitants, while Harare has a population of only two million. Two million that enjoy several magnificent parks and gardens, wide sidewalks and art exhibited in public areas, all over the city.

But let's not forget – Harare is a 'defiant' nation, a country that refuses to fall on its knees and to salute its tormentors. While Jakarta and Phnom Penh are the capitals of two market fundamentalist countries. They are choking on their own fumes, they have almost nothing that can be defined as public left, but in the eyes of the Western regime, they can't be as bad as Harare, Caracas, Havana or Beijing! They enjoy great immunity from uncomfortable questions; as well as full, hearty support from 'business-religion' publications like The Economist.

There are also almost no public spaces in other African capitals that have been serving as Western client states for year and decades, like Kampala, Kigali, Addis Ababa and Cairo, although, in the latter, at least, people are able to gather on the city's bridges.

But Harare, we are told, is the worst city on Earth!

There seems to be no crime in the city, and there are no disagreements about this. Black Zimbabweans and White Zimbabweans, foreign experts, cops and doctors – I spoke to all those groups – they all say that Harare is one of the safest cities on the African continent. In Nairobi or Tegucigalpa, in Port-au-Prince, you cannot walk down the street because of the fear of violent crime. The level of danger for Indian women in New Delhi and other cities of the Sub-Continent is almost as high as it is in war-zones.

But it is Harare – one of the safest cities in sub-Saharan Africa – that is depicted as the 'least livable' city on Earth.

I look around and I notice that the people lying on the grass, or, at least, many of them, are reading newspapers and magazines. Why do they do it? First of all, because they are literate, because this is the most literate nation, on the entire continent, from the Suez to the Cape of Good Hope. According to All Africa on 14th July 2010:

> "Zimbabwe has been ranked as the country with the highest literacy rate in Africa taking over from Tunisia, the latest UNDP Statistical Digest shows. Tunisia has held pole position for years with Zimbabwe second best and number one in Sub-Saharan Africa. Zimbabwe's literacy level currently stands at 92 percent, up from 85 percent while Tunisia remains on 87 percent."

"It shows how literate, how educated Zimbabwe is," I am told by a senior UN official working for UNEP in Nairobi, who for obvious reasons does not want to be identified. "When you work with Zimbabweans, things get done. Things are working there. It is real tragedy that so many top professionals had to leave for South Africa during the crises. Zimbabwe is a victim of a defamation campaign conducted by Western media outlets. The same could be said about President Jacob Zuma of South Africa."

* * *

Could it be that things are not so bad in Harare? There are several decent hospitals, preventive medical care, the highest literacy rate, some of the lowest crime rates on the continent, and public spaces all around.

Of course there are recurring electric blackouts in Harare, but not more frequent than in Nairobi, Kampala, Kigali, Lagos, Addis Ababa, Jakarta, Dhaka, Colombo, to mention just a few places. The water supply could be better, but it can hardly be defined as a tragedy as it definitely is in Indonesia, the Sub-Continent and most of Africa. The government is short of cash, and it has serious problems with garbage collection and recycling. But despite that, Harare still looks very clean by African standards and more at par with much wealthier Kuala Lumpur, than with cities like Manila or Surabaya.

Not influenced by horrible reports coming from the UK and the US, left to my own impartial judgment, I could easily believe that this is one of the most livable towns in the Southern Hemisphere.

But that's exactly the point: I am not supposed to be left to my own judgment. I am not supposed to evaluate objectively, what my eyes are seeing and my ears hearing. I am supposed to be pre-conditioned, told how to see things and even how to analyze what I see.

Mr. Hezekiel Dlamini, Advisor for Communication and Information at the UNESCO Office in Harare, is originally from Swaziland, but he was based for many years in Ghana, France and Kenya, before accepting a post in Zimbabwe. He blends in well with this country, which he finds 'beautiful' and 'comfortable':

> "It is much quieter here than in Nairobi," he explains. "In Harare, culture is very important and very diverse, and interesting. You can get true, vibrant and traditional local culture in the center and in other parts of the city, or you can drive to Borrowdale just a few miles away, as well as to other suburbs, and there you get what is common in the South African white suburbs or in Cape Town – all those luxury malls, movie theatres showing the latest releases, posh cafes."

We are sitting in a simple but comfortable café, near the glass wall of the National Art Gallery. It is quiet, almost serene here. Several impressive art exhibitions are taking place inside the institution, while the vast sculpture park is dotted with dating couples dressed in their best attire, sitting on the grass. Like in Nicaraguan parks, young people come here to hold hands and whisper intimate confessions in the shade of impressive artwork, instead of sitting in some stereotypical chain cafe in the middle of depressing and dull shopping malls, listening to banal music or loud announcements.

"You can eat local food, you can eat in several Chinese places, and there are Indian restaurants, Portuguese restaurants, and even a few sushi places."

"Are whites really suffering here, as we are told by the Western media?" I ask.

"Of course not!" Hezekiel laughs. "Just drive to any of their suburbs. Go to Sam Levy's Village or to any other big mall. You will see – things are still segregated, not because of the government, but because of the white minority. They have all they want in their suburbs; they have managed to create their own universe. If I bring my daughters to a white school, they will say 'no'. They will not tell me that it is because I am black African; they will argue that the school is full. And the government can do nothing about the situation."

I drive to posh suburbs equipped with golf courses, sports clubs, beautiful pedestrian malls, supermarkets stuffed with the most exquisite food products imported from South Africa and Europe, with elegant cafes and designer stores selling Hermes and LV garments.

It is all here. By then, I understand nothing.

Harare has everything! How could anyone think for one second that this is hell on Earth?

I said 'no politics'; not this time... But let me at least ask couple of rhetorical questions: is there any reason why this country is suffering from sanctions and humiliation, from vicious propaganda and demonization, other than because it has decided to re-distribute its land; or, because it made an attempt to stop Rwanda from performing yet another coup in DR Congo on behalf of Western companies and governments; or because it co-operates with China in the mining of diamonds; or because it is firmly rejecting Western imperialism?

"What about misery, what about slums?" I ask my friend Hezekiel, a few hours later.

"There is Mbare slum," he explains. "But it is not as terrible as Kibera or Mathare in Nairobi."

I drive there. Mbare is not a friendly suburb, but it is small, at most one-kilometer square but probably much smaller. It looks more like the South Bronx than Cité Soleil in Port-au-Prince. It has basic infrastructure, including sports facilities. While places like Kibera slum in Nairobi are housing hundreds of thousands, some say one million people, crammed in inhuman conditions; the population of Mbare must be at most ten or twenty thousand.

The historic Harare Mountain and Fort Salisbury are just a five minutes drive from Mbare. There is yet another public park there and a commanding view of the historic city center and the impressive city skyline.

There is an old, British commemorative sign, which refers to settlers as 'pioneers'.

"Pioneers!" laughs my driver, sarcastically. "Some pioneers!"

A few young men are busy doing push-ups. It is all very tranquil, and somehow comforting. I have no idea why, but it feels like being back in South America, in some part of it.

"No security issues?" I smile.

"Look," my driver gets started. He has a critical mind and a wonderful sense of humor. "In South Africa, if you pull out a 100 Rand banknote in some public place, you could get killed. There, that amount of money can fill a few shopping bags, easily. In Zimbabwe, you pull out 100 Rand note; people will laugh at you, because it is worth nothing. Things are so expensive." The group of athletes stops their push-ups and begins to laugh.

"You are right," one of them says. "You are so right."

Soon, a small circle is formed and people plunge passionately into discussion about food prices, security and the upcoming elections. There is no fear like in Rwanda or Uganda, no tension like in Djibouti, Kenya or Ethiopia; in all those Western client states.

Nobody calls me names, nobody points fingers at me; I am included in their conversation.

They love their country. Dollarization made prices high, and Western embargos crippled the economy. But people are resilient and tough, and very kind at the same time.

"Why have you come?" one of the athletes asks.

"Because they keep writing, in the West, that Harare is the worst city on Earth," I reply. "And I know it is a lie. So I came to write about it – to say that it is a lie."

"Why? What do you care? We all know it is a lie. This is a very nice city, isn't it? But we feel powerless. They write those slanderous things about us, and as a result, nobody comes... Tourism has collapsed. Our great ancient cities, our national parks – all are empty now. Who wants to come to a country with such a horrible reputation?"

"Why did you come to dispute those lies?" A second athlete asks.

I think for a while, I am silent. Then I tell them: "In Venezuela, far away from here, President Hugo Chavez died... Or he was murdered. We still don't know. When it happened, I was in Nairobi, but Nairobi is a Western outpost and to be there did not feel right. I needed to fight – to fight against so many things, especially against the propaganda that comes from the West. South America is very far, and I decided to come to Zimbabwe, at least for a few days."

There was a silence, long and deep. And then one of the athletes comes close to me, hugs me and says: "Good you are here. I understand. Thank you for coming."

At night I go to 'Book Café' to hear traditional Zimbabwean music. And close to Midnight I manage to get into the immense Harare International Convention Center (HICC), where more than 6,000 people are awaiting the appearance of one of the greatest South African artists – Zahara – a musician, songwriter and a poet.

In this 'most terrible city on Earth', those thousands of people are roaring and dancing to Zahara's rhythms, whispering her lyrics; while there are no fights, no skirmishes, no littering, no rapes, no violence.

I walk back to my hotel, in the middle of the night, alone, safe, endlessly impressed, suddenly in love with the city that has been standing tall despite the embargos, intrigues, and slander coming from the old and new colonial masters of the world.

As I stroll, briskly, through the wide and well-lit sidewalks of the Zimbabwean capital city, I think about the Cuban medical brigades. These people – brilliant and selfless doctors and medics – that have been deployed wherever the need for internationalist help arises, be it due to a conflict or a natural disaster.

This is exactly what we – writers, filmmakers, and journalists – need to create, to encourage, to staff: International Investigative Brigades, units that uncover the outrageous lies, propaganda and nihilism, those appalling byproducts of the regime and the Empire.

We need to form them very soon, before it gets too late.

Meanwhile, although I was walking alone, I did not feel lonely.

In my mind, I kept repeating to some abstract reader of mine: "Thank you for joining me; for taking this long and wonderful walk. Not everything is lost, yet. Not everyone is sold. There are millions of people, many countries that are still resisting, upright, not on their knees."

15 March 2013

*****

25

EAST AFRICAN OPPOSITION, REALLY?

In the three Western outposts of the eastern part of Africa – Uganda, Rwanda and Kenya – the opposition has either been totally smashed or is rotting in jail. Alternatively, it has 'ceased to exist'.

In East Africa, those who are in power and those who want to be, never challenge the supreme wisdom of market-fundamentalism.

There is no ideology here. Elections are fights between gladiators (Kenya) or of one gladiator against unarmed infants (Rwanda).

Corrupt politician A, or corrupt politician B (both campaigning along ethnic lines and on behalf of their mercantile interests), 'compete' over who will be the one to dip his snout into a generous portion of the caviar-seasoned feast at the end of the 'democratic electoral process'.

It is a well known fact that in Kenya, for instance, victorious politicians do not scream: 'Socialism or death!' or 'Let's liberate our people from misery!' They would not even dream of shouting something like 'Down with neo-colonialism; and down with the foreign bases that are scarring our soil!' The accepted phrase here is poignantly modest: 'It's our time to eat!'

In the recent Kenyan elections, not one single Presidential candidate dared to raise the essential issues that would most certainly cause the wrath of Western powers: comparing the virtues of capitalism versus the virtues of socialism in a poor country like Kenya, or unveiling the work of neo-colonialism on African soil; or, more concretely, opposing the RAF base in Kenya and the introduction of drones. Nor did they, the candidates, protest against the US, British and Israeli intelligence agencies that are allegedly kidnapping, even "disappearing", Muslim people – mainly fishermen – off the Swahili coast; nor did they promise to stop the senseless invasion by Kenyan troops of Somalia, something that has been fully orchestrated in Washington and London and dutifully implemented by Nairobi's political and military lackeys.

"Kenya is a hostage to foreign interests," I was told, in Kisumu, by one of the MP candidates, Edris Omondi, just a few days before the elections in March 2013. "We are suffering from a full-blown case of neo-colonialism here, in Kenya. If you want to know what Kenya is doing in Somalia, you have to first ask: "what are the interests of the West in this part of the world?"

Such 'revolutionary talk', however, would never reach the Kenyan electorate through their television sets and mass-circulated periodicals.

In Rwanda, where the fascist regime is co-responsible for the loss of 6 to 10 million human lives in DR Congo, there is, at least, no charade about democracy. Sugary and sentimental serenades sung to Rwanda, to RPF and to President Kagame by 'world leaders' like Tony Blair, Bill Clinton, Bill Gates, as well as by various high-ranking officials at the World Bank, are perfectly composed and orchestrated by leading apparatchiks and chief ideologists of the Western Regime. Everyone is so dreadfully sorry for 'doing nothing to stop the 1994 genocide', but the incomparably worse and still ongoing genocide perpetrated by Kagame, the RPF and his militias in neighboring DR Congo, is hardly ever mentioned by the establishment media.

The most prominent opposition leader in Rwanda, Ms. Victoire Ingabire Umuhoza, is in prison, locked away for 8 years after being accused of 'terrorism '. Her head is shaved and she wears the pink uniform of political prisoners; her main sin is her wondering out aloud: 'why are there only Tutsis who are commemorated at the Kigali Genocide Memorial, if even Paul Kagame admits that both Tutsis and Hutu were killed in those infamous 100 days, in 1994?' But her arch sin is that she dared to return to her country after 16 years in exile to compete against one of the most notorious mass murderers ever born on the African continent.

Ms. Victoire Ingabire could still be, in relative terms at least, considered 'lucky'. Lucky, because many other Rwandan opposition leaders and figures have already been murdered in cold blood, or at least forced into exile. The list includes several elite members of Kagame's RPF, those who dared to cross their supreme leader. It also contains the names of numerous journalists, and even one famous hotelier – Paul Rusesabagina – who was credited with saving hundreds of Tutsi lives during the 1994 massacres. His actions depicted in the movie "Hotel Rwanda", became part of the unchallengeable Western interpretation of the historical event. But now Mr. Rusesabagina, like so many others, lives in exile in South Africa.

Political prisoner Victoire Ingabire never became a sweetheart of the West, like, for instance, the Burmese opposition leader, Aung San Suu Kyi. It is maybe because Burma is not plundering an enormous country rich with natural resources, like Rwanda is plundering DR Congo on behalf of Western companies and governments.

The Rwandese opposition is expected to shut up and wait for a few more years at least. The booty is obviously not yet satisfactory, and the 6-10 million human lives lost in the Congo is still somehow tolerable for the politicians and the captains of the economy in Washington, London, Brussels and elsewhere.

The brutal reality is that most African countries are not in a position to decide anything. Their opposition leaders win when they are told to take power, when they are allowed to win by their foreign handlers. It is back to colonialism, minus those great African heroes of the past like Patrice Lumumba and Julius Nyerere.

When the West gets tired of Kagame it will simply depose him, or let him fall. And a new crony, some new gangster ready to serve the West, will get 'elected' through the 'democratic process', to a background of loud fanfare celebrating 'multi-party' democracy and the 'African renaissance'.

Heat wave or drizzle, almost every day – twice a day – on the road connecting Entebbe and Kampala, the sirens begin squeaking loudly and the convoy of armored and armed vehicles moves at breakneck speed, pushing all civilian traffic onto the shoulder, and if 'needed', into the ditch.

There goes the flamboyant Mr. Yoweri Museveni, the President of Uganda, and a strongman who has held the reins of power since 1986. He wears a cowboy hat, even though he rides inside a cool vehicle – to his office in the capital city or when returning home in the evenings.

It is quite an impressive sight to see that luxury, bulletproof Mercedes and the SUVs of Museveni's heavily fortified guards all flying past the decrepit and miserable huts and the destitute individuals who live in them along the main road of this conflict-torn nation, one of the poorest on Earth.

Uganda is a mess. A brutal civil war is raging in the north of the country. There, according to countless reports, HIV-positive military men are ordered, periodically, to rape rebellious soldiers and insurgents. Mr. Museveni hates gays, and he occasionally threatens them with capital punishment just for being what they are. But homosexual rape is clearly something he approves of, something he even commands.

He can get away with virtually anything. A loyal mercenary of the West in the region, Uganda is deeply involved in Somalia, Sudan and above all, in DR Congo.

The 'involvement' of Rwanda and Uganda in DR Congo is, of course, well documented, in the 2010 'UN Mapping Report" and in the conclusions of other investigations. But that does not prevent the West from using Ugandan troops as 'peacekeepers' all over Africa, particularly where their interests lie.

After the UN "Mapping Report" went to print, Mr. Museveni allegedly got very angry, which was enough to force the UN Secretary General Ban Ki-moon to fly to Kampala to shamefully beg the dictator not to abandon UN peacekeeping missions!

"Both Rwanda and Uganda are plundering DR Congo, killing millions. Museveni admitted it, Kagame never did. But both regimes are dictatorial, with close links to the West. And the Western public is unaware of what is happening", explained Nii

Akuetteh, Ghanaian political analyst during our meeting in Washington.

Paul Kagame was educated and groomed in Kampala and, according to former US Ambassador to Rwanda, Robert Flatten, he was even armed by the West in this city. Before the 1994 shooting down of the Falcon jet that had the Rwandan and Burundian Presidents on board, and the consequent genocide, Kagame was allowed and encouraged to train his brutal RPF forces on the territory of Uganda. For a long time he functioned as the head of Ugandan military intelligence, overseeing interrogations, cruel torture and even the murder of countless Ugandan political prisoners. I personally interviewed one victim in Kampala who testified about how he was tortured on Paul Kagame's orders.

Knowing the facts, it does not come as a surprise that the plundering and ravaging of DR Congo is not openly on the agenda of the Ugandan opposition. Any demand that the pillage stops, could easily lead to the straining of ties with North America and Europe.

Of course, there are other, 'domestic' calamities. There are child beggars on almost every corner in the center of Kampala, some as young as 3 years old. There are adult homeless people, even women, living on the pavement, with empty, resigned looks in their eyes.

As I drive through the capital, there are signs of discontent everywhere.

"The social situation in Uganda is terrible and continuously deteriorating", explains Mr. Kaliija James Kats, Program Manager of YLF Uganda. "People are at the edge."

It is true. And the leaders of the Ugandan regime are brutes, incomparably worse than those who governed the country during the infamous reign of Idi Amin Dada.

With cruel inter-tribal onslaughts, the old historic buildings of the Buganda Kingdom going up in flames in 2010, political violence, an aggressive foreign policy and appalling misery in both urban and rural areas, Uganda is hardly a place that one imagines would be supported by any sane government or influential individual abroad.

But it is supported whole-heartedly and has been for many years and decades, by several Western powers that use it as a trusted ally in their deadly geo-political games.

On top of that, this ally, occupying such an important position in such a mineral-rich part of the world, has to be well 'secured.'

"The opposition, the civil society, the government – everybody is getting money from the West", Doreen Nyanjura, a young Ugandan writer and activist and member of the opposition, tells me.

"Does it mean that whoever wins will be obliged to go to Washington and London for guidance?" I ask.

"This is a very poor country..." she replies.

To give credit where it is due, unlike in Rwanda, there actually is, at least, some opposition in Uganda.

Its members periodically protest; they write books and articles, arrange demonstrations, and even end up in prisons.

But they are also very careful not to alienate the West. There is very little talk about alternative political and economic systems. There is no naming names and, like in Kenya, no public exposure of the neo-colonialist and imperialist designs of foreign rulers.

"You write so often against the West; against imperialism," my Kenyan friends from the Left periodically tell me. "You stand by Venezuela, Cuba, China and Vietnam against Western ideological and real attacks. What kind of funding do you get from them"?

I say I get nothing. They don't believe me. They insist. Why would I work, why would I choose to stand in opposition to the Western regime, if the people I defended did not pay me a regular salary, or at least some substantial 'bob'.

In East Africa, being in opposition is often a job; sometimes lucrative, sometimes not too profitable, but always a job.

I mumble something about internationalism, about humanism, about duty. My friends listen, politely. After some time, they lose patience with me: "But who pays for your work?"

I tell them that I keep recycling almost everything that I earn from my films, books, articles, talks and my other work... I recycle it into more work. I don't save; I don't invest... I tell them that I almost never ask for funding; that I am scared of funding. They lose interest almost instantaneously. From there, our discussion often moves from revolution to the weather.

"We have to convince Venezuela and China to pay; to support us," I recently heard in Kenya from another candidate who aspired to a Parliamentary post. "They don't pay you anything?"

"Well, when they print my articles or show my films... or when I speak at their universities..."

He hit the table with his fist, outraged: "They have to pay. If they don't, nothing would change here!"

Before we parted, Doreen suggested: "Come to the high security prison with us, tomorrow. The leader of the opposition is there, his personal secretary is there, including the driver who was at the scene, during his arrest."

I agreed. We set up the time for the next day.

The night before our visit to prison, I met one of the ideologues of the opposition party, a bitter, aging man who did not consider China or Vietnam to be true 'socialist countries', who did not consider Latin American revolutions to be 'revolutionary enough'.

"I will tell you something," he insisted, although I was trying to get away from him. "I don't think that Bolivia or Venezuela are socialist countries. Actually, I don't think that even Cuba is socialist."

"You are pissed off about the Mao pants?" I suggested.

"What?" He did not understand.

"They don't wear blue Mao pants in China or in Latin America," I suggested. "And they travel freely all over the world if they can afford it. And, in most of these countries people want to be equally rich, not equally poor... And..."

The evening did not end well. I told him that not all socialist movements have to resemble the Western conception, that there are variations, like the Latin American interpretation of socialism, like the Chinese interpretation, like my own interpretation, like millions of other interpretations. And I suggested that he and Uganda start thinking about their own socialist concept, instead of digging into some fundamentalist, dusty, Western version from centuries ago.

The morning did not begin well either. Doreen could not get the car. My car was in Kenya. I offered my hired taxi.

She came with two young leaders of the opposition. We stopped at the market, to buy vegetables and meat for the prisoners, and then we drove towards the Luzira jail.

In case my readers have never visited any of the high-security prisons in Africa, here is a valuable piece of information about how to enter: 'Drive to the gate, get checked, get searched, get your car turned up-side-down, then leave your cameras and mobile phones at the guard's room. Leave all your money behind, even coins, and of course all sharp objects. Fill in some blanks on questionnaires. Present your ID, explain who you are, whom are you visiting, why are you here. Get checked again – metal detector, patting. It is a bit like taking domestic flight in India, but even worse.

There is a short interview... And then your request gets rejected at the end...

I had one official East African ID on me, and in the end they let us all in, together with the defense lawyers.

* * *

The leader of Ugandan opposition – Dr. Besigye Kizza – was released a day earlier.

"He wanted to stay, with the others, but they literally pushed him out, made him leave the jail," explains Doreen. "If he were to stay here, there would be a riot."

We go through several more layers of security and end up in a small room staffed with high-ranking jailers – 'officers' – watching our every move. There is also some European official there, almost licking the boots of the prison guards, smiling at them, cracking primitive jokes, flattering everybody around. He is an appalling type, a typical Euro bureaucrat; a collaborator, an individual one sees in all Western colonies like Cambodia, Indonesia, Thailand, Rwanda, or Djibouti. I always wonder where they manufacture them.

They bring the prisoners: Sam Mugumya, Political assistant to Dr. Besigye Kizzi, and the driver who was transporting the opposition during the arrest.

Sam is a socialist; that much I know. He is also a writer; he wrote a passionate book called "Road to The Revolution".

The driver is crying. He has obviously nothing to do with all this; he is just a minivan chauffeur, but the police grabbed him, brought him to the station, beat him up, took two of his mobile phones and all the money he had collected from fares for entire day – over US$100.

"They are beating me up all the time!" he keeps sobbing. "During the police raid against the opposition, a police SUV smashed into the back of my van. And now they want me to compensate for the loss. I have nothing. They have ruined my life..."

Sam is clearly one of the highest leaders of the opposition. He knows about me and about me coming to see him.

The next day I will be leaving Uganda and in one week I will travel back to Asia. There is no time to lose. We have plenty to say to each other.

Sam goes through the necessary routine, a testimony he is obviously not enjoying: "Prison is crowded, overcrowded. They treat us terribly. The driver is beaten every day. Those who are leading the investigations are actually criminals..."

At some point he stops. He suddenly grabs my hand.

"Chavez," he sighs. "How is Venezuela?"

"Coping," I reply. "It is not easy, but coping... There is an investigation..."

"I know," he says.

"I will go there soon."

"We will talk before you go..." Then he looks straight at me: "Before I die, I want to go to South America."

I nod. I don't want to tell him "You will not die anytime soon." This is Uganda. He fights. He is one of those very few people in eastern Africa who is fighting. I say nothing. I squeeze his hand briefly, and let go.

"Sam," I say. "Those millions in Congo... Is that on the agenda? On your agenda..."

"Of course we are aware that Museveni is playing a subservient role to the West," Sam speaks very fast, afraid to be interrupted by the guards. I take notes. He stops once in a while, to catch breath.

"Talk," I tell him. "Please".

"For the West, Museveni has been a very effective 'buffer' against Sudan. He was, of course, very useful for US interests in DR Congo. US give us – to Uganda – money and we give them the bodies that they want us to shoot. We are like a mercenary force – the whole country. The West talks human rights, and then it throws money at us. We take the money and we kill. The West is two-faced; it cares absolutely nothing about human rights. It only cares about its own interests."

"Are you going to change things?" I ask. "If your party comes to power... If Kizza wins, somehow... if they let him win... You know what I am saying, right?"

"Sure. I know perfectly what you mean... We have to be... we also have to be tactical. We just cannot directly confront the West... You see, Venezuela... There are different dynamics. In South America, there is great unity now, and people understand... they want independence. This is what is lacking here. And our social organizations – they are not where we want them to be, yet. Like this, we are not yet ready to go to direct opposition."

I realize he is not talking about his party here in Uganda, now; he is talking about the opposition that could be finally real, similar to the one which took power all over South America.

"We have to raise consciousness about the revolution," he whispers. "Revolution is inevitable, desirable... We are studying how to make it happen."

Soon we have to part. We embrace. They lead Sam away and I have to present my notes to the censor.

The censor is looking at the pages of my notebook. It is clear he understands nothing. There are no names and no numbers. There is only some theory, absolute worthless shit as far as he is concerned.

"All clear," he gives me my notebook back. "You can go now."

After leaving prison we witness a small riot at a fuel stop. One more riot, in a single day.

Some people joined us. Now I have half of the Ugandan opposition leaders sitting in my car, or at least that's how it appears. All of them are squeezed; all cursing Museveni.

I think about Egypt and about Indonesia; countries that each succeeded in forcing one man to step down, but where the regimes survived, regrouped, and became even more resistant to real change, to the revolution. Like roaches and rats, they have been digging holes and trenches, preparing to survive anything, even nuclear holocaust.

"Do you get some support from the West?" I ask one of MP candidates.

"Not necessarily support," he replies. "But we are given some money."

The road is blocked by several SUV's decorated by colorful flowers and paper lace. There is some loud music and the traffic is moving at a snail's pace.

"Is it a wedding?"

"Oh no," smiles Doreen. "This is a celebration for the former Minister of Health, who is being released from prison."

"Is he also from the opposition?" I ask.

"No. He is a corrupt bastard. And it was correct to put him to prison... But people are so fed-up with Museveni that anybody who ends up in prison in Uganda is seen as a hero."

"But the man is a thief, right?" I wonder.

"A thief," yes, everybody in the car confirms.

"And the country is celebrating his release..." I say.

They all nod.

When everybody disembarks in front of Parliament, my driver takes me to the hotel.

We have a long history together. He has driven me to several border regions with DR Congo, to dreadful refugee camps, to war zones. He helped me a lot when I was filming for my major documentary "Rwanda Gambit".

He does not speak much, he never does. But he is my friend; an old man who saw, it appears, all there is really to see.

"You have just listened to several opposition leaders." I smile. "Do you feel better about the future of Uganda?"

I know he hates the President. And I am surprised when he slows down and says, calmly:

"I heard all those things they were saying, before. But I did not hear what will really happen to my country when the old bastard steps down!"

29 March 2013

*****

26

Sulu Sultanate Contra Malaysia

THE GHOST OF BRITISH COLONIALISM HAUNTING SABAH

One ordinary day, precisely, February 9th 2013, a band of brigands (if you listen to the Malaysian authorities), or heroic liberators (as some nationalist Filipinos living in both the Philippines and in Malaysia would say), or simply mildly deranged and overly romantic buccaneers (according to most people on both sides of the Sulu Sea), landed their crafts on the green, palm-oil-plantation-covered shores of Sabah and immediately got themselves busily engaged in chivalrous warfare against the Malaysian nation, with the luminous goal of bringing the state of Sabah back under the reign of the Sulu Sultanate.

To be 'precise', it is often quoted that exactly 235 Filipinos (where that precision comes from is a mystery to me), some armed, some not, had travelled from Tawi-Tawi in the Southern Philippines, to the dormant, and, as many would say, god-forsaken town of Lahad Datu, in Sabah, Malaysia.

Their commander, Agbimuddin, is a brother of the self-proclaimed Sulu "Sultan", Jamalul Kiram III.

Those facts can be determined, confirmed and even re-confirmed; those facts alone, but not much more. After that, everything suddenly becomes a shadow play, something that would be more appropriate in the heart of Central Java in neighboring Indonesia, than in the grotesquely over-developed Malaysian-controlled Borneo, covered by a mono-culture of palm oil plantations.

Where did this romanticism come from? Sabah, with oil, palm oil and unbridled logging could easily be described as one of the most pragmatic, un-quixotic parts of Southeast Asia. And Sulu itself has been playing bizarre international games for years and decades.

But suddenly those few, those 235 maritime samurais, arrived from the isles, and from a different era, ready to fight for honor and even to die, facing the entire Malaysian state, one of the richest in Southeast Asia, with its 29 million inhabitants.

"How daring!" Some say, while others offer a more pragmatic view: "How idiotic!"

There are more questions than answers. Who is really behind this 'war'? Were leaders of the Sulu Sultanate calling for the attack; were they the ones who issued the orders? And while both Malaysia and the Philippines are presently submerged up to their ears in rather serious political crises, could that situation be somehow connected to the Sabah mêlée, and could some political forces be thinking that they might benefit from the conflict?

And what about the history; how is it interlaced with the present? The current geo-political arrangements are, undeniably, the result of British post – WWII colonialist schemes, just as they are the result of the brutal oppression of left-wing forces in the entire region.

Historically, Sabah used to belong to the once powerful but now defunct Sulu Sultanate, which is now part of the Philippines.

A leading academician, Eduardo C. Tadem, Professor from the University of Philippines in Manila, put things into perspective:

> "I have to highlight the principle of self-determination for the Sabah people. It is a historical fact that the Sabahans were never consulted in 1962 or 1963 as to whether they wanted to be part of the Malaysian Federation. The Cobold Commission may, in all

probability, have just fabricated the formula, '30-30-30'. As for the Philippine claim, it rests on the moribund Sulu Sultanate's assertion of sovereignty based on a grant by the Sultan of Brunei in return for a favor in helping suppress a native rebellion. In my book, while the transfer may have been 'legal,' there is no moral basis for it. Everything then turned murky. Arguing over whether the acquisition by the British of Sabah from the Sulu Sultan was a lease, or a cession, merely trivializes the whole affair."

There was an attempt at self-determination in 1962 when the left-wing Brunei People's Party led by Azahari launched a rebellion in an attempt to unify Sabah and Brunei under a nation-state independent of both Malaysia, and the Philippines. British forces with the help of Gurkha mercenary troops swiftly crushed this rebellion. Incidentally, at the time they launched the rebellion, the Brunei People's Party had popular support having won all the contested seats in the local legislature. Then President, Sukarno may have had a hand in this rebellion, as Azahari took refuge in Jakarta and died there years later. Then as now, therefore, what matters is what the residents of Sabah want, not what the Manila and KL governments, desire."

And one would hope, not what the Brits wanted... Although, in Malaysia, no matter how fiery and anti-imperialist the rhetoric of Dr. Mahathir used to be, the Brits never really left the psyche and imagination of a substantial part of the local 'elites'. This group of dogged anglophiles has been hopelessly enamored with the Empire; with their former colonial masters, even when the boot had been planted squarely up the behinds of the local people of the region.

The Brits naturally considered 'self-determination' to be one of the filthiest expressions that ever penetrated the English language.

The 'war' began as an operatic, even burlesque occurrence.

More than 200 men hid deep in the jungle, or in the rubber plantations, or in the dwellings in several stilt villages, ready to strike mighty Malaysia. Who could not immediately recall the iconic 1959 film with Peter Sellers: "The Mouse That Roared", about that tiny, poor, imaginary country in the middle of the Alps, called the "Duchy of Grand Fenwick", which declared war against the United States because the Empire refused to buy its 'Pinot Grand Fenwick' wine? Troops with bows and arrows were sent onboard a commercial flight to New York. Their mission is to get defeated and secure a miniature version of the Marshall Plan. Instead, through a terrible mistake, the army of Grand Fenwick defeats the Empire.

But in Sabah, the fun did not last long and there was no Peter Sellers to turn the whole thing into a circus.

People began dying. Clashes between the 'invaders' and the police began, and the Malaysian armed forces got heavily involved. Large areas were sealed off and declared out of reach for local and foreign journalists, for 'their own protection', naturally, Indonesian-style.

Tanks and armored vehicles were suddenly rolling down the roads of Sabah, and Malaysia scrambled fighter jets, relentlessly bombing the 'infiltrated' areas from the air, and then deploying heavily-armed troops to 'finish the job'.

The number of victims is absolutely unknown. Suddenly, all this turned into damn serious stuff, with tens of thousands of people displaced, on the move.

The Manila Standard Today reported that by the end of March 2013, at least 12 battalions of Malaysian soldiers and policemen, or more than 7,000 men, were searching for Agbimuddin and his men.

By the end of the month of March, according to official counts, at least 73 people died in the battles – 63 Sulu insurgents, eight Malaysian policemen and two soldiers.

Or this is what the public has been told.

Combatants were not the only victims, but official Malaysian statistics name no civilian casualties.

At least 4,000 Filipino men, women and children fled Sabah, fearing for their lives. From my own investigation, the real number of those who left Malaysia, as well as those who had been in hiding in Borneo, could easily at the most conservative estimate have reached the tens-of-thousands. "We are scared," whispered a lady selling basic foodstuff in the heart of a humble stilt village, which recently saw, a series of brutal exchanges between insurgents and Malaysian police.

"We are scared," whispered three boys, who were only in their early teens. They took me around, pointing at the places where some of the most gruesome killings took place. We flouted all security precautions, as we dashed into houses abandoned by their inhabitants, then walked on wooden, elevated walkways, some of them badly damaged, some still bearing clearly visible bullet marks and blood stains. This is where people, some militants and some police officers, had been shot, others hacked to death or decapitated alive. "We don't know who is watching us now, or who is listening," the boys murmured. "Just take photographs quickly, and let's get out of here, please!"

"I am scared,"the boatman shouted over the roar of his engine, as he navigated the small high-speed craft between seemingly endless forests of stilts. "I am not refusing to take you around; we can sail under the houses for hours, but I don't dare to land here. You can disembark one kilometer away and walk back to this town. Please understand: there are commandos inside this kampong. If they see me land, I could lose my license; I could be captured, questioned and interrogated."

"Could they "disappear" you?" I askeqd.

He pretended not to hear my question.

"Philippine people are scared and they had to flee," I am told by a driver who agreed to take me to the overblown police station on the outskirts of Semporna City. "Thousands of them had to flee. They have been petrified since 'the events'. It is like an exodus!"

In the morning, as I sat by the water, in a local café, an old man slowly walked towards my table. "What are you doing here?" He asked. I pointed at my massive professional camera resting on top of the table, making acquaintances with the fresh carrot juice. "So now it has come to that," the grandpa commented, sadly. "The international press in this town, a place that only used to be visited by divers, and adventurers."

"Are you also scared?" I asked him, because everybody else seems to be. "Yes I am," he nodded.

"Of whom?" I asked.

He did not reply.

"Of whom?" I insisted.

He left, abruptly.

The old man forgot to mention that for years and decades before the conflict, it was not just divers and adventurers, but mainly hundreds of thousands of legal and illegal migrant workers, predominantly from the Philippines, but also from India,

Indonesia, Bangladesh and elsewhere, who have been coming to Sabah, in search of relatively well-paid jobs.

He also forgot to say that this was not so 'unexpected', that it was not the first 'incident'. At least 21 Lahad Datu inhabitants were killed when Sulu pirates invaded the shores of Sabah, looted the local bank and Malaysian Airlines office in 1985. And there were kidnappings, later, from the Sandakan area.

Sabah, with its, by the region's standard, high salaries, has been like a strong magnet for migrants arriving from the Philippine islands of Mindanao, Basilan and Sulu, and from the Indonesian parts of Borneo called Kalimantan, both areas easily definable as some of the poorest in Southeast Asia. Remittance stores in Sabah's cities openly advertise the transfer of funds to the Philippines, India, Bangladesh, Indonesia and several other countries that regularly send millions of workers to much richer parts of the world.

Before the recent 'war', there was a Filipino migrant community living in Sabah over 800,000-strong, the majority without official papers and therefore vulnerable to exploitation and abuse.

All this created confusion, tension and even open hostility and discrimination, something that was always very well concealed.

There were anti-immigrant lobbies and pro-immigrant ones; there were those who wanted to keep Sabah predominantly 'native' and 'Malaysian', as well as those who were interested on getting their hands on as many immigrants as possible, in order to take advantage of cheap and badly organized labor.

Hardly anybody came here because of a love for the place: Sabah state is not only humid and hot; it is filthy, and outrageously boorish. Here, one could easily forget that this is Malaysia, a middle-income country that has aspired (for decades), to join the so-called developed world.

With garbage-covered streets, rubbish floating next to and off the seashores, with children begging at food markets and street corners, the cities of Sabah resemble some Philippine or Indonesian urban centers, with primitive or collapsed infrastructure, an acute lack of hygiene, public transportation and appalling social policies.

It is not only the outsiders that notice the rot. The opposition

State Reform Party claimed, recently, that Sabah health care is in a deplorable condition, everywhere; in some cases it says it is unacceptable. There is a feeling of thorough hopelessness here, mostly unknown in the rest of the country, especially in the glitzy and cosmopolitan Kuala Lumpur or elegant, historic and 'oh so' Chinese cities like Georgetown on Penang Island or Kuching in Sarawak.

Sabah used to be the second richest state in Malaysia, after Selangor, at least on paper, and mainly due to its unregulated logging and the later introduction of palm oil plantations. Those have been managing to ruin almost all of state's native fauna and flora, turning it into a near Indonesia-style environmental nightmare, but the earnings used to be high.

Lately the greed, mismanagement, and unequal distribution of wealth, has turned Sabah into the second poorest state of Malaysia. Apart from palm oil, Sabah also produces crude oil, but, like in the Gulf, the natural wealth of the area does not necessarily translate into prosperity for the majority of the inhabitants. Children here are often seen running barefoot and many adults appear to be illiterate. It is not only medical care that is in disastrous state; it is also education.

I get to work, trying to collect as many testimonies from the ground as possible. There seems to be no foreign press in the city of Semporna; all journalists left soon after the first wave of fighting subsided.

This is the area that registered the largest number of Malaysian casualties, most likely 6, but possibly much more.

There are several theories about what happened. The most accepted one is that on 2nd March 2013, ten alleged insurgents were holed up inside a house in a humble stilt village at Simunul, concretely in its dilapidated section called Lorong 5, and that they were discovered by police. That's what I am told by the locals; those few who are still left here; those who dared not to abandon their homes.

One of the local kids, Azman bin Ahmad is my self-designated guide. His grandparents came from Sulu, but he feels Malaysian. I don't ask for it, but he insists on flashing his official Malaysian ID at me, repeatedly, as if feeling the need to prove his own identity to himself, to me and to the world.

Azman and his mates take me through Lorong 5, to the house where the gruesome exchange took place. Elevated, stilt-supported walkways form a complex, fascinating labyrinth.

"There was a terrible battle right at this place," explained Azman. "Just look at those marks! They are all over and they are from the bullets. And, here – see the blood? At one point, police officers and insurgents all fell into the water... And the water was red from blood. It was just awful..."

I asked Azman and his friends to explain exactly what happened here.

> "There were some 10 or more people gathering here, inside the house. They were all from Sulu. During prayer time, between Maghrib and Isha (between 6:30pm and 7:30pm), they were conducting 'tahlil', a prayer for those who had died earlier in the battle at Lahad Datu, some 200 kilometers away from here; from Semporna. Then a group of police officers moved in; they were advancing towards the house, obviously tipped off by locals. The police were armed. One of them kicked the door of the house open... Then everything began happening with the lightning speed: several men were behind the door. They grabbed the nearest police officer and killed him on the spot. After that, many shots were fired. I don't know who was firing at whom, but I think that the shooting was coming from both sides. They say that six police officers died as well as three or more of the Sulu people. You can see there, and there, where the bullets hit the walls."

One of the boys jumps in, impatiently. He goes ballistic, arguing that the Sultan of Sulu is not really a sultan, and how the fighters who landed in Sabah had been fooled; how all that has been happening is one huge farce.

Whether it's a farce or not, the scene of the worst documented battle of this conflict definitely looks eerie. Stilt walkways collapsed; some parts are submerged, broken, and there is nobody around.

I peek into the houses and everything inside them is upside down, torn apart and smashed; in absolute disarray.

"Malaysian commandos came here on several occasions, and destroyed everything", explains," one of the boys.

There are some family photos on the wooden bench, left intact. These are images of content looking men, women and children, posing with warm smiles on their faces. 'What happened to them?' I think. This is the house where the killings took place. 'What is really going on?'

People in the photographs do not look at all threatening.

It appears that nobody in Kuala Lumpur and in Manila actually understands what is going on here. And it appears that it is supposed to remain like that.

Irwanizam bin Mad Jais, a Bajau native, is also confused by the present situation:

> "The majority of citizen of Semporna are Bajau and Suluk people. Many came from Sulu and then settled here. Some of them have already lived in Sabah for more than 10 years, and are in possession of ID (IC) cards. They are definitely not some kind of 'outsiders'."

When I ask about the battle in Semporna; at Simunul, Lorong 5, he immediately voices his doubts:

> "I heard that three or more policemen died in the fights at Kampung Simunul. They were sent here from Sarawak and from Kuala Lumpur. There are some things that I don't comprehend: the government has been saying that the attackers who died all came from Sulu, that they were followers of Sultan of Sulu. What I know is that Sulu fighters usually wear elaborate and scary uniforms, and they are armed. I saw with my own eyes those people who died in Lorong 5, and were later called 'Suluk fighters' by the government. They didn't wear any uniforms. Three dead bodies carried out of the village by the police were wearing traditional Malay clothes. It appeared as if they were just woken up from their sleep, killed, and immediately carried away. And there were no guns. I don't understand why the police killed these three men. Frankly, I don't think they were the insurgents."

I ask him about police brutality:

> "There is plenty of it now. I don't understand why police tends to be so violent towards the common people here? They are conducting frequent raids. And we are afraid because they are carrying guns. I am a citizen of Sabah. I have IC. I make money by driving my own car. But they are questioning me, and my friends, as if we were a bunch of criminals. Why don't they catch and punish real criminals and those who want to take over our State?"

I am told that Malaysian police brutality in Sabah is taboo; it is scarcely investigated and almost never mentioned in local media reports.

In Kuala Lumpur, a Malaysian college lecturer and filmmaker, Kia Meng Boon, later explained:

> "Peninsula Malaysians lack access to independent media in the country, where citizens could learn the facts and judge the real situation on the ground for themselves."

It is no secret that Malaysian media and intellectuals are not renowned for their courage. I was told by several of my friends and colleagues in Kuala Lumpur, that 'the government has really made this into a security issue' and commenting on the situation would 'not be strategic.'

Predictably, police and armed forces on the ground have their lips sealed. I visited both the gunboat docks and an enormous police station where a few dozens of the captured militia members are allegedly held. The answers were evasive:

> "We are very sorry, but we cannot talk about those incidents at all. There are people with more authority than us who can enlighten you. For instance, you can go to Police Headquarters."

I asked Nadira Ilana, a Malaysian filmmaker, who is originally from Borneo, whether the battles were actually 'real'. There are countless rumors in both the Philippines and Malaysia that political interests actually orchestrated the conflict.

"Not sure what the rumors are in Kuala Lumpur, but there are clearly many rumors in Sabah," she replied. "I personally don't think it was politically arranged. Both Malaysia and the Philippines are facing an election year. I can't imagine how this incident could help either party... Yes, the Sabah attacks were very much real. It's not the first time Sulus have attacked Sabah but it may be the first time we've been attacked over the Sabah claim..."

Then she concluded: "I think the Sabah claim was laid dormant after the formation of Malaysia, which unintentionally and perhaps indirectly sparked the Mindanao-Philippines civil war. If it were not for Sabah's Suluk Chief Minister Tun Mustapha, Malaysia and Libya, Mindanao would not have become an autonomous region. The Sulu claim on Sabah seems to fluctuate depending on Mindanao-Philippines relations, which is why I see these recent attacks as a spillover from Philippines' politics rather than a BN ploy."

It is quiet and peaceful at Café Melaka, on Semporna seafront.

Two ladies wearing headscarves are watching a soap opera, as if there was no drama, much more gripping than a television one, consuming their state.

The scenery around is fantastic; traditional structures emerge from the sea, built on wooden supports. There are entire man-made islands resting on stilts, mostly inhabited by native sea-bound people who only opted for this 'lifestyle compromise' in recent years and decades. Mountains encircle the cove. There is a constant flow of slow and high-speed boats shuttling people between the Borneo mainland and the islands in the bay.

As I clean my camera lenses, slowly sipping bitter coffee, the old man I had met earlier, returns. He is obviously eager to talk:

"It is terrible," he sighs, refusing to sit next to me, as if ready to deliver a memorized speech. "Here, we have no experience with such things. In other countries they would know what to do, but we are peaceful here. In Lahad Datu they had to face this situation in March, but we thought that here we would be spared. Suddenly, six police officers were murdered."

'Three or five or six', I think. They cannot even agree on the numbers...

The old man continues his lament: "My friend told me that one entire commando had to come to retrieve bodies, because police would not dare to rescue the corpses of their fallen comrades... I was also told that most of the officers were not shot; they were hacked to death, cut to pieces..."

In the end he gets philosophical: "In this part of the world, we may get the same color of hair, but who knows what is taking place inside our heads?" And he adds, laconically: "This also illustrates how thoroughly uneducated the attackers were. What did they think? That, they would manage to capture the entire State of Sabah with that little band and their bare hands?"

There is only one tiny step from outrage to bigoted talk, even to discrimination itself.

The Filipino people, both those who have lived here for generations and those who came illegally, have mostly left the area. Lorong 5 is now half-empty – only Malaysians and some Indonesians stayed.

I hired a boat and went to the biggest island in the bay – Palau

Bum-Bum – right across the water from Semporna. As I was arriving to jetty, mighty police speedboats were busy landing dozens of heavily armed men on the island.

I asked an Indonesian worker, a young girl named Zuraida, what happened to the Filipino people who have been living on the island for decades.

"Several of them used to work here, with us, but they are in hiding now. I have no idea where they went," she said. I got the feeling that even if she were to know, she would not tell, and for very good reasons.

The atmosphere, the mood all around Sabah is very bad. Most 'foreigners' have left, and some nationalist elements, are now on the loose.

Pulau Bum-Bum is no exception. In a very un-Malaysian and rude fashion, some minivan drivers speak to me in an obscene and insulting way: "Hey boss, hey you! Where you go?"

Heavily armed police move down the road.

Then the skipper who is taking me back to Sabah mainland is passing by 'ice village', where huge bricks of ice are waiting in the awful heat to be transported to towns and villages all over the bay:

> "People who are living in Lorong 5 have no clue about Malaysian law. They think here it is similar to what they have back at home – lawlessness. That's why they think they can just come over and try to take Sabah. They are coming here from their proud and isolated sultanate, and they think that we – Malaysians – are lower than they are... And on top of that, their leaders in Sulu have tricked them by making promises that cannot be fulfilled!"

He goes on and on. Finally he begins sounding approximately the same as German neo-Nazis, and he is carrying quite a similar message. Except that he is speaking Malay.

Yes, the fear is everywhere. I walk to a restaurant in a shack, near the road. One of the waitresses is married to a boy who used to live in Lorong 5.

I order a serving of awful fried noodles and ask her about her family. She studies me, for a while, then decides that I could be, most likely, trusted:

"My in-laws had to flee and to spend one entire week in hiding," she explains.

"Has it been tough here for you?" I ask.

She nods. "There were tanks here, big tanks, which you see in the movies... right here, on this road."

On the way back to Tawau Airport, all that could be seen are enormous palm oil plantations. Their size is monstrous. The land is terribly scarred. There is no native forest left in the entire area, everything is logged out, destroyed. It is almost one hundred kilometers of an uninterrupted and foreign monoculture.

"Do local people like this?" I ask the driver.

"Those who work in the industry – they do. The rest hate it. But what can they do?"

Tawau Airport is half-deserted. Like all over Sabah, people are sleeping with their heads on the table, including staff. A few kids are hanging around the untidy eatery:

> "With this conflict, I think business is down by 50%. You see that it is not as crowded as it used to be, and today is Friday, people used to travel a lot on this day... We have many Filipinos living here. We used to co-exist in peace. Now there are prejudices on both sides..."

I got bumped off the half-empty Malaysian Airlines flight. Their system jumped one month on my return ticket to Kuala Lumpur, not an unusual occurrence for this airline with an appalling customer service record. A check-in counter clerk shot his hateful glimpse at me, and then sent me, with spite, to the nearby ticket office. There, an inefficient and openly hostile agent began insulting me, before offering to re-instate the seat for approximately 300 dollars, three times the price of the original fare.

I flashed the gold card of One World alliance, which Malaysian Airlines recently joined, but they laughed in my face, and insulted me some more. I protested. Immediately, a couple of passengers stood up and threatened to call police. "There are children here," they shouted at me. To protest injustice is obviously illegal here. I bought a one-way ticket on the low-cost Air Asia and lost my Malaysian Airlines ticket altogether.

Sabah is overflowing with anger and bad moods, with bad will, frustration, concealed grievances, and both concealed and unconcealed violence.

The attacks were recent, but begging children, filth and destroyed environment are something that Sabah has been enduring for decades.

The medieval, feudal way in which the island of Borneo has been governed, as well as the cowardice of Malaysian intellectuals, many of whom are too comfortable, too lazy, too spoiled by Western funding and therefore thoroughly unwilling to address almost any of the uncomfortable issues in their country, are partially to blame for the set of nightmares that form the reality of the state of Sabah.

There are certain topics that are 'ignored' even by the opposition, unless some substantial financing from abroad is secured: like the savage logging practices exercised by Malaysian companies operating both at home and abroad, like the palm oil and ethnic/minorities issues. Naturally there are some exceptions; those individuals who are aiming at being a little bit more than just some supermarket toy coin-horses, but sadly, very few.

The British colonial madness is also hardly addressed here, and its legacy is seen as wise by some; even as a supreme type of guidance. This madness goes on and on, unchallenged and uncorrected.

The little invasion, the little war, will stop. Eventually, everything will calm down. After a year passes by, everything will be forgotten. Bizarre little wars and conflicts have a tendency to vanish from the memory of people, especially if their roots are not analyzed and publicly debated.

Palm oil trees will probably make it, eventually, even into some city parks and private gardens. I would not be surprised if the palm oil plantations will, one day, be declared as an inseparable part of Malaysian culture, as its heritage.

The Filipino community will keep enjoying the 'tolerance and lack of discrimination', it is told to be enjoying, by the Malaysian officials.

The regional political situation will continue to be confusing, even schizophrenic. To illustrate it: just a couple of days before the conflict, I was told by one of the Commanders of the Moro National Liberation Front (MNLF) that if the Sulu Sultanate ever demanded the return of Sabah to the Philippines, MNLF would fight the leadership of the Sultanate. Instead, at one point after the invasion, MNLF declared that they 'couldn't stop their own fighters from joining the insurgents, anymore'.

In Malaysia, there will be no referendum on the Sabah issue, or on any other essential matter. And there will be no serious revision of the colonial past despite the fact that it has been, periodically and nastily, merging with the present.

24 September 2012

*****

27

WHEN IS THE SYRIAN 'OPPOSITION', SYRIAN?

At the outskirts of the city of Adana in southern Turkey, is located an enormous US Air force base called Incirlik. It is actually only nicknamed 'the US base', in reality it is being utilized by the United States Air Force, the Turkish Air Force and by the British RAF. Of course for the United States it may be one of the key overseas military facilities; Incirlik is home to about five thousand US airmen, 'complimented' by several hundred airmen from the British Royal Air Force. But the primary unit stationed at Incirlik is the 39th Air Base Wing (39 ABW) of the US Air Force. One look at the map and the significance becomes obvious: several 'important', 'strategic' countries appear to be in a relatively short flying distance from here: Syria, Iran, Lebanon and Iraq to name just a few. But recently the base has been gaining a new infamy: "There is plenty of evidence that they are now training the so-called Syrian 'opposition' on the premises of Incirlik," I was told by the renowned Turkish investigative journalist Huseyin Guler in the city of Hatay, near the Syrian border.

The base propels the economy of the entire area, both formal and informal. We park at the entrance of "Mujda's Café & Restaurant", near the main gate leading to the base. At Mujda's, all prices are exhibited in US dollars, not in Turkish liras. Photographs depicting US military hardware, airplanes and the officers with all their decorations and medals on display are covering the walls. The exhibits are out of place alongside the kebabs, beer and yoghurt drinks. "Do people around here talk about the Syrian crises?" I ask. "They do of course," answers the waiter. "Do they talk about the training of the so called 'Syrian opposition'?" I press further. "Some do," he smiles evasively. There is a girl working nearby. We ask her about surveillance. "Of course my phone is tapped," she replies. "But that is nothing unusual. They are tapping everyone's phones around here. Other things happen as well, but I can't talk about them." My colleague and friend Levent (he has to be identified only by his first name, for safety reasons) joins the discussion: "Wiretapping is just one of the most innocent things this government does. It is not only used for collecting intelligence, but also for the character assassination of those who dare to stand in its way. For instance, the phones of the generals who declared their outrage and opposition over western involvement in Turkish affairs had been tapped, their conversation flow recorded, broken up and fabricated into ludicrous but extremely damaging sentences, electronically."

Incirlik however – is just the beginning of our journey. We drive 200 kilometers to the city of Hatay – a culturally and religiously diverse southernmost Turkish metropolis near the several border crossings to Syria. Most of the way the highway is suspiciously smooth and fast, perfect for the deployment of troops. It is clear that in Hatay almost everyone is afraid to talk, from the local barbers to shop owners, hotel receptionists or even the majority of common passers by. Suleyman, the owner of a huge coffee shop with several impressive water pipes is an exception, but even he prefers to keep his full name and the name of his business anonymous:

> "People that the west describes as 'Syrian opposition' are considered here, in Hatay, as just a bunch of renegades and bandits. It is hard to believe they actually call them refugees! Refugees with guns, roaming our streets; get real! They are not good people. Almost all of them wear beards, carry guns and make our citizens frightened."

A uniformed police officer appears at the door as we speak. He gives us an inquisitive look and disappears as suddenly as he entered. "90% of Syrian people are in favor of Assad's government, only countries like Saudi Arabia and Qatar are supportive of the 'opposition', and of course the West," continues Suleyman. Soon a small circle of people forms around our table. Once they hear that I am not 'one of those official media people', they begin gesturing and talking over each other, explaining that Hatay – the city they love and feel proud of – is renowned for the peaceful co-existence of various ethnic and religious groups. "There have been Syrians living here for ages, as well as Armenians, Jews and other diverse ethnic groups. There are Sunni, Shi'a and several Muslim sects. We used to all live in peace!" "Hatay is very close to Syria," explains an old man, sipping his strong tea. "90% of the people here are somehow linked to the major city of Aleppo just across the border. And this place – Hatay – even used to be an independent republic; it only joined Turkey in 1939."

Then Suleyman, who obviously has more on his mind, speaks:

> "People here believe that the US and the West in general are heavily involved in the conflict in Syria, and that they are grooming the opposition which is both very religious and very intolerant. Hillary Clinton was here in Turkey, and she openly declared that her country would be supporting the 'refugees'. Now, to make it clear, these people that are being called 'refugees' come to our city, and they rent houses here and then many of them walk around fully armed, waving their machine guns. What is on everyone's mind here is that they did not come here just to fight the war on the other side of the border – they appear to be quite ready and capable of igniting violence in Hatay itself."

But the right-wing, pro-government media in the country is using a rather different and more complicated language to justify the support Turkey is giving to the 'refugees'. Today's Zaman newspaper on August 29th, 2012 noted:

> "Exploiting the issue of Syrian refugees in domestic politics in order to criticize the government is a cause for concern, according to many analysts in Turkey, who believe that the tensions that have occasionally broken out in recent weeks between local Turkish people and Syrians who have taken refuge in Turkey should not be exploited by the opposition; nor should the issue be treated as one of internal politics."

***

We drive to the border. It is almost full moon when we arrive at the Cilvegozu crossing, barbed wires and watchtowers on both sides of the access road. There are a few cars with Syrian license plates in front of an enormous metal gate, and there are several Turkish taxis waiting seemingly idle by the side of the road. But periodically the gate opens and cars come in and out. My Turkish colleague inquires if we can pass to the other side and talk to the Syrian border guard. The answer is a resolute "No!" – No Turks and no foreigners are allowed to cross here. The border is open – 24 hours a day – but only for Syrian citizens and the 'refugees'. Mehmet is a local taxi driver who shuttles Syrian citizens between the two sides of the border. He is at first reluctant and suspicious, but eventually he agrees to talk: "Hundreds of people pass through this gate every day," he explains. "And this is not the only one - there are of course other crossings in the area. Some people who come here are injured. Syrian border guards are very lenient: if they see that civilians have been caught in the crossfire, they let them pass without any hindrance. And once in Turkey, they get registered, processed, and housed." He confirms that the border is only for Syrians and the 'others' (he does not elaborate, as we are supposed to know): "We can only take people to the other side, to the Syrian post, and then return having picked up others from there. Everything is organized; it is not like the spontaneous border traffic of the old days."

***

Apaydin village is just a few minutes drive from the road connecting Hatay and the border at Cilvegozu. There are refugee camps; at least two of them. Officially all these camps are supposed to be for the immigrants escaping the violence in Syria, but we are told that one camp is strictly for 'fighters' and the other one for civilians. "The nearest camp is for those who have been fighting against Assad," explains a fruit seller at the side of the road. "There is a constant military presence around that camp. We are so unhappy about the Syrians coming back and forth! We are afraid, but nobody will pay any attention to us."

As we make our way towards the Apaydin camp, we are in constant telephone contact with the investigative journalist, Huseyin Guler. He keeps sending warnings: "I went three times near those camps. Yesterday we tried to enter the Apaydin camp but the guards became aggressive and tried to grab my equipment and to delete the photos. We resisted! They tried to take my cameras by force, but we said: 'you'd have to fight us!' We will defend our equipment. In the end they backed up, but only after some physical brawling. And this time we just tried to photograph the camp from a distance. Before disappearing, I found a sympathetic soldier. I asked him: There must be some serious reason why we are not allowed to take photos."

"Yes," he replied: "There are commandos and soldiers from the Syrian opposition inside this camp".

Now we are here. I have plenty of experience with photographing army camps. Just in the last two months I managed to sneak into those near the war-zones in Africa: on the Ugandan and DR Congo border, as well as to the one near Gisenyi in Rwanda. But Apaydin Camp is different. To be precise, this is no Red Cross or UNHCR facility; there are no signs of normal refugees, like babyclothes drying, families sitting idly near the fence, or cooking fires sending smoke towards the sky. From the first glimpse, this is one heavy combat camp, surrounded by layers of barbed wire, with watchtowers, soldiers pacing back and forth along the perimeter. The tents are minimalistic and its entrance is like that to some military base.

We drive at a regular speed surveying all the possible angles for photographing. Then after a sharp 180-degree turn and we begin working: in a slow movement across the front of the gate. I use a very fast professional Nikon. All goes well, but the guard is also fast, and he begins to signal at us, trying to make us stop. We ignore him, making another fast 180-degree turn and hitting the dirt road along the perimeter, although at some distance from the soldiers. It is not much but it is something. I let the motor of the camera run and take a sequence of shots, from several angles. My Turkish colleague is at the wheel and he is as good and steady as one gets.

In several minutes it is over and I have some 100 images of Apaydin Camp. But what I have are just external photographs of the site. I want more; I want to know what is hiding behind the fence.

***

"I have been inside Apaydin Camp only once," explains Huseyin Guler, when we finally manage to meet in a safe place in Hatay. "I actually did not enter; I was dragged inside – I was detained! Others are luckier, but not many. For instance yesterday, a Russian journalist – Fatma – was for some reason allowed to go in. Later she said that those so called refugees are directly 'fed' with US intelligence."

Photo 8. Apaydin camp in Turkey where 'Syrian Opposition' is trained by the West.

"You see, I have been working here now as an investigative journalist for a year and eight months. I shuttle between the border and the camps. Fighters leave Apaydin Camp in the middle of the night. And they return before dawn. We did our surveillance. Local villagers are confirming that the armed groups regularly cross the border at Kizilcat, which is actually a Turkmen village in origin. They march with the weapons on their backs. Across the border from Kizilcat, there used to be a Syrian control post, but now there is none. So the fighters crossing to Syria are managing to train the locals and to return before dawn. Turkish border guards just let them pass. Four months ago a Syrian MP came to Hatay. He protested at the murder of 120 Syrian officials in his country. CIA, Mossad and MIT (Turkish intelligence) immediately began pointing the finger at Assad and the government, but in this part of the world almost everyone knows who is really responsible."

Huseyin Guler than recalls how he went, six months ago, to a meeting of the 'refugees' where he was told that they were invited there by the PM of Turkey himself – Mr Erdogan – and that if they were given money, weapons and training, they would be willing and happy to fight Assad's government. Mr. Guler filed the story for Aydenlik. And the Turkish government never disputed it. He added, “In another border village – Asagi Pullu Yazi – I once met people who were coming directly from the fighting. One of the fighters said his cousin had been injured and was in the hospital. He even insisted that I know and use his name – Ahmed Mullah Hassan.”

***

For months I have been meeting Mr Serkan Koc, a leading Turkish documentary filmmaker and the chairman of National TV (Ulusal TV) at the discreet café of Pera Museum in Istanbul. We have been exchanging our documentary films and at one point Mr Koc interviewed me for his television station. But mainly we discussed Syria. He offered great insight into the occurrences at the border; he even supplied me with his own photos taken in Syria, permitting me to use them in my reports. This time, when I went to the border, he was helping to coordinate my steps remotely, over the phone, and supplying me with the details of his investigation:

“Of course you do realize that those people are not really ‘Syrian opposition’. They are modern-day legionnaires collected from various Arab countries, including Qatar and Saudi Arabia, paid by western imperialist powers. Some are members of Al-Qaeda and other terrorist organizations. Most are militant Sunni Muslims. One could describe them as rogue elements hired to fight the Assad government. It is important to point out that some 90% of Syrian people are still supporting Assad and I think he is now actually winning the war, although reading the western media you would never think so. Assad is enjoying the support of China, Russia, Latin America, Iran, Hezbollah, and many other countries and movements world-wide. The Turkish government is clearly in decline, supporting those terrorist elements the West calls the ‘Syrian opposition’.”

***

We drive once again to the camps. A few kilometers from Apaydin, there is a large camp that is hosting Syrian civilians. In this one there are women and children in open view; elderly people are chatting in front of the tents.

According to an official media communiqué by the Governor of Hatay – Celalettin Lekesiz – 17 months have passed since the refugees began entering Turkish territory. 44,000 were accepted. Syrians with valid passport can enter Turkey for three months without a visa and extend their stay for five months. Syrians without a valid passport or those who overstay are taken to the refugee camps. No refugees are allowed to wear military uniforms... 1,980 refugees have been treated for gun-related injuries. 157 criminal cases accusing Syrian citizens have been filed in the last seventeen months.

The plush pastoral landscape around Hatay is charged with fear and uncertainty.

***

We are driving at an illegal 160km/h on the highway so that I can catch my evening flight to Istanbul. Levent is a friend of many years and this report was supposed to be signed by both of us, but at the last moment he decides that it would not be safe for him: over one thousand people in Turkey are already in prison, some have been tortured. The victims are nationalist (anti-western) military officers and generals, journalists and intellectuals. Levent is a young Turkish intellectual. After some hesitation he offers his theory:

> "I don't see all this as a regional problem. Syria is just one pawn in a tremendous game that is destroying nation-states worldwide. The US and the West are intervening in Iraq, Libya and now in Syria with absolute impunity. Syria and Iran are two obstacles to absolute control over the Middle East by predominantly western business interests. It is all about the control of the natural resources, of the people, the armies... A World government project, with the West giving orders exclusively."

Levent sees the Turkish government as a major and negative regional player:

> "The present Turkish leadership is clearly under the influence of western imperialist powers. But the way it behaves - is all very blurry and designed to confuse people. On the world stage, the Turkish government tries to portray itself as decisively anti-Israeli, but just look at the military arrangements between the two countries, including the air force base in Konya which is still helping to train Israeli military pilots!"

***

Returning from what could be described as the relatively new front of a global western neo-colonial war, it would be easy to feel disheartened. Just a few weeks before Hatay I was filming at the border regions of East Kivu, DR Congo, a country which has already lost close to ten million people. The screws of global control appear to be tightening. Human life seems to have become worthless, and the propaganda of the western mass media almost absolute.

But as I drove, I thought about Turkey, and the more I thought about it, the more I felt convinced that Turkey is not just some depressing place between the West and the Middle East – it is another staunch ally of the forces ruling the planet. Its population is well educated, well informed and full of life. For me, many Turks have been a great source of inspiration.

Many Turkish people are resisting and by doing so they are willingly risking their lives. They are fighting, with pride and determination, and lots of them are ending up in prisons for their beliefs; for speaking and writing the truth about the forces that have been destroying the region and the world. I find it natural to lean on many of them, as they lean on me, translating my books, constantly inviting me to speak, asking me to join the struggle. As we approached the airport of Adana, I suddenly felt more hope and more strength to continue my work than I had before this short but revealing journey.

24 September 2012

*****

28

IMPERIALISM IS NOW MURDERING STORIES

Nothing frightens fascism and its older brother imperialism more than real people and their honest stories.

It is because the ordinary stories of ordinary people are so genuine and so accurately reflect authentic human fears, desires and dreams that the ideologues and propagandists of the Western regime, which is supported by an unnatural hyper-pseudo-reality, feel, for their survival, that it is essential to annihilate those stories, to wipe them off from the surface of earth, even to erase them from our memories.

Real human feelings get in the way; they still resist, they block the path to the total commercialization of life and the full implementation of the perverse concepts introduced by the Empire. Such resistance is described and glorified in real stories, making them 'extremely dangerous' and potentially fatal to the regime.

Human nature is fundamentally optimistic and kind; it is mostly even-handed and sharing. If it is not grossly manipulated, fooled, even conned; it generally puts the life of others well above cold profit. It is disposed to be compassionate, forgiving and accepting. It is not perfect, far from it, but as the French philosopher and writer Albert Camus declared at the end of his brilliant novel "The Plague": "there is more to admire than to despise in humans".

That is all very bad news for market fundamentalism and for the masters of the world. They need to ensure that the majority of the human race consists of greedy individuals, aggressive people, people who do not think or feel but consume, and, if they do think, about how to amass more, consume more; definitely not about how to build a decent and egalitarian society.

* * *

Each human life is made up of stories, of true and sincere stories. Some stories are 'common' and can occur, with certain variations, in any part of the world.

A boy meets a girl, and their love is 'forbidden', because they belong to a different class, ethnicity, or religion. They fight for their future together, against all oppressive customs and taboos, and they win or they fall. But after their epic struggle for happiness, their village, or their clan, will never be the same.

The son of rich man walks down the road in a miserable village, right near his mansion. He meets an old man or a woman. They sit for a while and talk.

The poor peasant conveys a message to the young feudal lord. Later this provokes questions, doubts and thoughts; he studies. A decade later he joins the revolution, to overthrow his own class. Almost all men and women of the revolution have lived through that moment, when they were told the truth on some dusty country road: Che, Lenin, Engels, Marx, Mao, Fidel, and Chavez.

Some stories are extremely unique and powerful:

> "As documented in a great book written by Ron Ridenour "Backfire", several Cuban men and women are approached by the CIA and asked to destroy their own country, to kill innocent people, to cause explosions onboard civilian airliners in mid-flight, to assassinate Cuban leaders, to poison humans and crops with chemicals. They accept; they take money. Then they immediately join the Cuban intelligence and for years work as 'double agents', to protect, to save their beloved Cuba. There is not one moment of hesitation. Fatherland is not some commodity; it is not for sale! The personal lives of some of them are ruined in the process. They keep no money for themselves. They give their entire CIA pay to their country, to buy medicine

and other necessities. They feed North Americans with false information. Eventually the story is made public. They save Cuba."

Such, are the great stories of decency, of courage, of progress.

"My life is my story," the brilliant German film director, Wim Wenders, once uttered. The identity of each person, no matter how rich or poor, educated or simple, consists of memories and dreams, and of extremely complex and fascinating webs of stories.

Most 'real' stories are wise, and they contain unmistakable sparks of humanism. Many of them also aim at something that we are all secretly longing for from the bottom of our hearts: something very positive, warm, compassionate and tender. They are yearning for good conclusions, not for some toxic and pinkish Disney or Hollywood-style 'happy ending', but for solid, just, and decent finales.

That is exactly why real stories' are becoming the targets of hit men hired by the Empire.

In order to plunder unopposed, to control, and to manipulate, the Western Empire assumed that it has to give legitimacy to its own acts of terror. Those acts have to be elevated to the highest moral ground.

To do so, traditional, logical and philosophical thinking has to be decomposed, then 'new thinking' introduced. A thoroughly new breed of stories must emerge, and even how stories are told must change.

Some would ask: 'How could crime be packaged as altruism'?

It can, of course, in those societies that perceive 'reality' after getting stoned on huge daily doses of advertisements and propaganda, two sides of the same coin, two synonyms of lie and deception.

In order for the brutal Empire to pose and to be considered as the savior of the world, first the analytical thinking of people has to be damaged, their ability to think has to be sharply reduced. The stories they are told have to become 'light', 'entertaining', extremely far from the reality.

The human spirit has to be broken, human nature reshaped.

Then all that is real, decent and pure in people has to be dragged through a muddy and non-transparent bath of nihilism.

Things that used to be sacred have to be spat on, optimism humiliated, ordinary kindness and warmth, killed.

Instead, substitutes have to be injected, if needed, by force.

It is because the acts of imperialism, like constant plunder and the commodification of life itself are grotesquely unnatural occurrences; they are morbid and pathological. And the only way they can be accepted is if reality is canceled, and then substituted by a 'new', gruesome and irrational pseudo-reality.

* * *

If in thousands of brainless Hollywood films, millions of people continuously vanish, victims of mutants, robots, terrorists, giant insects or microorganisms invading the earth, then the public becomes hardened, and 'well prepared for the worst'. Compared to those horrors of pseudo-reality, the real agony of millions of men, women and children in places like Iraq, Libya or Afghanistan appear to be quite insignificant.

"Their children get cancer from depleted uranium coming from our bombs, or they get simply torn to pieces... well, guess what: our children are eaten by monstrous tarantulas or murdered by Arab terrorists..." Those words are not pronounced, of course. The monologue takes place in the subconscious realm.

If a false giant shark begins stuffing itself with actors depicting defenseless swimmers on a picture-perfect resort beach, such fictitious terror, shocks more viewers and at a much greater extent than the real violence unleashed against the prisoners at US torture and detention centers like those at Abu Ghraib or Guantanamo.

Pseudo-reality is designed to dwarf reality.

Using the same concept, the viewers tend to feel a much greater shock when California keeps falling off a cliff into the Pacific Ocean in one of those disaster movies, than when they read about dozens of real and decent governments all over the world being overthrown by the Empire for simply being 'too decent', even when millions of real people perish in the process.

Psychologically, for many people there is no border between reality and pseudo-reality, anymore. Consumers of blockbuster movies and the mass media have been made immune to the real terror the Empire is spreading all over the world, because they have already seen 'much more frightening' stuff beaming out from the box.

Simultaneously, indoctrination gets encoded permanently in people's brains; they cannot make the distinction, anymore, between some outright BBC propaganda against China or Cuba, and the reality they encounter when they visit those two countries.

Some now judge the world, then make political and other decisions strictly based on that hybrid of reality and pseudo-reality: "The Chinese brutally murdered several thousand people when they torpedoed some fictional ship, as was witnessed in the latest Hollywood blockbuster, therefore we have to finance their 'opposition' and send our battle ships to the East China Sea, to deter the potential expansion plotted by Beijing."

And if our film studios and pop writers keep demonizing Chinese people, South Americans, Russians, Arabs, Iranians, North Koreans and many others, the imaginary threat, in some very twisted but well calculated and effective way, suddenly begins to justify the real and countless aggressions by the military forces of the Empire.

* * *

The Empire that consists of Western fascist regimes that call themselves 'democratic' and 'free', have already murdered several hundreds of millions of human beings on all continents. They have dropped mountains of bombs and biological weapons on countless countries; they have experimented on people, and overthrew most of the governments that were determined to serve their own people. They murdered Presidents and trained gangsters, whom they elevated to the ranks of top military brass, as happened in Indonesia, Chile, Egypt, El Salvador and in many other places. These gangster-soldiers were then given training, on Western military bases, in the 'art' of interrogation, torture and punitive rape, as well as the 'disappearance' of the opposition.

No other system has spilled more blood; no other system plundered more resources and enslaved more people, than the one we are told to describe in lofty and benign terms like 'Western parliamentary democracy' or 'Western constitutional monarchy'.

But the writers of the 'new stories', and manufacturers of pseudo-reality, do their absolute best to block this line of thinking. There is no discussion about the fact that the world is now fully enslaved by Western neo-colonialism, that it is controlled and oppressed to the greatest possible degree.

The past has already been fully changed and re-written, with collaborators coming from the ranks of both academia and the so-called 'liberal' and 'creative elites'. Grotesque lies are repeated thousands of times and therefore, as was suggested by the chief ideologist of Nazi Germany, they have become reality, Joseph Goebbels, so correctly observed many decades ago: "If you repeat a lie often enough, it becomes the truth."

The lies are retold about China, the Soviet Union, Latin America, about Western colonialism, and neo-colonialism, the Cold War, Afghanistan, and so many other essential places and events. Almost all related stories, except those that have been pre-selected, approved, and are useful for propaganda, have been successfully eradicated, muted, or at least ridiculed.

Inside the Empire itself, almost nobody protests, except when it comes to demanding for higher wages and better benefits. The Western masses have become the most complacent, uncritical group of people anywhere in the world. It is obvious from the art they produce and consume, from their political affiliations, from their aspirations.

An amazing paradox has developed, without being noticed or commented on: 'the system, which professes both individual choice and extreme self-centeredness, has actually managed to reduce a substantial part of the human race into an obedient, thoughtless, submissive, and frightened mass of uniformed beings convinced about their own superiority.

The individuality of people has almost entirely vanished. Their identity is now closely-linked and fully dependent on the manufactured identity of television stars, pop musicians and footballers.

* * *

It is logical and essential that the Empire tries to make sure that real stories get discredited, destroyed, wiped out from the face of the Earth; in order to prevent lapses, in order to make sure that human brains stop doubting and accept what they are being served.

Even the closest historical allies of real stories have been kidnapped, corrupted, and forced against them: books, films, music, and theatres, even fairytales.

But to the dismay of their tormentors, while in terrible pain, abandoned and endlessly sad, the stories do not seem to yield. It is because they are brave and proud, as human beings essentially are, and they know that so much depends on them – they are holding one of the last lines of defense against the capitalist genocide, against the commercialization of life itself, against the attempt to exterminate the human species as we know it.

As a storyteller I know all this, because they, the stories, are always talking to me. I also know that we will hold that imaginary defense line until the very end, together, come what way, with others who are still capable of thinking and hoping, and dreaming.

We will never cease telling the stories, real stories, because that is what human beings have been doing for centuries and millennia; telling stories, listening, learning, reading, moving forward, reluctantly, stumbling but moving nevertheless. We will be holding the line of defense against cultural fascism, because to succumb would simply be like betraying everything that makes life worth living.

For centuries and millennia people have dreamt about justice and kindness, they have been fighting for a better world where everyone has a roof over their head, food, free education, and medical care, where there is no fear and no danger coming from beastly and greedy usurpers.

The 'real' stories have carried such dreams, in their core.

Several years ago I sat in an old Café, the Brasilero in Montevideo, Uruguay, with one of the greatest Latin American writers, Eduardo Galeano, a man who wrote some of the most magical and powerful stories in the 20th century.

Before we parted, he said:

> "I am a hunter of stories; I listen to the stories, then I give this back to the people after putting the stories through a creative process. My position is always that in order not to be mute, one shouldn't be deaf. One has to be able to listen in order to speak. I am a passionate listener. I listen to reality. Reality is a magic lady, sometimes very mysterious. To me she is very passionate. She is real not only when she is awake, walking down the streets, but also at night when she is dreaming or when she is having nightmares. When I am writing, I am always paying tribute to her – to that lady called Reality. I am trying not to fail her."

If the regime decides to starve us, the real storytellers, we will, as in the marvelous story of Gabriel Garcia Marquez, "No One Writes To the Colonel", rather "eat shit", than to betray that magic lady called Reality. In our stories, reality is not for sale, just as the truth itself is not for sale.

* * *

On the last page of an old copy of the novel "River of Fire", written by Qurratulain Hyder, there are letters and numbers entered with a simple pencil: D.K. 30-9-99 24036

I don't remember how I obtained that book, and I don't know what these numbers really mean. The handwriting is unfamiliar. But they certainly mean something; something very significant, one more story, a symbol penciled into one of the greatest tales ever written in India. Both 'River of Fire' and the penciled note make one to dream and use imagination – to be alive.

Just as pornography cannot be defined as love, the 'new stories' that shape our worldview and penetrate our psyche, are actually not true stories at all. They are substitutes that were implanted in order to permanently replace the real thing.

They kill life itself in real living beings.

Those endless car chases, the meaningless slaughters of thousands of humans in almost every film, never-ending computer-generated disasters and horror scenarios, all have very little to do with real life.

The 'new stories' are more like an addictive substance, be they narcotics, cigarettes stuffed with chemicals, or very bad booze.

All over the world, billions of hooked viewers, adult and children, women and men, even the elderly, are now watching the same rubbish, consisting of computer-generated plots and images, phantasmagoric scenarios.

As was the case with the CIA-run Paris Review, the storytellers have been encouraged to elevate form over substance. We are expected to 'become daring' by showing as many female genitals in our art, describing as many mind-blowing situations, inventing 'personal dramas' and epic quests for 'self-fulfillment'.

All calls for an egalitarian society, for rebellion, revolution, for the end of neo-colonialism, of state terror, of propaganda, have been turned into an absolute taboo.

'Politics is boring' is one of the main messages we are encouraged to spread around. Because people are not expected to mingle in 'what is not their business'. Ruling the world is reserved for corporations and a few gangsters with excellent PR. The voters are there only to give legitimacy to the entire charade. And if they don't, they get slaughtered like in that brilliant novel called "Seeing" by the Portuguese novelist Jose Saramago.

Or as in real life, Europeans were massacred in France, Italy and Germany after WWII, when they went to vote the Communists into power, but instead were confronted by old Nazis who had been put to work by the Western allies, concretely by the US and UK, to murder the leaders and supporters of the Left. Successful Nazis were then shipped, discreetly and with all that loot from their Jewish victims, to distant South America, where I met and interviewed some of them and their children – in Paraguay, Chile, and Peru. But don't you even think about writing stories about it.

"Colonia Dignidad!" I was then told by one of the editors of the major German Magazine Der Stern, when I presented him with damning photos and true stories about the murderous German colony in Southern Chile. At one point he burst out laughing: "Never again!"

Real stories have been ridiculing this arrangement of the world. True stories were always 'political', because everything that matters is actually 'political'. Education and medical care are political and so are housing, city planning, green areas, corruption, the arts, religiousness or secularism, and therefore even love and how it can or cannot be expressed.

Great novels have always been political, and what we see now, their de-politicization, is abnormal, even perverse, fabricated. Many great songs used to be political, and they still are – in Latin America, in Russia, or in China.

Even Hollywood used to go political in some of its greatest films like; All the President's Men, Marathon Runner, They Also Kill Horses, The Way We Were, Kiss of the Spider Woman, to name just a few.

French cinema was political almost by definition and so was almost everything great that came out from Latin American and the Italian studios, directly or indirectly. The Soviets told their stories about saving the world from fascism, and about their attempt to build a classless society.

All that had to be stopped, by every means.

Lenin very correctly pointed out that film is the most important art form that can influence the masses. He knew it and spoke about it, but the Western regime made perfect use of that fact.

To make the world fragmented, to control it easily, the Empire made sure that the intellectual exchange between the continents was decisively disrupted. Everything had to be re-routed through 'hubs', where the information and messages could be monitored, selected and finally modified. Such hubs were New York, London, Los Angeles, Miami; all depending on what parts of the world were to be influenced, and through what media.

Los Angeles is the center for visual indoctrination and de-intellectualization, while Miami is, among other things, the center for extracting teeth by turning Salsa, the most political music form on Earth, which originally came from Cuba and the rest of Caribbean isles, into brainless pop.

If not directly destroyed, most of the great mainstay stories from the different parts of the world had to be thoroughly 'retold', and only then be re-distributed widely all over the world, in their shiny, new and useless form.

The punch lines of Russian, Japanese and French film masterpieces have been amputated by pathetic Hollywood remakes. Anglo-Saxons were now the only ones allowed to present their version of the stories to the whole world. And they truly perfected that brainwashing, indoctrinating narrative for instant consumption by, by now, fully uniformed viewers all over the world.

The main goal is clear: to make sure that people do not think. They should not think when they read, when they listen to music, when they watch films. They should not think much at all: but just study in their specialized fields, work for companies, consume, vote as they are told, and obey. Or else!

Now people worldwide are being fed the same doctrines, as they were fed the same products. An entire new religion of 'coolness' and 'stigmas' has been born, propagated by electronic and social media, in turn fueled by the major multi-nationals.

To be 'cool' was turned into the very opposite of what 'coolness' meant to be for centuries. Now it means not to think, to be like the others, to be 'light', to chat, to exchange meaningless messages and information, to desire the same products, to look the same, to accept what the Empire and market-fundamentalism professes. Those few thinking beings have been booed and expelled to the margins, from a very young age; they have been humiliated and in the end forced into joining the ranks.

The concept was simple: "we will make you stupid, uniform, uninformed, and unimaginative. Then, we will give you free choice, and it is likely that you will demand even more empty entertainment, more uniformity, more social media, and more toxic dreams. You will not protest, you will not demand a change to the system. You will work hard to make the elites richer, and consume what you are told you should find desirable. Amen.

We – your regime and you – will then be locked in a perfect symbiosis.

It has gone even further. At some point, the Western ideologues and their media outlets awarded themselves the exclusive right to judge, and to erect moral concepts.

It is as if a gang of bandits invades some frontier town, kills hundreds of men, rapes women, and robs the bank. The next day, members of the gang catch some miserable bicycle thief who took advantage of the chaos. The thief gets tried and condemned to several years in prison for his 'terrible crime'. The bandits then pose as heroes and saviors.

This, actually, would be an extremely good story to tell. The whole charade is so ridiculous, so transparent. But, shockingly, nobody is laughing, definitely almost nobody is laughing in the West!

* * *

One of the greatest films ever made – Kurosawa's "Seven Samurai" – got swiftly overshadowed by a Hollywood remake, the "Magnificent Seven", because it had to be the American cowboys, not Japanese samurais, who had the right to demonstrate a true moral standard to the world.

Of course, Kurosawa was a socialist realist, and his early scripts were totally unacceptable to the Western regime. It is also important to recall that Kurosawa, after the war, was busy searching for ways to avoid the censorship imposed on Japanese art and media by the US occupation administration.

Like films, also all those brilliant fairytales from all over the world had to be kidnapped, recycled, their teeth extracted, their social messages reduced to zero. Disney had repackaged those mighty as well tiny creatures from all corners of the planet, into a horrid, fast food-concept of fairytales; it destroyed and humiliated them, and turned them into pinkish and yellowish kitsch.

Even in those countries with ancient cultures and folklore, like Thailand and Indonesia, there is hardly anything left of the original legends: children are growing up fully dependent on mass-produced toys designed in computer workshops in the United States, instead of relying on their own story-tellers and wonderful legends. It is the same as with junk food, and later, cigarettes.

All identity has been wiped out, all creativity and originality destroyed. Even original lullabies are now disappearing from many parts of the world.

* * *

Writers, thinkers, journalists, filmmakers – most of them, gradually – have become obedient propagandists of the regime.

Thus the horrid prophecy of Orwell and Huxley has materialized, quietly, without any major dramas or 'significant events'. Of course true drama – the slaughter of hundreds of millions of innocent men, women and children in all corners of the world – has been ongoing for centuries. But the victims were, as Orwell called them, 'un-people', so nobody cared.

Then all of a sudden, everything became constrained. The flow of stories virtually stopped. We don't know exactly when it happened. Nobody does.

* * *

I often think about true stories in these dark days of the Western 'Talibanisation' of the planet. I draw inspiration and optimism from them.

Not too long ago, just some twenty years back, in the early 1990s, I was just a kid, a young reporter, covering the South American continent.

I will never forget the dynamism, zeal and courage of the people

I encountered in Chile, Argentina, Peru and Colombia. My novel, my rebellious *Point of No Return* that is presently being re-introduced to English readers after being fully re-edited, was greatly influenced by those years spent in Latin America.

Chile and Argentina were just waking up from their terrible nightmares, from brutal dictatorships supported by the West. Both countries were trying to come to terms with their past, to rebuild their societies.

Peru was still consumed by a brutal 'dirty war'.

The stories were everywhere; they were searching for storytellers, competing for our attention, chasing us.

I was still based in New York then, where I knew dozens of aspiring writers and film-makers, many of them continuously lamenting about 'not knowing what to write'.

Those were the post-Reagan days; New York was atomized, fragmented, with miserable slums and homeless people everywhere; people rotting at the entrances to subways, men and women dying lonely deaths, abandoned by their families and society. But writers took the luxury of not knowing what to say!

This was the era when the Empire was consolidating its power abroad, from South and Central Africa to Southeast Asia and the Middle East. The Soviet Union, the country where I was born, was decomposing after the 'Afghanistan trap', under the terrible reign of one naïve nitwit, and then under another one, a brutal notorious alcoholic and a protégé of the West.

I was shuttling between the awakening in Latin America and absolute stagnation in the West, where the writers were too busy suffering from identity crises to notice what was happening in the world!

* * *

I remember how ecstatic I felt high in the Andes. Of course, not because of the war, but thanks to the stories, an incredible amount of them, of which almost all were genuine.

There, the air was thin and so was Anglo-American propaganda. There, the stories were firmly in control of life.

People talked. I listened. It was how it always has been, for millennia, and it all felt right. I learned how to tell stories in the

Peruvian and Bolivian Andes. I learned how to listen. Sometimes it took an entire night to hear one simple and short tale in a clay hut, but it was always worth it.

One night my English photographer and I left the city of Ayacucho in the middle of the night, both of us shaken to the core.

Just two days earlier we were stopped by the Shining Path, *Sendero Luminoso*, hastily tried at the side of the road, and then condemned to death. True, we managed to talk ourselves out of execution, explaining, honestly, our distaste for both the President Fujimori and Yankee imperialism. But we were still in shock, as our young lives could have just ended there, at the kerb, in one instant.

Ayacucho means 'corner of death', it is a beautiful but cursed place high in the mountains, very indigenous and battered by centuries of colonialism and consequent feudal mores.

It was pitch-black, and we turned all the beams of our Land Rover on, shaking from altitude sickness, driving fast in order to 'fly over' an uneven dirt road. We were on an assignment for a big news magazine, and we were young, and definitely not quitters.

At one turn, an indigenous woman dashed under our wheels. She jumped, and then knelt, begging. I slammed the brakes. This could have been a typical trap; and it could have been our end. But the woman was crying, in pain, she was heavily pregnant, indicating that she was entering labor. Then she joined her hands in a powerful plea.

We stopped. We had no clue what to do. Two hardened war reporters with a big car and all that equipment inside, totally helpless, clumsy, stupid when faced with a new life that was demanding our assistance.

We literally carried her to the car, put her on the back seat and played, for the sake of doing something, some Chilean ballads from the car stereo. We tried to make her feel better.

What followed was a mess, a total mess! And from that mess a child was born, a girl! She was born alive and she survived; we had all made sure that she survived. And the two of us, two not so tidy young men who were cracking terrible jokes just a few minutes before, while our eyes were glued on the dusty road at some 4,000 meters altitude, searching for deadly military patrols, were now jumping around that good-natured indigenous matron with red cheeks, cleaning sweat from her forehead, somehow trying to be at least useful.

Eventually we drove both of them – mother and her tiny daughter – to the next village, where we found a willing midwife. As birth-assistants we were absolute failures, but for weeks we felt endlessly proud and the girl – the baby girl – still lives in my memory, as the most beautiful and dearest child.

That was one of the greatest stories I have ever encountered, simple and pure as a creek, back there, high in the mountains.

Later I saw similar scenes in the movies. The men helping were always sensible, comical, and absolutely unrealistic.

We were not really sensible at all. It was a war, a brutal war, it was cold and the woman was probably abandoned by her man; kicked out from her house... It was not a happy story, but it was human and in the end, a good story, and it probably made both of us better men.

After that, I saw death on many, too many occasions, and it was necessary to see it. I don't regret seeing death, because that is how this world is arranged, and I can't write about things I have never witnessed.

Everyone who has been to war knows that how it is portrayed in most Hollywood films, is simply a lie. I described war in my *Point of No Return*, and I am describing it again, now, in detail, in my latest 1,000 page novel.

It is important to write about war, to tell the stories that one experiences during battle, in ravaged cities and villages. Because almost all wars in modern history are caused, are triggered by us, by the West: our 'culture', our brutality, our greed, have caused the loss of hundreds of millions of lives all over the world. And it is great duty of ours, of storytellers, to speak about those events.

Our 'real' wars have now become 'remote'. We invented carpet-bombing, we dropped the A-Bomb; we killed millions of men, women and children in Indochina. We killed them mostly with our flying monsters, dropping millions of tons of steel on poor hamlets and villages full of people who just wanted to be truly free – free from our diktats and from our terror.

And now we use drones. We don't even dare to fly that heavy metal shit, anymore.

All this, because we are cowards, and our culture is both that of despots and weaklings. And to realize it, the only way to understand it, is to read and to watch the real stories of those whom we have been brutalizing and torturing.

But we don't want to. We close our ears with the palms of our hands. We refuse to hear them speak and laugh, we make sure not to hear them cry and scream. We are killing them, but we are doing it 'surgically', long-distance, while watching tarantulas on television sets consuming our cities, while stuffing ourselves on pre-fabricated food and buying toys for tiny children – toys that have no heart and no soul, anymore.

We have turned into total idiots, and we even kill like idiots.

Oliver Stone has made films about how we 'fought' these wars. That was the closest to reality. It was also an exception, and many people did not like what they saw.

The Soviet people fought a real war and they saved our planet. They also helped to liberate dozens of countries from Western colonialism. Without them, there would have been no freedom in Africa, the Middle East and most parts of Asia. But those facts are suppressed and can't be mentioned.

What also can't be mentioned is the heroic, and at the same time humble, involvement of the Cuban people in Africa's liberation struggle.

The Soviets also made great films about fighting and winning the war, and about saving us from fascism. "The Cranes Are Flying", "The Ballad of Soldier", "The Dawns Are Quiet Here", just to name a few.

Those wonderful Russian stories remain completely unknown, from films to modern novels, even those brilliant cartoons they made for children.

The West which, in the beginning fought half-heartedly against the German Nazis while simultaneously committing crimes against humanity in Africa, the Middle East and Oceania, made sure that everything connected with the heroic struggle of Soviet Russia was dragged through the dirt. The same tactics were, for years and decades, used against China and Latin America, particularly Cuba.

Cuba is the greatest enemy, a country the West has demonized and tried to destroy by chemical warfare, embargo, terrorism and relentless propaganda.

Why Cuba? Because Cuba has three things that the Western regime does not have: it has heart, it has humanism, and it has guts.

* * *

Is there any true opposition, or even self-criticism in the West? Or is the West finally coming to resemble its ally from the old days – the Taliban?

No films depict the open racism of Winston Churchill and his theories regarding "the beastly lesser races", or many of the other colonial monsters like British PM David Lloyd George, who, while his country was bombing Iraqi civilians in the mid-1920s, killed an international proposal to ban aerial bombardment with the phrase "We have to reserve the right to bomb the niggers." Hardly any stories unveiling the terror unleashed against the colonies, in practical terms against the entire world, are being allowed to domesticate in the psyche of Europeans and North Americans.

Busts and monuments to the worst racists and criminals now decorate London and all major British cities, just as the statues of the Belgian King Leopold II, a mass murderer responsible for the slaughter of 10 million Congolese people and for the chopping off of the hands of those who did not work fast enough to fill up his coffers, are now scattered all over Brussels.

The greatest and the most frightening story: that of the enslavement of the world by European and later North American tyrants has never been told. The stories of resistance against this unprecedented and ongoing terror are perpetually suppressed.

* * *

So here I am again, in Egypt.

An ugly armored vehicle is moving its cannon from left to right, as if searching for something, for someone. It passed me and I could clearly see the inside of its muzzle. It did not stop; it ignored me, as I was not the one it was searching for.

I keep working, unhurriedly, photographing and filming, then photographing again. I work monotonously, each move calculated.

Then something hits my chest. I hardly feel any pain, not much pain at all, just some.

I thought it was a bullet; they say one does not feel much pain in the first instant, in the few seconds after being hit. I did not want to look down, because if I was really hit by a bullet through the chest, it would all be over very soon: my insane life, and all those adventures and battles I have lived through ever since I was a child. And so I kept on working, by inertia.

There was disgusting smoke all over the street and soon I realized that I was not hit by a bullet, but by an empty teargas canister.

I was alive, and suddenly, as if to celebrate the fact, that miracle, my brain recalled the handwriting penciled into the last page of The River of Fire.

And I recalled the face of a girl, a maid called Ratan, from "The Postmaster", the first of the "Three Daughters" trilogy directed by one of the most brilliant filmmakers of all times – Satyajit Ray. I recalled her story, originally written by Tagore:

"A new postmaster comes from Kolkata to a small village. Ratan, a maid, an orphan, is 'given to him'. He is kind to her; he does not beat her as the previous 'owner' did. But he is bored in the village. He begins to teach her how to read and write. He talks to her. They are scared of the terrible storm, together. He falls ill. She moves into his house; she stays next to him, day and night, awake, and saves his life. She falls in love with him, although not one intimate word is uttered. He recovers. He decides to leave. A new postmaster arrives. She meets her love, on an empty road, as he is departing. She looks at him, for the last time. He stops, and then moves on. This, outside of India, an almost unknown frame, is one of the most beautiful moments in the world cinema."

'What a story', I think. 'What a tremendous story!'

The smoke was now covering the entire surface of the avenue. "What am I doing here?" I thought, just for a fraction of a second.

But subconsciously I knew: I was at the frontline, as I had been for years, fighting for the survival of real stories. Those that are all around us: small but deep, frightened and humiliated by the multi-million dollar productions coming out of Hollywood and Disney, with all their false pathos and noise, and lies.

As I watched the cannon, I thought that philosophers, not only storytellers, were 'out of vogue'. Both were assigned the identity of wooden toys, made with love but now obsolete, pushed into oblivion by hyper-reality, by electronic media, which has reduced emotions and human interaction to just a few abbreviated incoherent barks.

I pushed the shutter. My heavy professional stills camera recorded a moment – a tiny girl clinging to her mom, teargas burning her eyes. But her story, her tiny and real story: how could it compete with giant insects invading the Earth; how could it compete with the horror of the entire California falling off over the edge of a cliff, in those doomsday Hollywood movies.

What I was actually doing here was desperately trying to record the last glimpses of humanity. The real pain, real longing, hope and yes, love.

In order to record all those disappearing stories, I kept moving between geographical extremes, in some of the most inaccessible parts of the world, in conflict and war zones. I was propelled by a thorough spite for virtual reality, which was attempting to murder compassion, hopes, dreams, even love. And it went without saying that virtual reality felt absolute spite for people like me.

I straightened my filthy shirt and checked my lenses. They were intact. My cameras were working. My body was working. The name of the girl in Ray's film was Ratan. The handwriting at the end of the River of Fire said: D.K. 30-9-99 24036; whatever that meant.

The gun moved again, this time from right to the left. Again it did not stop. I was alive. And my heart was still on the left, where it belonged, and it was beating regularly, pushing red blood through my veins. And I was not going to stop telling 'real' stories, for as long as there was that naturally left-centered movement inside my swelling chest.

3 May 2014

29

Misery is Like a War

A DISPATCH FROM THE TOUGHEST SLUMS ON EARTH

Nairobi.

They tell you 'peace', but you know you are living in a war-zone. You've known it from the start; you've sensed it ever since you were a very little boy or a girl. You wake up every morning, not certain whether you will witness another dusk, whether you will experience another sunrise.

A bullet can hit you at any moment while you are walking down the road. If you are a woman, you can be ambushed and dragged into a dark back-alley or a filthy shack along the way, and then raped.

The police are very hard to find, and are hopelessly corrupt. You prefer not to seek their 'assistance'. You are really on your own: you own no gun, you don't belong to a gang, and you are extremely poor.

You are exposed.

Around where you live, there are bullets flying and fires burning. Once in a while a gasoline truck explodes, or the entire gangway of some miserable hovel bursts into flames. Loud salvos of sub-machine guns often penetrate the night.

But they tell you 'peace'. Europeans and North Americans, all those people that are making great incomes running their countless workshops in your dilapidated villages and towns... They are talking about 'teaching you' and your fellow slum-dwellers. They are talking about educating you, so that you can continue 'living in peace'.

The companies and Governments of these 'noble men and women', those that are teaching you about peace, are all over your bleeding country. They even use it as a base to invade neighboring lands. They are actually doing many things, while you are eating shit. Well, maybe not literally, but stuff that you aliment yourself on is not really much better.

You have no access to clean water. You stink. If you are a man, you stink. If you are a woman, you are dying from shame, but there is no escape: you stink as well. Chances are you are functionally illiterate. Maybe you can read a few separate words, but the meaning mostly escapes you.

You vote for those who are offering you more 'bob', and then you feel proud when you are told, again and again, that you live in a flourishing democracy.

You scream at night. Not every night, of course, but most nights you scream. You are considering ending it all, you often wish you could die, to depart from this world, but you do not dare to kill yourself.

The more desperate you get, the more you are being told that you live in a 'peaceful' country. While everyone actually knows that you live in one of the biggest slums on Earth.

You don't resist. Foreign governments and companies hail you. You are their favorite subject. You are patient and submissive, as almost all people around you are. They kill each other instead of those who drag them into misery: foreign colonialists as well as local elites.

You are constantly publicized as a good example to others, all over the world, especially to those who are opting to fight for justice, dignity and a better society.

***

Kariobangi is a shantytown, near an enormous slum called Mathare, in the middle of the Kenyan capital, Nairobi.

Through the narrow gangways and filthy roads open sewage, I am being led to a meeting with "Fire", a fearless gang member who has spent ten out of his thirty years, in various notorious Kenyan jails.

"Fire" is robust, pensive and humble. He left the high-security prison just recently. He wants to start from scratch, once again, as he has so many times before.

We sit down on a concrete block. Soon there is a crowd of onlookers, mainly children.

"Do you think people here live in peace?" I ask.

"No," he answers. "Here people die every day. All my friends are already dead. Men here die before they turn seventeen; most of them die by the time they are sixteen."

"How does it feel?" I ask him. "How does it feel to be alive; to be the only one who has managed to survive?"

"I am scared!" He looks at me. I know what he means. I have heard similar stories in Honduras, El Salvador, Haiti, and Uganda, in so many other places. He knows that I know and that is why he speaks. He is not afraid of bullets hitting him, of daggers cutting him to pieces, of police torturing him; he is not afraid of dying. But he is scared of staying alive; alone!

He is not a coward; he is brave. He is bright. He may be a gangster, but he has plenty of dignity. His fear is not animalistic; it is existential.

"How does it all begin here, in Mathare?"

"Here we start very young; slowly. We start by stealing at home, little by little. Then it gets big: snatching phones and necklaces, buying guns. Eventually we get caught because we are young and have no experience. We go to prison and prison is both hell and the university of crime. You enter, you know nothing about crime; you leave and you know everything. You encounter people of all races and trades: bank robbers and serial killers. They tell you: it is better to die robbing a bank than snatching a wristwatch."

"How bad is prison, Fire?"

"They rape you. There are no women, so if you are a young boy, you have no chance. Young kids get sodomized. To survive, they have to prostitute themselves. In prison, men rape men. Some marry each other. You get beaten and humiliated; by inmates and by the police who are extremely brutal and sadistic. You learn how to get tough. If you survive, you are ready..."

I see a knife, sharp like a razor, shining in the sunlight.

I point at it: "Tell me about this."

"*Bila,*" he says. "It comes from Somalia. They are made for killing. The way they are shaped, look; you lose so much blood and you die. Here we call them *wambe*, which in Swahili means razorblade. But no matter how sharp it is; it is still a knife.

"What about guns?" I ask.

"They are all over the place. They are very cheap. Guns come with the refugees, and the refugees arrive from Somalia and Ethiopia."

"How do women survive here?"

"It is tough for them. Some are forced into prostitution; many join criminal gangs. Their boyfriends force them. Many women are submissive to 'their men'. They do what they are told. They are told to have sex and they succumb; they get into prostitution, and they even join the gangs. Whatever 'their men' order them to do. Women here are scared of losing their men." At some point, "Fire" becomes quiet. His eyes are fixed at some point in the distance.

"Talk to me" I say. "What is it?"

He looks somewhere else, but eventually he continues speaking. "My generation... I told you... All my friends are dead. All of them... all died... I feel a chill. But I can't leave the slum... It needs me... I need it... I can't run away from it, as I can't run from myself. The slum is the microcosm... it is..."

"Your Kenya?" I suggest.

"Yes," he nods. "I tell stories... I tell how I have survived up to this advanced age of thirty. I always tell stories, even to the government people. I tell them how lucky I am to be here... to be alive... I want to be good, but sometimes you can't sleep three nights on an empty stomach."

"We both tell stories," I say.

He does not hear me, anymore. "I wasted so many years... so many years," he repeats.

***

Those men of the slums, those boys! They play with guns, and they kill and rob. Like on the battlefields, their faces are resolute, serious. Even as they are doing the most insane things, even as they are rampaging and plundering, they look purposeful, as if their actions have some deep meaning. Here and in wars, the acts of pillage have an almost religious connotation.

Living in slums is like living in a war-zone: day after day, year after year, until one is hit, stabbed, burned; until one falls.

But what about the women of the slums, what happens to them? They become mothers at thirteen, prostitutes at fourteen; they get raped before their first period. Some go through an abortion at fifteen; others die of AIDS by the age of sixteen. Some throw their unwanted babies into the gutters, out of sheer thorough desperation.

Are the women of Mathare; are the women of Kibera, really living in peace? Are the women in the slums of Jakarta and Mumbai living in peace? Are the women in Haitian slums living in peace?

Ms. Jitne Watere has her 'boutique', in the middle of Kariobangi. It is just a small tent, next to a busy road, with some neat white clothes on show inside. I don't ask about her age; such questions are rude. I don't want to know any details; the most painful ones.

All I want to know: "Is this a war for you? Or is it peace?"

She avoids a direct answer. She looks at me straight in the eyes.

"If you are forced to become a prostitute at the age of twelve... if you get infected with HIV... if you are forced to... Can you call it peace?"

She is younger than me, but she looks at me as if I were a child.

I have seen a lot in this life and she was told that I had. But I sense that she has seen much more, and I lower my eyes instinctively, as she speaks.

"By the standards of the slum, I became a prostitute at quite a late age – I was sixteen. I lost many friends. One girl after another was falling, dying from AIDS, from 'bush abortions', from being beaten to death, even from poisoning. Others had fallen because of an overdose."

We are standing inside her 'boutique'. This is one of those moments when a writer sometimes cracks and just drops the notepad into the bag, waves his arms in desperation and says: "Let's go and get some beers... Let's get drunk... It is all damn screwed up!" But I get a hold of myself; I don't want to hear her stories through some unnatural filter.

And so, we keep standing, facing each other.

"Rape," she says. "It is often not even called rape here... And do you know what a 'bush' abortion is?"

I nod. I know perfectly well what it is. But I don't want to hear the details. I know I would not be able to put them into the pages of this brave publication. I stop her. I stop her.

"Fine," she says. "But one thing you have to know about a 'bush' abortion... It's that sometimes... very often... mostly... it doesn't succeed... If it fails, a woman dies. Or she doesn't die, but she wishes she did. Because if she doesn't, what comes is..."

Two of my acquaintances, one a local gangster and one local ambulance workers, both very strong men, are beginning to look away, in shock. My driver is waiting outside.

"The babies are thrown into the garbage," she says. "Some are alive, some dead. They don't tell you this in the newspapers... You are not supposed to talk about it... It is common here..." 'In Indonesia, too', I think. "As well as in some countries of Central America." I say nothing.

I ask no further questions. There is no point in asking anything else. She has said all there is to say, intuitively, and in summary.

But I was wrong: she had not finished, yet. She drills me with her eyes. I came here, I risked my life to come here, and I did more than what she had expected: I listened to her. Now she was going to give me her conclusion, her bottom line:

"Do you know why all this? Do you really... really... want to know?"

I know. She knows. I have written about it thousands of times. It is now her turn to say it:

"It is because we are all poor! Because we have nothing! We do not matter. That's why we die young. That's why our children die..."

***

Then, in the car, Douglas who now works for the St. John's Ambulance Service begins telling me his story:

> "There is nothing local people can count on... They are unprotected, totally on their own. Women suffer the most. 90% of women here are single mothers; there is nothing like marriage or loyalty in the slums. The family system has broken down. You go from door to door, and when you ask; you will be shocked."

Our car passes by Mathare. Almost all the children here suffer from malnutrition. Many have been working since an early age; pushing heavy carts, carrying loads, selling things by the kerb.

"What is the typical story here?" I ask Douglas.

"Fourteen year old girls get abused... or forced into prostitution... Mostly they become prostitutes for food. They go for about one dollar, out of desperation. One gets pregnant at the age of thirteen or fourteen, at most fifteen. Then her man leaves her. She is left with nothing; no education and no skills. These are girls who leave their children on the street... Others get abortions...

You were just told... many of them die."

"Very few men get married," the driver, Gilbert chips in. "Very few take care of their children and their women, everything has collapsed here. The entire structure is gone."

"I will tell you a story and then you tell me whether this place is a peaceful area or a warzone", continues Douglas. "One night I was forced to help my neighbor to give birth... It happened not far from where we are passing now. I was washing a car... My friend ran to me at 1AM, screaming that a woman who was living on our plot had entered into labor. We managed to get her to the car. There were three of us in the vehicle – two boys and the woman with labor pains. The child began coming out. I opened the window and began screaming: "Help!" I was begging for some woman to open a door and come out, to help us, because my friend and I had no idea what to do. Nobody came out; they were all scared. My friend ran away. In the end I dashed to the local store and bought a razor blade... I cut her umbilical cord. Then I drove her home. Her son was born. They both survived, miraculously, just like in a war!"

"Like in a war," I said, recalling a very similar situation, when an indigenous woman entered labor and gave birth in my car, in the Peruvian Andes, in 1992.

***

In Mathare 4A, the garbage is burning and child-scavengers are performing acrobatic somersaults. The ground is soft, swampy. The entire area consists of metal-sheet shacks, filthy stalls and a fast-moving polluted river. It is not as dirty and hopeless as those slums in Port-Au-Prince or in Jakarta, but it is still to a great extent, filthy.

"I grew up here," says Douglas. "I used to be like those kids. I used to play in the garbage; I used to swim in this river."

He waves at the kids. They wave back.

"Fortunately, I got some education. Now I do first aid and firefighting."

"Douglas, so what are you facing here?" I ask. "What casualties do they bring to the medical posts at night?"

"Victims of all sort of violence", he replies. "Machete wounds, gunshots... You know, police shoot gangsters and innocent bystanders, while gangsters shoot victims, and sometimes the police.

Everyday something terrible happens: people are shot, stabbed, and raped."

I am taking all of this in, then taking notes and photographing the somersaulting children.

"We have to go," says Douglas, abruptly. "They will soon begin closing on us."

"Wait," I say. He speaks better here than in the car. It is all flowing well, and coming out effortlessly.

"Ok," he says. "I know what you are trying to prove. And I agree with you a 100%. It is a war-zone, ok? It is a battleground. But now please listen to me: To me, to us here, it is normal. Totally normal, get it? Violence is normal... I know, I sense it is not good, but it is normal... I have buried many friends here. Every day, several people get assaulted, killed, shot. Nothing surprises me, anymore! It is normal! Many of my friends have died... many of "Fire's" friends have died. My cousin was recently killed... He was shot dead, at sixteen! Women... they get raped, brutalized, molested, insulted... At night... almost all of them here have experienced some violence, even at home... And at night, only those 'hardcore' ones dare to open the door... Men die because they fight back... You know, those gangsters who are assaulting people, they are not as brave as they try to look...Deep inside they are human, scared little kids, boys... They know they can die while stealing, and so they kill, because they are frightened... Despite everything, they want to live... They want to live desperately... and so they kill."

He said enough. He breathes heavily.

"Normal! All this is normal..." He repeats.

"So why are you crying?" I ask.

He does not reply. He looks around.

"We go!" He shouts at me. "Fast! They are watching us; they are coming. Here they can do anything they want to you... They can take anything..."

"Let's go," I agree. "We have photos inside this camera. No matter what, they can't take this one."

"We fight?" He asks. "If they come, we fight or we let it go?"

Gilbert, the driver, evaluates the situation. He steps on it, and drives the car towards us through the grass. Our feet are caught in the unstable, swampy ground. There are strange movements all around us, several people closing in on us. The river is on the left. I consider my options. The river seems to be one possibility.

"We will fight," I say in the end.

"Good."

The car is faster than the gang members. We dive in. Gilbert drives towards the road.

When we are inside, Douglas grunts: "You are tough."

That's all that matters here. My skin color becomes irrelevant and so does my work. The only thing that has value in the slum is whether one has guts.

***

Constable Bobby Ogola is based at Buru Buru Police Station. Buru Buru is one tough place and the constable is a tough guy who does not seem to like anybody, especially not the gangsters and Somali refugees. Anywhere else his attitude would be questionable, called racist. But it is again normal here, in the war-zone called the slum:

> "There are too many firearms in the hands of young people aged between sixteen and thirty. Most of the firearms come from Somalia. We have constant cases of car-jacking here, of violent robberies, rapes and murder. There are also abductions in Eastlands."

The doctor at the dispensary in the middle of Kariobangi calculates that on average, around ten people die a violent death during a weekend in this slum alone.

The majority of the people in Nairobi live in slums.

As we leave, Gilbert the driver concludes: "You have written about these places for years... It is absolutely clear that the people here live in a combat zone. You see their children go hungry everyday. There is no running water, no jobs, and no toilets. But there are bullets and knifes. And there is fear and violent death everywhere."

"You die if you get sick here," says "Fire". "Life is so cheap. Of course people die from cancer and other 'complicated' illnesses, because there is no way they would be treated for free. But they also die of easily preventable diseases like malaria. All we can get here are pain-killers, sometimes."

***

Is the system to blame? Everybody thinks so, but there is also that dogged belief that 'nothing can be done" and "nothing can be changed".

The elites are too powerful, and they are backed by several Western powers. Corruption is endemic, but the corruption is not homegrown; it came from outside, it was imported, and like elsewhere, it entered the 'culture' as local elites were encouraged to collaborate with colonial powers.

While the local MPs enjoy some of the highest government salaries anywhere in the world, almost no funds are allocated for the improvement of life in the slums.

"We have a program here, we formed an organization", says Ms. Jitne Watere. "We are trying to help abused women. But very few funds from above are allocated. And that little that there is, disappears in corruption. Women meet, they talk and then they ask: 'What next?' But there is nothing we can do."

***

While Venezuela, Bolivia, China, Vietnam and other socialist countries have managed to lift hundreds of millions of people out of poverty, those close allies or virtual colonies of the West, that include Kenya, Uganda, Indonesia, the Philippines and India, to name just a few, have developed and then perfected a total spite for most of their own people.

In Kenya, they hold elections, but no major political party represents the interests of the impoverished majority. The extreme capitalism serves only the very small minority, the immoral rulers. Statistics are manipulated and twisted, while the media is subservient to local and foreign regimes.

Nairobi, Kampala, Jakarta, Manila, Mumbai, Guatemala City – the same pattern of urban violence. Shopping malls and five star hotels surrounded by barbed wire and war zones.

Now there are organized tours, to the slums. Some Europeans like to see, to feel the thrill. One week in the national parks of Kenya and Tanzania, and then a few hours in Kibera, watching people starving and dying. It is the 'complete experience', something to show the neighbors at home or spread through social media. I saw this while writing about the Yugoslav War. I saw this recently at several Syrian borders. War tourism...

***

Some time ago, I was filming Kibera from the railway tracks; those that pass through this, the biggest slum on Earth. I put my professional camera on a tripod and began working.

An old man approached me. He was drunk, or he was high on *miraa (Khat).*

"I want your camera," he said. "I can kill you now, and I don't give a damn what will happen to me afterwards. I am HIV positive; I have nothing, I am dying."

But he could not kill me. He was weak and could hardly stand on his feet. My friends rushed to my rescue, but I didn't need any help. The man disappeared under the hill. He was destroyed, shaking, and alone.

After that, it was all totally peaceful. It was peaceful for me, for the Kenyan elites and for the global regime.

But soon, as the sun begun to set, down below there, in the middle of the slum, the first fires started burning and the first gunshots began resonating. Another battle was beginning, a battle between the victims and the other victims.

The poor have been obediently dying, as the Global regime has been consolidating its control over the planet.

24 May 2014

*****

30

Eight Days in the 'Land of Evil'

NORTH KOREA CELEBRATES ITS 60TH ANNIVERSARY OF VICTORY

As the plane – a Russian-built Tupolev-204 – was taking off from Pyongyang Airport, I felt nothing, absolutely nothing. The morning fog, that at first was covering the runway, then began to lift. The engines roared. Right after takeoff I could clearly distinguish green fields, neat villages and ribbons of ample and lazy rivers below the wing. It was undeniably a beautiful sight: melancholic, poetic, and truly dramatic. And yet I felt numb. I felt nothing, absolutely nothing.

The overhead monitors were beaming endless images of one parade after another, of endless celebrations and bombastic concerts. The volume was up, the women and men on the screen were singing enthusiastically, soldiers were marching; roaring jets and helicopters penetrated the blue sky. The conductor was waving his hands. The standing crowd was applauding. Emotions were brought to an absolute extreme; watering the eyes of the people, and the omnipresent pride on their faces.

Suddenly I felt empty, scared of something.

After visiting more than 150 countries, all over the world, after covering wars and conflicts, some of unimaginable intensity and brutality, I was suddenly longing for a rest, even for total silence.

60 years ago North Korea won the war. But some 4 million people died, many of them civilians. Maybe it was more than 4 million, nobody knows exactly. The capital city Pyongyang was totally leveled to the ground. I did not want to hear loud music and long speeches. I wanted to pay tribute to those who lost their lives, by sitting quietly by the river covered by mist, listening to the tall grass. But during my 8 days in North Korea, I had very few moments of silence, almost no opportunity to reflect.

What have I seen in those 8 days in DPRK – in North Korea? I saw an enormous futuristic city, Pyongyang, the capital, built from the ashes. I saw enormous theatres and stadiums, a metro system deep below the ground (public transportation doubling as nuclear shelters, in case the city came under attack). I saw trolley buses and double-decker buses, wide avenues, unimaginably ample sidewalks, roller-skating rinks and playgrounds for children.

There were statues and monuments everywhere. The size of some boulevards and buildings was simply overwhelming. For more than a decade I lived in Manhattan, but this was a very different grandeur. New York was growing towards the sky, while Pyongyang consisted of tremendous open spaces and massive eclectic buildings.

Outside the capital I saw green fields, and farmers walking home deep in the countryside. Clearly, there was no malnutrition among children, and despite the embargo, everyone was decently dressed.

I saw packed squares, with tens of thousands of people shouting slogans at the top of their lungs. I saw thousands of women in colorful traditional dresses waving their flags and ribbons, cheering when a command was given, welcoming us – the international delegates. Marching next to me for peace, was a former US Attorney General, Ramsey Clark, and on my other side, the leader of one of the Indian Communist Parties. There were human rights lawyers from the United States and from all over the world, Turkish revolutionaries, and, for hard to understand reasons, several heads of the Ugandan military.

But I did not come here to march. I came here to film and to photograph, to see the faces of local people, to read what was written on those faces, to feel, to sense, and to try to understand.

Instead of loud cheers, I came to listen to the whispers, hoping to catch understated facial expressions, tiny signs of fear, of joy, of love and even of existentialist confusion.

The West, its policy-makers and mass media, have succeeded in creating an image of a dehumanized North Korea. They did it by blurring the faces. For decades North Koreans were being portrayed as inhabitants of some monstrous hermit empire where men, women and children all look alike, dress the same, behave like robots, never smile and do not look into each other's eyes.

Before I came here, before I agreed to come, I explained to the organizers that I was not interested in all those elaborate fireworks and packed stadiums. I wanted to see a mom taking her child to school. I was longing to capture the faces of lovers at dusk, sitting side by side on some remote bench, whispering to each other those urgent words, those pledges that make life worth living; the same words, the same pledges, uttered all over the world.

Paradoxically, I was discouraged from doing so. Instead I was asked to march. From a storyteller and a man who is used to document the world, I was converted into a delegate. And whenever the crowd spotted me, it cheered, and then I felt embarrassed, I was longing desperately to become invisible, or to at least find some hiding place. Not because I was doing something wrong, but simply because I was unaccustomed to such naked outbursts of enthusiasm directed at me.

And so I marched, for peace and for the re-unification of the Korean nation. And while I marched, I kept filming and photographing. It must have looked awkward, I have to admit: a delegate who was filming a bunch of women who were dressed in their colorful traditional dresses, cheering him with their paper ribbons, and shouting at the top of their lungs.

I soon discovered that I was fighting for every glimpse of reality, of common life. Instead I was being fed with an extravaganza.

I was taken to those stadiums with 100,000 people, where children change the positions of their boards periodically, and the entire side of the tribune suddenly becomes like some colorful, living storyboard. I witnessed huge events, with thousands of dancers, with fireworks and multiple bands.

Yet what impressed me the most was an ancient and tiny stone bridge in Kaesong City, near the De-Militarized Zone. And the scene around the bridge: a tiny girl, perhaps three years old, her sock torn, crying, while her mother caressed her hair in the most tender, warmest way imaginable.

My hosts, they did not seem to understand. I explained to them, again and again, but my words sounded too foreign to them.

As far as they were concerned, I was just 'some famous writer, filmmaker, and journalist'. They needed me to show great support for their revolution, and deep reverence for their suffering during the Western onslaught more than 60 years ago.

Naturally I felt reverence and grief, but that was all that I was expected to feel. I felt much more.

But I fell in love, instantly with the North Korean countryside, and the faces of North Korean farmers and city dwellers. These were pure faces, honest and expressive. What could I do? Love is subjective; it is irrational. The exaggerated greenery of the fields, children playing at the roadside, soldiers returning home to their villages for a short home-leave, women facing the sun at dusk: it was overwhelming; love at first sight, as I said.

I was photographing through the windshield; I was annoying the organizers, demanding that they stop in the middle of the road.

Then on July 26th I met, together with Ramsey Clark and few other delegates, Mr.Yang Hyong Sob, the Vice President of the Standing Committee of the Supreme People's Committee. He looked like a very kind man, and I was given a chance to exchange some ideas with him. I explained that the best way to combat Western propaganda is to show to the world the faces of North Korean people.

"It is their common tactic," I said. "They portray the people of China, Cuba, Venezuela, Russia, Iraq, Afghanis-tan, Serbia, as heartless, as if they were some plastic androids. Then, subconsciously, compassion for the people of those nations vanishes from the hearts of the Western public. Suddenly it is fine to starve them, to bomb them, to murder thousands, even millions of those androids. But once their faces are shown, the Western public gets confused; many refuse to support mass murder."

The Vice-President nodded. He smiled at me. As we were leaving, he locked me in a bear hug, and said simply "Please come back!"

But even after that meaningful exchange, I was still marching. And the simplest images were continuously out of my reach. "For this trip only, as we are celebrating the 60th Anniversary," I was told. But I lived for now and now, I wanted to work.

I saw the De-Militarized Zone, DMZ, and the South Korean border post at Panmunjom. Twice in the past I had visited the same place, only from the opposite side. The DMZ is supposed to be the most fortified border in the world, as the two Koreas are still technically at war. The two armies are grudgingly facing each other, armed to the teeth, while the US forces are holed up somewhere underground on the southern side.

Yet The DMZ is like some eye of the storm, sitting in between all those nukes, tanks and rocket launchers, quietly and pristinely. The rivers flow lazily, and farmers grow ginseng, arguably the best in the world.

I endured endless security measures, and in the end I faced the empty South Korean visitor's terrace. There were obviously expectations of some hostilities on both sides of the line, and no 'ordinary' visitors were allowed to travel here.

It was all a big mess, and a never-ending drama. A divided nation; millions of deaths. I saw it all in the city of Sinchon. The tunnels where the US troops massacred thousands of civilians during the war, old veterans and survivors of the massacres spoke; recalling those gruesome events.

In 1950, at the beginning of the war, the city of Sinch'ŏn was the site of a massacre of civilians by the occupying U.S forces. The number of civilians killed over the 52-day period was allegedly over 35,000 people, the equivalent of a quarter of the city's population at the time.

It all looked chillingly familiar. I used to photograph the craters left behind after the carpet bombings of Cambodia, Laos and Vietnam. Brutality, brutality, brutality... Millions of faceless victims burned alive by napalm, 'bomb-lets' that explode decades later when children or water buffaloes are playing on the fields.

Ramsey Clark spoke about the horrors of the past, and about the brutality of US actions. An old man, one of the survivors of the mass killings of civilians in the tunnels, spoke about the horrors he witnessed as a child. The artwork in the local museum depicted the brutal torture and rape of Korean women by US troops, their bodies mutilated; with nipples penetrated by metal hooks.

In the West, the topic remains almost totally taboo. One of the greatest journalists of the 20th century, Wilfred Burchett, even lost his citizenship and became 'an enemy of the Australian people', partially because he dared to describe the suffering of the North Korean people, a few years after he had described the aftermath of Hiroshima bombing in his 1945 iconic report, "I Write This As a Warning To the World".

The brass band begins to play yet another military tune. I zoom on an old lady, her chest decorated with medals. As I get ready to press the shutter, two large tears begin rolling down her cheeks. And suddenly I realize that I cannot photograph her. I really cannot. Her face is all wrinkled, and yet it is both youthful and endlessly tender. Here is my face, I think, the face I was looking for all those days. And yet I cannot even press the shutter of my Leica.

Then something squeezes my throat and I have to search in my equipment bag for some tissue, as my glasses get foggy, and for a short time I cannot see anything at all. I sob loudly, just once. Nobody can hear, because of the loud playing of the band.

Later I get closer to her, and I bow, and she recipro-cates. We make our separate peace in the middle of the boiling-hot main square. I am suddenly happy to be here. We have both lost something. She has lost more. I was certain she had lost at least half of her loved-ones in the carnage of those bygone years. I lost something too: I lost all respect and belonging, to the culture that is still ruling the world; a culture that was once mine, but a culture that is still robbing people of their faces, and then burns their bodies with napalm and flames.

It is the 60th Anniversary of Victory Day in the DPRK. An anniversary marked by tears, grey hair, tremendous fireworks, parades, and by the memories of fire.

That evening, after returning to the capital, I finally made it to the river. It was covered by a gentle but impenetrable fog. There were two lovers sitting by the shore, motionless, in silent embrace.

The woman's hair was gently falling on her lover's shoulder. He was holding her hand, reverently. I was going to lift my big professional camera, but then I stopped, abruptly, all of a sudden too afraid that what my eyes were seeing or my brain imagining, could not be reflected in the viewfinder.

2 August 2013

*****

31

HAVANA, WHERE EVERYONE CAN DANCE

Havana, Cuba

It is crowded and loud. *La Froridita*, a famous old bar in *Havana Vieja* (Old Havana), is packed to the rafters. The patrons consist mostly of foreigners and some overseas Cubans. They are loud, trying to shout over the upbeat *son* music booming from an old stage where the confident lead singer of an all-girl band is threatening her boyfriend or husband, with a stunning re-arrangement of the old *bolero* 'Si Tu Te Vas' ('If you go away').

It is all very cool. This is the exact bar where Hemingway used to have his countless *Daiquiris*. Not those touristy and over-sugary ones that one gets anywhere in the world nowadays (even here, at *La Floridita*), but those very 'masculine' *Daiquiris*, bitter and unsweetened, made only from rum, squeezed grapefruits and crushed ice.

The waiters, all middle-aged men, work in unison, with perfectly coordinated movements, wearing "Havana Club" aprons.

Drinks here go for US$6, making them out of reach for most ordinary Cuban citizens. But this place is just a part of that huge hard-currency earning industry, which has countless outlets all over the island: beach resorts, clubs, restaurants, bars, and boutiques. Propaganda beamed from the North calls this arrangement 'cynical'. Some section of Cuban citizens, critics of the Communist system, as well as various revolutionary 'purists' also dislike the arrangement. But there is consensus among the rest of the population that this is the best way to maintain the free and excellent health system, education, housing and culture.

Clubs, theatres, galleries, are all powerful magnets for educated visitors from all over the world. Cuba has the reputation of being a cultural powerhouse. And unlike in any other nation in the world, Cuba's main attraction are its high-quality artists, and the main 'exports' are not manufacturing or agriculture; it is culture and the arts.

People from all over the world travel here to listen to some of the greatest music played anywhere on Earth, to visit countless research centers, art schools, to attend concerts and performances, or simply to stroll through the many magnificent cities, world heritage sites as declared by UNESCO, like those of Santiago de Cuba and Havana.

In Old Havana, the atmosphere is always electrifying. Unlike in Western Europe and United States where culture and the arts have become mostly decorative and 'form over substance', in Cuba, art is alive, it overflows onto the streets, and it is magnificently vibrant.

I lean over the bar and scream into the ear of old bar-keep whose name is Jose:

"They say this is like surrendering to capitalism. This bar; places like this bar..."

"Let them eat shit", he replies laconically, working his powerful mixer. "Look, do you see that door; the entrance door? It is open right? This place is air-conditioned but the door is open. All over the Old Havana, the doors and all those huge windows that grow from the floor are open. Do you know why? So everybody can hear the music. Windows here are like walls. And if they are open, it is as if there is nothing between the musicians and the street. Nothing at all! You just stand and listen, for free."

"And if they, the people, want to come inside?" I ask.

"So they come in," he replies. "They don't have to drink our booze here. It is their country. They can enter, and listen, of course. Do you see any bouncers here? Look, in this country we care about feeding people and curing the sick first... It is not easy with the embargo... We will make sure in the future that everyone can have a drink in places like this too. But for now, honestly, it is not a priority!"

At the end of the L-shaped bar, a bronze statue of Ernest Hemingway leans on a perfectly polished wooden surface. Several tourists take snapshots of the embracing great North American novelist, one of the best friends of revolutionary Cuba. Hemingway lived here. He donated money from his Nobel Prize for Literature, to this country.

Here, in this bar, Hemingway is not politicized too much. But it is clear what the Western establishment is ready to do to those who support Cuba and socialism:

> "The FBI tailed Hemingway, he was harassed and until now there are many unanswered questions regarding his death. Some suggest that his 1960 medical treatment was actually supervised by the government authorities and that he was given excessive doses of electric shocks that destroyed his memory and drove him to suicide."

This is of course not common knowledge embedded in the minds of North American and European visitors. They come here for the arts, for the unrepeatable atmosphere of lightness and good humor. They come here to listen to music and to dance. And to taste bits of 'forbidden fruits', and to break the US embargo here and there.

Very few can resist falling in love with the country, where entire streets and entire neighborhoods, are turned into concert halls and dance floors.

One of the iconic phrases symbolizing Latin American revolutions has always been: "Everybody Dances or Nobody Dances!"

In Cuba, music and dance are synonymous with life. Here, everybody dances, and that is how the revolution survives.

Yet things are not always 'light'. Cuba is under an embargo, *de-facto* under siege. It is often forced to literally fight for its survival. The East European bloc collapsed a quarter of a century ago. The Cuban economy was instantly pushed into a corner, it almost collapsed, as the 'newly capitalist' European countries almost immediately refused to honor trade agreements with its former ally, all too eager to join as quickly as possible, the club of global oppressors. And then, the brutal US trade embargo has been clearly geared, for decades, to destroy this proud Communist island-nation.

A short walk away from *La Floridita*, another iconic restaurant *La Bodegita de Medio* used to witness the indulgence and over-indulgence by Hemingway of yet another typically Cuban drink, *mojito*. And *La Bodegita* was just one of many places that were bombed by the Cuban exiles.

There were countless terrorist attacks against the island, coming from both the United States, and from the right-wing Cuban exiles settled abroad. Passenger airliners were blown from the sky in full flight, clouds were diverted to trigger draughts, crops were poisoned and tourist destinations were repeatedly bombed.

But Cuba stood proud and tall! It sometimes bled badly, its people had to get used to tightening their belts, but the country managed to survive the worst hours, and began growing once again.

Even in its most difficult hours, Cuba continued to help poor countries by sending there their doctors and teachers. Even when it stood, for several years, almost alone, it never abandoned its internationalist path.

Its culture and the arts became the main pillars of the fight for its survival, and for the nation's identity.

During my latest visit, Mario Hubert Garrido, Director of *Prensa Latina Television* (Prensa Latina is the Cuban and International press agency founded by Ernesto Che-Guevara, after the revolution in 1956), explained the role culture plays in his country:

> "Cuban culture has always had deep roots in the Cuban nation. And it is what feeds the spirit of resistance so embedded in the psyche of our people, always, but especially during the most difficult times. Here, people are united, because of the blockade, and because of the aggression against our nation. Here, culture means, above all, solidarity."

We talk. I agree to write for *Prensa Latina*. Here, interiors are simple. There are photos of Vietnam on the walls, the iconic villages of Ha Long Bay. There is some artwork and paintings depicting Fidel jumping from a tank. There are exposed, naked light bulbs. A pre-historic radio receiver broadcasts a program about Jose Marti and his long journey; I can't comprehend from where to where, really.

I feel at home here, inside this old dilapidated villa, very close to the statue of my great Chilean hero, President Salvador Allende.

"Do Cubans really hate North Americans?" I ask. "Do Cuban artists?"

He smiles. His smile is gentle, despite the fact that he is the director of an important revolutionary television station.

"No," he replies after a while. "Here, despite the political situation, we still maintain many vivid cultural contacts between Cuba and the United States. You know: writers, film directors..."

He looks at me, and he almost winks.

"It has never stopped. It will never stop. It never will... Even right now, as we are speaking, there is a meeting of Cuban and North American academics taking place in Washington D.C."

"Culture is solidarity," I smile.

He nods. Before I go, we embrace.

At the historic "Hotel Inglaterra" a band of local *salseros* is playing in the open, right on the pavement: nothing special, honestly, but good and authentic stuff, nevertheless.

Inside, in the restaurant, the ceramics are magnificent, but the food is mediocre.

But I am actually content as I am sitting at an enormous wooden table with my best friend, the Chinese concert pianist Yuan Sheng. He flew in to Havana all the way from Beijing, in order to participate in a festival of some of the best pianists from all over the world. His former professor from the Manhattan School of Music, the legendary Solomon Gadles Mikowsky, has organized the festival himself originally from Cuba.

"I am tremendously impressed by the cultural life and art scene in Cuba", explains Yuan, excitedly. "I traveled to and performed in so many countries in North America, Europe, Africa and Asia... But what I see here is unprecedented. Music, ballet, arts... Even the art objects that people sell on the street... It all shows how heroic the national character of Cuban people is.

Cuba is also very open-minded and receptive of international culture; there is a constant interchange with the world. The plane, which I took here was bringing an entire delegation of Chinese artists and performers. And that is at the same time as I was coming to take part in yet another festival, which was featuring top international pianists. Coming here, I am helping to deepen the understanding between China and Cuba. And you know, in the last years, many educated Chinese people are fascinated with this island and its artists. When I was talking to my friends back in Beijing that I was going to Cuba, their eyes widened. They were envious; they kept telling me how lucky I was. They wanted to know, to understand Cuba."

Later that night we ended up drinking beer with the renowned North American concert pianist Simone Dinnerstein, talking about the music and artwork of her famous father, Simon Dinnerstein.

We are in a café, in one of those beautiful squares, at night. Nearby, some band is playing old Mexican *boleros*. Simone, Yuan and I switch our discussion to the piano festival, but then, suddenly we all fell silent.

There is an unmistakable, confident, perfect sound coming from nearby. It's the Buena Vista Social Club! The stars are brilliant. Historic buildings are brightly illuminated. Two great classic pianists, one North American and one Chinese, are trying to catch the sounds coming from the *Taberna*. It is not difficult: all the windows and doors are open!

One night, Yuan and I go to the National Ballet of Cuba, to see a performance of "Shakespeare and His Masques" under the choreography of the legendary Alicia Alonso.

There are literally thousands of people queuing in front of the entrance doors. The tickets cost almost nothing, just a symbolic token; everyone here can actually attend some world-class performances.

But that very particular evening, something goes wrong. The doors do not open 15 minutes before the performance, as they should; they do not open even when it is time to begin.

The crowd mumbles, but stays calm. The ushers look indifferent. I knock on one of the glass doors and ask what is happening? The "electric system has collapsed," I am told. "Does it happen often?" I ask. Not often, hardly ever.

The usher is at first rude, but then I 'win her heart' by smiling and explaining that I am a writer and my friend is famous Chinese pianist, and we would actually like to wait inside, walk through the semi-darkness of this legendary theatre, and just dream.

She likes that. She obviously likes dreaming in semi-darkness, too. So, she lets us in.

"It reminds me of China, when I was growing up," says Yuan.

To some extent it also reminds me of Prague some time ago. But what exactly is it that we feel?

People are absolutely real here. They are not 'trained' to be servile, even in the service 'industry'. They are gloomy if they are in a bad mood, or cheerful when something good happens to them. They are not afraid of losing their job.

Cuban people are honest, sometimes brutally honest. They laugh when they are happy and they cry when it hurts. They show affection to those they love, and scorn to those they hate. It is a pure and sincere society. And in many ways much freer than those societies that promote their own freedom, as the only model for the world.

Eventually, the enormous space of the Nation Theatre fills up with thousands of people. The performance begins. It is powerful, and as expected sharp as a razor blade, unmistakably brilliantly choreographed and with excellent dancers.

Love stories and stories of death, of betrayal and hope. It is Shakespeare at his best, converted into classical ballet, on this green tropical island obsessed with artistic and intellectual excellence.

But at the end, the audience does not cheer. The applause is lukewarm. The long wait in front of the theatre was not forgiven. It is Cuba, after all, and in Cuba, one does not feel obliged to applaud, even when confronted by unmistakable greatness.

In the old lobby of the historic hotel San Felipe, in Old Havana, Solomon Mikowsky, continues to be impressed with Cuba, his native land:

> "Before, Cuba honored only great people, great artists like Jose

> Marti. But now, Cuba is honoring every single person, every single artist, who contributed to the creation of this great nation. Poets, musicians, actors, writers, alongside the great warriors... Now the history of Cuba has expanded to several hundreds of heroes who have made a true contribution... And by educating people, the government has made sure that so many citizens of Cuba are now thirsty for knowledge! Culturally, Cuba is to Latin America what Athens was to Europe. Cuban arts are not designed to 'please the audience'. They are designed to aim at excellence and creativity... they are geared to produce great poets in virtually every field of the arts."

Great bards and filmmakers, poets... That's Havana. Bookstores selling high quality, subsidized books...

I walk through the center of the city; I stop at an old and elegant bookstore. I decide to buy ten books of contemporary poetry. This store does not accept convertible currency (CUC).

"Please go next door and buy local pesos," I am told. I go to the bank. "What for?" the young clerk asks me.

"I need to buy books."

"How many?" Ten, I tell her. "Then change only 5 dollars and after you pay at the bookstore, you will get plenty of change for public buses, so you can ride for the rest of the week."

I talk to great artists, to journalists and students. For days I talk, and watch. I listen to music, day and night. I read.

"*Obama, give me 5*!" I see a poster on the wall. It is referring to the 5 Cuban patriots who have been held in high security prisons in the United States, for infiltrating the CIA, and for trying to prevent hostile, even terrorist actions, against Cuba. The posters are very artistic. But then, here, everything graphic could pass for art.

Then, one night, a young woman, a student, asks me about my impressions:

"What do you think about Cuban culture?"

We are in the old Basilica, where the piano festival is held. She is holding a small notepad in her hands.

"Do not think..." she smiles. "Answer quickly. Just few words..."

"Revolution... dignity... passion..." I shoot.

She nods.

I then turn the tables around:

“You? What is it for you?’

She thinks only for two or three seconds: “Everything... Life... Death... Love...”

Behind us, we hear Chopin’s Etude. And behind the walls of the Basilica, as the sun goes down, one of the most beautiful cities on earth is beginning to explode in a perfect harmony of sounds and rhythms.

This is not necessarily how revolutions are made. But this is how they survive!

23 August 2013

*****

32

SYRIA, PREPARE YOURSELF FOR RAPE!

Syria is next! She is already marked, cornered, psychologically ravished, and now petrified. She is tied, exposed, and told to expect the worst. She is where we tried to get her for years, where our regime has wanted her to be.

Well, actually, not yet, she is not there yet, but almost. She is still not on her knees, and that is what irritates our rulers endlessly! They like us all to be on our knees, paying for invented 'sins', for 'disobedience', for our desire to be what we really are.

For years she has been harassed, and beaten. Now there are no doubts that soon, very soon, she will be violated, in brought daylight, in front of the entire world, in front of television cameras, with no mercy and with attackers gluing cold and righteous expressions on their faces.

Her rape will be turned into entertainment, it will be orchestrated as a warning to all those who are still determined to follow their own and at least partially independent path.

It will be a punitive rape, like those used in the darkest moments of the history of human-kind.

It will be done, and nobody will be able to stop it. Because that gangster nature of global Western dictatorship is now so complete, and it is so frightening, that no country on earth would dare to intervene and then have its legs broken, face smashed, or eyes poked out. It is all down to a mafia approach, or inquisition, or the Crusades.

Many people recently asked me to write a commentary 'on Syria'. I agreed to do it, but now when I sit in front of my computer, I suddenly don't know what to say. I only feel fatigue and disgust. And I try to push away all those defeatist words that keep creeping into my brain: 'there is nothing that can be done, anymore... Humanism lost... Once again, awful and extreme dogmatists are in control of the world...'

I don't want to fall, to succumb to this way of thinking. I am a fighter, not some weepy café intellectual. But these days, one has to work very hard to remain an optimist, and to believe in a positive outcome for our planet.

***

If you are an absolute gangster, global or local, how do you make a woman marry you when everything else fails? You pay some thugs; they kidnap her, tie her to a post in some abandoned garage, and you rape her, to 'soften her up'. And after few weeks of agony and humiliation, you come to her with a huge bunch of flowers and propose marriage, so that once again she can become respectful, 'free' and 'liberated'. Sick? Yes, I agree it is sick, but isn't it, honestly, how the world is being governed these days?

How do you educate a child, if you want him or her to be an obedient servant, cleaning your crap forever, and respecting you, even if your only claim to fame is having been exploiting some buggers, miserable coolies, in your horrible pre-industrial age factory, in some awful country? The answer is simple: You hammer religion into your child's head, you spice it up with a monstrous fear of hell, archaic concepts of righteousness, and then you confuse servility with love, and rebellion with mortal sin. You brainwash the kid, and make your vision of the world the only one that is 'correct', and permissible.

This is the kind of education and 'culture' we are supporting in our colonies. And this is the kind of love and marriage we are offering to the nations that have fallen into our orbit.

In the West, on the surface, we oppose such scenarios. We even despise them; we consider them appalling, brutal, and incompatible with our 'values' and 'sophistication'. We fight for the rights of poor women living in 'underdeveloped countries', in those backward, grotesque, even retarded societies! We are so proud of ourselves, because we gradually became so undeniably noble, so refined, so sensitive, and so politically correct.

There are lengthy prison sentences for rape and sexual harassment, in both Europe and the United States. Our schools are mostly secular, and in some countries like France, they are secular even to the fanatical and religious extreme. Our family values are lax and it is easy for any child, any young man or woman to escape parental terror.

But the real issue is: what do we do to the world? How do we treat billions of people in the countries that we enslaved, both the poor and not so poor ones?

Remember Chile – country that I love with all my heart, which for many years had been my home. She did not want to love us, or to marry us. She was so independent, so creative, spreading new concepts of education, of the arts, of humanism all over the world. We tried to buy her, but she refused. She refused to be corrupted. She was beautiful, pure, proud and serene.

So what was done to my Chile? We paid those proverbial thugs; we kidnapped her, tortured her and finally raped her, on 9-11-1973. For years we ravished her, tied her to that post in some filthy garage, used dogs, used soldiers trained to rape, and used capitalist whips produced at the Chicago School of Economics. And we were broadcasting that rape all over the world.

"This is the way to love", we wrote in our mass media outlets. "Look, she is still bleeding, but we will now cover some parts of her body with Prada and Gucci scarves, and make her eat sushi with her broken, bleeding mouth!"

I am compelled to say: 'Fuck us for such love'! And I am not apologizing for my language. I am not your mainstream journo; for many years I have not been. Call me arrogant, novelist; fine with me, but fuck our culture of terror, nevertheless!

***

Now frankly: what are we going to do to Syria, dudes? This time, what torture should be applied? What sadistic methods used? Let's have it all in the open!

Is it going to be depleted uranium, like in Iraq? Are we going to starve hundreds of thousands of children? Or use drones like in Afghanistan and Pakistan, or maybe chemical warfare, for the sake of those good old Indochina days? Or perhaps we can use those precision bombs that are not at all so precise, and have a curious tendency to blast public television stations, private vehicles, wedding parties, and even entire villages?

Or maybe something new just to justify our over 1 trillion dollars "defense budget"?

Is the Libyan scenario going to be applied or something more 'innovative' and original? Is there some brand new "Syrian Concept" in pipeline, in development? And if yes, what will it consist of? How are we going to murder people this time; how many of them will lose their lives? Not that it really matters, as they are not white, nor Christian, and therefore "not people". But I am just being curious!

***

And so, now Syria is waiting for her turn, to be raped, tortured and humiliated... To be thoroughly destroyed! Our gangster global regime will call plunder "humanitarian intervention". Murder will be described as rescue.

We will also have plenty of those charity charades, later. We love charity; we love to give, don't we? It is our Christian duty! We first rob, loot, steal and plunder 100, and then, benevolently, after country is starving, give back 2... or maybe, maybe 4... if we feel very generous that day. It is like what is done by some factory owner somewhere in Honduras, who exploits his workers day and night, then gives them old clothes and food, and even builds the school that helps to brainwash them!

***

I have been there, recently; I have been to Syria! I have been to the Golan Heights, which is still, according to international law, uncontested Syrian territory. It is also a place that has been occupied by Israel for decades, where there are more armored vehicles now, than tractors. And we are talking about a part of the world previously known only for its delicious cherries and apples!

Oh River Jordan! Around 90% of the population had been forced to leave the Golan Heights, and villages were leveled, thoroughly destroyed, by the Israeli armed forces. Kibbutz after kibbutz grew literally on ruins of the original dwellings, producing wine, and growing food, right behind the barbed wire, high voltage fences and security towers!

I drove to the top of one hill, parked my car, and climbed onto the roof of one of the recently abandoned Israeli bunkers. In front of me – a huge Syrian flag and high voltage Israeli fences cut across this ancient and beautiful land. To make the scenery more diverse, there were some rotting tanks, and a huge United Nations camp, as there were remains of destroyed towns and villages all around, as well as Israeli commandos training inside abandoned Syrian structures...

Oh Syria! Now they are sewing your funeral gown, even as you are still breathing, still clinging to life!

***

I also went to the Syrian border, from the Turkish side... I went there twice in just one year, to the environs of the city of Hatay, historically one of the most tolerant places on earth, now terrorized by pro-Western jihadi cadres imported from Saudi Arabia and Qatar, on their Western-sponsored mission to destabilize the Syrian State.

I wanted to check on those 'refugee camps', which Turkey, that staunch member of NATO, has been recently building along its borderline with Syria. For instance, the *Apaydin Camp* is no refugee facility, but a tough military training boot camp, designed to prepare and further harden the already brutal 'Syrian opposition forces'...

I interviewed people at the border; it is common knowledge that Syrian opposition fighters infiltrate their country from Turkish territory, that they go back and forth, some return injured, get medical treatment, then go back again with fresh supplies of weapons and ammunition, to fight against the government forces.

I spoke to children just a few hundreds of meters from the borderline. It is a tough world at that border. They said that the Syrian opposition fighters steal at night, and that there is constant shooting all over the border area. The Turkish government does nothing to prevent it – the destabilization of Syria is the main and only goal.

Last time I went there in June 2013, to film for the Venezuelan television network TeleSur, accompanied by my Turkish translator. We were intercepted on several occasions by undercover as well as uniformed Turkish security forces, and most of our footage was deleted. We were lucky not to get arrested, or disappear. Many were less fortunate: thousands of brave Turkish men and women are now rotting in prisons for much lesser 'crimes'...

***

It seems that most of the countries of the world are now decisively against the pre-announced rape of Syria. Russia is standing firm, protecting Syria diplomatically, and in many other practical ways. China is also firm, and so is almost the entire Latin America.

Of course the global regime is regularly defining Russia, China and most of Latin America as evil, and 'undemocratic'. That is, because in the West, democracy ('rule of the people' in Greek language) means only 'rule of *our* people', like *cosa nostra* ('our thing') is the main definition of the Sicilian mafia.

Outraged citizens of the world are suddenly uttering many candid words, and media outlets like RT, *TeleSur* and China's CCTV, are now carrying them to all corners of the world. But that is not enough, not enough yet!

The outrage is boiling all over the world, as is the realization that our planet is being governed by sadistic maniacs, by mentally deranged beings who are sitting on nukes, warships and stealth bombers.

It is a horrifying reality, but at least some of us are now able to define it.

Western civilization and its followers all over the world need urgent mental, psychiatric help, instead of respect!

***

There is something heavy and 'crusade-style Christian' about the present situation. The way Syria has been treated, how Latin America has been treated, as well as Africa, and the entire Middle East and Asia!

No matter how secular the rhetoric is; it is all overwhelmingly twisted in a religious manner...

All the arguments for attacks against Syria, as were those for attacks against Iraq, Afghanistan, Venezuela, Cuba, Vietnam and countless other countries, are clearly religious, with absolutely no proof and no logic; no proof is offered, we only have to believe. All those actions are also illegal, by international laws effectively! Again, we are made to *believe*, not to think, not to use objective moral judgment, just some fully subjective and dubiously defined dogma.

***

Right after the Second World War, the great Swiss psychiatrist and psychotherapist Gustav Jung, connected the essence of Christianity to all those horrific crimes of conquest, colonialism and wars, committed by the West, in his little known book called "Essays on Contemporary Events":

> *The Christian Church should put ashes on her head and rend her garments on account of the guilt of her children. The shadow of their guilt has fallen on her as much as upon Europe, the mother of monsters. Europe must account for herself before the world...*
>
> And then again, summarizing what is clear and obvious to anyone who studies world history in detail, but very rarely publicly pronounced in this present era of absolute intellectual and moral submission:
>
> *It is after all only a tiny fraction of humanity, living mainly on that thickly populated peninsula of Asia, which juts out into the Atlantic Ocean, and calling themselves "cultured"...Viewed from a safe distance, say from central Africa or Tibet, it would certainly look as if this fraction had projected its own unconscious mental derangements upon nations still possessed of healthy instincts.*

And it is clear that the present crimes and horrors committed by the United States, have roots in that European colonial "culture" ('mother of monsters' according to Jung), and in the brutal Christian dogmatism of earlier days, or in the lunacy of fanatical sects and streams, found predominately in the United States and all over the poor world where fundamentalism (mostly exported by the United States), always manages to find extremely fertile ground.

***

If one looks really close, the foreign policy of the West is really full of clear psychological and moral derangements.

The world is run with a brutality that has the clear sexual overtones of those medieval Catholic and Protestant theological cadres obsessed with the 'sin' and 'guilt' of the flesh, but inside, bursting with oppressed sexuality. Many 'elites' in the United States and their local servants in colonized world are puritanical on the surface, full of 'moral rhetoric', but in constant need of the most violent, oppressive actions.

There is a total obsession with 'punishment', and with combating 'sin'. The result is the overflowing of prisons in the United States, as well as constant mass murderous actions abroad, which took directly more than 55 million human lives between Hiroshima and the present day.

But what is 'sin'? It is all that *we* disapprove of. There is no objectivity in defining it.

It is all very primitive, too. Like those "Shall I?" in the old English public schools, ruler in hand of some sadistic teacher, lifted over a pupil's shaking hand. And fear, fear, fear; and humiliation...

They have to rule: those puritans and Christian ascetics: they simply cannot live without ruling - over their children, over the countries, over the world! They cannot exist without constantly repeating to themselves and to others, even to their victims, that all that is done is for righteous reasons, for some greater good of the others. And that applies to torture, exploitation and killing!

"We destroyed the village in order to save it", was the old saying from the Vietnam War.

Go to Kampala or Manila, to see how such dogmas, brought to the extreme, function inside families, in politically and culturally oppressive societies. Or go to the Southern States of the United States. Then take that despotic family structure and imagine what would happen if it were allowed to govern the world.

Yes, you guessed it correctly. The result would be exactly what you see all around – the present global state of things consisting of intolerance, racism, bigotry, and extreme violence!

***

The conclusion, based on experience, is clear and shocking: The present global regime cannot 'love', it can only rape.

Abel Pose, the great Argentinean writer and diplomat, and my dear friend from earlier days, described the colonizing process of what is now Latin America in his brilliant novel, “Dogs of Paradise”.

When Western conquerors came, they carried heavy armor, even in the tropical heat. They were obsessed with the Christian dogmas of ‘guilt’ and ‘sin’. And they were sexually repressed, to the extreme, to insanity.

Local women were very kind and refined. They looked at those pathetic and barbaric creatures, at those religious fanatics and brutal primitives, and they willingly opened their arms, to embrace them, out of pity, to give them at some pleasure and relief at least.

But the conquerors had strict ‘values’, and ‘family and marriage’ dogmas. Their flesh was boiling, but their religious insanity prevented them from simple human joy. So what did they do?

They kidnapped those beautiful and gentle women. They dragged them to the bushes and tortured them for hours, for days. And then, when those poor women were destroyed, bleeding, hardly surviving – they raped them! Because that was the only love they knew, the only satisfaction they understood.

And it is the same now. The entire world, much more advanced than the West and than its open and subconscious religious dogmas, much more beautiful and kinder, on so many occasions, has opened its arms and whispered: ‘we forgave you for all those Crusades, for colonialism, for bestiality... Let us finally live in harmony. Just leave us alone; let us be what we are and what we want to be.”

But the West took it, in its pathologic mental state, as weakness. It continued its orgy of plunder and rape! And it is continuing it until now!

***

And so, Syria is next!

And I am sick of watching, as so many others are! I don't want to see blood running down her legs. I don't want to see her beautiful body ravished. I don't want to hear her screams, and witness her agony.

I don't want to pretend that this is a normal arrangement of the world. That rape is normal, that ruining millions of human lives is normal, that for one group of countries, for one race, for one religion, it is normal to commit endless crimes against humanity, with no mechanism that can put the end to this horror!

The great Sultan Saladin fought and stopped the Christian hordes of Crusaders at both Aleppo and Damascus. These days to fight Western invasions, is called terrorism, by the twisted logic of the Empire and its servile local elites.

What I suggest is maybe modest, but I believe it effective: let us not accept the linguistics and 'logic' of clearly disturbed, mad people, even if they are now ruling over the world. This is not the first time in human history: we had Caligula and Hitler, Calvin and Leopold II, to mention just a few. Let us go back to basics:

Rape is not love, and brainwashing is not education. Murder is not liberation and torture is not an act of mercy. Charity after theft cannot be called 'giving'. And denying one's identity can never have any righteous justification. And "war is not peace", as Arundhati Roy correctly pointed out on several occasions. And black is not white. And a cat is not a dog!

I don't give a damn whether Syria and its government are 'perfect', or even good. Not now, definitely not now. We have much more pressing issues, as human race, to deal with:

We have maniacs, control freaks, market, 'cultural', and religious fundamentalists, real Crusaders, running around our beautiful planet, armed with nukes, entire battleship fleets and air force squadrons

We have to help them and we have to help the world, urgently, immediately. They need some serious medical treatment, some prolonged rest in a mental clinic, some professional care!

And the world finally needs some space to breathe, some vacation from fear, real peace!

13 September 2014

33

Carnage Abounds

WHAT REALLY HAPPENED AT WESTGATE

Nairobi

Thick smoke hangs above the access road to The Westgate – the up-market shopping mall that serves mainly expats, UN staff and Kenyan elites.

Sporadic gunfire and explosions are clearly heard from the direction of the compound; overtaken on Saturday 21 September, by Somali fighters from the Muslim militant group Al-Shabaab.

Police forces and military duck for cover, and new troops are being bussed in, in order to take part in the operation.

Combat helicopters are circling around the site. Even higher than them, almost above the clouds, one can spot small airplanes. The sky is very busy. And it is overcast; the weather is gloomy and when the clouds are high up, aircraft are hardly visible.

Dozens of reporters, local and international, are shouting their dispatches into mobile phones. Some are Tweeting, or recording interviews with rescued hostages, nurses, and security officers.

Everything appears to be surprisingly well organized, including the supply of food, water and medicine. A Chinese clinic is offering help, as well as several voluntary organizations. People are donating blood. There are blankets and tents readily available.

But the gunfire keeps raging.

There are all sorts of speculations: the leader, the commander, is the 'White Widow', an English lady who was married to one of the Muslim attackers of the London Underground. Other 'unconfirmed reports' speaks about American jihadi fighters. And then, there is of course that semi-confirmed information about Israeli commandos, about US involvement and UK participation.

Who is inside that most luxurious shopping complex in East Africa? They say, there are no more than 10 attackers holed up inside, mainly Somalis, but there also others, some coming from outside the African continent. The rumors and official reports first speak about a few dozen hostages, then about 200. The number keeps swelling.

The armed forces and reporters are interacting.

"6 soldiers died", one army officer whispers into my ear. "They do not admit it, but I know, I was just there".

At one point I spot my Indian-Malaysian dentist, next to her son, also a dentist, who is said to have saved several people in the course of the first day. She is visibly shaken and her eyes are red, from lack of sleep, or maybe from tears.

It is all very emotional, very raw. Days and nights are blending together. Al-Shabaab is Tweeting. It tells the world that the pain inflicted during those days is just a tiny fraction of what Kenya is inflicting on Somalia. Twitter is quickly shutting down all the sites of Al-Shabbab, but new sites are being instantly created.

***

Since 2011, Kenya has been occupying a substantial part of Somalia, and many analysts are questioning the legitimacy of this action. Oil rich southern Somalia is perhaps seen as the trophy by both Kenya, and the Western powers.

For years and decades now, the West has been destabilizing

Somalia. Kenya and Ethiopia, two staunch allies of the West in the region, are playing a deadly game, incessantly. Thousands of civilians have already died.

Kenya is one of the closest allies of the West in Africa, with both US and UK military bases all over the nation, and with Israeli intelligence personnel on the Swahili coast and elsewhere.

That brutal invasion is not discussed, of course: in the Kenyan media and in the international press, the war and the attack on the shopping mall are carefully separated, disconnected.

And so is the brutality factor of the Kenyan troops in the territory of occupied Somalia: one can only judge from the stories told by refugees in Dadaab and other camps. The battleground is fully off-limits to foreign war correspondents – for our own protection, of course!

***

Efficiency appears to be only on the surface.

Dig deeper and chaotic pictures emerge.

Japanese acquaintances working for the UN, recalled how awfully unhelpful the local UN security system has been, since the attack:

"We were held in a bookshop, inside the Westgate." As the gunfight was raging all around, she and her little daughter were held for over two hours. She called the UN security. Their reply was chillingly laconic: 'stay safe!'"

It took the Kenyan police 30 minutes to get to the scene. Their excuse was; they got stuck in a traffic jam!

A retired Peruvian UNICEF staff member was shot to death while inside a car, and his 13-year-old daughter was shot through her arm. She had to remain inside the car with her dead father for two hours, before being rescued.

It had been common knowledge among the expat community in Nairobi that the attack against the Westgate Mall was very likely to come. Al-Shabaab had been threatening almost ever since the Kenyan invasion of Somalia, that it was ready to blow up tall buildings in the capital. All local media carried these threats. Still, the security at all the shopping centers of Nairobi remained ridiculously lax.

And how is it possible that it took several days for the entire army and police to defeat a small band of insurgents, and even after that, only after foreign forces got involved?

***

By the latest count, around 130 people lost their lives, but the real number could still be much higher.

Rumors are there, still. Interpol issued arrest warrants and the hunt for the 'White Widow' is just beginning. And that despite the fact that one body, of a white woman, an insurgent, has already been found.

More bodies are being pulled from the rubble. Some people working inside the compound said that they could not exclude the possibility that several insurgents are still hiding in the rubble of the Mall.

But the most important question now is what will happen to war-torn Somalia. And what will happen to over two million Somalis (exact numbers are constantly being disputed) who are living in refugee camps like Dadaab, behind barbed wire, as well as in depressing neighborhoods around the Kenyan capital and other cities.

27 September 2013

*****

34

Battleground Cairo

EGYPT: END OF HOPE

Cairo

Instead of passion and hope, all there is left on the streets of Cairo is depressing defeatism, frustration and hate.

Once there were heads and hands raised high, and the Egyptian flags flew proudly in the wind; there were fiery speeches, dreams of social justice, of a brand new country with an enormous heart and a distinct place for every citizen. Once it all was not unlike what has been taking place all over Latin America for more than a decade.

But it now appears to be over, burned down and in ruins. These days it is hate that has replaced hope, and there is so much of it, so much hate, all over the capital and all over the country!

And it is not a healthy, constructive hate pointed at savage capitalism or imperialism. It is a depressing hate, a defeatist hate; a hate that Egyptians are now showing towards each other. There is hardly any ideology left, except in the ranks of the Socialist Revolutionary Organization, and very few other groups and movements that are still fighting for the essential values of the

2011 Arab Spring.

There is still a core, a skeleton of the "Movement of the 6th Of April" – the organization that stood at the vanguard of the Revolution. But even that suddenly appears to be too weak – not strong enough to halt this depressing reverse trend.

As I look down from the bridge at Bulak neighborhood, the citizens are engaged at finder-pointing and loud shouting. Men and women are insulting each other, and soon there are skirmishes and fistfights. This is some sort of local-level settling of scores between the supporters of The Muslim Brotherhood and the followers of the military – that very same military which overthrew the moderate but inept Islamic government in July 2013.

Soon I am spotted and several fists are raised towards me, fingers pointed. One minute later, stones are flying my way.

"Get into the car!" My Egyptian friend shouts at me. "Get inside! If even one person attacks you, the crowd will get here in no time and they will take you apart... They will kill you."

"But why?" I wonder naively.

"These days they don't need any reason", he explains. "They hate foreigners. They hate each other. Don't you see what is happening in my country?"

I see. And what I observe, I don't like at all. The hope is over. What is left is a terrible hangover and a bad, dark mood.

But many rich urban dwellers are trying to convince each other that things will get better soon. The upper and upper-middle classes are openly supporting the military, not unlike in Chile, after the 9-11-1973 military coup' d'état in which the pro-Western faction of the army led by General Augusto Pinochet overthrew the progressive government of Salvador Allende.

Of course the Egyptian Islamist President Morsi and his Muslim Brotherhood had nothing in common with *la Unidad Popular*, but the willingness of the elites in the two countries to back the Western-supported military, is truly striking and revealing.

***

As I am photographing the ruined headquarters of the Muslim

Brotherhood in Cairo, a black limousine stops, the back window is open, and the upper class-looking woman begins shouting at me: "Morsi was a criminal! And I am forbidding you to photograph this building!"

"Who are you?" I wonder. "Do you have any authority to forgive anything, in this public place?"

"I am an Egyptian woman!" She spits at me with scorn.

"That is great", I say. "But I still don't understand what gives you the authority to prevent me from working?"

She begins calling someone frantically on her mobile phone. She is obviously reporting me, asking for reinforcements in her sacred fight against a dangerous foreign element.

"There is so much fear", my friend, a psychiatrist Mohammad Shafik, told me. "I love photography, but these days I don't even dare to take pictures of scenic spots in and around my own city – Cairo."

There is clearly something wrong with Cairo's residents. As supporters of General Sissi exchange punches with supporters of Morsi and his Muslim Brotherhood, women are running around and shouting frantically. Nile Street is blocked, as there is yet another bomb threat. Four people have already been killed recently, not far from here.

Vigilantes are controlling traffic. It looks like a state of siege in front of Sadat's old palace; there are tanks and sandbags everywhere, the military and police are pointing guns in all directions.

It is 6th October, Victory Day in Egypt, the day when, 40 years ago, the Egyptian military recaptured the Sinai Peninsula from Israel. Here it is known as the October War, or as the Yom Kippur War in Israel.

In 2013, this anniversary is the moment to show support for the Egyptian army apparatus. Never mind that the Egyptian armed forces have been getting 1.3 billion dollars annually from the United States. Never mind that for years and decades, it had been backing the brutal pro-Western regime of Mubarak. No matter that now it was clearly getting back into power.

"Prophet Mohammed said that the Egyptian army is the best in the region", reads one of the posters.

Even as the people are cheering the army, the canons on top of the armored vehicles point suspiciously at the crowd. Tanks are blocking all the streets leading to Tahrir Square. F-16 fighter jets are flying over the capital, and so are combat Apache helicopters.

There are slums are all over the capital, and more than 70% of the people of Cairo live in misery, as a sociologist Maher Abdelmalek tells me. But the misery is, suddenly, not on the agenda of either side. It is not discussed and it is not what people are fighting against.

I go to the slums and photograph there, but another set of vigilantes tries to prevent me from working. The same in Giza, where I attempt to film the clogged waterways.

There are insults and more insults, and there are threats. To be a foreign correspondent or a filmmaker working in Cairo, feels much more dangerous than working in DR Congo or in any other war zone.

***

Bombs go off at regular intervals. People are dying. The military has already murdered perhaps 2,000 people since the coup, but the numbers are not confirmed or trustworthy, and are most likely much higher.

Fear is now so potent that even members of the revolutionary movements and organizations do not dare to meet each other during the day, or at night. Several of my encounters are cancelled, despite the fact that I am not working for any Western media outlets – I am making a film for the Venezuelan television network "TeleSur", and reporting for RT and CounterPunch.

Nobody trusts anybody. Two of my main contacts are in hiding somewhere in the countryside. Members of several allied parties are now refusing to communicate with each other. It is impossible to plan anything, as all trust is broken and fear reigns over the capital.

But ask the elites and they will tell you that everything is great. I ask the General Manager of one of the major luxury hotel chains, whether things have really improved after the coup.

"What coup?" he looks at me in bewilderment. Then he gives me a big smile: "Oh, you mean after Egypt got liberated? Now things are fantastic! And they will soon get even better... Much better."

My driver laughs when I tell him that Egypt is doing well. He tells me about inflation and about him leaving his teaching position at a public school and becoming a driver: "I couldn't pay tuition for my two sons."

We drive to Giza, to the Pyramids, just to see what I had already suspected. The entire area is empty and there are only touts in front of the Sphinx. I see only one tourist bus, with somehow lost looking and confused Spanish visitors. And there are rumors of serious looting. The tourist industry has basically collapsed, but this is also not discussed openly, it is totally hidden. An insurgency is flaring in Cairo, in the Suez area, Alexandria, even in the Sinai Peninsula, which is the main center of the Egyptian tourist industry.

By 2:30PM on the 6th October, there is fighting all over the capital. But fighting is also not called fighting here. These are 'incidents', and there are some instances of 'terrorism'. 'Public order is being disrupted'. Again, the terminology is similar to that used in Chile in and after 1973, or in Indonesia after 1965. Except that in Chile, the great majority of the people had been aware of the situation and of cynical lies.

***

Clouds of teargas hang over the city. Once in a while, explosions resonate, from various directions.

The situation is becoming extremely confusing. There is so much shouting and so little information. I ask my driver to turn on the radio, but all we can hear are some militaristic and patriotic songs.

But everyone is aware of what will be happening after 15:30, when the Muslim Brotherhood cadres begin leaving their mosques.

It all looks grotesque: little children and women holding photographs of high army officials, even kissing their portraits for the cameras; the military pointing their cannons at civilians, as they have been doing for decades... They are aiming even at those who adore them.

Then some people begin to charge and the teargas canisters start exploding. There are several rounds of live ammunition fired into the air.

At 15:30, exactly as expected, the Muslim Brotherhood joins those Sinai celebrations, in its own – in its predictably heavy-handed way.

The battle begins. I see people climbing the walls, holding children to their chests. I see hard-core Islamists with green ribbons encircling their heads, slings in their hands. I see the armed forces charging, and shooting. I see people falling. Not for the Revolution, not for social justice, not for a better Egypt. I see people dying, on both sides, out of spite, from hate. I see human lives wasted. And I see the end of the Arab Spring nearing.

14 October 2013

*****

35

CHRISTIANITY, IMPERIALISM, CAPITALISM

This year as in every other year, Christianity and fundamentalist capitalism, two great allies, are joining their forces to extract billions of dollars, all over the world, mainly from the poor.

As money flies towards the coffers of the church and into corporate accounts, over-sugary, kitschy Christmas carols and gospels are soaring out from the audio systems of department stores and malls all over the Empire and in almost all of its colonies (Saudi Arabia being an exception).

'White Christmas' is re-enacted and faked in the steaming-hot tropical 'client states', into where Christianity with all its nomenclature was forcefully injected decades and centuries ago.

Christmas trees, colorful balls and stars camouflage the sharp teeth, swords, torture instruments and propaganda tools. This faith was built on all conquered continents, on fear, never on love! Righteousness, aggressiveness and intimidation have been some of the trademarks of Christianity, for centuries. The faith which murdered hundreds of millions of people worldwide, reducing hundreds of great civilizations to ashes, is, until now, unapologetic and self-assured.

It is no wonder, as the greatest pillars of the modern-day oppression support it: the Empire itself as well as its unchallengeable fundamentalist capitalist doctrines.

***

Dr. Carl Gustav Jung, a giant in psychology and psychotherapy, declared in 1942:

> *"The Christian Church should put ashes on her head and rend her garments on account of the guilt of her children. The shadow of their guilt has fallen on her as much as upon Europe, the mother of monsters."*

But was Jung only referring to the horrors of WWII? Definitely not! He viewed Christian dogma and especially its practices, as racist, intolerant, dictatorial and imperialist, and his conclusion and suggestion for treatment was clear:

> *"We are therefore forced to go back to pre-Christian and non-Christian conceptions and to conclude that Western man does not possess the monopoly of human wisdom and that the white race is not a species of 'Homo sapiens' specially favored by God..."*

***

But is the world really moving to embrace what Jung used to call pre-Christian and non-Christian conceptions?

The Empire itself is constructed on Christian dogmas, symbolism and practices. All of its leaders are Christians, almost all – Protestant. Every time they drag the world into war, their mouths are full of religious rhetoric and 'mysticism'. We are not supposed to question the logic of bombing some poor countries, into the ground. We are not supposed to question the morality of the societies that are abandoning the fate of people to private and voluntary charities, instead of giving rights to all citizens. We are supposed to 'believe', to 'trust'! And if we can't believe in such idiocy, then at least we are forced to be scared.

The dogmas of Christianity, of Western imperialism, capitalism, together with their brainwashing propaganda and 'education', have created one powerful entity. It fully controls the planet, allows no intellectual dissent, and destroys everything that dares to stand on its way.

By now, our minds are fully 'colonized', our morality twisted, our logic corrupted.

Only those who are by some 'miracle' spared formal education (read: propaganda) can see clearly.

Christian crusades and colonialist expeditions did not end with the military terror, with rapes, plunder and physical enslavement of the planet. They have continued spreading the most complete and complex net of indoctrination, aiming at ending intellectual diversity.

Those of us, who fell, at least for some time, into this machine of brainwashing, see the world with the same eyes, even if we are critical of it. And even those of us who call ourselves agnostics or atheists, have subconsciously been conditioned, at least partially, to see life through irrational and self-serving Christian lenses.

That is why we do nothing or very little, when millions of 'Others' are slaughtered by our rulers, when children are dying from depleted uranium left behind by our bombs, when the entire planet is 'sinking' as a result of our unbridled consumerism. That is why we just stare, like buffalos, when the group of twisted capitalist moguls is forcing entire nations to serve them like slaves, sacrificing lives for their wellbeing.

Christian logic, its dark dogma, millennia old, implemented and upheld, is the best guarantee that the world will never change, never improve, and never become egalitarian, a great place for all!

The terror spread to all corners of the planet by Christianity has been unprecedented, and it has to be remembered especially now, when the most celebrated Christian holiday is painting homes and shopping centers in that innocent and hypocritical white color, while hiding deep down the color red, that of spilt blood, as well as the color black, that of burned and ruined cities and nations.

After enslaving men, women and children, after taking away from them anything of any value, Christianity began 'converting', forcing people to accept all its gory symbolism, that of blood and pus, that of guilt and fear, and of a man nailed to the cross, as the very essence of their existence.

What a pathetic, sad and immoral world it became... But to refuse would have meant death!

Many have died. In Africa, South and Central America, in the

Caribbean, North America, Middle East, Sub-Continent, in Asia and Oceania. We will never know the exact numbers, but roughly, the victims of Christian terror can be counted in hundreds of millions.

***

I want to discuss the role of Christianity in today's world.

I want to know some practical things: about corruption, the embezzlement of billions by priests, I want to know about the Vatican Bank.

I want to have statistics that have been compiled about those rapes of children by preachers, and priests.

But above all, I want to see links between the most terrible chapters of modern history and Christianity.

I am extremely interested in the Pentecostal Protestant sects in Africa, Oceania, Indonesia and elsewhere.

I was recently told and explained to, about that grand design of Pentecostal churches, backed by the Empire, which is trying to destabilize many countries that are seen as adversaries of the West, from Eritrea to China.

In several old pro-Western fascist regimes, like those of Indonesia, Pentecostal religions thrive, are groomed and then exported to China and elsewhere, with a single goal – to destabilize and brainwash the nations.

Through US Pentecostals, the "Prosperity Gospel" is quickly becoming the most preached one, in cities like Kampala in Uganda, or Surabaya in Indonesia.

I want to know about those Pentecostal and other Protestant fundamentalist churches, all over Polynesia, Melanesia and Micronesia. I lived in Samoa, and I know all about the extortion, corruption and ignorance which they are spreading there. I know about child molestation and abuse committed by preachers and priests, with total impunity.

The poorer and more uneducated people are, the more they flock into the new Protestant Pentecostal churches, where the "Prosperity Gospel" is quickly becoming the most preached one, in cities like Kampala in Uganda, or Surabaya in Indonesia.

It is not just some religious fundamentalism, but it is also the market fundamentalism and the right-wing individualism: all walking hand in hand with those new pop, anti-humanist religious implants.

The new toxic, fluorescent wave of Christianity mostly comes from the United States, but also from Australia: prefabricated, shiny, ready to go directly into action, brainwashing people, and keeping societies stagnant.

In such churches, what is white and Western is fully and unquestionably admired. And there are even some Western preachers who are 'imported'.

Listening to their preaching, one really wonders whether they are working for God or for the intelligence agencies, or for both.

But that is no surprise. Christianity has always collaborated with oppressive right-wing powers: kings, aristocracy, banks, business interests, Nazis, slave owners, fascist dictators...

Family members and members of congregations are tied-up; they are psychologically conditioned to obey. They do not dare to leave, to rebel. They all become the same: they think the same way, they live the same way, and they desire the same things. Fly-by-wire lives are mass-produced. People are scared to dare, to dream, to 'fly', to fight, and to rebel! This ensures fully obedient, servile, uncreative societies: exactly what capitalism and the Empire want!

Everything is made primitive and commercialized: now, there are pop bands singing about Jesus in Manila and elsewhere, and there are entire melodrama-monologues delivered by preachers and their helpers, asking Jesus and God to solve all the financial and other problems of their congregations. It is the same idiocy as Televangelism in the West.

"God hates poor people and that is why they are poor. God loves those who are rich, and that is why they are rich", I recently heard at a mammoth service in a church that operates inside a mall, in one of the Southeast Asian countries.

But this is happening everywhere, in every miserable place on Earth. Malls and Christianity are merging, forming a great strategic alliance!

No matter where I have worked, on all the continents, there are those young determined men with a black name tag, 'spreading the gospel' among the natives.

I want to know who exactly they are and who is, exactly, behind them!

Michael Kafero, a Ugandan thinker and activist, explains:

> "Uganda traditionally had an alternative Christian tradition to the mainstream Church, the "Born Again Movement" or known locally as the "Balokole". These were historically a fundamentalist sects that stuck closely to Biblical teachings, interpreting them literally... In recent times they have been sidelined by the 'new wave' invasion of the American Pentecostals... Prosperity Gospel is now the most preached, and it has packed the churches to the rafters. In this sea of poverty, desperation has taken root, as opportunities are non-existent. Such hypocrisy sits nicely with the parked Humvees owned by pastors, paid for through donations called 'tithes', collected from the downtrodden, who believe that they are planting seeds for their own future prosperity."

Uganda is of course bleeding from its civil war, and so is the neighboring DR Congo, where around 8 million lives have already been lost, since 1995, because of the brutal plunder of its natural resources by Rwanda and Uganda, *on behalf of the West.*

The most heartless militia commanders in DR Congo are, of course, religious Christian leaders; some claiming that they are related to God, others 'serving God faithfully'.

In the meantime, the Church is sucking dry all poor neighborhoods in West Africa and East Africa, as well as in the southern part of Africa, in the process, keeping people as ignorant as possible, pillaging their meager resources, and blocking birth-control wherever it can.

In Latin America it was the same. The Church sided with all the monstrous regimes, from Chile (through 'Opus Dei') to Argentina, the Dominican Republic, Brazil, Paraguay and elsewhere. The Bishops supported the countless coups orchestrated by the United States. Yes, there were exceptions: the Jesuits, Bishop Romero, the Bishop of Linares, my buddy Padre Pepe in El Salvador, Dom Helder Camera, in Brazil, Gustavo Gutiérrez, the Peruvian priest who first formulated Liberation Theology, a pro-peasant, workers philosophy condemned by the Vatican, and others, but they were nothing else other than exceptions proving the rule.

It took great change in Latin American societies; it took true revolution, to put the priests where they belong, after addressing the past and the present.

To be a preacher is the guarantee of prosperity. Even the preachers in those 'poor' parishes live and enjoy life in 'gated communities'; they possess several cars and send their children to private (religious, of course) schools.

In many countries, even retired preachers are driven in chauffeured cars, something that is enjoyed, in places such as Europe, only by royalty and pop-stars. While the majority of people are resigned to the most appalling medical treatment in decrepit hospitals, the preachers are using the services of the best private medical facilities.

In Samoa where I lived for several years, I encountered priests and preachers who had entire armies of domestics: from drivers and cooks, to servants and gardeners.

Once, in Oceania, I caught my assistant stealing. She stole money, consistently, in all currencies. I confronted her. She fell on her knees, crying. "Punish me!" she screamed. By that she meant a beating, or perhaps something worse.

Horrified, I asked her to get back on her feet. After making her a cup of tea, I demanded only one thing: to know why she was stealing from me.

Through tears she explained:

> "I am poor, and a single mother, but we are managing to survive... But every week, when I go to my church, the preacher demands money in an open envelope. And when he sees how little I can give, he threatens me, humiliating me in front of everybody."

I know many stories like this. I know people who were molested and raped by their priests and preachers when they were children. I know people who were driven close to suicide by their parish. These stories come from all continents; they are uniform.

I want all of this to be discussed, openly!

I also want to discuss the political affiliations of the churches. Why most of them are right wing, and why so many of them are outrightly fascist?

***

Christianity supported the West during the Cold War.

I want to know more; also about that anti-Communist agent – Wojtyla. 'The Village Voice' in New York wrote in 2005:

> *"The public eulogies for Pope John Paul II may have ended, but another one lurks in the files of the Central Intelligence Agency. There, the Pope's fight against Communism is depicted not as a crusade of uncompromising moral force, but as a careful, calculated political campaign."*

We know that Christianity supported Fascists in Italy and Nazis in Germany, and Franco in Spain, it supported Pinochet in Chile, Videla in Argentina, Marcos in Philippines, Suharto in Indonesia, almost all Western implants and despots in Africa, to name just a few.

More, let us learn more! What have they done in Latin America, exactly? I investigated that Nazi territory in Chile – Colonia Dignidad – where they were torturing left-wing opposition, raping women with dogs and performing medical experiments on people. I fought against that imported hellish hoard, in the country that I love! I can testify about the involvement of the Church there, but what about elsewhere?

What about Cuba – was the Church trying to overthrow the government, there? Of course it was!

Christianity is heavily involved in China, Eritrea, Venezuela, and Indonesia – always on the side of Western imperialism. It supports every imaginable and unimaginable fascist and pro-western regime in Africa.

Those who say that 'all religions' are equally destructive are simply refusing to register the numbers.

During the last decades and centuries, Christianity is not acting independently in places like Europe or North America. It forms inseparable part of the regime, of the Empire. Or more precisely, the Empire is almost entirely constructed on Christian doctrines.

***

'White Christmas' is coming! This is announced in front of department stores and malls, not only in New York and Paris, but also in Manila, Lima, Suva, Johannesburg, and Nairobi, even in Beirut.

It is not really white at all, even where there is some snow around. It smells of gasoline, it is marked by global warming and by unbridled, energy-intensive consumerism.

I am actually writing this essay in Lebanon, where bullet holes in one of the buildings are clearly visible behind the figures erected to commemorate the birth of Jesus. The building and the figures are near the biggest and the most luxurious mall in Beirut – ABC.

Syrian refugees are overwhelming this tiny country – Lebanon. Officially 1.3 million are here, but a more realistic count would indicate well over 2 million desperate immigrants. Syrian children are now begging all over the capital. The U.N. is warning that it is running out of cash. I have just returned from the Bekaa Valley. Cold winter is approaching. Many people may freeze to death, or die from hunger.

Syria was destroyed by the modern-day crusades propelled by the neo-con clique, which consists mainly of the conservative Protestant fundamentalists and a powerful Zionist strain right in the heart of the empire's policymaking apparatus.

It is seldom put like this, but it is correct. As happened in the era of the crusades, a predominantly white and overwhelmingly Christian bunch of rulers —more precisely, Judeo-Christian—has gathered around the fundamentalist belief that their faith, the color of their skin and their 'culture', puts them well above the rest of humanity. And that the whole of humanity and the riches above and below Earth, have to be controlled by them and only by them, so help them God!

This belief has propelled many outrageous extermination campaigns against entire nations and cultures, during all the stages of European colonialism, to this day. The consistency and intensity of the onslaughts has been uniquely Western and Christian. Non-Christian countries like China travelled to the same places as the Westerners did, including Africa, in the same period of time or even earlier than Europeans. They came with much more potent weapons, but with no appetite to colonize and to plunder.

***

One of the main characteristics of Christianity has been its obsession with the total control over human lives, and over entire nations. Children have been literally enslaved by their Christian parents; and the entire continents, from Latin America to Asia, were not treated in any better way.

Disobedience had to be broken, rebelliousness oppressed.

Slavery in all imaginable forms was imposed.

It is little wonder, because both Old Testament and New Testament treat slavery as a given.

Turning conquered people into slaves was and to a great extent, still is, common practice of the Christian empires.

According to the African Holocaust Society:

> *"Slavery in various forms has been a part of the social environment for much of Christianity's history, spanning well over eighteen centuries. In the early years of Christianity, slavery was a normal feature of the economy and society in the Roman Empire, and this persisted in different forms and with regional differences well into the Middle Ages."*

***

No ideology, no religion, no calamity, killed more people on our planet than Christianity.

Year after year, wherever I happen to be and work on this planet, I'm waiting for these topics of utmost importance to be discussed. I am waiting in vain. With the exception of Latin America where many great thinkers like Eduardo Galeano or Abel Posse are relentlessly reminding the people about their past – about the horrendous crimes committed in the name of and under the shadow of the Cross – Christianity with the inexorable support of the Empire's propaganda is still managing to choke the memory of the world. It is also managing to break the ability of people to clearly analyze the horrendous past that is now effortlessly overflowing into the present, and poisoning our planet.

The past is intertwined with the present.

The crusades of the past, and the burning cities of Libya, Iraq and Syria now... The conquest of the entire (what is now called) Latin America, and the modern-day implementation of the 'Monroe Doctrine' (isn't that true Christian dogma?)... The Christian enslavement of Africa, the justification of slave trade and murder of millions of 'savages' neatly justified by Christian bigots, and the present day murder of the millions in DR Congo, Somalia, Mali and elsewhere...

Everything is connected, and I want to talk about it!

There was enough of the silence. Really enough...

We often say, correctly, in South Africa and in South America, that unless the past is addressed and fully understood, there can be no hope for a decent future.

Therefore, during these days when Christianity is flexing its muscle, when it is singing its gospels loudly, using thousands of choirs consisting of brainwashed individuals – military marches disguised as 'peace and happiness' hymns – let us demand that the whole truth and dirt hiding behind the cross gets exposed!

There can be no peace on earth until Christianity loses its grip on political and economic power. It can have no moral mandate, after all those crimes it has committed!

For endless centuries, Christianity was always allied with oppressive forces, be they big business, slavery, feudalism or capitalism. It has been marching hand in hand with despotic concepts like Western imperialism, racism and sexism, with royalism and colonialism. And it was not just a passive marcher: again and again it was pushing oppressors in the back, directly helping to construct the most horrendous models on earth.

Christianity blessed the ships sailing to distant shores, in order to colonize, plunder and destroy far away lands. It built its churches and cathedrals from the ruins of ancient temples in South America, forcibly converting broken and humiliated people. Much more than that – it actually invested in these expeditions of loot, it participated in them!

Offer another cheek? Metaphorically speaking: if someone were to as little as slap Christianity's refined cheek, he or she, or the entire village, would soon be showered with spears or bullets or missiles!

Let us talk about all this!

People burned alive, people tortured and raped by the priests in dungeons. They have been totally against sex, but they did not mind raping and torturing women! There are entire museums of Christian torture, of Inquisition; the most graphic one located in Lima, Peru, which was one of the headquarters of Christian barbarity.

It should all be discussed, and not just in this essay, which is too short for listing even the most essential crimes committed by

Christianity. We need hundreds of thousands of pages of books and hundreds of films to just touch on the very basics.

We need it, because this era of Christian dictate never really ended.

And let us never again accept that nonsense repeated by apologists: that the Christian religion is essentially good, but people, the followers, are bad! That is as insulting as if the Nazis declared that their movement was just fine, but very mean members managed to kidnap it.

Christianity, the concept, is brutal and wrong. People are just its victims!

Let us all read the Bible again, that horror of horrors of cruelty – the Old Testament. And then let's also read the New Testament, both books that accept slavery, and call for violence and the spreading of dogma.

Let us read very, very carefully. It is all there, black on white.

It is clear, it is obvious, that extremely destructive things are encoded in the dogmas of Christianity. Not 'in its people', but in the very dogma, in the essence of the religion, which has made people behave like monsters and worse, for centuries, for millennia. The Bible and the dogma actually inspired, allowed all those outrageous crimes, massacres, and genocides to take place.

We have to find, urgently, before it is too late, what exactly that toxic, violent stuff is.

On all continents, Christianity spread agony and corruption, theft and misery. It sided everywhere with the rulers, against the people. And it was the last one to support defunct regimes. All in the name of its perverse, false 'morality', all in the name of God, who it knows as little about as all the rest of us!

Morality... Rapes and indoctrination, fear... Always fear!

Let us talk, openly, because the crimes of Christianity were committed everywhere, because they still are committed everywhere. Because the Empire is Christian, and because the rulers are! We have to define what Christianity really is and what it has done, because there is no way forward for this humanity, unless this dogma is prevented from controlling the world!

Let us throw away clichés erected by the Empire and its

religion. Let us talk loudly, because Christians are in stupor: most of them have no clue that they belong to the most violent group on earth. I spoke to Christian men and women, in Europe and Asia, in the Middle East, Oceania and Africa, and in North and South America. Most of them, especially those who were educated in their lobotomizing private religious schools, have never heard about the onslaughts by their faith. They live in total darkness, in absolute torpor.

Let us open this difficult discussion, now, when Western neo-colonialism, a shadow and delayed twin of the Christian crusades, is trying to bulldoze out of its way, everything that may prevent it from taking final control over the world.

How is Christianity, which directly participated in colonialism, crusades, and extermination of entire nations, in Nazism... how is it still, now, shaping those brains of the neo-cons, of mass murderers who are leveling entire nations into the ground, at this very moment, as these words are being written.

Once again, I don't want to talk about 'bad Christians' who 'give Christianity bad name'. I want to talk about the dogma itself, about the essence of the belief, one which has created so many monsters, and so much suffering all over the world.

After hundreds of millions of deaths, I believe that such a demand is justifiable. Were Christianity to be a political party or a movement, it would be condemned, banned and declared to be the most brutal creation of humanity.

But it is hiding behind some abstract figure of God, of divinity, which it arrogantly claims it represents! It made itself 'untouchable'. It is not. It should never be!

Are some believers going to be offended? But of course! Their faith can murder the world, but others, even the victims, have to be 'sensitive'! But should some 'sensitivities' of those who believe in fairytales, and are willing to sacrifice hundreds of millions of human lives on the altar of irrational invents, be put above survival of humanity? By no means! Those who believe in the Christian doctrine, or in market fundamentalism, imperialism, slavery or racial superiority, should be questioned, challenged and confronted.

It is all very urgent, especially now when the Empire and its lackeys are once again threatening survival of our planet.

Let us talk, when there is still some time left, let us analyze, and let us contain the dogma, which has been poisoning this planet, by murdering, frightening and ruining human lives for endless centuries!

19 December 2014

*****

36

CHILEAN SOCIALISM 1 INDONESIAN FASCISM 0

Several years ago, I spoke to two members of Allende's government. Two who managed to survive. One of them recalled: "They used to threaten us, before the coup, before that terrible September 11, 1973: 'Watch out, comrades, Jakarta is coming!'"

"We did not know much about Jakarta then," he confessed. "Only that it was the capital of a far-away country called Indonesia... But very soon we found out..."

'Jakarta' is not just the capital of the fourth most populous country on earth; it is also the 'least habitable major city in Asia Pacific'. Jakarta is also a concept, an enormous experiment on human beings, which was quickly turned into a blueprint that has later been implemented by the West all over the developing world.

The experiment was about trying to figure out this: What happens to a poor country that is hit by a brutal military coup, then thrown to religious zealots, and forced to live under the heel of extreme capitalism and fascism? And what happens if almost its entire culture gets destroyed, and instead of education, some brainwashing mechanism perfected abroad, gets implemented?

What if you kill 2-3 million people, and then you ban entire languages and cultures, theatres, art films, atheism, everything that is to the left of center?

And what if you use thugs, paramilitaries, archaic family and religious structures and a ridiculously toothless media, to maintain 'the new order'?

The answer is this: You get your Indonesian model! Which means – almost no production, a ruined environment, collapsed infrastructure, endemic corruption, not even one sound intellectual of international caliber, and frankly speaking, a 'functionally illiterate' population, ignorant about the world, about its own history, and about its own position in the world.

But the most important conclusion of this 'research' is that after the orgy of terror in 1965 and 1966, after the millions that were killed, millions that were raped, tens of millions beaten and tortured, the result is the entire archipelago that is wholly silenced, and unable to organize any resistance. You get the archipelago that is unable to think, and which constantly repeats religious, pop and television slogans, instead of thinking about the past, present and the future.

If you are a corrupt and treasonous local ruler, or if you are the puppeteer that controls such a country from abroad, what you get is easy access to all its natural resources, a population unable to organize itself and fight for its rights, and voters indifferent to reality and unfamiliar with concepts such as dignity, and therefore ready to cast their ballot simply for a fee.

You get all this and more, and all you have to do is to make sure you butcher some 2-3% of the population, 40% of teachers, and that you rape millions of women and children, then terrify and silence all the minorities.

The West hailed this as a splendid success! It congratulated "Our Man – Suharto" (In 1995, a senior Clinton administration official, commenting on the Indonesian President, Suharto, then on a state visit to Washington, referred to him as "our kind of guy."). Murdering millions of 'Communists', was after all, the best way of gaining the admiration and respect of the US White House and Congress. And "selling" the country to Western companies was the most honorable and sensible path to gaining political and financial rewards from the 'free world'.

To terrify the country, to paralyze it by fear... To strip it of all real opposition, that was exactly what was needed! Suharto and his military cronies, his generals (one of them is presently the President of Indonesia), his thugs that murdered intellectuals, teachers, writers and union leaders, all became our 'buddies', our 'mates', our 'jolly good fellows'.

Like those guys, who dutifully cut people to pieces, raped 14-year old girls and terrorized those people who were still willing to think and to speak, everything was shown in detail in the award winning film by Joshua Oppenheimer: "The Act of Killing".

And what did the Indonesian viewers and TV hosts do when the thugs confessed to kill hundreds? They laughed, and cheered, and applauded!

In 1998, Suharto fell, but the 'model' survived, and it is still being promoted, and pushed down the throats of many countries all over the world. It is marketed as 'tolerant and democratic' by European and US government officials and certain NGO's. This I was told, recently, by members of the diplomatic community in Cairo, Egypt, the place where the revolution was successfully derailed and destroyed, mainly from abroad.

And why should it not be promoted? This is the masterpiece of Western domination: an enormous country, fully screwed and thoroughly ruined, plundered, abandoned to the market, robbed of everything... And the people here are so conditioned, so badly educated, so uninformed, that they are thoroughly unaware of how grotesque the state of their subsistence is.

In Indonesia, for years and decades, I have been interviewing hundreds of poor men and women who are living in a gutter, then shitting into filthy canals in cities like Surabaya, Medan and Jakarta, using the same water to wash their dishes and themselves... People who barely survive on a less than $1 a day, were proudly declaring on camera that they are not poor, that they are doing well, and that their country is just fine.

A few streets away, the newly rich, sit in their luxury SUV's in epic traffic jams, watching television, going nowhere, but proud that they have moved up the rungs on their class ladder.

What a success! What an absolute success of fascist, neo-colonial demagogy and the 'market economy'!

This 'success' was, of course, studied and analyzed in Washington, Canberra, London and elsewhere. It has been implemented all over the world, in different forms and variations, but with the same essence: strike and murder every thinking being, shock and brainwash... then rob the poor and reward a few criminals... from Chile to Argentina, Yeltsin's Russia and Rwanda, now again in Egypt.

It has worked almost everywhere. "Jakarta was coming", and it has been spreading its filth, its ignorance, brutality and compassionless way of 'thinking' all over the planet!

It seemed to be the most perfect 'treatment' for dissent and the dreams of freedom, all over the world. And the US has been busy administering it all over the Western hemisphere, but also in Asia, Africa, and everywhere. Death squads were trained in the North American military facilities, and then sent back to operate in Honduras, Guatemala, El Salvador, and the Dominican Republic and in many other unfortunate places.

Of course they could not fully compete with the insane sadism of the Indonesian butchers, but they did their best; they worked quite well, really... Blowing the brains out of rebellious priests during their sermons, raping teenage daughters in front of their parents, cutting people to pieces... slightly watered-down versions of the Jakarta scenario, but with some local 'cultural' flavors.

In Chile, in one of the oldest democracies on earth, the 9-11-1973 military takeover, brought new innovations to the established routine of horrors: women prisoners raped by dogs, prisoners with their hands tied, thrown alive into the sea from helicopters, while some were delivered to those old German Nazis inhabiting the so called "*Colonia Dignidad*" in the south of the country, for medical experiments.

It appeared that Western terror; its colonial tactics perfected and refined over centuries, will finally triumph, globally. It looked almost certain that no antidote would work: An antidote to the sadism and fear that has been paralyzing most of the subjects in the client states.

The Chilean military junta began with the same zeal as its Indonesian counterpart of eight years earlier. In Jakarta, religious Muslim cadres almost immediately joined the killing and torture, while in Santiago; it was conservative Christendom, particularly Opus Dei, which threw its support behind the murderers and rapists of General Pinochet. In both places 'conservative family values' were evoked, to justify the most appalling atrocities.

The streets of Santiago and other Chilean cities fell silent. Horror was omnipresent. Doors were kicked open by military boots and people dragged to dungeons, tortured, raped, murdered.

The National Stadium was filled with men and women. Like in Jakarta, noble, educated people were tortured and beaten, even killed with absolutely no scruples.

At one point, the soldiers came and arrested a bard; one of the most beloved singers of Latin America, Victor Jara. They broke his hands. Then they threw his guitar at him and shouted: "Now you can sing!"

This was the most significant moment – I would insist, the crucial moment. The moment when Santiago and Jakarta parted! The moment when in South America, an extremely long and difficult process began: the process, which could be described as the fight for freedom, for true freedom, not for that empty fake slogan that has been repeated over and over again by Western propaganda.

Because at that moment, Victor Jara stood up, in terrible pain but undefeated, full of spite, and sang to his tormentors, straight at their filthy muzzles, "*Venceremos*!"

He sang loud, and after a while, they were overwhelmed by his voice and the lyrics, they aimed at him and shot him dead.

But he did not die, instead he became the symbol of resistance, of the struggle against fascism and imperialism. He became the symbol of the struggle that is still continuing and gaining momentum in so many parts of the world!

In 1965, in Jakarta, there was no struggle. The victims allowed themselves to be slaughtered. They were begging for mercy as they were strangled, stabbed, shot to death. They called their tormentors, their murderers, their rapists, '*pak*' and '*mas*' (respectful form of addressing a man). They cried and begged for mercy.

In 1973, in Santiago de Chile, young men and women went to the mountains, to fight fascism, under the banner of MIR; some 10,000 of them. It was a clean and proud fight, as MIR decisively rejected all forms of terrorism, and concentrated on military targets.

Hundreds of thousands of Chilean people left the country,

scattering to all corners of the globe, from Mexico to Sweden, Canada to New Zealand. Wherever they went, they relentlessly worked on bringing down Pinochet and his US-backed *junta*. They wrote theatre and radio plays, made powerful films, wrote novels, arranged meetings and demonstrations in literally every major capital of the world. They never gave up. They dedicated their lives to the struggle. The millions at home and the hundreds of thousands of those forced to live abroad.

Eventually, Augusto Pinochet became a symbol of degenerate military power, of treason, of colonialism, of modern fascism.

In Indonesia, the victims accepted their 'fate' and with it, they accepted the most disgusting type of market fundamentalism. They accepted the fascist political system that stripped the poor (really the great majority) of all their rights. They accepted the thuggish, mafia-style arrangement for their country. They accepted a system where women are treated as the property of their fathers and later as the property of their husbands, while those who work and hold important positions are treated like whores, by their bosses, co-workers and even by their fellow Parliamentarians.

In Chile, nothing was really 'accepted'. Nothing was forgotten and nothing was forgiven. Instead of looking at the ruling 'elites' as heroes, the majority of Chileans saw them as a bunch of bandits. Instead of looking at their parents with servile submissiveness 'Indonesian-style', a great number of Chilean youth held them responsible for creating or at least tolerating this monstrous system.

While Indonesia became the second (after Nigeria) most religious country on Earth (despite the fact that Muslim and Hindu cadres were directly responsible for some of the most appalling atrocities, while Christians are lately professing the outrageous belief that God loves the rich, and hates the poor, participating in the segregation of society, and even in open racism), Chile reformed its laws, modernized its education, and sent Christianity where it belongs – to its churches and very far away from public eyes.

In Indonesia, Suharto stepped down, but the system survived; it even hardened itself. One of Suharto's generals is now serving as President of the country. And decades ago he was one of the leading military figures in occupied East Timor, during the most horrible massacres, during the genocide, in which some 30% of the local population lost their lives. The father of his wife was another general, who boasted that during the 1965 coup, they, the military, managed to kill around 3 million people.

In Chile, as in Argentina, most of those military leaders who committed crimes against humanity are now imprisoned, disgraced and despised.

Both armies, Indonesian and Chilean, of course, committed high treason, by selling their services to foreign powers, and instead of defending their citizens, fought for a fee, against their own defenseless women and children.

In Indonesia, many consider one of the worst butchers of the 20th century, and the most corrupt ruler of all times, General Suharto, a national hero! In Chile, General Augusto Pinochet is now clearly identified as a criminal, by a great majority of the people.

In Indonesia, between 2 and 3 million died in 1965/66. In Chile, the number was 3 to 4 thousand. Even adjusted to the dissimilar size of the population, the difference is overwhelming. Still, in Chile, there are hundreds of books written on the topic, dozens of powerful films made, and the topic is constantly addressed in newspapers, magazines and television programs – it is an essential part of the national memory. Without it, there seems to be a consensus – there is no way forward.

In Indonesia, there is an absolute blackout and silence.

The Indonesian population is fully loyal to the propaganda it has been fed for many decades. It is telling that at a recent attempt to resurrect the topic, at a screening of the documentary (unfortunately quite mediocre) called "15 Years After" (referring to numbers of years since Suharto's stepped down), there were only 5 people in one of the major cinemas in Jakarta... And it was a Saturday afternoon.

Saturday afternoon in Santiago de Chile and the entire city is getting ready for an extremely long night. Dozens of theatres offer everything from classical performances to avant-garde plays. Nightclubs are preparing for the latest bands that come from all over Latin America. The music ranges from opera and symphonies, to ballads, salsa and *cumbia*. Cinemas in all corners of the city are showing the latest releases, as well as Asian, Latin American and European art films.

There is some 'art for art', but plenty of it is deeply political; it is shaping the nation, addressing every important issue, including the past.

The same obsession with culture and knowledge is the norm in other cities of the 'Southern Cone', including Buenos Aires, Sao Paulo and Montevideo. To know is to exist. To understand the world is to be free, independent, and to be alive. Knowledge is valued; it is deeply respected.

Some 15 thousand kilometers West of Chile, in the Indonesian cities of Jakarta, Surabaya or Medan, there is close to nothing one can do on Saturday nights. There are restaurants, of course, and several cinemas showing the lowest grade of Hollywood films. But there are no art cinemas, no theatres (only maybe one theatre performance a month, in a city like Jakarta, with 12 million inhabitants). The only random concerts are those organized by the European cultural centers, and those very few ones for the 'elites' in some hard to get into private hall.

Life is extremely boring in Indonesia, with no variety and no intellectual inspiration. And that's how it was intended.

To get to the theaters, many citizens of Santiago opt for the metro system, one of the best and most efficient on earth. Each station is dedicated to local artists, many are equipped with public libraries, and one even has a free art cinema, where one can sit for the entire day for the price of one metro token, watching the greatest world classics.

In Jakarta, there is no metro at all, and almost no sidewalks, and there are only very few public parks. To cross the street, one often has to take a taxi. The city is approaching, and some people say it has already reached, a permanent gridlock.

Chile is embracing knowledge and everything that is 'public'. Indonesia is stuck in uncool, totally cheap pop, buried in depressing individualism, forced to admire all in 'private'.

The countries of South America that suffered from brutal dictatorships imposed by the West are now free and run by Socialist governments.

Indonesia is run by thugs, old generals and by a gloomy, degenerate, capitalist clique.

Women govern Brazil, Argentina and Chile, while a man who

was in charge of a military unit in East Timor, during the genocide, runs Indonesia.

Michelle Bachelet who is poised to win in the second round and return as the President of Chile (after being a head of UNIFEM) is a doctor, pediatrician, single mother of 3 and an atheist. Her father, an army general during Allende's administration, was murdered by Pinochet's regime, and Ms Bachelet herself was brutally tortured in detention. She left the country and was trained as a doctor in East Germany, before returning back home.

While Camila Vallejo (25 years old), and her fellow student leaders are ready to become MP's in Chile, many for the Communist Party. Indonesian women MP's face sexual harassment from their fellow People's Representatives, right on the floor of Parliament. And the Communist Party is flatly banned in Indonesia, just to make sure that nobody pushes for land reforms and social justice, anymore.

Chileans are now fighting for free education and for free medical care, and it is expected that their demands will be satisfied during the Presidency of Ms. Bachelet.

Indonesia is living with fully collapsed medical care and education systems, and everyone who can afford it, is leaving for hospitals in Singapore or Malaysia, and as far as possible for education.

There are countless private schools all over Indonesia, most of them religious. They specialize; it appears, in producing masses of young people unable to excel in anything at all, except in serving capitalist and religious dogmas, and in stealing for the sake of their family clans.

While Chile is fighting against poverty on all fronts, including by building high quality social housing, Indonesia has some of the most appalling inequalities on earth, and it even lies about the number of its inhabitants (it has over 300 million citizens, but only around 247 million are accounted for), just in case someone may demand, one day, that the poorest of the poor be housed, educated and healed.

Chile is one of the least corrupt nations on earth, while corruption in Indonesia is one of the highest on earth, with the former 'our kind of guy' Suharto entering the record books as the most corrupt ruler of all times.

Indonesia and Chile are two countries that went through a

fascist hell; but there are two totally different stories, at the end of that hell.

One country – Indonesia – submitted itself, collaborated and in the end failed, collapsed, became much like some of those unfortunate nations of sub-Saharan Africa.

The other fought, proudly, consistently, and won, becoming one of the most habitable nations on earth, with a quality of life comparable to that of the European Union.

One is not able to produce one single decent novel after its great Communist writer – Pramoedya Ananta Toer (a former prisoner of conscience, whose books and manuscripts were burned by Suharto's clique) – passed away. It produces nothing of intellectual value: no quality music or films, no scientific research, no ground-breaking educational concepts.

The other one – Chile – gave birth to some of the greatest modern writers, poets, filmmakers and architects. And some of the best wine!

The Indonesian model is frightening, but it can be defeated. It succeeds only when the people refuse to fight, when they submit to terror.

Indonesia, individuals are expected to surrender to brutal family and religious control. From birth, people here are conditioned: they live with fear, which is confused with 'love'. First it is the potent fear of father, then of the priest, of the teacher. And then it progresses to fear of the military and capitalist dictatorship. In the end it becomes a paralyzing fear of 'everything', which stops every rebellion at the embryonic stage.

It is pathetic and depressing. It is working. But definitely not everywhere!

Rebelliousness works better. It has been working all over Latin America, including Chile. 'Jakarta came', but was fought, and thrown to the dogs.

But, as a result of the joint efforts of local and Western propaganda, the success of Latin America is absolutely unknown in Indonesia. And there is no one screaming in Jakarta at those brutal faces of the elites: "Watch out, bandits, Santiago is coming!"

22 November 2013

37

Elites F*** Up Bangkok

DOWN AND OUT IN THAILAND

They really do, do it! And they are hard at work.

Sukumvit Road, the main commercial artery of the capital, is totally blocked. 'Protesters' are camped in the middle of it, basically taking it over, their tents, shops and eateries are spread all over the pavement.

In most true capitalist societies it would never come to this. Local businessmen, the city administration and the government by now would be worried silly about all those huge losses – of hundreds of millions of dollars disappearing because of the irresponsible actions of the ultra-conservative minority political movement.

Were this to occur in London, Paris or New York, police would have already moved in a long time ago, maybe even the army, and beat up hundreds of people, and arrested perhaps thousands.

And in Bangkok itself, it was done several years ago, and in a much more horrible way, when the Red Shirts (those who are now practically running the government after winning elections again and again) were massacred in the middle of the night, when the pro-elites, pro-feudal and pro-Western government of Prime Minister Abhisit Vejjajiva (born in England, and educated at Eton College and Oxford University) began using snipers to blow out people's brains.

Were Thailand to be some sort of 'mature capitalist society', things would have been a bit different. Not great, not good, but different...

But Thailand is the land of rumors and long silences, of unpronounced threats. And Thailand is not capitalist, not yet, far from it. Like the Philippines and Indonesia, it is a deeply feudal society, which has never really managed to reform itself, nor to progress. Don't be fooled by the boutiques, five star hotels and luxury restaurants. Don't think that Bangkok's cosmopolitan flair is something that has managed to change Thai society to its core.

Thailand has always 'served' those, whoever, that came. Be it the Japanese or Americans, or now the millions of foreigners that descend on the capital city for a variety of reasons.

Foreigners want their Latin American salsa clubs and traditional Indian eateries: and here they can have them and enjoy them! But there is still very little mingling between the locals and outsiders, and even when there is some contact, (at workplaces or during the 'client/service provider exchanges') real dialogue between the cultures is not common.

True changes, Latin American revolutions, the fight against imperialism – all these are unknown, totally foreign terms in Bangkok and in the provinces.

Here, things are mostly done because 'they are profitable'. Thailand is very pragmatic.

It was the same during the Vietnam War, when Thai airports were converted and expanded or built from scratch, to serve their neo-colonial masters. Millions of sorties were flown against Vietnam, Laos and Cambodia, spreading death and destruction all over the region. Millions of innocent men, women and children were massacred because of these airports, with Thai staff servicing them, even getting into the cockpits.

Then it was not about 'morality' or about what one actually believed (the West's fight against progress or against Communism): it was absolutely simple, practical. Air force bases were 'good business' for the elites. And if the price had to be counted in millions of human lives, so be it! Thais have always had an enormously high opinion of themselves, of their worth. Such an opinion clearly borders on racism. Therefore, if the millions who were dying (while Thailand was getting richer) were foreigners, and especially Khmers, Vietnamese or Laotians, then what was there to worry about?

Tens of thousands of young girls, even children, were brought from the North to Pattaya and to other bases, in order to 'service' those foreign men, who were so busy implementing Kissinger's dogma of using 'all that flies against all that moves' (read, massacring millions of civilians).

Girls were not allowed to say 'no', because of the structure of the Thai feudal society and its medieval family structure. Here, girls in the countryside could not say 'no' to their fathers, who could easily decide whether their children stay at home or leave home, even whether they should go and prostitute themselves, to send money back to the family.

And the most feared and revered 'father' was that man whose name we cannot even mention, that's if we want to stay out of prison.

He was born in the United States, brought back, and implanted into Thailand, when the institution of the monarchy by then had almost disappeared as a real force and as an alternative. The West needed him. It generously rewarded him and lifted him up to a divine level.

From then on, it was all 'unconditional love', between the Western regimes of neo-colonialism and this old twisted Southeast Asian culture. It is a culture that helped to spread terror all over the region, a culture that burnt people alive in oil barrels (those members of its own left-wing opposition, its own progressive youth).

It was a culture that had been massacring its own students, shooting them on the streets, or in the murky waters of the river near the Thammasat University in Bangkok. It was a culture that 'survived' several military coups with no major soul-searching afterwards, and with almost no criticism coming from abroad. This culture ruling over a country with a higher per capita homicide rate than the United States; but dubbed by the mainstream Western media and Western propagandists as 'The

Land Of smiles”.

This, one of the most feudal systems in Asia, was glorified as a democracy, while the man at the top (one of the richest monarchs in the world), was only described by the disciplined Western press as a ‘revered’ demi-god, and, a ruler ‘loved by his people’.

So what is really happening now in Bangkok?

It is simple, but it is not supposed to be spoken about.

Thaksin Shinawatra, the former Thai Prime Minister, a business tycoon of Chinese origin, committed the most unforgivable crime in the eyes of the Thai elites: Some years back he actually attempted to convert Thailand from a backward feudal nation, into some sort of a modern capitalist state.

Which under the circumstances, was actually an attempt to move his nation forward.

Mr. Shinawatra was not an angel, and when he was in power, I criticised him on several occasions. He ‘cleaned’ the Bangkok streets of homeless people, moving them to the suburbs. He was brutal towards the Muslim minority in the South. He was a real business tycoon.

But, he did some things, unimaginable anywhere in the region, except in Singapore and to some extent, Malaysia.

He introduced universal health care, virtually free, and excellent. He reformed education dramatically and so well that many of my friends, left-wing educators, were actually deeply impressed. He began housing the poor.

The elites in Bangkok hated this. The majority of them are not just after profits. They need to feel exceptional. They need ‘respect’. They need admiration and fear. They need weak, prostrated people; they need their feet to be kissed. They need to feel that the majority of the nation exists only in order to please them.

While Mr. Shinawatra knew that Thailand can only compete on the world stage and succeed, if its people are well fed, are healthy, educated and enjoy at least some of the basic privileges that are taken for granted in places like Singapore, Japan and Korea.

But the elites felt that if the ‘plebs’ got all those privileges, the gap between them would shrink, an unimaginable and most horrifying outcome!

And so they forced Mr. Shinawatra out from office, from Thailand, and in the end, they massacred those that demanded his return.

The Red Shirts they shot at actually consisted of individuals and movements as far apart as the Communists, and the moderate, pragmatic business folks. There were maids, peasants, as well as technicians and engineers in their ranks.

The massacres resolved nothing.

Soon it became obvious that the Reds represented the majority of Thais. Pro-Shinawatra and pro-reform forces kept winning election after election, democratically.

Then, a charismatic Ms. Yingluck Shinawatra, the younger sister of Mr. Thaksin Shinawatra, became the Prime Minister, following the 2011 general election.

The elites and the army, as well as the 'revered father', could not allow this course of action. People deciding the fate of the nation is something insane, even monstrous to them. And they are not hiding their thoughts; it is all in the open.

***

And here we are. Sukumvit Street blocked, every major intersection converted into a dormitory for the demonstrators. There are speeches and concerts. And there are also thousands of thugs, 'controlling' traffic and access to public places.

The iconic Bangkok Art and Cultural Center is closed down. No wonder, culture is dangerous. When the Red Shirts occupied this area in 2010, BACC was wide open.

Two days ago, 'protesters' blocked people from voting in a pre-election round. Photos showed one man, a potential voter, being almost strangled to death.

The Prime Minister confirmed that the elections would take place on February 2nd. Protesters have declared that they will boycott them, and do all they can to disrupt them.

One speaker after another declares that 'Thailand is not ready for democracy', and suggests that the country should first be governed by technocrats. "Otherwise the present government will keep winning". And that is, of course, 'unacceptable'.

It is clear that the present government is going to win again. Of course it will. People are not cattle. They know perfectly well that they have had all those feudal elites, 'up to here'.

To show the real state of marasmus in which Thailand exists, the army is sending messages that the possibility of yet another coup, should not be excluded.

So read well: if people vote for the existing government, there will most likely be a coup. The opposition will not accept the results, instead, suggesting openly and publicly, the abolition of democracy. And the West is listening to this crap, and is doing nothing to encourage one of its closest allies, in fact its 'client' state, to come back to its senses. Or more precisely, to discipline its collaborators, that fraction of Thai society, that is sucking blood from the open veins of the country.

"If the army takes over the capital, this time we will fight", I was told by my contact in the North, who did not want to be identified. "People will descend on Bangkok. This would be one coup too many... Thais will not allow this to happen. Enough is enough!"

A manager of one of the international hotel chains operating in Bangkok, Joseph Yamdee, explained:

> "I am sure that someone very big is behind all this. It is all organized so perfectly well. The guards and those who are sleeping on the streets; almost all of them are from the South. It is said that they are being paid 500 Baht per day (US$15). There is everything in place at the sites: huge electric generators, food and medical supplies."

I asked Mr. Yamdee, what impact Shinawatra's reforms on his hotel chain had, on the employees, and on the lives of ordinary people in Thailand?

"Huge," he replied. "The minimum wage was elevated to US$300 dollars a month. For instance, the receptionists used to make that amount in the past, and most of the receptionists belong to the middle class. We matched the wages of the cleaning ladies, to comply with the new minimum wage regulation, so suddenly everybody was making the same amount of money. Of course that was unacceptable for those who came from wealthy families... You see, it was not about receptionists making less money, but about others, those from the lower class, suddenly making the same wages."

Mr. Thon, one of the owners of café Bake & Brew, at the Bangkok Creative Design Center, commented:

"Now everything is closing down early. We used to be open late, but now we shut down at 7pm. People are scared. I am against Shinawatra. I don't want him to come back, although I can accept this government, the one led by his sister. But whatever I think about Shinawatra, I absolutely reject this blocking of elections, and bringing Bangkok to a full stop."

"Shut Down Bangkok!" the slogans all around the city shout.

There is clear impunity in the air.

The army is waiting. The elites are waiting. The government is scared. One false move, and there will be a military coup.

***

At the Foreign Correspondents Club of Thailand, the mood has been subdued. As always, almost nobody here would openly criticize the local elites, the Thai military or the monarchy. All three are fully allied to Western interests.

Instead of daily press conferences, the FCCT was showing, on January 27th, a BBC film about the child-victims of the Syrian conflict. That was one day after 'protesters' blocked access to several polling stations.

Bangkok is part of this bizarre new type of 'rebellions', simultaneously and very suspiciously taking place all over the world: Syria, Egypt, Ukraine and Thailand – everything appears to be inter-connected.

It is definitely not a set of uprisings that are supposed to improve the lives in all those above-mentioned countries. Instead it appears that these are events sponsored from abroad and their only goal is to bring politically, religiously or economically oppressive or regressive regimes to power: Mubarak and the military in Egypt, jihadi pro-Saudi cadres in Syria, pro-business and pro-Western market fundamentalists in Ukraine and now this feudal clique in Thailand trying to survive by all means.

What is striking is how uneducated, how ignorant the Western crowd visiting this city is. European tourists pose in front of posters, admiringly grinning at the 'protesters'. They have no clue what they are witnessing. And it appears that they have lost all interest, all curiosity about what is behind the propaganda with which they are being bombarded, day and night, from their own Western mass media.

Now Bangkok is getting ready for a showdown.

The depressing and oppressive feudal forces, all of them backed, paid and 'educated' by the West, are blackmailing that embryonic, fragile Thai democracy.

It is a really bizarre spectacle: A legitimate government, elected by the people, is too scared to strike back at hordes of paid thugs.

It is sickening. Once again, local elites are raping the country, in broad daylight, in front of the world. But suddenly there is nobody to say it. The local press and the international mass media are presently deep in thought, at how to package this shameful act, without insulting the sensitive Western regime and its local collaborators.

29 January 2014

*****

38

HOW THE WEST MANUFACTURES “OPPOSITION MOVEMENTS”

Government buildings are being trashed, ransacked. It is happening in Kiev and Bangkok, and in both cities, the governments appear to be toothless, too scared to intervene.

What is going on? Are popularly elected administrations all over the world becoming irrelevant; as the Western regime creates and then supports thuggish ‘opposition movements’ designed to destabilize any state that stands in the way of its desire to fully control the planet?

***

They are shouting and intimidating those who want to vote for the moderately progressive government that is presently leading Thailand. There is no dispute over the electoral process – voting is generally free, as both international observers and most of the local Election Commission members agree.

Freedom, legitimacy or transparency is not what is at stake now.

The rhetoric varies, but in essence, the 'protesters' are demanding the dismemberment of the fragile Thai democracy. Most of them are paid by the upper-middle and upper classes. Some of them are thugs, many hired for around 500 Baht a day (roughly US$ 15) in the villages of the restive southern provinces of the country. They are accustomed to the use of violence, their body language and facial expressions clearly show it.

Government officials of the legitimate government have to climb over blockades, or beg protesters to allow them to enter their own offices. People who came to vote in the pre-election round were intimidated and insulted, and one man was almost strangled to death.

While life in the capital has been fully disrupted, the government does not dare to send in tanks or the police to clear the streets. It should. But it is too scared of the army and the monarchy – two pillars of this outrageous hybrid of savage capitalism and feudalism – comparable only to even worse regional nightmares, such as Indonesia and the Philippines.

It is all in the open now: the government speaks of its fear, while the military sends poisonous threats through the lackey media and through 'leaks'.

What is happening and what is at stake? The Prime Minister's older brother, Thaksin Shinawatra, while he was PM himself, attempted to bring in a modern capitalist system to this submissive and deeply scared nation. And not only that: he housed the poor, introduced an excellent free universal medical care system (much more advanced than anything ever proposed in the United States), free and very advanced primary and secondary education, and other concepts deemed dangerous to the world order, and to the local feudal elites, as well as the army.

Thai elites, whose love of being obeyed more than wealth, admired and feared, reacted almost immediately. The PM was exiled, barred from returning home to his country, and smeared. There were military coups, mysterious 'alliances', rumours, and 'secret messages' coming from a 'very high place'. There was outright killing, a real massacre, when the so called 'Red Shirts', supporters of Mr. Shinawatra (ranging from moderate reformists to Marxists) were butchered by snipers, some shot in their heads.

Fascism is raising its ugly head, once again. And the West is fully aware of it, and in fact it is openly supportive of the regime that is now *de facto* governing Thailand from behind the curtains. Because it is the regime it helped to manufacture.

But the people, the poor, the majority of Thailand, particularly those from the North and Northeast, reacted in a stoical and most determined fashion. Whenever elections were called, whenever the regime outlawed the pro-Shinawatra political parties, the new ones emerged, and kept winning the elections.

In 2011, Mr. Shinawatra's sister, Yingluck, became Thailand's Prime Minister.

'Protestors' blocked several central arteries of Bangkok, declaring that "Thailand is not ready for democracy", and that "if elections should determine the country's future, pro-Shinawatra forces would keep winning".

That, of course, would be unacceptable to the elites and to many Western countries that have, for decades, benefited from the Thai feudal system.

One of Thailand's generals, 'refused to rule out the possibility of another military coup'.

What the opposition proposed was some hazy concept, of a government of technocrats, which would govern until Thailand 'is ready' to vote: read until people's power is broken and it would become certain that a pro-elites, pro-monarchy and pro-military government would be 'freely' elected.

In the meantime, thugs are blocking public streets; cultural centers but not malls. They are described as 'protesters' in both Europe and the United States.

And here we are coming to the core of things: The terror of the military and feudalism was dressed up in the clothes of rebellion, even revolution. It was given legitimacy, even a certain romantic flair.

Fascism is raising its ugly head, once again. And the West is fully aware of it, and in fact it is openly supportive of the regime that is now *de facto* governing Thailand from behind the curtains. Because it is the regime it helped to manufacture.

***

I left Bangkok and while in the air, one thought kept repeatedly coming to me: many of the places I had been writing about lately are living a very similar reality as Thailand is.

Those elected democratically, those progressive in their core, these governments all over the world have been under severe attacks by some armed thugs, bandits, and anti-social elements, even by outright terrorists.

I saw it on the Turkish-Syrian border. I heard the stories of many locals, in the Turkish city of Hatay, and in the countryside near the Turkish-Syrian border.

There, I was stopped, prevented from working, interrogated by the local police, army and religious thugs, when I was trying to photograph one of those 'refugee camps' built by NATO specially for Syrian fighters, who were housed, trained and armed in this area.

Hatay was overran by Saudi and Qatari jihadi cadres, pampered by the US, EU and Turkish logistics, support, weaponry and cash.

The terror these people have been spreading in this historically peaceful, multi-cultural and tolerant part of the world, could hardly be described in words.

Children from the borderline village described raids, theft and violence, even killing, by anti-Assad 'rebels'.

Here, and in Istanbul where I worked with Turkish progressive intellectuals, media and academia, I was explained to again and again, that the anti-Syrian 'opposition' has been trained, financed and 'encouraged' by the West, and by Turkey (a member of NATO), causing the death and destruction of millions of lives in the entire region.

As I write these words, RT is broadcasting an exclusive report from the Syrian city of Adra, the city that had been plundered and destroyed by pro-al Qaida and the pro-Western 'opposition' forces, including the Free Syrian Army.

This is the city where, allegedly, one month ago, people were murdered, stoned alive, burned in barrels, and beheaded.

Instead of stopping support for the racist, bigoted and extremely brutal Syrian 'opposition', Washington continues demonizing Assad's government, and threatening it once again with military action.

***

And those thugs, in the countries that elected their own patriotic or progressive governments, were hired by local elites on behalf of the Western Empire.

And before that, the so-called 'elites' were hired, funded, or at least trained/'educated' by the West.

On an 'intellectual' level, the private media outlets have been fiercely competing with each other, over which one would become more submissive towards the foreign handlers. The militaries and the most regressive feudalist, even fascist forces all over the world (see Ukraine, for instance) are clearly getting back into the saddle, benefitting and taking full advantage of the trend.

All this has been happening in different degrees and with variable levels of brutality, in Thailand, China, Egypt, Syria, Ukraine, Venezuela, Bolivia, Brazil, Zimbabwe and many other places all over the world.

Right after reading my article about the situation in Thailand, published on 30 January, my Brazilian reader reacted:

"Similar to our Brazil: though in a faded... somewhat lighter environment but substantially the same... the local elites, right now in January 2014, are doing whatever they can, to prevent the re election of Ms Dilma Roussef... You are an experienced Latin America´s observer, you know very well..."

The process, the tactics, are almost always the same: Western-paid media, or Western media directly, discredit designated popular governments, then 'scandals' are created, colors designated to some newly constructed 'opposition' movement, thugs selected and paid, and finally deadly weapons 'miraculously' appear at the 'protest sites'.

As long as the government is 'nationalist', really patriotic and defending the interests of its own people against international plunder, (not like the Abe's government in Japan which is peculiarly described as 'nationalist', but in reality it fully sides with US foreign policy in the region), it gets marked, and it appears on an invisible but powerful hit list, old-fashioned mafia-style.

As Michael Parenti correctly and colorfully described: "You do it our way, or we break your leg, capice?"

I witnessed President Morsi of Egypt (I was critical of his rule at first, as I was critical of the government of Mr. Shinawatra, before real horror swept both Egypt and Thailand), being overthrown by the military, which, while in its zealous over-drive, managed in the process to murder several thousands of mainly poor Egyptian people.

I was then in Egypt, in and out, for several months, filming a documentary film for the South American television network, *Telesur*.

In disbelief and dismay I witnessed my revolutionary friends going into hiding, disappearing from the face of the earth. This happened as outrageously arrogant families cheered on the military murderers with no shame, openly.

The logic and tactics in Egypt were predictable: although still capitalist and to a certain extent submissive to IMF and the West, President Morsi and his Muslim Brotherhood, were a bit too unenthusiastic about collaborating with the West. They never really said 'no', but that had not appeared to be enough for the Euro-North American regime, which, these days, demands total, unconditional obedience as well as the kissing of hands and other bodily parts. The regime demands old-fashioned, Protestant-style obedience, complete with self-deprecation and a constant feeling of guilt; it is ordering true and 'sincere' servility.

It appears that almost no country, no well-liked government can escape annihilation, if it does not fully submit.

It went so far that unless the government in a developing countries such as Philippines, Indonesia, Uganda or Rwanda, sends a clear message to Washington, London or Paris that "we are here simply to make you, in the West, happy", it would risk total annihilation, even if it was elected democratically, even if (and actually 'especially if') it is supported by the majority of the people.

All this is nothing new, of course. But in the past, things were done a little bit more covertly. These days it is all out in the open. Maybe it is done on purpose, so nobody will dare to rebel, or even to dream.

And so, the revolution in Egypt has been derailed, destroyed, and cruelly choked to death. There is really nothing left of the so-called 'Arab Spring', just a clear warning: "never try again, or else".

Yes, I saw the 'elites' of Egypt dancing, and celebrating their victory. The elites love the army. The Army guarantees their continuous place at the zenith, their power. The elites even make their little children hold portraits of the military leaders responsible for the coup, responsible for thousands of lost lives, responsible for breaking the great hopes and dreams of the Arab world.

What I witnessed in Egypt was chilling, and it resembled the 1973 coup in Chile (a country which I consider my 'second or third home'); the coup, which I am not old enough to remember, but footage of which I have seen again and again, in silent and never diminishing horror.

'Or else' could be the torture and murder of people in Bahrain. 'Or else' could be Indonesia in 1965/66. Or it could be the 'collapse of the Soviet Union'. 'Or else' could be civilian airliners exploding mid-flight; a Cuban plane was destroyed by CIA agents. It could be ravaged Iraq, Libya, Afghanistan, or Vietnam, Cambodia and Laos, bombed into the stone ages. 'Or else' can easily be some fully devastated country like Nicaragua, Grenada, Panama or the Dominican Republic. Or 'or else' could mean ten million people butchered in the Democratic Republic of Congo, for both its natural resources and for the anti-imperialist outspokenness of its great leader, Patrice Lumumba.

Now in Egypt, Mubarak's clique is rapidly coming back to power. He was a well-trusted 'devil', and the West quickly realized that to let him fall would be a serious strategic blunder; and so it was decided to bring him back; either personally, or at least his legacy, at the cost of thousands of (insignificant) Egyptian lives, and against the will of almost the entire nation.

The military of Egypt, of course, cannot be allowed to fall, either. The US has invested billions and billions of dollars in it, and the soldiers are now literally in control of half of the country. And it is a very reliable organization: it murders without scruple any being attempting to build a socially just society in this the most populous Arab nation on earth. And it plays with Israel. And it loves capitalism.

Two countries are separated by thousands of miles, and belong to two different cultures, located on two continents; Thailand and Egypt. In both countries, people spoke. They voted in their leaders. Not some Communist government, mind you: just a moderately socially-oriented one in Thailand, and a moderately nationalist/Islamic one in Egypt.

In both cases, the feudal and fascist elites went to work, immediately. Those that are behind them, that are financing them, and 'morally' supporting them, is, I believe, absolutely clear.

***

Ukraine is not a fresh victim of destabilization tactics of the European Union, which is so sickly greedy that it appears it, cannot contain itself anymore. It salivates, intensively, imagining the huge natural resources that Ukraine possesses. It is shaking with desire dreaming of a cheap and highly educated labor force.

European companies want to get into Ukraine, by all means. But one has to be careful not to allow the Ukrainian hordes to enter that sacred and thoroughly racist fortress – the European Union. Europe can plunder all over the world, but it is strict and brutal to those who want to get in and 'steal its jobs'.

Of course the EU cannot do in Ukraine, what it freely does in many places like the Democratic Republic of Congo (DRC). It cannot just come and pay some proxy countries, as it pays Rwanda and Uganda (that are already responsible for the loss of over ten million Congolese lives in less than 2 decades), to plunder Ukraine and kill almost all those people that are resisting.

Europe, again and again, for centuries, has proven that it is capable of massacring entire nations without the slightest mercy, (while showing almost zero historic memory) and with almost no moral principles, at least compared to the rest of the world. But it is canny, and unlike the United States, it knows plenty about tactics, strategy and PR.

What the EU did in Libya is clear. Anyone claiming that the United States is acting on its own, must be exercising enormous discipline not to see how closely linked are the interests and actions of the old and new usurpers of Africa, Asia, Latin America, Middle East, Asia and Oceania. France is acting, once again, as the arch neo-colonial thug, particularly in Africa.

But Ukraine is 'right there', too near geographically, to the EU itself. It has to be destabilized, but it all has to appear very legitimate. 'The rebellion', 'revolution', 'uprising of its people'; that is the way to handle things 'properly'.

More than a month ago, a bizarre deal was proposed, where European companies would be allowed to enter and clean Ukraine of its natural resources, but the people of Ukraine would not be allowed to even come and work in the EU.

The government, logically and sensibly, rejected the deal. And then, suddenly, Thai-style or Egyptian-style thugs appeared all over the streets of Kiev, armed with sticks and even weapons, and went onto trashing the capital and demanding the democratically elected government to resign.

The groups of thugs include many neo-Nazis, anti-Semites and common criminals. They are emboldened by the Thai-style fear of the Ukrainian government, to use force. They are setting on fire police officers, blocking and occupying government buildings, preventing the administration from serving the people.

Just as their 'orange' predecessors, they have been manufactured and carefully crafted, before being released into the wider world.

***

In Africa, just to mention a few cases, tiny Seychelles, a country with the highest HDI (Human Development Index by UNDP) has for years been bombarded with criticism and destabilization attempts. The Government provides excellent totally free (including medicine) medical care and free education. The people of Seychelles are well fed and housed. It is definitely not a perfect society, but, together with Mauritius, it is the best the African continent has to show. But that does not seem to be relevant.

Propaganda from outside, as well as the mainly British-sponsored opposition press, is trashing the system.

One wonders why, but then, on closer scrutiny and understanding of the Empire, things become clear: The Seychelles used to cooperate closely with both Cuba and North Korea, on educational fronts and in other fields. It was too 'socialist' for the Empire. And for those retirees seeking an exclusive hedonist lifestyle, it would be acceptable to be surrounded by blue and maybe even by brown, but definitely not by red.

Eritrea, dubbed as the 'African Cuba', may be a proud and determined nation, but it was designated as total pariah and outcast state by most of the Western powers. It was hit by sanctions and punished for who knows what.

"We are trying to be inclusive, democratic and fair", the Eritrean Director of Education recently told me, in Kenya. "But the more we do, the more we care about our people, the more infuriated Western countries appear to be."

He was a very wise man and so he did not appear to be surprised. Both of us were just 'comparing notes'.

Zimbabwe is another clear and extreme case. There, the West evidently and openly supports 'the opposition', against the government that is loved and supported by the great majority of citizens; the government of liberation struggle against colonialism and imperialism.

Provoked by outrageous lies disseminated by the mainly British mass media, I visited Zimbabwe last year, disputing point-by-point all the main propaganda points directed against Harare. Needless to say, my report, published by *CounterPunch*, created outrage against Western propaganda, all over the African continent.

The West builds and feeds 'rebellions' and 'opposition' against Venezuela, Bolivia, Cuba, Brazil, and Ecuador, to mention just a few countries high on its hit list.

In Venezuela, the US sponsored an aborted coup, and it directly pays for hundreds of organizations, 'NGO's' and media outlets, with the direct goal of overthrowing the revolutionary process and the government.

In Cuba, the people of this proud and humanist nation have been suffering for decades. They have been enduring what can only be described as terrorism against their beautiful country. The US and the West have sponsored invasions, terrorist acts, even attempts to influence weather patterns and cause devastating droughts. Crops have been poisoned.

Any Cuban 'dissident', any thug that takes up arms against the Cuban system and the government, would get immediate funding and support from the United States.

Even Western media outlets, performing secret polls in Cuba, often come to the conclusion that the majority of Cuban citizens support their system. But that only infuriates the West further. Cuban people are paying a heavy price for their freedom, for their pride, for their independence.

There are many other examples how the 'opposition' and terror against 'unpopular' (in the eyes of the West) governments are built.

Bolivians almost lost their 'white' and-right wing province of Santa Cruz, as the US supported, many say financed the 'independence movement' there, obviously punishing the extremely popular government of Evo Morales for being so socialist, so indigenous and so beloved. Brazil, in one great show of solidarity and internationalism, threatened to invade and rescue its neighbor, by preserving its integrity. Therefore, only the weight of this peaceful and highly respectable giant saved Bolivia from certain destruction.

But now even Brazil is under attack of the 'manufacturers of opposition'!

I don't want to write at length about China here, in this report. Readers are already familiar with my stand, but in summary: The more high-speed trains the Communist government builds, the more public parks, free exercise machines, more public transportation lines and wide sidewalks, the more it attempts to make medical care free for all once again, the more it attempts to make education free and public – the more it is being smeared and called 'more capitalist than capitalist states (while over 50% of country's production remains firmly in state hands).

Russia, like China, Cuba or Venezuela, is demonized relentlessly, every day and every hour. Any oligarch, any deranged pop figure, who criticizes the government of President Putin, is immediately elevated by the US, German and other Western governments, to the level of sainthood.

All this is definitely not because of the Russian human rights record, but because Russia, like the Latin American countries and China, is determinedly blocking Western attempts to destabilize and destroy independent and progressive countries all over the world. It is also due to the increasing influence of the Russian media, particularly RT (Russia Today), which became a commanding voice of resistance to Western propaganda. Needless to say, this writer is proudly associated with RT and its efforts.

***

It is certain that what the world is experiencing now, could be described as 'the new wave' of a Western imperial offensive. This offensive is taking place on all fronts, and it is rapidly accelerating. Under the proud Nobel Peace Price winner, Barack Obama and his closest European Neo-cons and 'socialists with brown insides', as well as the re-elected fascist Prime Minister of Japan, the world is becoming an extremely dangerous place. It feels like some frontier town invaded by violent gangs.

The biblical perception of 'those who are not with me are against me' is gaining new depth.

And be aware of the colors. Be aware of the 'uprisings', or anti-government 'protests'. Which one is genuine and which one is unnaturally created by imperialism and neo-colonialism?

It all appears to be extremely confusing to the majority of people who are getting stuffed on the corporate media feed. Actually, it is supposed to be confusing! The more confused people get, the less capable they are to rebel against real dangers and oppression.

But in the end, despite everything, on the 2nd of February, the people of Thailand voted! They climbed the barricades; they fought with those who were attempting to close polling stations.

And in Ukraine, the majority still supports their government.

And Venezuela and Cuba have not fallen.

And the jihadi cadres are not yet in control of Syria.

And Eritrea and Zimbabwe are still behind their leadership.

People are not cattle. In many parts of the world they are already realizing who their real enemies are.

When the US sponsored a coup against Chavez, the military refused to follow, and as a handpicked businessman was sworn-in as President, the military began moving tanks towards Caracas, in defense of the legitimate and elected leader. The revolution survived!

Chavez passed away, and some say that he was poisoned; that he was infected with cancer, that he was hit from the North. I don't know whether it is true, but before he died, he was photographed, bald and sweating, suffering from an incurable disease, but determined and proud. He was shouting: "Here nobody surrenders!" And this one image and one short sentence, inspired millions.

I remember, last year in Caracas, standing in front of a huge poster depicting his face, spelling out his words. I would thank him; embrace him if I could, if he were still alive. Not because he was perfect – he was not. But because his life and his words and actions inspired millions, pulled entire nations from depression, from gloom and doom, from slavery. I read from his face this: "They try to screw you by all means, but you fight... You fall but you fight again. They try to kill you but you fight... For justice, for your country, and for a better world." Chavez did not say this, of course, but that is how it felt, looking at his photograph.

By then, most of South America was free and united against Western imperialism, and hard to defeat. Yes, here, nobody surrendered!

The rest of the world is still very vulnerable and mostly in shackles.

The West is continuously manufacturing and then supporting oppressive forces, be they feudal or religious. The more oppressed people are, the less disposed they are to fight for justice and for their rights. The more scared they are, the easier it is to control them.

Feudalism, religious oppression and cruel right-wing dictatorships, all that serves perfectly well both the market fundamentalism of the Empire, and its obsession with controlling the planet.

But such an arrangement of the world is abnormal, and therefore temporary. Human beings are longing for justice and, in their essence, are a sharing and decent species. Albert Camus, correctly, arrived at the conclusion in his powerful novel "*The Plague*" (analogy to fight against fascism): "there is more to admire than to despise in humans".

What the West is now doing to the world; igniting conflicts, supporting banditry and terror, sacrificing millions of people for its own commercial interests, is nothing new under the sun. It is called 'ordinary fascism'. And fascism came and was defeated, in the past. And it will be again. It will be defeated because it is wrong, because it is against natural human evolution, and because people all over the world are realizing that the feudal structures that Western fascism is trying to administer all over the world, belong to the 18th century, not to this one, and should never again be tolerated.

3 February 2014

*****

39

JAPAN'S ODD PRO-WESTERN 'NATIONALISM'

Can one be a nationalist, while faithfully serving the interests of a foreign country or an empire? Anywhere else in the world the answer would be resolute and loud "No!"

It would appear as a clearly logical and linguistic contradiction. But in Japan, such a pirouette is apparently imaginable, acceptable and for many it is even perfectly *'normal'*.

At Nashappu Cape, which is right outside Wakkanai, the northern-most city of Japan, huge radars and military listening devices have been humming for decades, their low-key electronics resounding day and night. They are pointed directly at Russia and its remote island of Sakhalin, a huge isle taken over by the then Soviet military at the end of WWII, possibly because of Moscow's fear that Japan would soon become a US colony. Having huge US military bases not far from the cities of Khabarovsk and Vladivostok did not, obviously, appeal to the Soviet Union, which had just lost approximately 20 million people, fighting and defeating fascism.

On any clear day, Sakhalin is visible from the shore, or from the windows of any of Wakkanai's multi-story hotels.

Almost all signs in Wakkanai appear to be friendly towards visiting foreigners, as they are written in Japanese, English and Russian. But there can be no doubt: The city is firmly integrated into the massive imperial structure of the United States, based on the Asian continent. And Japan has been, since the end of WWII, the most important element of this arrangement.

In Tokyo, I asked David McNeill, leading expert on Japan and Professor at Sophia University, whether Japan is really an independent country, when it comes to its foreign policy. He got straight to the point:

> *"Critics would say 'no', and I would be among those people... Japan, after the Second World War, aligned itself very quickly with America... And Japan's military alliance with America is also accompanied with, what critics would say, its subservient attitude towards Washington."*

These days, Japan is in some sort of high or low level confrontational mode with almost all its neighbors. Cynics would say 'not surprisingly', considering that relations are strained between Japan's best friend the US, and China, Russia and North Korea.

Some 3,000 kilometers from Wakkanai, at the opposite end of Japan, the chain of Ryukyu Islands is totally militarized by the US air force and marines. In fact, the bases occupy some 19 percent of the land of Okinawa, and fences and barbed wire fragment much of the rest.

"We are colonized; our land and even our minds are now colonized," a leading Okinawan writer, Ms. Chinin Usii, explained.

On a normal day, from two major US air force bases located on Okinawan soil – Futenma and Kadena – jet fighters and surveillance airplanes take off with deafening regularity, unnerving both China and North Korea. Okinawa itself suffers: the F-15's fly at extremely low altitudes, their engines roaring. The island feels humiliated, used, sacrificed by Tokyo.

"This is where the Third World War could easily begin," I am told in a bar, one night, by one outraged Okinawan resident. *"And we have no say in the matter."*

The governor of Okinawa was supposed to have kicked the military bases off the island, but at the last moment, he succumbed to pressure from Tokyo and, according to most local residents, *'betrayed Okinawa.'*

The more it loses out economically to China and South Korea, and the more irrelevant it becomes politically, the more Japan becomes increasingly frustrated and aggressively pro-Western, particularly pro-United States. And what better way to show loyalty than by keeping those enormous US airforce bases on its soil, especially if the soil is one thousand miles from Tokyo, and belongs to islands with a distinct identity and culture.

'Becoming more and more pro-Western'

"There is this very strange mood in Japan these days", explains Osaka-based film editor, Hata Takeshi. *"Japan is becoming more and more pro-Western, while increasingly showing anti-Korean and anti-Chinese sentiments."*

This is reflected in several opinion polls, showing that most Japanese people now view the West favorably, and its North Asian neighbors negatively.

The incumbent administration is not only hawkish; it is brazenly insulting towards China and Korea. For example, Prime Minister Abe was unrepentant when he visited the ill-famed *Yasukuni* shrine recently, a place where many Japanese war criminals are buried.

Japan is increasing its military budget, and there is a strong drive to revisit, reverse, or at least to amend its peaceful post-war Constitution. Abe is talking tough; he is promising *'change'*. But the *'change'* could trigger conflict in East Asia.

Japanese Self Defense forces aircraft regularly fly over the disputed islands, outraging China. These dangerous games are backed by the US, which is backing Japan with strategic bombers.

In the meantime, the coverage of these events by most of the mainstream Japanese media is thoroughly one-sided and anti-Chinese as well as pro-Western, in its tone and core. China is accused of *'belligerence'* and *'aggressiveness'* when it comes to the recent events surrounding the disputed Senkaku Islands [known as Diaoyu in China] and such definitions are almost never challenged in public.

The fact that Japan is upsetting the fragile *status quo*, and according to many analysts based in Asia, is actually *'provoking China'*, is very rarely mentioned on Japanese TV or in the pages of its most widely read newspapers.

Reports by the Japanese media increasingly resemble a well-orchestrated propaganda drive. On February 13th, The Japan Times offered a predictable and stereotypical summary of the events related to China and the possible changes to Japan's Constitution:

> *"Prime Minister Shinzo Abe, pressed by China and seeking to strengthen ties with the US, is considering Japan's biggest change in military engagement rules since World War II. Having increased the defense budget two years running and set up a US-style National Security Council, Abe is now seeking to allow Japan to come to the aid of its allies. China's escalating challenge over the sovereignty of the Senkaku Islands has played into Abe's plans to strengthen the Self-Defense Forces",* says Liberal Democratic Party lawmaker Katsuei Hirasawa."

Militarizing Japan

A leading Australian historian and professor emeritus at Nagasaki University, Geoffrey Gunn wrote about the questions and answers sessions at the Japanese House of Representatives Budget Committee on February 12th, 2014, an event that had scant coverage in the local and international press. Gunn watched the session with his wife on local TV.

"Prime Minister Shinjo Abe sat in the front row, occasionally taking the microphone. Deputy Prime Minister, Taro Aso, reclined beside him. At the podium, following a round of applause, came Shintaro Ishihara, the unreconstructed neo-nationalist former governor of Tokyo. In his present incarnation, Ishihara enters the picture as member of recently resigned Osaka Mayor and right-wing ideologue Toru Hashimoto's Japan Restoration Party (Nippon Ishin no Kai). Also taking the podium was defense minister, Itsunori Onodera, fresh from a visit to India drumming up security and defense ties with China as the obvious target," Gunn said about the session. He noted that Ishihara is the one who, by threatening to *"purchase"* the Daoyu/Senkaku Islands, forced the hand of the then government

to nationalize them, thereby breaking with the *status quo* of recognizing a dispute with China as the other claimant, and setting up a dangerous escalation in tensions between the two nations.

"Far from backing off, the octogenarian Ishihara launched into a 30 minute harangue, denying the legitimacy of the Tokyo War Crimes Trials; calling for an expanded 'Self Defense Force' (the full nuance of his demands escaped my interpreter); making a pitch for the purchase of attack fighter aircraft; and virtually beating the drums of war," Gunn noted.

"For Prime Minister Abe, whose recent visit to the Yasakuni Shrine (inter alia, a shrine honoring A-class war criminals) offended both China and South Korea, Ishihara offered the soothing words, 'don't hesitate to visit again and ignore the words of neighboring countries'."

"Defense Minister Onodera, Prime Minister Abe, and Ishihara appeared to be in concord, a veritable cauldron of hawks. Gaffe-prone Taro Aso slumbered on, fortunately, perhaps, as the world cannot forget his statements of the previous year that a Nazi-style Reichstag would be the appropriate way to ram through constitutional amendments to better fit the Abe government's neo-nationalist agenda. All I can say is that if the military attachés of concerned states, Washington included, were not watching this show then they should have been," Geoffrey Gunn wrote.

The atmosphere in Japan at this time, as the Asahi newspaper reported, is that books and periodicals highly critical of China and South Korea are flying off bookstore shelves, prompting leading publishing companies to jump on the bandwagon to take advantage of the trend. But despite the undeniable turn towards the right, the Japanese public still disapproves of Abe's plan to change the pacifist course, and the Constitution. According to a poll conducted by Kyodo News, at the end of January 2014, approximately 54 percent of Japanese citizens expressed their dissatisfaction with the potential changes.

But while the majority of Japanese people would not like to see their country turning back and once again becoming a major military power, hardly anyone thinks of criticizing Japan's alliance with the United States.

In Okinawa, a former US marine who became a leading academic, Douglas Lummis, recently explained:

> *"The other day I heard, in open forum, two ladies discussing whether Japan's peaceful Constitution should be nominated and granted intangible world heritage status. They asked my opinion... I said: 'But while Japan has a peaceful Constitution, it allows huge US military bases on its territory. And these bases are anything but peaceful. And there is this military alliance between the two countries...' They could not understand my point: to them and to many Japanese people, challenging the US-Japan military alliance would be something thoroughly unthinkable. I totally confused them."*

It is perhaps not Japan itself, but its alliance with the West that is threatening peace in Northeast Asia.

The peaceful Constitution may still become, one day, an intangible world heritage. And Japan's self-defense force may not shoot at anybody abroad for some time to come. But what purpose would all this serve, if US strategic bombers take off one day and head towards China, North Korea, and even Russia, from those enormous military airports based on Japanese soil?

20 February 2014

*****

40

About Courage

I AM SCARED, THEREFORE I AM BRAVE!

Recently, my Italian translator, Giuseppe, wrote me an email. It was not a typical exchange, but quite an extraordinary personal query:

"Many see you as a very courageous person. They would like to imitate you at that, at least a little bit, but they feel they are not courageous, say, 'by nature' and they cannot learn courage. What do you think about that? Can people train themselves to be courageous?

I do not know how to answer this question in brief, and definitely not in the body of an email, not in just a few words. But the question is important, maybe essential, and so I decided to reply by writing this essay.

***

I have travelled the world, covering a myriad of conflicts, on all continents. I have written books, made films, and produced investigative reports.

I have seen fear on the faces of men, women and children, I

have seen misery and sometimes I saw what could only be described as absolute desperation. I often sensed fear 'in the air', in so many corners of the globe!

Fear has been, naturally, omnipresent at all battlefields and in the areas of carnage and plunder, but also at 'not so obvious places', such as churches and family homes, and even on the streets.

I have been 'studying fear', trying to understand its causes, its roots. I always suspected that to define what triggers fear, what produces it, would be like coming at least halfway to containing it, destroying it, freeing people from its tyrannical claws.

There are, of course, many types of fear: from rational fear of direct violence, to some abstract, almost grotesque fear that is imposed on people by our political regimes and establishments, by almost all religions, and by oppressive family structures.

The second type of fear is purposefully manufactured and has been perfected throughout the centuries. How to use it effectively, how to maximize it, how to inflict the greatest damage, all of that is passed on from oppressor to oppressor, from generations to generations.

Fear is administered in order to stop progress, in order to choke dissent and to keep people in a thoroughly submissive and servile position. Fear breeds ignorance, too. It offers a false sense of security and of belonging. Needless to say that one can belong to an extremely bad 'club', or to a family of gangsters, or to a fascist country. Fear manipulates masses to an ignorant obedience, and then threatens those who resist: "don't you see, that is what the majority of people want and think. Follow the others, or else!"

***

Almost several decades ago, thinkers like Huxley, Orwell and others prophesied societies in which we now live. We are still reading '1984' or 'Brave New World' with disgust, and with outrage. We read those books as though they are some imaginary, science-fiction horror, not realizing that those nightmares, actually, have already arrived in our countries, cities, even into our own living rooms.

As many nations, including those in Europe and North America, increasingly succumb to indoctrination and intellectual homogeneity, courage is vanishing. It is demonstrated very infrequently, and it clearly fails to inspire the majority.

It is not because 'people have changed', but because the world in which we are living is becoming increasingly compliant and restrained, and the main sources of information (mass media), as well as those sources that shape public opinion and the behavioral patterns of the citizens (social media), are fully controlled by corporate and conservative political groups and their interests.

While people used to be influenced and inspired by great thinkers, novelists and filmmakers, they are now being shaped by 160-character messages of social media, and by all those opinion-formers who try to make them shallow, unemotional, compliant and cowardly.

In much of the distant past, but before I was born, rebellions and revolutions were seen as something truly heroic; they were respected and seen as something worth living for, even dying for. That was still the era of true pathos, of struggles against fascism and against colonialism. And life was not stripped of all poetry, yet, not even of revolutionary poetry.

One's worth was defined by one's contribution to building a much better world, not by the size of his or her SUV.

In those days, entire nations rose up from their knees. Great men and women led some of the spectacular rebellions. Writers, filmmakers, even musicians joined the struggle, or often marched at the vanguard. The line between top investigative journalist work and the arts became increasingly blurry, as great personalities such as Wilfred Burchett and Ryszard Kapuscinski circled the globe, relentlessly identifying its plights and grievances.

Life suddenly became meaningful. Many, not the majority but definitely many, were ready to dedicate their lives, and even to die, in order to destroy that outdated and unjust world order; to build, from scratch, a decent and prosperous society for all human beings, or in brief, 'to improve the world'.

If you see some of the French, Italian, Japanese and Latin American films from that era, chances are, that you will get goose bumps. Such was the energy, the zeal, and determination to challenge the establishment and to improve life on the planet.

When Sartre spoke, even if on topics such as imperialism and colonialism, hundreds of thousands of people would gather in Paris, and he would often appear in places like the Renault factory, far away from those famous intellectual salons of the capital.

"I rebel, therefore I exist!" wrote Albert Camus, proudly. It appeared to be one of the main mottos of that era.

Then, suddenly, rebellion ended', it was 'contained'.

But the wars continued. Imperialism and colonialism regrouped. Media outlets were purchased, bought. Capitalism won, once again, despite all dialectic logic against such a victory. Progress was stopped, even reversed. Corporatism produced Thatcherism and Reagan-ism, and the world got its shackles and muzzles back. Then, that gangrenous 'War on Terror' was launched and fear began creeping back, even from where it had been expelled several decades earlier.

***

I do not consider myself 'brave', Giuseppe.

In fact, I am very scared, and that is why I rebel, and risk my life, constantly.

I am scared of what I see. I am also scared of not being able to see, to witness, to document.

I am scared when I see the desperate faces of women, holding photos of their disappeared or killed husbands and sons.

I am scared of the aftermaths of aerial bombardment and of drone warfare.

I am scared of overcrowded hospitals, with injured people screaming on the floor, drenched in their own blood.

I am scared when I witness how all those great dreams of, on paper, independent countries in Africa, Asia, Middle East and Oceania are vanishing into thin air.

I am scared of all the new forms of imperialism, of neo-colonialism, of buying intellectuals in poor countries, of manufacturing 'opposition movements' against the governments the West does not like.

I am scared of the irreversible destruction of our beautiful planet. I have seen how entire stunning countries, atoll nations, are becoming uninhabitable because of global warming and the rising sea level – Tuvalu, Kiribati, and the Marshall Islands.

I am scared when I see scars instead of beautiful rainforests, stumps of trees and black chemicals floating where once ran bubbly, happy rivers – in Sumatra, Borneo, and Papua.

I am scared of so many things!

I am scared of seeing women being treated like dogs or doormats, as possessions of their fathers and husbands, and even brothers.

I am scared when brutal, corrupt and ignorant priests ruin lives and spread grotesque fears.

I am scared when books are getting burnt, directly or indirectly, replaced by sheets of metal and plastic, with potentially controllable content.

I am scared when they are, metaphorically or in real terms, shooting people straight between their eyes, or in their backs, simply because they refused to kneel.

I am scared when people have to lie in order to survive, or when they have to betray their loved ones.

I am scared of rape, of people being raped; in any way that rape is performed – physically or mentally.

I am scared of darkness. Not the one in the bedroom, at night, but of the darkness that is once again descending on our planet, and on humanity.

And the more scared I am, the more I feel that I have to act.

It is just because sitting still is the scariest thing of all. Sitting still while this world, this beautiful world which I know so intimately; from Tierra De Fuego to Northern Canada, from the Cape of Good Hope to the tiny Pacific Islands, to PNG to DRC, is being plundered, violated, and intellectually lobotomized.

It is also because I am a human being, one tiny grain of sand in this tremendous mankind, and as Maxim Gorky once wrote "Mankind – that has a proud sound!"

I am not always scared.

When the muzzle of a gun attached to some tank, slowly moves in my direction, I am not scared. I have seen what happens, what can happen if it fires; unfortunately I have seen it too many times. The moment of pain must be very intense but extremely short – and then, there is nothing. I don't want it to happen to me, because I love this life so passionately, so much, but I am not scared of the possibility of death.

But again, I am extremely scared of 'not being there', of not witnessing and documenting life, in its full beauty, in its richness and its brutality.

I am scared, I am terrified, of not knowing, of not understanding, of not fighting, of not rebelling, of not loving, not hating, not running, not falling, not laughing or crying (as one cannot exist without other), of not doing the right thing, or not erring, of not existing!

***

To search for the truth, to educate oneself, that is already brave, it is very brave.

The way our world is structured nowadays, people are strongly discouraged from being different.

Most men and women, even children, are now conditioned in such a way, that it makes taking the first step away from the controlled mainstream, extremely difficult. To step out of that 'comfort zone', away from the swamp of 'commonly accepted and promoted values', of cheap clichés, and the outright lies, is brave, heroic.

As a result, while the world is in flames, while it is being plundered, very few are actually fighting for its survival.

Has courage disappeared from this world? Is cowardice what actually accompanies those cheap 'pop' values'? Does shallowness, intellectual and emotional, breed compliance?

Can there still be a struggle for justice? Is rebellion still possible? Of course there can still be, of course it is, and you are walking away, you are rebelling as well, Giuseppe, with every article that you translate, and with every question that you ask.

It is not necessary to always face a combat helicopter, in order to be defined as a brave person. Some do go to wars, of course. I do. Is it because I am brave? Or is it because it is sometimes easier to point my camera at some battlefield, than to deal with the gentle art of translation? I don't know. Let others judge.

But to answer your question, it is: yes, one can learn the trade, any trade. And one can also learn how to be brave, too.

However, courage just for the sake of courage is worth nothing. It is like bungee jumping, or driving at breakneck speed on some icy road, not much more. Just a strong rush of adrenaline...

Genuine courage, I believe, has to have a purpose, an important goal. And to risk one's life, one has to really and deeply love it, and to respect it: his or her life, as well as the life of others. Therefore, courage makes sense only if it is there to protect the life of other human beings. One has to love this life, passionately and madly, in order to fight for it, in order to fight for the survival of others.

A courageous person can never be a slave, to anyone or to anything. Maybe that is the best way to begin 'being brave': by realizing, by defying, by demolishing slavery, by fighting against it no matter where and in which form it exists. There is still so much of it, all around us... Not only that old-fashioned slavery defined by shackles, but all types of slavery, in so many forms.

Accepting slavery, but especially becoming a voluntary slave, is the opposite of courage.

To 'swim with the flow', equals to being a slave. To repeat pre-fabricated clichés, to refuse forming his or her personal opinion is nothing less than intellectual servitude.

Of course, to be courageous, one has to be informed, as one has to be able to analyze the world, to choose a personal set of values, to be secure. Then and only then can one fight, if there is no other way; to fight and to risk everything combating oppression and brutality, whenever human beings are being tortured and violated, anywhere on this planet.

In order to be informed, one should never 'believe', one should always demand to know! That is brave too, and not at all easy, but necessary. It is brave when one is determinedly demanding to study and to learn, when one dares to form his or her own personal opinion. Not some pre-chewed school curriculum, but real learning. That is actually immensely brave, and also the only way to help to move humankind forward.

That is why truly free thought has lately been directly and brutally targeted in the West, and in the other oppressed parts of the world. Because this present regime, this 'New World Order', which is actually not new at all, is doing all it can to reverse natural development, to lock us all back in the gloom and doom of some outdated religious-style dogmatism. We are forced; we are being conditioned to believe in capitalism, in a Western style of 'multi-party democracy', in the superiority of Western concepts.

But it is clear – more thoughts are there, more alternatives, options, more checks and balances, the safer our planet becomes. Needless to say, it is brave to fight for its safety.

***

There is perhaps nothing as powerful, as humble, as honest, as this quote by Bertrand Russell displayed in the office of Noam Chomsky, at MIT:

"Three passions, simple but overwhelmingly strong, have governed my life: the longing for love, the search for knowledge, and unbearable pity for the suffering of mankind."

This quote also helps to answer the question posted by my translator and friend from Italy:

When the desire for knowledge becomes truly overwhelming, one simply cannot stop, or slow down. The only way is to go forward, to absorb knowledge, to fight for attaining knowledge, to see the world, to understand, to feel, to listen; passionately and consistently. No fear can deter us, when we are avidly searching for truth. It is so proud, so brave, this desire to know!

When we feel 'unbearable pity for the suffering of mankind', when we witness how unjust is the arrangement of this world, when we truly internalize the suffering of others, of our fellow human beings living on all the continents of this beautiful but battered planet, then almost all of us, or at least those who are humanists in their core, become courageous, and brave. They suddenly know what has to be done.

As for 'the longing for love', it is there, it is always there, in all of us, in all human beings. To fight for love, when it comes, is brave, and to die for it, if risking all is the only way to save it, is courageous. That 'longing for love' is the most humble, most sacred, the most essential part of our nature, so rarely satisfied. It takes courage to love; it takes tremendous, indescribable courage!

As the Cuban poet Antonio Guerrero Rodriguez, one of those brave 'Cuban Five', imprisoned for defending their country against Yankee infiltration and terrorism, once wrote: "Love is either eternal, or it is not love." If it can vanish, it is not love. El amor que expira no es amor.

These words, a poem, were written in a brutal North American prison and what they mean is clear. It is brave to love. It is so easy to betray. But it takes real courage to defend love.

Such courage, Giuseppe, can be learned. Or it can simply be discovered and nourished, as it lives inside us: inside all of us it lives!

14 February 2014

*****

41

Open Letter to the President of Venezuela

SOON THE BATTLE OF VENEZUELA

They are already sewing your funeral gown, Venezuela. They are now ready to welcome you back to that world of the lobotomized, destroyed nations that are fully submissive to Western political and economic interests – Indonesia, Philippines, Paraguay, Uganda, Kenya, Qatar, Bahrain, and almost the entire Eastern Europe. There are so many places like that – it is impossible to list them all.

They want you back in their deadly embrace; they want you to be corrupt and hopeless, as you were before the "Bolivarian Revolution".

They want you to be the top oil exporter, but with all those horrific slums hanging, like relentless nightmares, over your cities. They want your elites and your military top brass to speak English, to play golf, to drive luxury cars and to commit treason after treason, as for decades they used to commit treason, before your brave predecessor, President Hugo Chavez, began serving and literally saving the poor, in Venezuela and all over Latin America.

Those who are planning to destroy you, those who belong to the so called 'opposition', in their heads, are already portioning you; they are dividing your beautiful body – fighting over which parts should be taken where and by whom. They are arguing which pieces of you should stay at home, and what should be taken abroad – a leg, an arm, and your deep melancholic eyes, the color of the profound pools under the mighty waterfalls of Canaima. They want to sell your jet-black hair, as black as those evenings in the mountains, or like that endless night sky above Ciudad Bolivar.

They want everything, all that is under your skin as well as what is deep inside your body. They want your skin, too, as well as your heart.

They want your dreams, which are almost everybody's dreams – the dreams of all those people from all over the world, people that have been oppressed, and humiliated, for centuries, up to today. They want to take your dreams and to step on them, dirty them, spit on them and to crush them.

But it is not over; it is all far from being over. You are loved and admired, and therefore you will be defended. By all means – we who love you will not be ungenerous; we will not be negotiating the price!

For many men and women, for millions all over the world, you used to be a girl; a brave, rebellious, wonderful young woman... then suddenly you became a mother and then you turned into a motherland – for all those who lacked one until this very moment. For me, too, you became a motherland... for me too!

***

I am not a Venezuelan citizen. I wish I could be, but I am not. But I have fought for Venezuela, in my own way, through my reports and speeches, through films and in my books. I fought ever since Hugo Chavez became the President, 'my President'.

And I am proud that I fought. And now, when Venezuela is once again under vicious attack, I want to stand firmly by her side, by the side of her Revolution, by the side of *El Processo*, and of her great Presidents – both Chavez and Maduro!

And I want to say this, and I will say this loudly, carajo: I don't care what passport is hanging from my pocket, but Caracas is now my capital, and Caracas is what we are going to defend, if we have to. Because in Caracas, we will be fighting for Havana, for Harare and Johannesburg, for Cairo and Calcutta, for the tiny atoll nations in the Pacific Ocean, for Hanoi, for Beijing, and even for Moscow, Asmara, La Paz, Valparaiso, Quito, Managua as well as for so many of the other independent, freedom-loving places of this wonderful world.

The violent activities undertaken by those so-called 'protesters' in Caracas have to be stopped, immediately, and if necessary, by force.

'The opposition' has been paid for from abroad, as it has been paid, in the past and now, in China, in Eastern Europe, in Syria, Ukraine and in Thailand, as it has been paid everywhere else in the world, where the West could not manage to easily strip those 'rebellious' countries of all their riches, while keeping them humiliated, and on their knees.

***

As you are contemplating your next step, Mr. President Nicolas Maduro, as Venezuela is once again bleeding, as none of us knows what the next day may bring, I am leaving Indonesia, flying to Thailand. (For now it is Thailand, but I soon may change my course).

Thailand is not Venezuela, but their government also introduced free medical care and free education, and other basic social services. People responded – by supporting progress. They have been supporting it for years, through ballots.

But the elites intervened and the army intervened. There was a coup, and there are now voices shouting that 'the people cannot be trusted', otherwise they will always be voting for this administration, read: for progress.

The West is firmly behind the elites and against progress. Thai feudal leaders are fully trusted in Washington, in London, and even in Tokyo. It is because they have totally sold out their souls, because they fully lost all their shame during the Vietnam War. They fully participated in the horrible slaughter of the Vietnamese, Laotian and Cambodian people, and they even eagerly murdered their own people: revolutionaries, Communists and students.

The West likes it when such despots hold the reins of power. They like people like Duvalier, Trujillo, Videla and Pinochet – and their equivalents – on all the continents and in every country.

In Thailand they are now supporting the 'opposition', as they supported the 'opposition' in Chile before 1973 or in China before Tiananmen Square. As they are right now supporting 'the opposition' in Venezuela! Everything that can damage or destroy a rebellious country, Communist or non-aligned, goes!

It does not matter how many millions will die in the process. As long as a rebellion, or a fight for independence, can be crushed, Western imperialism and neo-colonialism will sacrifice any amount of human lives, especially the lives of those 'un people', just to borrow from the Orwellian lexicon.

I will soon be leaving Indonesia, Comrade President Maduro. Indonesia is the country about which I have written books and made films, including a recent film for TeleSur.

Here, too, the West disliked the progressive President, Sukarno, who used to scream in the face of the US Ambassador: "To hell with your aid!" Sukarno was one of the founders of the Non-Aligned Movement. Some would call him the Asian Chavez, and they would not be too far off the mark.

And so in 1965, the West teamed up with the local military and religious cadres, supplying them with lists of those 'who had to be killed'. What followed was one of the bloodiest coups in human history: between one and three million Communists, intellectuals, trade unionists, teachers and people belonging to the Chinese minority, were slaughtered. Culture was destroyed. The spine of the country was broken. It is broken right to this day. It is terrible, a terrifying sight!

Now Indonesia is a servile, nauseating place, corrupt, both financially and morally. Its people are only there to supply multinational companies and the local 'elites' with raw materials, and a low quality uneducated cheap work force.

It is exactly what the West wants to turn Venezuela into – the Latin American Indonesia, or even more frighteningly, the Latin American version of an African horror story – the Democratic Republic of Congo.

Venezuela's riches under and above the ground, are so numerous, and its land so fertile, its rainforests endless. Foreign companies and governments from the North simply cannot stop shaking from the lowest type of desire; unable to contain their unbridled greed.

The West, of course, does not come and say: We will rob you

and rape you. They sing some stereotypical tunes about freedom and democracy. But anyone in Venezuela who wants to know what will happen to their country if the 'opposition' takes over, should go to Indonesia and see with his or her own eyes. Or should at least remember what occurred in the Chile of 1973, because in Chile, the US replicated its horrible Indonesian formula.

It is all connected and inter-connected, comrades, although Western mass media does not want us to know any of this.

***

Venezuela has to fight back! It is under siege and you were democratically-elected, Mr. President. You have a mandate, and an obligation to defend your people.

I have worked in almost one hundred and fifty countries. And I have seen the horrors of those places that fell into the hands of Western usurpers: directly or indirectly. I have worked in places as diverse but broken as Paraguay, Honduras, Egypt, Bahrain, Kenya, Uganda, Philippines, Indonesia, the Democratic Republic of Congo and the Marshall Islands.

Countries are so often punished for their great leaders!

In Congo, Patrice Lumumba decided to dedicate his life to feeding the children of the continent, to use the enormous natural wealth of his country for the good of his citizens. He despised colonialism and he openly repeated his accusations against the former colonial masters (the Belgians murdered ten million Congolese people during the reign of the Kind Leopold II) and against the neo-colonial clique. And he was murdered; after the Belgians, North Americans, Brits and others joined forces and decided that 'such behavior' could not be tolerated.

Now the DRC, a country that has some of the greatest natural wealth on this planet, has the lowest 'Human Development Index'. Brutal Western allies in Africa – Rwanda and Uganda – have plundered the DRC ever since 1995 on behalf of Western companies and governments. By now around eight million people have died. I made a film about it. Needless to say, nobody in Europe or in the United States wants to see it!

It is all because of coltan, diamonds, uranium and gold. But it is also, undeniably, because Congo once so proudly stood up against imperialism and foreign oppression. The Empire almost never forgives!

The Empire never forgave Yugoslavia, another founding member of the Non-Aligned Movement, breaking it apart and bathing it in blood. It never forgave Russia, supporting an awful despot and alcoholic, Boris Yeltsin in his determined efforts to ruin what was left of the Union of Soviet Socialist Republics, and by murdering thousands of Russian people during the siege of the Russian 'White House'.

It never forgave China, or North Korea, or Zimbabwe.

The list goes on, and it is endless.

Please, do not allow this to happen to Venezuela!

Allende, Sukarno and others, fell, and their countries fell, because they assumed that despite everything, despite the West murdering hundreds of millions of people all over the world, for many centuries, it would actually not be as brutal in this particular day and age, it would at least spare cities such as Santiago or Jakarta.

Then, when millions of Indonesian women had been gang-raped, when their breasts were 'amputated', when victims had to dig their own graves before being killed... when Chilean women were violated by dogs, under the supervision of 'English speaking investigators' as well as old German Nazis from Colonia Dignidad, when people were "disappeared", tortured, thrown alive from helicopters... Mr. President, it was too late... Too late to fight!

***

I saw enough of this. As a war correspondent, as a man who was searching for the truth on all continents, writing about the most devastated cities and nations, I managed to absorb so much pain and suffering that I hope it gives me at least some right to write this letter, this appeal, and to urge you: "Do not allow this to happen to Venezuela."

Those who are opposing you will not stop – they will go all the way, if allowed. They have been engaged in a disinformation campaign, suspiciously similar to the one before the "9/11" in Chile, 1973. The 'strikes' and 'insecurity' are also similar to those provoked in Chile and Indonesia before their coups. And like elsewhere, in Venezuela there is also a group of 'economists' and 'business people', ready to reverse the course of the country, immediately, were the counter-revolution to succeed.

It is great business to oppose you! Tens of millions of dollars are poured into the coffers of those who want to overthrow the government of Venezuela... of Cuba... of China... of Iran, Bolivia, Ecuador, and so many other countries...

But Venezuela is now so high, perhaps at the top, of the Western mafia-style hit list.

In my recent essay: "How the West Manufactures 'Opposition Movements'", I gave a list of countries where all this is happening right now – an attempt to use local gangs to overthrow totally legitimate governments only because they are defending the interests of their people.

Mr. President, your country – Venezuela – is much more than a beautiful place inhabited by brave people. It is also a symbol of hope, and as Eduardo Galeano once told me in Montevideo: "To take away hope is worse than murdering a person."

Do not allow them to choke this hope: the hope of the Venezuelan people, and the hope of millions all over the world.

If you have to fight, please fight! And we will join you; many of us will. Because, what your predecessor and friend Hugo Chavez, started, is what billions all over the world desire and dream of.

Venezuela, your Venezuela and my Venezuela, gave free books to the poor, free medical care, education, and housing to all needy people. Not as some sort of charity, but as something they deserve, have a right to. Venezuela has built cable cars, libraries and childcare posts to help working mothers, where only naked misery reigned before. Venezuela educated and inspired some of the greatest musicians on Earth. It stood against imperialism; it redefined together with Cuba, what 'heart' and what 'courage' is.

Now our Venezuela cannot fail. It cannot fall. It is too big, too important. Perhaps, the survival of the human race depends on the survival of Venezuela and the countries related to it.

After Hugo Chavez died, or as many believe was killed in cold blood, I visited TeleSur in Caracas. In the center of the city, there was a photo of Chavez, sweating, clearly suffering from chemotherapy, but clenching his fist: "Here, nobody surrenders!"

And a short distance away, there was another poster only showing a sprinkle of blood on a white background. 'Chavez from his heart', it read. Chavez was endorsing Maduro, posthumously.

President Maduro, let's defend our Venezuela! Please let us not allow this revolution to fail. Let us do it by reason and by force! Let us do it for every tiny village destroyed by drones, for children dying from depleted uranium, for the 'Cuban 5', for those who have died from the horrors of modern-day imperialism, in Congo, Angola, Vietnam, Laos, Indonesia, Iraq, Libya, Chile, and in dozens of other ruined countries.

Let us defend Venezuela for the sake of humanity. *No pasaran*! This time, let us make sure that the fascist forces will not be allowed to advance!

21 February 2014

*****

42

Brainwashed

THE INDOCTRINATED WEST

Is it really possible that the European public has no clue what is being done to Ukraine? Are the men and women of the continent that lives in hallucination, that it is well educated and well informed, really unaware how its own governments have created and are supporting that 'opposition movement' in Kiev; a movement full of fascists and bigots?

Unfortunately, it is possible, and it is to be expected!

After working in some 150 countries, in all the continents, I have finally come to the absolutely clear conclusion: there is no part of the world as brainwashed, so programmed, so indoctrinated, as are both Europe and North America.

There are no people so out of sync with the global reality; people so naive and willing to follow the religious doctrine of market fundamentalism and the self-righteous belief that they, and only they, are the sole guardians of democracy, freedom and virtue, on this planet.

The world is once again in flames, and both Europe and North

America (let us please not pretend for one second longer, that the Empire is actually somehow divided between that bad United States and that 'moderate' Europe) are bulldozing, demolishing, moving out of their way everything that is still standing straight and proud; everything that is defending those who used to be defenseless, everything and everyone who is dreaming about, and actually building egalitarian and decent societies.

And the great majority of Europeans are clapping. They read their propaganda sheets and they are clapping. And they are engaged in pathetic pseudo-intellectual discussions (while sipping, oh – in such a sophisticated manner, their refined wine and beer), while millions are being murdered by their implemention of their bigoted 'interests'.

Entire nations are, again, bleeding, in order to make sure that millions of French or Italian farmers can drive their luxury BMW's (oh, sorry, in Europe they are not marketed as luxury, but as 'reliable cars'), consuming enormous subsidies, for producing and often for not producing anything at all.

The subsidies are paid for with the blood of African and Asian people.

How many people in poor countries have to die, so some grandma in Germany or the Czech Republic can go to a doctor for free, again and again, simply because she is lonely or bored of staying at home?

Should there be free medical treatment for all? Yes! Yes. It should be free, and for all. But not just for Europeans, while the rest of the world has to pay the going rate!

How many countries in Africa, Asia, the Middle East and Latin America have to be destabilized, so that the Empire can enjoy its privileges? So that the rich there can be even more obnoxiously rich, and even the poorest citizens can afford to live way above those who belong to the middle classes in the countries that are still being plundered by the West?

***

Now, please, I am not trying to be funny and I am not trying to play with words: I am honestly wondering... I am humbly asking: "Are people in the West, particularly in Europe... are they pretending that they don't know what is happening in Syria, Venezuela, Thailand and now, particularly, in Ukraine? Or have they simply turned into a cynical assembly of brainwashed degenerates?

Where is that fabled diversity? Where is intellectual courage?

Where are huge demonstrations shaking Paris, Rome, Berlin; demonstrations trying to bring down governments that have been destabilizing a huge European nation – Ukraine, while provoking Russia, the nation that saved the world from Nazism and later helped to liberate many African and Asian nations from the claws of colonialism?

Where are those loud voices protesting against the antagonization of Russia? Don't Europeans know their own history? Russia is not an aggressor; it has been a victim, for at least a hundred years. Russia was attacked by Europe repeatedly, and in just one century, tens of millions of Russian people were slaughtered by European fascists, imperialists and 'democrats'.

Russia was attacked at the onset of WWI, then again, after the 1917 Bolshevik revolution, by a joint invasion of US and UK troops. Russia was also attacked by Czech legions, fighting their way to the front, against the Austro-Hungarian Empire (and getting there by circling the globe). Czech legions occupied almost the entire area surrounding the Trans-Siberian railroad, raping, looting, and murdering indiscriminately as they progressed.

Then WWII came, before which, both France and the UK sacrificed just about everything that stood in the way of the Nazis towards the Soviet Union. And yes, then the war itself took at least twenty million lives. Soviet people vanished in an enormous struggle against Nazism.

Half of my family, of my ancestors, vanished there too, during the siege of Leningrad.

The Cold War was next, and finally that most cynical and Machiavellian act by the West: dragging the USSR into Afghanistan, and destroying it, using jihadi cadres from the Middle East, from South and Southeast Asia.

Finally, the Western puppet – 'opposition democrat', Boris Yeltsin – an alcoholic with a clearly decomposing brain, was helped by Western powers, to grab power. And when the Parliament and the Russian people rebelled, Yeltsin sent the tanks in against both Members of Russian Parliament, and the people on the streets. The Western lackey mass media cheered:

"Democracy!"

"Victory!"

Thousands of unarmed people died. The "Fifth Column" smashed the Soviet Union to pieces, using lies, and using vicious propaganda that came from Washington, London and elsewhere.

And then the West stood suddenly unopposed. It appeared that there was nothing blocking its way, towards absolute control of the world, anymore.

Colonialist nightmares from the past returned. The world became mono-polar, with only one dogma, one ideology, and only one Empire.

And in just a few years after the Soviet Union 'collapsed', it became total... Total shit!

***

Is Europe so indoctrinated, is it so propagandized to the point that it really is not actually able to recognize, anymore, what their regime has been doing, all over the world?

For years, the West in general, and the European Union in particular, have been destabilizing Ukraine, paying for its 'opposition'... Wait; damn... what are we talking about? Everybody knows it, right? No? Really? Not everyone?

It is not about 'proof' or 'the avalanche of information'. For years, for decades I have been amassing proof and arguments about the horrendous and unthinkable crimes that the West has been committing on all the continents of the world. I have been painstakingly researching what has been going on, sometimes risking my life or ruining my health, sometimes doing it without being supported by anything or anyone... actually, that has been the scenario, most of the time.

I was doing it because I believed; I believed like an idiot, I believed day and night, that my findings would shock the world, particularly the West... That it would shame the European and North American dictators... That what I show will enrage the public... That the horrors that I had witnessed all over the world, will finally end... you know: That bloody idiotic fairytale world of mine:

"People will see the truth and force the monsters who are ruling them to stop killing human beings everywhere on this beautiful planet."

Today, I have to declare, publicly: I was a fool!

I failed to move people, of course! I tried. I even dropped the journalistic style in my writing, and I began writing as a poet, as the novelist that I am.

I did it because I realized that nobody cares only about facts! There are facts everywhere. Everything is documented. Coups all over the world financed and planned by the US – it is all available, easily accessible. Yet nobody bothers to read about it!

I tried other tactics – novels, films, journalism mixed with poetry. Nothing! Nothing pushed Westerners to the barricades.

Yes, people like me, we are failing to move, to touch, those who are committing crimes against humanity... and also those who are benefiting from the enormous plundering of the globe.

Those, mostly well-fed masses, don't give a shit: in Europe, or in the United States. Their governments and companies rule the world, and most of the citizens of those countries get some crumbs. Their level of understanding, their political awareness is way below those in Africa, Latin America and Asia, those very people who are being constantly robbed and sacrificed.

To know and to understand... would make many Europeans and North Americans uncomfortable... It would mean having to take responsibility; to be co-responsible for the crimes committed by Western governments and multi-nationals. It would mean, god forbid, taking action.

***

In a recent Reuter's article, an author argued that China is watching what Russia is doing. Of course, from the tone of the article, right from the beginning, it was clear, that what Russia, China, Iran and other countries that disagree with 'Western-style democracy and capitalism' are thinking and doing is absolutely wrong.

Without inviting Russian, Chinese or Venezuelan polemicists, the author selected the 'grievances' of the world, saying that the West should face criticism, by some, for Kosovo and maybe for Libya... although such criticism would be wrong...

Such a degree of self-discipline and propaganda would be fitting for the German newspapers of the 1930's and 40's. And it is becoming the norm in both Europe and North America, as well as in many countries in the 'developing world', where information is fully controlled by Western funding, training programs and other means of arm-twisting.

The propaganda coming out of Europe is so mighty, so potent, that it has blurred the eyes of even those that live in the former colonies of the West, including China, India and Indonesia.

It is not about Kosovo and it is not only about Libya, damn it!

In Yugoslavia, which I covered intensively from all sides, the West destroyed an entire country, a great country, one of the founding members of the Non-Aligned Movement (Indonesia had already paid the price in 1965, with between one and three million people brutally slaughtered, in an US-orchestrated coup performed by the military and religious cadres).

In Africa, an entire continent screams in pain. Since 1995, pretty close to 10 million people have been slaughtered in the Democratic Republic of Congo alone, by Uganda and Rwanda on behalf of Western geopolitical interests. DRC has uranium, Coltan, and diamonds... Its people do not matter. The Belgian King Leopold II succeeded in killing 10 million people there one hundred years ago, by chopping off their hands and burning people alive in huts.

France is involved in all of its former colonies. It is once again as sickeningly brutal as it was in the past.

Mali, the Central African Republic, and almost all the countries in that area have been destabilized and are close to total ruin.

The US-UK-Israeli coalition is undermining Somalia, using Ethiopian, Ugandan, Kenyan and Burundian forces. South Sudan, an artificially created entity, with oil but no ability to govern itself independently, is now on the verge of famine and civil war. And it is at the total mercy of the West.

Zimbabwe and South Africa are standing tall against Western imperialism, but in both places, the West directly finances the 'opposition', and propaganda viciously smears both nations.

Eritrea is facing a direct embargo and constant intimidation. For being what is called – The 'African Cuba' (of course nobody knows anything about Eritrea in Europe, except for some educated Italians).

Even the tiny and prosperous Seychelles, known for royal weddings and honeymoons, has to face an opposition that is groomed from abroad (particularly from the UK); revenge for its free, excellent medical care, and its Cuban-influenced education system.

In both Uganda and Rwanda, brutal and insane fascist regimes are clinging to power, coached openly by people like Tony Blair (advisor to President Kagame).

The 'Arab Spring' has been fully derailed in Egypt; a country with powerful labor movements, that have been openly murdered. In the process, thousands of people have died, as the pro-Western military and elites have overthrown a democratically elected moderate Muslim government.

The most horrendous religious regimes like those of Saudi Arabia, Bahrain and Qatar, are being pampered and defended by both North America and Europe.

In Latin America, the governments of Honduras and Paraguay have been overthrown; Venezuela has had to face coup attempts and its own brutal 'opposition', fully and openly financed by the West. Cuba has survived countless terrorist attacks from the North, and the 'opposition' there is also directly financed and supported from abroad.

Bolivia and even Brazil were targeted by malicious attempts to destroy their left-leaning governments, as is the case with Bolivia, even the geographical integrity of the country has been threatened.

In Asia, things go from bad to worse. Both China and North Korea are being literally provoked, often militarily, from US air force bases located in Okinawa and elsewhere. Countries like the Philippines are being openly pitched against China (PRC) by the US, while Vietnam is also being 'encouraged' to antagonize its enormous neighbor.

It goes without saying that the Chinese 'opposition' has been financed mainly from abroad, for decades. On the contrary, in pro-Western brutal regimes like Indonesia, the Philippines but also Thailand, the West is paying and helping the military and elites to actually control and if necessary, destroy the genuine opposition.

The 'opposition' has been clearly employed to ruin Syria (the West created refugee camps in Turkey and elsewhere, to train and arm the so called 'opposition' there), Venezuela, Ukraine and even Thailand. It has also caused some great damage to Russia and China, as well as countless Latin American and Caribbean countries.

The West is directly attacking foreign countries, by arming and indoctrinating thousands of people who are then paid to overthrow governments and political systems.

Not only is it illegal – it actually amounts to an act of war... undeclared, and covert, but war.

Are the citizens of Europe and North America ignorant of the fact that their governments and companies are fighting undeclared wars and committing acts of terrorism all over the world?

And it has been going on for decades, with total impunity, it is perfectly well-documented and it takes tremendous discipline to overlook it!

I have worked in almost all those places, making films, writing books and reports. I am intimately familiar with what the West has been doing in Venezuela, Syria, Turkey, China, North Korea, Vietnam, Thailand, Indonesia, Zimbabwe, Somalia, Congo, Rwanda, the Philippines...

I have proof. But have you noticed that proof is, these days, worth nothing? You can come with the most powerful, most damning and shocking proof, but it will move nobody, propel nobody to action... in the West, I mean. In that 'democratic' and 'free' West!

You can prove that 10 million people were slaughtered, and the response you will get, will be: "Thank you... Wonderful essay! Another cup of coffee?"

***

And even this incomplete but powerful list of horrors that the West is administering all over the world, is not something that could be defined as new.

It is simply a continuation of colonial culture, of the plundering and of mass exterminations, of genocides and holocausts, those that have been taking place for many centuries.

Look at the map of the world at the turn of the 19th and 20th centuries, and everything will be clear. The West basically occupied almost the entire planet.

It plundered thoroughly all that it controlled. It destroyed cultures, raped women, robbed all that it could get its hands on.

Ever wondered where all that wealth that allowed Europe to build lavish palaces, theatres, museums, public buildings, came from?

Of course it came, and is still coming, from the blood of oppressed people, from their hard labor for a pittance, from their sweat, from their humiliation.

And now, people from India, China, Indonesia, Peru, Nigeria, Senegal – they come to Europe and they sigh in front of those tremendous facades of enormous buildings, in the middle of well-manicured parks, on board fast moving trains.

And some say: "What a civilization! What a wonderful part of the world! Here they respect other human beings. Here they are kind to others."

Well, it is built from your wealth that evaporated, from the terrible labor of your grandparents, from the rape of your female ancestors, from the cracking of whips on the naked backs of your male ancestors.... It is built on the ruins of your culture, of your civilization. It is all built, because you were left with nearly nothing, and for decades and centuries forced to live in shit...

The majority of people of what is now Latin America vanished! Their religions were destroyed and so were their languages. The Inca people had to obliterate their temples, and from those stones, enormous Christian cathedrals were erected. And they were decorated with gold and silver, dug by once free but now enslaved Incas, in Cusco and Potosi, Quito and Cuenca, everywhere.

Slaves poured out from Africa to Latin America and to North America, as well as to the Caribbean! Entire states in Africa, entire families were ruined, destroyed, uprooted. Human beings were treated like animals, while literary salons in London and Paris enjoyed refined music and perfumes.

Countries like Germany and Belgium performed appoling genocides – the Belgians in Congo, and Germans in what is now Namibia.

There was no mercy then, as there is no mercy now.

The Christian religion, that outrageous machinery of terror has been part of this for centuries, walking hand-in-hand with the Conquistadores and Crusaders. Periodically it took the lead in the massacres. The Church had been greedier than monarchies, and it was power hungry, oppressive and brutal.

Christianity, that symbol of Western civilization, brought torture and slavery; it blessed the men and the deeds that murdered millions.

To date, there has been no attempt to declare Christianity illegal because of the genocides it perpetrated, or based on its other crimes against humanity.

***

And this culture is now scalding Russia, China, Venezuela, and Iran – this culture that has murdered billions. And nobody is laughing. No one is rolling around on the floor, dying from amusement.

In the Middle East, the Brits bombed and gassed 'those niggers' (both Lloyd George and Winston Churchill saw 'lesser races' as something worth exterminating, if 'necessary'), divided nations, manipulated and enslaved them.

'Divide and rule' led to horrific consequences later, like the 'Partition' of India and Pakistan, or genocide in what is now Bangladesh.

In Asia, just about everything was occupied, plundered and raped, including such enormous areas as the sub-Continent, or China and the archipelago that is now known as Indonesia.

All was neatly divided; French Indochina, British India, and Dutch Indonesia.

Western Empires fought over vast foreign lands and no Europeans protested (as they are not protesting now, against neo-colonialism) against the genocides that were committed by their rulers. Some countries like France 'successfully' exterminated a hundred percent of the people on some islands in the Caribbean, and came very close to exterminating the entire population of Rapa Nui in Polynesia.

Rape, looting, murder, have been all over the world. The West still feels that it has the full right to determine who lives and who dies, and who should live which way.

The great Swiss psychoanalyst Gustav Jung described European and Western culture as a 'pathology', as an illness. To him, as a doctor, Europe was a patient, a seriously ill one, in constant need to terrorize others, to control, to steal, and to murder.

And Jung was not the only one. J. P. Sartre's writing on colonialism is as damning, and also much more detailed.

But now, after decades of huge propaganda injections, everything is 'forgotten and forgiven'. But is it? Europeans 'do not know' what horrors they have been spreading all over the globe. Westerners in general do not know. They are conditioned not to know. They have eliminated almost all 'comparative thinking' in their own continent, and simultaneously in their colonies.

People do not know how to compare, anymore. The media and scholars are discouraged from comparing crimes and brutality. It is obvious why. No continent, no culture, has committed such monstrous crimes, perpetrated such horrible and unforgiveable deeds, as the Western 'cultures' and 'civilizations'.

They committed them and they are still busy committing them. Until this very moment!

***

This essay is just a brief reminder of 'who is speaking'! Who is pointing fingers at Russia right now, and who is demonizing China, and calling true Latin American democracies – 'dictatorships'.

One feels like paraphrasing an old Communist slogan, and shouting:

> "People of the world who still have some brain left – wake up and unite!"

It is clear that the West is on an offensive: as it tries to annihilate all the dissent that has grown since the destruction of the old multi-polar world.

But a new, perhaps better, multi-polar world has emerged.

Some parts of it are much more informed and educated about the horrific terror that comes with allowing the West to rule over this world, unopposed.

It is not Russia that is 'on the wrong side of history', as Obama recently declared.

It is the West, clearly and patently. And just to say; that it is not good enough... Not good enough, anymore!

7 March 2014

*****

43

SHAMEFUL, COWARDLY EUROPEAN ART

I searched for pain, and I found none.

In those enormous halls of the Louvre, I searched for reminders of the agony of the people from the Caribbean, from islands like Grenada, where the native people were entirely exterminated during the French colonial onslaught. I searched for at least one tear, one moan, one canvas saturated with sadness and remorse. I searched for confessions.

But I found none.

I was trying to catch a glimpse of the desperate, terrified facial expressions of North African women, dragged into some empty rooms, and raped brutally by French soldiers. I was looking for paintings depicting the torture of Vietnamese patriots, and their execution by decapitation, for nothing else other than fighting for freedom and for their fatherland, against the appalling French colonial rule.

No – I found nothing, nothing at all in the Louvre, or in any other major French museums.

I stood in front of bizarre, sick and cold religious artwork, full of adult looking, perverse baby Jesus's, or of some saints with daggers sticking out grotesquely from their heads. It was mostly total kitsch, created to order from the Christian church – a morally corrupt religious entity responsible for the extermination of entire nations, of entire races, worldwide!

I could find no paintings depicting the destroyed people of Rapa Nui, no killing of Southeast Asians, Africans and the islanders from both the Atlantic and Pacific oceans.

I have searched and searched, for years, during my ever decreasing in frequency visits to that old and sick continent, responsible for dozens of holocausts on basically all the continents of the Earth.

Then, one day, recently, when I was presenting my documentary film (on Western-backed tyranny in Indonesia) at SOAS in London, I asked my mother, a renowned painter and cartoonist, to join me, and to search some more, just in case I have been missing, or overlooking, something substantial.

***

We spent days, crisscrossing several major museums in Paris, but we found nothing there, nothing in the Louvre.

Earlier we had found nothing in the State Gallery of Stuttgart.

And I found nothing in the Royal Academy of Art in London, or in the National Maritime Museum, or in the National Art Museum in London.

Not one excuse, not one apology, not a glimpse of remorse. I found no soul-searching, not even an enormous, erect, shouting question mark.

Brainwashed, corrupt and arrogant, European art has stood proud and unapologetic, unmoved by the suffering of those hundreds of millions of people who lost their lives because of those who patronized and funded most of the artists for centuries – the Christian Church, and the European political and economic establishment.

There has been no artwork depicting the torture and humiliation of entire nations; the vanishing of numerous great civilizations in Latin America... as there appeared to be no canvases illustrating entire Ukrainian villages burnt to ashes during WWII, or of the savage bombing of Leningrad, or of the medical experiments performed by German Nazis on human beings. Enormous canvases showing the holocaust against the

Herero people of what is now Namibia were nowhere to be found.

I am not exaggerating, I honestly searched, but I found nothing remotely accusative, outraged, or furious at the Western torment of the world that has been going on for centuries, even millennia...

I found nothing brave or courageous, and nothing revolutionary whatsoever in the galleries of Stuttgart, or in the museums, exhibition halls, galleries of Paris and London.

I found no j'accuse. There was no scream and no agony, no suggestion that the West should be held responsible for all those crimes it has been committing. In all those European 'temples of culture' – all guilt was banished, as all the terror imposed on the world from Washington, London or Paris, was completely ignored.

I faced no images of the impact of the carpet-bombing on the Vietnamese villages, and no images depicting the rape of Algiers. I did not even see the suffering of Palestinian people – no artwork depicting it – or that total and quite well documented, recent destruction of countries like Libya, or Syria or the Democratic Republic of Congo.

On the paintings at the Tate Modern or at those countless Parisian galleries that I have been visiting, there were no images of women with their breasts cut off- a common occurrence during the Western-backed 1965 military/religious coup in Indonesia, which took at least one, but perhaps three million human lives – or of the women savagely gang-raped and mutilated in the DR Congo, where between six to ten million people have lost and are still losing their lives, in order to satisfy the unbridled greed of numerous Western companies, governments and consumers – greed for Coltan, Uranium, Diamonds and Gold.

Western art generously forgave everything; all the crimes committed by the Western Empire. Yes, everything is forgotten and forgiven... as it always is by the establishment itself; by the Western regime imposed so completely on our planet.

Bunches of forgiving blokes are now running museums and galleries. Stunningly 'forgiving', are the great majority of Western artists themselves, who are paid/rewarded generously and glorified relentlessly for such 'bigheartedness'. Just as they always have been remunerated for centuries, because, they agreed to put form over the substance.

Just keep painting countless cans of mass-produced soup, while your country is murdering millions of innocent men, women and children, and you will be elevated to a deity, by the regime.

Because the regime and the art establishment are one single entity! And they don't want you to be political, politicized, well informed, or angry with what your government is doing to the defenseless people of the world. And they don't want you to, god forbid; suggest that the masses should be informed and outraged!

Just entertain, spread your colors on huge canvases, and enjoy all those great privileges!

***

During my life, I saw many; too many destroyed lives, I saw craters and burning cities, and I saw women – too many women – victims of savage rapes. I saw pain and despair scarring countless monstrous, overpopulated cities, as well as vast and impoverished countrysides. I saw misery and indescribable sorrow on all continents, and on too many occasions.

But during these last ten days in Europe, I saw many endless lines, numerous ovals, and squares. I saw orange triangles and pink dots, as well as fluorescent disconnected words and grotesque bizarre objects... and I saw meditations on space and on failed erections... on multiple orgasms and on rubbish, shit and gore.

I observed ego trips and psychedelic LSD visions. I witnessed sex in many different forms. I saw countless studies on parents and their children: conflict between different generations... I saw emptiness.

I found it difficult to recognize the world, in which I was living – to recognize it in the Louvre, in British museums, and in several German museums... As I previously found it difficult to recognize it in Spanish museums, in Belgian museums... and in hundreds of contemporary art galleries all over Europe...

Nothing appeared to be recognizable.

I was not asking, I would not dare to ask, for outright realism, or naturalism... I was not demanding Socialist Realism. For now I was only longing for at least some links between the 'flights of insane fantasy' and the universe inhabited by human beings... I was yearning for some sense and some logic, for something that could serve our humanity, something that could enrich and improve the lives of millions of people.

But all that was flying into my face, were vulgar and egocentric concepts; art for art's sake... or some primitive and frivolous entertainment genres – the best allies of the Empire which was now willing to pay any amount of money just to convert human beings into some empty, emotionless and unthinking organisms.

***

For several long centuries, most West European art has been corrupt, prostituted and rendered toothless.

Lately, it has become out-rightly poisonous, anti-humanist and anti-human, deadly.

During those ten days that I spent in Europe searching for 'courageous art', I kept hunting for life, for real life, and for genuine feelings...

In between self-serving cacophonies of colour, I struggled to recognize some elements of great the Mexican murals and Soviet political posters... But there were no Diego Riveras and no Siqueiros.

Instead, there were countless phantasmagoric ego trips... There were lunacies and they were all supposed to entertain me, to impress me, to keep me floating in some abstract, cold but metallically cool, and always detached realm. But there was no strife for building a better world, no optimism, and enthusiasm, like in the great post-war paintings created in Vietnam, the Soviet Union and China.

Cynicism, detachment and selfishness – these were all promoted, paid for, and in vogue.

I desperately wanted to smell, I wanted to feel, to love fully and passionately, to hate, to struggle... I wanted all this, as almost every human being does want all this... as almost every man, woman and child wants to... even if secretly... even if shyly and subconsciously... in every society.

"We shall be returning to the simplest of the roses", a great Czech poet Jaroslav Seifert wrote in his unforgettable poem.

But almost all simple roses seemed to be gone; they have disappeared, faded away.

Everything was diverting me, taking me far away from reality... The art was grotesquely mutating into a social media form, and it was having dirty brutal intercourse with the lowest grade of pop 'culture'. I noticed that the colours were now increasingly fluorescent; while human lives were becoming increasingly blurry... before they began disappearing altogether in the distance... as they were decreasing in size and importance, as they were pushed further and further away... as it was becoming obvious that they were going to be gone, and disappear altogether... soon.

Modern European art was not dreaming about a 'better world'. It was hardly offering any social criticism.

But has it ever?

It was not calling people to the barricades... It was not dreaming about overthrowing the fascist global regime.

But after days in the Louvre and in the National Art Gallery, I was coming to a chilling realisation – it never has... Not in Europe... It was whoring here... For as long as we can remember, ever since we have been able to monitor...

Drunk, in fact totally stoned from an excessive intake of European classic and modern art, I struggled to remain firmly on the surface of our mother Earth.

The art was everywhere, all around me, and much of it was now absolutely free, here in Europe... But most of it was clearly on some sort of sinister mission – to simplify reality, to mute and humiliate all honest, positive and constructive emotions, to depoliticize societies, and in the end, to push people away from thinking and feeling altogether.

Perhaps it would have been better to have no art at all, than such art as this!

***

What was it that European propaganda was criticizing Soviet or Chinese art for? I recall words like 'censorship', and 'fear'!

The Louvre... Prado Museum... National Art Gallery... what else are those other than collections of incomparable and shameless orgies of submission, or servility, of cowardice, which would be inconceivable in any other culture on Earth?

Canvases of the Louvre: In horror, I observed the crawling infant Jesus depicted on every second painting... then crucifixions and of course countless resurrections... all with a frightening repetitiveness.

An image of baby Jesus with a perverse and adult face, crawling on the ground, while adults are watching with subservient admiration. There are images of some religious freaks with knives sticking out from their heads... There are bizarre angels flying, falling from the sky, fighting and threatening looking with their mean faces.

There are cardinals, bishops, and popes. And there are aristocrats, kings, governors and simply rich merchants who could afford to hire 'big artists'. All that creative prostitution; all those paintings produced to order, forming the essence of European culture; of European art!

I walked with my mother from hall to hall. "Great technique", she uttered sarcastically. Yes, I agreed, truly great technique... but the substance!

"All the might during those centuries was concentrated in the hands of the Church", commented my mother. "The Church was much more powerful than the throne and the aristocracy. And the church of course employed the greatest masters, such artists as Caravaggio, Leonardo da Vinci, and Rafael. And they were ready, happy, to be employed by the church, naturally, because the church paid them exquisitely, and because it was 'protecting them', making sure that they will not get burnt on the stake as so many others, and that they would not be tortured and murdered.... naturally, artists were not calling for rebellion, and there was no diversity of thought, no criticism of the system, or of the bestiality of the Christian dogma itself..."

In those years and centuries, Christianity murdered tens, hundreds of millions, of innocent people all over the world.

It financed 'expeditions' to what is now north and Latin America, to Africa, the Middle East, and to almost the whole of Asia.

Entire nations, countless great cultures were destroyed, and people of much more advanced civilizations, like the Inca, were forced to destroy their own identities, by ruining their own temples and dwellings, and then use the stones in order to erect monumental churches and cathedrals for the satisfaction of ruthless, merciless Christian invaders.

Where is all this being documented? Of course it can be seen in the great schools of painting: those of Peruvian Cusco and Ecuadorian Quito... but in the West?

Where in the Prado Museum in Madrid, are those sculptures and paintings depicting Christian barbarity? Where are those hundreds and thousands of artworks depicting Christian monstrosities: People being tortured for days and weeks, their bones broken on wheels, sharp objects inserted into their vaginas and rectums, men and women burnt on stakes? All this, so that they would admit that they are 'sinners', that they are 'evil'? That it is justifiable to murder them without remorse.

Where are those artists who would have dared to depict the results of the crusades – the bestiality, and the looting committed in the name of the cross? They are nowhere to be found – as they were all cozily copulating with the church, as they were paid by the church, and corrupted by the church!

Where are the paintings showing full Christian coffers, stretched from booty? And again, where are the images of the millions of victims, decapitated, cut to pieces, with their eyes poked out, tortured on stakes, burnt alive?

I walked slowly through the endless halls and corridors of French, Spanish, British and German museums. And I saw nothing, nothing at all, depicting crimes, genocides and holocausts committed by the most evil institution that ever existed on this earth; the most evil institution of all times – the Christian church.

This church, this horrific establishment which has been intimidating, scaring, and torturing billions of people worldwide, for millennia, is still 'morally' and 'intellectually' in control of the most powerful and the most destructive country on earth: the United States of America.

And it is still forming the cultural essence of Europe. It is – until now it still is!

In Europe, the majority of people may not go to churches, anymore, and it may not believe in Christian dogma... it may not believe in the religions at all, but its 'culture' is clearly shaped by aggressiveness, ruthlessness and the brutality of the Christian church and its realm.

It is not that 'people kidnapped good religion and made it monstrous' – it is religion that brainwashed people, entire nations, turning them into intolerant, bigoted murderers. But search for such thoughts on the canvases in the Louvre...

I saw almost no 'dissident' works in any of the major museums of Europe.

I felt shame. And I felt horror at the monolithic essence of such spinelessness.

I was walked through the Louvre and through the National Gallery in London, blushing like a little boy.

How could this 'culture' criticize great artists in China or Russia, or Latin America? How could such a submissive and cowardly culture dare to criticize anything or anybody at all?

There, in Latin America and Asia, art has been standing tall; it has been at the vanguard of all changes, of progress!

Even in Indonesia, the greatest post-war painter is Djokopekik... My friend Djokopekik... An 'outrageous' political artist, with a fabulous heart on the left politically, with guts and endless courage... He used to be a former prisoner of conscience in the Western-backed jails of fascist, post-1965 Indonesia... A painter who immortalized Suharto as a swine, and former President – Megawati – as a puppet! And his own, brainwashed, indoctrinated nation, as a horde of monkeys!

Where are those 'brave' European 'masters'? Where are they, damn it!

Paintings, murals, posters, songs, theatre and cinema – they have all been struggling and attempting to improve societies in many parts of Asia and Latin America, even in Africa. How socially-oriented the greatest Latin American and Chinese art is! How empty, submissive, irrelevant, is art in the West!

In Venezuela, Brazil, in Ecuador and Bolivia, in Cuba, Chile and Nicaragua, art is offering both beauty and hope; it is searching for new directions for their societies. So many songs that are sang there are deep, poetic, with stunning lyrics and music. So many of them are 'engaged'.

***

The art in the West is now trying to cover up, by its complex curves and uneven squares, its total impotence, its moral emptiness, as well as the frightening brutality of European and North American culture.

As I walked through Paris, from the Sorbonne University to the Musee Quai Branly (the one that the French wanted to name, originally and arrogantly, as the "Museum of Primitive Arts"), I passed literally hundreds of art galleries.

In those days, the West had been, as I described in several of my recent essays, involved in a deliberate and determined attempt to destroy almost all the countries and governments that were still resisting its fascist grip on the global power.

'Opposition' movements were consistently manufactured in North America and Europe, and then implanted into Venezuela, China, Ukraine, Russia, Eritrea, Cuba, Bolivia, Brazil, and Zimbabwe, and to numerous other nations, on all continents. The Arab Spring has been literally derailed and bathed in blood, as the fascist and pro-Western military juntas have been arresting and murdering the opposition, and former revolutionaries.

I saw not one reflection of this reality in the galleries of Paris!

At one gallery I observed several metal dogs on long metal leashes that were sticking out into space... I was confronted by hundreds of pop topics, ranging from Italian sausages, nude girls and Frankenstein...

On Rue Mazarine, I was expected to admire several black garbage bags and one carton box... and then much the same in countless galleries of Quai Voltaire, only with more subdued and expensive finishing.

By now, France was heavily involved in almost all of its former African colonies. It has been playing as distractive a role on African continent, as the United States.

But you would never guess it from its visual art – from its museums and galleries!

It was all totally intellectually empty... It was finished... indifferent... and embarrassing. There were almost no dissident voices that were audible.

I was instinctively longing to escape from the Parisian art scene, as I, two days earlier, literally ran away from the National Gallery in London, 'cornered' by Juan de Valdez Leal and his "Immaculate Conception of the Virgin, with Two Donors", and the portrait of a pompous and obviously well paid Don Adrian Pulido Pareja, painted by Juan Bautista Martinez de Mazo.

I ran earlier, two years ago, from Brussels, where I kept stumbling over another 'great artwork' – statues of the King Leopold II, a true Belgian hero, who ordered the slaughter of a total of ten million Congolese people at the beginning of the 20th century – those who were accused of being too slow while working on his rubber plantation. The typical form of killing was the chopping off hands, but millions were also burnt alive, after being locked in their huts. Confronted by such deeds, one can hardly argue against the refinement and greatness of Christian and European culture!

Statues of Sir Winston Churchill and Lloyd George, those jolly good blokes who murdered millions of 'those niggers' in the Middle East and Africa, are also considered as masterpieces of European art, not to speak of the sculptures of dozens of the vile monsters responsible for genocides in the Americas – those that dot both Madrid and Lisbon. And there is no graffiti in Europe that would add at least some color to those gray and bronze 'masterpieces', like: "assassins!"

***

Frankly, ten days of hunting for meaningful European art exhausted and depressed me to the extreme.

I came there to search, once again, for truth, but I found centuries of accumulated propaganda, layer after layer – piling on top of each other.

This was perhaps my last attempt, as I had already spent years and decades studying Western art, crisscrossing Europe and North America, visiting museums, galleries, concert halls, opera houses, as well as all sorts of tunnels decorated by graffiti. It was time to accept the obvious conclusions, and to dedicate my time to something more meaningful.

I searched for kindness, but I found intimidation, fear, and brutality.

I searched for answers to all those horrors that were spread by the Western way of thinking... I found only pompous sculptures and canvases, repetitive and made to order.

There were some, very few, painters, like Otto Dix in Germany, or the Norwegian Munch. These two at least managed to show the tremendous fear that has been spread by Christianity, the hypocrisy and perversions of Western dogmas.

At Tate Modern, in London, there was a substantial exhibition of Soviet poster art. And at the Pompidou Center in Paris, I visited a huge and impressive exhibition of Henry Cartier-Bresson, which confirmed, once again, that one of the greatest photographers of all times was actually a Marxist and very close friend of both the Soviet Union and Communist China.

But these were clearly some exceptions, and most of them were like an echo from the past. It is a well known fact that Western art exploded out for three decades after the WWII, attempting to join humanity... Yes, it exploded, but it burned itself quickly, way too quickly! Emptiness and soullessness quickly returned.

As the world has been, once again, screaming in pain; as neo-colonialism has again been murdering tens of millions of men, women and children in Africa, Asia and the Middle East (but also in such places as Venezuela, Egypt and Ukraine), Western art continued to do what it did best, for centuries – painting absolute shit, and strictly to order.

Be it the church, the throne, the merchants or now the multi-national corporations or conservative governments – European and North American artists are ready to serve them all loyally, as long as there is an uninterrupted flow of dough! And they are ready to compete for this money, and to even cut each other throats.

They are eager, 'technically and artistically capable' to deliver anything that would stop progress, to cover up all those monstrous crimes of religion, business and the state. They are ready to turn their trade into a deadly weapon, to stir people away from conscience, from rational thinking, from compassion, even from love and from basic kind human instincts and feelings.

The fluorescent lights, and huge art installations filled with plastic straws and blinking lights for idiots – that is what it is all coming down to.

Billions of those who are starving to death and living in a gutter, matter nothing. They do not pay – therefore they do not exist.

21 March 2014

*****

44

UKRAINE: LIES AND REALITIES

Kiev.

Two beautiful Slavic sisters, Ukraine and Russia, pitched against each other: long hair flying in the wind, gray-blue eyes staring forward accusatively, but in the same time with anticipation and love.

One single moment, one wrong move, one word, and two countries, two allies, two almost identical cultures, can easily dash at each other's throats... Different words, different gestures, and they can also fall into each other's arms, instantly.

Is there going to be a war, a battle or an embrace? Is there going to be an insult or reconciliatory words?

Ironically, there is no 'self-grown dispute' between two nations. The seeds of mistrust, and possible tragedy, are sown by the outsiders, and nurtured by their malignant propaganda.

As Sergei Kirichuk, leader of progressive movement 'Borotba', explained:

> "We have extensive invasion of western imperialism here. Imperialists were acting through huge network of NGOs and through the western-oriented politicians integrated into western establishment. Western diplomats declared that they invested more that 5 billions of dollars to 'development of democracy in Ukraine'. What kind of investment is it? How was this amount spent? We don't really know, but we can see the wide net of the US agents operating inside many key organizations and movements.
>
> We can see that those 'western democracies' had not been concerned at all about growing of the far-right, Nazi movements. They had been ready to use the Nazis as a real armed force in overthrowing of Yanucovich.
>
> President Yanucovich was actually totally pro-western politician, to start with. And his 'guilt' consisted only of his attempt to minimize the devastating aftermath that would come after implementation of the free trade zone with EU, on which the West was insisting."

***

Now *Maidan*, the main square of Kiev where the 'revolution' took place, is scarred, burned down, eerie.

Right-wingers, ultra-nationalists, young and not so young men with shaved heads, are watching pedestrians with confused, often provocative eyes.

Many of them are now controlling the traffic and, like in Thailand where the right-wingers also recently 'protested, are deciding who can pass and who cannot. The law is clearly and patently in their hands, or more precisely, in Maidan area, *they* are the law.

Religious symbols are suddenly everywhere, while monuments to heroes of the revolution and the WWII are desecrated.

At the makeshift stage used by right-wing extremists, there is a huge crucifixion as well as Virgin Marry.

But many right-wingers are at total disarray, they are outraged, as one of their leaders, Aleksandr Muzychko, was murdered just one day earlier.

Oleh Odnorozhenko is speaking. He is angry, irritated, accusing the state, the same government his people brought to power through the coup just a short time ago, of political murder. He is calling for 'the second stage of the revolution', as if one past stage would not be terrible enough, already.

My friend Alexander is explaining to me: "This is going to be a tremendous mess. The West used all fascist and ultra-nationalist forces to destroy legitimate government of Ukraine, but paradoxically, these ultra right-wingers are essentially against both NATO and all those agreements with the European Union."

Afghanistan, Al-Qaida, scenario, in brief and on smaller scale: use any force, any radicals, as long as you can manage to destroy the Soviet Union and later, Russia.

"They are going to get into each other's hair very soon", predicts Alexandr, former military intelligence officer.

***

The car is negotiating a bumpy four-lane highway between Kiev and Odessa. There are three of us on board – my translator, Dimitry from the *Liva.com* site, a driver, and me. Having left Kiev in the morning, we are literally flying at 160km/h towards Odessa.

The wide fields of Ukraine, formerly known as the 'breadbasket' of the Soviet Union, look depressingly unkempt. Some are burnt.

"What are they growing here?" I ask.

Nobody knows, but both of my friends agree that almost everything in Ukraine is now collapsing, after the decomposition of the USSR, and this includes both industry and agriculture. The roads are not an exception, either.

"They only built facades during the last decades", explains Dimitry. "The core, the essence had been constructed in the Soviet era. And now everything is crumbling."

***

I have no idea where the official numbers come from; those that say that Ukraine is evenly divided between those who support the West, and those who feel their identity is closely linked with

Russia. Maybe this might be the case in Western Ukraine, in Lvov, or even in the capital – Kiev. But Western Ukraine has only a few key cities. The majority of people in this country of around forty-four million are concentrated in the south, east and southeast, around the enormous industrial and mining centers of Donetsk, Dnepropetrovsk, and Krivoi Rog. There is Odessa in the south, and Kharkov 'the second capital' in the east. And people in all those parts of the country mainly speak Russian. And they see, what has recently happened in Kiev as an unceremonious coup, orchestrated and supported by the West.

***

Before reaching Odessa we leave the highway and drive northeast, towards Moldova and its small separatist enclave, called Transnistria.

There, the river Kuchurgan separates the Ukrainian town of Kuchurgan and the Transnistrian city of Pervomaisc.

I see no Russian tanks at Pervomaisc, no artillery. There is absolutely no military movement whatsoever, despite the countless Western mass media reports testifying (in abstract terms) to the contrary.

I cross the bridge on foot and ask the Transnistrian border guard, whether he has recently seen any foreign correspondents arriving from the United States or the European Union, attempting to cross the border and verify the facts. He gives me a bewildered look.

I watch beautiful white birds resting on the surface of the river, and then I return to Ukraine.

There, two ladies who run the 'Camelot Bar' served us the most delicious Russo/Ukrainian feast of an enormous borscht soup, and *pelmeni*.

Russian television station blasts away, and the two women cannot stop talking; they are frank, proud, and fearless. I turn on my film camera, but they don't mind:

"Look what is happening in Kiev", exclaims Alexandra Tsyganskaya, the owner of the restaurant. "The US and the West were planning this; preparing this, for months, perhaps years! Now people in Ukraine are so scared, most of them are only whispering. They are petrified. There is such tension everywhere, that all it would take is to light a match and everything will explode."

Her friend, Evgenia Chernova, agrees: "In Odessa, Russian-speaking people get arrested, and they are taken all the way to Kiev. The same is happening in Kharkov, in Donetsk, and elsewhere. They call it freedom of speech! All Russian television channels are banned. What you see here is broadcasted from across the border. They treat people like cattle. But our people are not used to this: they will rebel, they will resist! And if they push them to the edge, it will be terrible!"

Both women definitely agree on one thing: "We say, 'don't provoke Russia!' It is a great nation, our historical ally. It has been helping us for decades."

'A civil war', I hear in Kuchurgan. 'A civil war!' I hear in Odessa. 'A civil war!' I hear in Kharkov.

And the same words in Odessa are even written on huge banners: "Kiev, people are not cattle!"

Odessa city, that architectural jewel, an enormous southern port, is now relatively quiet, but tense. I speak to the manager of the historic and magnificently restored Hotel Bristol, but she is very careful in choosing her words. I mention Western involvement in the coup, or in the 'revolution' as many in Kiev and in the West call it, but she simply nods, neutrally.

I cross the street and enter the Odessa Philharmonic Theatre. A young lady approaches me: "Would you like to have my ticket?" She asks in perfect Russian. "My boyfriend did not show up. Please enjoy."

The performance is bizarre, and clearly 'un-philharmonic'. Some renowned folk ensemble performs old Ukrainian traditional songs and dances, but why here and why now? Is it a patriotic gesture, or something else?

The city is subdued, as well as those famous Potemkin Stairs: Renowned for one of the most memorable scenes in world cinema that of, the silent film 'Battleship Potemkin' directed in 1925 by Sergei M. Eisenstein.

As Helen Grace once wrote:

> The Odessa steps massacre in the film condenses the suppression, which actually occurred in the city, into one dramatised incident, and this remains one of the most powerful images of political violence ever realised.

One only hopes that Odessa never again falls victim to unbridled political cruelty, such as was visited on the people by the feudal, oppressive right-wing Tsarist regime, at the beginning of the 20thcentury!

***

Babushka looks exhausted and subdued. She is slowly digging into dark earth, all alone, clearly abandoned.

I spotted some collapsed houses in the village that we had passed just a few minutes earlier, and I asked the driver to make a U-turn, but he clearly did not see any urgency and continued to drive on: "You will see many villages like this", he explained. Dimitry confirmed: "Such villages one are all over Ukraine. There are thousands of them; literally, you see them whenever you leave the main roads."

This one, this village, is called Efremovka, and the name of a grandmother is Lyubov Mikhailovna.

We are somewhere between the cities of Nikolayev and Krivoi Rog.

All around us are the ruins of agricultural estates, of small factories, and houses that used to belong to farmers. Wires are missing from electric poles, and everything appears to be static, like in a horror science-fiction film. Only Lyubov Mikhailovna is digging, stubbornly.

I ask her how she is managing to survive, and she replies that she is not managing at all.

"How could one survive here on only one thousand Hryvnas per month (around US$80)?" she laments. "We are enduring only on what we grow here: cucumbers, tomatoes, potatoes..."

I ask her about the ruins of houses, all around this area, and she nods for a while, and only then begins speaking: "People abandoned their homes and their villages, because there are no jobs. After the Soviet Union collapsed, the entire Ukraine has been falling apart... People are leaving and they are dying. Young people try to go abroad.... The government is not even supplying us with gas and drinking water, anymore. We have to use the local well, but the water is contaminated by fertilizers – it is not clean..."

"Was it better before?" I ask.

Her face brightens up. She stops speaking for a while, searching her memory, recalling long bygone days. Then she answers: "How can you even ask? During the Soviet Union everything was better, much better! We all had jobs and there were decent salaries, pensions... We had all that we needed."

Looking around me, I quickly recall that Ukraine is an absolute demographic disaster: even according to official statistics and censuses, the number of people living in this country fell from 48,457,102 in 2001 to 44,573,205 in 2013. Years after its 'independence', and especially those between 1999 and 2001, are often described as one of the worst demographic crises in modern world history. In 1991 the population of Ukraine was over 51.6 million!

Only those countries that are devastated by brutal civil wars are experiencing similar population decline.

***

Krivoi Rog or Kryvyi Rih as it is known in the Ukrainian language – is arguably the most important steel manufacturing city in Eastern Europe, and a large globally important, metallurgical center for what is known as the *Kryvbas* iron- ore mining region.

Here Krivorozhstal, one of the most important steel factories in the world, it had seen outrageous corruption scandals during its first wave of privatization. During the second privatization in 2005, the mammoth factory was taken over by the Indian multi-national giant, Mittal Steel (which paidUS$4.81 billion), and was renamed Arcelor Mittal Kryvyi Rih. Since then, production has declined significantly, and thousands of workers were unceremoniously fired.

According to the Arcelor Mittal Factbooks (2007 and 2008), steel production decreased from 8.1 million tons in 2007, to 6.2 million tones in 2008. In 2011, the workforce decreased from 55,000 to 37,000 tons, and the management is still hoping that even more dramatic job cuts (down to 15,000) can be negotiated.

By late afternoon, we arrived at the main gate of the factory. Hundreds of people were walking by; most of them looking exhausted, discouraged and unwilling to engage in any conversation.

Some shouted anti-coup slogans, but did not want to give their names or go on the record.

Finally, a group of tough looking steelworkers stops, and begins to discuss the situation at the factory with us, passionately:

"Do you realize how little we earn here? People at this plant, depending on their rank, bring home only some US$180, US$260, or at most some US$450 a month. Across the border, in Russia, in the city of Chelyabinsk, the salaries are three to four times higher!"

His friend is totally wound up and he screams: "We are ready! We will go! People are reaching the limit!"

It is hard to get any political sense from the group, but it is clear that opinions are divided: while some want more foreign investment, others are demanding immediate nationalization. They have absolutely no disputes with Russia, but some support the coup in Kiev, while others are against it.

It is clear that, more than ideology; these people want some practical improvement in their own lives and in the life of their city.

"All we have heard, for the past twenty years is that things will improve", explains the first steel worker. "But look what is happening in reality. Mittal periodically fails to pay what is due. For instance, I am supposed to get 5,700 Hryvnas a month, but I get less than 5,000. And the technology at the plant is old, outdated. The profits that Mittal is making – at least if some of it would stay here, in Ukraine, and go to the building of the roads or improving the water supplies... But they take everything out of the country."

The next day, in Kharkov, Sergei Kirichuk, concludes:

"People all over the world are fighting against so-called 'free market', but in Ukraine, to bring it here, was the main reason for the 'revolution'. It is really hard to believe."

***

The border between Ukraine and Russia, near the town of Zhuravlevka, between Ukrainian Kharkov and the Russian city of Belgorod, is quiet. Good weather, wide fields and an almost flat landscape, guarantee good visibility for several kilometers. On the 28 of March, when Western and Ukrainian mass media were shouting about an enormous Russian military force right at the border, I only saw a few frustrated birds and an apparently unmanned watch tower.

The traffic at the border was light, but it was flowing – and several passenger cars were crossing from the Russian side to Ukraine.

What I saw, however, were several Ukrainian tanks along the M-20/E-105 highway, just a stone throw away from the borderline. There were tanks and there were armored vehicles, and quite a substantial movement of Ukrainian soldiers.

The local press was, however, not as aggressive, provocative:

"State of War!" shouted the headlines of Kyiv Post. "We lifted up to the sky 100 jet fighters, in order to scare Moscow", declared 'Today'.

***

The reality on the ground differed sharply from the 'fairytales', paid for and propagated by Western mass media outlets and by the 'free Ukrainian press'.

In Kharkov, Soviet banners flew in the wind, next to many Russian flags. Thousands of people gathered in front of the giant statue of Lenin on those windy days of 28th and 29th of March.

There were fiery speeches and ovations. The outraged crowd met the proclamations that the Western powers had instigated the 'fascist coup' in Kiev, with loud shouts: "Russia, Russia!"

Old women, Communist leaders, and my friend Sergei Kirichuk, as well as people from international solidarity organizations, made fiery speeches. Apparently, the government in Kiev had already begun to cut the few social benefits that were left, including free medical assistance. Several hospitals were poised to close down, soon.

People were ready to fight; to defend themselves against those hated neo-liberal policies, for which (or against which) none of them had been allowed to vote for.

"In Crimea, people voted, overwhelmingly, to return to Russia", explained a young man, a student, Alexei. "But the West calls it unconstitutional and undemocratic. In Ukraine itself, the democratically elected government has been overthrown and policies that nobody really wants are being pushed down our throats. And... this is called democracy!"

In an apartment of the *Borodba* movement, a young leader and history student, Irina Drazman, spoke about the way the West destroyed Ukraine. She reminded me of a Chilean student leader and now an MP – Ms. Camila Vallejo. Irina is only twenty, but coherent and as sharp as a razor.

"There is great nostalgia for the Soviet Union", she explains. "If only it could be re-shaped and the concept improved, most of the people in Ukraine would be happy to be part of it again."

And that is exactly what the West tries to prevent: A powerful and united country, one which can defend the interest of its people.

Standing in front of a police cordon in Kharkov, Alexandr Oleinik, a Ukrainian political analyst, explains:

> "The essence of what is now happening is based on the doctrine of the United States, which has one major goal: To wipe out from the globe, first the Soviet Union, and then Russia, regardless of its form; whether socialist or capitalist... As is well known, these goals were already defined in the early 1980's, by Zbigniew Brzezinski, in his report to the US Department of State, "*Game Plan: A Geostrategic Framework for the Conduct of the U.S.-*

Soviet Contest".

Besieged square in front of the court of justice may not be the most comfortable place for political discussions, but Mr. Oleinik has plenty to share:

> "After destroying USSR, the US is, until now, making enormous effort to, in accordance with the 'Brzezinski Doctrine', to drag Russia, Ukraine and other post-Soviet countries, into exhausting regional conflicts, in order to out root from the consciousness of the people of these nations all thoughts about reunification (be it a customs union, common economic sphere, etc.). Series of 'color revolutions' from so-called American doctrine of 'advancement of democracies' became a clear proof of the essence of the geopolitical interests of the US. Libya, Tunis, Egypt, Iraq, Afghanistan, Syria, and Yugoslavia – all this is from the same shelf."

"Venezuela, Cuba, Bolivia, Ecuador, Zimbabwe, Eritrea, even China", I continue.

Policemen are looking at us suspiciously, as both of us are naming dozens and dozens of countries located in all corners of the world.

***

In Kiev's Maidan, the main square where the 'revolution' or the coup took place, the right-wing groupings are hanging around, aimlessly. Some men and women are frustrated. Many now even feel that they were fooled.

Thousands were paid to participate in what was thought would bring at least some social justice, some relief. But the interim government began taking dictate, almost immediately: from the United States, from European Union and from the institutions such as IMF and World Bank.

Now thousands of disgruntled 'revolutionaries' feel frustrated. Instead of saving the country, they sold all ideals, and betrayed their own people. And their own lives went from bad to worse.

The tension is growing and Ukraine is on the edge.

There is growing tension, even confrontation, between conservative, oppressive forces and those progressive ones. There is tension between Russian speakers and those who are insisting on purely Ukrainian language being used all over the country.

There are political assassinations; there is fear and uncertainty about the future.

There is increasing and negative role being played by the religions: from Protestant to Orthodox.

Nobody knows what will follow the coup. Confusion and frustration, as well as social collapse, may well cause a brutal civil war.

Protesters are now, this very moment, occupying government buildings in Donetsk and Lugansk, demanding referendum. Majority of people in these and other cities would rather join Russia then to live in pro-Western dictatorship, which Ukraine became after the coup.

Same tactics that were lauded by Western propaganda during the Maidan uprising are now hypocritically condemned in the east and south of the country.

Russia gained greatly, especially in the non-Western world. It is now recognized as the center of global 'mutiny' against global dictatorship of the US and EU. It opened one more front of resistance, and it stands alongside countries of Latin America.

Its generally peaceful and measured approach is in direct contrast to brutal and destabilizing methods used by the US and EU all over the globe. Except in those few fully indoctrinated modern-day colonies (which the West calls 'democracies' just because the people there can stick a piece of paper to a carton box, and most are stupidly doing so), the world is waking up to reality that there actually is, suddenly, some strong and determined resistance to Western imperialism.

After decades of total darkness, the hope is emerging.

In the meantime, two beautiful Slavic countries are still facing each other. But the people, particularly those in Ukraine, are now waving Russian flags and shout to the faces of riot police that is obedient to Kiev: "Russia! Russia!"

No matter what the propaganda says, reality is well known. For decades, after destruction of the USSR, Ukraine mainly obeyed the West and Russia went its own, determinedly independent way.

The result is: Ukraine is on its knees (although not as horribly yet as some East European countries like Bulgaria, that actually became full members of the EU). Wages for workers and pensions for elderly are now approximately 3-4 times higher in Russia than in Ukraine.

And Russia has its own, independent voice, flying all over the world though the outlets like RT and Voice of Russia, while Ukraine is a clearly a colony.

It is obvious in what direction the majority of Ukrainians is now looking with hope. The government should listen. It should also call referendum, soon. It should use 'direct democracy', not some rigged multi-party charade like in Indonesia.

Two countries that share both history and the future, should embrace. And face the wind, and tremors, together! They should never fight each other – Russia and Ukraine are soul mates, not enemies. Those who are dividing them should be exposed, shamed, and expelled!

11 April 2014

*****

45

UNITE AGAINST IMPERIALISM!

In countless interviews, , in personal letters, in face-to-face discussions, the questions I keep being asked are becoming very similar: "Now that it is obvious that the West is ready and willing to destroy everything that stands in its way to the total domination of the planet, what can still be done?"

Some say: 'Nothing'. There are plenty of discouraged, scared voices of people who have already fully given up, and come to the conclusion that the Empire is too powerful, too determined, and therefore, unstoppable.

Others are praying. And there are also some, who are putting all their trust into those few brave ones that are 'still fighting'.

Hopelessness, fear and defeatism – this is how the Empire wants you to feel.

Do not! Defeat is only purposefully encoded in the propaganda that is being spread by the West. In reality, nothing is lost.

Actually, working all over the world, I am increasingly optimistic. People in the Middle East, in Africa, in many parts of Asia, are now waking up. People in Latin America woke up long time ago – they are alert, vigilant!

These are actually truly breathtaking moments in our human history. But nothing is free. To save the world, we will still have to stand firm against neo-colonialism, and all that insane propaganda that is being constantly disseminated by the West. We will have to be determined and strong. If we are, this is not going to be the end, but the beginning!

Of course if we just whine, everything will go to hell, and fall into the laps of the rulers of the world.

***

I actually think, and I have said it and written it on so many occasions, that right now there is absolutely no reason for nihilism.

Those dark days, some two decades ago, of disheartenment and gloom, are over. The era of the monsters like Reagan and Thatcher, the post-Reagan and post-Thatcher decades, of the Bush years, of the Yeltsin years, pre-Chavez years, pre-Morales years: Have all gone!

This is a new reality, and in many parts of the planet, it is quite a beautiful one!

Of course, most of the world is still extremely ugly, in pain and being governed by ruthless thugs, hypocrites, and even by mass murderers. Of course the West has not reformed itself, and it has never abandoned its ambition to dominate the planet. Of course there are millions of innocent people still dying, and the planet is being plundered by a bunch of degenerate morons belonging to the new religion called 'market fundamentalism'... as this is being written.

Of course the propaganda and brainwashing campaigns coming from North America and Europe are intensifying dangerously. Of course it is not 'the end of history', but 'the end of democracy' as we have always perceived it...

Democracy has been totally kidnapped, perverted and humiliated by the most cynical manipulations from Washington, London and Paris. It has nothing to do with the 'rule of the people', nor about sticking some piece of paper into a carton box, in order to legitimize an entirely illegitimate 'multi-party' (really multi-party?) regime.

And of course, if there is no determined resistance, or defense of the basic values on which humanity is based, there will soon be nothing except absolute slavery, market fundamentalism, in brief a society much more appalling than Orwell or Huxley could ever envision.

***

The good news is, that there is resistance!

And there are people who are standing tall and fighting for the survival of mankind.

But equally as important, or even more important, is the fact that now there are also several countries that are totally determined not to allow this neo-Nazi European and North American system to choke the world.

These countries are not 'perfect', as nothing on this earth is. But they are historically peaceful, even if dirtied by the relentless disinformation campaign carried out by the global mass media. And they are all, without exception, much more interested in the well-being of humankind, than in religious concepts attached to business doctrines or world domination.

These countries – they all have different histories, economic and political systems, but all of them are fundamentally against Western neo-colonialism and imperialism. Needless to say, all of them have suffered greatly from it in the past, so they know what they are fighting against.

I am talking about Cuba and Venezuela, Bolivia and Ecuador, Uruguay, China, Russia, Eritrea, Vietnam, Zimbabwe, Iran, and many other nations of our wonderful and diverse planet.

Each and every one of them has been attacked in the past, by either Europe or the United States, or both.

China, one of the oldest and greatest nations on earth, was tricked, occupied and divided; plundered... Barbaric French hordes ransacked its cultural treasures, while the British colonized its cities, and in fact entire areas.

Symbolically, as recorded, the invaders even looted Chinese cultural treasures. As written in 'The Telegraph': there are Chinese artifacts, "1.5 million artifacts... in museums and collections across Europe and America, including the British Museum and the Victoria & Albert Museum in London."

The West has been meddling in the internal affairs of China, financing, training and even arming its 'opposition'. The narrative over Tibet, as well as its mostly internationalist approach towards Africa (I have interviewed hundreds of African people on the ground, in twenty odd countries, and most of them were appalled by the Western anti-Chinese narrative), has been totally kidnapped by the propagandists in London and Washington. The country has been antagonized and provoked on various occasions, its neighbors pitched artificially against it, again and again.

The outrageous provocative military actions of the US, Japan and South Korea against China and North Korea, are continuously bringing the world somewhere close to WWIII, as I have been told by most of the leading academics specializing in the region, including many of those from the West. Europe or the United States would never tolerate even one percent of what they are subjecting China, Russia and other countries to, with deadly regularity.

Is there any rational, historical reason why the world should fear China or North Korea, or Vietnam? Of course not! Except that the world is constantly being bombarded by a 'religious' and impossible to prove demagogy, which describes China (not the West!), as the true aggressor.

The historical and present-day violence against Russia is even more extreme. In recent history, the West has openly attacked Russia, on countless occasions. To name just a few of the most deadly ones: WWI, as well as several incursions against the young Soviet State by the French, Czech and others. According to the BBC Russia Profile:

> "In northern Russia, British, French and US troops captured Murmansk and Archangel until 1919, while in the Russian Far East they occupied Vladivostok."

WWII terminated the lives of twenty million Soviet citizens, who in the end defeated Nazism and saved further hundreds of millions of people worldwide, from definite annihilation.

While the Soviet Union supported most of the liberation struggles in the fight against Western colonialism, it never directly attacked Western Europe nor the United States.

In the end, the Soviet Union was dragged into the Afghan conflict in 1979, and was financially and mentally exhausted, exactly in accordance with the plan created by Zbigniew

Brzesinski. As I was recently told, in the city of Kharkov, by a Ukrainian political analyst, Alexandr Oleinik:

> "The essence of what is now happening is based on the doctrine of the United States, which has one major goal: To wipe out from the globe, first the Soviet Union, and then Russia, regardless of its form; whether socialist or capitalist... As is well known, these goals were already defined in the early 1980s, by Zbigniew Brzezinski, in his report to the US State Department, titled: "Game Plan: A Geostrategic Framework for the Conduct of the U.S.-Soviet Contest."

But it is Russia, not the US, UK or France, which is constantly defined by Western propaganda as the aggressor! No facts are given, except for many pseudo-facts about the Ukrainian famine, which, this author is intending to re-visit from his previous essays, together with the other 'main pillars of Western anti-Communist propaganda' – the Chinese famine and Cambodian bloodletting (both triggered by imperialism – by the US and Japanese ones), but about these topics, a little bit later this year.

Could all these vicious lies and manipulations be created precisely because Russia has always fought against Western imperialism?

And what about the world? Just ask people from the Middle East, Latin America, and Africa: Many see both Russia and China as two giants, two heroes, not as 'aggressors'.

Iran: Is there any country (maybe except Cuba and Russia), which has suffered from Western terror more than this old cultural powerhouse?

Iran has been battered relentlessly! The democratically elected Prime Minister Mohammad Mosaddegh, a true patriot who introduced great social changes in his country, was overthrown in a CIA and MI6 arranged coup, in 1953. It is not even denied in the West. The New York Times in 2000, reported ("The C.I.A. In Iran") on that fact, and called the operation a 'success', lamenting 'mishaps':

> "The Central Intelligence Agency's secret history of its covert operation to overthrow Iran's government in 1953 offers an inside look at how the agency stumbled into success, despite a series of mishaps that derailed its original plans."

The West then pampered and supported its brutal implant, the Shah; his torture chambers, rapes, political murders and disappearances. And it armed and conditioned Iraq, which was under its close ally – Saddam Hussein – who invaded Iran in 1987, triggering a beastly war that took between 500,000 and 1.5 million human lives (historians can still not agree on the exact numbers).

Iran, naturally, has never attacked Europe or the United States, but we are told to fear its 'potential nuclear capability'! Of course it did something much more 'terrible' in the eyes of the West; it dared to, under Mosaddegh, to nationalize its oil reserves. For that, millions of people had to die.

I don't know about others, but while looking back at our planet's history, I'd feel calmer if Iran were to have nukes, than when I know for certain, that the UK, France or US, some of the most aggressive countries on earth, actually have them.

And Cuba! Assassination plots against its President, the bombing of a passenger airliner, the bombing of restaurants and hotels, a direct invasion, an insane embargo, and even attempts to trigger drought and poison its crops, not to speak about the direct financing of the 'dissidents'! The West, led mainly by the United States, did all that to Cuba. And it was done with absolute impunity.

All this because Cuba has been fighting, for decades, against imperialism and colonialism in Africa, because it helped to liberate Namibia and Angola, and tried to liberate the Congo; because it has been sending its doctors to the poorest parts of the world, because it has become a symbol of resistance against Western fascism...

Are we all scared of Cuba? Hands up who is! I am serious.

I can go on and on, about Venezuela and Bolivia, about Chile, even Brazil. But this time I just want to send a relatively short message: Just once, just for a few minutes, let us 'censor' our minds, to all the propaganda coming from the West. And let us, based on history and common sense, ask a very logical question:

"Would it not be better to give a chance to those countries that are now standing against the Empire?"

We let Europe, the United States and their religious market fundamentalists rule the world, for many long centuries, and hundreds of millions of people vanished. Just let us have a glance at the map of the world, the way it looked at the very beginning of the 20th century. Are we getting the point? Everything colonized by Europe, all divided, messed up and enslaved.

Let us try something else. Let us all join the fight against Nazism and imperialism. Let us at least try!

***

Slowly but surely, non-Western countries are joining hands: Russia and Latin America, China and Latin America (yes, it was China which bailed out and saved Cuba, when that traitorous alcoholic Yeltsin, was busy destroying his country and the world, while at the same time taking direct Western dictates). Russia and China are getting closer, while Russia declared that it would support and defend Iran, if necessary. Venezuela and Iran, despite their cultural and social differences, are now as close as possible, and so are countries like Brazil and China.

The world is changing.

New and powerful media has emerged, sheltering the world from the one-sided Western indoctrination, offering great alternatives:

> 'TeleSur' in Venezuela (for which we are laboring relentlessly and proudly!). Press TV. RT! And there is even CCTV of China, although it still has to shed its 'shyness'.

All this new and potent media is being read watched and relied on, by tens of millions of people starved of honest reporting and anti-imperialist stands! These media outlets are now standing tall and firm, alongside those several great opposition publications in the West (mainly in North America, very little in Europe) such as Counterpunch, Global Research, and Znet.

***

Public disobedience and "Occupy Wall Street" will definitely not save the world.

Whole countries, big and strong, will have to get involved.

There should be no appeasement. If the Empire dares to put its destroyers and military bases near Russia, China, Iran or Venezuela, these countries should do the same. And they are doing it, and they will.

The West is increasingly acting as a Nazi entity, and one does not do 'peaceful protests' in front of the Reichstag, when flames are consuming the world, when millions are being murdered!

Such protests will only be tolerated for as long as they are ineffective, but the moment when they truly become dangerous to the empire, they will be crushed. As they were!

I also believe that internal opposition in Europe and the United States should stop being so picky, demanding purity and perfection from the countries that are fighting against their own Nazi rulers, the system and the Empire. It's not the time to be too fussy.

Resistance forces are diverse, they are not always ideal and to everyone's taste, but they are already saving millions of human lives.

Let us first stop Western aggressions, imperialism and neo-colonialism, and only then, let us sort out our differences and determine the ideological way forward for the progressive forces on this planet.

Until then, to the barricades, to the battleships and to the television stations and magazines!

Of course we will win, but it will take some balls and ovaries, as they say in Latin America!

25 April 2014

*****

46

OBAMANIZED ASIA

Welcome to Asia, President Obama!

And back? Smiles and more smiles... Obama speaks Malay! Damn, he can manage "terima kasih" – Malaysian for 'thank you'! It is indeed very impressive, considering that G. W. was only able to manage this in Spanish, and at times, very rarely, in English.

Huge headlines were shouting from most of the Asian dailies... "Hello Malaysia", the 'Sunday Star' which is a self-proclaimed 'The people's paper', was depicting the beaming face of Barack Obama, adding its butler-esque comment:

> "Flashing his infectious smile, President Barack Obama stepped out of Air Force One, gave his customary right handed "hello" wave – and charmed every one of the dignitaries who met him as he arrived for his official visit to the country. It will be a busy day for him before he leaves for Manila tomorrow."

That was all taking place on the 26th and 27th April 2014.

Welcome Barack Obama! You are the top!

Trade agreements, new military bases – let's discuss anything, as long as you are here, our dear leader! We are open, wide open, for... business!

***

Of course, behind the curtains, things were very different.

Malaysia has become a brand new addition to the list of US 'allies' in the region, although, to what extent, still remains to be seen.

And how exactly will Malaysia be used, is not too certain either.

President Obama confused the local 'opposition' when he refused to meet Anwar Ibrahim, the Malaysian neo-con and free marketer, Deputy Prime Minister of Malaysia from 1993 to 1998 and Finance Minister from 1991 to 1998.

While the then Prime Minister Dr. Mahathir Mohamad was blaming currency speculators like George Soros for the 1997 Asian Financial Crises, Anwar Ibrahim was administering 'market forces', taking direct dictates from the IMF and introducing austerity packages. Eventually he fell out of grace, was accused of sodomy (the real one, not a metaphorical reference to the national situation) and corruption. Eventually he became a favorite betting horse for many Malaysian 'opposition figures' and NGO's, who saw him as a person supported by the West and therefore an excellent channel for substantial funding. Obama's refusal to an encounter with him means that he will soon be, and most certainly abandoned by many of his 'loyal' supporters.

***

As I landed at the habitually super-efficient KL International Airport on the 26th of April, long lines formed queues before the immigration counters, and arriving passengers were fingerprinted, something that is very rarely done in Malaysia.

The rail network had collapsed, express trains were running on local tracks, and I was told that many of the roads in the capital had been blocked.

Overall, in Malaysia, the entire 'Presidential charade' was thoroughly embarrassing, even from the point of view of the former ruler of the country, and one of the most outspoken critics of the West on Asian continent, Dr. Mahathir Mohamad.

The former Prime Minister particularly distrusted the proposed TPP or TPPA, which commits countries to lower import tariffs and therefore horrifies local producers.

A Malaysian filmmaker and TV producer, Ms Azreen Madzlan, shared her experience with me:

> "According to former Prime Minister of Malaysia, Tun Dr Mahathir Mohamad, during an interview with a local business channel Capital TV for a show that I was producing, Malaysia should not be compelled to sign the Trans-Pacific Partnership Agreement (TPPA) just because of President Obama's visit to Malaysia this weekend. Tun M who has openly roasted Najib's administration for its intention to sign on with the non-transparent deal continues to warn that TPPA is a controlled trade agreement put together by an impoverished nation trying to exploit the natural resources of other countries."

But the Malaysian media had chosen to welcome the supreme leader of the Western world, by loud fanfares and even using the most poetic words.

The Western media opted for a wide range of attitudes, from hard-core propaganda, to the phlegmatic style adopted by the New York Times:

> "On Sunday, President Obama visited Malaysia to underscore how much has changed in the past 16 years – not least in the country's attitude toward the United States, which has evolved from deep suspicion, verging on contempt, to a cautious desire for cooperation."

The legendary Malaysian political activist, Mr Hishamuddin Rais (he identifies himself as a 'non-government individual'), wrote for this essay:

> "Obama is trying to recreate the atmosphere of the Cold War in Asia in particular and globally... Obama's trip to Malaysia in particular is aimed at the Malaysian leadership to open up and allow access to the Malaysian market. At the same time America is keen to have a military arrangement with Malaysia, i.e. the possibility of having a base.
>
> This is a move partly to control the Southeast Asian market and also to contain what Americans term as the danger of China. Obama is trying to create a wedge between ASEAN nations and China.
>
> In Malaysia in particular, with the weak government of Najib Razak, Obama will force Najib to sign the TPPA trade agreement. It is a fact that TPPA will be destructive to the domestic market."

***

There was plenty of cliché propaganda talk from US officials, as always... about 'defending democracy', about freedom and trade, and about all those 'terrible countries' that the 'benevolent and wise West' has to 'deal with'.

Most of the Western media (widely distributed and reprinted all over Asia Pacific), had been actually painting President Obama as some peacenik, who is being criticized for not standing decisively and militarily against Syria, Russia, even China!

Not a word about the West creating, building and arming 'opposition movements' all over the world, attempting to destabilize countries like Venezuela, Zimbabwe, Ukraine, Russia, China, Syria and many others.

On May 1 2014, International New York Times wrote:

> "Despite his frustration, Mr. Obama had some small victories in Asia. The 10-year deal with the Philippines will give American troops, ships and planes expanded access to bases here, something that would have been unthinkable a decade ago, after fierce public opposition forced the United States to relinquish its naval base at Subic Bay."

'A small victory' is basically a willingness to rape the constitution of the Philippines, which prohibits the US military forces on the territory of the country.

Officially, it is all being justified by 'protecting' the Philippines from the rising 'threat' of China. Although many of the intellectuals in Manila, naturally, see the United States as pitching Southeast nations against its great neighbor and natural ally.

Eduardo C Tadem, a leading Philippine academic and professor of Asian studies at the University of the Philippines, commented for this report:

> "The Obama administration has not departed substantially from the policies of its predecessors as far as foreign policy is concerned. Given this, it does not possess the moral authority to lecture China on the proper behavior of a big power in the Asia-Pacific region. Granted that China has not been on its best behavior with respect to the territorial disputes it is embroiled within the region, it is the US, on the whole, that has done much more damage against Asian peoples and societies with its imperial policies in both the economic and political spheres. Neither does it have the moral authority to lead Asian societies in charting a new economic order given its own failed economy with high unemployment and continually rising inequalities."

***

The increasingly aggressive role of the United States and the 'Western world' has not been discussed in the suddenly over-polite local media outlets.

It should have been. Because between the lines, it was clear that the goal of Obama's journey was to flex muscles, and to show Asia who is still in charge here.

And of course, to re-pledge support for the most obedient ones, like South Korea and Philippines, over their policy towards China, or in the case of Japan, its open hostility towards the great neighbor.

It would be desirable that the Asian countries that are now willing to collaborate with the West, would realize that they are actually becoming co-responsible for what can be best described as the imperialist, neo-colonialist, even fascist adventurism of North America and Europe all over the world.

In the future, history may judge the collaborators as harshly as their masters!

***

There were speeches clearly aimed at swelling anti-Chinese and anti-North Korean sentiments, and there were promises to 'defend' certain countries, including South Korea and Japan, although both of them appear to be more belligerent than their alleged Communist adversaries.

There was an immediate reaction from Pyongyang, calling South Korean President Park Geun-Hye 'a prostitute', and there was an ice-cold reaction from Beijing, calling on the US and Japan to "abandon their cold war mentality".

The language of the Empire was, as always, patronizing, even insulting. As The New York Times reported:

> "Jeffrey A. Bader, who was the senior China adviser on the National Security Council until 2011, said: "The message is: Don't think that what Putin is doing in eastern Ukraine is so brilliant that you should be inspired by it. Don't think that this is a model that could work for you.""

This kind of unsavory preaching is naturally despised in China and in many other countries. It is provocative and insulting, and it should not be tolerated for much longer.

***

And so, Mr Obama, welcome to the continent that your country, and several other Western countries, plundered and ravaged for such long and arduous decades.

Here in Asia you get away with just about anything. Isn't it nice, Mr. President? You can spew any bullshit, tell any lie, and nobody will rebuff you, or laugh at you. With a straight face, you can call North Korea, a pariah state. And nobody replies: 'and what about your own country, Mr. President? What should your country be called?'

In Venezuela, Bolivia, even Brazil and Chile, you would be met by hundreds of thousands of angry people, who all remember that horror that the West had spread there, for decades and centuries.

Somehow, these days, suddenly, almost everyone in Asia is so nice and hushed about these crimes.

It is maybe because here, people are really scared to talk about the role that the Empire has been playing, and to write about it as well. In some countries, like the Philippines, outspoken individuals and especially journalists can easily disappear without a trace, as that 'democratic' nation has one of the most terrible records of violence against the journalists, anywhere in the world.

In Japan, to criticize the Empire would clearly mean losing one's job, as Japan has one of the most disciplined, obedient and servile mass media anywhere in the world. That is why it is designated to 'teach' – to basically brainwash – tens of thousands of students from the rest of Asia, giving them scholarships and turning them into lobotomized idiots with legitimate diplomas.

And so the media field is clear. The leader of the Empire – the Supreme Leader, Dear Leader – is here, with fanfare, facing almost no protests, and no criticism (except for not being 'martial enough').

In a way, he is quite an honest bloke. He is not hiding his goal to side with Japan against China, he sends strategic bombers – B-52's – to openly provoke the most populous nation on Earth, and if one reads between the lines, Mr. Obama is quite candid about his desire to re-introduce the Cold War to all regions of the planet.

But, these days, almost no one, in the West or here, is trained to read between the lines.

***

The West, including the United States, has embarked on all sorts of genocidal projects, all over Asia Pacific, for centuries. It has terrorized this part of the world, with tremendous force and determination, from Vladivostok to East Timor.

Be it not for the servility of Asian leaders, and for the total manipulation of history, Air Force One would have been met with jet fighters and interceptors, not with flowers, and national anthems.

The problem is that in Asia Pacific, in many parts of it at least, the countries are governed by thoroughly shameless 'elites' (read thugs, bandits), and these individuals are united with Western economic and political 'leaders', in their determination to plunder and mug everything, that grows, hides below the surface, and even that which walks and talks.

This is especially true about places like the Philippines and Indonesia, but also about Thailand, Cambodia, and even, to a lesser extent, South Korea.

Japan is an exception, as it has willingly and shamelessly been exchanging its independence for a rich and comfortable quality of life, willingly accepting the role of an obedient, sclerotic and depressed (but extremely well paid) servant of the West, on the Asian continent.

David McNeill, a leading expert on Japan and a Professor at Sophia University, recently explained during our conversation and the filming of my Okinawa documentary, in Tokyo:

> "Japan, after the Second World War, aligned itself very quickly with America... And Japan's military alliance with America is also accompanied with, what critics would say, its subservient attitude towards Washington."

***

Let's just revisit a few of the most horrifying atrocities the West performed in Asia Pacific, in the last hundred years or so.

Both British and US forces occupied, brutally, the city of Vladivostok, in the Russian 'Far East', after the Bolshevik Revolution.

China was plundered and colonized by European forces, brutally and relentlessly.

Korea was terrorized by mainly North American troops, with

the most horrific toll on the local, mainly civilian population, with an estimated death toll of over four million people.

During WWII, Japan endured firebombing and the carpet-bombing of its cities, including Tokyo, as well as basically, two nuclear experiments against its population in Hiroshima and Nagasaki.

The French barbarically tortured, raped, and mutilated people of Vietnam, but also those of Laos and Cambodia. The savagery exceeded even that of the later US 'involvement', as many local people, whilst I lived in Hanoi for three years, explained to me.

In 'Indochina', the US, of course, bombed to ashes entire cities, and it poisoned the countryside, raped the female population of entire villages, and committed atrocities comparable only to those they themselves had earlier committed in Korea. Historians are still arguing about the death toll: Was it six million or ten million, during what they called the 'Vietnam War' and the 'Secret War in Laos' (in that part of the world, that genocide is squarely identified as the 'American War')?

The US also made sure to open the doors to the Khmer Rouge in Cambodia (by carpet-bombing most of the Cambodian countryside into the stone ages), later vocally demanding their return to power, from the floor of the United Nations and other organizations. All that, of course, happened after the Vietnamese troops, had kicked out Pol Pot's boys and girls from power (the US considered it a great crime).

Kissinger had it very clear: He suggested that 'anything that flies should be used against anything that moves', and he had it his way. And, he never faced a firing squad for this, although his tactics were not too different from those employed by the German Nazis.

In the Philippines, the US committed much greater atrocities than Japan (including the Balanginga massacre), but a brainwashing campaign and the servility of most of the local media, made it impossible to discuss these topics openly.

The Philippines were brutally colonized by both Spain and the United States, but the US propagandists have managed to re-narrate the entire history of the archipelago.

British rule in what is now Malaysia and Singapore, was very far from benevolent.

The Thai Western ally murdered its Communists, as well as student protesters, and placed its territory at the disposal of the West, during the Vietnam War.

Indonesia was repeatedly attacked by the United States from its bases in the Philippines, during the reign of the progressive and anti-Western President, Sukarno.

A US-sponsored coup brought the military junta to power, and some 2-3 million Indonesians were murdered, mainly Communists, Chinese citizens and intellectuals. Fascist Indonesia then occupied (with the support of the West) tiny East Timor, where some 30% of the population lost their lives in a horrific genocide. Western media hushes up coverage of the ongoing genocide against the Papuan population, as it greatly benefits the interests of Western mining companies.

***

Still, collaboration with the Empire appears to be an attractive option to many governments in the region.

China is watching, and, not surprisingly, it appears that it does not like what it sees at all. Russia, another great 'Asian' power is even more outraged. North Korea is, as always, 'ready'.

Mr. Obama may count on weak and submissive allies. But Asia is changing, too. It is evolving. It is watching. It may soon begin saying "No".

Mr. Obama decided to visit South Korea, but not China.

Does it matter? Maybe... But for how long?

"If you come or do not come, we will be here," the Chinese foreign ministry spokesman Qin Gang, said.

***

Obama's visit was disastrous on many fronts. There were trade deals proposed but that never fully materialized, including those between the United States and Japan.

There were constant insults and provocations, double-speak, maneuvering and manipulations.

Those who had any illusions left about the Western press have, perhaps, finally lost them.

Perhaps the main reason why President Obama's visit felt so

unsettling was because the danger of what the West is trying to achieve on all the continents of the world is now so obvious, but also blurred by massive propaganda. People feel, they fear, but they do not fully understand – cannot fully define what is going on.

Mr Obama came as the head of a junta, of the regime, which is supervising the killing of millions, directly and indirectly. In Congo and Ukraine, in Syria and Iraq, Afghanistan and Libya, Somalia, South Sudan, Uganda, Papua, to name just a few places.

And the more crimes are committed; the more twisted the truth gets. Fingers are pointed at Russia and China, who are basically doing nothing, or Iran, which has never attacked anyone in modern history.

Would any other nation act the way the US does, there would be an immediate war.

If the mass media in any other part of the world, outside of North America and Europe, were to apply such self-censorship and use outright lies, it would be immediately accused of being nothing more than just a propaganda tool.

After decades of the absolute horrors administered by Western imperialism, much of Asia Pacific has turned into a spineless, scared group of nations. Tens of millions have vanished between Hiroshima and now. The racist spite with which the West has been exterminating local people has no comparison in modern history, with the exception of the Western annihilation of African people.

Despite all that flowery rhetoric that we have just witnessed during the visit of the US President to Asia, there were no traces of love, or friendship.

From Tokyo to Kuala Lumpur, it was tense maneuvering – very tense and very dangerous.

Terima kasih, Encik Presiden!

One should always remember: The West never came in peace here. Not once. Wherever it has engaged, millions have died... millions of, exclusively, Asian people..

2 May 2014

47

GENOCIDE IN INDONESIAN ZOOS

Indonesians are no amateurs when it comes to mass murder and genocides.

They managed to slaughter with their bare hands, between 1 and 3 million people in 1965/66, mainly those who belonged to the educated class, and of course the Communists, teachers, artists and members of the Chinese minority.

They butchered and tortured to death around 30 percent of the inhabitants of what is now Timor-Leste. And they have already exterminated at least 150,000 men, women and children in Papua, in an ongoing and totally hushed up genocide that allows Western countries to access its natural resources. 150,000 corpses is, of course, one of the lower estimates...

One could say that with such a record and such an absolute lack of compassion even towards their fellow human beings, the fate of the animals killed regularly all over Indonesia, should not come as something surprising or shocking.

In Indonesia, every creature of any commercial value is poached mercilessly and has virtually no protection. Even the few remaining elephants of Sumatra, whose habitat has essentially been ruined already, are regularly tortured and killed.

But what is happening right now in Surabaya, the second largest city of Indonesia, is shocking by all standards. Here, massacres in the local zoo do not involve 'just a few animals', but half of their entire population.

The magnitude of this crime against defenseless and captive animals is symbolic and in sync with other similar crimes that have been committed for decades against human beings. And as expected here, those responsible also enjoy full impunity.

In Indonesia, basic ethics have collapsed. The nation went truly bananas following the officially encouraged (and orchestrated by the West) and glorified to this day, orgy of bloodshed and rapes of 1965/66.

Here, killing, crime, looting and violence, pay. The only victims are: the great majority of impoverished Indonesian people, as well as creatures big and small, are still barely surviving among those black clogged streams, deforested mountains and poisoned seas. Here, both, people and animals were robbed of everything.

***

"Originally there were some 4,400 animals in the Surabaya zoo", explains Ms. Sybelle Foxcroft, Founder and CEO at Cee4life ('Conservation & Environmental Education 4 Life' located in the Melbourne Area of Australia). "Now there are only approximately 2,100 of them left..."

We are facing each other, sitting at the table of a restaurant in a bizarre and moderately kitschy 'Art Café' in the city of Surabaya. Sybelle is a scientist but also a former Medical Sergeant in the Australian Army. I have been a war reporter for many years. We understand each other very quickly and intuitively: she came here to save tigers, turtles and many other fantastic and endangered creatures. My duty is to shame those who are murdering them. It resembles a theatre of war. The genocides, misery, and total destruction of the environment – all these Indonesian realities are actually nothing else other than warzone scenarios.

I tell Sybelle that this country left Asia, psychologically, a long time ago: it resembles the Democratic Republic of Congo or at least Uganda. We both know Africa well, and she understands what I am saying.

Just recently, Sybelle finally met the mayor of Surabaya, Ms. Tri Rismaharini:

> "We had to push the mayor to bring professionals... this is ridiculous... The media put pressure on the Mayor... it was all totally political. I know that the zoo will be there for at least two more years. Some say that mayor cracked the deal with a foreign developer..."

She continues after a while:

> "They have this zoo where the animals are dying left and right, and there is no help for them? They cannot help them? At times it was if they did not want to help them? Now people like us, from outside, are helping... building an elephant enclosure for those poor creatures that are in chains, scarred!"

So what is really going on? Peter Dickinson, the owner and editor of Zoo News Digest in the UK, wrote:

"The real problem about Surabaya Zoo today is its location. This is prime development land. Its city central 'green' location has big business salivating in anticipation of the zoo failing. They want it to go. Every opportunity to muddy the Zoo's reputation is taken... There is corruption and big money at stake here."

Are animals being murdered to give space to developers? It is not pronounced publicly, but said over and over again behind closed doors.

Many had been criticizing the Mayor of Surabaya, and the critics included Dr. Tony Sumampau, the renowned director of Taman Safari Indonesia (a private safari park in West Java, with two other branches in the country), who was forced to leave his job at the Surabaya Zoo in June 2013, allegedly because he was actually trying to improve the conditions of the animals.

The accusations against the mayor have ranged from the inadequacy of her response to the crises at the Zoo, to allowing a deal with a foreign-based developer, which will within two years; effectively liquidate this historic zoo that was founded in 1916.

As always in Indonesia, there is no transparency. The Mayor and others are pointing fingers at each other.

The English language newspaper, the Jakarta Globe wrote on January 20th, 2014:

> "In response to the criticism, the mayor said she planned to

> report the Surabaya Zoo case to the Corruption Eradication Commission (KPK) over the alleged embezzlement of the funds overseen by the temporary management team. She also said the transfer of 483 animals out of the zoo was highly suspicious..."
>
> ...Rismaharini claims that some of the animals were traded by zoo officials for money or other items, including cars.
>
> "Trading the animals for cars or motorcycles is illegal. You can only exchange animals with animals...""

Sometimes, when translated from Bahasa Indonesia, some sentences and arguments sound simply weird, who knows why?

***

What is described in the pages of local newspapers, does not of course reflect the true nightmare of the extermination of half the population of the entire zoo.

Sybelle lists the horrors:

> "A giraffe dying with a 20kg bag in her stomach... Bear covered by sores... Malani, that wonderful Sumatran tiger, skin and bones from eating poisoned meat... another tiger that died a terrible death: Chandrika – dying in agony, with no anesthesia or pain relief... Animals failing constantly and all around: skinny and starving creatures! Animals from the Zoo and animals from outside: dead cats hanging from the walls... Every animal here has either Hepatitis or TB."
>
> "We thought, 'where does this come from'? I was informed by an Indonesian professional that 15 people/staff were tested for the diseases and 11 of them had TB and hepatitis. After that any further results were hidden...It's unknown which way the disease was passed, but it was passed on and many are suffering from disease. Even a hippo died from hepatitis here!"

The list is endless:

> "Green turtles, sea turtles, endangered ones, were found by us in the fresh water pond, with color changed and covered by fungus... In January 2014 someone told me that one turtle 'looked sick'. It sure was sick! It was dead. From the skin coloration it had been already, for 5 days! With a plastic bag sticking out from its mouth...choking it to death. Here, animals die under grotesque and unnatural circumstances."

***

Our several visits to the Zoo have been also truly Kafkaesque.

With an untrained eye it is obvious that something has gone terribly wrong.

One animal after another was dying, and those that were alive, camels, giraffes, apes and reptiles, even tigers, looked desperate, starving and resigned.

Once, we stopped an intern, Ms. Perina Thenesia, from Airlangga University, as she was throwing some food into the cages.

What does she think has been happening here recently?

"I think what happened..." She looked at us phlegmatically. "It is because the weather and the environment..."

"Were animals murdered?" I asked a keeper, without insisting that he identifies himself.

He does not say yes or no. Not for a while.

"Do you believe animals were killed?"

"Yes."

We approach several employees, hiding from the rain. We ask again and again.

"Ask Pak Agus" we are told.

But there is no Pak Agus, anywhere around.

Do they have any opinion?

"No."

Then one of the keepers utters: "We don't want to talk. If we say something wrong, it could cause us a problem."

His pal nods his head in agreement: "It has all been already taken care of by the management."

We go everywhere, but what we get is total silence. Ms. Penta from the data center suddenly has no data on how many animals are supposed to be in the zoo, how many were recently born and how many have died. It appears to be a top secret, a war and peace situation. There is only one portion of information that Ms. Penta happily shares with us: "Since July 2013, there is a regulation that forbids us talking to the press. Talk to Pak Agus..."

Several days later, we manage to locate Pak Agus, a

spokesperson of the zoo:

> "One Nilgai antelope was recently found dead and a Baboon died yesterday," Agus Supangat said it was a natural death because of age. "That Baboon was the last one Surabaya Zoo had... Now there is no Baboon anymore."

He refused to get more philosophical.

***

Again, on May 14th, 2014, I visited the Zoo. One would think that after all those campaigns and international coverage, things would have improved. But I saw again, the same bears covered with sores, I saw the babies of Komodo Dragons and Orangutans in horrifying conditions, and everywhere I went, there were empty cages.

"You want to see baby Komodo?" One of the keepers offered. He led me to a beat up wooden box. He unlocked it and let me peek in. There were some ten tiny and adorable creatures, crammed, clinging to each other.

"Here, look!" said keeper. He took long wooden stick and began poking into confused and scared dragons, some of the most endangered species on earth.

And everywhere I went, keepers were sitting in groups, doing nothing, just smoking and chatting.

How on earth could all this happen, in the 21st century, and in Asia?

How could be animals fed with rot penetrated with formaldehyde?

But then you think: in Jakarta and in fact in every city in Indonesia, there are constant reports of people, even children, being fed and poisoned by the same think. Formaldehyde, rat meatballs... Poisonous chemical drinks sold to children near schools...

Of course this was part of a much larger issue; Surabaya Zoo does not exist in a vacuum.

Indonesia has already collapsed, and only survives from the plundering of its own natural resources. The fourth most populous nation on earth is producing nearly nothing. The education level has hit the bottom.

"One Vet here asked me: how do we treat a tiger?" says Sybelle in disbelief. "This was a Vet! They had no idea a blood test was required, and did not want to anesthetize the tiger, nothing!"

Then she continues:

> "I am teaching against racism... I am also teaching about rights... people, animals... You know, in Indonesia I have to start from the very beginning: I have to tell my students that animals can also feel pain, that they have emotions..."

***

I face a black bear, with some fungus near its mouth, covered with sores all over its body.

I don't know why, but as the bear and I stare at each other, I suddenly remember all the horrors that I have witnessed around the archipelago: the aftermath of rapes in East Timor, being tortured for exposing them, Papua refugee camps, killings in Ambon, Aceh... horrors and horrors that I have described in my fiction, and non-fiction books... testimonies that I collected for my films...

"Look", I tell the bear. For some reason I speak to it in Russian, although it is definitely not from there. "It is all screwed up... but we will try to do something... to save your skin, so to speak..."

The bear pretends that it understands. It actually gets up on its two legs and grabs the bars. It is bigger than me. It is beautiful, beautiful creature, but they made him look like shit – defeated, broken, sick...

I want to scream, to run away from here, fast and far... to Venezuela or Chile... to places where fascism has been defeated... to those places where we have won. To that part of the world where there is, once again, light and kindness, and compassion.

But I stay. I know that the bear trusts me. And so do a few people in this collapsed nightmarish fascist country.

More than 2,000 creatures have died, in a terrible massacre. Hopefully their deaths will help to explain conditions in this country, which was designated as a place where people and animals are supposed to live and die for a few rich individuals and clans, and for market fundamentalism.

Hopefully these creatures did not die for nothing! In my mind, I consider them as fallen comrades.

16 May 2014

*****

48

More Than a Voting Booth

DOWN WITH WESTERN 'DEMOCRACY'!

A specter is haunting Europe and Western world – it is this time, the specter of fascism. It came quietly, without great fanfare and parades, without raised hands and loud shouts. But it came, or it returned, as it has always been present in this culture, one that has, for centuries, been enslaving our entire planet.

As was in Nazi Germany, resistance to the fascist empire is again given an unsavory name: terrorism. Partisans and patriots, resistance fighters – all of them were and have always been defined by fascist bigots as terrorists.

By the logic of Empire, to murder millions of men, women and children in all corners of the world abroad is considered legitimate and patriotic, but to defend one's motherland was and is a sign of extremism.

German Nazis and Italian Fascists defined their rule as 'democratic', and so does this Empire. The British and French empires that exterminated tens of millions of people all over the world, always promoted themselves as 'democracies'.

And now, once again, we are witnessing a tremendous

onslaught by the business-political-imperialist Western apparatus, destabilizing or directly destroying entire nations, overthrowing governments and bombing 'rebellious' states into the ground.

All this is done in the name of democracy, in the name of freedom.

An unelected monster, as it has done for centuries, is playing with the world, torturing some, and plundering others, or both.

The West, in a final act of arrogance, has somehow confused itself with its own concept of God. It has decided that it has the full right to shape the planet, to punish and to reward, to destroy and rebuild as it wishes.

This horrible wave of terror unleashed against our planet, is justified by an increasingly meaningless but fanatically defended dogma, symbolized by a box (made of card or wood, usually), and masses of people sticking pieces of paper into the opening on the top of that box.

This is the altar of Western ideological fundamentalism. This is a supreme idiocy that cannot be questioned, as it guarantees the status quo for ruling elites and business interests, an absurdity that justifies all crimes, all lies and all madness.

This sacrificial altar is called, Democracy, in direct mockery to what the term symbolizes in its original, Greek, language.

***

In our latest book, "On Western Terrorism – from Hiroshima to Drone Warfare", Noam Chomsky commented on the 'democratic' process in the Western world:

> "The goal of elections now is to undermine democracy. They are run by the public relations industry and they're certainly not trying to create informed voters who'll make rational choices. They are trying to delude people into making irrational choices. The same techniques that are used to undermine markets are used to undermine democracy. It's one of the major industries in the country and its basic workings are invisible."

But what is it that really signifies this 'sacred' word, this almost religious term, and this pinnacle of Western demagogy? We hear it everywhere. We are ready to sacrifice millions of lives (not ours of course, at least not yet, but definitely lives of the others) in the name of it.

Democracy!

All those grand slogans and propaganda! Last year I visited Pyongyang, but I have to testify that North Koreans are not as good at slogans as the Western propagandists are.

"In the name of freedom and democracy!" Hundreds of millions tons of bombs fell from the sky on the Laotian, Cambodian and Vietnamese countryside... bodies were burned by napalm, mutilated by spectacular explosions.

"Defending democracy!" Children were raped in front of their parents in Central America, men and women machine-gunned down by death squads that had been trained in military bases in the United States of America.

"Civilizing the world and spreading democracy!" That has always been a European slogan, their 'stuff to do', and a way of showing their great civilization to others. Amputating hands of Congolese people, murdering around ten million of them, and many more in Namibia, East Africa, West Africa and Algiers; gassing people of the Middle East ("I am strongly in favour of using poisonous gas against uncivilised tribes", to borrow from the colorful lexicon of (Sir) Winston Churchill).

So what is it really? Who is it, that strange lady with an axe in her hand and with a covered face – the lady whose name is Democracy?

***

It is all very simple, actually. The term originates from the Greek δημοκρατία (dēmokratía) "rule of the people". Then and now, it was supposed to be in direct contrast to ἀριστοκρατία (aristokratia), that means "rule of an elite".

'Rule of the people'... Let us just visit a few examples of the 'rule of the people'.

People spoke, they ruled, they voted 'democratically' in Chile, bringing in the mild and socialist government of 'Popular Unity' of Salvador Allende.

Sure, the Chilean education system was so brilliant, its political and social system so wonderful, that it inspired not only many countries in Latin America, but also those in far away Mediterranean Europe.

That could not be tolerated, because, as we all know, it is only white Europe and North America that can be allowed to supply the world with the blueprint for any society, anywhere on this planet. It was decided that "Chile has to scream", that its economy had to be ruined and the "Popular Unity" government kicked out of power.

Henry Kissinger, belonging, obviously, to a much higher race and country of a much higher grade, made a straightforward and in a way very 'honest' statement, clearly defining the North American stand towards global democracy: "I don't see why we need to stand by and watch a country go Communist due to the irresponsibility of its people."

And so Chile was ravaged. Thousands of people were murdered and 'our son-of-a-bitch' was brought to power. General Pinochet was not elected: he bombed the Presidential palace in Santiago, he savagely tortured the men and women who were elected by the Chilean people, and he "disappeared" thousands.

But that was fine, because democracy, as it is seen from Washington, London or Paris, is nothing more and nothing less than what the white man needs in order to control this planet, unopposed and preferably never criticized.

Of course Chile was not the only place where 'democracy' was 'redefined'. And it was not the most brutal scenario either, although it was brutal enough. But it was a very symbolic 'case', because here, there could be absolutely no dispute: an extremely well educated, middle class country, voted in transparent elections, just to have its government murdered, tortured and exiled, simply because it was too democratic and too involved in improving the lives of its people.

There were countless instances of open spite coming from the North, towards the 'rule of the people' in Latin America. For centuries, there have been limitless examples. Every country 'south of the border' in the Western Hemisphere, became a victim.

After all, the self-imposed Monroe Doctrine gave North Americans 'unquestionable rights' to intervene and 'correct' any 'irresponsible' democratic moves made by the lower races inhabiting Central and South America as well as the Caribbean Islands.

There were many different scenarios of real ingenuity, in how to torture countries that embarked on building decent homes for their people, although soon there was evidence of repetitiveness and predictability.

The US has been either sponsoring extremely brutal coups (like the one in Guatemala in 1954), or simply occupying the countries in order to overthrow their democratically elected governments. Justifications for such interventions have varied: it was done in order to 'restore order', to 'restore freedom and democracy', or to prevent the emergence of 'another Cuba'.

From the Dominican Republic in 1965 to Grenada in 1983, countries were 'saved from themselves' through the introduction (by orders from mainly the Protestant North American elites with clearly pathological superiority complexes) of death squads that administered torture, rape and extrajudicial executions. People were killed because their democratic decisions were seen as 'irresponsible' and therefore unacceptable.

While there has been open racism in every aspect of how the Empire controlled its colonies, 'political correctness' was skillfully introduced, effectively reducing to a bare minimum any serious critiques of the societies that were forced into submission.

In Indonesia, between 1 and 3 million people were murdered in the years1965/66, in a US -sponsored coup, because there too, was a 'great danger' that the people would rule and decide to vote 'irresponsibly', bringing the Communist Party of Indonesia (PKI), at that time the third most numerous Communist Party anywhere in the world, to power.

The democratically elected President of Congo, Patrice Lumumba, was murdered in 1961, by the joint efforts of the United States and Europe, simply because he was determined to use the vast natural resources of his country to feed his own people; and because he dared to criticize Western colonialism and imperialism openly and passionately.

East Timor lost a third of its population simply because its people, after gaining independence from Portugal, dared to vote the left-leaning FRETILIN into power. "We are not going to tolerate another Cuba next to our shores", protested the Indonesian fascist dictator Suharto, and the US and Australia strongly agreed. The torture, and extermination of East Timorese people by the Indonesian military, was considered irrelevant and not even worth reporting in the mass media.

The people of Iran could of course not be trusted with 'democracy'. Iran is one of the oldest and greatest cultures on earth, but its people wanted to use the revenues from its oil to improve their lives, not to feed foreign multi-nationals. That has always been considered a crime by Western powers – a crime punishable by death.

The people of Iran decided to rule; they voted, they said that they want to have all their oil industry nationalized. Mohammad Mosaddeq, the democratically elected Prime Minister of Iran from 1951 to 1953, was ready to implement what his people demanded. But his government was overthrown in a coup d'état, orchestrated by the British MI6 and North American CIA, and what followed was the murderous dictatorship of the deranged Western puppet – Reza Pahlavi. As in Latin America and Indonesia, instead of schools, hospitals and housing projects, people got death squads, torture chambers and fear. Is that what they wanted? Is that what they voted for?

There were literally dozens of countries, all over the world, which had to be 'saved', by the West, from their own 'irresponsible citizens and voters'. Brazil recently 'celebrated' the 50th anniversary of the US-backed military coup d'état, which began a horrendous 20 year long military dictatorship. The US supported two coups in Iraq, in 1963 and 1968 that brought Saddam Hussein and his Baath Party to power. The list is endless. These are only some random examples.

On closer examination, the West has overthrown, or made attempts to overthrow, almost any democratically elected governments, on all continents attempting to serve their own people, by providing them with decent standards of living and social services. That is quite an achievement, and some stamina!

Could it be then that the West only respects 'Democracy' when 'people are forced to rule' against their own interests? And when they are 'defending' what they are ordered to defend by local elites that are subservient to North American and European interests?... and also when they are defending the interests of foreign multi-national companies and Western governments that are dependent on those companies?

***

Can anything be done? If a country is too weak to defend itself by military means, against some mighty Western aggressor, could it approach any international democratic institutions, hoping for protection?

Unthinkable!

A good example is Nicaragua, which had been literally terrorized by the United States, for no other reason than for being socialist. Its government went to court.

The case was called: The Republic of Nicaragua v. The United States of America.

It was a 1986 case at the International Court of Justice (ICJ) in which the ICJ ruled in favor of Nicaragua and against the United States and awarded reparations to Nicaragua.

The judgment was long, consisting of 291 points. Among them that the United States had been involved in the "unlawful use of force." The alleged violations included attacks on Nicaraguan facilities and naval vessels, the mining of Nicaraguan ports, the invasion of Nicaraguan air space, and the training, arming, equipping, financing and supplying of forces (the "Contras") and seeking to overthrow Nicaragua's Sandinista government.

Judgment was passed, and so were UN votes and resolutions. The UN resolution from 1986 called for the full and immediate compliance with the Judgment. Only Thailand, France and the UK abstained. The US showed total spite towards the court, and it vetoed all UN resolutions.

It continued its terror campaign against Nicaragua. In the end, the ruined and exhausted country voted in 1990. It was soon clear that it was not voting for or against Sandinista government, but whether to endure more violence from the North, or to simply accept depressing defeat. The Sandinista government lost. It lost because the voters had a North American gun pointing at their heads.

This is how 'democracy' works.

I covered the Nicaraguan elections of 1996 and I was told by voters, by a great majority of them, that they were going to vote for the right-wing candidate (Aleman), only because the US was threatening to unleash another wave of terror in case the Sandinista government came back to power, democratically.

The Sandinistas are now back. But only because most of Latin America has changed, and there is unity and determination to fight, if necessary.

***

While the Europeans are clearly benefiting from neo-colonialism and the plunder that goes on all over the world, it would be ridiculous to claim that they themselves are 'enjoying the fruits of democracy'.

In a dazzling novel "Seeing", written by Jose Saramago, a laureate for the Nobel Prize for literature, some 83% of voters in an unidentified country (most likely Saramago's native Portugal), decide to cast blank ballots, expressing clear spite towards the Western representative election system.

This state, which prided itself as a 'democratic one', responded by unleashing an orgy of terror against its own citizens. It soon became obvious that people are allowed to make democratic choices only when the result serves the interests of the regime.

Ursula K Le Guin, reviewing the novel in the pages of The Guardian, on 15 April 2006, admitted:

Turning in a blank ballot is a signal unfamiliar to most Britons and Americans, who aren't yet used to living under a government that has made voting meaningless. In a functioning democracy, one can consider not voting a lazy protest liable to play into the hands of the party in power (as when low Labour turn-out allowed Margaret Thatcher's re-elections, and Democratic apathy secured both elections of George W Bush). It comes hard to me to admit that a vote is not in itself an act of power, and I was at first blind to the point Saramago's non-voting voters are making.

She should not have been. Even in Europe itself, terror had been unleashed, on many occasions, against the people who decided to vote 'incorrectly'.

Perhaps the most brutal instance was in the post WWII period, when the Communist Parties were clearly heading for spectacular victories in France, Italy and West Germany. Such 'irresponsible behavior' had to be, of course, stopped. Both US and UK intelligence forces made a tremendous effort to 'save democracy' in Europe, employing Nazis to break, intimidate, even murder members of progressive movements and parties.

These Nazi cadres were later allowed, even encouraged, to leave Europe for South America, some carrying huge booty from the victims who vanished in concentration camps. This booty included gold teeth.

Later on, in the 1990's, I spoke to some of them, and also to their children, in Asuncion, the capital of Paraguay. They were proud of their deeds, unrepentant, and as Nazi as ever.

Many of those European Nazis later actively participated in Operation Condor, so enthusiastically supported by the Paraguayan fascist and pro-Western dictator, Alfredo Strössner. Mr Strössner was a dear friend and asylum-giver to many WWII war criminals, including people like Dr. Josef Mengele, the Nazi doctor known as the "Angel of Death", who performed genetic experiments on children during the WWII.

So, after destroying that 'irresponsible democratic process' in Europe (the post-war Western Empire), many European Nazis that were now loyally serving their new master, were asked to continue with what they knew how to do best. Therefore they helped to assassinate some 60,000 left-wing South American men, women and their children, who were guilty of building egalitarian and just societies in their home countries. Many of these Nazis took part, directly, in Operacion Condor, under the direct supervision of the United States and Europe.

As Naomi Klein writes in her book, Shock Doctrine:

> "Operación Cóndor, also known as Plan Cóndor, Portuguese: Operação Condor) was a campaign of political repression and terror involving intelligence operations and assassination of opponents, officially implemented in 1975 by the right-wing dictatorships of the Southern Cone of South America. The program was intended to eradicate communist or Soviet influence and ideas, and to suppress active or potential opposition movements against the participating governments."

In Chile, German Nazis rolled up their sleeves and went to work directly: by interrogating, liquidating and savagely torturing members of the democratically elected government and its supporters. They also performed countless medical experiments on people, at the so-called Colonia Dirnidad, during the dictatorship of Augusto Pinochet, whose rule was manufactured and sustained by Dr. Kissinger and his clique.

But back to Europe: in Greece, after WWII, both the UK and US got heavily involved in the civil war between the Communists and the extreme right-wing forces.

In 1967, just one month before the elections in which the Greek left-wing was expected to win democratically (the Indonesian scenario of 1965), the US and its 'Greek colonels' staged a coup, which marked the beginning of a 7 year savage dictatorship.

What happened in Yugoslavia, some 30 years later is, of course clear. A successful Communist country could not be allowed to survive, and definitely not in Europe. As bombs fell on Belgrade, many of those inquisitive and critically thinking people that had any illusions left about the Western regime and its 'democratic principles', lost them rapidly.

But by then, the majority of Europe already consisted of indoctrinated masses, some of the worst informed and most monolithic (in their thinking) on earth.

Europe and its voters... It is that constantly complaining multitude, which wants more and more money, and delivers the same and extremely predictable electoral results every four, five or six years. It lives and votes mechanically. It has totally lost its ability to imagine a different world, to fight for humanist principles, and even to dream.

It is turning into an extremely scary place, a museum at best, and a cemetery of human vision at the worst.

***

As Noam Chomsky pointed out:

> Americans may be encouraged to vote, but not to participate more meaningfully in the political arena. Essentially the election is a method of marginalizing the population. A huge propaganda campaign is mounted to get people to focus on these personalized quadrennial extravaganzas and to think, "That's politics." But it isn't. It's only a small part of politics. The population has been carefully excluded from political activity, and not by accident. An enormous amount of work has gone into that disenfranchisement. During the 1960s the outburst of popular participation in democracy terrified the forces of convention, which mounted a fierce counter-campaign. Manifestations show up today on the left as well as the right in the effort to drive democracy back into the hole where it belongs.

Arundhati Roy, commented in her "Is there life after democracy?"

> The question here, really, is what have we done to democracy? What have we turned it into? What happens once democracy has

> been used up? When it has been hollowed out and emptied of meaning? What happens when each of its institutions has metastasized into something dangerous? What happens now that democracy and the Free Market have fused into a single predatory organism with a thin, constricted imagination that revolves almost entirely around the idea of maximizing profit? Is it possible to reverse this process? Can something that has mutated go back to being what it used to be?

***

After all that brutality, and spite for people all over the world, the West is now teaching the planet about democracy. It is lecturing Asians and Africans, people from Middle East and Sub-Continent, on how to make their countries more 'democratic'. It is actually hard to believe, it should be one of the most hilarious things on earth, but it is happening, and everyone is silent about it.

Those who are listening without bursting into laughter are actually well paid.

There are seminars; even foreign aid projects related to 'good governance', sponsored by the European Union, and the United States. The EU is actually much more active in this field. Like the Italian mafia, it sends covert but unmistakable messages to the world: "You do as we say, or we break your legs... But if you obey, come to us and we will teach you how to be a good aide to Cosa Nostra! And we will give you some pasta and wine while you are learning."

Because there is plenty of money, so called 'funding'... members of the elite, the academia, media and non-government organizations, from countries that have been plundered by the West – countries like Indonesia, Philippines, DR Congo, Honduras, or Colombia –send armies of people to get voluntarily indoctrinated, (sorry, to be 'enlightened') to learn about democracy from the greatest assassins of genuine 'people's power'; from the West.

Violating democracy is an enormous business. To hush it up is part of that business. To learn how to be idle and not to intervene against the external forces destroying democracy in your own country, while pretending to be 'engaged and active', is actually the best business, much better than building bridges or educating children (from a mercantilist point of view).

Once, at the University of Indonesia where I was invited to

speak, a student asked me 'what is the way forward', to make his country more democratic? I replied, looking at several members of the professorial staff:

> "Demand that your teachers stop going to Europe on fully funded trips. Demand that they stop being trained in how to brainwash you. Do not go there yourself, to study. Go there to see, to understand and to learn, but not to study... Europe had robbed you of everything. They are still looting your country. What do you think you will learn there? Do you really think they will teach you how to save your nation?"

Students began laughing. The professors were fuming. I was never invited back. I am sure that the professors knew exactly what I was talking about. The students did not. They were thinking that I made a very good joke. But I was not trying to be funny.

***

As I write these words, the Thai military junta has taken over the country. The West is silent: the Thai military is an extremely close ally. Democracy at work...

And as I write these words, the fascist government in Kiev is chasing, kidnapping and "disappearing" people in the east and south of Ukraine. By some insane twist of logic, the Western corporate media is managing to blame Russia. And only a few people are rolling around on the floor, laughing.

As I write these words, a big part of Africa is in flames, totally destroyed by the US, UK, France and other colonial powers.

Client states like the Philippines are now literally being paid to get antagonistic with China.

Japanese neo-fascist adventurism fully supported by the Unites States can easily trigger WWIII. So can Western greed and fascist practices in Ukraine.

Democracy! People's power!

If the West had sat on its ass, where it belongs, in Europe and in North America, after WWII, the world would have hardly any problems now. People like Lumumba, Allende, Sukarno, Mosaddeq, would have led their nations and continents. They would have communicated with their own people, interacted with them. They would have built their own styles of 'democracy'.

But all that came from the Bandung Conference of 1955, from

the ideals of the Non-Aligned movement, was ruined and bathed in blood. The true hopes of the people of the world cut to pieces, urinated on, and then thrown into gutter.

But no more time should be wasted by just analyzing, and by crying over spilt milk. Time to move on!

The world has been tortured by Europe and the United States, for decades and centuries. It has been tortured in the name of democracy... but it has all been one great lie. The world has been tortured simply because of greed, and because of racism. Just look back at history. Europe and the United States have only stopped calling people "niggers", but they do not have any more respect for them than before. And they are willing, same as before, to sacrifice millions of human lives.

Let us stop worshiping their box, and those meaningless pieces of paper that they want us to stick in there. There is no power of people in this. Look at the United States itself – where is our democracy? It is a one-party regime fully controlled by market fundamentalists. Look at our press, and propaganda...

Rule of the people by the people, true democracy, can be achieved. We the people had been derailed, intellectually, so we have not been thinking how, for so many decades.

Now we, many of us, know what is wrong, but we are still not sure what is right.

Let us think and let us search, let us experiment. And also, let us reject their fascism first. Let them stick their papers wherever they want! Let them pretend that they are not slaves to some vendors and swindlers. Let them do whatever they want – there, where they belong.

Democracy is more than a box. It is more than a multitude of political parties. It is when people can truly choose, decide and build a society that they dream about. Democracy is the lack of fear of having napalm and bombs murdering our dreams. Democracy is when people speak and from those words grow their own nation. Democracy is when millions of hands join together and from that brilliant union, new trains begin to run, new schools begin to teach, and new hospitals begin to heal. All this by the people, for the people! All this created by proud and free humans as gift to all – to their nation.

Yes, let the slave masters stick their pieces of paper into a box, or somewhere else. They can call it democracy. Let us call democracy something else – rule of the people, a great exchange of ideas, of hopes and dreams. Let our taking control over our lives and over our nations be called 'democracy'!

23 May 2014

*****

49

Time to Listen

HOW SHOULD WE WRITE AND FIGHT?

Why are the streets of New York, Washington D.C., London and Paris so orderly, so quiet?

Are we – opposition investigative journalists, philosophers and documentary filmmakers – doing such a terrible job? Are we not providing the North American and European public with enough information, enough proof about the monstrous state of the world? Enough so they – the citizens of the Empire – finally get thoroughly pissed off, detach their backsides from their couches and chairs, and flood the capitals and business centers with their bodies, demanding change, demanding the end to atrocities that are being committed all over the world... the end of this imperialist and neo-con madness?

Are we failing, squarely and patently, to give examples and proof of the pain this world is suffering because of the bestiality of market fundamentalism, because of unchecked neocolonialism and shameless Western supremacy? Are we not providing enough stories and images, enough footage, to convince the citizens of the countries that are ruling the world, that something has gone awfully wrong?

The answer is yes, and also, no.

Yes – we work relentlessly and, frankly; we work well... we fight well, day and night, often 25/8 (overtime, 24/7), forgetting about exhaustion, personal life, even our health and danger.

On the side of reason and decency, on the side of the resistance against the oppressive and murderous Empire, are the brightest minds of this world.

There are great philosophers and thinkers like Eduardo Galeano, Alain Badiou, Naomi Klein, Arundhati Roy, and Noam Chomsky, who clearly and precisely define and critique the essential concepts that govern the world.

There are brave international lawyers like Christopher Black, and celebrated economists, including the Nobel Prize laureate, Joseph Stiglitz.

Almost all the great writers are part of the resistance, including those – the greatest ones – who have just recently departed: Jose Saramago, Gabriel Garcia Marquez and Harold Pinter.

And there are, of course, investigative journalists, on all the continents, those who are risking their lives, often with no institutional support, working mostly against all the odds.

***

So Yes – we are providing plenty of information, plenty of images, plenty of proof, that the world is in flames, that tens of millions are dying, that true democracy everywhere is being raped and the natural resources of poor countries are being plundered, so that Western capitalism can flourish.

But No – we are not managing to improve the world. All those tremendous efforts are failing to ignite even those few millions of educated and concerned citizens in the West, to organize and rebel, to demand the end of the global imperialist onslaught.

All the information mentioned above, about the horrors of imperialism and market fundamentalism, is easily available on-line, "just one click away", to use corporate language.

But nothing is happening. The majority of Europeans and North Americans appear to be thoroughly apathetic towards the state of the world. They keep stuffing themselves on cheap, subsidized food; amusing themselves with the latest gadgets (including smart phones, sated with Coltan taken from the Democratic Republic of Congo, where some ten million people have died since 1995). They keep voting in those right-wing governments and they believe, increasingly and blindly, that their societies are an inspiration to the rest of the world as the sole examples of democracy and freedom.

The citizens of the Western Empire are actually so lethargic and indoctrinated, that even when billions are stolen from them (not just from the people in their colonies), when banks get bailed-out after their speculative orgies, or after so-called elections get fully subsidized and manipulated by the corporate mafia, they do nothing; absolute nothing!

Go to a pub in the UK or Germany, and 'everybody knows everything'. You will hear it repeatedly: 'politicians are swine', 'corporations are controlling elections'. If you stay long enough, after several pints of beer someone will perhaps slam his fist on the table: "We need revolution!" Then everybody agrees and they all go home... and the next day – nothing.

'Occupy Wall Street' activists got rouged up by the police... And nothing. Everybody goes home. And shouts at the television.

***

Is there still anything that will outrage people to the point that 'they would actually not go home'? That they would stay on those bloody streets, build barricades and fight, as they did in the past, even as recently as in 1968?

How many millions have to die in the Western colonies, before the people in Europe and North America pay attention, recognize the massacres and admit that they are actually citizens of a fascist empire, and that it is their moral obligation to fight it and dissolve it? Is 10 million in the DRC not enough? Is one coup after another that the West openly orchestrates, not a sufficient eye opener?

***

As President Obama pointed out, honestly, on May 28 2014, at West Point, NY:

> "In Egypt, we acknowledge that our relationship is anchored in security interests – from the peace treaty with Israel, to shared efforts against violent extremism. So we have not cut off cooperation with the new government."

Or, to put this into perspective, to quote The Economist (May 24, 2014):

> "Prodded by a fawning reporter to reveal the extent of American plotting in support of the Muslim Brotherhood, a theory much harped on by Egypt's xenophobic post-coup media, Mr Sisi disarmingly confessed that the only interference he could recall was when the American ambassador requested that last year's coup should be delayed for a day."

But it is not just in Egypt, although Egypt as well... It is one coup after another, these days, all over the world. Coups financed and arranged by the US and Europe... and all those countries ruined, bombed or run to the ground. We can see them clearly, as we are shown images (with twisted commentaries) every day: from Egypt to Ukraine to Thailand. Destroyed Libya and crippled Syria. Bleeding Bahrain. Countless attempted coups against any progressive Latin American governments. A multitude of African nations terrorized by the West – from Mali to Somalia, to DRC to Uganda.

France is increasingly behaving like a bandit nation. Entire regions covered by blood and pus, governed by gangsters who are maintained and armed by the Empire, decades after many great leaders had been either assassinated or shamelessly overthrown.

There is plenty of evidence and information about all that I am talking about.

If the West cannot murder or overthrow a government in a powerful country, it risks lives in its client states: I have just left Manila, Philippines, where two leading academics, Eduard and Teresa Tadem, explained to me how the United States is pitching Southeast Asian nations against China; their historic and natural ally.

The country's press is servile and so, all the terror of European colonialism and of the US extermination campaign against the Philippine people has been miraculously forgotten. Propaganda works. China is the villain! Western propaganda is brilliant, professional, and deadly. Nobody knows anything about the disputed islands; nobody studies history or legal documents. But China is simply wrong. It must be wrong, because that is what has been repeated on television and in the newspapers every day, for years.

The West is antagonizing China, relentlessly, while spreading anti-Chinese propaganda everywhere, totally discounting the country's enormous achievements and the fact that it is undergoing some profound socialist reforms, related to medical care, education, housing, arts and public transportation, just to mention a few. Of course, any notion that China is a successful socialist state has to be destroyed (it either has to be a failure, or it has to be portrayed as capitalist).

These provocations, many of them of a military nature, are now using the old regional imperialist power, Japan (and its extreme right-wing Prime Minister), which is in sudden need of 'protection'. Needless to say, all this can easily lead to WWIII.

The same provocations are taking place against Russia – against Latin America...and Zimbabwe, Iran, Eritrea – basically against any country that is unwilling to succumb to intimidation, or to sacrifice its own people and lick the boots of the Empire.

And the Western public is blind and deaf. Or it pretends that it does not know and does not see.

There are two possibilities why: either, as I wrote in my earlier analyses (including "The Indoctrinated West"), the Western public is totally lost and overrun by corporate propaganda (it appears to be the most ignorant and misinformed public I have encountered anywhere in the world). Or it simply pretends to be like that, because the status quo suits its interests – it can take advantage of the looting and plundering done by its governments and companies, while pretending that it is still morally superior to the rest of the world... with hardly any feeling of guilt.

***

We write and write, film and talk... Huge accusations are made, crimes confirmed... But again: nothing happens!

The most disturbing fact is that no revelation, no discovery of crimes committed by Western governments and companies is upsetting enough, or monstrous enough, for the men and women of the Empire, to demand the immediate resignations of their governments, or of the changing of their entire political and economic system.

Genocides are apparently not sufficient reasons to demand the disbanding of the regime.

The overt nature of thieving, the perverse, nihilist economic and social system controlled by kleptocrats, provokes no major revolutionary actions, no nation-wide rebellions. Even demonstrations are diminishing in size. If there are actually any demonstrations, they tend to be of a pathetic caliber – for higher wages, for instance, but hardly ever for ideological reasons.

How often, do we see huge protests in Europe, against the plundering and murdering of people in Africa or Asia... or against, say, the "French New Wave" of imperialism? Or against the monstrous AFRICOM that sits right in the middle of Europe – in the city of Stuttgart? That monstrosity is, according to its own words: 'responsible for U.S. military operations and military relations with 53 African nations – an area of responsibility (AOR) covering all of Africa except Egypt', and it is crammed into the Kelley Barracks, on the outskirts of the city of Stuttgart... which in turn produces all those Mercedes and Porsche cars for the corrupt elites and their children, all over the world.

Nobody protests and nobody gives a damn. I have witnessed some demonstrations against a new train station in Stuttgart, because a few trees had to be cut down in order to build a new terminal... there were demonstrations against the destruction of the 'historic character of the station', but I never saw any substantial demonstration against AFRICOM or against the destruction of millions of lives, all over the world, by German companies.

Europeans (and North Americans) appear to be totally 'bullet-proof' against any information that could lead to making them feel co-responsible for the plunder and devastation that their Empire is and has been spreading, for years, decades, even centuries, all over the world.

As there is hardly any retrospective feeling of guilt, outrage and horror for colonizing, raping and looting basically the entire planet (including North America, as the killing of native people there was done mainly by the first and second generation of European migrants), there seems to be very little chance that Westerners will now rise and demand an end to the terror they are responsible for having imposed on Africa, Asia, Middle East, Latin America, including Oceania.

Great proof was provided by John Perkins when he wrote, "Confession of an Economic Hit Man", a book that made it to The New York Times bestseller list. Several million copies were sold in various languages, and... nothing!

I met John at the studios of INN in New York City. He was interviewed about 'Confession' and I was interviewed about my documentary film "Terlena – Breaking of a Nation", which was about the insanity and brutality of the Indonesian regime after the US-sponsored coup of 1965/66.

We exchanged notes. In his book, John wrote a first-hand account about his former activities and duties. Working for the State Department, he used money, sex and alcohol to corrupt governments in places such as Ecuador and Indonesia, so they would accept totally useless and unserviceable loans that would disappear into the deep pockets of the elites, and bring nothing else other than total misery to the poor and middle classes. Why? The answer was simple: Because indebted countries were easier to control.

Of course, in any normal country or society, such a revelation would bring down the government along with the entire political and economic system. There can be no question that this is the pinnacle of 'immorality', and a system that produces this kind of global scenarios, should never even be trusted with governing, its own nation.

But nothing has happened in the United States. As far as I am concerned, there were no major demonstrations triggered by Perkin's book.

In Budapest, much, much less, triggered the 'uprising' of 1956 – an uprising that was partially provoked by the West (including by the propaganda arm of the US government – 'Radio Free Europe'), and later glorified as the fight against Soviet rule in Eastern Europe.

An extremely uncomfortable but definitely honest conclusion is that the citizens of the West are incapable of, or unwilling to fight and defend the lives of those whom their Empire destroys. They cannot be trusted, anymore. They have failed for centuries.

People all over the planet have waited and hoped that opposition will come from within the Empire.

It took China to rise up, in order to stop military attacks against its territory. Russia had to regain its strength and to get rid of all the horrible rot that was turning the nation into yet another "client state" of Washington – from naïve nitwits like Gorbachev to the tyrant and alcoholic, Yeltsin. And it took Latin America several decades of fights and revolutions, and hundreds of thousands of martyrs, to finally forge a huge united front against the colonialists and fascists from the North.

***

But what I want to ask today is: how, if until now, nothing has worked... how do we deal with the Western public; how do we address it?

Does it really make any sense to speak to them, to appeal to them, even after they had shown such ignorance, such vicious stupidity, indifference and servility?

Would bombarding them – Europeans and North Americans – with facts change anything?

If I show them what they have done in Eastern and Central Africa, would they rebel? We know the answer, and it is: no, they will not.

If we tell them what they are doing to Ukraine, would they demand that all aid to those gangsters who are now holding power there (including that 'newly elected President'), stops? Definitely not! For most of them, Ukraine is nothing else other than a bit of titillating news they watch in the evening, while stuffing themselves at their dining tables.

Most of them do not pay attention. They do not know and do not want to know... all the while pretending that they are the best-informed part of the world. That's not good enough for the citizens of the countries that are ruining the world.

I do believe in collective guilt and collective responsibility. The more I see of European culture, its evasiveness and deception; the more I believe, the more I am convinced that it has to be insisted on. They don't like it, naturally. Tell them about collective guilt and they turn against you like a mad bunch of pit bulls... for very logical reasons. To be a citizen of the continent that is guilty of the destruction of the planet, for many long centuries, is not a joke; it is quite a serious responsibility, and burden... Tell a rapist that he is a rapist, and he breaks your skull. Tell a gangster that he is a gangster and just wait and see what will happen.

***

So what to do? Should we stop writing? Of course not!

There are decent people out there, too. Our readers... For them, and only for them, we write, we labor and risk our lives.

But how and where do we go from here? What is the strategy?

Frankly, I think that facts wrapped in academic writing can change nothing. Absolutely nothing. They can get someone a tenure or even put things 'on the record', but do not expect that those facts and 'records' could trigger a revolution, real change.

As it is, all the crimes of the Empire are already very well documented. Information can be effortlessly accessed, read and understood. So we can very easily conclude that pure facts are not moving anyone, anymore. Otherwise the whole field, the entire situation would be quite different by now.

'Facts' are now effectively used only against Communist countries and parties by the elaborate and pointed Western propaganda machine, and here we are talking about inflated, exaggerated and twisted 'facts'. They are repeated thousands of times, over and over again, and as in Nazi Germany, they became truth: the globally accepted truth.

But even many left-wing intellectuals, as Badiou confirms, are readily accepting those re-invented and re-conditioned 'facts', although they also claim that they also know that the individuals and companies that are spreading them have a clear interest in perverting the truth through their corporate media and corporate universities, which makes it all one great contradiction.

Working in all those places that are used as examples, as the 'proof of evilness of Communism', I can testify that the 'facts' presented by the Western propaganda apparatus, range from being inflated, to being absolute lies. That goes for Ukraine (including the 'famine' of the 1930's), Cambodia, and North Korea, the Soviet Union's gulags, the Chinese famine and the Cultural Revolution. Half-truth is, as we know, much more dangerous than outright falsehood.

To contradict those fabrications in one or two publications is pointless. It would be just you, and a couple of those who know what you know, and are ready to risk everything and go public with it, against those hundreds of thousands repetitions and reprinted falsehoods, against their trolls, even their establishment academia and press. You cannot win.

I tried with the Rwanda genocide: that outright complex lie, manufactured by Western propaganda, which I have perfectly documented. You cannot win – trust me, even if you have unlimited evidence.

Then what else?

Would the books of confessions of those Western apparatchiks help? If Perkins failed, who can do better?

Investigative journalism? The same as academic writing: it does not seem to move anybody, anymore. Definitely not to 'move them to action'...

I personally went through hell, through fire, and a few of those sniper attacks, through death sentences and through being tortured, even being "disappeared" once... all this, in order to inform, to fire-up people, to outrage them, to piss them off. So they do their part and help to stop the genocides that I witnessed all over the world. But did I change much? Did I manage to stop Western invasions or to prevent their 'coups'? I don't think so...

***

I am giving up on journalism and on academic writing. I actually gave up on them, totally, at least two years ago.

I am back to where it all used to be, before corporate journalism. I am a left-wing writer and a filmmaker. I do not hide it; do not lie. That is what I am, and proud of it. Tradition is great, and I am honored by our tradition, too: from Hemingway and Orwell, to Ryszard Kapuściński and Wilfred Burchett!

I go to warzones to fight for revolution, to be in the resistance against imperialism. I don't go there to 'write objective articles' (that stuff is total lunacy, 'objective reports'). Tripods, computers, cameras, recorders – all of them are my weapons; our weapons.

In many of the places where I go, people are dying. Many of them are dying. Women are being ravished, villages and cities bombed and burned.

All of us, including Hemingway, Orwell and Burchett were, of course, artists and poets. And this is how they wrote.

And this is the conclusion to which I am now arriving:

When in war, when defending revolutions, when fighting imperialism: one has to be, and to write as a poet... Each report has to be part of a great novel which will be written in the future, or which is being written right there, as one prepares his or her reports. Otherwise it is all shit, and will touch nobody and change nothing.

This is where our only advantage is, against those corporate whores: we are human and alive and we have a heart that is on the left and blood that is red, and all that we do is because we love this world passionately... we love this humanity... and we fight and are ready to die for it.

Every report should have at least one poem hidden inside it. It has to touch. It has to offer warmth and relief, and it has to outrage and lead people onto the barricades.

We have to learn how to write like that, again. Otherwise everything is really lost!

And then, instead of recycling as those corporate scribes and academia do, we have to listen to the people, and not to the establishment, not to each other.

The greatest Latin American storyteller, Eduardo Galeano, once told me, deep in the wilderness of his old café in Montevideo: "Why do I write like this? Because I am a passionate listener."

Yes. Human stories are subversive, honest and mostly revolutionary. If a writer truly listens to the people, he knows what to write and how. And he knows how to fight for the people and how to defend them, instead of serving corporations.

I listen, too. Wherever I go, I listen. I don't watch television. Instead I listen to stories.

I have asked many questions today. I'm not sure I know the answers:

How to be effective? How to move people? How to inspire them, so they join the struggle for a better world, even if it were against their own immediate interests and privileges?

What I write is for you, my readers. I do not write in order to hear myself speak, but to convey to you what others have said, as well as how others are suffering and dreaming.

To quote a great poem and song by the Chilean artist, Violeta Parra:

> Thanks to life, which has given me so much
>
> It gave me laughter and it gave me longing

With them I distinguish happiness and pain

The two materials from which my songs are formed

And your song, as well, which is the same song

And everyone's song, which is my very song

I want you to talk to me, my readers. I have written so much; you have read what I have written, patiently. Now write to me. I want to listen. How do we go forward? You and I, together... What touches you? What makes you cry? What would make you rise up and struggle for a better world? How do we coordinate our steps and walk forward, together?

30 May 2014

*****

50

BEWARE OF KICKING THE DRAGON AND THE BEAR

It is not prudent and it is not safe to stick an iron rod into a dragon's mouth. Whatever they say in the West about dragons... but here in Asia, the dragon is revered as the greatest fabled creature on Earth and in the sky. The dragon is wise and patient, and it hardly ever uses force first. But if treated with disrespect and aggression, it is capable of retaliating in a deadly, determined and powerful way.

It is also thoroughly idiotic to go and start terrorizing a sleeping bear. It is obvious what would follow if one descended into a bear's hole and then started poking a hibernating creature in the head. Nothing good would follow, nothing good at all.

But it appears that those who are ruling the Empire are not obsessed with prudence. They seem to be tired of tiny conflicts, which they are continuously stirring all over the globe. Libya is not enough and Congo is not enough. They need something big, really big; even much bigger than what they had already 'achieved' a few decades ago – like the destruction of the entire Indochina or Indonesia.

The Empire needs a mortal fight with mighty opponents.

Instead of helping to build a decent and peaceful world, it needs to cover our planet with innumerable corpses.

This time, if it will be allowed to do it, like it was some 70 years ago, tens of millions, and maybe many more, will vanish.

Once again, it would have to be a dragon and a bear, this time in unison, facing fascism and fighting for the survival of the world.

***

The anti-Chinese and anti-Russian propaganda howl is reaching a deafening crescendo, especially in Asia. Western media outlets are in the highest gear, spreading propaganda through both their own outlets and through their local media affiliates in the client states, mostly owned by big business.

China and Russia are now vilified, openly insulted, and blamed for the escalation of tensions in the Asia-Pacific region, and for the military build up. The entire mighty Western propaganda machine is now at work, demonizing China, Russia and other independent countries.

It is because the West is obviously pushing this planet towards the war. Not to see it would require truly great discipline.

Politicians are parading, one after another, in front of television cameras, pledging allegiance to capitalism, the Western-style regime or simply put, to the Empire. All those derogatory and inflammatory speeches against their 'enemies' are embarrassing, see-through, but nobody in North America and Europe is laughing, as they are becoming the norm.

Many are warning that this can lead to a world war, that the West has lost all restraint and is ready to bathe the planet in blood, once again. A quarter of century ago it appeared that with the destruction of the Eastern block and with China then increasingly on a capitalist course, the West had finally got what it had fought for centuries for – the total and absolute control of the planet.

But recently, something went 'wrong' for the West. Latin America rose and most of it gained freedom, then spat on the Monroe Doctrine. China began pushing for socialist reforms in medical care, education, culture and many other spheres. And Russia refused to get bullied and humiliated, reminding both Europe and North America that it is as always powerful and will not be stepped on as happened in the era of Gorbachev and

Yeltsin.

North Korea and Iran (countries that have never attacked anyone in modern history) realized that the only way to survive and not be reduced to dust is by having their own nuclear capacity.

And all these nations: several in Latin America, China, Russia, Iran, joined forces and decided: "Never again!" Never again will they allow the world to descend to the horrors of Western colonialism.

The wet Western dream of unopposed rule over the world is beginning to disappear into thin air. Is the West going to risk the destruction of our planet simply because it cannot own it?

***

"Stephen Harper attacks Vladimir Putin and 'evil' communism", reported the Canadian news outlet, CBC News on 31 May 2014, in reference to the "lengthy keynote speech" at a fundraising event that the right-wing Canadian PM gave in Toronto. The speech was spiced with "language reminiscent of the height of the Cold War".

Grotesquely, the President of the most aggressive country on Earth, the United States, Barack Obama, was promising to 'curb the aggression' of Russia and China, two countries that have not invaded anywhere in the last few decades.

In a speech clearly aimed at provoking China, the US Defense secretary Chuck Hagel, spoke more like a thug than a politician: "The United States will not look the other way when fundamental principles of the international order are being challenged."

'Which order?' Some would ask. Was he talking about the order that is being imposed on the world from Washington and European capitals and has been for centuries, at the cost of hundreds of millions of human lives? Quite an order!

Christopher Black, a leading international criminal lawyer based in Toronto, provided an analysis for this report:

> "The speech made by President Obama at West Point, the American military academy, that the fulcrum of American policy will be to curb the "aggression" of Russia and China immediately followed by his Defense Secretary Hagel in Singapore accusing China of destabilization in the South China Sea, rightly characterized by Lt. General Wang GuanZhong as "threats and

> intimidation", express the clear intent of the United States to wage war in all its aspects against the two most powerful nations that dare to develop independently of American domination.
>
> The United States has attacked China several times since World War II, first in the Korean War, followed by decades of attempted sabotage and isolation and then by the NATO bombing of the Chinese Embassy in Belgrade in 1999. It now has continued that pressure by trying to destabilize China internally through various mechanisms of infiltration of "human rights" groups into Chinese society and within China's military and administrative mechanisms and a constant propaganda campaign to defame China and its people around the world. The momentum of this strategy has been stepped up with the recent attacks by fanatical Muslim groups from western China against Chinese civilians in key cities and transportation hubs and use of provocateurs to attacks Chinese interests in Vietnam, Thailand, the Philippines and Africa and the recent absurd charges against Chinese military officers for cyber attacks.
>
> The recent events in Ukraine show that the pace of this aggression is accelerating as America attempts to complete the encirclement of Russia and China by advancing NATO to Russia's borders and by repositioning of 60 per cent of US military assets to the Pacific.

But now the true aggressors are blaming the victims for 'aggression'. And it is nothing new under the sun. Nazi Germany and its propagandists employed the same 'logic' and arguments, before and during WWII. And the French used it in Algiers and their other colonies, as did the Brits all over their 'dependencies'.

***

In Asia, on a local level, the servile press in countries like the Philippines is taking orders and often surpasses its handlers in the West by its zeal.

On May 25th 2014, The Philippine Star began with lashing out at China, continued by quoting the words of Admiral William Locklear III, the commander of US Pacific forces, that "Russia has its own 'pivot' in Asia". Then the newspaper finally produced a few pieces of 'brilliant' analyses: "Official sources said Russia's incursion into Ukraine has raised concern in Washington that China may try something similar in staking its territorial claims, in the guise of protecting its citizens overseas."

'Russian incursion into Ukraine?' That sounds more like

propaganda shouting from the pages of the North American or European daily press. In some 15 years of work in the region, after interacting with hundreds of media people from all over Southeast Asia, I have to testify that such a thought as quoted above, could never have come from a local journalist. Here, knowledge about Eastern Europe is very near absolute zero. And after being brainwashed in London, New York and elsewhere, local journalists *do not compare*. Someone else wrote it. Who did it? We all know it. It is the same source, which sends trolls biting at all my reports written for RT.

Most of the local Philippine press generally concluded that the US has basically no choice but to expand militarily, because of 'China's aggressive moves.' Almost all the newspapers mentioned the high cost of the permanent US military bases in the region, also arguing that 'spokes', bases belonging to local countries but wide open for use by US forces, are the real way forward. Such bases would also be located on Australian and Japanese territories, and possibly in Singapore and Thailand, as well as Malaysia.

Now Thailand is certainly 'secured', after the army that has been killing millions in the region on behalf of the West, overthrew the progressive and elected government, and took control of the country. The coup is truly timely, isn't it?

As if it would not already be enough to have countless bases in Africa, the Middle East, Japan, Oceania and those few client states that are still left in Latin America. But of course, those are too far from the main targets – China and Russia.

The mainstream Philippine media is not even bothering to question the integrity of such a military agreement, which is in direct violation of the nation's Constitution. It is because the journalists in Southeast Asia are not paid and flown for training abroad, to moralize. They are paid to write what suits the elites and their foreign handlers.

Eduardo Tadem, Professor of Asian Studies at the University of Philippines, explained, during our recent conversation in Manila:

> "The recently signed agreement between the Philippines and the United States is called EDCA (Economic Defense Cooperation Agreement). In this agreement the Philippine government offered virtually all the military bases in the Philippines for total access to American soldiers, for a ten-year period. But who

> knows for how long, really... This is very dangerous, because all military installations of the country are now open for 'entry' of the US forces. And this certainly goes against the Philippine Constitution, which bars the establishment of foreign bases on our territory."

Then what really happened? Why the sudden change?

> "It has to do with certain factors. One, of course, is the factor of the so-called 'US pivot' to Asia. Under Obama there is this strategy of 'pivoting to Asia'. Second has to do with the so-called Trans-Pacific partnership proposal of the United States; to build some sort of integrated market in the Asia Pacific region. Except that the Philippines is not part of it for now... The third one has to do with the territorial disputes that are taking place in this region, both in the South China Sea and the North China Sea."

China.

> "It is mainly an issue of nationalism. And it is also because here they were always asking for more assistance, including military assistance. And this is the way to get that assistance. Also remember that Philippine Presidents were consistently supportive of the US. You probably saw the survey that shows that the Philippine people love the United States more than Americans love themselves. So for the Americans it is easy to get support for their China policy here."

I asked both Teresa Tadem, Professor of Political Science at the University of Philippines, and Professor Eduard Tadem, how was it possible that a country, the Philippines, that suffered so severely during its occupation by the United States, during the colonial era, when there were human rights violations, massacres... How come it feels so positive towards its former brutal colonizer?

> "It has to do with the extremely intensive American propaganda machine, which depicted the colonial era as a benevolent type of colonialism. Atrocities during the Philippine – American War at 1898–1901, which saw 1 million Philippine people killed, which was then almost one tenth of the population, were made to disappear from the consciousness of the people... the genocide, torture... The Philippines was known as the 'first Vietnam'... all of this has been conveniently forgotten, hidden in the history books. And then of course the image of Hollywood that we are bombarded with...

How dangerous is it to antagonize China and even Russia? For centuries, China had been a very peaceful country, and it still is to this day. Many Filipinos come from China; it is a natural, historical ally... While the West is liquidating, and bombing entire countries into the ground, overthrowing governments, China pulls one oil-rig into disputed waters, sprays a few boats with water cannon, and it is immediately defined as the aggressor.

"It is again all about propaganda. They depicted China as Communist and here they always attach a negative connotation to that word", said Professor Teresa Tadem. "

"For me the most dangerous country on Earth now is the United States", continues Eduardo Tadem. *"It has been the most aggressive... intervening in many countries all over the world, thousands of miles from its shores, trying to impose on the planet its vision of a global capitalist system. So, if you compare what China is doing in the vicinity of its territory, and compare it to what the US is doing in all parts of the world, on every continent... then you clearly see the disparity in the image that has been created, depicting China as a danger to peace in the world."*

Both professors then expressed deep concern over the fact that the Western propaganda is igniting Sino-phobia in the Filipinos and in other Asians. They pointed out that what the US is doing is actually fanning ultra-nationalism, which can easily mutate into fascism. This is, according to them, an extremely dangerous situation – planting seeds of Sino-phobia all over the continent.

"This can lead to a point of no return", explains Eduardo Tadem. "I am afraid that this is what is happening now in the Philippines, as well as in other parts of Asia where territorial disputes are taking place."

And it is clearly not only Sino-phobia that can lead to the destruction of the world, although Sino-phobia is partially, definitely is. Stirring hatred against Russia is also clearly on the menu of the Western masters of propaganda. Stephen Harper of Canada, Polish and Baltic politicians and their irrational anti-Russian speeches, is all leading to a frightening outcome: manufacturing racism against those nations that are standing in the way of US and European domination of the world.

Dehumanizing a potential enemy, unleashing racist and derogatory sentiments against him or her, is the first step in the Western 'art' of war, the first step towards a confrontation.

One should seriously question what is being planned? One

should demand to know, because what is being planned is most likely really awful.

***

People are beginning to speak up. Geoffrey Gunn, a prominent Australian historian and Professor Emeritus at Nagasaki University in Japan, wrote to me, for this report:

> "The international media big notes the "China threat," yet who is the provocateur? We observe the Japanese Prime Minister in Singapore (May 30) offering to lead an international coalition to check Chinese aggression offering 'quality' Japanese naval vessels to obliging clients as with the Philippines and Vietnam. This is madness coming from a nation without official contrition seeking as well to unpick its god-save, the "peace constitution." Meantime, the neo-con government in Australia overreaches with matching rhetoric, together snaring the US Defense Secretary to offer his own "pivot" to the South China Sea. My spin is to let Asian nationalisms (China, Vietnam, Japan, Korea) resolve their own problems diplomatically – after all the central kingdom has been in place for several millennium – outsiders keep out, militarists watch your step, and China rise peacefully."

From Vietnam, saddened by the new wave of hostilities between two Communist neighbors, Vietnam and China, a renowned Western artist who did not want to be identified, explained the situation:

> "I have no doubt the West is delighted at the turn of events and will do all it can to further exacerbate the China-Vietnam etc. rift. Of course it serves the pivot to Asia and other nasty USNATO agendas. But the Vietnamese are just angry at bully China and one can't argue with them about it. The Vietnam's PM has been sending text messages to the entire mobile network warning people not to listen to "bad guys" and to only protest within local and international law..."

It is striking how emboldened and self-assured Vietnam is becoming, lately, considering that it is actually doing an identical thing as China is – drilling in the disputed area.

Many see tensions between Vietnam and China as dating back to the Chinese punitive expedition to Vietnam (after Vietnam entered Cambodia and deposed the Khmer Rouge), known as the Sino – Vietnamese War of 1979. And it is almost bizarre to observe how unforgiving Vietnam is towards China, but how reconciliatory it has become towards the United States.

During the Sino-Vietnamese War some 10,000 Vietnamese civilians lost their lives – definitely not an insignificant number. But how could it even be compared to the millions of Vietnamese civilians who died in the "American War" (or the "Vietnam War" as it is known in the West). During the American War, entire cities were leveled into the ground, fields poisoned, women raped and people burned by napalm and other chemicals.

But, as in case of the Philippines, the creeping Western propaganda erased many of the horrors from people's minds.

I spent 3 years in Hanoi. Holding US citizenship, I was treated with respect and never insulted. In a stark contrast, now Chinese businesses are being attacked and going up in flames, while Chinese people (from Mainland China, but also from Taiwan and elsewhere), are being chased, beaten, and even killed.

In the meantime, RT reported:

> "Visiting Washington, General Fang Fenghui also blamed the Obama administration's "pivot" to Asia as a reason for heightened tensions in the region. He said some Asian nations have used the strategic shift to create mischief in the South and East China Seas."

***

Are we being dragged into the final global confrontation, to a possible WWIII? Observed from Asia Pacific or from Ukraine, it clearly appears so.

Christopher Black has no doubts that provoking, antagonizing and insulting powerful independent countries like Russia and China may be the next step towards the destruction of our human race:

> "All these actions are preparations for war. In fact, the positioning of American anti-ballistic missile batteries in Eastern Europe is in preparation for a nuclear first strike on Russia. Those batteries are deployed solely for the purpose of trying to intercept a retaliatory strike by Russian nuclear forces after a US first strike. They have no other purpose. These preparations for a war of aggression, in fact nuclear war, are a clear violation of the UN Charter and all international laws and can rightly be characterized as war crimes. But since the United States has contempt for all international laws and civilized standards of behavior we can expect these preparations to continue.
>
> Mankind rests on the brink of annihilation for no other reason

than the American pursuit of unlimited profit. They are the extremists of the capitalist system. We must hope that the skillful diplomacy we have seen employed by both Russia and China, the increased pace of their bilateral cooperation with each other and their increased steps to achieve multilateral cooperation throughout the world from Latin American to Africa and Europe and Asia will change the power dynamics of the world sufficiently to prevent the Americans and their allies from achieving their aims so that the peoples of the world can live in peace and devote their energies to solving mankind's pressing problems."

6 June 2014

*****

51

THE LONELINESS OF AN ANTI-IMPERIALIST FIGHTER

It is late at night and you cannot sleep. *Ebrie Lagoon* is right behind the window of your hotel, but it is hardly visible at this hour. You are in Abidjan, Côte d'Ivoire, West Africa.

You are here because you were informed that the President of Ukraine, Petro Poroshenko, also known at 'Chocolate King', has been getting his cocoa from the fields of this country. You are also convinced by several of your sources, based all over the world, that his confectionary empire, *Roshen*, is receiving its basic product from some of the most terrible plantations in Côte d'Ivoire that are still using child labor. You decided to come here, to investigate...

You feel sick, really unwell. You caught some intestinal virus, some terrible infection, while staying for a month in the Indonesian city of Surabaya. There was no time to cure it, or even properly diagnose it. You had to go and work in Jordan, on the Syrian border, between your engagements in Indonesia and Africa.

During nights like this, you feel alone. Totally alone... After each of your books that goes to print, after each film, or essay from some battlefield or other dreadful part of the world, you get many emails; readers are thanking you and encouraging you to write... to write more and more. You are grateful for each letter of support... But you actually cannot increase volume of your writing.

There is no one behind you – no government, no organization and no institution. You are 'senior fellow' at a respectable institute, but it really does nothing for you... it does not even ask you how are you doing, or whether you are alive. They have your name there, on their website, because it is convenient, good for them... That's all.

You know that if your stomach gets worse, you are on your own. You know that if you are going to be arrested or even "disappeared"; you are on your own.

In Surabaya, sick and broken, you were alone. Nobody even cooked and delivered a simple and honest chicken soup to you; nobody stayed by your bed in the evening. You were discouraged to call, to Skype, locally... Your presence there was inconvenient.

You were encouraged by everybody to write. To write more and more... The tone of emails has been suggesting that it is your obligation... You accepted it... Fine... Yes. As an internationalist and fighter, you accepted.

There was a massacre of animals in Surabaya... You were sick. But you went. You covered the story. For free; an entire week of voluntary work... You connected the genocide of local animals, with three genocides that Indonesia has committed against its people, since the 1965 coup. One reader was so impressed that he offered financial support. You thanked him, not really expecting anything. He kept asking you for banking details. You provided them. One week later he informed you that he had instead sent support to some well-funded animal-rights group, as it was easier to transfer funds to them.

While based for that terrible month in Surabaya, you also went back and forth to Thailand and the Philippines, in order to cover events there. After each journey you calculated how to make it through the next month or two, as what you had been producing was funded, from, only what you earned from you work, your several books and countless documentary films.

You are not complaining, not at all. But you want those who keep writing to you... those who keep asking how to be like you, how to be tough and brave like you... you want them to know how it really is. How it is at night... All about loneliness, all about sadness... You want them to think twice, before they embark on the same road.

***

Ok, so it is myself I am talking about, right? We all know that... So I better switch the grammar.

I even paid a salary. Not high, but by local, Surabaya standards – substantial. I wanted to make sure, I hoped that my interviews, those I conducted in Ukraine, Okinawa and the Philippines, would be trimmed and uploaded on YouTube at least. People were dying, and countries ruined by Western imperialism... I was going all around, documenting the struggle and disasters.

But nothing, absolutely no interview, was edited and uploaded. The editor was too busy with her little world and personal issues.

My Japanese editor was also too busy with some local feature film, and the film – debate – between Noam Chomsky and I – had already got delayed by two years. While the book ("On Western Terrorism, from Hiroshima to Drone Warfare") is available through Pluto, London, the film is far from being finished, and I was told that it might actually never be. In 2012, I travelled to war zones to get the footage, again with no outside funding, to illustrate with images, what Noam and I were expressing verbally. I was shot at in El Salvador, a military plane I was on board of, almost crashed in Bolivia. I spent all my savings... The editor kept telling me, that he knows the importance of this discussion, between Noam and I. He insisted on becoming a co-director. But the film was never completed. Just like that: no explanation given whatsoever, except that he is 'lately very busy'.

"Rwanda Gambit", a film about how the West twisted the entire narrative regarding the Rwanda genocide, and then used both Rwandan and Ugandan fascist regimes to plunder The Democratic Republic of Congo, has been rotting at Press TV, totally delayed, as they keep losing the copy somewhere between their London and Teheran offices. 10 million people died so far, the contract is signed, but there seems to be no urgency to air it.

And the television station that is very dear to me (the reason why I do not want to name it here), postponed work on my Okinawa film (about the US air force bases, that can easily trigger

WWIII), because of the World Cup.

***

This essay is not intended to sound like some desperate lament. But it is an honest and sad account, which is trying to demonstrate to readers, that those few of us who are still fighting and bringing to the world detailed investigative pieces that are highly critical of the Empire, are actually totally on our own and almost extinct. I met a few others, recently, and the conclusion is very straightforward: we are all walking on a tightrope, with no security and no protection. Much of our work is not remunerated, anymore. If we fall, then we fall. It is 'our problem'. Many already have. Most of us have.

Often, the regime does not even bother to take us down. We are sitting ducks. We are exposed. We can be 'taken care of' at any moment.

All we get is a steady flow of supportive emails. And plenty of insults, of course...

What I am trying to say is that it is often quite scary at night.

Most of us carry all this, locked inside our hearts. I do. It is bit embarrassing to write about it, openly. But I receive hundreds of emails a month, often asking me 'how do I do it', and 'where I get strength'. So, once every few years, I decide to share with my readers, how it really feels, and what is going on deep inside.

***

Back to what I wrote earlier: it is late at night and you cannot sleep. I am sure something similar used to happen to Ryszard Kapuscinski, as he was on his own in Africa and Central America. I bet Wilfred Burchett went through something similar during the Korean War or while he passed through those dark railroad tunnels, as he approached the devastated city of Hiroshima.

Nights are the worst. Because that is when it all hits you and, no matter whose fault it is, you feel concerned, guilty and often extremely frustrated.

It is not really about you... It is about the films and books, and about all that work that you have done but others refused to polish and bring to the world. It is all about the urgency, because you know that you did something that can easily save many lives, but those you work with are too lazy or too selfish to spend few days doing their job, actually just doing what they are paid to do, anyway... and they are paid from your meager book and film royalties, because that is all that you have... these books and films are results of your sweat and blood, and often of unimaginable risks that you take.

Of course when it comes to a technical piece of work, you do not work with the best. You cannot afford the best... You work with those who wrote to you, stuff like "we admire your work and we want to fight for humanity, along your side..." They come and have some thrills, you trust them... again and again the same game... You want to trust and so you trust... you even begin paying them something, regularly... Then, when they get enough of your world – when they 'have already experienced a bit fun of being part-time revolutionaries' – they leave you, unceremoniously.

And you are alone, with the footage and with the work that was supposed to be distributed... work that was supposed to help the world... help people in different countries, to survive.

You do not ask much, anymore... One interview may take a day to edit, if one is dedicated. You stopped asking much from people, a long time ago. And you stopped, altogether, asking for anything at all for yourself.

"Please, please do not leave this work unfinished", you beg. You never beg anybody for anything, except when it comes to work that could save human lives.

At night, you are scared: "what if it happens again? What if interviews do not get edited... what if films do not get finished... what if, what if..." And it happens like that... It always happens exactly as it happens in your worst nightmares.

And all you dream about, every night is that someone says, kindly: "I will come... You just rest on the couch, not far from me, so you can hear clicking of my keyboard... get some sleep... you fought enough. Now just rest... I will edit those few things for you; for the humanity... It will take just a few days."

***

It is night again. The Ivorian authorities have detained me for several hours, every day. There was some visa screw up... An Internet site said I do not need a visa, another site said I could get one on arrival. Others: French and Americans, were in the same shoes, but after being arrested and threatened with deportation, were soon released.

My local contact is snitching, reporting on me, he is informing on me both to the US embassy and to the local authorities. Like most of the local elites, he is doing it to make his name known to the real rulers of Côte d'Ivoire: those who sit inside the French and the US embassies... and also because he loves to feel important.

The local police does all it can to slow me down. In order to be issued a visa (they insist it has to be a biometric one, so high-tech that even my thick passport has nothing similar glued into it), I have to fill out papers, to be intimidated and harassed by an aggressive female officer, then photographed and fingerprinted.

That's fine, except that the fingerprinting machine and their cameras do not work. Naturally they do not work, as I notice that the plugs to the computer are pulled out. They make me stand for ten minutes each time, maybe 20 times, in front of the camera, in a booth. They scream at me. Then they 'fingerprint me'... For hours... "Your fingers are not good..."

I was fingerprinted in the last 2 weeks in Jordan and Thailand, as well as Kenya: no problem.

"You are in trouble! You go to hospital. Go to a dermatologist and get a certificate that your fingers are no good!"

But they are good.

They grab almost 100 dollars in local currency for the visa but do not give me my passport back.

My contacts inform the US embassy. The embassy sends a car together with their local officer. I demand that I am fingerprinted in front of him. The police refuses: "We already locked the system for your case", which is obviously a literal translation from French. The embassy official is clearly on their side: "We have to respect and follow local procedure". It all drags on for days.

Every day I sneak out and drive to plantations, interviewing people and conducting my research, in this horrid neo-colony of the West, in this police state.

I photograph an enormous French military base "43 Bima". I go to several slums and work there. I talk to the people who are brought to Abidjan from the provinces, mainly children injured on cocoa plantations. The picture is becoming clear.

"They love French people here," I am told.

"Why?"

"Because the new President... he was supported by the French... So now he is pumping pro-Western propaganda to the country..."

I finally give up and go to a dermatologist. It takes the entire half of a day. State clinics are horrid; I am told people die there. The private one is just semi-horrible. I am first made to pay the equivalent of US$60, the monthly salary of the majority. That does not include the 'services'. Water and electricity – all has been privatized: all belongs to the French, the former colonizers – de facto present-day colonizers.

Just as in Senegal, the supermarkets are full of French food; at between 2 and 4 times Parisian prices, with salaries about 30 times lower than in Paris.

"What happens if you get sick and can't pay this clinic?" I ask a lady who is sat next to me.

"You die", she says.

I wait, for about one hour. Then I am led to an office of an ageing and noble looking lady-doctor. I explain everything to her. She listens carefully.

"I do not even have to look at your fingers, right?"

"No", I reply. "This is all because I write against imperialism."

"Imperialism", she replies, with sad expression on her face. "Imperialism, neo-colonialism... You know, here everything is hopeless, because the minds of our people have been colonized. They are serving the West, not their own country..."

She wrote me a paper, stamped it several times, and signed it. It said that my fingers are not good enough to be fingerprinted. She refused to take money. "I am sorry, this is the least I can do."

My driver and I left. We dived into his old Peugeot, but before departing, we saw the doctor running down the stairs, at her age...

"I am so sorry", she said. "The clinic told me that I have to charge you another 60 dollars. For the paper."

We drove to police headquarters, where the same vulgar and monstrous woman began smiling sadistically, even before opening an envelope.

"I don't think we can give you your passport... Maybe not today, anyway... The letter has to be certified."

***

There are assignments when everything goes wrong; everything fails. The place is just totally hopeless, totally sold out.

As I said, in Côte d'Ivoire, my local contacts snitched on me, delivered me to the authorities. My London-based and Ghana-based contacts that were supposed to be arranging details of this work (and thanking me in advance for helping their country) did, eventually, absolutely nothing.

At one point I had only two options: to abort my mission, which was to expose the cocoa trade and its connection to neo-colonialism, or to start from scratch, from the very beginning, alone. As always, I had chosen the latter.

First I made eye contact with a young receptionist at my Pullman Hotel, the only one who was not mean to me, at least so far. I dragged her to a cafe and just trusting my instinct, told her everything: what happened to me, as well as what I was trying to achieve here. "I need a car", I concluded.

"I will get you a good one", she said. "I will also get you a great driver... This is so cool... what you are doing."

It was not cheap but it was worth it. She got me the son of a plantation owner all the way from the Liberian border. He knew all about cocoa. He knew all about child labor... He spoke English. He was an honest Muslim man, happy to exchange ideas about the world. Ten minutes later, we hit the road. This is where the things turned around.

Then I was totally alone in this world – just my driver/translator and me. Nobody knew where I was going.

Soon, I was facing machetes, local workers, as well as bizarre wooden sticks with razor-sharp blades on their end, razors that are causing so many terrible injuries on the cocoa plantations. Soon I will taste the sweetness of cocoa fruits and see tears on the faces of people who would be sharing their stories with me...

As most of the time, I will be unprotected and alone. But as they say in Chile: 'It is better to be alone than badly accompanied'.

***

I got enough information to write several essays on the topic. I also managed to get away, to survive.

While in the Ivory Coast, my latest book "Fighting Against Western Imperialism" had been published.

I am writing this on board Ethiopian Airlines, taking me from Abidjan to Accra and further, to Addis Ababa.

I am crossing the African continent – from West to East. I am glad that I am. And I am glad that I am alive.

I am happy that I am doing exactly what I am doing. I would never trade my life with anyone else.

But then a night will come once again, and with her, a recollection of so many broken hopes and dreams, and promises. And desire; longing, for something permanent and solid. For something that every fighter, every revolutionary desperately needs – a home base and unconditional support.

30 June 2014

*****

52

Mass Murderers are Ruling

INDONESIA, A PROUDLY NAZI NATION?

Indonesians have voted and what votes they have cast! Either they have chosen an outright Nazi, or a populist supported by a bunch of Nazis!

The results are actually too close; it appears that almost half of the active Indonesian voters have endorsed either the Mayor of Jakarta – a former furniture salesman and populist known as 'Jokowi' – or a former general of the National Special Forces – Prabowo Subianto.

Incompetent according to some, populist, if you listen to others, or fierce 'reformer' for quite a substantial group of his supporters, not long ago Mr. Joko 'Jokowi' Widodo appeared to be running almost unopposed. But then the state, intelligence and corporate apparatuses went into gear and the gap 'miraculously' closed.

The 'military camp' deployed nationalist speeches, insults, and flag waving...

And now it is almost even...

Both candidates have declared victory.

Propaganda and 'manipulations' cannot be blamed for everything. There could hardly be any excuse for the great part of the nation being poisoned by racism, a nation submissive to anybody who wears a uniform, who has some power; a nation submissive to market fundamentalism.

Without any doubt, Prabowo Subianto is all that the Indonesian public that desires the continuation of fascist rule can dream of. He is a perfect 21st century Nazi.

He served in the Indonesian National Army Special Force *Kopassus (as*commander of Group 1 *Komando Pasukan Sandhi Yudha (Kopassandha))* during the brutal 1976 occupation, and the genocide that Indonesia committed in East Timor. In that ruthless sadistic orgy of killing and rape, a third of the local population of the tiny nation vanished.

As a reward from his handlers, Mr. Prabowo was later trained (in the 80's) at Fort Benning, in the United States, the country that he is really serving.

And to show his zeal, he was then involved in yet another (and ongoing) genocide, that in Papua.

But even that did not wear him out. In 1998, according to Adam Schwartz, (*A Nation in Waiting)* in a private conversation with Sofyan Wanandi, Prabowo said he was willing "to drive all the Chinese out of the country even if that sets the economy back twenty or thirty years." That's the spirit of a good Indonesian racist!

In the same year – 1998 – troops under his command were busy kidnapping and torturing opposition figures. Countless Chinese women were publicly gang raped.

Prabowo never went to jail.

Those that yearn for fascist continuity in this confused nation can now truly rejoice, by studying their candidate's biography. Prabowo's clan is all about that 'continuity'.

His grandfather was a founder of Bank Negara Indonesia, his father was a cabinet minister in Suharto's government, and as an exemplary son of a... dictatorship, Prabowo himself managed to wed one of Suharto's daughters.

Not that his history is all that different from the biography of the present President Susilo Bambang Yudhoyono (SBY), who was also a general under the Suharto regime, got his 'education' in Fort Benning, USA, in 1976 became a platoon commander in ravaged East Timor, and married the eldest daughter of retired General Sarwo Edhie Wibowo, the very same Indonesian 'hero' who was unable to stop bragging that his military managed to butcher 3 million people during the massacres (or call it again, a genocide) of 1965/66.

Mr. Prabowo and the present Indonesian President, Susilo Bambang Yudhoyono, also studied at the same military academy, in the city of Magelang, as have many other Indonesian leaders. They, most likely, studied the same things, at home and abroad.

***

Many Indonesians are fond of acts of murder and mass murder in general (the homicide rate in Indonesia is twice that of the United States, per capita) and those committed in the 1965/66 in particular, as was clearly shown in the recent documentary film "Act of killing", directed by Joshua Oppenheimer.

After these 2014 elections, Anwar Congo, *jagal* ("Butcher"), one of the main protagonists of the *Act of Killing*, is most likely rejoicing.

In the film, he admitted, looking straight at the television cameras in one of the major Indonesian television studios, that he murdered 1,000 people with his own hands.

As a reward, he received loud applause from the audience, and an admiring grin from the lady moderator.

For sure, *Kopassus* murdered many more people and managed to gain even greater respect...

War criminals and mass murderers are, of course, all over the place, in all national and local Indonesian elections.

To make it 'diverse' ('Unity in Diversity', is a national motto, after all), for instance, General Wiranto is one of the strongest backers of 'Jokowi'; and Wiranto is the same general who on February 24, 2003 was indicted for Crimes against Humanity by a joint UN-East Timorese court.

According to John M. Miller from the "East Timor and Indonesia Action Network":

> *"Others in the 'Jokowi' campaign team are also accused of serious violations of human rights. General AM Hendropriyono has been implicated in the 1989 massacre of civilians of Central Lampung, in the assassination of human rights lawyer Munir while head of Indonesia's intelligence agency (BIN), and in the forced deportation of over 250,000 people from East to West Timor in 1999. Former BIN deputy chief retired Major General Muchdi Purwoprandjono also stands accused of the murder of Munir. A U.S. Department of State cable described Muchdi, a career Kopassus officer, as "one of Indonesia's most vindictive public figures to justice" and placed him "at the heart of one of the nation's human rights tragedies–the 1998-99 abductions of student and pro-democracy activists.*
>
> *Former Jakarta Military Commander Lieutenant General Sutiyoso is accused of torture in Timor-Leste. In 2007, an attempt by Australian investigators to question him about the October 1975 murder of five Australia-based journalists in Balibo, Timor-Leste, caused a diplomatic incident. Sutiyoso was Jakarta's military commander when thugs backed by troops and police attacked the headquarters of the Indonesian Democratic Party in 1996. Retired General Ryamizard Ryacudu is a hardliner known for his xenophobic remarks and criticism of rights activists. As Army Chief of Staff, he oversaw the implementation of Martial Law in Aceh beginning in May 2003."*

***

And at this point, I have to ask one simple if maybe a rhetorical question:

Would many of my readers consider going on vacation, or for work, to Germany, in 1961, just 16 years after 'Adolf Hitler was made to step down'? Would they go there if half of the German folks would have cheerfully cast their ballots in favor of a Nazi candidate, who had been, on top of it, married to a daughter of Hitler (if Hitler had one)? And if that candidate had been a general, or a *Sturmbannführer* of the SS or SA forces, responsible for murdering, torturing and raping civilians somewhere in Ukraine or the former Yugoslavia, or "disappearing" the opposition in his own city, Berlin?

Would that be even thinkable?

Would they close their eyes and ears to the fact that anyone who did not look German and dared to just walk down the street, would be called names (at least in the capital city's suburbs and in all major cities even in the center), had fingers pointed at them... blacks, Chinese, Papuans, even whites?

In Indonesia, everything is being tolerated, because Indonesia is just a myth – a grotesque product of the Western media, while the local media is trained to repeat exactly the same lies, only on a much more primitive level.

'A democracy, a tolerant nation.'

In mythological Indonesian 'democracy', the mainly uneducated population (the Indonesian education system is a disaster) votes for parties that do not represent the majority and belong to the same corporate, feudal and military clique.

Its economic growth is a myth, too. What has grown is the plunder of raw materials, while the country produces close to nothing. Now it even imports rice from abroad. And its official poverty rate is one grand myth – if international norms were to apply, well over 80% of population would be defined as poor.

In this fictional country, in 1965/66, the top Indonesian military brass is true hero! In reality, it committed treason and triggered the killing of 2-3 million of its own people, mainly Left-wing intellectuals, the Chinese minority and atheists, on the explicit orders of the West. Suharto and the others around him were always just the lackeys.

Of course, the religious cadres, Muslim, Hindu and even Christian, had settled their scores with the moderate and constitutional Communists (PKI), simply because they were advocating for social justice and land reforms (religious cadres in Indonesia double as *latifundistas*, historically).

How do I know? I was told by my friend; the former Indonesian President, Abdurrahman Wahid (Gus Dur), who also happened to be a progressive Muslim cleric, and the head of the biggest Muslim organization in the country (NU). Gus Dur was not a 'fictional figure' for a change; he was real! He was also a closet socialist and the only person with great vision, although he was almost blind. Therefore, the elites and the military got rid of him, in a well orchestrated coup.

***

I have covered Indonesia for 15 years. I have written books about this country including *"Indonesia – The Archipelago of*

Fear". A book about this nation, with sub-Sahara African social indicators, but with the inflated pride of a well fed and protected lion. I have made films. I have written countless reports, essays and studies. I also co-authored the last book written by Pramoedya Ananta Toer, the greatest Southeast Asian novelist of all times, "Exile"; the book in which Ananta Toer openly calls Indonesia a fascist state, a collapsed and immoral nation, and a shame.

Pramoedya Ananta Toer was the only Indonesian who ever came close to receiving the Nobel Prize... for anything. Year after year, this former "prisoner of conscience" in the Buru concentration camp was nominated, but the academy would never give the prize to this 'Indonesian Solzhenitsyn', who rotted for years in a horrid pro-Western gulag. When he died, his family gave him a Muslim funeral, although he was an atheist. His comrades sang, like beggars, the International, at the curb. Make-believe place!

***

For 15 years I have listened to farmers in dozens of god-forsaken villages, and even to a bunch of Indonesian businessmen.

One tycoon told me, in Sumatra:

> "We need Adolf Hitler! In order to fully restore law and order."

He loved Adolf... Many in Indonesia do.

For all those years I could not stop writing and researching! Despite all those trolls deployed by the Indonesian regime and the West, to discredit me and anybody who dares to shout that the 'emperor has no clothes.'

To write about Indonesia is a totally ungrateful job. They spit at you there and abroad, if you dare to write the truth. That is why almost nobody does.

But I kept writing, as a warning to the world (an example of what happens to a country fully abandoned to a perverse bunch of looters, and to Western neo-colonialism; a concept of extreme brutality) because what I have seen, witnessed and heard, was bordering on the 'impossible'. I kept thinking: "a country like this cannot really exist on this planet. And if it does, it cannot really get away with it, can it?"

But it really exists and it gets away with everything. Especially the elites do! Local elites – that perfect Nazi, racist (now all ethnicities belonging to that gang have become hopelessly racist), brainwashed gang, consisting of angry serfs, full of arrogance but also of inferiority complexes. More insecure, more brutal and murderous...

This gang kills people, poisons rivers, conducts full deforestation, poisons the air, robs cities of parks and sidewalks, as well as of any cultural institutions... It privatizes all public assets and throws the nation to an absolute dark nihilism, insecurity, ignorance and indefinable fear.

And it rules the country. And it gets elected!

And for the poor, the great majority of Indonesians, what is left? It is the Democratic Republic of Congo (DRC) slammed onto the extreme of Southeast Asia. Similar, but with luxury hotels and malls, and with corrupt leaders, with the local and foreign media (and the Australian National University next door, with its 'Indonesian lobby' and shameful lies that Indonesia is a 'normal country', like Brazil...) covering the entire insanity of it all, presenting it as a 'normal country' to its own people and to the world.

My Ugandan colleague who proofreads my essays, always comments: "It is like Uganda; damn, exactly, exactly like home!"

Uganda is, of course, yet another horrid and Fascist client state of the West, which is devouring its own people, and alongside Rwanda, murdering millions in the neighboring DRC.

It is all so similar. It is exactly the same. Indonesia devoured between 1 and 3 million of its own citizens in the 1965/66 cleansing period, and then committed two monstrous genocides in the neighboring countries that it shamelessly occupied – East Timor and Papua. Papua is an on-going genocide, committed in full view of the world, and totally under-reported, for obvious reasons...

Any sanctions against Indonesia, for the genocide? ...For the third genocide in just half of century? No?

As I was writing this, my friend, a leading Australian historian and Professor Emeritus at Nagasaki University, told me over a coffee:

> *"The question is; what is the United States doing right now, in Jakarta? What is it doing, inside those 300 rooms they have inside the embassy – the CIA, the Pentagon, the economists?*

> *There are huge interests at stake there, right now! What protagonist would fit the best to their interests? Is Washington favoring old military elites dating to Suharto, or an unknown populist? All we know is that Washington and Canberra revoked visa restrictions on Prabowo. They prepared for his Presidency, in case it happens... We all know how closely he is linked to the US, through Kopassus..."*

Identically, like the Rwandan leadership and the ongoing genocide in DRC it is committing, the Indonesian military is covered, given immunity by the West, because it is killing and plundering (Papuans and others, now and in the past) on behalf of Washington, London and Canberra.

You cannot touch the Indonesian elites, and you cannot touch the Rwandan ones. You cannot touch them; and you cannot cover them or expose them, fully, in the mainstream.

Therefore, mass murderers are ruling with no fear in Jakarta, Kigali and Kampala.

So back to the original question: would my readers consider going on vacation to a country where half of the people had just expressed their support for the Nazis?

11 July 2014

*****

53

The New Cold War

MH17: SACRIFICED AIRLINER

The special train carrying refrigerated corpses from the MH17 catastrophe has left the station of Torez, just a few miles from the crash site. People, who died a terrible death onboard the Malaysia Airlines Boeing 777-200, will soon be reunited with their grieving families. They will receive a proper funeral, and will be laid to rest in the Netherlands, Malaysia and several other countries. They are on their way home, at last.

The Ukrainian rebels handed over the black boxes to international authorities. The investigation can begin. It hopefully will begin, unobstructed by political maneuvering.

Will the Empire allow the investigation to follow its course? The Western propaganda machine is in full gear. The twisting of facts, obscuring of evidence, and maneuvering public opinion all over the world: all this is being done with determination and routinely applied precision.

So much is at stake! Increasing cooperation between Russia, Latin America and China could mean the end of Western neo-colonial control of the world. The creation of alternatives to the

World Bank can free billions of human beings from market feudalism and its slavery. Powerful news organizations broadcasting from Russia (RT), Venezuela (TeleSur) and Iran (Press TV) are consistently breaking the depressing and nihilistic monopoly of Western propaganda and control of people's brains all over the world.

The more liberating these trends and waves are for the world, the more panic there is in Washington, London and Paris, but also on Wall Street and in the City, as well as in the newsrooms of the corporate media.

The West is terrified. Its 'exceptionalism', tremendous profits from controlling everything that moves on this planet, the kick of being in charge and holding the whip, all this can disappear if these waves of resistance are not reversed!

And the villains are damned Russia and Putin, who is refusing to yield. Putin is despicable, and a real nuisance in the eyes of the Empire, because he is unwilling to sacrifice, or to destroy his own country as Yeltsin had done two decades earlier. The villains are also those bloody Chinese, because they are sticking to their ideals, to socialism the Chinese way, while lifting hundreds of millions of people out of poverty. The other villains are those bastards from Latin America, with their big dreams and humanism, their revolutions and sudden refusal to sacrifice their own people for the wellbeing of the Western elites.

And all of them – these three disobedient parts of the world, three cohorts – are now getting closer and closer together, forging an as yet undefined alliance, but an alliance nevertheless, increasing cooperation, signing treaties, creating alternative organizations, and saying "No!" to the world order. And more countries are looking at all this with hope; more are joining the club of the free. Not absolutely free, but free from Western colonial terror, which is now perhaps the worst kind of terror that exists on this planet (including those horrid derivates of the regime, implanted all over the planet).

To fight these dissident nations openly, to do it on ideological or moral grounds, is impossible. They would most certainly not lose! By now it should be too obvious, it should be too clear who is on the 'right and wrong sides of history'.

Therefore, the "smear" is the only way for the Empire to advance its destructive cause. Or at least it is the most effective way. The good old way of discrediting one's enemy, was by dragging him through filth, by turning his achievements into failures, his heroic resistance into hideous crimes. The Brits perfected this, ruling their colonies for centuries, by deceit and perverse philosophical concepts. The German Nazis were fairly effective as well.

The way it stands, there is nothing good that Russia can do. There is nothing decent about China (it is Communist when it suits Western propaganda or 'more capitalist than traditionally capitalist countries are', when it fits the bill). Venezuela with its direct democracy is dictatorial. And so on.

And now the plane... The second Malaysian Boeing 777 lost in one single year... Both belonged to one of the best airlines on earth, with a great maintenance record for its equipment! Strange, very strange... But Russia is certainly to blame. Because the President of the United States said so, because the British PM said so... No proof is needed. The Western public is extremely obedient.

Now the bodies are going! From a small Torez station, they are going home, wrapped in bags.

They are victims of something that many decent people all over the world are even afraid to formulate in their minds.

The area of Eastern Ukraine that they – the corpses – are now leaving, is full of local victims, too – those civilian victims of ethnic cleansing, whose only fault is that their maternal tongue happened to be Russian, or that they do not or cannot live in a country run by the pro-Western fascist dictatorship of the 'Chocolate King', Poroshenko, and his gangsters.

Now civilians are dying, every day. That does not bother the Western regime. Killing the rebels, their families and neighbors, is encouraged. Burning people in Odessa, burning them alive, is not even criticized in the lackey corporate media. The entire debate and coverage of events has become grotesque and sick.

More then 100,000 people have recently crossed into Russia, seeking refuge from Ukrainian bombers and rockets, or perhaps more, most likely much more.

Russian lives do not count. Asian lives do not count. African lives do not count. Middle Eastern lives do not count. The lives of Latin Americans do not count. That is why the West so freely and without hesitation has murdered tens of millions of 'unpeople', for decades and centuries.

The formula is simple: Dutch tourists do count. Ukrainian villagers don't. It was quite similar during Nazi control of Europe.

***

Right after the tragedy, the legendary thinker and Chief Editor of "The Greanville Post", Patrice Greanville, summarized the events and predicted what is coming. He did it with deadly accuracy:

> *"The US TV networks —the West's Ministry of Truth organs— and other media have been blabbering almost nonstop for the past few hours about the Malaysian airliner down in Ukraine.*
>
> *In the early reports on CBS, ABC, etc., I perceive a marked tendency to suggest "Russia or her proxies did it", in this case also involving the "Pro-Russia separatists" in East Ukraine, who supposedly "have been shooting at planes" (the implication is indiscriminately) in their struggle against Kiev's all-out military offensive.*
>
> *As you probably agree, this is either an outright blatant provocation by the West, or a direct result of Washington's criminal policies in Ukraine.*
>
> *It's easy to determine several scenarios in varying degrees of plausibility and culpability. While it's plausible the plane was shot down by Eastern Ukraine separatists, it's also obvious they (and Russia) have little to gain from such an act. So at worst, it can be argued it was simply an error on their part.*
>
> *Indeed, if the plane was shot down by a missile, it* could *have been fired* accidentally *by the East Ukraine rebels—perfectly understandable given the horrible pounding they've been taking by Kiev's air force, etc.*
>
> *The second type of suspect involves not error but direct intention and therefore full moral culpability. Here the lineup is clear, as the shot could have come from Kievan forces in the region, seeking to heighten tensions as per script, or [from] a third party working for the West...*
>
> *As usual, the larger context, that the US is the principal and very real meta-cause of this tragedy, will be lost to most in America...*
>
> *Welcome to the new, even higher stakes Cold War, courtesy of the usual bastards in Washington, and their accomplices around the world.*

> *The problem for us now is how to counter the inevitable propaganda wave sure to follow. Brace yourselves for the barrage of hypocrisy and sanctimonious accusations to pour out of Washington's mouthpieces."*

All this was happening while I was working in Cambodia, trying to counter another fully perverse narrative manufactured by the West in this tortured country, several decades ago.

I met my friend, a fellow war correspondent, Andrew Marshall, and asked him, theoretically, about the coverage of similar events. Andrew is the former head of *Reuters* in Iraq, who later resigned from the agency because it refused to publish his critical findings about the Thai establishment and its 'elites' (I will be soon publishing my full interview with him). He offered his thoughts on the issue of the downed passenger jet. The point he was making: whatever the answer to 'The question' is (who is responsible for the act itself?), it does not change the wider geopolitical and ethical issue:

> *"There is a tendency in the 21st century World of 24-hour rolling news coverage to overemphasize and dramatize individual incidents in a conflict, subjecting them to intense coverage, while at the same time failing to analyze the underlying causes and patterns of conflict. The task of analyses is to focus on the "signal", not the "noise", but most modern media do the opposite. It's also clearly true that powerful global interests seek to control the narrative by staging events to drown out the signal with noise. Some opponents of this strategy seek to create their own "noise", trying to undermine the dominant narrative. In many instances it is justified, but a focus on the noise rather than signal can be counterproductive.*
>
> *For example, I believe the overwhelming evidence of what happened on 9/11 is that men associated with Al Qaeda flew planes into the World Trade Center and the Pentagon. This was then exploited by the United States to justify a disastrous "war on terror" in the Muslim world.*
>
> *The modern news media seize on incidents such as MH17, or 9/11, to exemplify a wider struggle. But in fact, in conflict, all sides tend to commit atrocities sometimes, and all sides make mistakes. In any conflict, innocents on all sides, and innocents unconnected with any side, routinely suffer. This is tragic. But sensible analysts need to avoid conflating the horror and blame of specific incidents within a conflict with the overall moral calculus of the conflict. The two are totally unconnected."*

***

Soon, things began to crystalize. As Western propaganda howling reached a crescendo, I contacted another trusted source, Sergei Kirichuk, the leader of the 'Borodba' movement, an influential left-wing organization in Ukraine, which is fully opposed to the Kiev junta, but at the same time maintains its independence, and cannot be defined as fully 'pro-Russian'. He replied at length, and I have translated most of his quote for this essay:

> *"Without any doubt, the tragedy of the Malaysian airliner has become the most significant political event of the last few years. The tragic death of innocent people shook public opinion in Ukraine and in the entire world. Unfortunately, the circumstances of the tragedy and the information related to it, offers more questions than answers. First, and the most important question, is how did a passenger airliner happen to be in the epicenter of the military conflict? In all those days leading to the tragedy, the mass media was carrying stories about attempts by the insurgents (both successful and unsuccessful attempts) to down airplanes belonging to the Ukrainian military. Earlier it was announced that the airspace was declared closed for civilian aviation. Besides, MH17 deviated significantly from its usual flight path; routinely it was flying more to the south. Answers to these questions should be given through an international investigation.*
>
> *The second important question is based on the claim by the Ukrainian security services, related to some "intercepted communication of the terrorists", that the 'terrorists' were the ones who downed the plane. This communication appears to be a clear fabrication, fake, but were it to be genuine, it would provoke even more questions towards the Ukrainian security services: would it mean that they were able to monitor the communications of their adversaries, were familiar with their plans, but did nothing to prevent the tragedy?*
>
> *The most terrible thing is that the tragedy of innocent people who lost their lives is being used by Ukrainian mass media as some sort of justification for the loss of lives of the civilian population in Donbas. The onslaught of the Government forces began with renewed zeal, not caring at all, anymore, about the losses among the armed forces or civilian population.*
>
> *Besides that, pro-NATO elements now believe that there is solid justification for the invasion of Ukraine by Western forces..."*

***

But a leading international lawyer, Christopher Black (he has investigated genocides and crimes against humanity all over the world), based in Toronto, Canada, went even further, and declared in a letter to me:

> *"The downing of the Malaysian airliner was either an accident by the Kiev forces or the anti-fascist forces of the Donetsk Republic, in each instance targeting the plane because they thought that it was a military and therefore a legitimate target, or it was a deliberate attack on a known civilian aircraft. If it was deliberate then it is a case of mass murder and a war crime since it took place in the midst of hostilities. I wouldn't call it an act of terrorism as some have said as an act of terrorism is designed to create fear and panic in a population. Clearly those who downed the plane had other motives than creating fear and panic among civilians.*
>
> *Many writers over the past few days have commented that neither the DPR forces nor Russia had either the equipment in place to hit neither the plane nor the motive to deliberately shoot it down. But there is strong circumstantial evidence that the forces of the Kiev regime had the means, the opportunity and the motive. They had the equipment and engaged in very suspicious actions; they had BUK anti-aircraft systems in place for unknown reasons since the DPR forces have no aircraft, the Ukraine Air Traffic Control ordered the plane's crew to divert from the regular more southerly route to go north over the combat zone, a Ukraine jet fighter was recorded by Russian radar climbing rapidly towards it just before it went down, and, within minutes of the crash, it was the Kiev regime and its masters in Washington and London who cried loudly that it was the DPR and Russians who were to blame without a shred of evidence to support the claim. And now we know that the Ukraine SBU immediately seized the ATC radar tapes and do not appear to have handed them over to international investigators.*
>
> *Kiev and Washington also had the motive: to smear Russia and the anti-fascist forces and to provoke the EU to abandon its political and economic relations with Russia. It does not take a Hercule Poirot or Sherlock Holmes to conclude the most likely suspects are in Kiev and Washington not in Donetsk and Moscow.*
>
> *President Putin has insisted on an objective international investigation since the news broke while President Obama and his minions in Kiev have done nothing but call for the head of Putin. History shows that President Putin has insisted on*

> *adherence to international law and civilized behavior consistently throughout his terms in office. His integrity is unquestioned, whereas President Obama has been consistent in his calls for war, war and more war in every region of the globe and insists that the Americans are "exceptional" and above the law and judgment.*
>
> *It may be that the results of an independent investigation of this tragic and terrible event will have consequences for the United States that are beyond its imaginings and that will erase any remaining influence or credit that it may still have in the world. They have committed many crimes. This may be the one crime too many."*

***

The presentation of logical arguments and proof, by Moscow, by the rebels, and even by some dissidents inside the Western regime, has not changed the dogged and extremist position of the Empire. But why should it, really, if the entire scenario had been, most likely, manufactured (or at least manipulated) by the neo-con mafia in Washington and by their counterparts in European capitals?

At some point, The Wall Street Journal reported in its article, "Russia Presents Its Account of Malaysia Airlines Flight 17 Crash," and it was refreshing that at least some quotes 'from the other side' were able to make it into the mainstream Western media:

> *"Russia's Defense Ministry on Monday presented its first detailed account of the final moments of Malaysia Airlines Flight 17, saying Russian radar had spotted a second aircraft in the vicinity shortly before the crash and that satellite imagery showed Ukraine had moved missile systems into the area before the incident.*
>
> *At a news conference, air force chief Igor Makushev didn't say who the ministry thought had fired the missile that apparently brought down the airliner on Thursday.*
>
> *In an elaborate presentation displaying radar and satellite imagery, Mr. Makushev said it was likely that the second airplane was a Ukrainian fighter jet. He also showed satellite photos allegedly portraying several Buk ground-to-air missile systems in the area close to where the plane crashed. The systems, he said, could only belong to the Ukrainian military. Ukraine has accused Russia of giving the rebels a Buk system, with which they then shot down the passenger jet.*

> *Mr. Makushev said the airplane deviated from its course by 14 kilometers, but then attempted to return to its course, before crashing shortly after.*
>
> *He said Russia is prepared to hand all of the information it has to European authorities, which included satellite imagery and data from its own radars."*

***

But there was much more to it – proof after proof painstakingly put together by the Ministry of Foreign Affairs of the Russian Federation. And one is only left to wonder how many 'objective' and 'well-informed' European and US citizens ever read these accounts.

It is becoming clear and obvious, that even at the height of the so called Cold-War, citizens of the Soviet Union, even countries like Romania, were much better informed and knew more about the lines of thought of their adversaries, than the arrogant and thoroughly brainwashed Westerners now know about the points made by the people in the countries designated as their enemies.

But back to the Russian response:

The Wall Street Journal was referring to what occurred on July 21, 2014, at a Special Briefing by the Ministry of Defense of the Russian Federation on the crash of the Malaysian Boeing 777 in Ukrainian air space, the speech was given by the Deputy Chief of the General Staff of the Armed Forces of the Russian Federation, Lieutenant-General A.V. Kartapolov. For those who are interested in what Russia has to say, these briefings are indispensable.

I worked for several hours, on improving the original translation, while trying to keep the original tone in which this was presented.

General Kartapolov argued that:

> *"After the Malaysia Airlines Boeing-777 accident on July 17, studying the international flight-plan for, Amsterdam – Kuala Lumpur, we can find a quantity of conflicting information. In this case, the Russian Federation Ministry of Defense considers it necessary to submit the information which is at the General Staff's disposal. On the scheme you can see the international flight-path. The Boeing-777 was supposed to fly on this flight-path. Draw your attention to the fact that the aircraft was flying inside the specified air corridor to Donetsk, but then it deviated north from the route. Meanwhile the maximum*

> *distance from the left border of the air corridor was 14 kilometers.*
>
> *Then we can see that the Boeing-777 turned back to the borders of the specified air corridor. Nevertheless, the Malaysian aircrew didn't perform the maneuver successfully. At 17.20 the aircraft began registering a rate reduction, at 17.23 the aircraft's point blinked off on the radar. Why did the aircraft cross the border of the air corridor? Was it a navigation mistake, or the aircrew following the Dnepropetrovsk ground control orders? We will find out the answers after the decoding of the "black boxes" and communications. According to our information on the day of the accident, the Ukrainian Armed Forces deployed 3 to 4 artillery batteries of Buk-M1 missile systems not far from Donetsk. The system can hit targets at a distance of up to 35 kilometers, and at an altitude, up to 22 kilometers. Why did the Ukrainian Armed Forces deploy these air defense units in the Donetsk region? As we know militants don't have any aircraft.*
>
> *On the scheme we can see that both the projected impact point and the flight-path are inside the air defense battle zone of the Ukrainian Armed Forces' Buk-M1 missile system. We have satellite photos of the Ukrainian Air Defense systems deployed in the Southeast of the country."*

Then the photos of the Buk are shown, near Luhansk and Donetsk. The first three photos are dated July 14, 2014. There are photos from that day to the day of the accident: launchers, radar, all belonging to the Ukrainian military.

After the painstaking photo presentation, the General continued:

> *"I want to expose the airspace situation in the Donetsk area that day. In the picture you can see the information of the objective air traffic control between 17.10 to 17.30 Moscow time.*
>
> *During that period, there were 3 civilian aircraft:*
>
> *Flight from Copenhagen to Singapore at 17.17;*
>
> *Flight from Paris to Taipei at 17.24*
>
> *Flight from Amsterdam to Kuala Lumpur... Beside it, the Russian system for air traffic control detected a Ukrainian Air Force aircraft, supposedly a Su-25, moving upwards towards the Malaysian Boeing-777. The distance between two aircraft was 3-5 kilometers.*
>
> *The Su-25 can gain an altitude of 10,000 meters in a short time.*

It is armed with an air-to-air missile R-60, which is able to lock-on and destroy a target at a distance of 12 kilometers, and destroy it definitely at a distance of 5 kilometers. What was the mission of the combat aircraft, in the flight-path of civilian aircraft, almost at the same time and same altitude with the civilian craft? We want to have this question answered.

The video of the Rostov Aerial Center of the Joint Air Traffic Management System can provide the information. The Chief of Staff of the Air Force, Lieutenant-General Igor Makushev, will comment on the video."

Then the Chief of Staff of the Air Force of the Russian Federation, Lieutenant-General I.Y. Makushev presents his arguments:

"Today the aircraft Air Traffic Control has acquired some objective control materials from the Rostov Aerial Center of the Joint Air Traffic

Management System. The video presents the air control information on the airspace situation in the region of Donetsk in the period from 17.19 P.M. to 17.25P.M., Moscow time, on July 17, 2014. In the upper left corner there is a Boeing-772 mark, as it was following the route from Copenhagen to Singapore. Under this dot, there is another aircraft – it is marked as Boeing-777, which is on its way from Amsterdam to Kuala Lumpur. And on its right there is a Boeing-778 mark making its way from Delhi to Birmingham. All these three aircraft have been steadily monitored by the three radar stations of the air traffic control of the Ministry of Defense of the Russian Federation. The Boeing-777 is moving towards the Russian Federation state boundary, and is to cross it at the point of «TONAK». An air traffic control officer has been controlling the aircraft flight and keeps on enquiring for its flight variables to compare them with the given ones. At 17.20 P.M. at a distance of 51 kilometers from the Russian Federation state boundary and the azimuth of 300° (degrees), the aircraft started to lose its speed inexplicably, which is to be seen quite distinctively on the table of the aircraft characteristics. At 17.21.35 (seconds) P.M. with the aircraft at a speed of 200 km/h, at the point of the Boeing crash, there is a new mark of an aircraft to be seen. The radar stations of Ust-Donetsk and Butirinskoe, during the 4 minute period, steadily monitored the aircraft. The Air Traffic Control officer, having enquired for the characteristics of newly appeared aircraft but couldn't possibly get them, because it is in all likelihood that the aircraft had no secondary deduction system mounted on it, which is typical of military aircraft. The early detection of this aircraft appeared to be quite impossible because those radars work in a standby mode and usually perform the air situation control. Detection possibilities at the given distance are over 5000 m altitude.

The detection of the aircraft turned out to be possible as soon as the aircraft ascended.

The further aircraft flight variables changed. It was now flying in the area of the Boeing crash and was monitoring the situation. Earlier the Ukrainian officials reported that on the day of the Boeing-777 accident, there were no military aircraft flying in the region. So, as you can see, it does not appear to be true.

...We also have some questions for our US partners. According to the statement of the US representatives, they have some pictures from space supporting that the militants launched the missile. But nobody has seen these pictures.

According to our records from 17:06 till 17:21 Moscow time on the July 17 over the Southeastern territory of Ukraine, a US space satellite flew overhead. This is a special device of the experimental space system designed to detect and track various missile launches. If the US party has photos made by the satellite, please let us ask them to show them to world community for further investigation.

Is it a coincidence or not? However, the time of the Malaysian Boeing-777 accident and the time of the observation done by the satellite over the Ukrainian territory are the same. In conclusion, I would like to mention that all the concrete information is based on the objective and reliable data of the different Russian equipment, in contrast to the accusations of the US against us, made without any evidence. A good example of such facts is that some mass media showed the transportation of a Buk-M1 missile system from Ukrainian to Russian territory. We can clearly see that it is a frame-up. These pictures were taken in the city of Krasnoarmeisk, which is confirmed by a banner situated close to the road. This banner has an address of the car shop situated at No. 34, Dnepropetrovskaya Street. Since May 11th, the Krasnoarmeysk city has been under the control of the Ukrainian Armed Forces. That is why we have some questions. What kind of launching system is it? Where is it being transported? Where is it now? Why is it completely unloaded? What was the last time it launched missiles? To end my speech I would like to emphasize that the Russian Federation did not deliver any Buk-M1 missiles systems to the militants, and any other such equipment. All the data compiled by the Ministry of Defense of the Russian Federation will be transmitted today to the experts of the European countries and Malaysia...

The Ministry of Defense will continue to inform you about the newly revealed facts connected with the air disaster of Malaysian Boeing-777.

***

Now why on earth should we not believe this presentation, backed by facts, images and concrete analyses?

Western and Ukrainian lies are piling up: wobbly explanations or no explanations at all for change of 777's course, lowering altitude, 'bad weather', and revealing testimony of the Spanish traffic controller working in Ukraine...

And why should we believe people like the current President of the United States, who openly bragged about US 'exceptionalism', at the military academy, which has been responsible for producing countless mass murderers?

And for the sake of objectivity, why would we not listen to the Russians, before imposing sanctions on them, for something that we are, most likely, responsible for, ourselves?

And although it is most likely that the pro-Western Ukrainian military shot down the plane, even if it were to be the other side that did it, the entire conflict began with the EU and the US destabilizing Ukraine, overthrowing the legitimate government, and igniting the war.

Angry Dutch families of the victims should stop pointing fingers at Russia. Instead they should go to Brussels and Washington to express their wrath and to demand justice.

***

And what about Malaysia and Indonesia? Indonesia lost 12 people on that ill-fated flight.

Most of the Southeast Asian countries are historically "client" states of the West, with hardly any independent, non-corporate media. Indonesia has been exactly that since the 1965 'events'. Malaysia, pushing for an independent course under Dr. Mahathir's rule, is presently being lured by the US, which is trying to establish military bases there, or to at least gain access to existing Malaysian ones.

Suddenly, a great amount of US funding has been unleashed, to win over Malaysian intellectuals, some of the most shamefully subservient in the region. Several have already began departing for conferences, cultural exchanges and writer's retreats, to destinations all over the United States, all expenses paid.

In Kuala Lumpur, there was deadly silence after the downing of MH17. Not one writer or filmmaker that I know and contacted wanted to go on record. One mistaken word and the entire rosy dream of Western 'funding' would go up in flames.

Only the official anti-Russian narrative was available.

Two filmmakers spoke, but off the record:

> *"To be honest, Malaysians are completely out of touch with what's happening or even with the political consequences of the 'deal' that our Prime Minister had made to bring the bodies back. No one has even questioned what the deal was. There is no discussion whatsoever, even in the educated circles as it's taboo to even start talking about anything other than the people who died. All Malaysians care about is that it's tragedy and that we should feel sad. But largely, Russia and Putin are the villains in the mind of Malaysians."*

In Indonesia, theories vary. Some are far, remote from the war in Ukraine.

Mr. Agus Suhartono, a former aeronautical engineer at PT. Dirgantara Indonesia, thinks that Malaysia has been punished for creating an alternative banking system for the Muslim world:

> *"I think it is bit strange. How could a plane at an altitude of more than 30,000 ft be a mistaken missile target? At that altitude, the plane identification should be very clear. Whoever fired knew perfectly well what he was doing. The question should be why MAS (Malaysia Airlines) again? Did they rub somebody the wrong way? Why was Malaysia the target twice in a row? I think maybe because the financial turnover of the Arab world is centered in Kuala Lumpur. Malaysia is the gate. The sharia gate of the Arab financial world."*

***

New sanctions are being leveled against Russia. "Cold Warriors" in Canada, Australia, UK and US are back in their saddles, like Major Kong in the unforgettable film, "Dr. Strangelove, or: How I Learned to Stop Worrying and Love the Bomb", they are ready to cover their skulls with cowboy hats, and stick A-bombs between their legs. Time to 'go and bomb the Russkies'.

Arabs are not tough enough adversaries, and most of the Muslim world is now in ruins anyway, thanks to the 'War on... ehm... terror'.

Russia and China are again blocking the West from fully controlling the world. 'How dare they?'

The most frightening thing is the state of the self-righteousness and self-deception of the Western public. One wants to scream: Don't they see? Do they refuse to see? Is it more comfortable not to see? How long are they going to pretend that they are blind? Or maybe they are blind...

After the MH17 tragedy and after the way it has been handled by the Western mass media, there is no doubt that we are back to the Cold War again. It is not just a war against Russia. The war is reflected in the arms race that is being accelerated by the US in Asia, from the revolting, racist anti-Chinese propaganda, and from the attempts to overthrow our socialist governments in Latin America.

We should never forget that Western imperialism murdered tens of millions of innocent people all over the world, after the Nagasaki 'A-bomb' and the official end of the WWII: all those crimes and horror to satisfy its unbridled obsession with controlling the world.

Tens of millions of lives already lost.

Why should they spare some 298 of those on MH17?

25 July 2014

*****

54

CAMBODIA AND WESTERN FABRICATION OF HISTORY

As we enter the small city of Anlong Veng in the Dângrêk Mountains, located in the northwest of Cambodia, it begins to rain. The rain is powerful, but it is, after all a tropical rain, and it ends as unexpectedly as it begins.

We drive over the bridge, over some sort of dam, and suddenly, there is a beautiful but eerie lake in front of us.

"Just few years ago, this was the last stronghold of Khmer Rouge", explained my friend, Song Heang. "Then, it was impossible to drive here just like that. There were no houses around. And the lake was like a swamp, impossible to cross."

We drove all the way here, to visit the compound of the last military leaders of the Khmer Rouge, Ta Mok, the military chief, known as "Brother Number Five" or "the Butcher". This is where he lived and this is where he commanded his troops from.

Ta Mok, the right hand of Pol Pot. Ta Mok, who split the movement, put Pol Pot under house arrest and most likely poisoned him. Ta Mok who commanded the army of several thousand Khmer Rouge loyalists, between 1979, when the Vietnamese forces ousted his movement from power, until 1999, when he was captured by government forces. Ta Mok died in custody in 2006, without ever being properly tried, or sentenced.

Ta Mok's personal security man, his bodyguard who lived with him for years, San Reoung, is expecting us.

He is missing his left leg, and that is common among Cambodian civilians and combatants of his age. Ta Mok also lost one leg in the fighting.

There is actually only one thing that I want to know: how Communist was the Khmer Rouge, and was it the ideology, the Marxist ideology, that drew farmers to the ranks of the movement?

San Reoung thinks for a while, then replies, weighing each word:

> "It was really not about the ideology... We did not know much about it. I was, for instance, very angry with the Americans. I became a soldier at the age of 17. And my friends were very angry, too. They joined Khmer Rouge *to fight Americans*, and especially the corruption of their puppet dictator Lon Nol, in Phnom Penh."

Were people in the countryside aware of what was going on in the capital, before KR took power?

"Of course they were. The US gave so much support, so much money, to the corrupt Lon Nol regime. Everybody knew where it all went to: to countless lavish parties, to fancy prostitutes... The US bombed our countryside to the ground. Hundreds of thousands of people died. People went mad, they were indignant. And so many of them joined Khmer Rouge as a result."

"Not because of Marxist ideology?" I asked again.

San Reoung replies, immediately:

"Of course not. The great majority had no idea about Marxism, they had never heard about it".

I visit the compound of Ta Mok. I enter an old wagon, a communications center, used by Pol Pot a few decades ago. It is now empty and rusty. The entire compound has become some sort of an informal museum. I refuse to go to the former living-quarters of Ta Mok. I don't see the point of doing it.

Instead, I stare at the lake for quite some time.

Having worked for many years in this part of the world, I got to understand that all the answers to the important questions about Cambodia and its past, lie in its countryside. The West, for decades, managed to corrupt Phnom Penh, by paying almost everyone that matters there, to repeat and to perfect a twisted and clichéd narrative.

The NGOs, journalists – they are all shouting about the "Communist" genocide in Cambodia. It has become a well-remunerated job, the source of an incessant flow of funding, a complex lie backed by the Western propaganda machine, academia and the mainstream press.

The Khmer Rouge was a brutal force, of course, but definitely not a 'Communist' genocidal monster. And it did not appear out of the blue.

***

I ask Song Heang whether what we heard in Anlong Veng was correct. We are slowly gaining speed, on the way to the disputed and bloodstained temple, Preah Vihear, on the Cambodian-Thai border.

Song Heang works for a small Australian charity organization, which is building little rural libraries for children. He hates the Khmer Rouge. But he readily agrees that there was very little that was 'Communist' about them:

He is good natured and even-headed:

> "As a child, I lived along the Mekong River, in the village of Prek Tamak, some 65 kilometers from Phnom Penh. When the Americans were bombing, everything stopped and people got petrified... There, they used those very fast planes; jetfighters, and local people called them 'Amich' – fast ones... Many people then joined Khmer Rouge. They did not know what Communism was. They only knew how horrible the pro-Western government in Phnom Penh was."

"Why do people in Phnom Penh keep repeating that Pol Pot conducted 'Communist Genocide'? Why, like in the rest of Southeast Asia, is China being demonized? And why is Vietnam demonized ?" I ask.

"We are a very poor country", replies Song Heang. "And if our people in Phnom Penh get money, they just like the money, and say exactly what they are paid to say. And the US and the European Union are pushing lots of money for certain statements."

***

In Phnom Penh, there are new malls now, and countless new and second-hand luxury vehicles, for the very rich and very corrupt.

The city has embarked fully on the savage capitalist road, not unlike Jakarta, another Asian urban nightmare. Except that Phnom Penh has at least some impressive French colonial villas, a beautiful riverfront and several good galleries and museums.

But its urban area of around 2.2 million people has no public transportation system (except a few buses), and its public health system and education are in an appalling state.

Its long-serving, dictatorial and brutal Prime Minister, Hun Sen, is both a former Battalion Commander of the Khmer Rouge, and, "free market and multi-party liberal democracy" champion. Although periodically criticized by the West for human rights violations, the West is generally happy with the market fundamentalism applied here, as well as with the virtual absence of coherent social policies.

For years, I have observed a great number of 'advisors', particularly from the European Union, 'shaping the course' of the Cambodian economy, and of its society in general.

Which, of course, includes its history. Advisers say certain things in public, and others behind the closed doors.

Eight years ago I wrote:

> "In one of the terrace cafés frequented by foreign experts, the atmosphere is relatively relaxed. Men from the U.N. and E.U. drink beer, hand in hand with their local "second wives," unwinding after a tough working day in this chaotic capital. They perform diverse tasks in this country, which used to be marked by some of the worst violence known to humankind. Some are in charge of de-mining the countryside; others attempt to convince locals to turn over their weapons, which are still in abundance, one of the reasons for the high crime rate."

But many are here to advise the government and countless NGO's, how to run the economy, and the state. It is clear that such advice mostly leads to 'projects' strictly based on pro-market theories. As a result, a very small percentage of the economic growth ends up in the pockets of the poor, which is the great majority of Cambodian people.

Marijuana smoke lazily moves through the humid and stale air. After several years in Cambodia, these experts are tough and cynical — every day is a battle. To achieve anything in this country, one has to bribe and compromise. Polite speech has been fully forgotten; conversations are brutally direct and frank.

Common clichés reserved for the public in the U.S. and Europe are targets of ridicule and open scorn at these informal gatherings.

"Khmer Rouge killing more than a million Cambodians? Impossible!" frowns one of the middle-aged Europeans who has been living and working in this country for more than ten years. "They had no capacity to kill so many people. Sure, between one and two million people died between 1969 and 1978, but that number includes 500,000 or more of those massacred by the U.S. carpet bombing before Khmer Rouge took over."

"Most of the people died because of starvation and illnesses," he continues. "Furthermore, terrible massacres did not happen because of the communist ideology of Khmer Rouge. It was not on that level. U.S. carpet-bombing and Lon Nol's brutal dictatorship supported by the West pitched local people against each other. Killings were performed out of vengeance, not on ideological bases. Peasants went insane from enduring B-52 carpet bombings. Many were tortured, massacred and "disappeared" during Lon Nol's reign. Country folks hated city-dwellers, blaming them for all the misfortunes and horrors they had to endure. And most Khmer Rouge soldiers and cadres came from the countryside."

Just half a mile from the café and the detached conversations of hardened expats, the Tuol Sleng Museum (Museum of Genocide), based in a former secondary school, speaks to the unbridled brutality and sadism of Khmer Rouge cadres. In 2009, The United Nations Educational, Scientific and Cultural Organization (UNESCO) declared Tuol Sleng Museum the "Memory of the World".

After April 17, 1975 the classrooms of Tuol Svay Prey High School, became the Khmer Rouge's main torture and interrogation center, known as Security Prison 21 — or just S-21. This is where men and women were shackled and severely beaten, where women had their nipples torn-off by pliers, where electric wires were applied to genitals. After the confession (and one had no option but to confess in order to stop the unbearable torture), most of the men, women and children who went through this institution of horror ended up in the extermination camp Choeung Ek, facing almost certain execution. It is said that 20,000 died after being interrogated at S-21.

In an insane attempt to give structure to the savagery, Khmer Rouge documented each case, photographing all the men and women detained right after their arrest, and before torture, then taking pictures of some after the savage interrogation.

Some of the most terrifying images are those created by Vann Nath, a painter and former prisoner of S-21, one of the very few who managed to survive because of his talent and ability to draw complimentary portraits of Pol Pot, and of the officials who were in charge of the interrogation center. After the Vietnamese invasion, Vann Nath transferred the most terrifying memories onto canvas; a mosaic depicting the barbarity and insane brutality of the interrogators — a mother whose baby is being assassinated in front of her eyes, a man whose nails are being extracted by pliers, a woman having her nipple cut off.

But even Van Nath, in a conversation we had some fifteen years ago, insisted that the Khmer Rouge killed around 200,000 people during its reign, a number which he also uses in his book "A Cambodian Prison Portrait: One Year in the Khmer Rouge's S-21" (White Lotus Press).

And among most of the Khmer survivors that I spoke to, there is a consensus that the majority of people died not because of Communist ideology and not because of direct orders from Phnom Penh to exterminate millions, but because of officers and local cadres in the provinces who ran amok, taking their personal vengeance on deported city-dwellers and "elites" whom they blamed for both the savage American bombing from the past, and for supporting the corrupt and savage pro-Western dictatorship of Lon Nol.

There can be no doubt that the great majority of those who died during that era (between one and two million people) were victims of the US bombing, of famines related to these bombings and of becoming internally displaced people (around 2 million became refugees in their own country, lacking medical care, food, and enduring despicable living conditions).

The fact that a substantial number of people vanished as a result of the U.S. carpet-bombing is very rarely mentioned in the mainstream Western media. But among academia it was understood that the U.S. Air Force had been secretly bombing Cambodia using B-52s, since May 1969. It was called "Operation Menu" (Breakfast, Lunch, Dinner, Snack, Dessert, and Supper). Although now, new evidence, from declassified documents (in 2000 by the Clinton administration), shows that the Air Force had already began bombing the rural regions of Cambodia along its South Vietnam border in 1965, under the Johnson administration. The "Menus" were just brutal escalations of the mass murder of defenseless civilians.

Facing defeat in Vietnam in 1973, the ruthless carpet-bombing was performed in order to support Lon Nol's regime. Historian David P. Chandler writes:

> "When the campaign was stopped by the U.S. Congress at the end of the year, the B-52s had dropped over half of a million tons of bombs on a country with which the United States was not at war — more than twice the tonnage dropped on Japan during WWII."

The war in Cambodia was known as "the sideshow" by journalists covering the war in Vietnam and by American policy-makers in London. Yet the intensity of U.S. bombing in Cambodia was greater than it ever was in Vietnam; about 500,000 soldiers and civilians were killed over the 4-year period, in the territory of this small country. As mentioned before, it also caused about 2 million refugees to flee from the countryside to the capital.

The barbarity of the bombardment, the displacement of millions of people, and resentment towards the corrupt pro-Western regime in Phnom Penh, paved the way for the Khmer Rouge's victory and the campaign of ferocious vengeance.

It was not the "Communist Genocide", but the Empire murdering millions in Indochina, with absolute impunity and complete spite for the 'unpeople', followed by blind and brutal revenge of those desperate people who lost everything.

***

I enter the market place, a lane of eateries 50 kilometers from Phnom Penh, on the Bassac River. I came with my driver and interpreter, who is a former de-mining expert for CMAC (Cambodian Mine Action Centre).

We approach two old women, both in their late 70's.

In Phnom Penh, almost nobody wants to speak about the US atrocities. But all over the country, in the countryside, people are still outraged, and at the same time grateful to anyone who is ready to listen to them.

I see the tears in the eyes of one of the women. Her name is Tang Vilim, a seller. She begins her speech, het lament, speaking fast, as if afraid that we will interrupt her and go away:

> "I lost relatives during the bombing of 1972. I still feel anger; I feel outraged! I am still waiting for the answers, so many years later. I want to know why? Why did Americans drop those bombs on us? Their bombs killed so many people! I still remember it: I was a young woman then, now I am 76. What had we done, what was our sin? Until now... Until now – wherever I go, I feel upset! I keep asking these same questions in my mind."

And the same lament from the second lady:

> "People still don't understand... They want to know why? They want the US government to take responsibility! There are craters all over the countryside. Some are filled but others are still open. This entire country is dotted with craters."

We drive further, all the way to the border with Vietnam: to the beautiful crossing on Bassac River, at Chrey Thum.

Right next to the border post, there are several craters, but guards do not like to discuss the topic. We walk on the borderline, and my guide once again remembers his days working for de-mining agencies:

> "Cambodia is still dotted with bombs, 'bombies' and mines. Some are from Khmer Rouge days, but most are from those carpet bombings by the USAF. You find them all over, from here to the areas in the West of the country – around Siem Reap and north..."

Understandably, this topic is explosive and still evokes passionate outbursts and tears.

After returning to Phnom Penh, I am welcomed by one of the managers at The Plantation Hotel. It is already dark, but he has heard about my work in the countryside, and decided to wait for me.

"I think what you are doing is very important", he begins. "We should investigate why our country was bombed so brutally. In my hometown, we had so many bombs, so many craters. Please go there, if you have time: Chea Lea Village, Chealea Commune, Bateay District, Kampong Cham Province..."

***

On the other side of the world, in Toronto, Canada, a leading international lawyer, Christopher Black, wrote for this report, echoing what the victims in Cambodia said:

> "The UN-backed war crimes trials of Khmer Rouge leaders are show trials designed to once again demonize communists, and to scapegoat them for the millions of Cambodians who were killed by the American bombing of Cambodia. What the world needs are trials of the American leaders and officers for war crimes for the carpet-bombing of Vietnam, Laos and Cambodia. (We had the Bertrand Russell war Crimes Tribunal in the 70s but it could not enforce its judgments)."

At the end of July 2014, the United Nations-backed tribunal held an initial hearing against two former high-ranking leaders of Khmer Rouge: Head of State, Khieu Samphan, 83, and Nuon Chea, 88, right-hand man to Pol Pot.

Of course, nobody would be so naive as to expect that the US leadership could one day stand trial for murdering millions of people all over Indochina.

***

A prominent Australian historian, an author of several books on Asia, Professor Emeritus at Nagasaki University, Geoffrey Gunn, put Khmer Rouge into historical context, for this essay:

Bookending an era as it were, on July 12, 2014, in a ceremony attended by Sihanouk's widow Queen Monique, current King Sihamoni, Prime Minister Hun Sen, cabinet members, and foreign diplomats, the King-father's ashes were interred in a stupa in the Royal Palace.

"Having led his country to independence in 1954, Sihanouk's neutral foreign policy was never acceptable to Washington. Following the US-backed coup in Phnom Penh in March 1970, US Secretary of State Henry Kissinger/ President Richard Nixon unleashed the most intense and deadly bombing campaign in human history upon the Cambodian countryside and people. Viewed from the air some years later, this normally verdant land presented itself as a ruined moonscape. Sihanouk, accordingly, endorsed the rural-backed guerrillas (the Khmer Rouge) – notionally Marxist – but fanatical in their rage duly turning Cambodia into a "killing field."

The wheel of history has turned but what are the lessons here if it is not that full justice has to be served, not only in the Extraordinary Chambers (the UN-backed "genocide court" in Phnom Penh), but also by roping in the perpetrators on all sides."

Albert J. Johnman's "The Case of Cambodia", Contemporary Genocides: Causes, Cases, Consequences defined the movement by following words:

> "The Khmer Rouge's ideology combined elements of Marxism with an extreme version of Khmer nationalism and xenophobia. It combined an idealization of the Angkor Empire (802–1431), with an existential fear for the existence of the Cambodian state, which had historically been liquidated under Vietnamese and Siamese intervention..."

That "Marxist element" rested mainly at the very top, particularly with Pol Pot, who got radicalized in Parisian cafes, although it is not clear how well he himself was versed in Marxist theory. Generally, his academic performance in France was so pitiful, that he never came close to graduation, and was forced to return to Cambodia without a diploma. Although, as noted by Geoffrey Gunn, some members of the Paris circle managed to produce political economy dissertations, namely Khieu Samphan, Hu Nim, Hu Yuon, Phouk Chhou (Pol Pot's secretary), KR was really far from versed in any ideology.

Based on my conversation with one of the prominent professors at Beijing University (who did not want to be named), China was never embracive of the Khmer Rouge 'Maoist' brand:

> "It was somehow embarrassing... both theory and the practice, like their determination to send rice to us, while their own people were starving..."

The British investigative journalist and former head of 'Reuters' in Iraq, Andrew Marshall, made Phnom Penh his home. He has a clear opinion about the Khmer Rouge and how they were misrepresented by Western and Asian propaganda:

> "Khmer Rouge was never a socialist or a communist movement. It was built on genuine anger of the poor against elites in Phnom Penh, who were always treating the poor like dirt. And it was built on anger against the United States that bombed Cambodia as no other country was ever bombed before. It was a movement created by popular fury. Abused became abusers, longing to destroy 'elites'. Families that were razed, killed, wanted their revenge... And after it was over, 'the example' of Khmer Rouge was used by the elites all over Southeast Asia to demonize people's power, especially in Thailand, but not only there."

Eventually, Western propaganda went into total over-gear, using the Khmer Rouge as one of the cornerstones of its global anti-Communist crusade.

The frustrated, rural, ragged and a thoroughly uneducated force of victims of the Western carpet-bombing, torture and displacement, the Khmer Rouge, were 'elevated' into a mythical and perfect Communist killing machine.

The paradox remains that the closest ally of the final years of KR was not China or any other Communist country. It was the United States, which was fighting the Cold War with the Soviet block, as well as its terror war against Vietnam and Laos. After distancing themselves from Leninism, and at least theoretically embracing Maoism, the Khmer Rouge received full diplomatic and other support from Washington.

After Vietnam liberated Cambodia, following the Christmas Offensive of 1978, saving perhaps millions of lives, the government of the United States took a decisive stand, 'demanding the return of legitimate government' in Phnom Penh. That legitimate government was, in Washington's eyes, no one else other than Khmer Rouge.

The erroneous punitive invasion by China of Vietnam came next, followed by anti-Vietnamese propaganda sponsored and in fact manufactured by the West.

The crimes against humanity committed in Cambodia by the United States managed to be fully whitewashed. While they live in vivid memory all over the countryside, Phnom Penh conveniently forgot all about them.

As Andrew Marshall and I were having lunch in Phnom Penh, with a local star journalist, Ms. Bopha Phorn, Andrew asks her directly: "What nation do people of Phnom Penh hate the most?"

With no hesitation she replies: "Vietnamese."

***

I do this almost every two years. I come to Cambodia and I search for answers. I hire a car, an interpreter, and I go very deep into the countryside.

Almost no one else does. Most of the 'academic work', as well as that of 'investigative journalism' is done in the bars and offices of Phnom Penh, as most of the similar work on Indonesia is created in Jakarta and Bali.

Outside the capital, people are open and ready to talk. In fact, they are desperately in need of talking. And unlike in Phnom Penh where people only ask questions but hardly give answers, the countryside of Cambodia knows how to reply.

In July 2014, as we drove towards Anlong Veng, I did an experiment: I asked my friend to just stop at any village along the road, some 100 kilometers from the capital. I only later found out that the name of the place where we broke our journey this time was called Prei Saak.

We entered the humble hamlet and I asked the first woman that we met on a narrow path leading to the fields, whether there are still some unexploded mines or bombs in this area.

"Of course", she replied. Her name was Ms. Leoun. "2 days ago, they exploded 8 mines. A mine-clearing agency... Since then we found more. Here, the children can take you there."

Did any of her relatives get injured?

"My husband had an accident. And my brother-in-law was injured. He was clearing the forest for a tapioca plantation, and something exploded under his feet, and he lost one leg. My husband got both his face and body destroyed by an explosion, few years ago."

I asked her whether these were the US 'bombies', sitting in the fields since the carpet-bombing of Cambodia, or the landmines left by Khmer Rouge?

She was not sure. She thought these were US devices, but she couldn't be certain.

But what is certain is that almost every town and every village of this country has been suffering for decades, after the US unleashed its monstrous military and de-stabilization campaign.

***

Back in 2006, I hired a sturdy car, and a recommended driver and translator all in one person, and we headed south on Route 3, then going further south on 31 as far as it took us, then turning left, towards Vietnam. This is not the main border crossing, not even a crossing which foreigners are allowed to use. There is no asphalt road here, just a dirt path with deep potholes, surrounded by rice fields, miserable villages and water buffaloes. Ours was the only passing car in this area; locals were walking or riding ancient bicycles. Just like in 2014 when I visited a few other rural border crossings with Vietnam, it was raining and the bottom of the car was scraping against the sand. My driver was swearing, having no idea what we were really doing in this god-forsaken place.

Then we came to the end; a lazy river, a dormant town, the last border checkpoint, with a sleeping guard — Prek Kres. Just a few yards further, the houses of the first village in Vietnam began.

This is where, in the past, the first skirmishes between the Khmer Rouge and Vietnam began, and one of the points where the Vietnamese army invaded, as mentioned earlier, most definitely saving further millions of Cambodian people from certain death. But the West decided to see this action as an invasion and occupation, to turn all the facts on their head. In the Cold War climate and from the point of view of its geopolitical interests, it was more acceptable for the U.S. to sacrifice further millions of Cambodian lives than to allow Vietnamese (and Soviet) influence in the region.

I had no problem finding Mr. Sek Cuuin, the mayor of Prek Kres. We sat down at the outdoor table of his house and he seemed to be happy to share his memories.

"This huge puddle which you see in the middle of the road is what remains of the U.S. carpet bombing", he explained. "We filled the hole, but when it rains, there is still a puddle there, I don't know why. This area was heavily bombed during the war, by B-52s. If you enter the fields, you will see small lakes all over. It's what happens during the heavy rains. These lakes are bomb craters."

We walked around the village. Barefoot children were staring at us. People were gathering, wondering what had brought us here.

Makeshift vehicles were parked next to a primitive jetty where a traditional merchant boat was being unloaded.

"There were always conflicts here," explained the mayor. "There were border skirmishes during Lon Nol's regime and after, when Khmer Rouge took over in 1975. We had 700 families living in this town; 400 were forcefully relocated. When Khmer Rouge entered, I just jumped into the river and swam for my life. Most of the remaining 300 families tried to escape to Vietnam, and Prek Kres became a ghost town — an outpost for the Khmer Rouge's army which began attacking Vietnamese villages across the border."

I asked him about the Vietnamese Christmas offensive in 1978.

"The Vietnamese army crossed this border in 1979. No matter what they say now, almost everybody was happy, welcoming their troops. Those who survived and stayed in this town simply lined along the road, waved at Vietnamese soldiers and cried. The entire area — entire country — was ravaged; destroyed by the Khmer Rouge and earlier by U.S. bombing and by the movement of refugees. The Vietnamese saved this nation from complete annihilation. And when they took Phnom Penh, it was obvious that the mass killing and torture would stop. But you know what happened later; the gratitude evaporated and nationalism gained ground. And the foreign countries insisted that this was not liberation, but an occupation. If you repeat what rulers want to hear, you get paid. But you can ask anybody, except members of the Khmer Rouge, how they felt in 1978 and 1979 — we felt liberated, we were saved and we suddenly realized that we might survive."

I asked the mayor how he would compare Vietnam and Cambodia now. After all, on paper, Cambodia is a success story, a multi-party democracy. He grins sarcastically. "Yes, now we have many political parties. But you can't eat political parties; they don't fill your stomach. Everything here is corrupt. The Vietnamese government has managed to give a much better life to its people. Especially to poor people, and in this part of the world almost everybody is poor. All I can tell you is that when we are hungry and when we are sick, we don't go to Phnom Penh; we cross the border and go to Vietnam. They know we are Khmers but they don't care; they help us. They believe — over there — that if you are hungry or sick, you have to be helped, no matter what your nationality is. People there have a big heart."

***

It is now 2014, and I ask a question to my friend, Song Heang, as we are driving through the night, through the countryside of western Cambodia.

"Tell me, did Vietnamese soldiers kill Cambodian people in 1978 and 1979?"

"Yes", he replied.

"Did they kill many?"

He is silent for quite some time. He is reflecting: "It was a war... But honestly: not many. There was some fighting... As a rule, Vietnamese did not target civilians."

"Then why?" I ask. But both of us know that this is just a rhetorical question.

At some point, as it is getting closer to midnight, we stop in some dark village in order to buy water and some local fruits.

Something breaks in Song Heang, and he begins to speak in an urgent, agitated tone of voice:

> "You don't understand, you don't know how terrible this country really is... How terrible it has become. The rich are so rich. The poor are so poor and they are totally uneducated now, so much that they don't even know anything about corruption and the hedonism of the 'elites' in Phnom Penh. It is the same now again, as it was over 4 decades ago. Do you know how schools look here? Sometimes there is just only one teacher for a class of 100 pupils. And medical care: it is simple here – if you are poor – you die. And some of our 'traditional families': they amputate the legs and arms of their children, of their babies, and then they take them, across the border, with those terrible infected wounds, to Bangkok, to beg."

We drove in silence for quite some time.

"What kind of Cambodia do you want?" I ask him.

"A Cambodia where children get a free and great education, where people get free medical care, where culture is important and supported by the state, where people are equal..."

"That is socialism", I say. "A Socialist or a Communist Cambodia..."

He hesitates. "Is it?"

"Yes. This is what they are trying to build all over Latin America, in China..."

"But that is not what the Khmer Rouge was trying to achieve, right?"

"Of course not", I reply.

It is pitch-dark outside.

"I see... It is not what we are being told by Westerners... So... It looks that... it is all fucked up," he concludes.

I agree with him.

At the next village we stop, buy some Angkor beer, and get more philosophical at the side of the road, the old Soviet style.

1 August 2014

*****

55

WHY DO THEY HATE US?

They hate us, because we are alive, and because we are walking and moving forward, sometimes stumbling, sometimes unsteady, but walking nevertheless.

All the while they are dragging all of humanity back into, dark nihilism, into terrible moods, dark sarcasm, and a feeling of hopelessness.

They hate us because we insist on doing things our own way, and because we put our people first, and sometimes we put deprived people all over the world, first. We do it more and more, often, whenever we can afford it.

While 'they' are putting their economic interests first, and in doing so, they torture, destroy and humiliate those that refuse to succumb, to kneel and to lick their boots.

For ages they have been trying to destroy us, but we stood firm and we fought back, proudly. They invaded, ruined, burned our lands, and they murdered the people of Russia, of China and of the entire part of the world now called Latin America. They, of course, also murdered and destroyed tens or hundreds of millions of people in the Middle East, in Africa, Asia and Oceania.

When I say 'they', I mean the West, and once again I refuse to make any distinction between the old colonial devils, Europe, and the new ones that come from the same roots, the same 'culture', but kill under the shade of their relatively new flags.

They hate us because we bled and cried over our dead, but we never gave up the struggle.

They only 'acknowledge' and glorify those who accept their regime, who have decided to collaborate, partially or fully: countries like India, Indonesia, the Philippines, Japan, South Korea, Saudi Arabia, Qatar, Kenya, and dozens of other 'client' states, countries that are feeding that horrendous capitalist monster with the flesh of their own citizens.

'They' even invented 'political correctness' so the 'culture' of the oppressive and brutal regimes loyal to neo-colonialism, would evade being criticized or ridiculed in those 'polite circles' (lackey academia, mass media, etc.). Political correctness is not there to protect the majority of Indian or Indonesian people, but to shield their usurpers and exploiters, who wrap themselves hypocritically in their flags, as well as religions and cultural gowns.

They hate us for our dreams and for our laughter, for our confidence and determination. We are often hated not only by the Western global regime, but also by the majority of Western people, who are part of the system or at least to some degree, are beneficiaries of it.

The more they steal all over the world and the less evil we do then them, the more they smear us and claim that 'we are the same', robbing and 'pushing for our interests' in Africa and elsewhere. They own the mass media and they spill the poison of their lies through their press agencies and television networks, as well as the Internet. Elites all over the world, owners of most of the local media, are then happy and always ready to disseminate these lies.

They hate us because they actually suspect that we are different, and the more they suspect it, the more they hate us; then the more they shout and scream that we are exactly like them, and perhaps even worse!

If the world they have created is total shit, then, they insist, the entire universe, even humanity itself, has to also swim in the excrement.

But we are not like them.

They may be masters of propaganda, great puppeteers, but we, most of the time, refuse to lower ourselves to their level. We are trying to play fair, fighting fair and honest battles. We are trying to win honestly, not like the deceptive and sadistic scum. It is simply because we do want to play fair and also because we are so horrified by their bloodstained hands and mouths that we simply do not want to be like them, even when they are fighting us with all their might; even when they are trying to wipe us out, off the face of the Earth.

For that, they hate us, too.

The more sincere we are, the more they slander us.

The more considerate we are, the more they accuse us of demagogy and deceit.

The more peaceful we are, the more they accuse us of being the aggressors.

The more pure our goals, the dirtier their comments about our deeds are.

Those right now that are collaborating hate us for not surrendering, because the collaborators always hate those that are free, proud, and resolute.

Cowardly angry servants, and slaves, are often much more vicious than their masters; not always, but they often are.

The more comrades we lose, the more they hate us, because we refuse to kneel, and to beg them to stop killing us. We just grin through our teeth and keep walking forward. For humanity, for our beloved people...

The more united we are, the more they hate us. Latin America, China, and Russia, are now together. And several other great nations are joining us. We embraced. We embraced standing, proudly, voluntarily!

The nearer we are to achieving our main goal – the creation of a socialist, more humane and decent society on this planet – the more they hate us.

They would rather obliterate our countries; even destroy them – nuke us – the entire planet, instead of accepting a global egalitarian society built on principles of social justice, true respect and non-interference.

The more reasonable and egalitarian we are trying to become, the more they hate us. We may not always succeed but they still hate us even when we try, but fail. But when we get it right, when we succeed, then they go into top gear in their odium, assassinating our leaders, manufacturing and funding 'opposition' in our countries, preparing and executing military coups against our leaders. How many 'successful' and failed coup attempts have we had, recently? Let us just recall a few: Honduras, Paraguay, Venezuela, Syria, Ukraine, and Libya...

But back to the main point: we do not yield! Not anymore. We refuse to yield. Their grotesque, idiotic, nihilist turbo-capitalist, neo-colonialist system and other fundamentalist dogmas, are as terrible as death itself. We are working night and day to resist it, to expose its maliciousness. We feel obliged to work and to fight, not because we are always so great and honorable ourselves, but simply because they are so horrid, murderous, cynical and inhuman!

Photo 9. Memorial to the victims of pro-Western military regime in Buenos Aires

And so they bathe us in dirt, they vomit their toxic poisons at us, pitching our neighbors against us, planning and triggering coups and 'opposition movements', as well as 'student revolts' and 'color revolutions'. The targets are China and Russia, Cuba and Venezuela... Bolivia and Ecuador. Smeared are Brazil and South Africa, Argentina and Zimbabwe, demonized are Eritrea and North Korea...

In a way, they – our enemies – are pathetic, ridiculous and sad... For those who know the world, they are just a bunch of sadistic lunatics... mighty but uncool, stinky echoes of previous loud and toxic colonialist/imperialist/racist farts.

But they are managing to scream louder. They are publishing billions of sheets filled with lies. They are using their money (mostly stolen from us and others) to twist all logical observations and analyses, presenting the emptiness they are spreading, with their soulless gadgets and consumerism, as something hip and human. And so the new generations in their countries and in their colonies are being manufactured and shaped – they are confused, tired ever since their cradles; empty, lacking poetry and creativity, obsessed with form whilst rejecting substance.

We keep telling them what they are doing to the world, and the more we tell them, the more they hate us.

But what do we really want? What truly unites countries as diverse as Cuba and China, Russia and Venezuela, Bolivia and South Africa?

It is a great desire for freedom. Not 'their' twisted concept of freedom! But the freedom to choose our own path, to use our resources to feed our children, to heal our sick, and to educate both adults and children! All for free. All as our patriotic and humanist duty!

We want our countries to exist only in order to create, to facilitate a good, healthy, meaningful life for their citizens. We want people to wake up and not to be scared that they will end up on the street, or that if they get sick, they will die just because they can't pay their medical bills. We want people to think about the journey, about where they are going and what they will do at their destination, instead of constantly agonizing over where they will they get the money to buy a new car!

We want people to be free and to have the time to decide 'where they are going', and to have knowledge, to release their creativity and energy for the improvement of life, all over our beautiful planet.

And the more we want that, the more they hate us.

We want to be; many of us want to be, 'naive' again... to be able to dream, to communicate with each other, to work with our hands and our brains, to put our entire hearts into this life. And we want people to feel safe, not to be scared of waking up every morning, of being ridiculed for simply being good, decent; for being human!

This is what socialism or communism mean to me. This is what it meant to Chavez and what I think it means to Evo. This is what it means to my dearest friends in Beijing.

Venezuela, Bolivia or China are not perfect, damn it! We are all human; we all make mistakes. But we are trying. We are doing our best. We want to pull hundreds of millions out of poverty and we are doing it, step by step. Each of our countries is doing it in its own way, depending on its culture and history. And we want to do it our way and only in our own way, and that is why they hate us!

I don't care or mind if someone runs his or her private hotel, or restaurant, or a newspaper... I don't mind at all. I am not some dogmatic freak. But I do mind when entire nations are destroyed simply because they want to go their own way!

I do mind when 'democracy' is reduced to only what the Western bullies say it should mean. I mind when people are converted into serfs for the rich in their own countries, and then into serfs for the Empire. I do mind when they have no choice. I do mind when they are constantly fearful of something, when they get humiliated again and again. And not only do I mind, I want to clench my fists and fight for justice.

The more I mind, the more others like me mind, the more they hate us.

More and more of us actually do mind.

Now we have this great new wave of cooperation between four wonderful parts of the world. Soon we will have an alternative to the horrid institution called the World Bank. And eventually we will create an alternative to the United Nations, which by now has become a toothless, kidnapped institution, unable to punish or even name those true gangsters and true terrorists!

They hate us! But we do not like them, either! How could we like fascists and bigots?

They run this world by employing fear, just as for centuries, they used to run their colonies. They killed hundreds of millions, perhaps billions, in the last millennia. They would not think twice of killing a few hundred million more.

On top of it, they are also scared, and the more scared they are, the more bellicose and aggressive they are becoming. They suspect that this cannot last – this twisted, psychopathic arrangement of the world. They just hope it will last for another few decades, while they are still alive.

The more scared they are, the more they are trying to scare others, too... to provoke conflicts, to antagonize people, to spy on them, to lock millions up, to brainwash billions worldwide.

Those corporations of the Empire, the governments that they select... they make normal people want to puke. And we tell them this, straight to their faces! Now we have our own block of countries, our organized resistance, our media, (this publication is an integrated and strong part of it)!

We tell them who they are.

And they hate us for that.

We tell them: you do what you want at home. As long as your people tolerate it, accept it, or even endorse it. We will not be attacking you or 'liberating you'. But do not dare to come to our homes again, to plunder and corrupt.

If you do, our nations and our people will fight.

They know it, and they hate us for that!

We tell them: Our people will fight against you and for what is human, and for the normal development of mankind – development, which you have derailed in such a brutal, Machiavellian manner, for centuries.

For centuries, you used slavery in order to accumulate your riches. You are enslaving billions of men and women even now, although you do not use that "s" word.

Our people will fight against you if you try to impose slavery on us once again.

We will also fight for kindness, poetry – for that dreamy, naive and at the same time creative and secure world, which almost all of us humans desire from the bottom of our hearts.

And this is why 'they' really hate us – we want to stop this horrific experiment on human beings. We want human life to be much more important than the profits of some corporations and twisted individuals. We want to be proud again of being part of the human race.

They want us to produce and to consume, submit to their designs and on top of it, stay quiet and scared.

While we want to build and we want to sing, to dream and to invent, for other people, not just for cash. We want to help each other. We do not want to succumb to a system where those who are brutal and aggressive are enslaving those who are gentle and kind.

We want to prove that humans are not just cynical and selfish beasts. They are not! They only behave like that when they are injected with high doses of repulsive psychological toxins.

We want the end of this corporate and colonialist tyranny. Millions have fought it for centuries, and millions have already died, fighting for a much better world.

We are not going away! We are not deserting. We are not scared, anymore.

Before falling, Hugo Chavez shouted: "Here nobody surrenders!" Well said!

We feel the same. Aqui no se rinde nadie!

And that is why they hate us!

And we should be proud that they do.

8 August 2014

*****

56

DO NOT DILUTE BRICS!

There is a growing danger that BRICS – the club of the nations that are holed up at the frontline, in the trenches, facing global Western imperialism – could one day be diluted and weakened if some radically right-wing Western allies, such as Indonesia and Turkey, were to be allowed to join.

BRICS consists of Brazil, Russia, India, China and South Africa, and it was originally supposed to be just an economic bloc, but in recent years, Western attacks against countries with independent political and economic systems, has pushed most of the BRICS nations into a powerful political alliance, even an embrace.

With the exception of that staunch ally of the United States and a capitalist zealot – India – all the other member countries are standing defiantly and proudly against the latest wave of a Western neo-colonialist onslaught. They may have diverse political and economic systems, but anti-imperialism is their essential common denominator.

All of them, again with the exception of India, are under severe propaganda attacks from the Western mass media.

For the last few years, China and Russia are being encircled militarily, and openly provoked. South Africa is being demonized and ridiculed, while Latin America has endured countless attacks, and gross interference in its internal affairs: the progressive governments in Honduras and Paraguay were overthrown, and many 'opposition movements' have been persistently manufactured and financed from the North.

But the bloc that embraces roughly 40% of the global population has been moving forward, creating the much needed diversity and, once again, a bi-polar world.

On 15th July 2014, Pepe Escobar wrote for the Asia Times, from Brazil where the leaders of BRICS countries met, incorporating into these encounters, other Latin American nations. Grandiose plans were defined, and it has, once again, become clear how close China and Russia are to the progressive Latin American nations; how fast they are all moving towards each other politically, strategically and economically:

> "The headline news is that this Tuesday in Fortaleza, northeast Brazil, the BRICS group of emerging powers (Brazil, Russia, India, China, South Africa) fights the (Neoliberal) World (Dis) Order via a new development bank and a reserve fund set up to offset financial crises.
>
> It's been a long and winding road since Yekaterinburg in 2009, at their first summit, up to the BRICS's long-awaited counterpunch against the Bretton Woods consensus – the IMF and the World Bank – as well as the Japan-dominated (but largely responding to US priorities) Asian Development Bank (ADB)."

These are great times, without any doubts.

***

Where India stands is unclear. I recently visited this the second most populous nation and after travelling there, intensively, I came to the conclusion that its elites, its military and the religious cadres that are running what the West cynically calls "the world's largest democracy", are definitely much closer to Washington and the 'Chicago School of Economics boys', than they are to Moscow, Brasilia, Pretoria or Beijing.

I also established that the overwhelming majority of Indian people are told very little about developments in Latin America, China and Russia, and that they have almost no influence on the direction in which their country is developing.

I will soon release my report on India in the BRICS's context, but what I can say now is that it is obvious that this complex country is not at all a driving force in the alliance.

It is also clear that this new, powerful and important (for the survival of mankind) bloc does not need in its ranks more 'client' states handled by the West. For that very reason, the 'dilution' of BRICS countries and of their determination is exactly what the corporate and neo-colonialist world is trying to achieve.

There is an entire group of lethal candidates, ready to join BRICS at any moment, in order to torpedo the movement. And there are several different packages of extension on offer, from a 'small enlargement' incorporating Indonesia and Turkey to a much bigger one, the inclusion of an entire group called MINT, an abbreviation for Mexico, Indonesia, Nigeria and Turkey.

If such an expansion occurs, it would, most certainly, destroy the entire political direction in which the BRICS are moving.

It has to be averted by all means.

***

MINT countries range from those that are simply right-wing, to those that are openly fascist. All of them are staunchly pro-Western, and governed by the elites. Mexico is the most reasonable and benign of them. Indonesia is the 'deadliest' one, as it is not just a country but it also an entire concept. In 1965, the West teamed up with the corrupt Indonesian elites, the military and religious cadres, and overthrew the progressive President Sukarno, father of the Non-aligned movement.

At least 1 million Indonesian Communists, intellectuals, union leaders, teachers and members of the Chinese minority were murdered, but the number may well have been much higher; as high as 3 million. Mass 'punitive' rapes and the destruction of Indonesian culture took place simultaneously. Books were burned. Almost everything was privatized and offered up for foreign exploitation.

Two brutal genocides followed: those against the people of East Timor and, an ongoing one, against resource-rich but poor and tribal Papua. In the first one, one third of the local population vanished, and in the second, even according to Western human rights groups, at least 120,000 people died. More are dying as this is being written. There are no discussions and no protests against the slaughter.

'Concept Indonesia' (just murder indiscriminately, spread fear, paralyze the entire nation and then let the private sector grab everything) has latterly been implemented with varying success in numerous countries around the globe, including Chile (Allende's people were told again and again, before the 1973 coup: "Watch out comrades, Jakarta is coming!"), Russia under Yeltsin, and in the Democratic Republic of Congo, to name just a few.

Suharto's 'stepping down' and the 'return of democracy' was just a cosmetic maneuver. Savage capitalism has clenched its fists and survived, in Indonesia, virtually nothing public remains. There are hardly any public parks, public cultural institutions or even modern public waste management. If international statistics were to apply, then more than half of the population would be deemed as living in misery. Creativity has been reduced to almost zero, with the fourth most populous nation on Earth showing hardly any scientific or artistic achievements, hardly any research. And the economy is growing only due to the severe plundering of what is left of its natural resources, and due to high global commodity prices.

In the recent Presidential elections, two candidates ran neck-and-neck: a retired general, an alleged war criminal with a bunch of his buddies behind him, and a populist with another set of military cronies backing him up.

With all the mass media being owned and controlled by business interests, and with virtually all the political parties serving local oligarchs, 'democracy' is just a word with which the West is covering up all those past and present horrors of one of its most brutal and grotesque 'client-states'.

It is also important to mention, that in 'democratic' Indonesia, the law bans atheism and Communism, and many gatherings that are aimed at discussing the reintroduction of at least something 'public', are brutally broken up by religious zealots and by the cronies that serve corporate interests.

It is easy to imagine what impact there would be, if Indonesia were to be 'invited' to join BRICS!

***

It would be naive to think that a country like Indonesia is a natural ally of, for instance, Latin America, just because it is located in the 'South', and because it is not near the West, geographically. Its direction of 'development' and the mentality of its rulers, are the exact opposite of what countries like Venezuela, Cuba, Bolivia, but also Brazil or China, stand for and are fighting for.

Countries like Indonesia take dictates not from their people, but from their corrupt business cronies and their Western handlers.

Turkey is somehow better, but it is also implementing a savage capitalist system, and it has allowed itself to be used as the main Western ally in the Middle East, with its RAF and USAF air force bases, with 'refugee camps' that are training Syrian 'opposition' fighters including ISIS, and with clearly distractive policy towards Lybia, Iraq and Syria.

Turkey is an important member of NATO, and many 'opposition intellectuals' there (even those who claim to be from the Left), particularly those in Istanbul, still see their country joining Western alliances (including the European Union) as the main goal.

Nigeria is, in many ways, the same as Indonesia: a country that gulps down its own citizens. There seems to be no ideology there, but plenty of market fundamentalism, ego-trips of the elites, of religious fundamentalism (and Islam is definitely not the only religion that goes overboard), and of serving foreign interests.

And, just as in Indonesia, in Nigeria there is an absolute and endemic spite for the poor people – for the majority of the nation.

A Ugandan left wing opposition figure, Arthur Tewungwa, commented on Nigeria for this essay:

> "There is a veneer of competence masking an underbelly of business as usual, plain uncaring corruption. Is the present government in Nigeria pro-US; pro-Western? It is; very! The current Finance minister, for instance, is a former World Bank big-wig. BRICS have to be wary – too many fifth columnists!"

Mexico used to be a revolutionary country and it is still a nation with both a big culture and a tremendous heart. But it is not certain yet which direction it will take, under the stewardship of its young President from PRI, Enrique Peña Nieto. However, of all the MINT countries, Mexico has the most humane social system and it is certain that if accepted, it would hardly steer BRICS off its present foreign policy course.

***

The BRICS are moving forward and it is mainly the quality of their designs for a much better world, not just the number of its members that matters.

It is not, and it should never function, like a commercial club that tries to attract a broad membership base.

BRICS developed, evolved, from an economic group, into the leaders of the truly free world; of course together with their great allies like Cuba, Venezuela, Ecuador and Bolivia.

As has been said many times, they are not perfect, but they are all that we have, and they are constantly improving.

Among the BRICS, there is no place for countries that are siding with the colonialist powers, as there is no place for those nations that are tormenting and sacrificing their own people. For now it is still just an acronym of the countries, its members. But soon, who knows, it may be interpreted as the Broad Revolutionary Internationalist Causeway towards Socialism.

The BRICS should be very careful, very selective, whom they invite and whom they accept into their ranks. They are the vanguard of the new world. And they are what the "Old World" (or call it the 'world regime') wants to destroy, by all means.

It is their duty, their obligation to live, to survive.

Each country that wants to join should be asked to prove that it exists solely in order to serve its own people, as well as our great humanity!

15 August 2014

*****

57

India is Where?

ON TWO CHAIRS!

India, where are you? Are you really in the BRICS camp, fighting for a new, free world, or are you now in bed with your former colonial master and her mighty offshoot? India, a BRICS country, is actually nowhere to be seen while Brazil, South Africa, Russia and China are increasingly facing hostile attacks. India is not helping, as the United States and Europe are now manufacturing all sorts of 'opposition movements' inside countries that are still in the West's path to total and unopposed global dominance.

India, a BRICS country, is silent as both China and Russia are being encircled, provoked and stabbed; at a time when their neighboring countries are constantly being pitched against them, ideologically and militarily.

India, a BRICS country, does not seem to mind as the US increases its military presence in Asia, from Okinawa to the Philippines and Qatar, or when Russia is being demonized and provoked by insane propaganda and by lunatic sanctions, imposed by the West which is actually the one that overthrew the Ukrainian government, putting in place a brutal fascist dictatorship.

And as the Western mass media outlets are now in top gear,

spreading propaganda all over the world; the Indian newspapers, magazines and television stations, are dutifully reprinting and repeating the many vitriolic lies and fabrications, in exactly the same way as the Philippine and Indonesian business-owned media outlets are doing. But the Philippines and Indonesia are the West's client states, and they do not belong to BRICS, while India does, at least on paper.

In the *Economic & Political Weekly*, published in 2013, Atul Bhardwaj wrote:

> *"India has got itself trapped into an anti-Chinese matrix set in place by the United States. This has led to a situation where the military is increasing its say in foreign and domestic policy and pushing aggressive postures on to the civilian government. Unless India abandons its aspirations to great power status and pursues a foreign policy which builds on Asian cooperation and strengths, it will continue to become cannon fodder for western strategic aims."*

That's correct, but it is not only the anti-Chinese matrix; it is the staunchly pro-Western matrix that is serving India's ruling elites, and it is the matrix of disinformation and ignorance imposed on the members of the underprivileged majority.

I went back to India to see where the country really stands in relation to BRICS. I opted for a very much unplanned, chaotic, jazzy and spontaneous journey. I wanted to speak to those of the Indian majority; to people in the villages and towns, to ask them what they really know about BRICS, about the new winds of freedom and progress that are blowing all over Latin America, about tremendous social changes in China, and about their own lives in the country, which the West continually defines as 'the largest democracy on earth'.

***

Two village women are covered from head to toe in colorful fabric, and unlike in Saudi Arabia where only the eyes are visible, but totally. They are carrying huge crooked tin plates on their heads, and those plates are full of cow dung.

The village is called Karora, it is located almost 200 kilometers north from New Delhi, in Haryana State.

It is here that, in 2007, a newlywed couple was murdered in cold blood, after the assembly of village elders, *Panchayat*, passed 'the verdict'. Both the girl (18) and boy (23) were only 'guilty' of belonging to the same sub-clan.

The Deccan Herald reported then:

> *"In June 2007, the couple was dragged out of a Karnal-bound bus by the girl's relatives and was brutally murdered. Their bodies were paraded in the village and then dumped in a canal."*

We did not come here to only discuss honor killing and the horrible lot of Indian women; we came here to this remote corner of Haryana to discuss what the West calls 'the biggest democracy on earth', and above all, how India really fits into the BRICS, and to their determined fight against Western imperialism and market fundamentalism.

Yes, India is part of BRICS; but it is feudal in the countryside and capitalist in the cities. It is increasingly close to its colonial master and to the grand Empire.

We could not see the expression on the faces of the two Karora village women when we asked them about democracy, voting, women's rights, caste oppression and honor killing. But the first female began speaking, bravely if reluctantly, in front of an entire army of onlookers:

> *"I'm only a poor village woman, how can I know such things? I have to work for 14 hours every day to make out a living for my family. My husband doesn't have any regular work, and he is an alcoholic. I'm constantly worried about my children going hungry. The government doesn't care about people like us and I don't know who else could help. I'm very afraid so I can't talk more about the caste system or honor killings. Women have no freedom here. "*

The second lady echoes her, and then adds:

> *"I know the family of the eloped couple who suffered at the hands of Panchayat but I can't talk about it. I'm afraid of such things. Women have no freedom here. Most of us are struggling to survive and I don't know how things could be better, anytime soon. About democracy: I don't know how the election could improve living conditions in this village and I don't know about people's movement in other countries or about things that are happening elsewhere."*

Soon, the crowd of onlookers begins to participate in the discussion.

The youths surrounded us to find out the reason for our sudden appearance in their village.

A boy named Biswan, wearing a black T-shirt, explained:

> *"My impression of what they call 'Indian democracy' and of the political parties that are participating in this game is... that it is a pattern of appealing for votes by some political party, with the inducement of local liquor by their men to the villagers, one day before every election day, then disappearing, to be never seen again for the next 5 years. We don't have work here nor can anyone make a decent living with earnings here. I don't feel this type of democracy works for us... We still haven't got real freedom."*

Then the village youths begin speaking over each other:

> *"Money talks here, we are all educated to some degree, but only those who can afford to bribe some officials manage to get regular employment. We are poor villagers and unaware of developments in our own country, then how can we know about China, Latin America or other countries?"*

The forlorn expression on the faces of the villagers showed their frustration, even resignation. Most certainly, we saw no hope and no enthusiasm here.

India is feudal in the countryside and capitalist in the cities.

Our driver, Sunil, appeared to be extremely unhappy to be here. "In these villages, they have already torched so many cars belonging to those who came to ask questions!"

I insist that we have to finish our work here, in the heart of Haryana State. The driver fumes. He drives us around, missing the motorway a few times, but after we activate our navigation system, he gives up and just gets us where we want to go.

Later, in Delhi, my good friend and colleague, Anish, calls me and explains:

"Before he dropped me home, he said that he was so mad at you, he was ready to drive into a tree and kill us all.

"Kill us?" I thought I misunderstood.

"Yes. You may want to know that he was a soldier, serving in

Kashmir... He told me that much, just a few minutes ago. We had a chat... He said he was court-martialed, because he killed a few civilians there. In Kashmir, in 1996, he was on a mission to capture members of some insurgency group, but things went wrong and the people he was after, had fled... So he opened fire on civilians, killing several of them. He said he used a LMG inside the house, emptying 2 magazines of ammunition, killing at least 3 civilians... Just like that!"

"Why is he driving a taxi?" I asked. "Isn't he supposed to be in prison?"

Anish just commented, laconically:

> "When we discussed this, he was depressed. Not because of what he had done, but because he was caught and punished. He said to me: 'was I to have managed to kill at least one insurgent, then even if I killed dozens of civilians, I would never have got court-martialed."

I wondered whether this approach is one that would really serve as an inspiration for the BRICS countries.

***

Some 1,500 kilometers from Karora Village, in Mumbai, a monster building belonging to the richest man in India, Mukesh Ambani, is allegedly the most expensive dwelling ever constructed on this planet.

Arundhati Roy describes Ambani's home in her book "*Capitalism A Ghost Story*":

> *"...The twenty seven floors, three helipads, nine lifts, hanging gardens, ballrooms, weather rooms, gymnasiums, six floors of parking, and six hundred servants... In a nation of 1.2 billion, India's one hundred richest people own assets equivalent to one-fourth of the GDP."*

But to own all those billions is not enough. In order to rule, in order to fully control society, this small group of modern day rajas has to always find a way to morally justify their medieval, feudalist behavior.

The most effective way to do it is through almost total control of the media. Arundhati Roy continues:

> *"Mukesh Ambani is personally worth $20 billion. He holds a majority-controlling share in Reliance Industries Limited*

> *(RIL)... RIL recently bought 95 shares in Infotel, a TV consortium that controls twenty-seven TV news and entertainment channels, including CNN-IBN, IBN Live, CNBC, IBN Lokmat, and ETV in almost every regional language. Infotel owns the only nation-wide license for 4G broadband, a high-speed information pipeline which, if the technology works, could be the future of information exchange."*

The criticism of Indian elites does not only come from the Left. The Conservative British news magazine, *The Economist*, recently ran its cover story about Ambani: "*An Unloved Billionaire*", making the rhetorical suggestion, "Why Mukesh Ambani, India's richest man, needs to reform his empire":

> *"Reliance's relationship with the government is even more troubling. Anti-corruption campaigners claim Mr Ambani is the power behind the throne of India's political leaders..."*

In Indian 'democracy', the real rulers of the country pay politicians, to get to the top, while the voters get paid to vote a certain way, which is suitable to the regime. Mass media shapes public opinion constantly, so it stays exactly where the elites want it to stay.

From an amazing tolerance level for medieval oppressive 'cultural practices', to the gross cruelty towards women and ethnic/religious minorities, India is hardly a beacon of light for other BRICS nations, or, for the rest of the world. The way its economy, election practices, foreign policy and government systems are structured, the Indian state is much closer to MINT (Mexico, Indonesia, Nigeria, Turkey – although in this group, too, there is Mexico, which is, despite everything, culturally and historically, in the Social Democratic camp), a group which, if allowed to join BRICS, would surely destroy their political and social direction: (http://www.counterpunch.org/2014/08/15/the-challenge-to-the-west/).

But the West is always extremely generous towards its allies and economic cohorts. It promotes and glorifies those countries that are willing to sacrifice their people, throwing them on the sacrificial altar of global market fundamentalism.

Therefore, for the West, both Indonesia and India, two enormous and impoverished countries, are the true democratic and economic stars!

***

DLF Promenade in Vasant Kunj is a symbol of new wealth, hosting some of the top international retail brands, from Armani to Prada.

There are literally armies of guards, some in their white butler informs, others armed with guns. Photographing is prohibited. Surveillance is constant, just as in every place frequented by the elites.

Situated right near the DLF Promenade is the Khushampur Pahari slum, a place that is miserable and rough. Children move around aimlessly and barefoot. It is not as dirty as many of the much bigger settlements in Mumbai or Calcutta are, but still, people here are clearly desperate and deprived.

Mr. Jagdish is a 'wage laborer', not permanently employed:

> "I have no regular work and the system is geared for the rich. We, poor people who form the great majority in India, don't count."

I ask him about the mall, but he insists on calling it 'that huge building':

> "There is that huge building, but I don't go there. They built it nearby, but I would never be allowed to enter. I would be beaten up if I try to go there."

He looks into the distance:

> "We are struggling here to meet basic needs. We don't have clean drinking water and before each election they offer us free electricity supply and water. Promises that are never fulfilled; they lie to us. And they have always lied, whether it is the Congress Party or BJP..."

Electric poles and wires hang loosely above the roofs of the settlement. I ask whether people here are managing to get free electricity supply, by simply stealing the juice as they do in Peru or in Haiti, but the answer is resolutely 'no'. They check on them, constantly. In fact, people here suffer from gross overcharging by the private company, *Reliance Energy* (owned by Anil Ambani, brother of the richest man in the country, the abovementioned Mukesh Ambani), which supplies power to this entire area.

"We are receiving a 1,000 Rs (approximately US$16) bill, every month", explains an old couple next door. "On top of it we have to bribe employees of the electric company, to keep the connection. We have to go begging to more fortunate neighborhoods for water, and it is not always that the people there are willing to help us."

An old man in the house actually follows what is happening in the world:

> "I am aware of changes that are taking place in China, but our government is not doing the same things for us. Here, things are so bad that if we fall seriously ill, we simply die."

"What about democracy?" I ask.

"Democracy is for the rich."

Mr. Jagdish chips in: "As you heard, political parties come here, and they promise us free electricity and water, but nothing happens after the elections. Democracy is not working for us; it is the tool for the people with money to keep in power."

Down an alley, a lady with a child confirms that there is no supply of clean water to this settlement.

Eventually, small barefoot children begin begging.

***

The ITC Hotel manager in Jaipur, Rajasthan, philosophizes:

> "Arvind Kejriwal from AAM Admi Party (AAP) was very critical of the private media, and the mass media got extremely angry with him... You see; Arvind Kejriwal could become the Indian answer to the Latin American leadership!"

So I go to see him and his people.

On 3 August 2014, at the ancient star observatory, Jantar Mantar, in New Delhi, Aam Aadmi party held a mass gathering consisting of around 5,000 local residents, who were demanding fresh elections. There were fiery speeches coming from the podium and the AAP's leader, Arwind Kerjiwal, agitated the dense crowd with anti-corruption slogans, swearing he would implement reforms, were he to be voted in, back into the office. He was also promising to improve the lot of the common man. The reigning cry of the day was of getting rid of the oppressor ruling class through the democratic contest of the ballot boxes.

Here, surely, people knew something about BRICS and the Latin American revolutions?

But it was not the case. The campaign was almost exclusively about corruption.

Mr. Pawan Das, a cable manufacturer from the Shahdara constituency, spoke about the impact of AAP and the ex-chief minister, Arvind Kejriwal, and his former 49 days rule in Delhi:

> *"I noticed the policeman in our factory who used to extort Rs.300 bribe money from me every month, didn't turn up for 3 months. I egged him on to collect his extortion dues on coming across him, and enquired as to why he didn't come to get the money, to which he replied, evasively, that he was posted on an election duty. I retorted: 'were you really engaged in any election duty or got scared by the fear of prosecution instituted by Arvind Kejriwal's strong anti-corruption measures?'*

But BRICS or the fight against Western imperialism – definitely not!

"On asking about their stance on India's strengthening alliance with the American government and India's unassuming posture at BRICS meeting, all of them expressed their unawareness about such matters", explained Anish, in rather decorative language.

Then, at Jantar Mantar, we encountered several individuals who clearly demonstrated the art of sitting on two chairs.

Both Mr. Deepak Lal and his wife voiced their favorable opinion about the strengthening of ties with America:

> *"It's in the interest of India to be a great partner in creating alternatives to the dominant paradigm offered by the U.S., but at the same time India-US relations should remain unaffected".*

Another old couple went on in an even more Kafkaesque manner:

> *"US-India relation is the way to the rise of India along with creating alignments leading to a multipolar world".*

***

At the May Day Bookstore in New Delhi, after an avant-garde theatre performance, I met my friend Sudhanva. Comrade Sudhanva Deshpande, is the editor of *LeftWord Books,* as well as a famous Indian intellectual and actor. He explained:

> *"You are absolutely right posing the question: "Where is India in all this? It is very a good question because it is well known that for the last several years, a decade or more, Indian foreign policy had turned more and more towards the US. A few years ago, India conducted the Indo-US nuclear deal. That led to a lot of opposition back home, here in India, but the government went ahead with the deal. The Hindu right became more and more oriented towards the US. The government also argued for*

> *much closer ties with Israel. As you know, India is the biggest buyer of Israeli arms in the world today."*
>
> *"Earlier this year, in May, in the general elections, the party of the Hindu right, which is Bharatiya Janata Party (BJP), came to power. It is led by Narendra Modi, the man who is widely seen as being complicit in the pogrom of Muslims, in his homestay, Gujarat, in 2002, when he was a chief minister. His campaign was a very muscular campaign, a very macho campaign... He presented himself and his party as aggressively nationalist. The pre-election campaign was marked by anti-Muslim violence and rhetoric. As for foreign policy, there had been a long-term trend for more and more orientation towards the West, towards the US. In the current aggression on Gaza, for instance, the Indian government took the stand of so-called 'equidistance' from both Israel and Hamas, and this is really... this is compromising India's long-term commitment to the cause of Palestinian independence. And this goes back to even the 1940's, when India was not even independent.*
>
> *The fact that India itself was a colony, and that it fought an anti-colonial struggle – it all seems now as a distant memory."*

I asked Sudhanva about BRICS, concretely: "Is it even possible that India, where it stands right now, could and should be considered as a member of BRICS?"

"I think right now, Indian foreign policy is trying to calibrate its position", he replies".

And he continued:

> *"On one hand there is a trend towards more and more alignment with the US, and on closer and closer ties with Israel. So that's on the one side. On the other side there are also hard economic realities. And that is what forced the Indian establishment to look towards formations like the BRICS. If indeed it so happens that BRICS will not be just an economic club, but if it starts taking a more determined anti-imperialist position, then the Indian establishment would have to really decide, where it stands. I don't see India taking an anti-imperialist stand anytime soon, beyond some lip service."*

We talk about the past, about India's determined anti-imperialist stand in its post-colonial period. Nehru brought this country to Bandung, Indonesia, in 1955, where the Non-Aligned movement was created.

Sudhanva explains:

> *"India abandoned the Non-Alignment movement, effectively, in the late 80's. In some sense you can say that it happened in Delhi, in the early 80's, that it was the swansong of the non-alignment movement... The fact was that India became more and more ambivalent towards the idea of non-alignment, which helped to terminate the movement, because India was such an important part of it."*

And then India took a neo-liberal turn, in the early 90's, and even the past was forgotten.

***

What can be expected of the present nationalist government of Narendra Modi, in relation to BRICS?

Benny Kuruvilla is from Kerala, a recognized expert on BRICS, and political lead at the 'South Solidarity Initiative'. I met him, and his Chilean wife, Susana Barria, a labor organizer, after a demonstration in support of Palestine, in front of the Kerala House, in the center of New Delhi.

Benny readily clarified:

> *"Modi and his government would be happy to be part of the Western alliance and of the BRICS... This is really an ultra-nationalist government, and it has to reassert its ideology... In the past it was all very different: during the Cold War, India was very close to Cuba, and to the USSR. Now that India has a very pronounced right-wing government, it is very reluctant to side with the anti-Western block. I don't think India will go along with the idea that the Western concept should be cancelled. Indian Left-wing forces are very weak now, and this government is so happy to be part of big-boy's club; for them it is the place in the sun! What is happening in BRICS and in Latin America is mainly monitored by the local intelligentsia; mainly by the upper class."*

Susana appeared to be more optimistic and hopeful, believing in change, and in a way she echoed what Noam Chomsky told me about the Arab world, several years ago:

> *"Look, some 5 years before Hugo Chavez came to power in Venezuela, everything was bleak, in many parts of Latin America. We did not think that everything would be reversed so fast. We should not underestimate that things could change very fast."*

But India is not Venezuela. All three of us agreed that the Indian Left is too 'purist'. It is stuck in theoretical definitions of what Communism or Socialism should be. For its taste, China is not socialist enough; most of the Latin American countries are not really strictly Marxist. In the end, much is being discussed here, but very little achieved.

The next day I asked my friend Anish Gopinathan, a former international banker who spent several years working in Dubai, before returning, disgusted, back to India and began studying the Chinese language, and culture, whether all that I asked and heard so far made any sense. He replied:

> *"Yes. In 2002 MP Modi was the Chief Minister in Gujarat, during the pogrom. For years, there was a US ban on him, a refusal to issue him an entry visa. That ban was lifted around the time of elections..."*

The same happened in Indonesia, against Prabowo, an ultra-nationalist who was accused of crimes against humanity in Indonesia and blacklisted by the US Department of the State, but was quickly rehabilitated when he almost won the presidential elections earlier this year.

Anish concluded:

> *"Modi is pro-business and pro-West. But in a way, he can also sometimes stand against the West, and for India. You often mentioned the Indian colonial hangover, when Indian elites shamefully idealize the colonial era. Well, Modi is one politician who does not have this hangover... For instance, he insists on using Hindi at international meetings. All our elites were conditioned in the West: Nehru, Indira Gandhi, Rajiv Gandhi, Manmohan Singh... But not Modi! In fact he represents a big break against that colonial hangover... But the price is – he wants his Hindu state!"*

***

Hindu state... We flew to Varanasi, to the 'holy city' built on the banks of Ganga River. It is a depressing, oppressed and miserably poor city, but at the same time it is the place that the current MP – Mr. Modi – was elected from.

We went to Kashi Vishwanath Temple, to talk to Brahmin priests, about their vision for India.

The results were shocking.

Mr. Pandey spoke to us in front of two military sentinels guarding the entrance to the temple. He was a Brahmin priest, associated with this place of worship since his childhood:

> *"I am here, I am a priest, because... actually... I couldn't get a job anywhere else. Really, no regular employment for me... And so, this is how I make a living... To me, religion is important, because it gives me some income... I like Americans, because they come here, and give us money... Somehow I sense that they feel good, giving us money... I have no idea about the developments in China, Russia or Latin America... I really don't care."*

Mr. Shyama Prasad Sharma who also works for the temple, clarified his views:

"Latin America? BRICS? No, we don't have time for stuff like that. We are busy here, at this temple, with business, with trade."

What about something higher, more enlightened than that?

He walks away.

Anish is outraged:

> *"This is like some market place; market mentality. It is like some fish market or vegetable market, or stock market! No time for any big questions in life! This is what BJP is fighting for. Hindu state... It is exactly what the mullahs in Pakistan are trying to create in their madrasahs. A cold, religious society; the code of primitive society..."*

Desperate, we approach a simple man, a vegetarian food vendor. His name is Mr. Anoop Upadhyaya and he somehow brings things into perspective:

> *"I voted for Modi because my parents ordered me to do it. I don't expect much improvement from his government. If they deliver even some 25% of what they were promising us, I would be satisfied. We are always 'Bhajpa' (BJP)... That is what we are. We don't think about it, don't question it."*

We ask about BRICS.

He does not react, as if we were talking about some distant planet.

***

At some point I had had enough and I expressed a desire to visit some old-fashioned school to talk to teachers who were already there, teaching, before India entered the pragmatically-oblivious realm.

I was taken to Bhigan, just across the border from the capital, on the very edge of Haryana State, to a well-organized, clean and optimistic looking primary school.

I don't know if what I saw was true or whether my friends were just being too kind to me, creating a spectacle, similar to that in the film 'Goodbye Lenin'.

The educators and the principal – Mr. Kuldeep Singh Chavhan, as well as the history and physical education teacher – were extremely kind, knowledgeable and supportive.

We all expressed our admiration for the Soviet Union, and then we condemned Western imperialism.

"Friendship with Russia!" screamed one of the teachers.

"Israel is the oppressor! US are behind Israel!"

Then the Principal spoke:

"We are very well aware that the US is trying to buy India through its multi-national companies!'

Then I spoke.

It all felt like a scene from a long time ago, even before I was born...

We did not hug, kiss or embrace. We did not sing. But it all felt fantastic.

A dog barked outside.

Children began leaving the school. We were still speaking.

Then I asked about BRICS.

"There is an issue," the Principal admitted. "I am not really aware of the BRICS's cooperation with India."

"But..." I howled: "India is member of BRICS."

Silence.

"But Modi went to Brazil!"

"I don't know", said the Principal, sadly.

'It's better if we sing!' I thought.

***

From the other geographical extreme of the country, in the

poorest Dalit villages around Kanchipuram in Tamil Nadu, my dear friend Venkat (he wanted to use only his first name for this report), a Cambridge-educated Brahmin, who was so appalled by the helplessness of the poor people, that he went against all that the upper cast and the elites represent, wrote to me:

> *"The Indian social and political landscape hasn't changed in years. Like the distant mirage, new governments come and go giving hope to the parched souls who are soon left out to die with still hope in their eyes!*
>
> *The new middle class, thanks to the growth of IT, has often been praised and written about but this is only a small percentage although in a country of this size even such small percentages works out to be huge in numbers!*
>
> *An average rural person is still struggling to make ends meet and still hoping for the "paradise' that every politician promises! There is no time to read, think, discuss about other issues that affect the nation or the world. Cricket stars, film stars and sleazy politics conveniently fascinate Indian media, as the mass media are only concerned about TRP ratings and not about what people think and want!*
>
> *So, discussions about BRICS or what happens in Syria or Iraq doesn't really matter. Many villagers accept the stereotypes that the western media has painted. For example – the US is the land of wealth; China means cheap goods, Latin America – Che on your T-shirts and Cigars, Africa- famine and dangerous diseases, Middle East- only war!*
>
> *The education system is being so commercialized that Indian youth are actually produced in large numbers, lacking even the skills that Industry wants!*
>
> *Unless 'real' education is given to our children, we may not have a 'thinking' population in the future. But only if people are educated, can we hope for a greater critical mass of intellectuals who can guide the country."*

***

After having our boarding passes scanned at the gate and before entering the airplane, passengers had to go through three more military checkpoints. The entire state of affairs appeared to be thoroughly Kafkaesque. This confused, frustrated 'police state' was using its military, cops and other armed forces to intimidate and to keep at bay its own citizens. It has been doing it, for decades, in the most open and despicable way.

I still remember how in Gujarat, after that horrid sectarian pogrom of 2002, the Akshardham Temple killing and both (then) Prime Minister Atal Bihari Vajpayee, and Sonia Gandhi, decided to visit the area. A huge crowd gathered, to welcome the politicians. It was a very peaceful crowd, consisting mainly of poor onlookers. But the police began beating the people with batons, savagely, just 'preventively' I was told, as if it were the most natural thing on earth: 'The largest democracy on earth at work'. Nobody dared to protest against such treatment.

After talking to many, it appears that the poor see it all very clearly now: in the villages and in the slums, they laugh and cry or gesticulate angrily whenever the word 'democracy' is uttered in front of them. Most of the poor (that is the great majority of the country) have no doubts that they are living in a country whose rulers and oligarchs, backed by the security apparatus, are alimenting on their sweat, misery and blood.

Those 'educated classes', including most of the intellectuals from the Indian 'Left', live in a continuous and great deception. Most of them are desperately clinging to the notion that has been spread by the old and new Western colonial masters: that India is actually the largest democracy on earth.

Even those individuals in India who see clearly that both European and North American 'democracies' are increasingly becoming nothing else other than a grand farce, do not dare to admit that their own, Indian, multi-party system (aped from the West) in which all major political parties are controlled by corporate interests, as most of the mass media is, have been totally failing to represent the interests of the Indian majority.

'Democracy' is not a secretive and complicated scientific formula. It only means, in Greek, 'the rule of the people'. And it goes without saying that most of the long-suffering Indian people that I spoke to, do not feel that they are ruling their own country!

***

Just before I took off from Delhi, I found myself sitting right next to a member of the new local elites. A Sikh man, who began with the usual line of interrogation: where am I from, where do I live, what is my line of work? Dutifully and calmly, I replied. Then he offered his short biography: he was a manufacturer and owned 3 homes in 3 different parts of the world: one in India, one in Bangkok and one in Vancouver. "I am taking my family back to

Bangkok, now", he explained. "I have a wonderful house there. It is such a great place to live."

"It is quite complicated there, lately", I suggested, neutrally. "After the coup..."

My statement shocked him: "Why do you say that? It is all very simple. One and a half months ago it was complicated, but after the army took over, everything is great."

"For you, maybe", I said, "And for the Thai elites, as well as for their Western handlers."

He gave me that look, indicating that I was actually nothing more than a piece of dirt to him; that very look, which has increasingly began appearing on the faces of the new Indian 'elites', in those 5 star malls and hotels, in both India itself, and in countries like Thailand and Malaysia, which are now inundated by corrupt Indian officials and businessmen.

The conversation ended: from then on, arrogantly, he refused to reply to anything that I uttered, ignoring my attempts to be at least essentially civil and polite to someone who was occupying the seat next to me.

I did not ask about BRICS. I knew what he would reply: "They should all go to hell!" or something of that nature.

***

BRICS countries have to maintain high standards, if they are to make a significant difference in this world. Their determination to fight against colonialism, imperialism and for true freedom for countries worldwide cannot and should not be diluted.

If states like Indonesia, with governments full of war criminals and mass murderers, and one of the most inhumane economic/social systems on earth, are allowed to join, if Turkey, a member of NATO and one of the closest allies of the West in the Middle East, with several Western air force and military bases, is allowed to join; if India, which is openly and shamelessly collaborating with the West while sitting on two chairs is allowed to maintain its membership, then BRICS will soon lose all of its clout as well as its moral upper-hand.

If such a scenario takes place, the world will lose an alternative, and that would be an enormous tragedy.

India matters. Its people matter! It is a great and important nation. It used to be 'our nation'. It used to stand firmly against colonialism and imperialism. In many ways, and in many of its parts, it still does.

India should wake up. It is needed. It should rebel against the oppressive system, both domestic and global. And it should become a proud BRICS nation: with all its heart, and not just on paper!

22 August 2014

*****

58

FREEDOM FOR PALESTINE! AND PAPUA! AND CONGO!

This is not an easy essay to write. I have been postponing it for several weeks. But I have many readers all over the world who trust me, and they encourage me to tell the truth, as I perceive it. And I will continue doing so, for them, even when the topic is complex and somehow uncomfortable.

Let me begin by saying that I fully support freedom for Palestine; I demand that the Palestinian people be allowed to have their own state, and to have their pride and dignity restored. Not 'soon' but now, and even 'now' is too late!

I condemn Israel, for being the Rottweiler of the West in the Middle East, for its bellicose approach in the region, for its brutality towards the Palestinian people, and for its endemic dishonesty.

I have stood by the Palestinian people on several occasions: In Gaza and the West Bank, in Hebron and Bethlehem, in the Rafah Refugee Camp. I have stood by them physically, not just in an abstract way, fighting, at least verbally, with the Israeli border guards, having rubber-coated bullets flying all around me, dashing illegally from Jerusalem to Bethlehem with my Israeli activists and

Marxist friends.

But that does not seem to be enough. Lately, I am constantly being 'encouraged', even 'ordered' to 'go immediately to Palestine', as if I were a bunny rabbit operated via remote control by some couch potato who has just realized, sitting in front of his television set, that Israel and its handler, the West, are committing an on-going crime against humanity. And instead of going there himself, he begins demanding that I (and people like me) go, immediately, 'or else'!

'Or else' – meaning that I will be exposed and discredited (yes, by some part-time couch-bound living room fighter for the freedom of oppressed people) as someone who is, perhaps, not really too loyal to the cause, and not really a genuine internationalist or revolutionary.

I detest those 'or else' letters. I feel indignant. And I will respond to them, once and for all, now, aboard this four-hour flight from Nairobi to Johannesburg.

For years I have not stopped. No weekends or vacations for me. I have been fighting for oppressed people all over the world, and keeping absolutely nothing for myself. Once I get paid for my films or my books, everything I earn goes back into my work, to my struggle. I have no support whatsoever; there is no institution backing me, no 'protection' is offered or given to me.

Often, the 'thank you' from my readers, that 'you are making big difference' has been my only fuel, when things at times get totally messed up, very scary and very lonely.

The fact is: I cannot be everywhere. I am a lone fighter, my resources and time, are limited.

I cannot jump on a plane and fly to Tel Aviv, hire a car and dash to the border with Gaza, every time Israel begins to run amok. I wish I could.

Palestine has many friends, and I am aware of the fact that I am only one of many.

Some of the greatest thinkers of our time, from Noam Chomsky to Naomi Klein, are standing by it, solid as a rock. Many people, who are otherwise politically apathetic, are ready to get involved any time the Palestinian people get attacked (although one could argue that what is done against the Palestinian nation is a constant onslaught).

There are also some great Israeli men and women who are constantly engaged in reporting on the situation, shaming the Israeli state. I know some of them personally. They are fighting against their own country, because their country is wrong, and because they want it to change, to improve.

It does not make the suffering of the Palestinian people less horrible, but at least one could say that their defense is always in very good hands: in the hands of their own leaders and in the hands of true internationalists from all over the world.

But please understand that I am often stuck reporting from places that are almost defenseless, and with a level of suffering that is unimaginable to people living somewhere in Europe or North America.

I have spent years, going back and forth, to the Democratic Republic of Congo (DRC). Between 8 and 10 million people there have lost their lives, from 1995 to this day. That is as many as the same unfortunate country (unfortunate because it is so rich in minerals and raw materials, which the West needs for its communication equipment and weapons) lost during the reign of one of the most appalling monarchs in human history – Belgian king Leopold II.

I made a film – a feature documentary film – that is now being aired by Press TV. A film about how Rwanda and Uganda, on behalf of their European and North American handlers, are plundering and massacring millions of people in DRC.

Even the UN in its 'Mapping Report' spoke about alleged genocide. It is not some lunatic conspiracy theory. It is real and it is happening now. And two horrible fascist dictatorships, those of Rwanda and Uganda, are persistently supported and glorified in Washington, Paris and London. And the entire 1994 genocide narrative on Rwanda has been twisted and manipulated, so as to give Tutsis some moral legitimacy for the genocide they are presently committing in the DRC.

Yes, I spent more time in Rwanda, Uganda and East Kivu, lately, than I am spending in Gaza or in West Bank. I am sorry. But please see for yourself, how many people are really involved in bringing to the world some objective information about the Great Lakes region of Africa, and about this greatest episode of bloodletting in post-WWII history.

10 million people! Entire communities destroyed. There are hundreds of thousands of child soldiers, perhaps millions. The land is scarred and robbed of all its resources. There are Christian fundamentalist fanatics running private armies, torturing and mutilating, executing people, simply for pleasure.

There are rapes. Millions of women have been raped – from babies to 80 years old or more, grandmothers. And the way they rape there, is also absolutely unimaginable. After being gang-raped, many women have their faces slashed open with razor blades and knives, they have their rectums and vaginas cut mercilessly, just in case they were hiding some diamonds between their teeth or inside their private parts. Men do not even bother to kill them before they mutilate them.

And there is absolute silence about this, in Europe and North America, where Kagame and Museveni are portrayed as reformers and close allies.

You know, honestly, it is easier to fly to Tel Aviv and to protest there, than it is flying to and investigating in Kigali or Goma. Honestly, I would rather go to Gaza, but I have often felt that I am needed much more in East Kivu.

I spent some time in detention, deep underground, in a Congolese intelligence bunker in East Kivu, and I would rather restrain myself from supplying you with the details.

Rwandese and Congolese soldiers once pulled me in two different directions, right at the borderline. If the Congolese soldiers had won, I would now be dead.

I also work in Indonesia, making films and writing books.

In the West, the governments and mass media want us to think that Indonesia is synonymous with those few (quite polluted) beaches of Bali, during sunset. Hilary Clinton even claimed that Indonesia is proof that Islam, democracy and women rights can go hand-in-hand.

Indonesia is easily one of the most brutal countries on Earth, with a homicide rate twice that of the US (per capita), with its feudal system, and with social violence unimaginable anywhere else, except in sub-Saharan Africa.

Between 2 and 3 million people vanished during the US-backed coup in 1965, perpetrated by the military and by the religious cadres. That was the first genocide in the modern history of the country.

Soon after, there followed a second one, that of East Timor, where approximately 30% of the population lost its life. Almost everybody who means anything in the present political hierarchy of Indonesia was involved in the East Timor massacres – from the President (SBY), to the Presidential candidate Prabowo and his entourage, as well as the entourage of the President-elect, 'Jokowi'.

I used to smuggle myself into East Timor during the occupation, but there was zero interest or appetite in the West, to support its fight for independence.

There, in 1996, I was kidnapped by the Indonesian intelligence services and tortured. My films were developed and destroyed. I was unable to use my left arm for a year after that.

The on-going genocide in Papua is as appalling as that of East Timor. Like DRC, occupied Papua is one of the richest places of the world, in terms of its natural resources. The corrupt elites in Jakarta are allowing the total plunder of that complex cultural area, by countless Western multi-national companies. Indonesia produces almost nothing, and it lives off the pillaging of raw materials on its fringes and occupied territories.

According to Western human rights organizations, at least 120,000 people have lost their lives, but it is common knowledge among those who are investigating the genocide, that at least a quarter of a million have died.

In Indonesia, to even show the independent Papua flag is punishable by life imprisonment. To even speak about independence brings long prison sentences for locals, and deportation for foreigners. And foreigners are actually not allowed to travel to the territory, except to its capital, where intelligence agents follow them closely.

In Papua, local people are now in the minority, due to the Jakarta-implemented 'trans-migration' policy, and through the outright killing of the natives. The native population has been transformed into beggars and renegades in their own land, and is forced to adopt Islam as their religion, if they want to survive.

Local girls are regularly kidnapped by the TNI (Indonesian

military), raped and tortured – their nipples and clitorises are cut off by soldiers who consider these savage act to be "entertaining" – as I was told by a former Minister of Education of the neighboring Papua New Guinea (PNG). If the girls speak out, their villages are burnt to ashes.

While Indonesians regularly protest against the situation in Gaza, there are absolutely no protests against one of the most brutal occupations on Earth – that of Papua, by their own, Indonesian fascist state.

Apart from a few dedicated and brave people, including John Pilger, nobody speaks about the Papuan genocide. In fact, Westerners do not consider it weird travelling to, and spending money in Bali, now, just as they never considered it strange during the genocide in East Timor.

***

I work all over Africa and all over Indonesia. I mostly work in those places that are far from the radar of mass media, even off of those largely progressive media outlets.

I don't ask for recognition or support.

I only ask for some basic respect. For myself, but above all, for those defenseless people whose plight I am trying to define and to highlight.

Please try to free the Palestinian people and to support them. I will also do my very best to participate in this noble undertaking.

But please, do not insult, do not humiliate and do not doubt those of us who are trying to highlight the unknown and horrendous plight of the Congolese people, of Papuan people, or of Somali people.

Do not insult us for trying to tell the stories, of Cairo and Alexandria where the West has managed to derail the so-called Arab Spring, or from the Turkish/Syrian and Jordanian/Syrian border, nor from Thailand where the elites have once again sidelined their own people.

Your support is often all that we have. And where we are, where we operate, it is an often extremely cold and horrendous world.

And like cats, we, war correspondents and insane writers and filmmakers, also 'only' have a few lives. Most of us have spent most of them already and now, sometimes, are even running on reserve.

***

During the last Intifada, I worked all over Gaza, including at the Shifa Hospital, which was then overwhelmed by casualties. Howling ambulances kept bringing wounded Palestinian men, women and children into the bloodstained emergency rooms and corridors.

After I left, we drove towards the Rafah Camp. There was an open stretch of the road.

Suddenly, I spotted two Israeli helicopter gunships flying at a very low altitude. They flew over the roof of our car (a local hired taxi), then, a few seconds later, there was a tremendous explosion and our car jumped forward. I looked back and saw that a car that was moving behind us had been hit and destroyed, it was in flames.

I don't know who was inside that car or how many people were killed, but it was very clear that the attack was a random one. I could have been killed on that road with the same ease as those people that had been driving behind us. I could also have been easily killed, at different times and in different places; in Peru, Sri Lanka, Bosnia, East Timor, DRC, Kenya, and Paraguay, as well as in many other places.

The world is in flames. It has been, for centuries.

Our decisions – where to get physically engaged – are not easy to make, not easy at all.

Most of the time it is not about 'where we would like to be', but 'where it is our duty to be', where we will be the most effective.

I mostly aim for the most unprotected zones – not always, but mostly.

Palestine is now one of those priorities and I will try to return there, soon.

But please, help us out elsewhere, too. In Papua and DRC, in the Somali camps of Kenya where an entire generation of young people have never seen anything other than a dry desert and barbed wire, as a result of the West's total destabilization their country.

Each human life has the same value, the same weight. Be it the life of a poor Palestinian girl or an upper class Israeli boy, of a Papuan woman from a remote tribe, or an Italian aristocrat. We know that this is the objective and universal truth. We know that the entirety of humanity stands on this perception. And the moment this ceases to be understood as essential, the entire human race will regress, immediately, by moving back several centuries.

We know all this theoretically, but practically, the way this world is arranged; this principle has very rarely been implemented.

It should be.

And that is why the Israeli occupation has to stop, immediately.

And that is why, I will continue risking my life, writing about those people whose names we can hardly pronounce, and whose culture and lifestyles we often cannot comprehend. I will do it simply because they are human beings, because they are in pain, because they are our brothers and sisters, because our greed is murdering them, and because almost nobody gives a damn.

5 September 2014

*****

59

ARE EUROPE'S HORRID CRIMES FORGIVEN?

Many North American intellectuals have this ongoing love affair with everything that is European, particularly with the European 'social system' and 'European culture'.

It is a deadly, shameful obsession; partially based on a desperate desire to maintain the belief that the West is not finished, yet, and that to a great extent it is still superior to the rest of the world. Europe is portrayed as 'unique', as different to the United States, as something that is worth admiring... or at least its past and its essence.

It is never propounded or defined like that, of course, but this belief (and yes, it really resembles a religious faith) indirectly points out that it is quite legitimate that the West (or at least a big part of the West) continues its rule over our planet.

It is obvious that many men and women of the Left, living in North America, actually believe in Western "Exceptionalism"; not that of the United States, but that of Europe.

North American Eurocentric intellectuals tell us indirectly or even directly, that the US is some kind of desperado, which is derailing that wonderful, that glorious, centuries old, European cultural process, and the quest for egalitarianism.

Europe is often shown as a contrast, or counter-pole, to the United States; to its brutal selfishness and turbo capitalism... This is how the reality is depicted in so many progressive films, books and essays.

This view is somewhat romantic (in a Wagnerian way, searching for the idyll), but it also fully ignores clear historic facts, and defies essential logic.

It also blurs reality, doing tremendous harm to any sincere attempts to solve the present global nightmare, which has its roots exactly in the domination over so many long centuries, by European brutality and greed.

It is also arrogantly racist. Instead of US 'exceptionalism', it is advancing a clear and vulgar 'Euro-exceptionalism' and Euro-centrism. Everything has to be defined and judged by 'European logic' and measures, from Chinese socialism, to 'human rights', as well as 'democracy' and the entire scale of other essential issues.

***

But let us go back to that European 'social system' – the holy cow of the great majority of North America's left:

It has not been built by the exertions and honest labor of the European people. Anyone who bothers to look and study those maps of the world depicting our planet up to WWII would understand the reality, in just a few seconds.

That famed 'social system' is built on the enslavement of colonized peoples; it is built on the unimaginable horrors visited on those hundreds of millions of men, women and children, who were slaughtered mercilessly by the colonial European powers. It is built through oppression, terror, and almost exclusively, on theft and plunder.

To admire it, is like admiring some brutal thuggish oligarch, who has amassed huge wealth by extortion and open plunder, built a gigantic palace and provided his family or his village with free medical care, education, some theatres, libraries and parks.

European colonialists 'opened the veins' of Latin America. They stole everything they could lay their hands on; in what is now Peru, Bolivia, Ecuador, Brazil, Chile, Mexico and so many other places in Latin America.

They murdered everybody, unlike the US neo-colonialists, but 100% of the people, as happened during the French reign of places like Grenada or (near 100%) in the Polynesian Easter Islands.

Europe committed slaughters that are unimaginable in today's times, like those by the Belgian king, Leopold II, who was responsible for around 10 million lost lives in Congo, in the days when Congo had just a fraction of the population that it has now.

And at present again, EU companies are responsible, together with US companies, of course, for another bloodletting of nearly 10 million Congolese people (in DRC); simply because that unfortunate country is very rich in strategic minerals like Coltan and uranium, that those greedy Westerners simply cannot control their cravings. The West supports murderous regimes in Rwanda and Uganda that are killing and plundering on its behalf, by manipulating mass media, and creating insane historical narratives about the 1994 genocide... The French are openly plotting to carve off the mineral rich East Kivu from DRC, and to give it to Rwanda, so it could be ravaged in a much more organized way.

When it comes to the list of crimes against humanity committed by Europe, in the past and now, I never know where to begin and where to end. The list is so long, so horrible, that an entire book would, perhaps, be needed to simply compile the most exhaustive list.

But just to give a short summary, such a list would have to include the German holocaust against the local people of what is now Namibia; Belgian super-genocides in all of their 'dependencies', Dutch plunder of what is now Indonesia, Portuguese 'activities' in Brazil, India and China, Italian barbarities in Africa, British and French holocausts and devastation in basically all the continents, which goes on to this day, unopposed and ignored.

European companies have been so 'deeply involved' all over the world, that it is often impossible to separate their corporate activities from the worst fascist nightmares that have been taking place on our planet Earth, from the above-mentioned DRC, to Mercedes factories in Argentina, or, in Southern Chile, the German Nazi 'Colonia Dignidad' (a huge builder of motorways), where prisoners were savagely tortured, and women raped.

***

The perception of Europe being somehow more 'progressive' than North America is clearly manufactured by Europhiles and Eurocentric groups in New York, Toronto, San Francisco and elsewhere.

Yes, Europe has social nets, and in many of its countries decent subsidized medical care systems and education, but, but... once again, these have not been built or sustained from its creativity and production, instead, it has mostly come from the colonial and neo-colonial plunder perpetrated all over the world.

How many Asian and African families have to starve, in order to have some early-retired, still strong, German man or woman farting deep holes into his or her sofa, immobilized in front of the television set?

How many Senegalese farmers have to lose their livelihoods and go totally bust, so that French and Spanish farmers get their 'subsidies' and drive those latest BMW's? A generous compensation for 'not producing' or a great incentive to produce more, depending on the year.

And where did that theory come from, that it is only the US companies that are plundering the world? It almost appears like an extremely simplified formula: 'the multi-nationals = US based corporations'.

I have seen German pharmaceuticals in action during the civil war in Peru – what horror and spite for the local population!

I have studied French food giants and their actions in Indonesia, West Africa and elsewhere.

And some of the most horrendous genocides in the world, including those in the Democratic Republic of Congo (DRC) and Papua are fueled and propelled by many European-based conglomerates, not just those with US headquarters.

Yes, the United States behaves like a global thug, like a bandit, but it is definitely not alone, and its behavioral patterns clearly come from the colonialist culture and mentality of the 'old continent'.

And Europe is unrepentant, just as arrogant as in the days when their armies marched through all the continents and capitals of the world, which really, was, not too long ago.

When the Namibian government decided to move 'The Horse'

(a statue erected in tribute to German colonialism, which was responsible for two genocides in Africa) out of sight – to the courtyard of the old wing of the National Museum – the German community protested, loudly. They felt no shame!

As a European UN permanent staff member in Windhoek told me, during my visit there just a few days ago, the statue actually stood right above what used to be one of the first concentration camps on earth, built, of course, by the Germans.

To this day, the government of Namibia is still negotiating with Germany for the return of the skulls of local people who were decapitated and their heads flown to Germany for 'research' that was supposed to 'prove' that Africans are inferior to that great German race!

When I was filming my documentary film – "Rwanda Gambit" – about two outrageously brutal puppets of the West in Africa, Kagame and Museveni, I visited Brussels, among many other places, realizing in shock, that the city is still full of statues and train/subway stations named after King Leopold II, the butcher of Congo. This was the man under whose command, people who 'did not produce fast enough' on his rubber plantations, had their hands cut off, and their entire 'lazy villages' were burnt to the ground, with the inhabitants locked inside their huts.

King Leopold II – one of the great 'European heroes'! No repentance.

Winston Churchill – the butcher of the Middle East, as well as a self-proclaimed racist – is one of the symbols of the 'greatness of Europe', to this day!

Spain, the 'mother country', is dotted with statues of the most outrageous bandits, responsible for the plunder of the 'New World', or what is now called Latin America. And not long ago, before this great Revolution that swept through almost an entire continent, gangsters like Francisco Pizarro proudly decorated the main squares of Lima and other capitals. What a horrible insult to the hundreds of millions of local people who were literally exterminated by that European colonial power!

All this is hushed up by European cultural propaganda. In some countries and parts of the world (those that gained real freedom and independence), these facts are known, but in others, like in Southeast Asia, the brainwashing campaign has been much more 'successful' and complete.

The grooming of collaborators – local elites from Africa, Asia, the Sub-Continent and the Middle East – is mainly performed in the European capitals, be it London, Paris, or lately, Berlin.

Europe, not the United States, has developed an incredible propaganda system, effectively justifying its colonialist onslaughts, its crusades, its control and plunder over virtually the entire planet, a system implemented with deadly consistency and predictability, for centuries. This system has been evolving and 'perfecting itself' ever since the Middle Ages, and even in ancient times. Machiavelli was, of course, just one of the minor demagogues, not the main culprit.

US propaganda is fully transparent and thoroughly vulgar. To control the world, it needs more 'refined' and 'culturally sophisticated' supervision – in short, better formulated lies.

That is why it is actually pathetic and ridiculous to call Europe a 'junior partner in crime'. It is not 'junior' at all. It is just really old, lazy and vitriolic; therefore it is letting its outgrowth do all the shooting and yelling. But it is ruining the minds and brains of the people worldwide. The demagogy and real propaganda comes from London, Paris, Madrid and Berlin.

European 'culture' is behind the crimes, and it is in charge of the propaganda, by its justifications, lies and disinformation.

Europe is also grabbing great chunks of the booty.

In this Imperialist and neo-colonialist game, there are no major and minor roles. All roles are essential, and they are divided masterly.

***

In Europe, it is often repeated that the guilt for imperialism and neo-colonialism lies with the United States, and that the rest of the world agrees.

That is absolute rubbish.

In the past I lived in Hanoi, Vietnam, for several years. Holding US citizenship, I was often shocked by how friendly and forgiving the Vietnamese people were. Once, over a mug of beer, I asked my good friend: "Don't you hold any grudges against the US?"

The answer shocked me, but very soon I understood.

"We fought the United States. It was a terrible war, and millions of our people died. But in the end, we won. We forgave... But we could never forgive the French. They did not really fight us, except at the end of the colonialist period. But they humiliated us, plundered our land, and raped our women..."

It became clear to me that to those proud Vietnamese people, it was easier to forgive napalm and carpet-bombing than broken bottles inserted into the vaginas of their women, the common method of torture in Indochina. It was better to die proudly than to suffer constant dishonor.

Ask people from the sub-Continent, where they would most like to go, if they decided to leave India. Europe, with the exception of London, would hardly be on their priority list. Yes, one could argue that India is a very unusual place, and has, lately, become excessively chummy with the United States. I criticize it for that. But the reason why a great majority would choose to migrate to the US, Canada, Australia, New Zealand or South Africa, is simply because they feel more at ease there, where they are treated much better, because Europe is, honestly, outrageously racist. It is the continent of milk and honey if you are a white person, particularly if you are white from the 'West'.

The colonial master – the United States – murdered one million Philippine people. But there is no animosity towards the country. It is bizarre, I know, and it is partially due to brainwashing and propaganda. But there is also a certain logic to it – Spanish conquest and rule was, incomparably worse.

Europeans spilled blood everywhere. And their arrogance left a terrible aftertaste all over the world.

The ransacking of Beijing by the French, the colonization, plunder and division of China by the British, French, Portuguese... All this is forgotten in Europe, but not in the most populous nation on earth.

The Dutch and their countless crimes – that insane plunder of what is now Indonesia has never been forgiven, or forgotten on the archipelago, but in Europe is muted.

***

Who built the European palaces, theatres, hospitals and schools? Whose blood was spilt so that Europeans could have their 'social net'? Whose lands were robbed? Whose labor utilized?

I have repeated many times and say it again here: I am totally appalled, absolutely against all those 'free medical schemes' in Europe; I am against their 'social schemes', as long as they are paid for by the blood and tears of people in the poor countries.

I hail them – these or similar schemes – when they are implemented in Cuba or Venezuela, China or South Africa, because there they are 'by the people' and 'for the people'. But not in Europe! The way their economies are structured, it is clear that for some grandmother in Germany to have free and long chats with her doctor, dozens of people in Africa and elsewhere have to starve and live in servitude.

The best scenario would be universal and global free medical care, education, and many, many other social projects.

But that is not how Europeans envision the world. They want to be 'unique'; they want to be the 'chosen' ones. They don't give a damn how many people die to provide them their sheltered and sclerotic lives.

On top of it all, European countries come to their former colonies and lecture them about 'good governance', giving scholarships, and teaching young people about 'democracy'.

'Good governance' is of course nothing other than the implementation of systems that will continue to serve the business and geopolitical interests of the West. 'Democracy' is a political concept that would never allow real change.

You never hear about the Goethe Institute or Alliance Française arranging a series of lectures in Africa or in Indonesia, about free medical care or free education.

And the people from Africa or Indonesia travel to Europe and say: "My god! What a great social system. Why have we never managed to build it ourselves?" Well, why not? You did build it! But not for yourself! You built it for the Dutch and other Europeans!"

***

The North American Left is doing a tremendous disservice to the world, with its staunch Euro-centrism!

It may actually be the greatest single reason why the "Left" lost in so many places.

The world is measured and analyzed by Western, mainly European logic, which is absolutely foreign, even hostile to the people of the rest of the world.

The arrogance and provinciality of these analyses are pushing away people from some of the greatest cultures and societies on earth, including those of China, Russia, the Middle East, Africa, but also to some great extent, of Latin America.

And we are actually talking about societies where the Left – their own, home -grown Left – has lately been victorious!

But this Left is not good enough for most Europeans and their North American admirers. Chinese socialism is not really socialism, because it is not based on European 'culture'. Unless it gets that seal of approval from the intellectuals in Paris, London or Rome, it is not real socialism, not at all!

For years, since the beginning of the Process, I had been fighting for Chavez. I even began working for, and making films for Telesur. I am a firm *Chavista*, not because I believe that his governance was flawless, but because I am convinced that it was pulling the country and the world in the right direction. And because his people had chosen him, again and again! But it took more than a decade before the West's left, and even then just a small part of it, began taking the Venezuelan revolution seriously! And they are still trashing Cuba!

I am behind China with all my heart. I have seen how Chinese socialism is transforming the country, and I have also witnessed the great work it is doing abroad. But the more socialist China is (and it is, once again, increasingly), the more spite it gets from the Western, particularly European intellectuals, who lost, flatly and patently, in their countries, and are now bitter about every nation on earth where that young, progressive, healthy spirit is propelling millions towards constructing new schools and hospitals, high-speed railways and metro systems, public parks and social housing. They would never accept the leadership of some Asians! They would rather bury the entire spirit of the Left, which, in a way, they are actually doing.

I see the same now, here, in South Africa! The more this wonderful country is changing, transforming itself, the more it does for its people – the more it comes under fire, and the more it is being spat at.

It is different here, damn it! It moves on through very different dynamics than those in Europe. China is thoroughly different, and so are its culture and its way of doing things. And thank God it is different! People worldwide have had enough of European cultural chauvinism, which always leads to the same result, in the end – the seeking of exceptional privileges for the people whose greatest 'achievement' was the most efficient, intensive plunder and murder seen on our planet!

Ask Africans, whether they trust and want the Chinese here, or the Europeans? Despite all that vitriolic BBC propaganda, the great majority all over this destroyed continent will say that they trust Beijing much more than London, Paris or Brussels!

But they do not count! How many African voices (except the collaborative ones) are carried by European media, or by progressive North American ones?

You see, foreigners, the majority of the world, cannot be really trusted. Look who writes about China, Russia, Latin America or Africa? Just look at their names! How many Chinese, Japanese, Korean, African names do we see even in progressive Western publications? How many Latin names are allowed in?

India is an exception. Indian intellectuals speak English and many of them (although not all) are part of this Western game: from the Right, Left, and from the Center.

Everybody in the West is passing judgment on China and Venezuela or Africa; especially Europeans or those who take the European uniqueness and its cultural exceptionalism as their basic platform.

I have very unpleasant but honest news for the North American Eurocentric left: people in many countries worldwide, where socialism is actually being built and fought for as we speak, want nothing to do with the Western left, anymore, exactly for the reasons I have spelled out above. They see it as patronizing, hostile and extremely unhelpful.

Many Chinese comrades that I know in Beijing feel indignant. They feel that their country, which has done so much for its people and for the world, is being insulted, dragged through dirt, and smeared... often by the Western, mostly European, left!

I feel the same anger in South Africa.

And I have to declare here, that I share these emotions. If I am forced to choose, to take sides, I would not hesitate for a single moment: my allegiances are with Latin America, with China, Russia, Eritrea, not with the Western Left, and not with those European analyses of the world.

No other continent or part of the world ever damaged, or harmed our planet as much as Europe; not even the United States. And all the foundations of terror that the US and its allies have been spreading all around lie in the long and horrid centuries past, depicted so well by the historical world maps.

I do not want the world to be judged, defined and ruled by European ideas and perceptions. I do believe in collective guilt and responsibility, and I am holding Europe accountable for most of the conflicts, divisions and nightmarish scenarios that we have on this planet Earth right now.

We need unity, and we are working on it.

It is unthinkable for China to begin trashing South African or Brazilian concepts.

Venezuela would never start criticizing Russian culture or the way Russians are doing things.

Before my latest documentary film was broadcast by *Telesur,* throughout Latin America and the world – a film about the horrific slums in Nairobi that were created under the Kenyan capitalist nightmare – one of the leading figures of the network asked us to remove from the film both the Venezuelan Ambassador and some Kenyan politicians who kept repeating that only adopting the Venezuelan way would save their country.

The argument put forward by the most influential television channel in Latin America was clear: "It is an insult to put a high ranking Venezuelan official on air... The great Kenyan nation knows and will find its own way forward."

To some extent I disagreed, but I saw the point. The argument was full of respect for that far-away suffering African country and her people.

Venezuelan comrades were refusing to dictate the way forward to their brothers and sisters in Africa.

China is adopting exactly the same attitude: "if you need us, we will help, but do not expect us to come and push our system down your throats! And we will not judge you. We will not tell you who you are and what to do!"

***

The Western, pro-European Left, may actually cost some terrible harm to all progressive countries, governments and movements, worldwide. By stubbornly embracing and endorsing the continent (and its schemes) that is seen by majority of the planet as the most merciless, arrogant and brutal, it has actually already alienated many genuine revolutionaries in non-white and non-Western countries.

To observe this love affair between the North American Left and Europe – to see it from some none-Western city or village, is thoroughly grotesque, confusing, even insulting. It appears to be millions of miles from true and honest Internationalism. And it is strategically suicidal and morally chauvinist.

Europe is fully behind all crimes committed in early days of the United States, Canada, Australia and New Zealand. Murdering of indigenous people was done, mainly, by the first, second and third generation of the European settlers. The 'Old Continent' introduced the US exceptionism, and the same goes for slavery, apartheid and brutal discrimination. The same is apparently true about what was done to the territory now called Latin America.

And colonialism and neo-colonialism, as well as the spite for non-white human beings all over the world, came, most clearly, from the logic and concepts that originated in the UK, France, Holland, Belgium, Spain, Portugal and other European countries.

After exterminating hundreds of millions of 'lesser people', and after plundering natural resources all over the world, using local slave labor, the European conquerors awarded their own nations with internally egalitarian social systems, which, the North American left-wing intellectual elite cannot stop admiring, until now.

For centuries, the aristocracy, royalty, Church and merchants, were hiring and prostituting court musicians, to bang into their harpsichords and to sing on the stages and in the theatres built on corpses from foreign lands, and amalgamated by blood. They also employed painters to depict the 'noble faces' of the elites, the saints, the Jesus and the countryside. That has been the core of that fable European culture!

No horrors, no genocides were depicted or described by that 'culture', despite the fact that the entire continent was built on the genocides and plunder committed all over the planet.

'The European intellectual elites' have been, historically, the most silent and servile, of any part of the world.

And these facts are totally overlooked, even censured, by most of the North American 'left-wing' admirers of Europe.

I believe it is time to revisit both history and the 'culture' of Europe.

And it is time to re-visit the sources that are fueling its 'social system'; to see who is really paying for those agricultural subsidies, early retirements and free medical care all over the European Union.

***

I am writing this in Maseru, the capital of Lesotho, which has just suffered from an abortive coup. I am sitting in the Alliance Française cafe... There are three white men sitting at the next table, speaking German. Unfortunately, I do understand.

They are talking about how pathetic, how useless the African Union and SADC is. They despise this part of the world. They came here to preach. They are full of 'ideas' about how to change Africa – pushing her in their direction. I don't know if they work for some bank, or for the EU.

I have nothing to do with them. I don't want this world to be run by them, anymore. They are vitriolic, toxic.

A few minutes' walk away; there are men and women of South African police force. Pretoria took immediate action after the coup in the neighboring country: on request, it sent the elite police force to protect the government and key institutions. Like Brazil in South America, South Africa is taking direct actions to improve life in its part of the world.

Spontaneously, I approach a woman selling fruits at the corner, as if trying to cleanse myself from that Euro-neo-colonialist talk.

"Whom do you trust more: South Africans or Europeans?"

She laughs, thinking that I am joking:

"But... These are our brothers and sisters", she points her hand towards the South African police. Two of my sisters live in their country. We follow all that happens there.... All their victories and problems..."

As I board my shuttle to the tiny Maseru airport, for some reason, I feel light and happy and full of hope.

12 September 2014

*****

60

GERMANY'S AFRICAN HOLOCAUST

How outrageous, how heartbreaking, how truly grotesque! Windhoek City – the capital of Namibia – is, at one extreme full of flowers and Mediterranean-style villas, and at the other, it is nothing more than a tremendous slum without water or electricity.

And in between, there is the town center– with its Germanic orderly feel, boasting 'colonial architecture', including Protestant churches and commemorative plaques mourning those brave German men, women and children, those martyrs, who died during the uprisings and wars conducted by local indigenous people.

The most divisive and absurd of those memorials is the so-called "Equestrian Monument", more commonly known as "The Horse" or under its German original names, Reiterdenkmal and Südwester Reiter (*Rider of South-West*). It is a statue inaugurated on 27 January 1912, which was the birthday of the German emperor Wilhelm II. The monument "honors the soldiers and civilians that died on the German side of the Herero and Namaqua 'War' of 1904–1907'".

That 'war' was not really a war; it was nothing more than genocide, a holocaust.

And Namibia was a prelude to what German Nazis later tried to implement on European soil.

A European expert working for the UN, my friend, speaks, like almost everyone here, passionately, but without daring to reveal her name:

> *"The first concentration camps on earth were built in this part of Africa... They were built by the British Empire in South Africa and by Germans here, in Namibia. Shark Island on the coast was the first concentration camp in Namibia, used to murder the Nama people, but now it is just a tourist destination – you would never guess that there were people exterminated there. Here in the center of Windhoek, there was another extermination camp; right on the spot where "The Horse" originally stood."*

"The Horse" was recently removed from its original location, and placed in the courtyard of the old wing of The National Museum, together with some of the most outrageous commemorative plaques, glorifying German actions in this part of the world. Nothing was destroyed, instead just taken away from prime locations.

Where "The Horse" stood, there now stands a proud anti-colonialist statue, that of a man and a woman with broken shackles, which declares, "Their Blood Waters Our Freedom".

***

A visit to those German genocidal relics is 'an absolute must' for countless Central European tourists that descend every day on Namibia. I followed several of these groups, listening to their conversations. Among these people, there appears to be no remorse, and almost no soul-searching: just snapshots, posing in front of the monuments and racist insignias, pub-style/beer jokes at places where entire cultures and nations were exterminated!

Central European, German-speaking tourists in Windhoek, appear to be lobotomized, and totally emotionless. And so are many of the descendants of those German 'genocidal pioneers'. Encountering them is like *déjà vu*; it brings back memories of the years when I was fighting against the German Nazi colony, '*Colonia Dignidad*' in Chile; or when I was investigating the atrocities and links, of the German Nazi community in Paraguay to several South American fascist regimes that had been implanted and maintained by the West.

And now the German community in Namibia is protesting the removal of "The Horse". It is indignant. And this community is still powerful, even omnipotent, here in Namibia.

Almost nobody calls the 'events' that took place here, by their rightful names, of holocaust or genocide. Everything in Namibia is 'sensitive'.

But even according to the BBC: "In 1985, a UN report classified the events as an attempt to exterminate the Herero and Nama peoples of South-West Africa, and therefore the earliest attempted genocide in the 20th Century."

On 21 October 2012, The Globe and Mail reported:

> *"In the bush and scrub of central Namibia, the descendants of the surviving Herero live in squalid shacks and tiny plots of land. Next door, the descendants of German settlers still own vast properties of 20,000 hectares or more. It's a contrast that infuriates many Herero, fuelling a new radicalism here.*
>
> *Every year the Herero hold solemn ceremonies to remember the first genocide of history's bloodiest century, when German troops drove them into the desert to die, annihilating 80 per cent of their population through starvation, thirst, and slave labor in concentration camps. The Nama, a smaller ethnic group, lost half of their population from the same persecution.*
>
> *New research suggests that the German racial genocide in Namibia from 1904 to 1908 was a significant influence on the Nazis in the Second World War. Many of the key elements of Nazi ideology – from racial science and eugenics, to the theory of Lebensraum (creating "living space" through colonization) – were promoted by German military veterans and scientists who had begun their careers in South-West Africa, now Namibia, during the genocide..."*

The Namibian government is still negotiating the return (from Germany) of all skulls of the local people, which were used in German laboratories and by German scientists to prove the superiority of the white race. German colonialists decapitated Herero and Nama people, and at least 300 heads were transported to German laboratories for 'scientific research'. Many were 'discovered' in the Medical History Museum of the Charite hospital in Berlin, and at Freiburg University.

Leading German doctor, who was working on 'the pure race doctrine' in Namibia (the doctrine later used by the Nazis), was doctor Fisher. He 'educated' many German physicians, including Doctor Mengele.

It is all to a very little surprise, considering that the first German governor of the colony was the father of Hitler's deputy Herman Goering.

Germany never officially apologized for its crimes against humanity in what it used to call German South-West Africa. It did not pay reparations.

Germany's holocaust in 'South-West Africa' is, among other things, a proof that the common Western theory about how German Nazism came to existence before the WWII was totally wrong. According to that theory, after the WWI, defeated and humiliated Germany got radicalized and 'reacted' monstrously to its condition.

But in reality, before and during the Second World War, Germany simply decided to behave in Europe exactly as it was behaving in its colonies, for many decades.

***

There are Robert Mugabe and Fidel Castro Streets in the center of Windhoek. And there is that tremendous National Museum, commemorating the national-liberation struggle and the role of the heroic Cuban and North Korean troops in their fight against Western-supported apartheid.

Bizarrely, German pre-Nazi/WWII monuments and insignias literally rub their shoulders alongside those great liberation struggle tributes.

Divisions are shocking: ideological, racial, social.

In Namibia, there is segregation on an enormous scale, everywhere.

While neighboring South Africa is moving rapidly away from racial segregation, introducing countless social policies, including free medical care, education and social housing, Namibia remains one of the most segregated countries on earth, with great private services for the rich, and almost nothing for the poor majority.

"Apartheid was even worse here than in South Africa", I am told by my friend from the United Nations. "And until now... You go to Katutura, and you see who is living there, they are all local people there, all black. Katutura literally means 'We have no place to stay'. 50% of the people in this city defecate in the open. Sanitation is totally disastrous. Then you go to Swakop city, on the shore, and it is like seeing Germany recreated in Africa. You also see, there, shops with Nazi keepsakes. Some Nazis, who escaped Europe, came to Windhoek, to Swakop and other towns. In Swakop, men march periodically, in replicas of Nazi uniforms."

***

Katutura is where the black people were moved to, during apartheid.

My friend, a 'colored' Namibian, who fought for the independence of his own country and of Angola, drove me to that outrageous slum which seems to host a substantial amount of the capital's population, with mostly no access to basic sanitation or electricity.

He has also chosen to remain anonymous, as he has explained, in order to protect his lovely family. To speak up here, unlike in South Africa, which may, these days, be one of the freest and most outspoken places on earth, can be extremely dangerous. But he clarifies further:

> "In Namibia, it is very rare for people who used to suffer, to speak about it publicly. In South Africa, everyone speaks. In Angola, everyone speaks... But not here."

Then he continues:

> "What we can see in Namibia is that many German people are still in control of big business. They are ruling the country. They have hunting farms and other huge estates and enterprises. Germans bring money to Namibia, but it stays with them, and it consolidates their power – it does not reach the majority. You cannot even imagine, how much local people working on their farms, are suffering. It is still like slavery. But it is all hushed up here."

***

"Sprechen Sie Deutch?" A black Namibian man intercepts me, as I am walking down the Fidel Castro Street.

"I do, but I would rather not, here", I explain.

"But why not?" He grins at me. "You know... It is not only them... Germans... I grew up; I was educated, in East Germany during our fight for independence. And my friend that you see over there – he was flown to Czechoslovakia and he went to school there. Communist countries did so much for us, for the Africans: Cuba, North Korea, Soviet Union, Czechoslovakia and East Germany. We are so grateful!"

"Yes", I say. "But it is over, isn't it? Czechoslovakia, East Germany... They joined the imperialists, the rulers. They exchanged ideals for iPads."

"Yes", he said. "But one day... who knows... things could be different, again."

Yes, definitely, I think. But most likely not in Europe...

***

At the new and lavish National Museum in Windhoek, I salute the Namibian and foreign fighters against apartheid – those who struggled and died for freedom, and the independence of Africa.

Then, I descended to the "Goethe Institute", the German cultural center, a colonial building surrounded by barbed wire.

There, a local starlet is loudly rehearsing for something called 'a night under the stars', or something of that sentimental, over-sugary pop nature. These are basically evenings designed to bring together the pampered international crowd and those 'feel-good-about-life' local elites.

I ask the starlet, whether this institute is trying to address the most painful issues of the past and present, all connected to Germany, of course.

She is black but she speaks and behaves like a German. She gives me a huge and pre-fabricated smile:

> "At Goethe we don't want that... We are trying to get away from all this (meaning colonial and segregation issues). We are just trying to get Germans and Namibians together, you know..."

I later peek at those Namibians who are being brought together with the Germans. No Katutura here, naturally...

And for some reason, what came to my mind is a conversation I had, on the phone, many years ago, with one of the editors of the German magazine, Der Stern, after I offered him my findings and photos from Nazi *Colonia Dignidad* in Chile. He said: "Oh, Colonia Dignidad! Hahaha! Never again, ja?"

***

One evening I eat at Angolan/Portuguese restaurant in Windhoek, *O Portuga*; an institution known for its great food and mixed crowd. What an evening, what a place!

After dinner, I dive into German 'Andy's Bar', a nearby place that was described to me as "An institution, which not even a black or a colored person from the embassies or the UN would dare to enter".

Photo 10. SWAPO and fight for freedom, Namibia.

The Beer is flat, but the conversation of the local crowd is extremely 'sharp'. Patrons are freely giving black Namibians names of local farm animals. Their spite is open and sincere. I listen, I understand. Eventually I leave.

I catch a taxi, driven by a corpulent black man. The radio is blasting and I hear the socialist, anti-imperialist lyrics of 'Ndilimani', a brilliant local political band.

It is now well past midnight, and despite the warnings from all those 'well-meaning Germans' that I met in Windhoek, I feel much safer in this taxi than in Andy's Bar and in so many other similar institutions.

"Is this country really governed by Marxist SWAPO?" I wonder aloud.

"No way", the driver points back, towards the bar. "'They' never left. 'They' are still controlling the country. The revolution is not over."

I tell him that I am beginning to understand what drove Robert Mugabe mad and angry, in Zimbabwe. The driver nods. I push my seat back, and make it recline.

"It is all fucked up", I say.

The driver thinks for a while, but then replies, using almost the same words as the man who spoke to me on Fidel Castro Street: "Yes, brother, yes! But one day... who knows... things could be different, again."

19 September 2014

*****

61

They Are At it Again

SYRIA, THE LATEST CRUSADE

The West is striking again; it is stabbing the very center, the heart of the Arab World.

This time it is targeting the group – ISIS – which it created itself, and which it had been arming, feeding and pampering until just very recently.

Airplanes and missiles are flying, and bombs are falling. The war has begun.

But is it really a war, or just a brutal game, a gigantic PlayStation operated by thousands of hooked-up maniacs in the Pentagon and all over Washington, Brussels and some servile capitals in the Middle East?

A war is, after all, when two sides are facing each other, when two sides fight, when two sides are risking their lives.

In this surreal and post-modern 'war', the only victims will be the people of the Middle East, most likely civilians. Their lives will be risked by those who are sitting, in safety, on their destroyers and in control rooms, hundreds and thousands of miles away, drinking coffee and cracking jokes.

The *Übermenschen* of the West will not descend from the sky, in order to fight, – man to man – in order to minimize the casualties of a peaceful population. The killing will be done by Tomahawks and F22's (at least those have real pilots), and by drones.

This is actually not a war but a massacre, a mass murder.

Another massacre. This one may last very long and take millions of human lives in the most brutal circumstances.

Western leaders are ready... to sacrifice the lives of the "others"; the regime is ready. You can read it on Obama's face, and on the face of Cameron.

***

The Empire began attacks against its own creation – the Islamic State or ISIS as it is known here in the Middle East. Countless ISIS cadres were armed and trained in the NATO-run refugee camps in Turkey and Jordan, right on the Syrian border. And the main purpose of ISIS was to destabilize and destroy Bashar al-Assad's Government in Damascus.

ISIS did not fall from the sky. Nor is it some sort of spontaneous movement. Like the Mujahedeen forces in Afghanistan, which fought both, the Democratic Republic of Afghanistan (DRA) and later the Soviet Union, ISIS were paid, armed and trained by the United States and its allies.

It is a common tactic used by the West, to identify and groom the most radical forms of Islam, including Wahhabism, which is now choking Saudi Arabia and other countries in the region.

I was told in Istanbul by a leading Turkish documentary filmmaker from Ulusal TV, Serkan Koc, who has produced several ground-breaking works on the subject of the 'Syrian opposition':

> "Of course you do realize that those people are not really 'Syrian opposition'. They are modern-day legionnaires collected from various Arab countries, including Qatar and Saudi Arabia, paid by western imperialist powers. Some are members of Al-Qaeda and other terrorist organizations. Most are militant Sunni Muslims. One could describe them as rogue elements hired to fight the Assad government."

I have covered those border camps for more than two years,

often risking my life, occasionally being harassed and detained by Turkish intelligence.

In 2012 and 2013, I visited the areas around the Turkish city of Hatay, and camps like Apaydin, where various ISIS fighters were being trained by Western and Turkish intelligence. I investigated the situation at the border and also around Incirlik air-force base near Adana, which both the RAF and USAF use. And I worked in Jordan, at the camps that are openly utilized for the training of the 'Syrian opposition', a fact that is not concealed, even by the regional press.

I thought that my reports, and the reports by Serkan Koc, Huseyin Guler and others, dispersed the myth of a 'spontaneous uprising against the President al-Assad'.

But obviously our efforts could not match the tremendous propaganda and brainwashing campaign unleashed by Western corporate media.

In a totally irrational, logically bizarre pirouette, the US accused Syria of not destroying Islamic State, that unsavory offspring of Western imperialist policy.

As reported by Reuters:

> "In a letter to U.N. Secretary-General Ban Ki-moon, U.S. Ambassador to the United Nations Samantha Power wrote, "The Syrian regime has shown that it cannot and will not confront these safe-havens effectively itself."

The strikes were needed to eliminate a threat to Iraq, the United States and its allies, she wrote, citing Article 51 of the U.N. Charter, which covers an individual or collective right to self-defense against armed attack."

To interpret what was written above: 'Bashar al-Assad, we helped to create ISIS in order to overthrow you... Now we hold you responsible for not managing to destroy our offspring... Therefore, we are going to bomb your country, kill thousands of your people, and possibly overthrow you in the process.'

The Western public is fully ignorant; it is indoctrinated and brainwashed, otherwise hundreds of millions of European and North American citizens would be now rolling around all over the streets, many dying of laughter.

The statements made by Obama and Power are so absurd and

philosophically foul, that they would make even Orwell and Huxley blush in embarrassment. Even the most brilliant of novelists could not invent such twists of logic!

The Middle East is well informed, it is aware of the game, but people in so many countries here are too scared to protest, or even to speak up. The West overthrew progressive and truly patriotic governments, and upheld the most oppressive tyrannies.

There is some commonsense left, of course. In Lebanon, Hezbollah snapped back, most likely expressing the feelings of a great number of the people living in the Middle East. In its televised address, the leader of Hezbollah, Sayyed Hasan Nasrallah, clearly stated his position:

> "The U.S. isn't qualified morally to lead an anti-terrorist coalition. In our view, America is the mother of terrorism and the cause of terrorism in the world... Everyone knows that Hezbollah is against ISIS and Takfiri groups and is fighting them... However, that doesn't mean we support U.S military intervention in the region. Hezbollah is against any US-led coalition that uses terrorism as an excuse for a military intervention in Syria and Iraq."

And one could add: and most likely, one day, in Iran...

It is clear that in this region; almost nobody is fooled by empty clichés and the twisting of language. ISIS is a multi-purpose, flexible stick in the hands of the West. It is also 'helpful' when it operates on its own, when it 'gets out of control'. It served as a weapon against Mr. al-Assad and now it is turning into a perfect scarecrow, a justification for the direct invasion of Syria, for redeployment, or more precisely for an increase of the Western military might in the region, for the creation of a pro-Western puppet Kurdish state, and quite likely, for deposing the government in Damascus.

The trigger-happy Turkish government is already making noises, promising to get involved, militarily, but only if the goal is defined concretely and openly: to overthrow Mr. al-Assad.

To overthrow the government in Damascus is, of course, the main goal of Washington, as well, but Mr. Obama is not as honest and open as his counterpart and ally in Ankara.

***

All this can be, of course, only the beginning of something truly horrendous. One should never forget that the Empire and its Saudi, Qatari and Israeli allies are always 'thinking big'.

There is always more to destabilize, to ruin, and to conquer – there is Iran on the horizon, and much more.

To them – to the Empire – places like Syria or Iran do not constitute some of the oldest and greatest cultures on Earth, inhabited by gentle and peaceful people. To the Empire, these places are only booty, consisting of natural resources and strategic locations.

People mean nothing. If one million die, if two or three millions vanish, it makes absolutely no difference. Cultures mean nothing, as they are not Western, as they are not Christian ones, as they are not 'white'.

Obama and Cameron are building on that grand old tradition of the deranged British colonial empire. It was, after all, only 80 years ago when then British Prime Minister Lloyd George commented on Britain's success in undermining a disarmament conference— which would have barred the use of air-power against civilians, particularly those in the Middle East. He pointed out that it was a success. His secretary and second wife Frances wrote:

> "At Geneva, other countries would have agreed not to use aeroplanes for bombing purposes, but we insisted on reserving the right, as D[avid] puts it, to bomb niggers! Whereupon the whole thing fell through, & we add 5 million to our air armaments expenditure..."

Decades later, the Empire retains this and many other similar 'rights'.

***

What is left, how much is left, of the Arab world?

And I don't mean those few flashy airports, complemented by '6-star hotels', shopping malls for the elites, and European limousines. I don't only mean those oil wells and artificial islands with palm-tree-shaped villas.

This part of the world used to be a beacon, one of the light-houses of humanity. This is where the first universities were erected, the first public hospitals, and this is where the very ideas of 'social', of 'egalitarian' and of 'compassionate' values, came to life.

The Arab world and Persia were where the greatest doctors, architects, astronomers, scientists and poets used to reside and create.

This is where many great men like the first Sultan of Egypt and Syria – Ṣalāḥ ad-Dīn –defended the world against those brutal European hordes, invading in the name of the cross, while being obsessed with looting and rape.

After centuries of colonial wars, Western cruelty and militarism finally won. They conquered Arabia, as well as the rest of the planet.

The Arab world was reduced to subservient kingdoms and states, ruled by a few outrageously rich and ruthless families.

In Egypt and Iran, the heroic attempts to create egalitarian and socialist societies in the post-WWII era, were brutally crushed by the Western powers. Nihilism, cynicism, corruption and militarism were introduced and upheld.

In modern days, even those relatively socially-oriented states like Iraq and Libya, were annihilated, at the cost of hundreds of thousands, even millions of human lives. Oil had to belong to the international corporations, not to the state, not to the people.

Now what is here, are a few countries in total ruins, including Iraq, Libya and Syria. There are several staunch allies of the West, states like Qatar and Saudi Arabia, governed by secretive and oppressive monarchies that are spreading the most tyrannical form of Islam all over the region, and as far away as Southeast Asia, while enjoying the full support of the West, as well as impunity.

What else can be seen in this devastated part of the world? Egypt where pro-Western elites and the military managed to choke all hopes of what used to be called the 'Arab Spring', that strife for social justice and true freedom from foreign diktats.

There is Bahrain, where a Shia majority is immobilized by fear, Yemen once socialist but now repressive, 'extremist' and miserable. In places like UAE there are pockets of luxury for the rich and hell on earth plus humiliation for the migrant workers who built the place but are left with almost no rights. Palestine is bleeding from its wounds, as it has been, for countless decades. Israel and its backers are blocking all solutions for full Palestinian independence. Almost the entire world votes in support of Palestinian state, almost the entire world condemns Israel. But it clearly shows, who are in charge of the planet and the region: the Empire determinedly vetoes all resolutions and blocks anything that could lead to justice for the Palestinian people. Jordan has become something of a huge refugee camp for Palestinians, Syrians and Iraqis, as well as the service station for Western interests, from the military ones to those of the 'development agencies'.

Lebanon, once the jewel of the region, is suffering from spillovers of various conflicts, as well as from Israeli incursions. It has basically no functioning government, and the socially-oriented and anti-Western Hezbollah has been placed on the "terrorist list" by the US and that of several European countries. This is of course consistent with the twisted logic of the Western regime: caring for the welfare of one's people is seen as the worst imaginable crime, punishable by death.

***

This is all consistent with the legacy of colonialism, neo-colonialism and imperialism.

The Empire has entered its final gaga stage. In the youngest and the mightiest part of it – a nation that came to life through people like Jefferson and Lincoln (not saints, but at least giants), has now ended up by being controlled by the souk, by the market vendors. And it shows.

If one were detached, it all seems so comical, so grotesque.

It is also tremendously vulgar.

One feels like laughing, like cracking sarcastic jokes.

But then, laughter freezes in our thoughts. It does, when we suddenly realize that all this is actually for real! Missiles are flying towards Syria, and so are the bombers.

And children are howling in horror. And bodies are torn to pieces. Millions of refugees are on the move. Millions of men, women and children have lost their homes. Women are being raped. Entire communities have ceased to exist.

There used to be countries like Iraq, like Libya, like Syria. True, Iraq was shaped by British colonialism, and so was Kuwait, but it was there for decades. It is no more. Now Western imperialism is reshaping the region again, at a horrendous cost to the local population.

The Empire is 'experimenting'. It uses 'trial and error' tactics. 'We created the Syrian opposition and now let us see what will happen. The 'opposition' mutates into a militant regional force, which dares to cross our interests? Let's bomb it and let's also arm the Kurds so they can form their own, pro-Western state, in the middle of the region. Let's see how it goes... Once we are on the move, we can also, perhaps, overthrow al-Assad... And who knows, maybe we can also find a reason to invade Iran.'

The Empire is using people as if they were guinea pigs. There is no consideration for the well being of the Arab population, there is no respect for human lives. All basic human rights chapters are being violated; most of the Geneva Convention clauses are spat on.

The world is so conditioned, so shackled, that this latest attack is being accepted without any major protests or debates.

If questions are being asked, publicly, then there are no essential questions. Entire debate is twisted. It is presumed that the West is doing right thing, that it is defending the world against terrorism.

It is also accepted by a great majority of people and countries, that the Empire enjoys absolute impunity, that it is above the law, that there is no international body that can challenge it, or to make it reverse its devastating and destructive course.

The West has finally reached the highest level of 'freedom'. It is a freedom for itself – a terrible freedom to play with the world as if it were a ball, a cheap and insignificant thing.

***

As al-Qaeda is derived from the US-backed Mujahedin fighters in Afghanistan, so ISIS was a part of the anti-Assad 'opposition' supported by the West and its regional allies. The West played masterfully on local intolerances: Syrian President Bashar al-Assad is generally secular, but belongs to the Alawite sect, which is considered to be heretical in some Sunni Muslim circles, especially in the most radical ones. That helped to mobilize and recruit extreme religious cadres. And religious cadres historically, are very determined fighters.

The Empire groomed both al-Qaeda (or more precisely, its predecessors) and ISIS as true 'multi-purpose' groups. One helped to destroy the Soviet Union and the other mortally wounded Syria and then, they became the justification for the 'Global War on Terror' and in the latest case, for an attack against Syria.

Both could be described as the 5th columns of the West in the Arab world. Just like the West, they care nothing about the welfare of the people in this region. The true socially-oriented groups here, like Hezbollah, are actually fighting against ISIS, but are designated by the West as 'terrorist organizations'.

And so the Kafkaesque destruction of the region by Western lunatics continues.

Of course all this is nothing new. This is how, for centuries, the European and later North American colonial terror functioned: divide and rule, destroy all that stands on your way. Sacrifice millions of people for your economic and geopolitical goals, even if you are not yet fully certain exactly what your goals are.

Without the Western gaga/racist/PlayStation/genocidal realm, there would be no al-Qaedas and no ISISs. There would be, however, several authoritarian but rich and socially-balanced countries like Iraq and Libya, as well as well-educated and secular Syria. If the West had not battered the region with its invasions and coup d'états after WWII, there would have been at least two powerful and socialist countries here: Egypt and Iran. In fact, most likely, entire region would be by now socialist.

ISIS is an implant, which is now serving as the justification for an invasion.

It is so obvious. Not to see it requires great discipline. But the world, or at least both Europe and the United States, appears to be increasingly disciplined, obedient, even submissive.

And so the Western crusaders are again, as they had for centuries, riding their horses, spreading devastation and fear wherever they pass.

But now, there is no brave, enlightened and compassionate Sultan – no modern-day Ṣalāḥ ad-Dīn – to stop them: in the name of life itself, in the name of justice and of our entire humanity.

26 September 2014

62

IN SOUTH AFRICA, AFRICA IS RISING!

Soweto is not just a suburb of Johannesburg located right near the mining belt; it is an enormous urban sprawl, with over 1.2 million inhabitants. It is more populous than Boston or Amsterdam.

It used to be a place synonymous with misery, with sadness, with the depravity of apartheid.

This is the township where Nelson Mandela lived with his first family and then with his second wife, Winnie. This is where he was forced underground in 1961, before being arrested one year later and sentenced to life in prison by the pro-Western apartheid regime.

And this is where, in 1976, a student uprising against apartheid erupted, and up to 700 young people lost their lives, among them the 12-year-old-boy Hector Pieterson, whose death became a symbol of regime's savagery.

Soweto, which gets its name from 'South Western Townships', with its tin roofs, unpaved roads and excessive crime rate had been, for many years and decades, an emblem of poverty and hopelessness.

But since the end of apartheid, South Africa has become a totally new nation – progressive, socialist and increasingly compassionate. Two decades after the new rainbow flag was raised, Soweto looks cosmopolitan, upbeat and forward-looking.

Most of the roads are now paved; a commuter train system transports tens of thousands of people between Soweto and the center of Johannesburg. There are elegant, South American-style bus lanes, as well as a super modern motorway ('Soweto Highway', which branches from the N1) with dedicated lanes for public transportation.

Soweto counts an architecturally stunning stadium, with enormous playgrounds for children, new green areas, and countless lanes of high quality social housing. Not far from 'Mandela House', which has been converted into a museum, there are countless hip restaurants, cafes and art galleries.

There are also two modern medical facilities: the Baragwanath hospital, and the new Jabulani, 300-bed hospital that was handed over to the Gauteng health department in 2012.

New schools are opening their doors.

As was written by Bongani Nkosi in 2011:

> *"The community of Soweto now has access to a state-of-the-art higher learning facility, following the multi-million rand upgrade of the University of Johannesburg's (UJ) campus in the township.*
>
> *Formerly known as Vista University, the UJ campus is now of the same stature as universities in South Africa's more affluent towns. It sports a more exciting look than Vista, which was built by the apartheid government to prolong racial segregation in tertiary education.*
>
> *The university was transformed at a cost of R450-million (US$62-million), a sum allocated by the government in 2005. Science and Technology minister Naledi Pandor commented that the design "inspires creative thinking"."*

This is Africa; this is a proud and determined African nation rising, taking off.

It is not perfect; this is no paradise. But those of us who are well acquainted with hell; with those African countries that were forced to become client-states of the West, all over East, West and Central Africa, where the poor are literally made to eat shit, where the sick are dying in agony, where there is no justice for the under-privileged majority... for those of us who know, South Africa is a tremendous force of enormous hope and true pride! This is BRICS, or more precisely, BRCS.

A few weeks after being told by slum-dwellers in New Delhi (the capital of 'democratic' India) that they would never dare go near 'that enormous building near us' (they were referring to the luxury mall), because the guards would beat them up, I saw several old women in Soweto pushing huge shopping carts out of the elegant, marble-glass-and-fountains, Maponya Mall.

Yes, in Soweto they now have malls and the huge Virgin Active Health Club.

I asked one of the ladies, whether she can really afford shopping here.

"It is cheaper here," she explained. "Small shops are bit more expensive. And... it is very clean and nice here".

Does she have any problems with the guards?

She does not understand my question. We smile at each other, and then she leaves.

But by now, there is a small group of people that has formed around me. Men and women are curious; they want to know why I find it so surprising that they are shopping here. I explain that in many capitalist countries like India, Indonesia or Kenya, people like this gentle old lady would never have been allowed to enter, or would never be able to afford to shop in a place like this.

There is laughter coming from the group, but it is friendly, encouraging laughter. People have finally realized that I am a foreigner, and that I came here to understand and to write about their country.

"This mall was built for us," explained an elderly man. "And in South Africa, we can go wherever we want and nobody would dare to stop us. We fought for this, and we won."

I suddenly realize that at one of the entrances to the mall, there is a statue of a young boy, being carried...

"Who is it?" I ask, although I know the answer to my own question almost as soon as it leaves my lips.

"Hector Pieterson," I am told. "He is the boy who died in 1976, fighting against apartheid."

Outside, after I enter a hired car, my Burundian driver explains as we begin driving towards Pretoria:

> *"South Africans have no fear. They can talk about anything here; they are very brave. They can praise or insult, they can criticize President Zuma or the police, military... no problem. It is a very free country. Before I only knew Burundi, Rwanda, Tanzania and Kenya – I could never imagine what it is to be free, to have no fear. A country where you can say what you think, go where you want to go, do what you want to do... In South Africa you see the guards, but they would never stop you... Poor people, black people: they can go to any of the expensive shops, even to the privately-owned platinum mines, and no one would stop them. Nothing would happen. Here, you can photograph anything, discuss anything... I never thought that such country could exist."*

***

I test that freedom on many occasions, during this latest visit of mine to South Africa. I test it at the platinum mines, near the military installations during clashes between protesters and the police. South Africa passes all the tests gracefully and confidently.

One day I go to the Constitutional Court of South Africa, in Johannesburg. It is not in session, but there are judges and clerks present there.

In front of the building, a young woman is shouting insults directed at the government of South Africa. She is very vocal and very vulgar, and her 'audience' consists of several confused and titillated foreign visitors (they perhaps feel that they are 'witnessing a piece of history in the making').

I knock at the door. The door opens. "I would like to enter the Court," I say.

A security personnel officer looks at me, embarrassed. "Could you come back in a few minutes? We are bit... concerned that the lady outside will try to enter and will try to shout inside, disrupting work..."

"But I have nothing to do with her..."

"Oh, OK then..." They let me in. I only have to put my phone and cameras through an X-Ray machine. Security procedures are lighter here than when entering a Kenyan supermarket. Then, soon, I am in. No questions are asked.

"A Luta Continua" is written on the wall. A revolutionary slogan, that means "The Struggle Goes On!"

I enter the courtroom. Nobody cares what I am doing or where I am going. I photograph and again, nobody cares.

I don't know why the lenses of my glasses suddenly become foggy.

I talk to a judge... I am not supposed to be talking to a judge, on the record...

We manage to get around the restrictions: I don't ask his name, and he talks.

I ask about President Zuma, about that endless, toxic propaganda howls against him, coming from abroad.

"He was acquitted," says judge. "The entire world, even the West, keeps repeating that South Africa has the best, or at least one of the best and freest, judiciary systems on earth. But when a decision is made, as in the case of President Zuma, and it is not to their liking, they are suddenly questioning the integrity of our entire judiciary system."

'President Zuma taking shower after unprotected sex', or 'President Zuma allegedly involved in corruption'. Over and over again, the same old tune.

One never hears: 'The President of Indonesia used to be an army general responsible for atrocities in East Timor during the occupation, and then in charge of the on-going genocide in Papua... he is also unwilling to stop the plundering of the natural resources of the country...' We never hear that 'Both the presidents of Rwanda and Uganda are responsible for much of those 10 million deaths in the Democratic Republic of Congo; people butchered on behalf of Western governments and multi-national companies'. That is because all of them – SBY, Kagame and Museveni – have been dutifully serving the interests of the Empire.

While presidents Zuma, Mugabe and Afwerki, are committing the highest crime in the eyes of the Empire – they are trying to serve the interests of their people.

***

More obvious is the progress in socialist or socially-oriented countries/societies that are trying to improve lives of their people – such as South Africa, China, Brazil, Eritrea or Venezuela – the louder and more vitriolic become the insults by the Western mainstream/corporate propaganda media.

Realizing that 'socialist' is once again seen as something positive, at least by billions of people all over the world, the Western propaganda is now using a very effective weapon of deception – it portrays countries like South Africa and China as 'not socialist enough', or even as 'more capitalist than those countries in the West'. Unfortunately, it is an extremely effective tool of trickery.

On the other hand, brutally capitalist or feudal countries like India or Indonesia are hailed as 'democratic' and tolerant, even if these countries are openly devouring their own miserably poor majorities.

In Indonesia or in India, governments and the private sector can get away with just about anything – from genocides (in Papua and Kashmir) to corruption on an epic scale – as long as they are loyal to market-fundamentalist doctrines, and as long as they are willing to sacrifice their own citizens for the interests of the Empire.

Countries like South Africa or China are constantly under the microscope. They can get away with absolutely nothing.

***

South Africa is not unlike Brazil, its fellow BRICS country, as it used to be a decade or so ago. It is a rich nation with excellent infrastructure, but with deep social problems. It is a great multi-racial and multi-cultural society with enormous potential.

It is a beacon of hope, not only for the African continent, but also for the entire world.

South Africa matters! If it succeeds as a country, with a progressive political and social system, then it will deliver to its long-suffering people what they fully deserve: true freedom and prosperity. It would also offer another great alternative model for humanity. If it fails, much of the African continent will lose trust in daring and fighting for a better world. That is why South Africa should never be allowed to fall!

Chris Lwanga, Political Assistant to leading opposition politician, James Akena MP who is a son of the late progressive President of Uganda, Milton Obote, expressed his opinion about South Africa, for this report:

> *"Potentially South Africa is the true engine and hope of Africa. This is in terms of resources both developed and un-developed. That potential couldn't be fully tapped because the ANC went into talks for ending apartheid minus a global ally standing on her side. The formation of the BRICS states is good news for ANC/South Africa and Africa! It shall enhance the role of South Africa. It is supposed to play to realistic levels. Africa feels proud of the younger rainbow nation and treats South Africa as her newly-born child that is destined to defend and promote Africa in a hostile global world. A newborn child after the dismantling of apartheid and attainment of majority rule since 1994! Majority rule can be viewed as that of a child's growth and development, one that must be nurtured! The emergence of the BRICS grouping is a move in the right direction that South Africa, Africa and the rest of the progressive world must support. And if South Africa matures into a socially responsible state, that would be a development the imperial and colonial forces don't want to happen, hence an early attack on South Africa, its policies and membership of BRICS."*

Yes, hence an early attack! The usual strategy of the Western propaganda system: to vulgarize all genuine attempts to improve the lives of people in Latin America, China, Russia and Africa; to inject nihilism and to spit on enthusiasm.

In Kenya, Edris Omondi, who is a lawyer and Editor-in-Chief of Frontline International Magazine, is clearly inspired by South Africa and its prominent Marxist, Joe Slovo:

> *"I draw inspiration from Joe Slovo the then General Secretary of the South Africa Communist Party, that a party such as the ANC should consider the complex social fabric, ranked from communists, non-communists, workers, capitalists and middle class in designing its policy. He said: "It's a forum of the people, the whole people, whereas the party goes beyond just the struggle against racism and believes that in the end the only rational form with which humanity should order its life is through a system in which one person can't live off the labor of another, a system of socialism. And we don't postpone the advocacy of that until after the ANC flag flies over Pretoria. We regard it as our independent task as a party to begin to explain, to get acceptance for the doctrine of socialism and its ultimate implementation in South Africa." These words of Joe Slovo are*

the ultimate critical truth to salvage tribal politics in Kenya and any part of Africa and every political party work should embrace the same in their manifesto for ultimate party and national success."

South Africa is increasingly inspiring the continent's 'Left', which has been for decades derailed, beaten, manipulated, even murdered, mainly by the outside forces of former and present (European and North American) colonialist powers.

My friend, Mwandawiro Mghanga, opposition leader and Chairperson of the Social Democratic Party of Kenya (Marxist), a poet and former prisoner of conscience under the pro-Western dictatorship of Moi, explained to me, on several occasions:

"We are in contact with the leftist movements of Africa... we are actually connected to the South Africa Communist party... ANC is truly progressive nationalist political party. It consists of the COSATU and the South African Communist Party. They call it the Tripartite Alliance – ANC, COSATU and the Communist Party. The ANC is the great hope for Africa. It is serious and it is a progressive socialist party."

I mentioned to Mwandawiro Mghanga, that South Africa in general and President Zuma in particular are steadily demonized in the West. He replied, passionately:

"They are! Very much so... but the only thing they, the West, can do is to bark to deal with it, because it's the only party that is controlling the government; it was elected by the people, it's in power, and they are very much alert about being constantly undermined. I have been reading and also receiving direct information from South Africa... You know we are partners to the likes of COSATU. Communists dominate it; even President Jacob Zuma is coming from there."

Wherever I went, the eyes of Africans were pointing towards South Africa – be it in Ivory Coast, Uganda and Kenya, in Namibia and in Lesotho.

I witnessed the deployment of the South African police force, in Maseru, Lesotho, after the aborted coup there. Again, what came to my mind were Brazil and its acts of regional solidarity towards countries like Venezuela and Bolivia.

Even in Namibia, a country that had been occupied and battered by South Africa during the apartheid regime, most of the people see their big neighbor now as a country in transition, a nation that is taking off, and becoming a thoroughly sovereign and free homeland for all of its citizens.

"They do things well there," a man who fought for both the independence of Namibia and Angola tells me in Windhoek, the capital of Namibia. "It seems that the welfare of their people is the most important thing for the government."

In front of the Constitutional Court of South Africa, the promise of the future, Preamble to The Constitution, is engraved in stone:

> *"We, the people of South Africa*
>
> *Recognise the injustices of our past;*
>
> *Honour those who suffered for justice and*
>
> *freedom in our land;*
>
> *Respect those who have worked to build*
>
> *and develop our country, and*
>
> *Believe that South Africa belongs to*
>
> *all those who live in it, united in its diversity..."*

***

South Africa is not a 'perfect country', because there are no perfect countries in this world.

But it is one of those very few places on earth, which manages to cover my body with goose bumps whenever I arrive, and encircle me with great sadness, whenever I have to leave.

It is a country that is capable of evoking great and pure emotions – a country worth fighting for.

My South African friend who works for the United Nations and therefore is not allowed to speak on the record, expressed his outrage over the treatment his country is receiving abroad:

> *"The West ran out of its propaganda ammunition against Zuma. They tried to smear him by all means: calling him a polygamist, ridiculing his sexual practices. But despite everything, he is still there and under his leadership, his country, our country, South Africa, is clearly improving."*

I mention that it is so obvious that huge progress has been made, all over the country.

"But of course there is!" Proclaims my friend, who is actually white, but to whom being African and South African in particular, means much more than the color of his skin. I don't even know whether he voted for Zuma, it is irrelevant. What is essential to him is that his country should be judged and portrayed fairly:

> *"There is enormous progress, and people voted for Zuma again... Zuma came from the grassroots of the ANC. Some may say that ANC itself is not necessarily a left-wing party, anymore... But its youth-wing and its women league, its alliance with COSATU and the Communist Party – because of them its politics are left wing.*
>
> *What irritates me the most is that Western media is using totally different measures and language, when it comes to South Africa. They don't care what is happening in the political space of South Africa. They are just throwing stereotypes at Africans. I always feel like saying: 'you propagate for democracy, but when it happens in countries like South Africa, you cannot accept it'. They refuse to understand that as in any other country on earth, there are social classes in South Africa. They do not judge us with the same measures as they judge themselves.*
>
> *Some South African media outlets are also treating South Africa unfairly. It is because foreign interests own several of those outlets, and local elites and their interests own many. And the 'elites' have lost!"*

***

Not to see how South Africa has progressed on the social front requires huge discipline.

I witnessed cheering children from poor neighborhoods taking a ride on that new legendary Gauteng Train, which now counts on three lines, connecting at the speed of 160km/h, the cities of Pretoria, Johannesburg and O.R. Tambo International Airport. What I saw was part of a school excursion, something one sees in the countries like Venezuela.

I saw people painting their fences and beautifying their streets, on so-called Mandela Day.

I traveled to Alexandra that in the past used to be one of the most terrible townships in the country, and atop it the posh suburb of Sandton is located nearby. Now, everything here is in transformation, with several new areas dedicated to state-subsidized social housing, like Bothabela Village.

In the middle of Alexandra, I asked Richard Baloist about life in the township, and he answered without any hesitation: "Things are much better now. We are free now... and we are supporting this government... There is sanitation here, electricity and water..."

Ms. Irene passes by and when she overhears our conversation, she decides to join in. She is against Zuma and his government: "There is no change," she utters.

I begin asking her practical questions and she replies, honestly:

> *"Yes, they dropped school fees... yes they supply children with school uniforms, notepads, books... We have clinics here, and yes they are free, and so is medicine for the poor. We have 'medical cards', and the quality of medical care is OK... All mothers in South Africa get around $30 dollars a month per each child, and giving birth here is free, for both South Africans and foreigners."*

I ask Ms. Irene why she is against Zuma, and she replies: "I simply am... But most of the people here are voting for him."

In almost every town of South Africa, there are public libraries, sport facilities, and playgrounds. In every township there are clean shopping centers and medical posts. And slums are undergoing great transformation, mutating into livable neighborhoods, from what had been something that could easily be described as hell on earth.

On the outskirts of Alexandra, there is still the appalling Mokuku slum, located right next to the river. But immediately across the bridge, there are entire neighborhoods of high-quality social housing and green areas.

I speak to a security guard of the Bothabela compound, which is part of a Johannesburg Social Housing Compound. He explains:

> "Here, people are paying what they can afford, and they get all necessary services. As you can see, construction of social houses is everywhere – here or in Soweto, everywhere... Many people who live here are working, but there are also unemployed people living here, as well as single mothers. People are really happy to live here."

Is crime an issue?

"In social housing, there is almost no crime. Crime is now generally much lower than 20 or 10 years ago. Even crime in the center of Johannesburg has gone down, dramatically."

A man wearing a Zuma T-shirt approaches us, grinning happily.

I shout at him: "Are you supporting President Zuma?"

He looks at me as if I'd have fallen from the Moon: "But of course I support him!"

And he smiles and poses.

I feel like I am in Venezuela.

***

South Africa is becoming a true Rainbow Nation, a real tolerant and multi-racial, multi-cultural society.

It is not fully there yet, of course. The horrors of apartheid, its 'boxing of people', dividing them, has created a legacy which will take many years to fully dismantle.

As I am about to board my train from Cape Town station, bound for Simon's Town, I hear some loud screams and I see two black women and a man being pushed by police off the station. There is actually no police violence; the officers are black and white, men and women. People being pushed off are shouting a few insults, trying to throw plastic boxes at the law enforcers.

I asked what happened. Police pointed at a convenience store owned by a man of Indian descent.

I go there.

"What happened?" I wonder.

"I can tell a thief before he or she begins stealing from me," he begins shouting. "They came here for nothing good!"

I am beginning to understand that he called police simply on suspicion that something could be stolen from his store. There was no theft, no action.

A white man who entered the store begins shouting: "I already left this shithole country twice. I should have never returned!"

The violence of those outbursts truly shocks me. Especially considering that nothing really happened.

Buying my ticket to Simon's Town, I get into a conversation with a local 'colored' (as people of mixed blood are called in Africa) girl. Soon she detects from my accent that I am not from South

Africa.

"You know," she tries to explain, "Things like this happen, but this not a norm, anymore. There has been great progress. People of different races now get along really well... most of them."

"I know," I say. "I have travelled all over South Africa..."

"And how do you find it?"

"I love it," I reply, honestly.

"Really? That makes me... so happy."

"I really do. I feel at home here, just as I feel at home in Venezuela, Cuba, China and Russia."

She gives me a big smile. Then she pokes me on the shoulder: "Welcome to South Africa!"

***

On commuter trains in South Africa... here, along these lines it shows, it is so evident, how South Africa is struggling, how it is trying to fly high and to become a wealthy nation for all... But it cannot fly too high yet, although it will, soon, no doubt. There are still too many weights it has to shake off, too many ropes and bandages that it has to cut off. It is trying so hard, its muscles are working to the extreme, its brain is working, and its heart is pounding.

Cape Town stations, still painted with graffiti, still scary and tough... still barbed-wire... still the desperate look in the eyes of cornered teenagers.

Better, yes, much better, but still...

Steenberg... Almost there, to that cozy middle class neighborhood, but not yet there... too many fences and the pavement is too broken. Nearby are standing new and modern, elegant houses. Then suddenly a lake appears, and the lakeside, so similar to neighborhoods in Australia or New Zealand... rugby fields and suburban 'bliss'. We laugh at suburbia in the United States or in Canada, but here it is not funny; it is millions of people rising up from poverty and for the first time, given a chance to live! Not really rich, but definitely 'First World'. The population here is mixed, totally mixed. Finally! Oh South Africa! What a fight, what a struggle, what heart, what courage!

Then the train hits the coast, and suddenly it is moving along some of the most beautiful scenery on earth. It is bit like Chile, my faraway imaginary homeland.

Kalk Bay... Beaches and beaches all along the track... all the way to Simon's Town... and beyond that, there is no train, only a road, just the marvelous wilderness until the very end, the very tip of Africa – the Cape of Good Hope.

On the opposite seat, a father, a white man, is playing with his two sons. One son is white and one is black. Perhaps they are from two different marriages. He is spoiling them both, corrupting them with candies and his love. He looks at both children with equal pride. Soon, one forgets that the children belong to two different races.

This is the new South Africa. This is Africa rising!

***

And here it is – that damned Lonmin Marikana mine; the mine strikes of 2012... the massacre that took 44 lives in total, and made South Africa 'notorious', just two years ago.

I don't want to go into the political details of the tragedy, as they are too murky.

But I have to testify that this terrible drama was once again twisted and exploited by the foreign media and those who wanted to discredit South Africa.

The mine, let us not forget is owned by a giant British mining company, not by the ANC, not by the South African Government, not by President Zuma. The fact that some ANC cadres have stakes in that mine is not proof of anything: the mine is one of the biggest in South Africa, employing tens of thousands of people. Many, many people have investments in it.

Then, it should be remembered that the AMCU (union organization) is the one that ordered the strike. And AMCU is a breakaway faction from NUM (that is COSATU-affiliated, therefore to a large extent, Marxist). AMCU proudly claims that it is "apolitical and noncommunist".

Many believe that if the strike was organized by NUM, there would have been no bloodshed.

The Communist Party of South Africa strongly criticized AMCU for the way it was conducting the strike. It even called for the leaders of AMCU to be arrested.

Furthermore, the British owners of the mine kept the working conditions of the miners (at least until the 2012 strike and the massacre) at an appalling level, and they refused to accept the conditions of the strikers and to negotiate, which led to the escalation of tensions.

The South African Trade and Industry Minister, Rob Davies, testified that "the conditions in the mines was "appalling" and said the owners who "make millions" had questions to answer about how they treat their workers."

I drove to Rustenburg and to Lonmin Marikana in order to speak to the miners.

I wanted to hear directly from them what really took place in 2012.

To my great surprise, this was the only place in South Africa, where fear was clearly detectable.

While the entire world 'knows what happened', or more precisely was made to consume a well-massaged digest of the events that took place two years ago, at Marikana itself, an investigator who dares to ask direct and 'uncomfortable' questions is greeted with blank faces and sometimes with a chilling silence.

Mr. Leonard is a 55 years old miner and he has worked here for 15 years:

> *"The company warned us not to touch or damage anything. The company was of course involved in the killing. I don't know about the government. I was there when it happened. It was horrendous. All we wanted was to be paid a bit better and to have our conditions improved. The company refused. We were paid then, some US$500 (5,000 Rand) a month, for an 8h45min working day, and for 6 days a week labor. People here are getting sick from overwork. The working conditions are really poor. Now we are paid 7,000 Rand, an increase, but not a really dramatic one. We know it is a foreign – British – company. And it is only interested in profit and production, not the people. In 5 years from now, after I retire, I will most likely have nothing."*

I speak to a lady-miner. She refuses to provide her name. But she is pessimistic:

> *"Our working conditions have not improved. I have worked here for 3 years and it is now the same as before. I don't understand anything: our country is improving, working conditions are improving everywhere... but not here."*

And then it comes: two miners, one after another speak to me, anonymously:

> *"We think that it was the company that paid the police and security forces to kill the workers, not the government. We actually think that the government in the end pushed for and secured many changes here, on our behalf. We are afraid to speak openly... Because the killings are still going on... if we talk, we could disappear..."*

This is not the South Africa that I know and admire. This is not that brave and fearless country. This is a country that is still under the colonial boot. Here it is capitalism, exposing its sharp and ugly teeth, corrupting and murdering in the process.

After Marikana, I drove further, to the luxury and private resort, Sun City, a complex of casinos, resorts and hotels. There, for the first time in this country, I was stopped, right in front of 'The Palace of the Lost City', a six-star hotel

I asked the guard who is usually accommodated there.

He looked uncomfortable. "Some stars," he answered. "And..."

"Some executives from mining companies, foreigners?" I asked.

"Them too," he replied.

The nightly rate in this hotel goes for between 1,100 dollars and 10,000, I was told.

The increase in the monthly wages of the miners was, on average, 200 dollars.

Situations and scenarios like this exist, of course, even in Latin America. It is clear that the private sector, particularly multi-nationals, want to tie-down, to enslave progressive governments, and to make them dependent. We all know, and it was so well described by Naomi Klein and others, what blackmail and tricks were used by the multi-nationals and Western powers against the young and inexperienced South African State, and its leaders, right after the country broke off the shackles of apartheid.

And once someone stumbles, Western and local right-wing propaganda go into top gear, claiming that the entire South

African Left is 'corrupt, money-hungry and essentially the same as the previous regime'.

For one week in my hotel in Pretoria I sat next to a judge who has been investigating the Marikana case. I knew who he was and I knew how respected he is in his country. I also knew how exhausted he must have been. I was also aware that even if he'd want to, he would not be able to speak on record, while he was involved in the case. But at the end of my stay I approached him, and we spoke for one hour.

He spoke about his country with love and with passion.

At the end I gave him my full report on Marikana; I told him what I had heard and saw. I also pointed out that there is fear. Those who have something negative to say about the ANC or the government are not afraid – they freely put their names on the record. But those who believe that the company orchestrated the killings are petrified.

The Judge listened to me. Then he said: "But there is no investigation related to the government or ANC. There was no case brought against them in relation to the Marikana killing..."

***

I could talk for much longer about South Africa.

About entering the "Joburg Theatre", without being stopped, and about just sitting in darkness admiring the rehearsal of a Brazilian play.

I could write about the bands playing on the historic Waterfront of Cape Town. About the great overhaul of public transportation, about new hospitals and schools, about so many things...

I could say many more great things about the country, and also pass some critical observations, like the one concerning the new immigration law from 2013, which could be considered as biased. And I could comment on some discrimination of foreigners, particularly Zimbabweans, who come here with great education, ready to take low-wage jobs, but encounter hostility, even violence.

I could talk about land, and how arduous the land reforms really are.

But no country is perfect, and immigrants face much worse

violence in Italy, France, Australia and the United States, than in South Africa.

I could talk about BRICS. Here, unlike India, almost everybody knows what BRICS is. While in India BRICS is an abstract concept, more masonry than political, South Africa is fully with this proud and progressive project, and often on its vanguard.

My friend in Pretoria, Ibrahim, regularly watches RT.

"I love that station," he says. "It is so objective; a real breath of fresh air!"

He follows and supports BRICS and their stand against the West. He says that many South African people feel this way.

At the Pretoria Art Museum, a huge event is taking place. There are several openings. *Vernissages* are for invited guests only. But when I mention that I make films for Venezuelan Telesur TV and write for RT, all barriers disappear and I am warmly welcomed to "come and see how we are doing." Someone pats me on the back. The color of skin matters nothing. This is, after all, the rainbow nation. What I do matters.

In South Africa, everything is in motion; everything is changing. It is a peaceful but nevertheless determined and socialist revolution.

Once, one of the most oppressed nations on Earth is becoming one of the freest. One of the saddest countries is now one of the most vibrant, optimistic and onward looking. One of the most segregated places just twenty years ago, South Africa is now receiving its strength and brilliance from all the races and cultures of the world that proudly call it home.

3 October 2014

*****

63

VENOMOUS EUROPEAN JOURNEYS!

It was noxious. On a poster, a young African woman is resting on the ground, her breasts are exposed, one leg bent suggestively. Right behind her, a wild-looking black girl with red hair is wagging her hips.

What I am observing is not an ancient pornographic cartoon. It is an old, official poster, which is advertising a so-called 'human zoo', or as it used to be called in French: 'Jardin Zoologique D'Acclimatation'. And it is not hanging somewhere around Pigalle, but in the highly 'respectable' Army Museum, Musée de l'Armée, in the enormous palace – Hôtel national des Invalides – near the Military School, Napoleon's Tomb and the headquarters of UNESCO.

On this matter, Iman Hassan wrote for 'Africa Matters' in 2013:

> "In the 19th and 20th century, Human Zoos were public exhibits of indigenous people to demonstrate the customs and lifestyles of the 'uncivilized' in comparison to the 'civilized' western nations. The infamous 'Jardin Zoologique d'Acclimatation' was used as a means for the imperialist tyrants to feed their fascination with pseudo-scientific studies. In particular, surrounding racial differences amongst them and the indigenous nations they

> colonized. The Jardin Zoologique d'Acclimatation housed various ethnic groups who had all been subsequently taken from their homelands and relocated to Paris as species for the human exhibit. As I began to read more and more about this institution, I came across an article titled 'Les Somalis au Jardin Zoologique d'Acclimatation' which elaborated on the experiences of the Somalis inhabiting the exhibit in Paris. The zoo was one huge scientific exhibition to reaffirm the ignorant belief that Western culture was the pinnacle of social evolution. The zoo housed a caravan filled with twenty-six Somali children, men and women, who all belonged to various tribes, including the tribe my father belonged too..."

The Army Museum in Paris is also where posters that glorify the mass murder of African people are still proudly hanging on its walls, side by side with the 'artworks' celebrating the French conquest of Madagascar.

I spoke to the museum guards. I wanted to know whether there was more information available inside this museum – about the colonial onslaught and the countless genocides.

I searched for some monument, or at least for a glimpse of repentance. With all those massacres, rapes, even genocides that France performed (and in some places is still performing) – in Africa, in the Caribbean, in the Americas, in Oceania and in Asia – there surely must be at least one huge hall reserved for the mourning of all their crimes against humanity; crimes that actually paid for those enormous French cathedrals and churches, palaces and schools, hospitals and theatres.

But I found nothing of that nature; just an orgy of patriotism, and a vulgar glorification of French military might. There was the armor of medieval knights; there were countless historic weapons and armored vehicles, as well as banners. But there were no depictions of the millions, in fact of tens of millions of victims, of the French colonial terror.

The museum guards kept smiling at me, repeating that there is absolutely nothing related to imperialism and colonialism in this tremendous ensemble of palaces, maintained by the government, in order to boost national pride and to thoroughly pervert French, European and world history.

Those human zoo posters were there, but they had nothing to do with repentance, and they were obviously causing no outrage. African people dragged to Paris, stripped naked and exhibited like animals. Who would be surprised?

They reminded me of those pre-WWII Italian fascist posters, explaining pedantically to the young recruits who were selected for the occupation of Ethiopia, the anatomy of African women – their future booty!

In the meantime, the decay of Paris was omnipresent and shocking.

There were two beggars right next to my hotel in the relatively posh 15th arrondissement. One of them was an amputee, exposing his terrible wound while leaning his back against the wall. Both were French and white.

One of my French translators was just in the process of leaving the apartment where he had been living for 30 years. The search for a new place was traumatic, as prices in Paris had reached yet another unrealistic peak.

Everything appeared to be broken, from the trains to hotel lifts. In order to connect to 'free internet' in my hotel, I had to constantly watch an appalling advertisement – recruiting young people to join the French air force.

"Ten, even five years ago, The French government at least pretended that it cared about its people," explained my translator. "Now they just don't hide it, that they don't care."

We were having one of those 120-euro-dinners-for-two, but sitting at the bar, because there was no table available. I was told that the place was actually 'reasonably priced'. I felt somehow embarrassed to mention that an average set-price dinner in Tokyo goes usually for 10-15 dollars per person.

"Nobody complains," continued my translator. "People used to... They don't, anymore... As if they had totally given up... Almost all critical thought has disappeared from French mass media, and there are very few alternatives... That is why people now read critical publications produced in the United States, a country which has a much greater variety of thinkers than France and the rest of Europe."

'All the While in the United States, the majority of left-leaning intellectuals admire the 'refined and cultural' Europe', I thought.

Both sides of the northern Atlantic Ocean have been, of course, blissfully and determinedly ignoring the fact that real change –

true revolutions – are taking place, successfully and right now, in Latin America, Asia, and even Africa, but definitely far away from those intellectually corrupt and nihilistic centers of imperialism and neo-colonialism.

Of course the Europeans and North Americans never took the revolutions in Venezuela, China or South Africa seriously, as those revolutions were following 'indigenous' paths, and homegrown concepts.

Revolutionaries in Caracas or Beijing were not begging for advice from Paris and New York, or Madrid and London; they did not have to; they were better, more brave and successful. And no matter how 'Left' some Western intellectuals claimed to be, most of them have been suffering from a chronic cultural superiority complex, unable to admit their own pathetic defeat at home, let alone to follow the leadership of Asian and Latin American comrades, from the countries where socialism has clearly and patently won.

Relatively small acts of defiance and opposition by Western leftists and anarchists against the regime are seen, at least in the West itself, as epic and heroic battles.

In Venezuela, China, Cuba, Russia, Eritrea or South Africa, their entire foreign policy is designed to counter the murderous designs of the Western fascist regime. Battleships and airplanes are on the ready to defend their countries and sometimes even their neighbors. Hundreds of millions of men, women and children are being elevated from poverty. New mass media outlets are proudly offering the world alternatives to Western propaganda. There is the new great solidarity of BRICS countries. It is all happening. It is happening now!

But you would never guess it reading the headlines of Parisian dailies. The European public, most of it, is cynical, sarcastic, and even hostile towards countries like China, Russia, and those in Latin America.

The ignorance is striking. And it is ignorance in its purest, most toxic form. It is not passive ignorance; it is active, dragging the world back to the dark ages.

***

At Les Halles in Paris, an anti-war exhibition is both naive and deceiving.

At first sight, everything appears to be just fine, and honorable: there are drawings of bombs and there are cartoons depicting embedded journalists. The Palestinian 'issue' is addressed, and there are plenty of images of tormented children.

Parisians change trains and shop at Les Halles. They visit the art cinema and a media library. And these days, whatever they do here, they can see all around them, huge posters, drawings and other images, that depict the absurdity and maliciousness of war.

But if one stops and really takes a closer look at the art displayed, the integrity of the exhibition quickly crumbles. What is it really trying to say? That any war is wicked and that all sides involved are wrong?

It is all 'safe' and 'mainstream' with just a few soft politically risqué images, just enough to create a moderate atmosphere of daring. Israel and Palestine: the Israeli military and Palestinian 'extremists' pull a rope in two different directions, as if the two sides were equally guilty of the war. The Middle East as a whole: the West and jihadi cadres are depicted as two equally malicious forces, as if there was no horror of the US and European destabilization of the region, and as if none of those long centuries of colonialism existed, plus the decades of neo-colonialism.

"What do you feel about this exhibition?" I asked an elegantly dressed girl. She is window-shopping in front of the Japanese 'Muji' boutique, while throwing side-glances at the bombs hanging from the high ceiling.

She smiles at me, charmingly: "Terrible, no? All these wars... and killing of people, no?"

In Stuttgart, a middle-aged woman sat cross-legged on a cobblestone in the central square, Schlossplatz. The upper part of her body was fully exposed. She was staring emptily into the distance. She looked confused, scared and unwell. Somebody called the police and she was arrested; ordered to pick up her things, to get dressed and to enter the vehicle. She did not fight; she just did what she was told, slowly and mechanically.

A few steps from where she had been sitting before, a group of young people was setting up their stand, 'exposing the capitalist system' and 'educating the public'.

I tried to speak to them, but it was very difficult to find a common language, or to even figure out what exactly the point was that they were making. They were critical of banks, but they also believed that it would take the United States to save the global economy. I introduced myself, but they had very little interest in any of the points that I was making. They were here to 'educate' about the greatness of their hero – JFK – and other 'progressive US Presidents'. They began lecturing me. After a while, after their arguments became desperately confusing, I left.

***

That same night I received an email from Berlin, where a group consisting of German and French intellectuals was asking for permission to translate, and to disseminate my article on the German holocaust committed in Southwest Africa at the beginning of the 20th century.

"I discovered your article "Namibie: L'holocauste Africain de l'Allemagne" and it was like a kick in my face. I would like to share it with our community... your article is a bomb!"

Obviously, there has been very little knowledge in Berlin about those horrible deeds committed in Africa by the pioneers of German Nazism.

***

The entire Europe is pregnant with pseudo-knowledge and with arrogant assertiveness. It appears that everybody knows everything. But behind the self-confident façade, there is often only the gaping emptiness of ignorance.

Not long ago, in Germany, I was engaged in a conversation with two university-educated persons, about the political situation in Bolivia and Ecuador. Only after an hour of listening to their arrogantly self-assured tirades (they were defining the Bolivian, Ecuadorian and Venezuelan governments as 'dictatorial'), did I realize that they could not even name the capital cities of the countries they were judging, nor their Presidents.

I have lived and worked on all the continents, and I have to testify that Europeans are easily the most indoctrinated and the worst-informed people on the planet. They only know about their tiny playground and almost nothing about other much greater cultures than their own: those of Asia, the Middle East, South America and Africa. Such ignorance and spite towards others comes, as a result of the brutal European military conquests, and, the rapes and plunder of the entire planet. It is the attitude of thugs who have just finished ransacking some unfortunate village.

Europe is clearly the most dangerous continent, and it feels like that: aggressive, jumpy, and confrontational.

While the United States is lately doing most of the shooting and bombing, Europe is still firmly in charge of the ideological concept. It is indoctrinating the world, through its media outlets, its propaganda, and 'education'. Even its 'cultural centers' (including French and German ones) function as propaganda hubs, something that I am planning to address in one of my upcoming essays.

***

My ten-day visit to Europe culminated in Pilsen ('Plzen' in Czech). I accepted an invitation to speak at the Faculty of Philosophy and Arts, at the University of West Bohemia.

The invitation came from the faculty's head, my friend Milan Kohout.

A former signatory to Charter-77 and a leading dissident during the Cold War, Mr. Kohout emigrated to the United States, where after being confronted by the 'capitalist paradise', he became a powerful activist, turning against the capitalist system, imperialism and Christian terror.

For personal reasons, he had to return temporarily to the Czech Republic, but since then he has been counting the days that were left for his return to Boston:

"The Czech Republic is so right-wing, so brainwashed and so racist," he lamented over the endless pints of beer we downed during my first night in Pilsen: "I miss the multi-culturalism of the US, and I miss the diversity of opinions."

Like my translator in Paris, Milan was clearly convinced that 'as bad as the US is, and it is very bad, the real opposition to the regime there is definitely not to be found in the servile and indoctrinated Europe.'

And so I ended up facing some 150 students from the Faculty of Philosophy and Arts, in the city that has been immortalized in my memory as synonymous with hell. This is where, after being born in the Soviet Union and having a Russian/Chinese mother, I had to fight for my life from the first grade, after each class, for being Russian, for having 'Asian ears', for 'being different'.

This is where, during the winters, when I went to play badminton in a gym, I had my shoes pissed into, and then thrown out into the street, with the urine turning to ice.

This is where I had to face, periodically, a gang of local kids, several times a week, being beaten up mercilessly, for years, for being 'Asian' and 'Russian', while at the same time gypsy kids were being terrorized and beaten up all over the country, all over the continent... All this, before I managed to team up with 'fat Karel', a kid who was overweight and therefore like me, terrorized and humiliated for being different... Then Karel and I became hardened, like steel, we learned to fight back, and we stopped being scared – a counterpunch, straight back, with no mercy!

This was Pilsen, where someone shot at my face with an air gun, and missed my right eye, only by an inch.

"Andre grew up here," said Milan Kohout when introducing me. "But do not expect any sentimental feelings..."

I got out of that bloody place – from Pilsen, from Czechoslovakia and from Europe – as soon as I could, which was damn soon... Damn soon!

The students actually knew very well, who I was. To give them credit, they had researched my work: my books, films, and reports...

"They have never really heard any alternative ideas here," I was told by Milan, before my lecture began. "Here, it is total ignorance... only a one-sided, pro-capitalist, pro-Western narrative. During Communism, people were much better informed: they went out of their way to get alternative information, and they treasured whatever they got. Now, they just accept, they don't challenge whatever they are told."

I recalled how the Prague Post newspaper managed to misquote my friend and mentor, Noam Chomsky, on 6th June 2014, twisting what he said while he was visiting the Czech Republic:

> "Hundreds of thousands of people were killed by terrorists, part of whom, were trained in Russia and who committed murders in Latin America, the Philippines and Southeast Asia, he told journalists".

Chomsky was, of course, talking about the death-squads trained by the West, nothing to do with Russia! The Prague Post did what the servile, collaborationist press in Prague had been doing, for decades and centuries, under every regime: it was serving its masters, openly lying and twisting the truth, even changing the quotes!

I told them – the students – plenty about ISIS. How the West trained them and armed them in Turkey and Jordan, in the so-called refugee camps, so that they would help to destabilize al-Assad's government, and later, after they got, as it was predicted that they would, 'out of control', how they were to be used as the justification for Western 'intervention' and for the creation of 'independent Kurdistan', servile and full of oil.

I told them what I learned from Christopher Black, a leading international criminal lawyer based in Toronto, who clearly defined the possible endgame for our planet:

> "The Ukraine is the latest theatre of operations in the world war that erupted with the collapse of the Soviet Union and the drive thereafter by the West to dominate world resources and markets. The first theaters of operation in this global war were Africa and Yugoslavia. In Africa, America ejected France from Central Africa and turned Rwanda into a military state used to maintain a state of deadly chaos in the Great Lakes region of Africa."

The destruction of Yugoslavia during the same period culminated in the final brutal NATO attack of 1999 and the overthrow of Milosevic in 2001, Black wrote to me. In rapid succession the NATO states attacked Afghanistan, Iraq, Yemen, then Libya and Syria. The ultimate target of these wars is, of course, Russia and its vast resources, and those countries such as China, Iran, and of Latin America that insist on maintaining their independence and sovereignty.

"But these wars cannot be conducted without propaganda, and as the wars themselves are total wars – that is, wars targeting civilians as well as military forces – so the propaganda techniques used are total, using every aspect of communication and penetrating all levels of society. Important elements of this propaganda are the various war crimes tribunals whose primary function is the dissemination of false histories of the wars concerned, and criminalization of those who resist," Black told me.

I spoke to students about how the West has lately been manufacturing 'opposition movements', on all the continents, wherever political leaders decide to defend the interests of their people.

I told them about the horrid European 'new wave' of neo-colonialism, particularly represented by France in Africa, and by the United Kingdom all over the world.

I told them about the concept of 'people' and 'un-people' – those who matter and those who don't matter.

They were sitting there and listening; quite attentively, I have to admit.

In the end, after some 100 minutes of my bashing Western imperialism and fascism, the questions arrived, and they were relatively polite.

But I was told later, as students were leaving, some voices were less flattering: "What the fuck is he talking about?"

***

Before leaving the Czech Republic, I was invited to one of the studios of Czech Radio. The long interview was pre-recorded, and I was told that most likely, some parts would have to be cut out.

Then, it was time to go – I had to drive some 400 kilometers to Stuttgart, return the car, and fly back to the Middle East via Paris.

These entire ten days – what a bizarre, chilling feeling.

As I drove, I kept recalling details of this collapsing, unkind, depressed and depressing continent.

I kept the stereo system blasting, listening to Peruvian tunes from the Andes, and to Russian ballads.

I was thinking about those gloomy and unfriendly, very aggressive people, about crumbling infrastructure, about whole days without public Internet. I was thinking about 'public' toilets on the highways where one has to pay 70-euro cents just to take a piss, and about airport lounges stuffed with newspapers and magazines in several languages, almost all with fascist-sounding headlines, pointing their fingers against the 'enemies of the regime'.

This was definitely not the continent or culture qualified to lead the world.

Instinctively, I was longing for optimism, for a 'nation and character-building' attitude, for human kindness and warmth.

I wanted to fly back, very quickly, to Venezuela or Cuba, China or Vietnam, to South Africa.

In Europe, I felt scared, I felt humiliated, exactly like when I was a child; I felt unwanted and unloved. Exactly as I felt in those countries that had succumbed to Western terror and diktats: including those such as Indonesia or Kenya.

It is hard to explain all of this in a scientific manner, or by using an investigative journalism style.

I have written a lot of 'serious' books and essays about imperialism and colonialism, plenty about the brutality of all those European empires and their culture. I have written amply about European ignorance.

But this is simply an intuitive piece. And one should be allowed to write intuitive pieces once in a while.

As I was driving on the motorway, away from Pilsen, I was trying to imagine a world that is not owned, not controlled by Europe, by the West, and Christianity. I was imagining all those European countries having to suddenly rely strictly on their own natural resources and on their increasingly lazy and spoiled labor.

In the Czech Republic someone told me: "Well, I don't want people to work too hard..."

And I thought: "Well, why should they work hard? The West has made sure of installing a global system in which a few millions of 'un-people' die constantly in order to support the lethargy of Europeans!"

I thought if they have to fight, as they always do, they should fight each other, not to use the entire world as their murderous Gameboy or Playstation.

I thought: how long, how arduous a struggle it will be for the world to get rid of European cultural colonialism, of its global capitalist system, of its fundamentalist, depressing and murderous religions, that have been strategically implanted all over the world!

But the struggle had to begin and it has already begun. One country after another has been rejecting the grotesque arrangement of the world; an arrangement that was first designed in Paris, Madrid, London, Berlin, Brussels, Amsterdam and elsewhere in Europe, then adopted and modified by Washington.

I stopped at a service station, took one more 70-euro cent piss, drank an espresso macchiato and brought my powerful rented Volvo into the left lane of the Autobahn, stabilizing its speed at 220 km/h.

As I was approaching Stuttgart Airport, a huge military Hercules was taking off. Stuttgart is not only the home of the Porsche and Mercedes factories, but also of The United States Africa Command (USAFRICOM or AFRICOM). It is deadly; it is murderous. But of course, in Stuttgart, nobody really knows or cares what it really is!

17 October 2014

*****

64

'Pro-democracy Protests' in HK:

THEY RAN OUT OF COLORS – NOW IT'S AN 'UMBRELLA REVOLUTION'

For decades Hong Kong has been a turbo-capitalist, extremely consumerist, and aggressive society. Its people are facing some of the most unrealistic prices on earth, particularly for housing...

What is it? It is not orange or green, and definitely not red! It has an umbrella as its symbol. 'That humble umbrella', as many people in Hong Kong are often saying.

But is it really benign?

We are talking, of course, about the 'democracy protests' in Hong Kong, also known as 'the Umbrella Movement'; the latest addition of the 'popular uprisings' promoted by the West!

At the North Point in Hong Kong, near Kowloon Ferry, a middle-aged man is waving a banner that reads "Support Our Police". On the photo, the tents and umbrellas of the 'pro-democracy' 'Occupy Central' protest movement (also known as the 'Umbrella Movement') are depicted in sepia, a depressing color.

“Are you against the protesters?” I ask the man.

“I am not for or against them”, he replies. “But it is known that they have some 1 million supporters here. While all of Hong Kong has over 7 million inhabitants. We think that it is time to clear the roads and allow this city to resume its normal life.”

“On the 28. September”, I continue, “Police fired 87 canisters of tear gas at the protest site, and now this fact is being used in the West and here as some proof of police brutality and of Beijing’s undemocratic rule. Protesters even commemorated this event few days ago, as if that would turn them to martyrs...”

“They are spoiled”, a man smiled. “They mostly come from very rich families in one of the richest cities on earth. They don’t know much about the world. I can tell you that the students in Beijing know actually much more about the world... 87 canisters of tear gas are nothing, compared to what happened in Cairo or in Bangkok. And in New York, police was dragging and beating protesters, even female protesters, during the endgame of the Occupy Wall Street drama.”

Earlier I spoke to my friend, a top Western academic who is now teaching in Hong Kong. As always, he readily supplied me with his analyses, but this time, he asked me not to use his name. Not because of fear of what Beijing could do, but simply because it could complicate his position in Hong Kong. I asked him whether the ‘opposition movement’ is actually homegrown, or supported from abroad, and he replied:

> *“To answer the question as to foreign interference in Occupy Central, we would have to answer yes. As a global city par excellence Hong Kong is more than exposed to international currents and ideas and, historically, that has also been the case. Doubtless as well certain of the pan-Democrat camp have shaken hands with international ‘do-gooders’, a reference to various US or western-based ‘democracy endowments’ or foundations active across the globe. Taiwan may have a leg in. A British Parliamentary Foreign Affairs Committee seeks to wade in. But “foreign interference” is seen here as Beijing’s call echoed by C.Y. Leung and with the letter holding back from naming the culprits.”*

The protesters have an alarmingly skewed view of “democracy”. Western propaganda has penetrated deeply. Spitefully, they regard Venezuela, Bolivia and Ecuador as “dictatorships.”

Protesters may have some legitimate grievances. They want direct elections of the chief executive, and there is, in theory, nothing wrong with such a demand. They want to tackle corruption, and to curb the role of local tycoons. That is fine, too.

The problem is, that the movement is degenerating into a Beijing bashing mission, happily supported by both Western and local (pro-business and pro-Western) mass media.

Several students that I spoke to, at Admiralty and Mong Kok sites, did not even bother to hide their hatred towards the Communist system, and towards the government in Beijing. All of them were denying crimes that are being committed by Western nations, all over the world, or they were simply not aware of them. 'Democracy' to them means clearly one and only thing – the system or call it regime, that is being defined, promoted and exported by the West.

"China is surely on the right side of the history", I tried, at Admiralty, when I met protesters on the 31th October. "Together with Russia and Latin America it is standing against the brutal Western interventions worldwide and against Western propaganda."

I was given looks of bewilderment, outrage and wrath.

I asked students what do they think about Venezuela, Bolivia, or Ecuador?

"Dictatorships", they replied, readily and with spite.

I asked them about Bangkok and those 'pro-democracy movements and demonstrations' conducted against the democratically elected government; demonstrations that led to the coup performed by the elites and the army on behalf of the West.

I asked about 'pro-democracy' demonstrations against democratically elected President Morsi in Egypt, and about yet another military and pro-Western coup that brought army back to power. In Egypt, several thousand people died in the process. The West and Israel rejoiced, discreetly.

But the Hong Kong students 'fighting' for democracy knew absolutely nothing about Thailand or derailment of the Arab Spring.

They also could not make any coherent statements about Syria or Iraq.

I asked about Russia and Ukraine. With those topics they were familiar, perfectly. I immediately received quotes as if they were picked directly from the Western mass media: "Russia is antagonizing the world... It occupied Crimea and is sending troops to Ukraine, after shooting down Malaysian airliner..."

Back to Hong Kong and China, two girls, protesters, at Admiralty, clarified their point:

> *"We want true democracy; we want rights to nominate and to elect our leaders. Local leader now is a puppet. We hate communism. We don't want dictatorship like in China."*

I asked what do they really want? They kept repeating "democracy".

"What about those hundreds of millions that China raised from misery? What about China's determined stand against Western imperialism? What about its anti-corruption drive? What about BRICS? What about its attempt to rejuvenate socialism through free medical care, education, subsidized culture, transportation and mixed/planned economy?"

Is there anything good, anything at all, that China, the biggest and the most successful socialist country on earth, is doing?

Brian, a student at Mong Kok, explained:

> *"We want to express our views and elect our own leader. It is now dictatorship in China. They chose the committee to elect our leader. We want to have our own true democracy. Our model is Western democracy."*

I asked at both protest sites about brutality of British colonialism. I received no reply. Then I noticed quotes by Winston Churchill, a self-proclaimed racist and a man who never bothered to hide his spite for non-white, non-Western people. But here, Churchill was considered to be one of the champions of democracy; his quotes glued to countless walls.

Then I noticed 'John Lennon Wall, with the cliché-quotes like': *"You may say I'm a dreamer, but I'm not the only one"*.

The Hong Kong protest movement reeks of upper middle class bourgeois consciousness, including its cloying cheap sentimentality and unexamined worshipping of Western "heroes", like Churchill.

What exactly were they dreaming about, I was not told. All I saw were only those omnipresent banalities about 'democracy' and 'freedom'.

There were Union Jacks all over the place, too, and I even spotted two English bulldogs; extremely cute creatures, I have to admit, but explaining nothing about the aspirations of the protesters.

While hardly anyone speaks English here, anymore, all cultural, ideological and propaganda symbols at the demonstrations and the 'occupy' sites, were somehow related to the West.

And then, on the 29 September, in the evening, near Admiralty, I spotted a group of Westerners, shouting and getting ready for 'something big'.

I approached one of them; his name was John and he came from Australia:

> *"I have lived in Hong Kong for quite some time. Tonight we organized a run from here to Aberdeen, Pok Fu Lam, and back here, to support the Umbrella Movement. Several foreigners that are participating in this have lived in HK for some time, too."*

I wondered whether this could illustrate the lack of freedom and Beijing heavy-handedness?

I tried to imagine what would happen under the same circumstances, in the client states of Washington, London and Paris, in the countries that are promoted by the West as 'vibrant democracies'.

What would happen to me, if I would decide to organize or join a marathon in Nairobi, Kenya, protesting against Kenyan occupation of Somalia or against bullying of the Swahili/Muslim coast? What would they do to me, if, as a foreigner, I would trigger a run in the center of Jakarta, demanding more freedom for Papua!

Thinking that I am losing my marbles and with it, objectivity, I texted a diplomat based in Nairobi. "Wouldn't they deport me?" I was asking. "Wouldn't they see it as interference in the internal affairs of the country?"

"They would deport you" the answer arrived almost instantly. "But before that, you would rot for quite some time in a very unsavory detention [spot]".

I thought so...

In the meantime, protests are causing chaos; dramatically increasing commuting time and damaging businesses.

Even the great number of Hong Kong professionals now wants protestors off the streets.

The *South China Morning Post*, reported on October 29, 2014:

> *"Protesters criticized by Bar for flouting court orders, as doctors sign petition to end sit-ins."*

But some people actually see demands as genuine and legitimate.My friend, Mr. Basil Fernando, head of the Asian Human Rights Commission (AHRC), wrote to me:

> *"As for Hong Kong protests, they are very genuine local protests over serious local concerns. People of Hong Kong in their recent history acquired many rights, which people in other Asian countries have only in name, but not in real life. Reason is independent and functioning public institutions. The beginning of them can be traced to the Independent Commission Against Corruption (ICAC), which started in 1974. It was a success and as a result, Hong Kong is quite a bribery and corruption free society. Having lived 25 years [in there] I can confirm that.*
>
> *People have genuine fear of losing these and that is why they want a greater say, to elect the Chief executive. This is a genuine local movement with limited political objectives."*

But one week later, when Basil and I met, face-to-face, in Hong Kong, he admitted:

> *"Many students in Hong Kong are uninformed, and some are spoiled. They never had to undergo any hardship in life. This is one of the richest places on earth. Some kids are scared of China. Ok, we can say that some of them are reactionaries... But it is understandable; there are those whose families fled Mainland China, in the past... The parents and grandparents were feeding their kids with all negative things about the PRC."*

Few minutes later I am having lunch at Cafe de Coral, a local chain. A young man walks in, wearing a T-shirt, which proclaims: "Real Time NAVY. US Military Base."

In Hong Kong, it means nothing. It is not even a political statement, just a T-shirt.

As long as the city remains rich, anything goes. And it has been rich for many years and decades; under British rule, and as part of

China.

The question is, if they don't care about politics, why do protesters block important arteries of the city, and for more than a month demand direct elections and 'democracy', whatever democracy means to them?

Or could there be something hiding underneath all this, and also, 'in between the lines'.

"We have also our own poor people" I am told by Brian, one of the protesters at Mong Kok.

The truth is that Hong Kong is not a social bastion like the neighboring Macau, former Portuguese colony. And, tellingly, while visiting Macau just a few days earlier, I was explained by several people that what is happening in Hong Kong, could never happen there, because in Macau, people feel 'very close to Beijing', have closer ties with PRC, and feel more satisfied with their lives'.

Hong Kong, for decades, is a turbo-capitalist, extremely consumerist, and aggressive society. Its people are facing some of the most unrealistic prices on earth, particularly for housing. It is not at all the land of milk and honey; it never was – under British colonial rule, or now.

There is also great frustration over losing that 'uniqueness' and the cutting edge. Several Mainland Chinese urban centers are now becoming more attractive, with greater cultural life, bigger parks, more daring architecture, and more extensive public transportation. Quick trip to Shenzhen or Guangzhou, Beijing or Shanghai, and it becomes clear where the future and vibrancy and optimism really are.

It is likely the recent protests are ventilating the general frustration of many Hong Kong residents, not only with Beijing, but also, or mainly, with Hong Kong itself.

Lacking ideology and political awareness, and for decades being bombarded with Western anti-Communist and anti-socialist propaganda, protesters simply blame Beijing for everything, even for what they should be blaming its own extreme capitalist system.

There are some exceptions. At the protest sites, there are several small groups demanding social justice. Not many of them, but there are some Marxists and Trotskyists, even urban anarchists.

My academic colleague remarked:

> *"Their agenda is professed democracy and direct elections of the chief executive, but the social demands highlighted by Occupy Central cannot be ignored, namely extreme income gaps, property prices out of reach for the young, and generally an uncertain future..."*

But overall, frustration here is walking hand in hand with apathy. There is nothing revolutionary about this city or the movements it produces.

I used to drink, heartily, with Mr. Leung Kwok-hung (known as 'Long Hair'), who has a reputation for being the only prominent left-wing politician here. Long Hair is a member of the Legislative Council of Hong Kong. But being 'left-wing' did not prevent him from being admired and constantly interviewed by the right-wing press in the East European countries, as 'Long Hair' did not only criticize the West, he was also persistently trashing the People's Republic of China. I never really figured out where exactly does he stand and at some point he and I lost contact.

A 'progressive' professor of a prominent university in Hong Kong once confessed to me, in the wilderness of a noisy drinking establishment, and well after midnight, that her greatest achievement in life was to have had some lesbian sexual experiences, and admitting to herself that she was bisexual. That came just a few hours after I showed at her school my documentary film about Indonesian massacres of 1965, in which 1-3 million people lost their lives.

"Let's have dinner tomorrow night", I was told, a few days ago, by another lady academic. "But under one condition – this time no politics." I cancelled.

Perhaps unwillingly, or maybe some of them willfully, protesters are playing to the hands of the West, which is presently busy antagonizing, demonizing and bulldozing its way over all countries, governments and movements that are resisting its quest for global dominance.

For years, Western propaganda has tried to convince the world that China is actually 'not communist', not even socialist. A highly successful communist nation would be the worst nightmare to the Empire; it would torpedo Western dogma about the ideological victory over non-capitalist and non-imperialist forms of government.

So far, the propaganda has been extremely successful. If people were asked in Berlin, London or Paris, many would make ludicrous statements that 'China is more capitalist than many openly capitalist countries.'

By provoking China, directly and through its client states like Japan, Philippines and South Korea, the West hopes that the big dragon will eventually lose its patience, will snap, and consequently gain a reputation as a highly aggressive creature. That could, in turn, 'justify' another arms race, perhaps even a direct conflict with China.

The more socialist China becomes, the more the West panics. And China is becoming increasingly socialist: by maintaining the central planning system, by holding in state hands its key industries, by commanding the private sector what to produce, or by declaring that if the people would not be given free medical care and free education, the country would lose its right to call itself communist. The more public parks are built, the more high-speed trains and urban subway lines, as well as theaters and cultural centers, the more terrified the West becomes.

Now the revanchist students in Hong Kong admit that China (PRC) actually is a communist nation, but from their lips comes something extremely negative. And they declare openly how much they hate communism.

It all goes really well in the West, because China, together with Russia, Venezuela and Iran, are on the top 'hit list'.

Protests in Hong Kong surely came in at an extremely opportune time, for the Empire.

Although China is acting with tremendous restraint (much greater than the US, France or UK have shown towards their own protesters), it has become a target of yet another smear campaign in the Western mass media outlets.

Even if the Hong Kong protesters had only one goal, which is direct elections of their top executive, this is not the way to accomplish it.

Bringing out dirty laundry, when China, together with other BRICS countries is facing intimidations and direct provocations, is not going to evoke much sympathy in Beijing, or arouse desire to compromise. These are tough and dangerous times, and everyone is edgy.

The mistake of the protesters is that some of them are attacking directly the entire Chinese system, instead of concentrating on local and practical demands. Or maybe, if the goal is to actually destabilize China, then it is a well-planned move, not an error. But it will and should backfire.

In a way, Hong Kong's 'Umbrella Movement' is doing to China what the 'Euro Maidan' did to Russia, or what the right-wing protesters in Caracas did to *'El Processo'*.

Willingly or unwillingly, the Hong Kong protest movement joined the network of the color and other 'revolutions' designated to destabilize opponents of Western imperialism: those in Syria and Ukraine, in Cuba and Venezuela, in Thailand, Egypt and all over Africa.

When asked, many Hong Kong protesters say that 'they are not aware of that'. One could state that it would do no harm if they could get at least some political education, before erecting the barricades and 'unwillingly' joining the global battles—on the wrong side of history.

***

On the last nigh before leaving Hong Kong, I visited the Mong Kok protest site.

It was tense, but not because police would be bothering to intervene and clean the streets, but because many protesters had been drinking. Stench of alcohol was felt at the 'frontline', near the barricade that was separating protesters from police.

"Any developments?" I asked one of the cops.

"Nothing", he replied. "We are not supposed to do anything."

"How do you feel about all this?" I asked him, frankly.

"I am not supposed to say anything", he replied. "Or to do anything."

But there was one squabble after another among the protesters; not a lovely site, a bit like on Maidan in Kiev.

An old man was yelling at the protest leaders, who felt embarrassed, trying to first push the old man away, then to ridicule him, publicly.

"What is he saying? I asked.

"Nothing!" screams one of the leaders, who did not look much as a democrat. He said his name was Benny. "Don't worry! You can just leave. We will take care of this ourselves."

"Take care of what?" I wondered.

"The old man said that he is going to call the People's Liberation Army on us", someone whispered into my ear. "Then he suggested that he is going to fight the organizers, kung fu style."

It said 'occupied' on several tents. That was supposed to be quite funny, or witty, or something... Few meters away was a store advertising Rolex watches, next to it a massage parlor.

'A Rolex revolution', I thought.

The mood on those protest sites was truly sordid; nothing grand, nothing optimistic, nothing really 'revolutionary'.

For many long decades, Hong Kong has been busy becoming obnoxiously wealthy by serving faithfully British and other Western colonial and neocolonial interests. It readily betrayed, again and again, its Chinese and Asian identity, siding with the political, military and economic imperialism of Europe and the United States.

It showed no mercy towards the nations destroyed all over Asia Pacific. As long as money flowed, Hong Kong was in business. Money, money, money! Its wealth was often built on the suffering of others. The city was servicing anyone who ruled here, and paid, no matter how appalling were his pains for the rest of Asia.

Of course many of its citizens hate socialism, and especially socialist China, as it is fighting against Western imperialism, alongside Russia, Latin America, South Africa and other nations undergoing true social transformations.

Seeing great Chinese cities grow, all over the mainland, citizens of Hong Kong, or at least some of them, realize that one does not have to rob or to side with the brigands, to become wealthy.

Even those who are fully indoctrinated are subconsciously realizing that something went very wrong with their 'territory'.

As the waterway between Hong Kong and Kowloon is shrinking due to unbridled development, as new and new malls where almost nobody can afford to shop are growing; as the real-estate is now out of reach for the great majority of the population, Hong

Kong now has only two choices: to rethink its own political and economic system, or to sell itself even further, serve the mammon and then bark at the moon or at Beijing!

7 November 2014

*****

65

DO WESTERN LEFTISTS HATE SOCIALIST COUNTRIES?

The multitudes in Europe and North America did not really pay attention, did not notice, but in so many parts of the world, the Left was elected or it fought and won revolutions that propelled it to power. This is a totally different world than it was some twenty years ago; we are living in increasingly optimistic times, full of wonderful alternatives.

For the first time in centuries it seems possible to dream about a world that will not be defined by Western imperialism and colonialism!

In so many places, people are once again in charge of their countries, standing tall, building their cities and villages, erecting towers and bridges, putting to work mighty turbines, giving light to the poor, healing the sick and educating those who were kept in darkness, for decades and centuries, as a result of Western colonialism and savage capitalism.

Entire modern and ecological neighborhoods are growing up all over China; entire cities are being built, with enormous parks and public exercise grounds, with childcare centers and all the modern sanitation facilities, as well as wide sidewalks and incredibly cheap and super modern public transportation.

In Latin America, former slums are being converted into cultural centers, connected to the rest of the other urban areas by super modern cable cars.

Cuba, despite its extremely low (national) income (if measured in dollar terms), joined the exclusive group of countries with a 'very high development index', as calculated by the UNDP. That group also consists of other Latin American countries with socialist-leaning governments – Chile and Argentina.

Many things that would be unimaginable just a decade or two ago, are now considered normal. The Chilean President, Michelle Bachelet, has been elected for a second time. During the Western-backed Pinochet's dictatorship, she was held prisoner and brutally tortured. Her father, a military man loyal to Allende, was murdered. She was eventually exiled and became a doctor in East Germany. Ms. Bachelet now governs from the same palace – La Moneda – that was bombed to ashes during the fascist onslaught. Her country with only 18 million inhabitants, is an intellectual powerhouse, as are Argentina, Brazil and Uruguay. Chile is not 'purely' socialist, but it is implementing sweeping socialist reforms. Now it is so rich that tens of thousands of jobless Europeans are seeking work in its cities and countryside.

In Brazil, a lady, a former guerrilla leader, is lifting tens of millions out of poverty, while turning her country into one of the most important and loved nations on earth. It is one of the pillars of BRICS. Its intellectuals, filmmakers, and writers, are stirring emotions and giving birth to dreams about a much better world.

It is all thoroughly breathtaking, if one really pays attention, if one is there, if one goes out of his or her way to follow the events!

In South Africa, formerly hopeless slums are now full of life and hope, and initiatives, many connected by modern bus lanes and trains. They have stadiums, malls and fitness centers, modern hospitals and schools. By many measures, socialist South Africa is a super first world country, but still with terrible social problems. But each and every problem it has is discussed, openly and honestly, and thousands of impressive initiatives are moving this awesome country forward! As I wrote in my recent report from there, in South Africa, the African continent is rising!

Eritrea, Iran, and North Korea, are standing defiantly against Western embargos and intimidation. Their people work hard in order to maintain their freedom to move forward their own way, without taking diktats from the same nations that used to plunder and humiliate them.

And Russia, the mighty Russia that was once on its knees, during that monstrous government of the pro-Western puppet Boris Yeltsin, is now back in its saddle, standing on the side of many progressive nations, all over the world. It has forgiven a tremendous, multi-billion dollar debt to Cuba, it is forging powerful alliances with Venezuela, Brazil, and other left-wing nations, and above all, it is finally creating a grand alliance with China.

The world has never been so close to a real breakthrough – to true freedom.

***

But much of the Western Left refuses to acknowledge that this is a great opportunity for mankind. It is because it feels left behind, humiliated by the tremendous defeat on its own turf.

It is because, despite all the rhetoric and political correctness, many of its members are actually chauvinists, and even racist. And many thinkers in China, Russia, Africa and Latin America, are actually aware of it.

The perception of the Western Left is that a revolution – a true and pure revolution – has to always come from Europe or North America. It is the West that has to liberate poor Asians, Latin Americans and Africans.

The Chinese revolution is 'impure'. Who cares that hundreds of millions, the majority of the country, are now eating healthy and nutritious food, live in good housing with high quality services, travel on modern modes of transportation, and getting a very good education? Who cares? It is 'not real communism', according to most of the Western left-wing gurus, or it is not even socialism, according to some!

Only the Western thinkers can define such things as 'socialism' or 'communism', not Asians, and 'Chinese socialism' means nothing to them; it is just a pose, a charade.

Several years ago, in Venezuela, I traveled with a very

prominent Western intellectual who had been reporting, very well I have to admit, on the events that have been taking place in the Bolivarian Republic. One evening, after several pints of beer, we began talking about China.

"I hate China", she said. "I don't trust Chinese people."

I told her that I had travelled all over PRC and that I am extremely impressed and convinced that China is actually a very successful socialist, even Communist, country. She began arguing with me, passionately. I asked her whether she had ever visited China.

She replied, loudly and clearly: "I would never go there! I hate the place and I hate the people."

Her statement impressed me: at least she was brutally honest and it was all in the open. Racism against Chinese people is hardly ever pronounced in Western 'progressive' circles. It is there, inside all that biased set of 'analyses'. But it is never admitted. All is covered up by the 'objective criticism'.

It begins with "can you imagine what would happen to our planet if every Chinese were to have his or her own car and television set, like us in the West?" and ends with "The Chinese are as brutal as we are and they have the same imperialist tendencies".

While China's transformation into a middle-class socialist society is clearly a miracle (but more than a miracle, it is actually proof of the superiority of central planning, and of the general excellence of the system), perhaps the single greatest success on our planet in the last 100 years, the Western Left mumbles something about what has happened is actually not pure, that it is not really Communist, and that in many ways it is all extremely sinister.

It is because, from their point of view, only what is designed and implemented in the West can be trusted. They would never say so, but it is by now so obvious! That scorn is directed at the great non-Western societies of China, South Africa or Venezuela! That black sarcasm. That overall lack of support for countries that are truly trying to take care of their people!

To most Western intellectuals, one billion human lives that have become comfortable and full of dignity, means nothing! It is because to them, Chinese people mean nothing, as individuals or as a group.

Instead of talking with pride and encouragement about the enormous parks and green areas of Chinese cities, all that is repeated ad infinitum is Beijing's pollution, or the destruction of some 'hutons' – those filthy and unsanitary hives where dozens of families used to shit into one hole. That, to Western eyes, was good – stereotypical and typical of 'ancient' China, full of poor people. On the other hand, those proud, modern, high-quality housing towers with all their modern facilities, that are now the norm in all corners of the country, are 'annoying', even disturbing. And the fact that Chinese people want and have phones, good clothes, even cars, is seen as a proof of 'consumerism' and is used as an argument that China is not socialist, anymore! Because for many Western leftists, while they themselves have nothing against having villas by the sea, those living in the non-Western world have to be pure and poor, functioning like some sort of guinea pigs, if they want to be called Marxist.

No comrades! It is total bullshit! And by now it is clear who really cares for the people.

The goal of socialism or un-dogmatic communism is simple and clear – a better life for the people. Better cities and villages, less fear, more culture, education, dignity and yes, more fun!

And that is clearly what China is achieving, as well as South Africa, Venezuela and other socialist countries!

***

In the past few years, it has become evident that the West is ready to destroy everything that is standing in its path to the total dominance of the planet.

But suddenly, four powerful countries have refused to tolerate such banditry, and have become determined not to allow the global dictatorship to succeed. These countries are China, Venezuela, Cuba and Russia. There are more states joining, gradually, but this is the core.

The West has attempted to destroy Venezuela, openly and shamelessly, on several occasions, through orchestrated coups and by financing and supporting the 'opposition'; some believe, even by assassinating the President of the nation.

The smear campaign that was directed against Caracas became epic! I have made several documentary films for Telesur, and I will never forget the words of one of the editors there, during the height of the anti-revolutionary riots sponsored by the West: "We are all working under the barrels of guns!"

It was a war then, and it still is, now. It is a war against fascism, and for humanity. Those who have not noticed should pay better attention.

And in a war, one has to choose sides.

The Western rulers also see China and Russia as the arch-enemies. Day and night, these two giant and mighty countries face vicious propaganda, smear and hate campaigns, provocations, and indirect attacks.

In Asia, the Empire's goal is to isolate China, to provoke and to challenge it. The West is literally sticking a hot iron rod into the dragon's mouth. This is common knowledge in the academia in both Philippines and Japan, two client-states of the West in the region. But it is a very little known unknown fact among the Western public.

So where is the mobilization by Western left-wing intellectuals, in support of China, which is clearly being threatened by the United States and its allies?

There is no such mobilization! Instead, some of the left-wing intellectuals are actually repeating, like parrots, most of the lies invented by the mass media outlets in both Europe and North America! All that nonsense about China having imperialist ambitions, in Asia and Africa!

If they would only bother to speak to the African people, they would hear that China is admired and seen as the hope, by the African majority. They will hear that "Chinese people are the first foreigners who treat Africans as human beings, even as equals", as I was repeatedly told at infrastructure construction sites all over East Africa.

But the propaganda invented in the colonial centers like London, Paris or Berlin, is actually consumed and trusted, even disseminated further by many from the ranks of the Western Left! The West plundered, raped and destroyed tens of millions of African people. It hunted them down like animals, and turned them into slaves. It has perpetrated countless genocides, from those in which 10 millions died during the reign of the Belgian King Leopold II, to the German holocaust against the native Namibian people, or the present 8 million murderous drive to secure the supply of coltan and uranium, in DR Congo, using their Ugandan and Rwandan allies, and their deranged armies. Somalia is destabilized, Mali; tens of countries are screaming and bathed in blood. But 'China has the same ambitions'!

And the Western Left is silent or complacent. A great majority of its members do not even bother or dare to travel to places where China is doing a great good.

When the US and Japanese air force flies over what China claims is its territory, when new military bases are built surrounding PRC, the Western Left does nothing, absolutely nothing, to support Beijing!

But when Russia was confronted, smeared and provoked, over Ukraine and Novorussia, there was actually almost immediate mobilization. It is good, very good, that there was one. But why did the Western Left suddenly opt for supporting the Russian government, which is actually not even socialist (although, by inertia from the Soviet days, it is still doing some great things for the nations oppressed by Western imperialism)? Why Russia and not others? Why Russia but not dozens of really socialist countries that are in great need of support?

Could it be that it is because Russia is a predominantly Western and 'white' country, while China, Venezuela, Bolivia, Cuba, South Africa or Eritrea, are not?

There should be serious and honest soul-searching, answering these questions. And soon!

***

These days it appears that most Western left-wing intellectuals are not even seeking power, anymore. They are comfortable with their feeling defeated and powerlessness. They appear to enjoy hopelessness and gloom. They constantly describe the faults and crimes of the Empire, but are unwilling to really confront it, in any determined way. They do not build barricades and they hardly fight intellectually.

It actually gets much worse than that: there is an easily detectable and open hostility from the Western Left towards most of the left-wing and anti-imperialist governments, all over the world, be it Cuba, Venezuela, Bolivia, China, North Korea, South Africa or Eritrea.

Those trusted and supported are only underdogs – those who already lost. That is the company in which many Western progressive intellectuals feel good and cozy.

The strength of those who fought, proudly, against the neo-colonialism and corporatism, and who are now actually governing their countries (or at least some of them are), is being ridiculed, at times even demonized. Nothing is good enough and nothing is 'sacred' for the Left in Paris, Berlin or London: definitely not Cuba and Eritrea, South Africa or China.

Again, that 'religious' search for the ideal movements, parties and societies!

It is like trashing the French resistance or Serbian partisans, during WWII, for not being fully 'democratic' or considerate. Of course they were not! Because there was no time to try being perfect: they were not faultless, they were not ideologically refined; they were single-mindedly fighting a war against great evil.

The Western Left is playing safe, even when it comes to world history. Some are (have for decades now) even comparing the Soviet Union to Nazi Germany, that greatest of brainwashing propaganda scoops invented by the chief propagandists of the Empire! They are actually talking about that very Soviet Union, which helped dozens of enslaved nations to attain their independence from Western imperialism, that very Soviet Union which actually, almost single-handedly, defeated Nazi Germany at the price of more than 25 million of its people; that Soviet Union which helped to build and to educate newly independent countries on all continents. Such comparisons are not only historically ludicrous; they are insulting and outrageous! If the Western Left needs to compare something to German Nazism, it should be the European constitutional monarchies and the Western 'democracies' themselves, as well as Western colonialism – all these institutions and political/ideological concepts have been destroying hundreds of millions of lives on all continents, for centuries, and until now!

***

Chinese intellectuals are indignant. I spoke to some, in 2013, when Tsinghua University in Beijing held a seminar on my work.

All that I am writing here is actually well known in China,

South America and Africa!

The arrogance and self-righteousness of the Western Left is infuriating and the result is that there is very little of a working relation now, between the European/ North American left-wing movements and the PRC. Predictably, again, the Europeans will say, "Because China is not left wing enough". Rubbish! Ask Fidel Castro whether China is socialist. Ask the government of Venezuela, or South Africa.

The main problem actually is, that the Western Left is not internationalist enough, or not internationalist at all! And to me, and to so many other comrades worldwide, internationalism is the essence of true socialism.

What is the European Left fighting for? It fights primarily for the privileges of its own people, not for the privileges of the other people of the world. It cares nothing about who actually pays for that free medical care or free education, or for the subsidies that the European farmers get.

During the colonial era, hundreds of millions of destroyed and enslaved people in the colonies paid for all those palaces, theatres, railroads and parks of Europe. Not much has actually changed, even to date. Ruined West African farmers are dying so those French farmers get their subsidies, and drive BMW's and other luxury cars for producing or not producing, depending on the year. Hundreds of millions of destitute, overworked people in the neo-colonies, with no medical insurance at all, pay for those old people in Europe so that they can have free clinics/hospitals/social clubs.

And the Western 'Left' is fighting for more privileges for the European people. China is nothing to them. China or Vietnam... Just some annoying Asian nations that are 'taking 'their' jobs away'! Chinese or Vietnamese people are just the multitudes and are un-people.

While China is reintroducing free medical care, it pays for it by the labor of its own people. And so do of course Cuba, Venezuela, Chile, Argentina and South Africa.

***

The Western Left is narcissistic, undisciplined and arrogant, self-righteous and morally defunct. That is why it lost. That is why it has no spark. That is why it does not inspire people.

And the less people it inspires the more bitter it gets, more vitriolic.

It attacks the Soviet Union (post mortem), it attacks China, and it is buying into yet another Western propaganda scoop, that the Khmer Rouge were Communist genocidal forces, not a band of deranged rural desperados that came to power after the US murderous carpet-bombing of the Cambodian countryside. It attacks Cuba and Venezuela for being 'undemocratic', and with unforgiveable and sickening consistency, it attacks South Africa.

And even when China fights malaria in Africa, and builds schools and hospitals, when it defends tiny nations in Oceania from total destruction, due to the rise of the ocean level by building sea walls and by planting mangroves (I saw all this with my own eyes, as I have lived in both Oceania and Africa), it is still wrong, because the entire world has to be shit, just because the West and its policies are! This nihilism is sickening, it is defeatist and it is having a vile effect even on the people in the West itself.

One has to conclude, with shock, that most of what remains of the Western Left is actually anti-leftist!

As a result, the people of Latin America, of Asia and Africa, feel much better in each other's company than with the progressive wing of their former colonizers, and they are increasingly seeking and finding inspiration in each other.

***

Russia has joined, too, in her own way. The more the merrier!

Almost 2 billion people are now living in or building their own socialist homelands. Each country is different in terms of culture and political models. Not one single country belonging to this group is perfect, but all of them are attempting to build a much better future for their citizens, and they are fighting against Western imperialism and fascism – for centuries now, really the only serious threat to the survival of our human race!

The world is now full of hope and optimism. The cranes are helping build and turbines are humming, new television stations and publications are inspiring billions to reject and fight the old colonialist propaganda.

It will be a good world in the foreseeable future. Maybe after some battles, but in the end, it will be.

Instead of preaching, the Western leftists should admit that they have failed, together with that aggressive Western culture, once described by the great Swiss psychiatrist Carl Jung as pathology – a culture that has been enslaving the entire world for centuries.

Then, they should go and learn from the countries where the people have won, countries that are fighting for the survival of mankind!

14 November 2014

*****

66

ISIS, Destroyed Iraq, and the Kurdish State

'IRAQI KURDISTAN' – WESTERN FIFTH COLUMN IN THE MIDDLE EAST

This report is dedicated to Serena Shim. Because both of us, had been covering an almost identical story. Because she is dead and I am still alive. Because she was brave. Because even as she was being threatened, and scared, she did not stop her dedicated quest for the truth, and as long as people like her live, work, struggle and die for our humanity, all is not lost, yet!

***

The weather is gloomy; it is drizzling and heavy fog is covering the entire countryside. After leaving Erbil, the capital of the Kurdish Autonomous Region of Iraq, large and small military as well as police checkpoints appear; like ghosts, on both sides and in the middle of an old, dilapidated motorway, which was built during Saddam Hussein's years.

There are huge Kurdish flags waving above the checkpoints. Small ones are attached to the bumpers of cars.

"We cannot slow down, unless the guards order us to stop",

explains my driver, as we pass by the mountains of sandbags and the aggressive black muzzles of machine guns. "They have orders to shoot without warning."

We don't stop, but I photograph whenever it is possible, even through the windshield.

We are driving on the road that leads straight to Mosul, the city that was taken by ISIS, or as it is known here, in Arabic, Da'ish, in June 2014.

My driver is scared. The entire region is tense and this time even the city of Erbil (also known as Arbil) has not been spared. On the 19th of November, a car bomb exploded in front of the Governor's office, killing at least 6 people, and injuring dozens. Almost immediately, ISIS took responsibility, declaring their aim to spread insecurity in the Kurdish, which is pro-Western, enclave of northern Iraq.

As our car literally flies over the bumps and potholes, on the right-hand side of the road, stand huge oil-drilling installations and refineries that are barely visible, belonging to KAR, the Kurdish oil company. The flames of the refineries burn confidently, and there are countless tanker trucks with Turkish license plates, parked or driving all along the main and secondary roads.

We soon pass Kalak Town, also known as Khabat. This used to be a major checkpoint; this is where refugees from Mosul used to stream through into the Kurdish region, by the thousands daily, after the ISIS surprise offensive. There used to be posts of several UN agencies here, as well as staff from all sorts of NGO's, spies from countless countries, and armed forces wearing different uniforms.

Now – there is just the road and some desperate makeshift fruit stalls. The road has been destroyed, broken, much the same as almost the entire country of Iraq has: battered, bleeding, and hopeless.

Soon after, there is a huge checkpoint, which ends with a wall made of concrete blocks. Now that is the end of the motorway. All around are antennas and watchtowers, SUVs and military vehicles.

"We cannot go any further", says my driver. "ISIS is just a few kilometers away from here. Nobody can go any further."

But I have everything arranged. A few minutes of talking, a few hot cups of tea, and from the post I go in further, in a Toyota Land Cruiser, driven personally by a Kurdish battalion commander of the Zeravani militarized police force (part of the Peshmerga armed forces), Colonel Shaukat.

We drive towards the massive concrete wall, and as we get very close, I realize that there is a small tunnel wide enough for military vehicles. We pass through it, and then the countryside opens up, becomes open and wide, and we speed towards the city of Mosul.

The road is totally empty and eerie. There are a few machine guns scattered leisurely around the cabin of the 4WD. There is one under my feet; I actually have to rest my shoe on it. Mechanically, I make sure that it is secured.

A few kilometers from the post, and there is a huge sand wall, then, a little bit further along, another one. The walls cut across 4 lanes of the motorway, leaving only one narrow passage.

"These used to be border lines between us and ISIS", explains the colonel. "You can see how we are gradually pushing them further and further back, towards Mosul."

War mementos dot the highway:

"This car blew up; exploded by a suicide bomber", the colonel continues. "ISIS also detonated the tanker truck over there, as we were forcing them towards Mosul and the hills."

And suddenly, the road ends. There is a river and a totally wrecked bridge.

"Khazer River!" the colonel gets emotional. "They –ISIS – were all over this area. They blew up the bridge... They destroyed my checkpoint, see over there?"

It all looks desperate around here, totally ruined. But there is a new military bridge, a metal one, just one lane wide. A few fighters approach us.

"We pushed ISIS from here" I am told again.

"How far is Mosul?" I ask.

"7 kilometers", they say. "At most 10."

I don't think so. I have a navigation system in my phone, and it appears that we are at least 15 kilometers from the doomed city.

"And where is the nearest position of ISIS, now?"

The Kurdish military men take me to the provisory military bridge, and wave their hands towards the hills, SSW from our present position.

"They are there, on those hills. And they are still shelling us, day and night?"

"Mortars?" I wonder.

"Not those. Mortars would not make it that far. They are shooting artillery rounds – 155 calibers. They get that stuff from Iran."

"Are you sure it comes from Iran?" I wonder.

"We are told..." I don't ask by whom.

Next to the bridge there is Sharkan Village, totally empty, and de-populated.

The colonel comes back to me: "I will drive you through the villages", he says. "We will make a detour. The US bombed ISIS into the ground, here, on the 9th of September. Then we attacked, and recaptured this territory. We lost some people... We lost Captain Rashid... We lost a soldier whom I knew – his name was Ahmad. ISIS also killed many Peshmerga troops. Several soldiers died because everything around here was mined."

We drive straight to that mess: Sharkan Village, then Hassan Shami.

"This is the village of the former Minister of Defense", the colonel tells me. "This used to be his house."

Almost everything has been flattened, but the mosque stands. The bombs penetrated countless houses and there is debris all over the place.

"How many civilians died?" I ask instinctively.

"Not one", I am told. "I swear! We provided great intelligence, so the US forces knew what to bomb."

I wonder... House after house: all destroyed.

Soldiers of the Kurdish army keep emerging from the fog, as we drive through this desolated land. There are many different uniforms being worn here, but everyone salutes the colonel. Some even come up and kiss him.

No one lives in the villages, anymore. The villages were 'liberated', but destroyed. People were killed, or they escaped. Or maybe something else happened to the survivors: I do not ask because I know that I would not be told.

"Do you also plan to liberate Mosul?" I ask.

"We are not going to take Mosul", says the colonel at one of the stops and consequent military gatherings. Others nod in agreement. "We have nothing to do with that city... We just want to recapture what is ours."

As we drive back to the Khazer base, I am told that the ISIS contingent, fighting around here, is truly 'international'. Recently, the Kurdish forces killed 3 Chechen fighters, 4 Afghanis, 2 Germans and 2 or 3 Lebanese.

I suddenly realize that the colonel speaks perfect English, something very unusual in this part of the world. And he only identifies himself with a single name.

"Colonel Shaukat", I ask. "Where did you learn to speak English so well?"

He gives me a big and bright smile: "In the United States and in the UK. I spent 2 years in the UK and 14 years in the US, where I was trained. I was also trained in Austria..."

"Where exactly were you trained in the US?"

"In North Carolina", he replies.

At the base, we sit on some rugs: with about ten Kurdish officers and me. Again, we drink tea. I pass my name cards, but the colonel only gives me his phone number: "No time for the internet, but come back, anytime! We like real war correspondents, here."

I interview two doctors in Mosul, a long-distance call, as we drive back to Erbil; the mobile phones are still working:

> "ISIS do not kill anymore", I am told. "Those who had to die are already dead. Now you smoke, and they cut off your finger. You work during the time for prayer, and they punish you. They have killed Shia Muslims, Kurds, and Christians... They had their list of the people to murder... Now Mosul is screaming from pain: we are out of medicine, milk formula, pampers for children, food..."

***

In the evening I have a cup of tea with an old scientist, a nuclear physicist, called Ishmael Khalil, originally from Tikrit University, now a refugee. We are in the ancient tea-room in the center of Erbil. He speaks:

> "All that I had was destroyed... Americans are the main reason for this insanity – for the total destruction of Iraq. Not just me, ask any child, and you will hear the same thing... We all used to belong to a great and proud nation. Now everything is fragmented, and ruined. We have nothing – all of us have become beggars and refugees in our own land."

Machko Chai Khana is a true institution: an old, traditional tea-room carved into the walls of the ancient Citadel of Erbil. This is where many local thinkers and writers gather; where they sip tea and play cards.

Now local intellectuals rub shoulders with refugees arriving from all over Iraq, and from as far away as Syria.

"I used to teach and to create, I used to contribute to building my country. Then Iraq was invaded and destroyed. I can do nothing, now... I have nothing... Now I only sleep and eat. And that is exactly what the West wants – they want to destroy our minds!"

As he speaks, Professor Khalil browses through his smart phone, showing me photos of his university, of his office and his former students.

"I escaped five months ago, after my university was devastated by ISIS. And we all know who is behind them: the allies of the West: Saudi Arabia, Qatar and others... I often dream about my country, as it used to be, during Saddam Hussein. The infrastructure was excellent and people were wealthy. There was plenty of electricity, water... There was education and culture for all..."

***

Now the Autonomous Kurdish Region of Iraq (with Erbil as its capital) is trying to promote itself as relatively stable and increasingly prosperous, 'unlike the rest of Iraq'. It has some of the greatest oil reserves in the world, and therefore attracts huge investments from the West. While the rest of Iraq is bathing in blood, decomposing economically and socially, this part of the country is 'not allowed to collapse', due to the strategic importance it has to the United States and Europe.

There are foreigners everywhere. As I find myself detained at a checkpoint, for an hour, just before the city of Kirkuk, allegedly for routine questioning and 'for my own safety', I see a convoy of several white government Toyota Land Cruisers speeding towards Erbil, with a Western man wearing sunglasses, sitting behind an enormous machine gun mounted on the back of the leading vehicle.

In a luxury hotel, the Rotana, I share an elevator with a British bloke walking barefoot, his filthy boots carried by a butler.

"I ruined my boots in the desert!" The Westerner confesses, smiling at his servant. "I teach people how to shoot, you know? Do you like shooting?"

"Oh yes, sir!" The man carrying the pair of dirty boots replies. He is most likely from Syria, a refugee. He is very eager to please. "I love shooting so much, sir!"

Foreigners are in control of oil production, they are 'dealing with the military issues', they run hotels, and they even work here as masseuses, waiters and domestic servants. Westerners are in charge of business, and there are Turks, Lebanese, Egyptians, Syrians, Indonesians, and people from the sub-continent, doing all sorts of managerial, skilled as well as menial jobs.

Turkey is investing heavily, and it has been building everything here, from shiny glass and steel office towers, to the brand new international airport on the outskirts of Erbil. It is Iraqi Kurdistan's most important trading partner, followed by Israel and the United States.

Turkey, a staunch ally of the West and of Israel, is also deeply involved 'politically'. Some of my academician friends in Istanbul actually claim that it is running almost the entire Iraqi Kurdistan.

Despite all that positive propaganda and hype that is being spread about Iraqi Kurdistan by the Western mass media, the place feels chaotic, even depressing. As any country or region of the world, which is under the total control of Western business and geopolitical interests, Iraqi Kurdistan is mainly geared towards the exploitation of natural resources and the neglect of its own people. While the income disparities are growing, there is very little done to improve the living standards of the impoverished, uneducated and deeply frustrated majority.

As a top manager (he is from an Arab country, and is afraid to reveal his identity on the record) of one of Erbil's luxury hotels explained:

> "We were young and ready for any adventure; we wanted to experience the world. And we were told: 'grab the opportunity and come to Erbil! It is soon going to be another Dubai! But look at it now, after all these years: the people are very poor, and there is no infrastructure. Basically, there is no drainage and the electricity is constantly collapsing: we have blackouts for long hours every day, and all the hotels have to use their own generators. Can you imagine, a country with so much oil, but with constant blackouts? They want to be independent from Iraq, but they have ended up in the deadly embrace of the foreigners: Westerners, Turks and Israelis are running their country. It is perfect for the rich, for the elites. Only the rich and corrupt are benefiting from the way this country is structured. There is not a single solid factory here... I am just wondering what they going to eat after they run out of oil."

I drive to the Erbil Refinery, belonging to KAR (a local oil conglomerate), located in Khabat district, at Kawrkosek town (also known as Kawergosk), just 40 km west of Erbil city. The army, police and paramilitary are everywhere, protecting the installations. There are Turkish tanker trucks parked all along the road. But as I drive just a few minutes further, up to a hill, the misery screams out loudly in my face.

I speak to Mr. Harki, whose house faces the refinery. He is indignant, like most of the common citizens:

> "All this is for the rich... All this is for the corporations and nothing for the people. This oil company has taken our land. It said that we would get compensation: money, fuel, jobs... But until now, we have got nothing! I am very angry. Now my family is sick: we have respiratory problems, the air is just terrible."

A few kilometers further, away from the motorway, the entire area is contaminated with garbage and filthy scrap yards. All types of fences, some even high-voltage ones, partition the land, just as in the rest of 'Iraqi Kurdistan'.

In the town of Kawergosk, I see several Muslim women picking up some roots, right off the road, obviously in order to fill the stomachs of their families.

Not far from them, I spot a public elementary school. It is

dilapidated, and extremely basic.

This Muslim community is obviously neglected, despite the nearby oil basins and refineries. No wonder: the pro-Western regime in Erbil is openly anti-Arab and pro-Western. President Barzani repeatedly speaks about the Eurasian character of his enclave, disputing that it has anything to do with an undesirable Middle-Eastern Arab character.

A school principal, erect, beautiful and proud, wears a headscarf. I dash into her office, and then slow down and apologize. I have only one question for her: 'Do any of the proceeds from those oilfields and refineries outside, end up here, in her school, in the education sector'?

Her reply is as short and precise, as my question: "No, nothing! Our people and our schools get absolutely nothing!"

But the number of Kurdish millionaires is growing, as is the number of luxury limousines and SUVs, as are the flashy malls for the elites, as are the armies of arrogant security guards, local and imported.

Like in so many 'client' states of the West, in Iraqi Kurdistan it is uncertain whether all those men flashing their machine guns are actually protecting the country from terrorists, or whether they are guarding the elites from the impoverished masses.

***

Not far from the oilfields, there is a massive refugee camp; this one is for the Syrian exiles.

After negotiating entry, I manage to ask the director of the camp – Mr. Khawur Aref – how many refugees are sheltered here?

"14,000", he replies. "And after it reaches 15,000, this place will become unmanageable."

I wanted to know whether all the refugees housed here actually come from Syria?

"They are all from the northern part of Syria; from Kurdish Syria. Almost all of them are Kurds; we have very few Arabs."

I am discouraged from interviewing people, but I manage to speak to several refugees anyway, including Mr. Ali and his family, who came from the Syrian city of Sham.

I want to know whether all new arrivals get interrogated? They do. Are they asked questions, about whether they are for or against the President Bashar al-Assad? Yes they are: everybody is asked these questions, and more... And if a person – a truly desperate, needy and hungry person – answers that he supports the government of Bashar al-Assad, and came here because his country was being destroyed by the West, then what would happen? His family would never be allowed to stay in the Iraqi Kurdistan.

***

Inside the magnificent Citadel, one of the longest inhabited places on Earth, and now a World Heritage Site, so designated by UNESCO, Mr. Sarhang, a curator at the impressive 'Kurdish Textile Museum', is as discontented with his country, as are almost all people in and around the city of Erbil:

> "We are supposed to be safe, but just a few days ago, on the 19th of November, a bomb blast killed 6 people, just a few minutes walk from here. ISIS claimed responsibility. Now as you can see, nobody dares to walk around here, and the museum is empty. But that is not the only problem that we are facing. Look at the outskirts of Erbil: they are building brand new posh apartments for the local elites and for foreigners. A flat goes for around US$500,000! Who can pay that? Money that is made here is siphoned out, by foreigners and by our corrupt officials and businessmen. There is almost no public transportation here, and extremely bad infrastructure..."

Back in Machko Chai Khana, Professor Ishmaeal Khalil raises his voice, as the owner of tearoom blasts old tunes by the great Egyptian singer, Am Khalthom:

> "Kurdish people are playing it both ways: they say one thing to the West, another to the Iraqi government. France, Germany, US – they are clearly betting on an 'independent' Kurdistan. The West wants to break Iraq, once and for all. They have already created a deep divide between the Shia and Sunnis, and they will go much further. Saudi Arabia, Qatar, Jordan, Egypt, Turkey – those are all close allies of the US and they are involved in the project. You speak against the plan – and you get killed."

He suddenly stops talking and looks around. Then he changes the subject:

> "Today, again, there is no electricity in Erbil."

I recall some of the last words of the Kurdish Colonel Shaukat, uttered near the frontline with ISIS: "Our allies are the US, the UK, France, and other Western countries."

As if to confirm his words, some 40 kilometers away, at the gates of Erbil International Airport, there are jets that have just come directly from Frankfurt, Vienna, Ankara, Istanbul and many other 'friendly cities': Lufthansa, Austrian Airlines, Turkish Airlines, also some unidentifiable 747s.

***

There is an increased nervousness in and around the city of Kirkuk, which sits on tremendous oil deposits, and which has been for several months now, governed by both the Kurds and the Iraqi government in Baghdad.

"Some anti-Western forces are operating there, right now", I am told.

It appears that almost no one likes the government in Baghdad, and no one, except some Kurds in Iraqi Kurdistan likes Westerners.

It is no secret that ISIS was welcomed in Mosul and other places, by desperate citizens. But many, or most of the educated Iraqi citizens, see them as some sort of routine nightmare – an offshoot of the US and European client-movements, created and armed in order to destroy President's al-Assad's Syria.

All of this is an extremely dangerous game. Millions have already died over the last few decades, in all parts of the Middle East; victims of the barbaric Western geopolitical games, victims of the West's allies: in Iraq, Iran, Syria, Lebanon, Palestine, and all over the Arab world.

People like Serena Shim, a Lebanese-American journalist who had been covering these horrendous events for Press TV, get intimidated. If they don't stop working and telling the truth, they get liquidated, murdered – exactly as happened to her.

In the meantime, corrupt businessmen and local officials, but mainly foreigners, are stripping Iraqi Kurdistan naked, systematically.

And there is very little left in the rest of Iraq.

As has become extremely common, thieves and murderers are now calling themselves 'liberators' and good Samaritans.

Iraq is bleeding, but almost nothing of the truth has been allowed to penetrate the rest of the world, about the awful fate of this country once known as the cradle of our civilization.

26 November 2014

*****

67

Eritrea

AFRICAN IDEOLOGICAL EBOLA FOR IMPERIALISTS

Qohaito is a mysterious, ancient, pre-Aksumite settlement in the Eritrean highlands, with several impressive monolithic columns rising towards the sky. It is said that right there, under the surface, exists another entire lost city. As you walk, the earth shakes, and somewhere deep below; you can hear the echo of your footsteps.

Just a few minutes drive from the columns, the plateau suddenly ends. There is a cliff and a breathtaking view into the deep valley. This place is called Ishka. And this is where thousands of Eritrean freedom fighters and civilians used to hide from the brutal Ethiopian occupation forces.

I set up my cameras right near the cliff, asks my local cameraman to roll, and then put the first question to a local mountaineer, Mr. Ibrahim Omar: "How was life here, for you, before and after the independence?"

"There were two separate lives", he explained. "The first one, before independence – that was harsh, brutal. And then came the other life, a totally different one, after we won. This is when our basic human rights got recognized and respected. The schools, health posts and roads were built. Everything was suddenly transformed."

I ask Mr. Omar for an example and he readily replies:

> "Before, a pregnant woman would have to ride on a camel, for long hours, to reach some medical post, in order to give birth. Many women would die during the journey. Now medical posts are readily available in this area..."

He thinks for a few seconds, then adds: "And this is what I call life."

As we drive back to the capital city – Asmara – we can see new roads, some paved, some not yet, cutting through the rugged, mountainous terrain. And parallel to them, new electric wires are stretching out towards the horizon.

In the car, I am thinking about what Mr. Omar defined as 'human rights'. Here, it is in direct contrast to what the expression stands for in the West. In the United States and in Europe, 'human rights' were created as an ideological tool, a weapon in the Cold War period. In Eritrea, it has a very simple meaning: feeding the people, giving them free education and medical care, building new roads, supplying them with electric power.

***

To understand Eritrea is not easy. But outside Asmara, everything is exposed; nothing can be hidden. Both poverty and the heroic attempts to eradicate it are right here, in my face. Farmers are working hard; many roads and electric grids are under construction.

But Western propaganda against Eritrea is so mighty, that often even I catch myself recalling its slogans, instead of concentrating on observing the reality with my own eyes. And I am professional: I have dedicated my life to uncovering Western indoctrination campaigns!

I film and photograph, in order to capture the truth, through my lenses.

After just a few days, a very clear portrait emerges: Eritrea; the African Cuba – country that stands on its own feet.

Eritrea – a proud and determined nation, which fought for a long 30 years for its independence, and in the process, losing hundreds of thousands of its sons and daughters during the struggle.

Eritrea – a country with its own egalitarian development model, working relentlessly for the welfare of its people.

Eritrea – a nation unwilling to sacrifice its citizens for the whims of the Empire and its corporations.

All this is in direct contrast to the propaganda that is emanating from London and New York, smearing the country, and trying to portray it as an outlaw state which supports terrorist groups in East Africa, oppresses its citizens, and violates all basic 'human rights'.

On this journey, on my search for the truth through the country which the West describes as perhaps the most hermit place on earth, I am accompanied by only three people – Ms. Milena Bereket, (Director of "African Strategies", an independent research and outreach think tank based in Asmara), by a local cameraman Azmera, and by a driver.

African Strategies is hosting me in Eritrea, but practically it is responding and accommodating my requests, arranging interviews and transportation to the places that I want to visit. We are planning together, working shoulder to shoulder. African Strategies is an independent research think-tank, established online in 2011, initially created to respond – virtually – to the growing demands of the Diaspora and continent-based Eritreans, as well as other Africans for fact-based and localized information regarding the Horn of Africa region, and more specifically Eritrea.

In a relatively short time, I have managed to visit three regions (zones) of the country, and I would have been allowed to visit all six of them, were I to have more time. As it is, in eight days in the country, I hardly sleep, but I encounter people from the mountain villages and from the port city of Massawa, I lead a roundtable discussion with several prominent young intellectuals, and I discuss politics and the development model of Eritrea with officials from the Ministry of Education and Health, as well as with former liberation fighters, and Eritrean diplomats.

All of my encounters are spontaneous. Eritrean people are well informed and educated. Our political discussions are open and often passionate. I cannot believe my own eyes, or more precisely: I cannot believe the lies that are being told about this country.

***

In the Hotel Asmara Palace (former Inter-Continental) I met a distinguished Ethiopian author and researcher Dr. Mohamed Hassan, a former Ethiopian diplomat in Washington, Beijing and Brussels, as well as an MP representing the militant Belgian Labor Party. He now spends a substantial amount of time in Eritrea, which is extremely close to his heart and to his ideological beliefs.

Without wasting much time on formalities, we began working together, almost immediately, filming and recording the discussion.

Dr. Hassan offered his well-defined thesis, right from the start:

> *"I am from the horn of Africa, and I saw the of Eritrea's point of view, even in the time of their struggle, which was not just the national independence struggle for Eritrea, but for the whole Horn of Africa in general. It is true that Eritrean people's strife for freedom had been denied and the Eritrean people had to embark on a very long journey to reach their independence... it took them 30 years to defeat the enemy, which consisted also of my country – Ethiopia – that was supported by many powerful forces... At one point it was the United States and all other Western countries... then Israelis supported special troops fighting against Eritrea... In 1991 the struggle ended, and we thought that we would build, all of us together, the new Horn of Africa, on the basis of equality, as brothers and sisters, with no differences between us and no hierarchy... 1991, I thought, was the best moment that our region ever had. Eritrea defeated the neighboring regime, and it was supporting revolutionaries in Ethiopia; people like us... There were great changes taking place in Ethiopia, then. We hoped that our economies would get integrated, and that we would establish new people to people relations..."*

But it was not meant to be. There were huge changes in the world, as Mr. Hassan recalled. The Soviet Union disappeared and the balance of power had tipped to one side.

Mr. Hassan continued:

> *"Suddenly, in the United States, an officer, one of the very important officers in the Pentagon, wrote for a military journal called "Parameters", his memoranda and his understanding of what should be done to Africa. It described the US interests in Africa, and it divided Africa into 4 regions... One region was to become the Southern part of Africa, all that huge area from South Africa to Congo; the region full of minerals; that region*

> *that was 'very important for the US military and the US companies... Second region was Horn Of Africa, which was supposed to be integrated with East Africa and 'greater Middle East', which G.W. Bush was later trying to create. Western military bases located in the Horn of Africa were supposed to be ready to intervene in the Middle East and in other African countries..."*

The 3rd zone was to become West Africa; rich in oil that is extracted in order to satisfy demand in the North America. 4th zone was to cover North Africa, from Egypt to Mauritania.

All 4 zones had to be, of course, fully controlled by the West.

> *"Immediately after this document was published, Mr. Anthony Lake, who was then a national security advisor under Clinton Administration, published his new theory called 'Anchor States'. He also divided the African continent into 4 bases; defining 4 'anchor states'. One: South Africa, 'responsible for southern Africa, two: Ethiopia, 'responsible' for the Horn of Africa, three: Egypt for northern Africa, and four: Nigeria 'in charge of' western Africa. Very soon, Nigeria intervened in Sierra Leone and Liberia, and Ethiopia accepted its role as well, becoming the base for Western aggressiveness in the region."*

Eritrea never sold out. It did not accept the imperialist's games in the region. It stood patently in the way of the Western domination of the region, because of its principles of national independence, non-interference, no military bases in the Horn of Africa, and its desire to build the new Horn of Africa... All this was considered by the big powers as 'negative', according to Dr. Hassan. This is why Eritrea was identified as pariah state.

***

How brutal, how consistent could the punishment be – retribution for attaining independence and for taking care of the people, for social justice?

Embargos against Cuba are a very good example of how far the Empire is willing to go. Or 'making the economy scream', under the socialist government of President Allende in Chile, who was obviously having an extremely 'bad influence', according to Mr. Kissinger and the corporate bosses, on the entire Latin America and even on the far away Mediterranean countries. Or maybe direct military attacks, as those that were performed against Indonesia during the reign of the independent-minded President Sukarno.

Both Indonesia (in 1965) and Chile (in 1973) were bathed in blood, in the Western-orchestrated coups. Chile recovered recently, Indonesia never did. Cuba stood firm, at a tremendous price and with incomparable determination and courage.

And so Eritrea has been as well– standing and fighting against constant subversions, attacks, propaganda, embargos and provocations.

That is why it is often called the "African Cuba". Or maybe it should be compared to Vietnam, or to both. But to be precise, Eritrea has developed its own model of resistance. Its courage, its struggle, is its own. It is a totally unique place, and its people are proud to be distinctive.

But can Eritrea survive, while much bigger and richer countries, like Libya, Iraq, and Syria are falling one after another, simply because the Empire decided that they were giving too much to their own people, and too little to its corporations?

***

"We do not want to be boxed", I am told over and over again, whenever I ask whether Eritrea is a socialist country.

"Look at Amílcar Cabral, from Guinea-Bissau", I am told by Elias Amare, one of the most accomplished writers and thinkers of Eritrea, who is also a Senior Fellow at the 'Peace building Center for The Horn of Africa' (PCHA). "Cabral always said: 'judge us on what we are doing on the ground'. The same can be applied to Eritrea."

Most of the leaders of Eritrea, most of its thinkers, are either Marxists, or at least their hearts are very close to socialist ideals. But there is very little talk about socialism here, and there are almost no red banners. The Eritrean national flag is in the center of all that is happening, while independence, self-reliance, social justice and unity could be considered as basic pillars of the national ideology.

According to Elias Amare:

> *"Eritrea registered success, substantial achievements, in what the United Nations defines as 'Millennium Development Goals', in particular ensuring primary education for all, free-of-charge; ensuring women's emancipation and equality of women in all fields. In healthcare – it achieved a dramatic reduction of infant mortality, as well as the reduction of*

maternal mortality. In this regard, Eritrea is considered exemplary in Africa; few other countries have attained that much. So, despite all the obstacles that the country faces, the picture is positive."

"Eritrea continues on the national independent path. It has progressive view in building national unity. Eritrea is a multi-ethnic, multi-religious society. It has 9 ethnic groups, and two major religions: Christianity and Islam. Two religions co-exist harmoniously, and this is mainly due to the tolerant culture, that the society has built. There is no conflict or animosity between the ethnic groups or religious groups. The government and the people are keen to maintain this national unity."

This is in stark contrast to the rest of Africa. Ethnic and religious conflicts are plundering Sudan, Kenya, Congo, Uganda, Rwanda, Burundi and many other nations. Behind them often stand the old colonialism and neo-colonialism.

What Eritrea has accomplished is not some minor achievement, but an essential breakthrough.

Then why, I ask Elias, is the West so aggressively against the Eritrean path? He replies:

"I go back to Noam Chomsky's view on this: whenever a small country tries to pursue an independent national path, and does credible work on development, Western countries do not like it. They want their 'client states'. They want states that are submissive to the global capitalist interests.... All this is no-no in the eyes of the Western imperialist countries. They want neo-colonial regimes that obey the diktats of the World Bank, IMF, WTO, and so on."

***

The port of Massawa, is still in ruins. Ethiopia bombed this historic city to the ground, during the last stage of the Eritrean war for independence.

Since then, the reconstruction work is progressing, slowly but surely. And the port is now functioning well; it is modern and efficient. Cargo vessels are sailing to all corners of the globe, while passenger ferries are connecting the mainland with the Dahlak Islands.

Still, in this city itself, the horror of war is visible at every step. Many historic buildings stand like ghosts, with nothing inside. At the entrance to the port, there is a massive stand. I ask, what statue used to be placed on it, in the old days? "Haile Selassie", I am told.

We stop at the ancient coffee shop, which is known for its lengthy coffee ceremonies. Life is slowly returning to normal. People are drinking, and chatting.

Two ladies are cooking in front of their house. We approach them. I want to know whether their life has been improving.

Ms. Maaza, 55 years old, replies:

> *"It is definitely better than when the Ethiopians were here. Adults are being educated... Kids are being educated as well: all for free. Medical care is also provided, when we get sick. We are optimistic, hopeful about the future."*

Then she invites us home, for lunch.

Massawa is, once again, waking up to life. There is a new college (College of Marine Sciences and Technology), new international airport, and a free-trade zone.

Hotels are opening their doors.

The countryside is still dotted with war relics, with monuments, with destroyed tanks and armored vehicles.

What this country went through is mindboggling. The fact that it is here, that it survived, that it won, managed to move forward, is itself a miracle. Or more precisely: it is proof of the heroism of its people.

***

In Asmara, I sit down for a talk with a senior Eritrean diplomat, Tesfamichael Gerahtu, a former Ambassador to the United Kingdom. But Mr. Gerahtu is not just a representative of Eritrea abroad; he is one of the national heroes, who fought, for long years, for the independence of this country, against all the odds. And he has been helping to build his nation, to this day:

> *"Eritrea is peaceful and stable because of the government's 'integrated development paradigm' – equal opportunities for all, with a special concentrated focus on rural areas and areas that were previously particularly disadvantaged. We are improving the general and overall quality of life... we are working on a cultural transformation that would lead to the creation of a 'knowledge society', where every person is an owner of the development process. We are trying to build*

cooperation based on dialogue, respect and ownership of the development programs and the process."

I ask about the way the United States has been treating this country – this African rebel.

"The US pattern of behavior towards Eritrea over the years has been full of conspiracies."

He quoted the then US ambassador to the UN (later to become US Secretary of State) John Foster Dulles: "From the point of view of justice, the opinions of the Eritrean people must receive consideration. Nevertheless the strategic interest of the United States in the Red Sea basin and the considerations of security and world peace make it necessary that the country has to be linked with our ally Ethiopia."

I mentioned that the United States used and continues to use different pretexts and mechanisms to destabilize Eritrea, to which Mr. Ambassador replied, passionately:

> *"They have actively promoted an economic blockade ... when that failed the US used Ethiopia to start the war in 1998 ... when that failed, it injected political dissent and tried to create divisions and cleavages along ethnic lines... when that failed, it used religion – Pentecostals ...when that failed, it actively began luring youth out of the country, even issuing visas, illegally, to people without the passports ... and then it turned around and accused the government of "human trafficking" ... when that failed, it actively pushed different neighboring countries to pick fights with Eritrea and also to encouraged them behind closed doors to encircle Eritrea out of IGAD ... It used the 'client' states to promote its own strategy for this region... And when that also failed, it used the infamous "terrorism" label to engineer illegal and unjust sanctions ... Finally, when everything failed, it used and continues to use "human rights" and "democracy" as a battle cry for intervention..."*

***

"See what we are doing and tell us whether we are socialist country or not", is repeated to me, by many.

The more I see, the more I am convinced that the Eritrea's plan, its process, its revolution, are extremely close to what is being fought for in Cuba, in Venezuela or Ecuador.

But there is great pride and also great modesty, here. The Eritrean process is shy, unvocal. As a result, the world knows very little about this remarkable country.

***

Dr. Taisier Ali is a Sudanese who lives in Eritrea for 15 years. He is the director of PCHA. We sit down in his office, and try to analyze, why the Eritrean model is so misrepresented abroad, or why it is ignored by the Western mass media:

> *"When you talk about Eritrea, to the international community and the outside world, I think it is one of the most misunderstood countries on the whole globe... After coming here, I soon realized that here, they have a sense of purpose, a 'national project', conceived and developed during the 30 years of struggle. We don't have to accept it, but at least they are determined to take their country from the point A to point B. They face many challenges, but they have always stayed on course. The rest of Africa is similar to my country – Sudan – no sense of purpose."*

> *"One disturbing factor in Sudan and in Africa in general, is corruption. Eritrea is nothing like that. For me it was always a reminder that if Eritrea could focus on its development; bottom-up development, rising from the real needs of its people, then why can't we, the rest of us, do it, too?"*

I asked, "Is the national project and 'purpose', what is actually bothering and scaring the West, the most? The fact that Eritrea could influence, positively, the rest of the region?"

> *"The international community, imperialism, neo-colonialism – they cannot perpetrate any society, unless the society is divided, unless it is weak, and clueless about where it wants to go; unless it does not have a national project. The national project galvanizes all natural resources, national actors, the human capital, to achieve the level of development that would improve the living standards of the people."*

"Like in Cuba?"

"Cuba is a very good example, yes! I also think that one of the reasons for this misunderstanding of Eritrea has to do with the self-reliance attitude of the party and the ordinary citizens. It is simply not seen almost anywhere in the world."

Mr. Ali says that many other countries have talked about self-reliance, including Tanzania, but it was mainly rhetoric. Eritrea did it. And when he speaks to local comrades, they realize that with this approach, the journey will take longer, but it will be achieved on Eritrean terms.

And that is definitely not what the West wants.

***

"Eritrea is not a neo-colonial state. Eritrea is an independent state. Eritrea does not host any military bases, any external forces. Eritrea has the vision, and not only for Eritrea, but also for the region. It is also promoting self-reliance and regional integration. It is also built on the ideal: 'let us use our own resources, and let us build our independence. It means elevating the life of Eritrean people, particularly those in the rural areas. This approach was considered in the West, as Chomsky said, as 'a rotten apple'."

There is Dr. Mohamed Hassan, again.

I ask him as well: Is it the main thing that the West is afraid of? A domino effect: an influence Eritrea could have on the rest of Africa?

"Of course", he replies. "Africa has some 50% of the world natural resources... Then consider this: the leadership of this country – they don't steal. They are living a normal life, that of normal people. No leadership in any other country in Africa lives like ours here. You go next door – the Prime Minister of Ethiopia who just died, left his family some 8 billion dollars."

I see the point: the lack of corruption could also considered be as 'very dangerous'. John Perkins explained to me, a long time ago, that corruption is one of the most effective tools used by the West in its quest to control the entire planet. It gives power to the elites, and it makes indebted and divided countries totally defenseless.

"Eritrea didn't attack anybody. But their views were considered very dangerous. And as you said, Eritrea is considered a virus contaminating much bigger nations," concludes Dr. Hassan.

A great Eritrean intellectual, Elias Amare, adds more, along the same lines:

> *"Eritrea has been insisting that its independence would be a genuine independence. It insists on self-reliance." It doesn't mean that Eritrea rejects direct foreign investment, for example. No. But when direct investment enters, Eritrea wants it to be on equitable terms. For example: Eritrea has huge*

> *natural resources. Gold, copper, zinc to name just a few. But it does not want to replicate what happened in DR Congo, or in Zambia. It wants an equitable partnership. Many Western countries do not see all this favorably. And that's the main reason for the hostility Eritrea is facing."*

But Elias, the West is also constantly using the accusations that Eritrea is supporting terrorist movements all over the region.

Elias replies vehemently:

> *"That is totally baseless and false. First of all, because of the nature of how Eritrea gained its independence, the country is totally against any religious extremism. It has been actually targeted by Islamist extremist groups for many years. Eritrea is a secular state: it does not mix politics with religion. It had been proven by many credible investigative journalists, that there is no support for terrorism, coming from Asmara; no support for Islamic extremist groups, or for Christian extremist groups."*

> *"Big powers do not want the Eritrean example to be replicated in Africa. I say again, Africa has huge natural resources. Big powers are now trying to grab these resources. What will happen if other governments in Africa were to try to follow Eritrea's example? It would definitely not be beneficial to great powers."*

***

In the days that I am spending in Eritrea, I see dams and irrigation systems, villages working and the building of strategic food reserves. I see schools and medical posts, new roads.

I stop the car and talk to several girls walking on the new Domhina Road, some hundred kilometers from Asmara. They are all from the 5th and 6th grades; cheerful, laughing, optimistic:

> *"In our village we already have an elementary school, and now we are walking to a secondary school, in a bigger village. We are good at school; we love English and math."*

The girls want to be teachers and doctors, but one resolutely aims at becoming an engineer, in order to build bridges, roads and power grids for her country.

Eritrea is still very poor, but it is neat, and orderly.

Crime is extremely low. I spoke to a Laotian eye surgeon, Dr. Soukhanthamaly Phonekaseumsouk, who has been performing cataract surgeries, for many years, in the deep countryside of

Eritrea, where batteries that are charged using the solar system have been mainly powering her equipment. Eritrea is number 2 in the world, per capita, in terms of the use of solar energy. The Doctor explained that she never felt unsafe, living alone, in the countryside or in the city; she was never harassed.

The adviser to the Minister of Health, Dr. Ghebrehiwet Mismay, took me on visits to the hospitals in Asmara. The neat institutions were in shocking contrast to the monstrous hospitals that I saw in several turbo-capitalist countries like Kenya and Uganda.

In Eritrea, medical care, including medicine, is virtually free. Wards are clean; those hosting children are overflowing with stuffed animals.

The country has managed to dramatically reduce child mortality through vaccination programs and constantly improving medical care.

China has just completed several specialized blocks of the hospital in Asmara, including those for cancer treatment and for heart surgery. Several Cuban doctors are teaching here, and treating the patients.

New housing projects are going up in several parts of the capital city, as well as in Massawa and elsewhere.

The day before my departure I met 2 education experts from the government, Mr Tquabo Aimut and Ms Mehret Iyob, who explained to me, clearly, how seriously adult literacy is being taken here.

Eritrea is now one of very few African countries that will be able to meet many of the Millennium Development Goals.

At Independence, life expectancy stood at only 49 years, at the last census it was up to 63 (very high by African standards). In 1991 adult literacy stood at between 20% to 30% and only 10% for women. In 2008 it climbed to 65% and in 2010 to 74%, 2015's (realistic) goal being 80%.

We are talking about post-literacy and functional-literacy programs, but above all, about how democratic the system really is. Not 'democratic' in terms of the Western perception, but democratic in terms of the participation of the people in decision-making; in developing the curricula, and the blocking of projects that would bring no benefits to the communities.

Both ministries – those of Health and of Education – agree that while Eritrea is repeatedly praised by several UN agencies, including UNDP and UNESCO, very little of it is ventilated in the mainstream Western press.

***

For all these days, it has not always been a smooth ride. One evening I hold a round-table discussion with young intellectuals. We shout, argue: about socialism, about the fight against imperialism, about whether Eritrea should be more engaged; whether it should be closer to the socialist countries or not.

I film, photograph and record.

I am introduced to Mr. Zemhret Yohannes, Director of the Research and Documentation Center at PFDJ (People's Front for Democracy and Justice), and we have a long discussion about the turbulent Eritrean history and on the country's right to improve the life of its people. We talk into the night, until the tapes are gone and my memory cards are full.

During my last night I speak at a hall full of people. I address the local intellectuals and youth. And just few hours earlier, the ERI-TV interviews me.

It is all totally interactive; it is all one huge "process"; nothing is staged, everything spontaneous.

***

Eritrea is under fire; it is clearly on the hit-list of the West, because it serves its people, and because it is refusing to aid the Empire and the corporate world.

The West is using its toxic propaganda to the maximum, in order to smear the country.

It is also systematically boosting, financing and manufacturing 'the opposition', as it does all over the world.

Periodically, huge campaigns from the BBC and other sources of Western propaganda get pointed, directly, at Asmara.

For instance, at the height of the "coup" that never was (January 2012), African Strategies served as a defying force that helped patriots around the world counter the barrage of disinformation regarding Asmara and the Government of Eritrea spread by the so-called "experts".

That is the time when the Western news channels and Al-Jazeera were reporting on the 'rebellion' in the capital city.

My local camera-person, Mr. Azmera, summarized the event:

> *"As the 'coup' was taking place, I was just leaving the Presidential compound, after working there for some time. I walked out, ate lunch... Then at 4PM I was called and told: 'Al-Jazeera is reporting that there was a coup in Asmara!' I just ignored them, and walked home."*

***

After my intensive work in Eritrea, I testify: I came to my conclusion: the country is socialist!

It is socialist, if the definitions of Latin America were to be applied.

At the same time, it is socialist in its own way. It will never take any diktats from anybody: from the West, or even from the friendly countries of Latin America, South Africa, China or Russia.

Eritrea belongs to its own people.

I have worked in 150 countries of the world, and I never encountered a nation like this.

My first three days there were confusing. I tried to place Eritrea in a box, somewhere. Later, I just let go and smiled... And enjoyed the ride, so to speak.

What a beauty she is! And what strength, courage, and resilience she radiates!

As my plane was taking off, for Cairo, at 4 in the morning, I was humming some tune, happily. I was leaving behind a country that I truly could admire.

Inside, in my heart, I felt much richer than when I arrived.

If this was, for Western capitalism and imperialism, a virus – political and economic, social Ebola – then I was ready to be infected by it, gladly over and over again!

12 December 2014

68

The West is Manufacturing Muslim Monsters

WHO SHOULD BE BLAMED FOR MUSLIM TERRORISM?

A hundred years ago, it would have been unimaginable to have a pair of Muslim men enter a cafe or a public transportation vehicle, and then blow themselves up, killing dozens. Or to massacre the staff of a satirical magazine in Paris! Things like that were simply not done.

When you read the memoirs of Edward Said, or talk to old men and women in East Jerusalem, it becomes clear that the great part of Palestinian society used to be absolutely secular and moderate. It cared about life, culture, and even fashion, more than about religious dogmas.

The same could be said about many other Muslim societies, including those of Syria, Iraq, Iran, Egypt and Indonesia. Old photos speak for themselves. That is why it is so important to study old images again and again, carefully.

Islam is not only a religion; it is also an enormous culture, one of the greatest on Earth, which has enriched our humanity with some of the paramount scientific and architectural achievements, and with countless discoveries in the field of medicine. Muslims have written stunning poetry, and composed beautiful music. But above all, they developed some of the earliest social structures in the world, including enormous public hospitals and the first universities on earth, like The University of al-Qarawiyyin in Fez, Morocco.

The idea of 'social' was natural to many Muslim politicians, and had the West not brutally interfered, by overthrowing left-wing governments and putting on the throne fascist allies of London, Washington and Paris; almost all Muslim countries, including Iran, Egypt and Indonesia, would now most likely be socialist, under a group of very moderate and mostly secular leaders.

***

In the past, countless Muslim leaders stood up against the Western control of the world, and enormous figures like the Indonesian President, Ahmet Sukarno, were close to Communist Parties and ideologies. Sukarno even forged a global anti-imperialist movement, the Non-Allied movement, which was clearly defined during the Bandung Conference in Indonesia, in 1955.

That was in striking contrast to the conservative, elites-oriented Christianity, which mostly felt at home with the fascist rulers and colonialists, with the kings, traders and big business oligarchs.

For the Empire, the existence and popularity of progressive, Marxist, Muslim rulers governing the Middle East or resource-rich Indonesia, was something clearly unacceptable. If they were to use the natural wealth to improve the lives of their people, what was to be left for the Empire and its corporations? It had to be stopped by all means. Islam had to be divided, and infiltrated with extremists and anti-Communist cadres, and by those who couldn't care less about the welfare of their people.

***

Almost all radical rightwing movements in today's Islam, anywhere in the world, are tied to Wahhabism, an ultra-conservative, reactionary sect of Islam, which is in control of the political life of Saudi Arabia, Qatar and other staunch allies of the West in the Gulf.

To quote Dr. Abdullah Mohammad Sindi:

> "It is very clear from the historical record that without British

help neither Wahhabism nor the House of Saud would be in existence today. *Wahhabism is a British-inspired fundamentalist movement in Islam. Through its defense of the House of Saud, the US also supports Wahhabism directly and indirectly regardless of the terrorist attacks of September 11, 2001. Wahhabism is violent, right wing, ultra-conservative, rigid, extremist, reactionary, sexist, and intolerant...*"

The West gave full support to the Wahhabis in the 1980s. They were employed, financed and armed, after the Soviet Union was dragged into Afghanistan and into a bitter war that lasted from 1979 to 1989. As a result of this war, the Soviet Union collapsed, exhausted both economically and psychologically.

The Mujahedeen, who were fighting the Soviets as well as the left-leaning government in Kabul, were encouraged and financed by the West and its allies. This horrible conflict, totally manufactured by Washington, was the "Soviets' Vietnam", in the words of Zbigniew Brzezinski, its principal architect. The Muslim faithful came from all corners of the Islamic world, to fight a 'Holy War' against "Communist infidels."

According to the US Department of State archives:

> "Contingents of so-called Afghan Arabs and foreign fighters who wished to wage jihad against the atheist communists. Notable among them was a young Saudi named Osama bin Laden, whose Arab group eventually evolved into al-Qaeda."

Muslim radical groups created and injected into various Muslim countries by the West included al-Qaeda, but also, more recently, ISIS (also known as ISIL). ISIS is an extremist army that was born in the 'refugee camps' on the Syrian/Turkish and Syrian/Jordanian borders, and which was financed by NATO and the West to fight the Syrian (secular) government of Bashar al-Assad.

Such radical implants have been serving several purposes. The West uses them as proxies in the wars it is fighting against its designated "enemies" – the countries that are still standing in the way to the Empire's complete domination of the world. Then, somewhere down the road, after these extremist armies 'get totally out of control' (and they always will), they can easily serve as scarecrows and as justification for the 'The War On Terror', or, like after ISIS took Mosul, as an excuse for the re-engagement of Western troops in Iraq.

Stories about the radical Muslim groups have constantly been paraded on the front pages of newspapers and magazines, or shown on television monitors, reminding readers 'how dangerous the world really is', 'how important Western engagement in it is', and consequently, how important surveillance is, how indispensable security measures are, as well as tremendous 'defense' budgets and wars against countless rogue states.

***

From a peaceful and creative civilization, that used to lean towards socialism, the Muslim nations and Islam itself, found itself to be suddenly derailed, tricked, outmaneuvered, infiltrated by foreign religious and ideological implants, and transformed by the Western ideologues and propagandists into one 'tremendous threat'; into the pinnacle and symbol of terrorism and intolerance.

The situation has been thoroughly grotesque, but nobody is really laughing – too many people have died as a result; too much has been destroyed!

Indonesia is one of the most striking historical examples of how such mechanisms of the destruction of progressive Muslim values really functions:

In the 1950s and early 1960s, the US, Australia and the West in general, were increasingly 'concerned' about the progressive anti-imperialist and internationalist stand of President Sukarno, and about the increasing popularity of the Communist Party of Indonesia (PKI). But they were even more anxious about the enlightened, socialist and moderate Indonesian brand of Islam, which was clearly allying itself with Communist ideals.

Christian anti-Communist ideologues and 'planners', including the notorious Jesuit Joop Beek, infiltrated Indonesia. They set up clandestine organizations there, from ideological to paramilitary ones, helping the West to plan the coup that in and after 1965 took between 1 and 3 million human lives.

Shaped in the West, the extremely effective anti-Communist and anti-intellectual propaganda spread by Joop Beek and his cohorts also helped to brainwash many members of large Muslim organizations, propelling them into joining the killing of Leftists, immediately after the coup. Little did they know that Islam, not only Communism, was chosen as the main target of the pro-Western, Christian 'fifth column' inside Indonesia, or more precisely, the target was the left-leaning, liberal Islam.

After the 1965 coup, the Western-sponsored fascist dictator, General Suharto, used Joop Beek as his main advisor. He also relied on Beek's 'students', ideologically. Economically, the regime related itself with mainly Christian business tycoons, including Liem Bian Kie.

In the most populous Muslim nation on earth, Indonesia, Muslims were sidelined, their 'unreliable' political parties banned during the dictatorship, and both the politics (covertly) and economy (overtly) fell under the strict control of a Christian, pro-Western minority. To this day, this minority has its complex and venomous net of anti-Communist warriors, closely-knit business cartels and mafias, media and 'educational outlets' including private religious schools, as well as corrupt religious preachers (many played a role in the 1965 massacres), and other collaborators with both the local and global regime.

Indonesian Islam has been reduced to a silent majority, mostly poor and without any significant influence. It only makes international headlines when its frustrated white-robed militants go trashing bars, or when its extremists, many related to the Mujahedeen and the Soviet-Afghan War, go blowing up nightclubs, hotels or restaurants in Bali and Jakarta.

Or do they even do that, really?

Former President of Indonesia and progressive Muslim cleric, Abdurrahman Wahid (forced out of office by the elites), once told me: "I know who blew up the Marriott Hotel in Jakarta. It was not an attack by the Islamists; it was done by the Indonesian secret services, in order to justify their existence and budget, and to please the West."

***

"I would argue that western imperialism has not so much forged an alliance with radical factions, as created them", I was told, in London, by my friend, and leading progressive Muslim intellectual, Ziauddin Sardar.

And Mr. Sardar continued:

> "We need to realize that colonialism did much more than simply damage Muslim nations and cultures. It played a major part in the suppression and eventual disappearance of knowledge and learning, thought and creativity, from Muslim cultures. The

> colonial encounter began by appropriating the knowledge and learning of Islam, which became the basis of the 'European Renaissance' and 'the Enlightenment' and ended by eradicating this knowledge and learning from both Muslim societies and from history itself. It did that both by physical elimination – destroying and closing down institutions of learning, banning certain types of indigenous knowledge, killing off local thinkers and scholars – and by rewriting History as the history of western civilization into which all minor histories of other civilization are subsumed."

From the hopes of those post-WWII years, to the total gloom of the present days – what a long and terrible journey is has been!

The Muslim world is now injured, humiliated and confused, almost always on the defensive.

It is misunderstood by the outsiders, and often even by its own people who are frequently forced to rely on Western and Christian views of the world.

What used to make the culture of Islam so attractive – tolerance, learning, concern for the wellbeing of the people – has been amputated from the Muslim realm, destroyed from abroad. What was left was only religion.

Now most of the Muslim countries are ruled by despots, by the military or corrupt cliques. All of them closely linked with the West and its global regime and interests.

As they did in several great nations and Empires of South and Central America, as well as Africa, Western invaders and colonizers managed to totally annihilate great Muslim cultures.

What forcefully replaced them were greed, corruption and brutality.

It appears that everything that is based on different, non-Christian foundations is being reduced to dust by the Empire. Only the biggest and toughest cultures are still surviving.

Anytime a Muslim country tries to go back to its essence, to march its own, socialist or socially-oriented way – be it Iran, Egypt, Indonesia, or much more recently Iraq, Libya or Syria – it gets savagely demonized, tortured and destroyed.

The will of its people is unceremoniously broken, and democratically expressed choices overthrown.

For decades, Palestine has been denied freedom, as well as its basic human rights. Both Israel and the Empire spit at its right to self-determination. The Palestinian people are locked in a ghetto, humiliated, and murdered—with almost complete impunity. Religion is all that some of them have left.

The 'Arab Spring' was derailed and terminated almost everywhere, from Egypt to Bahrain, and the old regimes and military are back in power.

Like African people, Muslims are paying a terrible price for being born in countries rich in natural resources. But they are also brutalized for having, together with China, the greatest civilization in history, one that outshone all the cultures of the West.

***

Christianity looted and brutalized the world. Islam, with its great Sultans such as Saladin, stood against invaders, defending the great cities of Aleppo and Damascus, Cairo and Jerusalem. But overall, it was more interested in building a great civilization, than in pillaging and wars.

Now hardly anyone in the West knows about Saladin or about the great scientific, artistic or social achievements of the Muslim world. But everybody is 'well informed' about ISIS. Of course they know ISIS only as an 'Islamic extremist group', not as one of the main Western tools used to destabilize the Middle East.

As 'France is mourning' the deaths of the journalists at the offices of the satirical magazine, Charlie Hebdo (undeniably a terrible crime!), all over Europe it is again Islam which is being depicted as brutal and militant, not the West with its post-Crusade, Christian fundamentalist doctrines that keeps overthrowing and slaughtering all moderate, secular and progressive governments and systems in the Muslim world, leaving Muslim people at the mercy of deranged fanatics.

***

In the last five decades, around 10 million Muslims have been murdered because their countries did not serve the Empire, or did not serve it full-heartedly, or just were in the way. The victims were Indonesians, Iraqis, Algerians, Afghanis, Pakistanis, Iranians, Yemenis, Syrians, Lebanese, Egyptians, and the citizens of Mali, Somalia, Bahrain and many other countries. Many of their homelands have been turned to rubble.

The West identified the most horrible monsters, threw billions of dollars at them, armed them, gave them advanced military training, and then let them loose.

The countries that are breeding terrorism, Saudi Arabia and Qatar, are some of the closest allies of the West, and have never been punished for exporting horror all over the Muslim world. The kept Western media naturally never mentions such an obvious fact.

Great social Muslim movements like Hezbollah, which is presently engaged in mortal combat against the ISIS, but which also used to galvanize Lebanon during its fight against the Israeli invasion, are on the "terrorist lists" compiled by the West. It explains a lot, if anybody is willing to pay attention.

Seen from the Middle East, it appears that the West, just as during the crusades, is aiming at the absolute destruction of Muslim countries and Muslim culture.

As for the Muslim religion, the Empire only accepts the sheepish brands – those that accept extreme capitalism and the dominant global position of the West. The only other tolerable type of Islam is that which is manufactured by the West itself, and by its allies in the Gulf – designated to fight against progress and social justice; the one that is devouring its own people.

9 January 2015

*****

69

2015 Will See Decisive Battles

THE EMPIRE IS CRUMBLING, THAT IS WHY IT NEEDS WAR

Last night in Beijing, I sat in a historic Szechuan restaurant with a friend who happens to be a Chinese diplomat. We exchanged some stories, ordered food, and then, suddenly, my throat felt dry and my eyes got misty.

I bowed and thanked her for the heartfelt offer China made to rescue Russia.

Just before leaving my hotel, I read the news on the RT:

> *"China's foreign minister has pledged support to Russia as it faces an economic downturn due to sanctions and a drop in oil prices. Boosting trade in Yuan is a solution proposed by Beijing's commerce minister.*
>
> *'Russia has the capability and the wisdom to overcome the existing hardship in the economic situation,' Foreign Minister Wang Yi told journalists. China Daily reported Monday: 'If the Russian side needs it, we will provide necessary assistance*

within our capacity.'"

By no means was I representing the Russian Federation here, in Beijing, nor was my friend representing China that night, at the dining table. It was an informal meeting attended by just a few friends, nothing more.

Not to mention that I am not really, 'technically' a Russian. Yes, I was born in Leningrad but almost my entire life I spent elsewhere... all over the world, to be precise. And in my veins, not that it really matters; it is also all confused... there circulates an explosive mixture of Russian, Chinese and European blood.

But lately, to be Russian, to me and to many others, is much more than just about blood. 'I am a rebel; therefore I am Russian', to paraphrase Albert Camus. Or: 'I am Russian because I refuse to abandon the struggle.'

'Ya Russkii!' or 'Cubano soy!' It simply feels good, and makes one proud, and stronger.

***

The world is in turmoil. Like in the early 1940's, something tremendous is gaining shape, something irreversible.

Almost all of us who have been analyzing the Empire fighting against the propaganda and nihilism it spreads, and its venomous tentacles extending to every corner of the globe, know that 'appeasing' Western imperialism is clearly impossible, as it is impractical, and even immoral.

Just as George W. Bush (clearly borrowing from fundamentalist Christian rhetoric), liked to say: "You are either with us or against us". Countries are now evidently put on the spot: 'they either accept the Western neo-colonialist doctrine', or they get destroyed, one after another, as were Iraq, Afghanistan, Libya and Syria.

No logic can help, no negotiations, no international mediation from the United Nations. The willingness to compromise is mocked. Appeals for simple human compassion do not move the rulers of the Empire even an inch.

It is clear that the Empire is preparing for the final assault. It will not back down. It will attack, destroy and annihilate. No idea when, but it will. And it will happen sooner rather than later, and with tremendous force.

Some would ask, why now? Why is there suddenly such a rush to fight the final battle for the total control over the planet?

The answer is very clear: for the first time disgust with the Empire is widespread, and worldwide. Many people are getting cured from blindness.

The mask of benevolence and rationality has been torn off by powerful media outlets based in the countries of Latin America, in Russia, China, Iran, but also in North America where the independent media is playing an increasingly important role. It is not even a matter of some elaborate 'objectivity', anymore. To get things right, it is enough to call fascism by its real name, as it is sufficient to identify mass murder perpetrated by the Empire on all continents!

The mask has fallen and what is now exposed is horrifying: the face of a monster, with blood and pus, a greedy grin and merciless fangs. It is a monster that is still in love with itself, unable to see its dreadfulness. It remains proud of its fundamental religious dogma, which it often doesn't even see as 'religious'. It dwells on self-righteousness, and at the same time, on its twisted market-fundamentalist faith that everything and everybody are for sale. It is a monster full of complexes – both those of superiority and inferiority.

It is not a happy monster and the people it produces are mostly miserable, lonely and scared. But it cannot change, it cannot back-up, it cannot let go. It would rather destroy its children and the world, than to admit that it went totally wrong, for years, decades and centuries.

Now many people have had enough, and some have even forgotten how to be scared! And the monster knows it, and it is actually scared itself, of those who are not scared of it.

The voices of the voiceless are now resonating louder and louder – we make sure that they are!

Except in the countries where the intellectuals and 'elites' have totally sold out, like in Indonesia or Malaysia, the horrendous deeds of the colonialism and neo-colonialism of Europe and North America, are finally being discussed, analyzed, and understood.

And the monster, the Empire, knows that it is the beginning of the end.

It cannot live as an equal. Therefore, it will fight its final battle. It will try to win. Or, it will try to destroy the world. Because life is not worth living for it, if it is not in full control; if its God is not in control, if it is not perceived as the enforcer of the divine manifesto.

***

When I visit a barbershop in Beirut or Amman, and am asked 'where are you from?' (It used to be a painfully confusing and complex question to answer, just a few years ago), I now simply reply: "Russia," and people come and hug me and say, "Thank you."

It is not because Russia is perfect. It is not perfect – as no country on Earth could or should be. But it is because it is standing once more against the Empire, and the Empire has brought so many horrors, so much humiliation, to so many people; to billions of people around the world... and to them, to so many of them, anyone who is standing against the Empire, is a hero. This I heard recently, first hand, from people in Eritrea, China, Russia, Palestine, Ecuador, Cuba, Venezuela, and South Africa, to name just a few places.

And that is why the Empire is now 'in such a hurry', unwilling to wait any longer, trying to provoke Russia, to bring it, metaphorically speaking, into yet another open epic battle, like the one that was fought in ancient times, on the thick ice, by Alexander Nevski.

The Empire is in too much of a rush, it is too scared to think, to understand, to remember, what every invader had to learn the hard way: Russia can be attacked and the Russian people can be murdered by millions. There can be devastation and fire; there can be ruins, tears and graves, graves, graves... Mothers burying their sons, and sons returning back home, to only encounter ashes. But Russia cannot be defeated. When the survival of the world is at stake, Russia stands up, enormous, powerful and frightening. And it fights as no other nation can; it fights for humanity, not only for itself. And it wins.

When such a moment comes, there is only one possible way how to defeat Russia: it is to destroy the entire world.

Are you ready for that, Mr. Obama? Are you ready for it, corporate America and Europe? Are you ready for it, Pentecostal Christians, Televangelists and other morally defunct beings?

Think twice. One more step, and you will find yourself facing two enormous nations, and dozens of smaller ones, ready to fight for the survival of mankind.

Your only strength is in your weapons of mass destruction, and therefore in spreading fear. And most of your arguments have no foundations in truth, only in deception and lies.

This year, I witnessed your deeds in Iraq, in Eritrea, China, Ukraine, all over Africa and the Middle East.

This year, somehow, it appears that you went too far, that the proverbial drop has fallen on Earth.

Stop! And stop torturing this Earth. Do not provoke, do not trigger yet another world war!

Stop, or there will be a fight. And you will lose, or we will all lose, but you will lose no matter what, because this time, Russia and China, Venezuela and Cuba, and others and many others, will not back down, anymore, while others will join.

***

Despite all of its terror, propaganda and brainwashing called 'education'—or news, or entertainment—the Empire is well aware that it is losing its grip on global power. And it is horrified, because it does not know how else to live, except with a whip in its hand. Planet Earth realizes that the ruler is sinister, ruthless and degenerate – some people realize it clearly using logic, others just sense it, intuitively. If there was really a global democracy, the people of our planet would throw the existing power structure straight to the dogs. But there isn't, there still isn't! Just look at the toothless, constantly humiliated United Nations. Almost everywhere, voting has become nothing more than an act of sticking a piece of paper into a box, and not much more.

***

The year 2015 is approaching. During that year, it will become clear who is fighting for the survival of our human race, and who is on the side of oppression, of imperialism, and of the Empire.

Next year, more and more countries will get destabilized or attacked. Perhaps millions of people will get killed, as they get killed every year, but most likely, this time, many more will. The 'opposition movements' manufactured by the West, as well as various Christian groups and other right-wing religious factions, will continue standing firmly on the side of imperialist oppression and market fundamentalism. The conservative petite bourgeoisie in the West and in almost all 'client states' will be battling to uphold their privileges. Fascist family structures and cultures will continue intimidating children and young people, preventing them from thinking, from rebelling and from living.

The Empire has many allies, all over the world, but most of them are of an extremely sinister nature. But their closest allies are always ignorance, servility and fear.

While our revolutions, the true ones, as well as the resistance and battles for a better world, are always based on knowledge, and in summary are nothing else other than an act of love.

***

The fight ahead of us will be extremely tough; it will be an epic struggle, involving great nation states, as well as groups and movements.

As the grungy Russian bear is being battered and provoked into a military conflict, great Chinese dragons are determined to form a protective circle, and this time, are declaring indirectly but clearly that they will come to the rescue of weaker nations attacked by the West. As even The New York Times reported:

> *"Mr. Xi did not mention the United States by name but took an unmistakable jab at Washington, saying, 'The growing trend toward a multi-polar world will not change', a reference to the Chinese view that America's post-Cold War role as the sole superpower is drawing to a close."*

The goal is to never allow Western imperialism and colonialism to take control over the planet again, as it mercilessly did at the end of the 19th century and at the beginning of the 20th, at the cost of tens of millions of human lives.

After centuries of plunder, rape and occupations, the West has no mandate to govern the world.

After constantly justifying and glorifying its terrible deeds, brainwashing our planet into believing that it actually brings progress and rationality to the savages (the rest of the planet), it cannot be trusted with 'informing' and 'educating' the people.

That is why we now have independent media, as well as powerful state-controlled media outlets based in the countries that are not willing to succumb to European and North American propaganda and indoctrination.

These media and education institutions should and will redraw the entire historical and contemporary narrative.

Some examples?

Instead of glorifying the wisdom of Founding Fathers of the United States, we should recall that North America was created on the unimaginable suffering of the indigenous people, on Christian bigotry and forced conversions, on genocide, and on theft of the land. And that it was not done by some new and extraterrestrial breed or race called 'Americans', but by the same European puritans and religious hordes that had already murdered for centuries, all over Asia, Africa and the Middle East—not to mention each other.

'New America', both North and South, was predictably created on fear, violence, glorified superstition, and theft.

We should recall the slaves who were brought in shackles from Africa. Most of them died when traversing the Ocean, women raped and humiliated, children raped and marked forever, men with their dignity taken away from them.

Women and young girls were then chained in the fields, becoming sexual toys for those 'puritan' white farmers. Men and children, at least those who survived, were made to work days and nights, until falling dead from exhaustion.

All this done under the shadow of the cross, progress, and 'democracy'!

This is how America was built. This is the true story, the true narrative, of those 'great beginnings of the land of the free'!

And those theatres of Europe, cathedrals and churches, palaces and parks –far too many created from loot and genocides, colonialism and the Crusades, 'military adventures'.

This is how the regime, how the Western establishment always functioned. Rape is love. Indoctrination is education and information. Fear is belief. Slavery is freedom!

Do we want this kind of world for several more decades, even centuries?

I am not asking Parisians, Londoners or New Yorkers. I am not asking corrupt businessmen in Jakarta or deranged preachers in Kinshasa, top military brass in Kigali or the murderous feudal lords in Guatemala.

No humanist, no compassionate human being wants this sort of shit!

And for the first time, people are not afraid to say it, or at least to hear it, or read it!

I am not afraid to write this. Are you scared to read it? I don't think so.

***

The 'peace', we were told about again and again, is something that has to be achieved and upheld by all means.

But what kind of peace are we aiming at, and peace for whom?

The Empire wants a 'peace' arrangement, in which countries like Cuba and Russia, Venezuela and China, just back down, give up, and surrender. That is not peace!

We are asked, ordered, to live peacefully in a world ruled by European and North American masters, as some slaves crawling in filth.

Are we expected to succumb to the one and only religious dogma on which this entire racist, imperialist and capitalist system is built?

What a prospect, what a peace!

To them, to the imperialist West, peace means only one thing: unopposed rule over the planet.

If one fights for his people, he is a terrorist, a bandit. Then, it is a war!

The Nazis called resistance fighters in Ukraine or France, 'terrorists'.

The Israeli military calls Palestinian resistance by the same name.

The West calls any legitimate rebellion, 'terrorist'. Even MRTA in Peru was a 'terrorist group'; MIR resistance against Pinochet was 'terrorist'. The mainly social movement in Lebanon – Hezbollah – is defined as 'terrorist', and so is the entire proud Eritrean state.

Shia Muslims are 'terrorists', because the West is supporting Sunni monsters in the Gulf.

Che Guevara was a terrorist, and so were Fidel and sub-commandant Marcos. So was Lumumba.

To the West, to its lackey regimes and NGOs, true peace will come only if all natural resources were offered to the multi-national companies. All left-wing, Communist and socialist movements would be butchered, if Russia were to return to that humiliated and shapeless shit it was converted into, for a short time, under the sneaky and brutal alcoholic Boris Yeltsin, if China turned back to the Deng Xiaoping days of only providing cheap products, labor and almost no global fight against imperialism! If Venezuela was to supply crude and fuck its own people, as it used to, before the heroic revolution of Hugo Chavez, if Cuba sold its women and booze and cigars for a pittance, before its most dignified revolution took place!

'Peace' would be, if billions of miserably poor people were quietly and un-confrontationally dying in their slums, while the capitalists, preachers and landowners several neighborhoods further were enjoying their private clinics and private schools!

But such peace will never again be accepted!

To fight for a better world, and for the oppressed, is like writing a poem.

War is when you plunder and rape, when you murder in order to oppress, and to control others!

Peace can only be based on justice, on social justice especially; otherwise it is not peace.

***

Russia and the Union of Soviet Socialist Republics fought for its survival on many occasions. Germans attacked it, then after the

Revolution in 1917, the West Europeans and North Americans attacked, and then the Germans again. Tens of millions vanished defending the Motherland. Not one apology ever came from Washington or London!

China was forced open, humiliated, ransacked, including its capital city Beijing. Those who did it, the Brits and French, are now lecturing China about 'human rights' and 'freedom'. It is truly grotesque!

Look at the other nations that are now standing up against Western imperialism!

Iran, colonized, destroyed when it took a socialist path, and then infected by a Suharto-style maniac, the Shah, later attacked by Iraq, after the West had armed Baghdad.

Latin America – was ruined by colonial and neo-colonial expeditions, for centuries, reduced to nothing by the 'Monroe Doctrine', with death squads trained in the US; trained how to kidnap and torture, and how to rape children in front of their parents.

Should we go on? Korea: tens of thousands of civilians were burned alive by US troops in tunnels. It was one of the most brutal wars in the history of mankind, aptly described by the most brilliant investigative journalist of the 20th century – Wilfred Burchett.

Indochina – 7 million were killed, bombed to death, or burned alive. Will we ever know how many? Vietnam is now an ally!

South Africa, Zimbabwe, Eritrea...

Yes, this is our alliance. Some 2 billion people who are living in the countries that were terrorized, brutalized, reduced to ashes, but that stood again and decided to fight, rather to live like slaves.

These are all imperfect countries, but countries peaceful to the core, countries that exist mainly in order to improve the lives of their men, women and children... and those all over the world.

And look at the other nations that are resisting Western attacks *against their sovereignty*– Cuba, North Korea, Eritrea – ostracized, surviving countless terrorist attacks, subversions, propaganda, and destabilizing campaigns. And then, when they mobilize, ready to protect themselves, they are designated, and defined as 'hermit states' or 'beastly dictatorships'!

Who forced them into a corner?

It is all twisted. Never again! Enough!

***

Do you hear that silence, after the US decided to 'normalize' its relationship with Cuba? We all know why there is such a terrible silence, don't we? Because we realize that, based on the centuries of US involvement in Latin America, this will be part of a new destructive tactic, a new attack: that Cuba may now actually be facing the greatest danger in decades! We don't know exactly what will happen, but we are somehow certain, that something very terrible will.

Is the West going to manufacture a 'Cigar Opposition Movement' in Cuba? Or is it going to be yet another color?

2015 will see many battles.

But the most important first step has just been made.

China made a great symbolic gesture: calmly, respectfully, but decisively. The message is clear: "You shall not be allowed to destroy others!" Not anymore.

The Empire is decomposing; it is sick, unsustainable.

But it is also toxic, and its illness is contagious. Its propaganda is mighty and its dogmas are violent.

Let us make sure that it goes away, crumbles, step by step, without destroying the world, without dragging it into WWIII.

Let us unite, individuals and nations, movements and parties. At least until the most dangerous period passes.

26 December 2014

*****

ABOUT THE AUTHOR

Philosopher, novelist, filmmaker, investigative journalist, poet, playwright, and photographer, Andre Vltchek is a revolutionary, internationalist and globetrotter. In all his work, he confronts Western imperialism and the Western regime imposed on the world.

He covered dozens of war zones and conflicts from Iraq and Peru to Sri Lanka, Bosnia, Rwanda, Syria, DR Congo and Timor-Leste.

His latest books are *Fighting Against Western Imperialism* and *On Western Terrorism* with Noam Chomsky.

Point of No Return is his major work of fiction, written in English. *Nalezeny*, is his novel written in Czech. Other works include a book of political non-fiction *Western Terror: From Potosi to Baghdad* and *Indonesia: Archipelago of Fear, Exile* (with Pramoedya Ananta Toer, and Rossie Indira) and *Oceania – Neocolonialism, Nukes & Bones*.

His plays are *'Ghosts of Valparaiso' and 'Conversations with James'*.

He is a member of Advisory Committee of the BRussells Tribunal.

Investigative work of Andre Vltchek appears in countless publications worldwide.

Andre Vltchek has produced and directed several documentary films for the left-wing South American television network teleSUR. They deal with diverse topics, from Turkey/Syria to Okinawa, Kenya, Egypt and Indonesia, but all of them expose the effects of Western imperialism on the Planet. His feature documentary film *'Rwanda Gambit'* has been broadcasted by Press TV, and aims at reversing official narrative on the 1994 genocide, as well as exposing the Rwandan and Ugandan plunder of DR Congo on behalf of Western imperialism. He produced the feature length documentary film about the Indonesian massacres of 1965 in *'Terlena – Breaking of The Nation'*, as well as in his film about the brutal Somali refugee camp, Dadaab, in Kenya: *'One Flew Over Dadaab'*. His Japanese crew filmed his lengthy discussion with Noam Chomsky on the state of the world, which is presently being made into a film.

He frequently speaks at revolutionary meetings, as well as at the principal universities worldwide.

He presently lives in Asia and the Middle East.

His website is: http://andrevltchek.weebly.com/

And his Twitter is: @AndreVltchek.

"Vltchek speaks with authority and knowledge about an extraordinary assortment of topics that embraced the entire global scene, something few of us would have the nerve to attempt, much less manage with such verve, insight, and empathy."

~ *Richard A. Falk*

“André Vltchek is a writer, the real thing, of the same calibre and breed as Hemingway and Malraux.”

~ *Catherine Merveilleux*

“Unlike mainstream media and even many "progressive" journalists, Vltchek regularly crosses into forbidden ideological territory and comes up with deeply revelatory scripts, insightful scenarios, telling details, and comprehensive analyses.”

~ *Michael Parenti*

Printed in Great Britain
by Amazon

57653269R00466